POLITICS

{ POLITICS

second edition

AN INTRODUCTION TO THE MODERN DEMOCRATIC STATE }

Larry Johnston

broadview press

BROADVIEW PRESS, LTD.
is an independent, international publishing house, incorporated in 1985.

North America
Post Office Box 1243
Peterborough, Ontario
Canada K9J 7H5

3576 California Road
Orchard Park, New York
USA 14127

tel (705) 743-8990
fax (705) 743-8353
e-mail customerservice
    @broadviewpress.com

United Kingdom and Europe
Turpin Distribution Services, Ltd.
Blackhorse Rd.
Letchworth, Hertfordshire
SG6 1HN
tel (1462) 672555
fax (1462) 480947
e-mail turpin@rsc.org

Australia
St. Clair Press
Post Office Box 287
Rozelle, NSW 2039
tel (02) 818-1942
fax (02) 418-1923

www.broadviewpress.com

Broadview Press gratefully acknowledges the financial support of the Ministry of Canadian Heritage through the Book Publishing Industry Development Program.

Art Director
    Zack Taylor
    Black Eye Design, Inc.
    Cover image © 2000 Stone.

Printed in Canada

CANADIAN CATALOGUING IN PUBLICATION DATA

Johnston, Lawrence Walker, 1955–
    Politics: an introduction to the modern democratic state

2nd ed.

ISBN 1-55111-369-4

1. Political science.   2. Democracy.   I. Title

JA66.J63 2000   320   C00-930258-1

contents

Preface to the Second Edition   11

one getting started   15

1   THE STUDY OF POLITICS, AND ITS OBJECTS   17

1.1   Initial Definition   17
1.2   Community and Society   19
1.3   Nation and State   21
1.4   Power and Authority   22
1.5   Obligation and Legitimacy   25
1.6   Justice and Democracy   27
1.7   State and Government   29
1.8   The State and Civil Society   33
1.9   Beyond the State   37
1.10   Conclusion   39

2   METHODS AND APPROACHES   41

2.1   Introduction   41
2.2   Politics as Philosophy   42
2.3   Politics as Social Science   45
2.4   Units of Analysis: Individual, Group, or Class?   49
2.5   Politics as Anthropology   53
2.6   Authority and Power Revisited   59
2.7   Politics and the Study of Politics   61

3   THE EMERGENCE OF LIBERAL DEMOCRACY   63

3.1   Introduction   63
3.2   Classical Antiquity   64
3.3   Feudal Society   66
3.4   The Reformation   69
3.5   The Enlightenment   71
3.6   The Market Economy   72
3.7   The Liberal Revolution   75
3.8   Liberal Democracy   77

two ideas 83

4 POLITICAL PHILOSOPHY 85

4.1 The Nature of Political Philosophy 85
4.2 Plato and Aristotle 90
4.3 Aquinas and Machiavelli 96
4.4 Hobbes and Locke 101
4.5 Rousseau and Burke 108
4.6 Marx and Mill 113
4.7 Conclusion 117

5 IDEOLOGY 119

5.1 Ideology Defined 119
5.2 Classic Liberalism 122
5.3 Traditional Conservatism 125
5.4 Socialism 128
5.5 Shifting Contexts 131
5.6 Reform Liberalism 133
5.7 Liberal Conservatism 136
5.8 Socialism: Communism and Social Democracy 140
5.9 Beyond the Consensus 145
    5.9.1 Anarchism 145
    5.9.2 Populism 147
    5.9.3 Feminism 149
    5.9.4 Environmentalism 151
    5.9.5 Nationalism 153
5.10 Beyond Ideology? 155

6 POLITICAL CULTURE 159

6.1 Definition 159
6.2 Beliefs, Attitudes, Values 161
6.3 Mass Culture and Socialization 165
6.4 Mass Media 169
6.5 The Politics of Public Opinion 178
6.6 Conclusion 182

three **institutions** 185

7 THE STATE: FUNCTIONS, INSTITUTIONS, SYSTEMS, CONSTITUTIONS 187
- 7.1 Introduction 187
- 7.2 Functions of the State 188
- 7.3 Institutions 190
  - 7.3.1 Legislatures 192
  - 7.3.2 Executives 193
  - 7.3.3 Judiciaries 197
- 7.4 Systems 199
  - 7.4.1 Concentrated powers 200
  - 7.4.2 Separated powers 204
  - 7.4.3 Comparing systems 209
- 7.5 Constitutions and Constitutionalism 211

8 PARLIAMENTARY SYSTEMS 217
- 8.1 Introduction 217
- 8.2 Majoritarian vs. Proportionate Systems 219
- 8.3 Majority, Minority, and Coalition Government 222
- 8.4 Formation and Dissolution 226
- 8.5 The Head of State 235
- 8.6 The Prime Minister and Cabinet 238
- 8.7 Policy-Making: Executive Dominance 242

9 PRESIDENTIALISM 247
- 9.1 Presidentialism Defined 247
- 9.2 Presidentialism with Separated Powers: The United States 248
- 9.3 Presidentialism in Parliamentary Systems: France 253
- 9.4 An Exceptional Case: Switzerland 257
- 9.5 Conclusion 258

10 FEDERALISM 261
- 10.1 Federalism Defined 261
- 10.2 Why Federalism? 263
- 10.3 The Division of Powers 265
  - 10.3.1 Legislative powers 265
  - 10.3.2 Administrative powers 270
  - 10.3.3 Fiscal powers 271
- 10.4 Bicameralism in Federal States 276
- 10.5 Constitutional Amending Formulas 282
- 10.6 Quasi-Federalism, Home Rule, and Decentralization in a Unitary State 285
- 10.7 Supranational Federalism 289

four **the political process** 293

11 DEMOCRACY 295

11.1 Introduction 295
11.2 Democracy Defined 296
11.3 Distrust of Democracy 298
11.4 From Representative Government to Representative Democracy 300
11.5 Representative Democracy Considered 304
11.6 The Costs and Benefits of Democracy 308
11.7 The Prospects for Democracy 310
11.7.1 Enriching democracy 311
11.7.2 Consolidating democracy 315

12 CLEAVAGES 319

12.1 Cleavages Defined 319
12.2 Cleavages Examined 321
12.2.1 Religious 321
12.2.2 Ethno-linguistic 322
12.2.3 Centre-periphery 323
12.2.4 Urban-rural 325
12.2.5 Class 325
12.3 Reinforcing and Cross-Cutting Cleavages 327
12.4 Case Study: Quebec within Canada 329

13 ELECTORAL SYSTEMS AND PARTY SYSTEMS 335

13.1 The Basics 335
13.2 Electoral Systems 338
13.3 Majoritarian Electoral Systems 341
13.3.1 Single-member plurality 341
13.3.2 Single-member majority 344
13.4 Proportionate Electoral Systems 346
13.5 PR: The "German-Style" System 351
13.6 Party Systems 359
13.7 Conclusion 365

14 PARTIES, ORGANIZED GROUPS, AND DIRECT DEMOCRACY 367

14.1 Introduction 367
14.2 Political Parties 368
14.3 Organized Interests 379
14.4 Pluralism versus Corporatism 382
14.5 Direct Democracy 384
14.6 Conclusion 388

five **governing** 391

15 PUBLIC POLICY, LEGISLATION, AND THE BUREAUCRACY 393

15.1 Public Policy Defined 393
15.2 Policy Communities and Policy Networks 395
15.3 Elements of Policy-Making 397
    15.3.1 Agenda formation 397
    15.3.2 Decision-making 399
    15.3.3 Instrument choice 402
    15.3.4 Implementation 404
    15.3.5 Evaluation 405
15.4 The Legislative Process 406
15.5 The Bureaucracy 413
15.6 Conclusion 416

16 JUSTICE, LAW, AND POLITICS 419

16.1 Justice Defined 419
16.2 The Rule of Law 422
16.3 Rights 428
16.4 Equality 432
16.5 Justice and Institutions 434
    16.5.1 Parliamentary supremacy 434
    16.5.2 Judicial review 435
    16.5.3 Balancing Parliament and the courts 438
16.6 Conclusion 440

17 THE RISE (AND FALL) OF THE WELFARE STATE 443

17.1 Introduction 443
17.2 Market Society 444
17.3 Liberalism and *Laissez-faire* 447
17.4 Critiques of Market Society 449
17.5 Ideological Compromise: The Welfare State 460
17.6 Rolling Back the Welfare State 464
17.7 After the Welfare State? 468

six **concluding** 473

18 POLITICS IN A GLOBAL CONTEXT 475

18.1 Introduction   475
18.2 The "End" of Empire?   476
18.3 Haves and Have-Nots   479
18.4 A Clash of Civilizations or a Convergence of Cultures?   486
18.5 Sovereignty, Security, Sustainability   491
18.6 Conclusion: Smashing the Crystal Ball   493

appendices 497

A The Canadian Constitution (Selections)   499

1. The Division of Powers   499
2. The Charter of Rights and Freedoms   505
3. The Constitutional Amending Formulas   514

B Canadian Federal Election Results, 1867-2000   518

INDEX   521

preface to the second edition

A second edition implies that much has changed in the intervening years, or that aspects of the first edition needed improvement. In this case, both are true. A book such as this is an extended discussion of ideas and a presentation of data to illuminate those ideas. In terms of concepts, the changes made for this edition have largely been additions, and these are intended to situate the discussion of Western liberal democracy more firmly within a global context. This has meant revisions throughout, new sections added to some chapters, and an expansion and thorough rewrite of the last chapter. Although globalization is a much overblown and inconsistently used term, there is a reality standing behind it that cannot be ignored, not least because in this age of the Internet, our students are part and parcel of it.

A fresh edition was also desirable given the amount of empirical data in the text and the speed with which such information quickly becomes dated. A Canadian general election within six months of the appearance of the first edition is a prime example of the challenges of keeping current. For this edition, virtually every set of election results in Chapter 13 required updating, as did the economic statistics in Chapter 17, newly supplemented by income and distribution data in Chapter 18. Of course, one problem with data is that what is up-to-date at the time of writing is only a snapshot that starts fading as soon as it is developed.

It may be that down the road we will look to texts like this primarily for the ideas, some of which ought to have a very long shelf-life. The data that confirm or refute hypotheses, or illustrate propositions, are increasingly available on-line, and on good Web sites are kept constantly up-to-date. Within the life of this edition

I hope to post a Web page on Broadview's site that will allow users to find updates to the data presented in this book.

In keeping with the notion that one should declare one's biases at the start, students and instructors are warned that the premises of this book, as with its predecessor, are fourfold.

First, it is written in the conviction that everyone can benefit from a basic knowledge of the political world. Within the liberal democratic tradition, political education—like participation—is voluntary, but within all societies, liberal democratic or otherwise, one cannot escape the consequences of political decisions. Somewhat paradoxically, in a world where more and more countries are at least formally democratic, and where information is ever more widely available, the political sophistication of citizens has not kept pace. The lack of depth to our everyday knowledge of the political world is compounded by the degree to which we often depend on mass media (shaped by the imperatives of entertainment and profitability) for our political information. In short, this text is written for students who will be citizens in a modern world, some of whom may go on to a more intense study of politics.

Second, in the knowledge that our students live in a liberal democracy, and in the expectation that most will continue to do so, this book makes no claim to deal as adequately as might be done with the problems of the developing world or with issues of international relations. Nonetheless, this edition has addressed such questions more squarely, albeit mainly from the perspective of what globalization and the effects of technology on nature mean for the liberal democratic world.

Third, just because this book intends to impart to students a basic understanding of their political surroundings and the pre-liminary tools for a more in-depth study of the political world, it makes no claim to present the complete and final word on any topic. Insofar as it is written for entry-level students (to the university or to the discipline), it does not try to cover the vast liter-ature on each topic, although further sources of reading are indicated to give some exposure to the broader scholarship that exists in each case. Every attempt has been made to avoid that trap into which too many texts fall: namely, to write for those least likely to read it in any detail—the instructors who assign it.

Finally, the approach taken here is avowedly eclectic, giving privilege to no particular school of ideology or methodology. This book demonstrates, one hopes, the value of appropriating from a variety of approaches, perspectives, and even disciplines in the attempt to make sense of political phenomena. I have also assumed from my own experience that no instructor will rely on only one text, and in this I rest confident that any lacunae may be easily filled by other treatments. This is not intended to be an introductory overview of world politics, but rather an introduction to the study of the political world.

The material has been organized into six sections, although cross-referencing within the text indicates that these are not "water-tight compartments." Section I (Getting Started) introduces students to the language, methods, and historical contexts that provide the background for studying politics within today's liberal democracies. Similarly, Section II (Ideas) offers the principal themes and substantive issues that have occupied normative political discourse, and that continue to animate discussions of the purposes and applications of authority and power. Section III (Institutions) introduces and explains the common institutional components of the liberal democratic state (e.g., executive, legislature, and judiciary), and explains the principal variations in how these are structured and co-ordinated.

In Section IV (The Political Process), the popular foundation of liberal democratic government is explained, compared in its various institutional forms, and assessed with regard to the degree to which it satisfies democratic principles. Section V (Governing) continues with an examination of the contribution of institutions of the state to actual government, and thus closes the loop by exploring what the state "returns" to the populace. A brief examination of the dynamics of public policy-making is followed by a study of the experience of the welfare state in the second half of the twentieth century. The concluding chapter (Politics in a Global Context) speculates on the future of the liberal democratic nation-state in a post-Cold War era of globalization, economic inequality, and ecological crisis.

I wish to express my thanks to Michael Harrison of Broadview Press for his encouragement and support, and to my various colleagues at the University of Toronto and Ryerson Polytechnical University. I remain particularly indebted to Ron Blair, Joy Esberey, and Jack McLeod. Above all, I must acknowledge an ongoing debt to all those students who endured the teaching that has been the basis of much that follows, and to Ailsa, for everything else.

GETTING STARTED

Politics is a discipline with its own vocabulary, its own methods, and a particular subject matter with which it is concerned. This opening section is something like a tool-kit, designed to prepare students for what comes after, by providing:

- an explanation of key terms;

- a basic introduction to various approaches;

- an overview of the historical underpinnings of the contemporary political world in which we live.

1 the study of politics, and its objects

The world we inhabit is political. We may choose to study politics or not, or having studied politics, decide that we will do so no more, but *we cannot choose to opt out of the political world*. Just as the sky rains upon us regardless of whether we understand why it rains, so, too, no matter how well or poorly we understand political events, however much or little we choose to participate in political activities, our lives continue to be shaped by political circumstances, changed by political decisions, and limited by the political possibilities left to us and others. Understanding the political realities we confront is no guarantee that we can alter them, any more than understanding tornadoes allows us to prevent them. It is nonetheless true that making sense of the political dimension of our lives may help us to influence their future course. When Aristotle began his *Politics* with the observation that we are "political animals," he was claiming not only that we live in political societies, but also that it is in our nature to be active in the politics of our community. Often, though, our stance is passive rather than active; others take the political actions, and we cope, one way or another, with the consequences. Indeed, much of what we do in society consists, however indirectly, of dealing with the consequences of political actions others have taken.

Our world is inevitably political because we share space with others. Our lives are essentially and not accidentally social: we live in neighbourhoods and communities; we work and play and communicate with others. A feature of all collective activity is that it requires some degree of regularity or order, or else there is inefficiency, miscommunication, or even chaos. Regularity and the way it is maintained is at the heart of the political dimension of our social existence. Not surprisingly, many definitions of

1.1 INITIAL DEFINITION

1.1   Initial Definition
1.2   Community and Society
1.3   Nation and State
1.4   Power and Authority
1.5   Obligation and Legitimacy
1.6   Justice and Democracy
1.7   State and Government
1.8   The State and Civil Society
1.9   Beyond the State
1.10   Conclusion

DEFINITIONS OF POLITICS

"We can define politics as the way in which we understand and order our social affairs especially in relation to the allocation of scarce resources, the principles under-lying this, and the means by which some people or groups acquire and maintain a greater control over the situation than others."
— Ponton and Gill, 1982: 5-6

"Among the common definitions of *politics* are these:

Politics is the exercise of power.

Politics is the public allocation of things that are valued.

Politics is the resolution of conflict.

Politics is the competition among individuals and groups pursuing their interests.

Politics is the determination of who gets what, when and how."
— Danziger, 1991: 5

"Politics, then, refers to all activity whose main purpose is one or more of the following: to reshape or influence governmental structures or processes; to influence or replace governmental office holders; to influence the formation of public policies; to influence the implementation of public policies; to generate public awareness of, and response to, governmental institutions, processes, personnel and policies; or to gain a place of influence or power within government."
— Redekop, 1983: 149

FIGURE 1.1

politics begin by talking about **POWER**. We, also, will find it useful to talk about power, but also to compare it with and distinguish it from **AUTHORITY**; both are fundamental political concepts. And, to remake the point with which we began, regardless of whether we understand power or authority, we cannot escape being subject to them.

Does the presence of power or authority in itself define politics? Or might politics not rather be, as one political scientist has argued, "any mixture of conflict and cooperation" (Laver, 1983: 1; see also Figure 1.1)? It is hard to know what kinds of human interaction would be excluded by such a definition, and surely not all interaction is properly identified as "political." Our working definition of politics, which I will explain further as we proceed, is the following:

> Politics concerns the formulation and execution of decisions binding upon the population of a communi-ty or society, and the relationships between those who make or implement such decisions and those who are affected by them.

This definition attempts to be comprehensive without including all human activity in the class of things political:

- it allows us to recognize politics where there is nothing we would call a "state" nor anything we might call a "government" (see Chapter Two);

- it reminds us that politics has to do with social wholes (community, society) and the way they are organized or ordered; and

- it also recognizes the common (but not inevitable) division of a society or community into those who make the rules and those who are ruled, and asks about the kinds of inter-action that occur between these two groups.

Besides investigating the relationships between the state and/or government and the people, the objects of political study we will be concerned with include **INSTITUTIONS**, **PROCESSES**, and **IDEAS** (see Figure 1.2). Parliament, for example, is an institution where laws are made through the legislative process; in that most

18

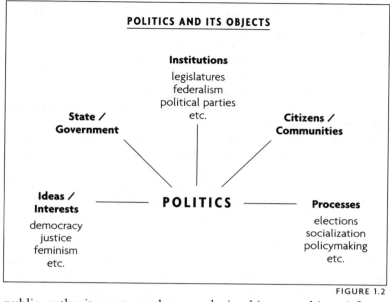

POLITICS AND ITS OBJECTS

Institutions
legislatures
federalism
political parties
etc.

**State /
Government**

**Citizens /
Communities**

**Ideas /
Interests** ——— **POLITICS** ——— **Processes**

democracy
justice
feminism
etc.

elections
socialization
policymaking
etc.

FIGURE 1.2

public authority rests on laws made in this way, this satisfies a normative idea or principle known as the "rule of law."

COMMUNITY and **SOCIETY** are terms used to describe the social whole within which individual life is experienced. All human life occurs within such wholes—something which exceptions serve only to confirm. Robinson Crusoe, for example, is interesting not just because he is an individual removed from his accustomed environment, but also because he behaves in his new setting as a product of a certain (European) society. Although "community" and "society" are often used interchangeably, the former can indicate a specific type of society, or more accurately, something that is present in societies to a lesser or greater extent.

Communities are marked by homogeneity and cohesiveness; their members share language, culture, and beliefs of a moral and religious nature, and their lives are governed by common norms and customs. A particular way of life, such as farming or fishing, may also be shared. Membership is more or less total (one belongs or one doesn't), and often requires a commitment, some participation or performance of duty. Communities are conservative in the sense of attempting to maintain the integrity of what is held in common, and collective in the sense that the welfare of each

**1.2
COMMUNITY
AND SOCIETY**

member is of interest to others. These characteristics suggest that community is like family, only on a larger scale (some families, at least: families and communities both are sometimes dysfunctional). Like families, too, communities are formed involuntarily. One is born into a community, and although one may repudiate it, one is unlikely ever fully to escape its influence.

Evidence would appear to indicate that, initially, humans lived in communities, or to put it another way, human societies were originally characterized by strong degrees of community. As societies become less homogeneous and more differentiated, they lose the cohesiveness of community. Members may differ considerably in their values and beliefs, and the sense of a common life in which all participate may lose its meaning. Societies without community are more like collections of individuals; you may choose to live in a society in a way that is not possible as a member of a community (the community may refuse to have you, while a society is less likely to do so). If belonging to a community is analogous to membership in a family, then living in a society without community is more like participating in a voluntary association, like joining a campus club or the auto league.

To distinguish between communities, on the one hand, and societies without community, on the other, can be misleading; it may be more accurate to talk about varying degrees of community within a society. Clearly, as communities become larger, cohesiveness and homogeneity are more difficult to maintain. But it is not just that community dissolves as societies grow and change, but rather that societies sometimes fragment into distinct, even hostile communities. Or, for any one of several reasons, two or more communities may be forced to share the same territory. In fact, to the degree that most contemporary societies no longer have the characteristics of community (or have them weakly), it may be difficult for students to appreciate fully the distinction we are making. This is because community is typically associated with conditions less likely to be encountered today. Community is more likely or possible in societies that are small (both in population and extent) and in societies of lesser rather than greater complexity. Modern societies generally are extensive, populous, pluralistic, and complex in their organization or structure. They may often contain the remnants of several communities. On a very basic level, the difference that matters is that community is personal and familiar, while society is impersonal, and in a curious way, invisible. Members of community, for example, can usually articulate what it means and why it is important to them; each of us is in many ways the product of the society in which we have lived, but we often fail to recognize the ways in which this is so. It is probably not too broad a generalization to say that the sweep of human history has been a movement from simple communities to complex, pluralistic societies.

This distinction between community and society, and the observation that community is often lacking in contemporary society, are of considerable political significance. Laver suggests that we need government when community fails (1983: 46). The more cohesive and homogeneous a people, the more united they are in their beliefs and committed to them, the greater the likelihood that these beliefs will effectively guide their actions and thus provide order and regularity. Conduct will be regulated here by customs, tradition, and religious beliefs, all of which exist as part of what the people hold in common. In these societies where community is strong, politics will be very much bound up with religion, moral beliefs, customs, taboos, etc. One may not even encounter specifically political institutions like law or government. Where community is weaker or fragmented, the political realm will be more detached from religious or ethical spheres, and correspondingly, the division between public and private spheres becomes very real in societies as community wanes. Conversely, the separation of the political from the religious or moral realm allows a society to accommodate communities that dispute or differ on religious or moral questions. As we have noted, the effect of history, of social and technological change, has not been simply to dissolve community, but also often to bring communities together, or to fragment one community into several. Canada was at Confederation an almost uniformly Christian society, but today presents considerable religious diversity; in many other respects, too, Canada accommodates a far broader range of communities than it did in 1867. Such reflections prompt a different set of questions of particular and ongoing relevance: how does one accommodate diverse communities within a single political society? These distinctions about community and society *and* their political significance are matters we will explore in greater detail in Chapters Two and Three, when we turn from the abstract to observations from the fields of political anthropology and history.

Just as at some stage in human social history something we call a state emerges to organize the collective experience of the

**1.3
NATION AND STATE**

CLARIFYING TERMS

NATION, refers to a people united by a collective identity and,

is distinct from

STATE, which indicates the ongoing institutions of government for a particular territory, and

is distinct from

JURISDICTION, which defines the people and territory over which a state has authority, as well as the nature of that authority, and

is distinct from

COUNTRY OR NATION-STATE, which indicates the conjunction of a particular state, territory, and people, and may be referred to by some political scientists as a polity.

FIGURE 1.3

community, so at a similar point human communities come to identify themselves with a specific domain, and eventually may attempt to enforce a title to it. This is the beginning of territoriality and from this develops a variety of relationships between peoples and territories and their governments. One result is a confusing vocabulary in which common terms may be used to refer to quite distinct entities (see Figure 1.3). The terms **NATION** and **STATE**, for example, are sometimes used interchangeably, but should be considered distinct concepts in political science:

> **NATION:** a people whose collective identity is based on common descent, language, religion, sense of history, customs and traditions, who usually (but do not always) inhabit a specific territory.

> **STATE:** a structure of power and authority organizing the political community that inhabits a given territory.

Thus, a state may include within it several nations, or parts of several nations: Belgium comprises the Flemish and the Walloons; Zimbabwe the Shona and Ndebele; within Canada the Québécois claim to be a "distinct society" or nation, just as in Spain the Basque and Catalonians express nationalist aspirations. At the same time, a nation may be spread through several states. The Kurds, a homogeneous people who regard themselves as a nation, are nonetheless spread through parts of Iraq, Iran, Turkey, and Syria.

Interestingly, just as politics puts us at the intersection of people, territory, and authority/power, each of these has also served as the basis for political conflicts. A people with a strong identity may fight for independence from a dominant or foreign power, thus seeking their own autonomous territory and state. Within states, the struggle between nations for power and/or territory has often led to civil war. Between states, competing claims of jurisdiction or of territory may lead to tensions, conflict, and even war.

1.4 POWER AND AUTHORITY

Power and authority are key terms in political science that are often used interchangeably, but they represent two distinct phenomena. As noted, all social existence requires some degree of order and regularity, and both authority and power refer to ways

THE PEOPLE

Terms like *the people* or *the public* or, to a lesser extent, *society* present a special challenge to the social scientist. These phrases have no immediate counterpart in reality; they are abstractions that help us make sense of reality, general terms that stand for collections of particulars.

In the real world our immediate experience is *only* of particulars. You have never encountered a society, heard "the people" speak, or confronted "the public." It is misleading to say "the people are represented," or "in the public's mind," especially if we give the impression that "the public" or "the people" is a singular entity with one view or interest or will. At the same time these terms are employed because they do make sense when used properly, namely to indicate aggregates of particulars (the people) or complex wholes (society) which do in fact exist, but do not exist separate from the particulars or simple parts of which they are made. A society is real, and consists of a diversity of structured roles and relationships, but a society does not act, or think, or desire; only individuals do. The same can be said of terms like "a people," "nation," "class," "interest group," "party," "the public," etc.

To insist that the reality of these terms is inseparable from the reality of the individuals of which they are composed is not to deny that the whole may be greater than the sum of its parts, or that the collected activity of particulars or the aggregate of relations among individuals may have different properties than these activities or relations considered singly. For example, a baseball team does not exist without the nine individuals who take the field and come to bat, even though the actual players may be frequently changing.

Similarly, recognizing that we do not *immediately* encounter "society" or "the people" should not blind us to the ways in which we indirectly encounter "society" or "class" or "interests" in the immediate relations we do have with other individuals. Each of us reflects in varying degree the society in which we have been raised, our family's wealth, religion, the schools we attended, etc. It is simply a matter of not conferring the attributes that properly belong to individuals to those broader terms that allow us to talk of people collectively. Concepts very often serve as a useful shorthand to describe or indicate in a simple way phenomena that may be very complex; it is important not to lose sight of the complexity that may lie behind such apparently familiar and simple concepts such as "society" or "the public." For example, in modern nation-states, "the public" or "the people," insofar as it exists, is a fragmented, pluralistic aggregation of different, often competing interests, groups, identities, and classes. Phrases like "the public" or "the people" suggest a unity and coherence that may have no reality at all.

decisions are made and enforced within a society or community. The difference between them is crucial to the politics of societies. We will use **POWER** primarily to refer to *the implementation of decisions through force*, where force ultimately involves physical coercion (though often merely the threat of force is sufficient to obtain compliance). To exercise power means to impose decisions upon people who might not otherwise accept or obey them. Consequently, having power means being able to impose one's will upon others. Those who are subject to power face real consequences of an unpleasant or painful nature (such as imprisonment, loss of property, or even death). For this reason, power requires possession of means of coercion, without which it cannot be said to exist.

By contrast, **AUTHORITY** is said to imply **CONSENT**. Decisions that are implemented with authority do not involve force, and therefore are not imposed upon people. When people

INFLUENCE AND CUSTOM

Some might object that our discussion of power and authority oversimplifies matters. In addition to being forced to do something and doing it willingly, there are some less clear-cut examples. What about *persuasion?* Presenting you with a compelling set of reasons for doing something may be a case of gaining your consent, but if those reasons involve a threat of unpleasant consequences, you may feel that your consent has been somewhat forced. So too, *bribery* or *reward* may be seen as coercive, or not, depending on the context, and people may be manipulated into consenting to decisions on the basis of misinformation or *propaganda*. It is also obvious that our behaviour is often a product of *habit* or *custom*, rather than conscious deliberation or consideration of consequences. This is why the way we are socialized, or learn to internalize the norms of our community or society, is so important. These observations reinforce the conclusion that our distinction between authority and power is most useful when people have the opportunity (and willingness) to make informed, rational decisions about politics. Only then can we hope to distinguish between when they have freely consented to authority and when they have unwillingly submitted to power.

FIGURE 1.4

willingly obey or accept a decision we say that they recognize the authority of whoever has issued the command or order. This does not necessarily mean that people agree with the order or are happy with what it commands them to do, but that for some reason or another they see the command as "right," or one that the author has a "right" to demand of them. The reasons why people grant or recognize the authority of a person or group of persons are various, and we shall consider several of them shortly.

Power is attractive because as long as the necessary means are available, one is sure to get one's way. With power we do not have to convince or persuade others, or wait for their consent; we merely impose our will upon them. On the other hand, power is expensive, because it not only requires possession of the means with which to force others (such as police, military, secret police, jails, money to pay all these agents), but demands their continual implementation. If I have to force you to do something in the first place, then, once I no longer have the means to force you, or stop employing them, you will cease to do what I have demanded. Unforced, you may be no longer willing to comply.

The advantage of authority, then, is that once established, it does not require a constant expenditure of means. Authority has its way not once, but continually. Your present consent to my command is likely to entail your future consent, all things being equal. This advantage of authority over power means that governments will seek, wherever possible, to establish authority rather than simply to employ power. Power invites opposition in an expensive way that authority does not. If the inefficiency of power is the expenditure of means it requires for enforcement (maintaining and employing an army, a secret police, prisons and labour camps, etc.), the drawback of authority is that it must establish and maintain consent for its actions. Thus, in cases where governments cannot maintain authority, or are unwilling to take the necessary steps to establish it, they frequently resort to power. Although power is expensive to exercise, and relatively inefficient because it uses resources that could be much more productively used elsewhere, it is in some ways or in some cases easier to obtain than authority (see also Figure 1.4).

The discussion so far may make it obvious that the politics of societies is always a mixture of power and authority. To rely solely upon authority, a regime would have to be a perfect community—all would agree about what each should do, and everyone would do his or her part. Failing that, power remains necessary in order to enforce rules upon those who fail to recognize authority, or who are otherwise tempted to do what they may very well know is illegal or wrong. Many of us abstain from driving while under the influence of alcohol *not* because we are afraid of the punishment, but because we accept the law as a legitimate rule that ought to be obeyed. At the same time, we want our government to have the power to punish those who do not recognize the authority of the state to make such rules. Without power to enforce rules, those who recognize authority are often at the mercy of those who do not. It is equally clear that those regimes that ultimately rely on power are nonetheless concerned to establish authority to whatever degree this is possible, and to minimize by doing so the actual expenditure of force they must make. What they claim, and hope to establish, is the legitimacy of their actions.

OBLIGATION and **LEGITIMACY** are two sides of the same coin: if you recognize the legitimacy of government, then you are obliged to obey it. Conversely, if you feel obliged to obey, then you have conceded legitimacy. Obligation is a statement about what you feel you "ought" to do, but in a special sense of the word "ought."

Let's suppose the penalty for petty theft is the loss of your hand; you are likely to conclude that in this case you ought not to steal. Here the "ought" is tied to a punishment; if the penalty for petty theft were a very small fine, you might well calculate that theft is worth the risk of being caught and punished. The point of obligation, by contrast, is that you feel there is a good reason not

1.5
OBLIGATION AND
LEGITIMACY

to steal, regardless of the magnitude of the penalty. When you are obliged, you have concluded, for one reason or another, that the rule "do not steal" is a legitimate one. We have said that authority implies consent, in other words, authority rests on a foundation of obligation; for some reason or another people accept the legitimacy of the decision, and obey because they believe they "ought" to, no matter what the penalty for disobeying. Conversely, it is where judgements of obligation are lacking, or legitimacy is denied, that power—the implementation of force—is required.

So far we have been vague about what informs or causes the consent people give to authority, that is, about why people feel obliged to obey, or to recognize the state as legitimate. One influential treatment of this topic was provided by the German sociologist Max Weber, who suggested that three grounds of legitimacy are present in different societies.

The first of these is **TRADITIONAL** legitimacy, that is, rule which is justified on the basis of its long history and a "habitual orientation to conform" (1958: 79). In other words it is custom, and the fact that things have always been done this way makes them right under traditional legitimacy.

Second, there is **CHARISMATIC** legitimacy, where it is believed that the ruler possesses extraordinary personal qualities which justify his/her rule. This is more than the view that such individuals are gifted; it is the claim that they are *uniquely* gifted, and those who have convincingly claimed to be divinely chosen have been among the most successful charismatic leaders. At any rate, Weber's special use of "charismatic" here is altogether different from what we indicate by calling politicians "charismatic" who are able to ignite public emotion.

Finally, Weber spoke of **LEGAL-RATIONAL** authority, where legitimacy derives from "belief in the validity of legal statute and functional 'competence' based on rationally created rules" (1958: 79). Where authority is sanctioned by its basis in law, and assumed through a rule-governed process, such as an election, its legitimacy is legal-rational. Thus, while Pierre Trudeau was characterized as a "charismatic" politician in 1968, the legitimacy of his government (like that of all Canadian governments) rested on a legal-rational foundation.

Legal-rational authority grounds the claims to obligation of most contemporary states, although, in the past, states or their rulers frequently claimed authority on traditional or charismatic grounds. There is, though, a deficiency in Weber's categories. In the first place, they tend to emphasize *who* has power (as in charismatic and traditional authority), or *how* they have acquired it (as in traditional and legal-rational authority), rather than *what* they do with it. Weber's categories are silent about the content or substance of authoritative decisions, and in this respect present us with a paternalistic understanding of authority—as if it never occurs to citizens to question the legitimacy of *what* governments do, only who is doing it, or how positions of power came to be filled. Weber's categories may well be useful for distinguishing between authority in different *types* of societies (which was his point), but within contemporary societies, the discussion and understanding of legitimacy often proceeds on a different basis.

As noted, the authority generally exercised within contemporary states is of the legal-rational type, for a variety of reasons. Traditional authority is most appropriate within relatively static (unchanging) communities, and the fluid, pluralistic nature of contemporary societies means that they are commonly not characterized by a high degree of community. Similarly, the rise of universal literacy and public education means that people cannot be relied upon to accept things simply because "that's how they've always been done." Finally, the role of religion in attributions of charismatic (and some forms of traditional) authority means that these avenues for securing political legitimacy are generally closed in secular societies. (By contrast, the few contemporary examples of "charismatic" authority are found within religious communities, or societies where religious fundamentalism is entrenched.)

In addition, the questions "who will rule?" and "how will they rule?" are not answered in modern legal-rational states by just any set of rules or any kind of rationality, but in certain recognizable ways, and not others. Authority in legal-rational states can be characterized by terms more specific than those which define legal-rational authority, and more recognizable to citizens. Most people do not say to themselves "the state is okay because it's a legal-rational state." The notion of the "legal-rational state" doesn't tell us what is most important about modern states. Here, typically, justification (the theory explaining obligation) makes reference to more specific concepts, such as the "rule of law" or "accountability." Today, most rulers claim two things about their state or government: that its decisions are "just," and secondly,

1.6
JUSTICE AND
DEMOCRACY

27

that its decisions and/or the composition of the government in power reflects the will of the people. In short, within most legal-rational states today, justification of authority rests on two concepts: **JUSTICE** and **POPULAR SOVEREIGNTY**.

Justice means different things to many people; here it refers to norms describing the way authority is or should be exercised. Within many contemporary states, justice has come to involve three ideas or norms: the **RULE OF LAW**, individual or group **RIGHTS**, and **EQUALITY**. To take just the first of these, the rule of law is a norm of justice concerned with the proper use of law as an instrument of authority, and with the ways law is made, interpreted, and administered. Justice rooted in the rule of law may find expression in notions such as *constitutionalism* (the belief that the ultimate power/authority of the state should be subject to fundamental rules typically articulated in a constitution), or may stress concepts such as the "presumption of innocence," or "due process." Of course, justice is not *only* about law, but much of the discussion of justice in contemporary states concerns law and who is responsible for it. (For a further discussion of justice see Chapter Seventeen.)

Popular sovereignty is a concept which claims that the ultimate source of any legitimate authority exercised by the state or government is its citizens. That is, governments are legitimate because (or to the extent that) they have the consent of the population. This is clearly incompatible with the view that time or custom confers authority, or that only some individuals are divinely chosen or endowed with special gifts that entitle them to rule. The form of popular sovereignty with which modern students are likely most familiar is **DEMOCRACY**. Although popular sovereignty is not confined to democracy, our discussion will focus upon various models and institutions of democracy, and examine the degree to which they actually deliver popular sovereignty.

Thus within legal-rational states, when the question is asked "what makes authority legitimate?", part of the answer is provided by the concept of popular sovereignty—it is legitimate because it is exercised by individuals the public has chosen, or given its consent to—and part is provided by the concept of justice—it is legitimate because it is exercised according to the rule of law, respecting rights, etc. These are powerful arguments for the legitimacy of government; if you accept that authority is just and something to which you have given your consent, it is difficult to imagine a basis on which you might consistently challenge that authority. Conversely, the legitimacy of the state will remain unchallenged only as long as its actions are seen to be just and to reflect the public will. One problem, as we shall see below, is that most expressions of the public will are at best indirect, and open to considerable interpretation. Another is that there are competing notions of what justice or democracy entails. Nonetheless, justice and democracy are very powerful concepts which rulers use to try to secure legitimacy for their power (thus establishing their authority), and which critics use to argue for change or reform in the politics of a given society.

We noted earlier that human history has witnessed a move from familiar communities to increasingly impersonal societies, something reflected in Weber's successive categories of legitimacy: from traditional to charismatic to legal-rational. In ways that will be discussed more fully in Chapter Two, as societies become larger and more complex, power and authority are increasingly depersonalized. Modern societies are governed by something we have been calling the state, by which we mean the permanent institutions and structures of authority, distinct from the actual individuals who control or populate them. For example, the legislature is, on the one hand, an institution in which certain processes (such as making law) are carried out, and, on the other hand, is a collection of individuals who perform the function of legislator. Parliament endures while MPs (Members of Parliament) come and go. Similarly, we can distinguish the office of the prime minister from the particular individual who currently occupies or "holds" that office. The depersonalization of the form of government known as the state means that power or authority are more properly seen to be properties of institutions rather than belonging to the individuals who occupy those institutions or exercise their powers. The institutions continue to exist and function as individuals come and go. In order to be clear about whether we are talking about the institutions or the individuals it is useful to distinguish clearly between state and government. **STATE** will be used generally to refer to *the enduring complex of institutions and processes by means of which authority and power are exercised in a society.* This complex of authority and power is impersonal and relatively permanent. By contrast, **GOVERNMENT** refers collectively to *the individuals entitled to employ the power and authority of the state.* In Canada, "the government" is often used to refer to the

**1.7
STATE AND
GOVERNMENT**

party in power, although technically this is more accurate when indicating the cabinet currently in office (see below, Chapters Seven and Eight). In the broadest sense, power and authority are exercised not only by elected officials but also by public servants in their work of carrying out or implementing the policies or programs established by present and past governments.

So to say that modern societies are characterized by legal-rational authority is to indicate two things: (1) that the state is justified in terms of its legality (that is to say, its grounding in and use of *law* as the primary instrument of authority), and (2) that the government is chosen by a legal, rule-governed process such as an election. We can go further and note that where governments are determined by popular political processes, such as elections, the state endures while governments come and go. An election is a device that allows the public to challenge the legitimacy of the (current) government, while respecting the legitimacy of the state. We can now be more specific with our suggestion above that *justice* and *popular sovereignty* are modern measures of legitimacy, which is challenged where decisions are seen to be "unjust" or contrary to the "popular will." To claim that the *state* (rather than the government) is unjust or undemocratic is to argue that the *institutions* and/or rule-governed *processes* by which authority is gained and/or exercised are in some way inadequate. Such a challenge calls for the reform or elimination of institutions, or for the creation of new ones. Challenges to the legitimacy of the state thus call for constitutional change or reform (see Chapter Seven). The tremendous changes in Eastern Europe and the former Soviet Union since 1990 may be seen as responses to challenges of this kind. Challenges of constitutional legitimacy question the *way* authority or power is exercised.

Sometimes, however, what is questioned is not the way authority or power has been used, but *what* has been done. In other words, it is not the means but the end or the *substance* of what has been done that is problematic. In these cases what is challenged is the use that the *government* has made of the authority of the state, rather than the existence of that authority. What is distinct about the kind of legal-rational state we know as liberal democracy is that these kinds of challenges are usually pursued in one of two ways. One is to challenge the validity of the government's actions with respect to some existing definition of the state's power, as found in a constitution. Here the claim is made that the government's action has exceeded the proper authority of the state. This is not a challenge of constitutional legitimacy (i.e.,

AN UNCOMFORTABLE DISTINCTION?

The distinction between "state" and "government" is not commonly made in North America, especially by non-political scientists. This may in part be because of the use of the term "state" to refer to the subnational units of authority in the United States.

It is, though, an important distinction because it recognizes the permanence of government (i.e., the state) versus the limited term of those (i.e., the government) who control it. In Canada's largest province, the governing Conservatives in the late 1990s have said "we are not the government, we are here to fix government." Of course, they are in fact the government; their task (as they see it) is to fix "the state" and the use that those *in* government make of the state.

FIGURE 1.5

of what is the proper authority of the state), but a claim that the government has acted unconstitutionally (beyond the authority that the constitution grants the state). As we shall see, in some states it is possible for citizens to challenge the exercise of authority by government through the courts, where the courts are empowered to uphold the constitution. In such systems, the constitution embodies the accepted statement of the legitimate powers of the state, and a challenge to government action amounts to a claim that the government has exceeded the legitimate powers of the state. This represents a specific kind of claim that the government's actions are *unjust*—unjust because acting beyond the authority granted by the constitution.

In some cases, though, government policies or actions may be challenged as unjust, even though they are fully legal and constitutional. In part this may be because there are limits on what can be specified in constitutions, in part because justice is broader than the rule of law or rights, and in part because in any given society there may be a plurality of notions about what is just. A good example concerns taxation. On one view of what justice requires, taxes should be progressive; that is, there should be a direct and increasing relation between the rate of taxation and the level of means of the individual taxed. On this basis, for example, a sales tax is regressive, because its burden falls most heavily on those whose income is most committed to expenditure on consumption—those with the least income. (One way such taxes can minimize their injustice is by offering a tax credit to low-income consumers.) Similarly, those who believe in progressive taxation would regard the introduction of a flat rate of tax on income as unjust. On the other hand, some believe that progressive taxation "unfairly penalizes" those with higher incomes, and others still believe that all taxation is unjust. To take another example, many Canadians believe that a law outlawing abortion would be unjust; many others believe any law permitting choice in this matter is unjust. In either case, these individuals would continue to believe certain laws to be unjust, even if the courts were to rule them constitutional.

In situations where the government is acting constitutionally, but individuals believe it is not acting *justly* (that is, the justice issues are not constitutionally addressed), the principal avenue of action is the **POLITICAL PROCESS** (see Section IV). Here individuals or groups attempt to persuade the government to take a different course of action. Failing this, they try to change the government. Again, it is not the state that is under suspicion, but those individuals exercising its authority, and the most important function of electoral democracy is that it provides citizens with an opportunity to replace the government of the day. The political process generally, and elections specifically, are means by which citizens express their will. Indeed, the political process is not only a means of challenging the claim of government to be acting justly, but also (and perhaps principally) to challenge its claim to be doing such things as promoting economic growth or maintaining social order—more generally, its claim to be carrying out the popular will through the policies it implements. We should be clear that these are often distinct concerns. While the public may protest the legitimacy of government actions on the basis of norms of justice about which the constitution remains silent or neutral, it may also express a discontent not conceived or presented in terms of justice. At issue in the Canadian general election of 1988 was the issue of free trade. Although this issue could be approached in terms of social justice, it is probably accurate to say that for most participants in the debate, justice was not the predominant concern.

To summarize, then, within the framework of legal-rational authority, contemporary problems of legitimacy can address either the state or the government, and be primarily conceptualized in terms of justice/injustice, or democracy/undemocracy. Challenges to the legitimacy of the state amount to demands for constitutional change—that is, for a redefinition of the institutions by which authority and power are exercised, and of the limits confining this exercise. Challenges to the legitimacy of the government, on the other hand, accept the existing constitutional order, and proceed in one of two ways. One is to claim that the government has somehow violated the constitutional definition of its authority. In some polities at least, this proceeds by way of legal challenge through the courts. The second route of challenge occurs through the political process, through which citizens aim ultimately to replace the current government with one more representative of, or responsive to, their will.

Our discussion so far might well prompt some questions: What is the relationship between democracy and justice? Can one have a state that is just but not democratic (or vice versa)? Would such a state be legitimate? This book is informed by the belief that legitimacy requires *both* justice and democracy, though many may wish to debate this. Certainly history confirms that justice has often been conceived as independent of (if not opposed to) democracy. This is least problematic where there is agreement on what is and what is not just. Where community is strong it may well be that justice is possible without democracy: rulers and ruled alike will agree on the appropriate norms and follow them. In modern pluralistic societies or societies where there are competing notions of what is just, which conception or whose conception of justice should prevail? That which is more "rational?" Who would determine this? Answering these questions leads us back to the notion that democracy may be an important means of securing justice in modern societies. Certainly the premise followed in this book is that in a society where democracy flourishes (see Chapter Eleven), justice is more likely to be obtained than in a society without democracy.

Ⅰn all political systems, a considerable sphere of citizen activities falls outside the authority of the state. This is the realm of **CIVIL SOCIETY**. What we think of as our private lives falls within civil society, as do many of our public actions and our relations with others. The one exception to this division of state and civil society, in theory at least, is the **TOTALITARIAN** state, which recognizes no limits to the reach of its power. We say "in theory" because no state has the will, let alone the means, to govern everything its citizens do, all the time. In totalitarian (and many authoritarian) states, there is a civil society, but its boundaries are uncertain and insecure. In states with effective constitutions (see Chapter Seven), the boundaries of civil society are more secure, and the existence of civil society may come to be so much taken for granted that even to talk about it seems strange. In these countries an expectation of civil society is implicit in the political culture.

Comparing states reveals that what falls within civil society can vary widely. In most so-called Western countries a separation of church and state means that religion and its institutions (the church, the synagogue, the temple, the mosque) fall within civil society. In other words, the state neither enforces nor do its policies reflect the precepts of any particular religion. (Again, this may be more true in theory than it turns out to be in practice.) The rise of the Taliban to power in Afghanistan illustrates how civil society is greatly diminished in a theocratic state (i.e., one where church and state are united, or very closely entwined): moral precepts governing matters so simple as growing facial hair become legal precepts backed up by the force of the state. Having a beard

1.8
THE STATE AND CIVIL SOCIETY

(or not) ceases to be a personal decision. The well-known opposition of a substantial portion of the citizens in the U.S. to any form of gun control reflects the view that gun ownership is something that should not fall under the authority of the state but remain in civil society. Some Americans even take the dubious position that this division between state and civil society is contained in the Second Amendment of the U.S. Constitution.

Some general considerations are worth keeping in mind, and the first is that this distinction between civil society and the state is rarely absolute or clear-cut. In addition to religion, in Western societies at least, two important areas of civil society are the family and the marketplace (i.e., an economic system based on private transactions). Yet, obviously, both of these are circumscribed to various degrees by regulations of the state. In the one case, the rules of marriage and divorce, of family support and child welfare, and to a certain degree of education, are all subject to laws, and violation of these can lead to state intervention. The "free" exchange of goods and services in a market economy clearly occurs within the framework of countless laws and regulations. And so, the existence of civil society is always a matter of "more or less," not "is or isn't."

Generally, too, we can suggest that the more populous, the more geographically extended, the more culturally diverse, and the more technologically complex a political community is, the larger the role occupied by the state vis-a-vis civil society. This has been a theme of political experience in the twentieth century, and it is an open question whether it will continue to be such in the twenty-first century as environmental, population pressure, and economic development issues command attention.

In Chapter Two we will examine briefly the experience of pre-industrial societies without formal governments or anything like what we call the "state." In these communities the maintenance of well-being falls to civil society or its institutions. This points to two more important generalizations, which are themselves connected. The first of these is that the distinction between civil society and the state is not a simple one between where or when we are free and where or when we are not. Our existence as social beings is always constrained, even if it is only by the values and customs of our culture. Within the family, or as members of a religious community, or by occupying a place within a particular economic system, we are subject to rules, are limited in our choices, or must accommodate the interests and desires of others. This is life. What distinguishes the institutions of civil society is that they do not have at their disposal the same range of coercive sanctions that the state can ultimately draw upon to enforce its laws.

The second and perhaps even more important observation is that civil society is not just another way of regulating our behaviour. It is within civil society that we are cared for and receive support, love, encouragement, and assistance. This is particularly the function of institutions like the family and the church (or synagogue, temple, or mosque), and of countless clubs, associations, fraternal organizations, etc. And just as our social being must always endure regulation, we are rarely so self-sufficient that our welfare has no need of others.

We noted earlier Laver's observation that "we need government when community fails." In part, the tremendous growth of the state in the twentieth century has been a response to the inadequacy or decline or changing character of the institutions of civil society. Consider the great changes that the forces of modernization have made to that very central element of civil society—the family. The extended family of multiple generations living under one roof or in close proximity gave way to the norm of the nuclear family (two parents with children), and more recently to the common existence of one-parent households, same-sex partnered households, and other "non-traditional" families. Add to this the increasing commonality of divorce, of common-law unions, and of marriages producing fewer children or none at all and the overall trend has been a fragmentation (or "desegmentation") of "the family." When elderly family members can no longer rely on children or grandchildren to care for them in their declining years, the existence and level of pensions or income supplements become significant, as does the number of retirement homes or long-term care facilities. When parents cannot afford to withdraw from the labour force and have neither parents nor siblings who can look after their children, the availability and quality of child care becomes critical. Into the late nineteenth century, churches and benevolent organizations provided the bulk of assistance to the economically unfortunate or to those disabled in one way or another. Combine the decline of the church with the growth of egalitarian expectations that all have a right to at least a minimum standard of well-being, and the increasing inability of private charity to meet these demands is not surprising. On any number of fronts, the state, generally in the form of what has been called the **WELFARE STATE**, took up the slack. Apart from the large military budgets of some states (particularly the U.S.) in the Cold

War era, the major expenditures of governments since 1950 have been on health, education, and social assistance. This highlights that the activity of the state is not just about regulating our behaviour, but may also be about providing us with some very essential goods and services.

The relationship between the state and civil society is something we will touch upon throughout this text. At this point, though, two propositions are worth pondering. One, popularized by Robert Putnam in *Making Democracy Work: Civic Traditions in Modern Italy* (1994), is that a sustainable, healthy democracy requires a healthy civil society. Put generally—and we will discuss this in greater detail below in Chapters Three and Eleven—the idea here is that people bring to the political realm the habits, behaviours, values, and skills that they learn in the non-political spheres of life. Democracy is not simply about the existence of free elections; it is about working with others, being able to compromise, learning realistic expectations of efficacy (i.e., what one can expect to accomplish by participating), accepting defeat, seeing beyond one's own interests (narrowly defined), developing a sense of obligation to participate or take responsibility even when it is inconvenient or not "fun," etc. These life skills are often imparted through the activities and institutions of civil society, in school and church groups, clubs and associations, the workplace, the labour organization, the boardroom, and yes, in the family. Acquiring these skills and transferring them to the political realm are what make us citizens and not simply subjects (those who are ruled). Passive, solitary activities such as watching television or surfing the Net probably do very little to teach us how to be citizens.

The other, more controversial, proposition is that civil society no longer possesses the resources to ensure the well-being of all within the political community. Whether or not this is true is critical in light of the effort in the last two decades to scale back the welfare state created in the 30 years after World War II. In Chapter Seventeen we trace in greater detail the social and political reasons for the rise of the welfare state and the economic conditions that have caused governments of almost every political stripe to seek to bring about a smaller, more efficient state. Strong ideological currents have also fuelled these developments. But if one basis for the growth of the state in the middle part of this century was to make up for the inability of civil society to provide those things that we cannot provide for ourselves, such as education, health care, and social security, how well equipped is civil society to resume responsibility for these public goods? Many advocates of a smaller state see a larger role for the private economy here, and this is logical to the degree that the family and the church show little sign of recapturing their once central position in our society. Not surprisingly, then, we hear much more discussion about charter schools, private health care, and other market-based approaches to social policy.

To the degree that a market economy distributes wealth unevenly (see Chapter Seventeen), turning to market-based solutions for social policy issues enhances the possibility of an unequal access to (or access to an unequal quality of) social goods such as education, health care, and income security. Students need only reflect how reductions in the level of state funding for higher education have pushed up tuition fees and student debt levels. Public opinion sampling in Canada reveals that the same citizens who want smaller government and lower taxes continue to expect adequate state funding for health care and education.

The appropriate balance of roles for the state and for civil society, and the compatibility of such a balance (whatever it might turn out to be) with values such as equality, fairness, and democracy, will continue to inform political debate over the coming years.

The discussion so far—like much of what follows—has been about what transpires within entities such as the state, the nation, or the union of these two in the modern nation-state. The reason for this is simple: politics is about the regulation of our interactions with others. For most of us, our relationships are mostly with our fellow citizens. But in recent decades, the increasing **GLOBALIZATION** of economics, culture, and communications means that a growing proportion of what we do involves or affects the citizens of other states. More and more, politics must address issues that no longer respect the borders of nation-states.

There has long been a discipline within political science, called **INTERNATIONAL RELATIONS**, concerned with world politics, or what some call "geopolitics," in which the primary actors are countries. International relations has studied the conflicts between nation-states, the alliances they form, and their diplomatic and military manoeuvres—what is commonly known as "foreign policy." The study of international relations is no less

1.9
BEYOND THE STATE

authority
charismatic authority
civil society
coercion
community
consent
country
democracy
equality
globalization
government
ideas
institutions
international relations
jurisdiction
justice
legal-rational authority
legitimacy
market-based solutions
nation
nation-state
obligation
political process
politics
polity
popular sovereignty
power
processes
rights
rule of law
society
state
territory
totalitarianism
traditional authority
welfare state

important in today's world, with almost 200 countries, than it was a hundred years ago when there were less than 80.

In today's world, citizens expect their governments to tackle problems that do not recognize borders, on topics from the economy to the environment, world health, regulation of the Internet, and the preservation of human rights. This means that the modern state must be concerned not just about what happens within its territory, but also about how its own policies affect the well-being and activities of its citizens in the wider world. Similarly, decisions taken abroad may have a local (i.e., domestic) impact. Will enacting tougher environmental protection laws increase the costs of goods and services for consumers or make it difficult for domestic firms to compete in the global marketplace? Will higher taxation rates cause companies to relocate to less restrictive regimes, or will they provide the state with the means to deliver good social programs and sound infrastructure, which in turn might attract investment from abroad?

In a world of freer trade, international finance, and multinational corporations, an increasing array of subjects invites response from multinational bodies, international organizations, or countries acting together. Internal conflicts that threaten to disrupt the global economy or send streams of refugees abroad cannot be regarded simply as civil wars. The state is *not* (as some would have it) becoming less relevant in the era of globalization, but as its challenges change, so, too, must its responses.

Interestingly, it might be argued that globalization will exert pressure on all countries to adopt at least formally democratic political systems. This poses the greatest challenge in those states where autocratic rulers show little inclination to surrender power. In newly democratized countries, where political practice and political culture have not been democratic, the immediate task is to consolidate popular sovereignty by developing the institutions and habits that make democracy work (see Chapter 11). In all democracies, even the most "advanced," the challenge is to ensure that citizens have the knowledge, the tools, and the will to keep government representative and accountable. In the age of globalization, democracy is threatened by the fact that our lives are increasingly shaped by forces, institutions, and actors over which or whom we have, at best, a very indirect measure of control.

This chapter has introduced some of the concepts and ideas most basic to the study of politics. What they have in common is a concern with the development and exercise of power and authority within the various kinds of community and society that humans inhabit. The foundational character of these ideas means that we will have occasion to refer to them again and again in the chapters that follow. Although the purpose of Chapter Two is to discuss different approaches within political science, a significant portion of that chapter will expand upon the relationship between the changing nature of human community and the emergence of the modern state as a product of that evolution. In Chapter Three, the particular character of liberal democracy, or what is sometimes called the politics of advanced industrial societies, will be situated within its historical context.

SOMETHING TO CONSIDER

What impact are continued modernization, globalization, and population growth likely to have on the nature of modern government? What are the implications for democracy?

1.10 CONCLUSION

REFERENCES AND SUGGESTED READING

Benn, S.I., and R.S. Peters. 1959. *Social Principles and the Democratic State*. London: Unwin.

Crick, Bernard. 1964. *In Defence of Politics*. New York: Penguin.

Danziger, James N. 1991. *Understanding the Political World*. New York: Addison-Wesley.

Johnson, Nevil. 1989. *The Limits of Political Science*. New York: Oxford University Press.

Laver, Michael. 1983. *Invitation to Politics*. Oxford: Basil Blackwell.

Ponton, Geoffrey, and Peter Gill. 1982. *Introduction to Politics*. Oxford: Basil Blackwell.

Putnam, Robert. 1994. *Making Democracy Work*. Princeton, N.J.: Princeton University Press.

Redekop, John, ed. 1983. *Approaches to Canadian Politics*, 2nd ed. Toronto: Prentice Hall.

Weber, Max. "Politics as a Vocation," in H.W. Gerth and C. Wright Mills, eds. 1958. *From Max Weber: Essays in Sociology*. New York: Oxford University Press.

2 methods and approaches

The exaggeration in saying that there are as many ways of doing political science as there are political scientists is only slight, particularly in an age that encourages and rewards specialization. The longer or more intensively one studies politics (or almost anything) the narrower the focus becomes, the more esoteric the subject matter, and the more technical the language and procedures. One virtue of textbooks is that they must necessarily remain more general and more accessible for readers who have yet (indeed, may never choose) to specialize. This chapter is an introduction to some of the principal variations in the way political science is studied, primarily so that students will have a background to some of the material that is presented in the remainder of this text, and to introduce the rich diversity of political literature that is available.

It is perhaps useful to keep in mind that while political scientists (like other academics, intellectuals, or scientists) often engage in primary research of one kind or another, students of political science (and often their teachers, too) are mainly involved in *reading about* the primary research done by others. Chances are that you or I will not perform a sophisticated study of voting behaviour, or a cross-national comparison of electoral systems, but read instead the published reports of such studies or comparisons. To be able to understand and critically assess the work of political scientists it is useful to know something about their methods and approaches, even if they are not methods and approaches we directly employ ourselves.

We can meet Bismarck half way and say that the study of politics is *both* a science *and* an art, because it is a discipline with two dimensions: the **NORMATIVE** and the **EMPIRICAL** (see Figure

2.1 INTRODUCTION

"Politics is not a science ... but an art."—Bismark, 1884

2.1 Introduction
2.2 Politics as Philosophy
2.3 Politics as Social Science
2.4 Units of Analysis: Individual, Group, or Class?
2.5 Politics as Anthropology
2.6 Authority and Power Revisited
2.7 Politics and the Study of Politics

41

2.1). This is one basis on which political study has diverged in its methods, political philosophy in particular focusing upon the normative dimension of the subject matter, political science being more directed to the empirical puzzles of political reality. This distinction begs further explanation.

**2.2
POLITICS AS
PHILOSOPHY**

A century ago, to study politics involved specializing in a branch of moral philosophy, a method of study reflecting the normative dimension of politics. Moral philosophy presents systematic reasoning and argumentation about *what ought to be*: the normative dimension of politics engages beliefs about what ought to be the case regarding political objects and interests. This does not mean that all moral theory is political, nor even that the normative dimension of politics requires us to become moral philosophers. Nonetheless, the study of politics has traditionally engaged questions that were once studied under the heading of moral philosophy. Many of the authors studied by students of politics are philosophers who dealt with politics in their investigation of moral theory (see below, Chapter Four). This close association of politics with normative discourse is not a historical accident or a matter of preference, but an inescapable feature of the study of politics.

Normative discourse involves critical, rational debate about the ends of human life, viewed as goals or states of being to which humans (ought to) aspire, and about the means of achieving such goals. Statements or propositions about the end(s) of human life are often based on appeals to our understanding of what human nature is, should be, or could become. In this way, claims about the good life seek a foundation in our experience of human life, or in expectations of what that experience suggests is possible in human life. Our beliefs about the lives humans ought to lead and about human nature carry implications for the politics of the societies in which we live, and for the policies of governments exercising authority.

Aristotle is famous for the proposition that man is a specifically political animal. The word "political" is derived from the Greek word *polis*, which refers to the community in which one is a citizen. In saying that man is a political animal, Aristotle may be saying simply that all humans live and take part in the life of a community, that this is what it means to be human. But it is also possible that Aristotle means that man is an animal governed not by instinct, but by politics. That is, our actions are not simply responses to ingrained biological imperatives, but are consciously regulated. This is a consequence of saying that humans have free will, or the ability to choose, or, in more technical language, that human behaviour is intentional. Not only does this mean that our actions are deliberate, but also that the regulation or prohibition of actions is deliberate, done by means of rules or laws rather than automatic instinctive checks. Rules or laws are specifically human devices that presuppose matters such as language and culture—in short, the community life that humans share. They also represent decisions made by someone about what is or is not to be done. When we discuss, debate, or deliberate about such decisions, we engage in normative discourse. Since politics is concerned with decisions to regulate human behaviour, it is inescapably normative in character. As discussed earlier, many contemporary states are societies containing more than one community, or are no longer communities in any meaningful sense: that is, there is no longer a shared set of values, norms, or beliefs that unites all members. In these societies, normative debate is necessarily persistent, as various groups, communities, and sub-cultures attempt to influence decision-makers about the right choices for society at large.

Whatever else they do, governments make decisions and enforce them upon populations; in this way governments address ends. Certain views about the good life for man, or about what it means to be human, are logically tied to certain kinds of government, or to specific government policies. For example, the belief that all individuals are basically rational, self-interested actors more readily disposed us towards democratic government than the belief that there is a natural hierarchy of rulers and ruled. Similarly, the priority attached to certain views of liberty or security, respectively, may lead to opposition to or support for gun-control policies. The reverse is also true: certain actions or decisions by governments presuppose beliefs about the good life (mandatory childhood education) or about what is proper for humans (anti-discrimination legislation). Just as our actions always have consequences, regardless of whether or not we foresee those consequences, government decisions, because they are binding on a society, entail a view about what is proper for the members of that community. Government decisions always have normative consequences, that is, they always affect the kinds of ends humans may pursue, and what kinds of human life it is possible to have. Politics (and society) is inevitably about norms, and about

EMPIRICAL VERSUS NORMATIVE

EMPIRICAL refers to the data of experience, meaning that which happens and is subject to observation and sometimes to measurement. For example, the existence and operation of institutions; the behaviour of political actors; the existence of ideas, attitudes, and values; all this is empirical, and the empirical dimension of political inquiry seeks to explain such phenomena.

NORMATIVE refers to beliefs we hold or judgements we make about what the political world should be like, or conversely, about how the existing political world falls short of that ideal. What is the good life for humans; the best kind of state or government; or the relative weight of equality and liberty in the scales of justice; these issues (and many others) are normative, and normative discourse seeks to justify a state of affairs, or present a case for its reform.

The distinction between empirical and normative should not be mistakenly identified with the distinction between fact and theory. *Both* empirical and normative inquiry are theory-laden, and necessarily so. To deal with "just the facts" in the absence of theory would be like trying to talk about objects or people without using names for them. Facts may be the raw data of experience, but to describe, record, or make sense of facts (phenomena), we need concepts, and a theory is an organized body of concepts. All knowledge has an essentially theoretical component.

FIGURE 2.1

normative outcomes, which require selection by some means from the normative options available.

To be sure, not everyone will want to study the body of normative discourse that comprises political philosophy from Plato to the philosophers of our own day. It is nonetheless important that all students of political science understand the normative character of their discipline *and* have a basic familiarity with the normative problems and issues that underlie the institutions and structures of government today. Consider terms like liberty, equality, rights, sovereignty, justice, democracy, the common good, opportunity, fairness, welfare, authority, and power. It is hard to imagine a sustained political discussion or inquiry which did not make reference at some point to one or more of these terms. They are so imbedded in our understanding of political life that even those who have never studied politics use at least some of them quite regularly. Each has a normative component: it involves beliefs about what is right or proper, and each is difficult to use without implying a statement about what is right or proper. Most certainly, when we wish to make a statement about what ought to be, we will use one or more of these terms or words like them. It is also the case that each of these terms has several possible meanings. For one person, freedom may mean the *absence* of a law or restraint upon their behaviour. For another, freedom may very well *require* the presence of laws and restraints for protection from other individuals. For a third person, freedom may mean participating in making the laws to which one is subject. Accordingly, when a political candidate promises to reform government on behalf of individual freedom, we may well want to ask "What kind of freedom or whose freedom do you mean?"

The ubiquity of normative terms—the impossibility of avoiding them—and their flexibility mean that before we proceed very far we have to clarify or explain them. This means taking terms that in everyday use are very general, and making them more specific. Instead of ambiguity, we look for precise, definite meanings. When we become more specific about our understanding of these terms, we often find contradictions or inconsistencies. We might find, for example, that our understanding of liberty conflicts with our understanding of equality, or that we have defined justice in a way that tolerates certain situations we would normally regard as unjust. The rules of good reasoning and of clear communication ask us to try to resolve contradictions or remove inconsistency.

As political scientists, but as educated citizens, too, we use the critical faculties of our reason and the analytic skills they allow us to develop in order to increase our understanding of each other. We seek precision, coherence, and consistency in the use of normative terms like freedom or justice so that we will understand the normative outcomes involved in their use, whether this is to promote a political position, advance a policy decision, or propose legislation that will bind each of us. The better we understand what is at stake in these matters, the better we will be able to judge if they are consistent with our interests, or with our conception of "what ought to be."

As a science, political inquiry is concerned with explaining the objects of political experience. This empirical dimension has increasingly displaced political philosophy in the twentieth century for two reasons: one negative and one positive. The negative reason was an increasing dissatisfaction with the ability of a philosophical approach to investigate adequately the increasingly complex political world, especially with the development of democratic politics and the growth of the modern, bureaucratic state. The positive reason for a scientific approach to politics was the development of methods patterned after the natural sciences and with much borrowing from other social scientific disciplines such as psychology, sociology, anthropology, and economics (none of which existed as recognizably separate disciplines prior to the nineteenth century).

Controversy has often accompanied the adaptation of scientific methodology to political inquiry, but that is a debate largely beyond the scope of this text. Whatever the methods employed, students of political science should be concerned with acquiring an accurate representation and understanding of political reality. The clearest goal of the *scientific* approach to politics is to be able to make accurate observations and reliable generalizations about political phenomena. The most enthusiastic supporters of a scientific approach to politics have argued that to some extent these phenomena are subject to laws, rather as physical phenomena are subject to the laws of thermodynamics or gravity. Politics is about human behaviour, though, and social phenomena are often overdetermined; that is to say, there is such a multiplicity of causes involved in the creation of each outcome, and it is so difficult (if not impossible) to isolate causal factors, that very few law-like

2.3
POLITICS AS
SOCIAL SCIENCE

generalizations have been successfully demonstrated. Nonetheless, positing a more modest goal, such as explaining political phenomena through the identification of causal tendencies, is reasonable and realistic. Empirical accuracy remains central to good political study, and in this sense politics is legitimately a social *science*, even if it is not an exact or "hard" science like the natural sciences.

Because politics is normative, and because it often involves a clash of competing interests, it is controversial, which sometimes leads to heated discussions or emotional discourse. Consequently, there is an understandable tendency—reinforced by liberal ideas of tolerance—to urge respect for the opinions of others and in this way defuse the potentially explosive atmosphere of politics (like religion or ethics). One virtue of remembering that politics is a social science is the reminder that there is a dimension to the political world that is not merely "opinion," that there *are* matters here about which it is possible to be right or wrong. The functioning of electoral systems, or the review of legislation by the courts, or the role of bureaucrats in implementing public policy— these are not just matters about which one can have opinions; they are also subjects about which one has knowledge, or is ignorant. And most citizens are probably as ignorant about vast areas of the political world as they are about the activity of enzymes or the relationships between sub-atomic particles. By analogy, just as we understand that the weather is ultimately explicable in terms of basic laws of chemistry and physics, so too the outcomes and effects of government are explicable in terms of the behaviour of political actors and the functioning of institutions.

A post-war push for a more rigorously scientific approach to politics culminated in the 1960s in behaviourism or **BEHAVIOURALISM**. This was a movement for a **"VALUE-FREE"** political **INQUIRY** patterned on the natural sciences, and focusing on the observation and measurement of political behaviour of individuals, in the hope of generating law-like generalizations that would lead to successful predictions about future behaviour. Like many movements, behaviouralism probably went too far in some respects, and may have been misguided in others. It was criticized for being too abstract and for being empirically conservative. Certainly, it became apparent that a "value-free" political science is not possible (let alone desirable) given the ineradicably normative character of the subject matter, and of its investigators. Behaviouralism in the strictest sense focused attention on individuals and their behaviours at the expense of institutions or social

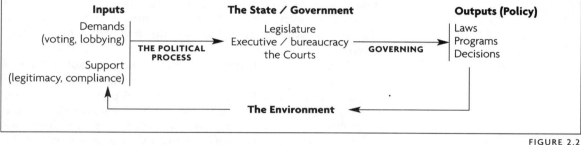

FIGURE 2.2

processes, and perhaps for this reason flourished in sub-disciplines such as political psychology and political sociology. Nonetheless, the behavioural approach made political scientists self-conscious about scientific methodology, developed a considerable body of empirical theory (including the enduring notion of "the political system"—see Figure 2.2) and encouraged interdisciplinary linkages with other social sciences. To some degree, when the popularity of behaviouralism waned, so, too, did the methodological self-consciousness of politics as a social science.

It would be a mistake, though, to assume that behaviouralism is the only empirical approach to political inquiry; an alternative method of considerable popularity is comparative analysis. Comparison is an important feature of any analysis we perform, and in politics the possible objects of comparison—from the political systems of nation-states, to specific institutions like legislatures, to political actors like prime ministers or presidents, to ideologies or popular values—are countless. The challenges of comparative politics are several. One is to make sure that we are comparing comparables. For example, we usually compare political systems of countries in the developed world with the systems of other countries in the developed world rather than with developing world systems. It usually makes sense to compare parliamentary democracies with each other rather than with presidential democracies, and to compare democracies with each other rather than with totalitarian or authoritarian regimes. A second challenge is to separate the significant from the trivial. It is not enough to identify similarities and differences: Which similarities matter? What are the differences that make a difference? Third, comparative politics ought to move beyond **DESCRIPTION** of differences and similarities, to their **EXPLANATION**. It is much more satisfactory if, in addition to telling me that coalitions survive longer in some countries than in others, you can identify some features or factors that account for this difference. If we change the constitutional provisions concerning the legislature or the electoral system in a given country, can we have any reasonable expectation as to what the outcome(s) might be for the political system of that country?

As implied, comparative politics is only fruitful if there is something in common between the objects under examination; if they are completely different, then the comparison will be not only brief, but uninteresting. Most comparativists operate on the assumption (a) that a political system performs specific functions within a society or community, (b) that this is generally true of the political systems of all societies, and (c) that the more societies are alike the more similar their political systems and the functions these systems perform will be. We will talk below at greater length about the kinds of functions governments and states are seen to play within societies, and about the way institutions provide the structures to perform these functions. It is also clear, though, that every political system, every society, is in significant respects unique, respects often bound up with a history, a culture, traditions, and customs. For this reason, part of the politics of each society will resist explanation in terms of functions or institutions common to other societies, and will be explained better in terms of the mix of cultural factors unique to that society.

Ultimately, the goal of politics studied as a social science is to sort out the linkages explainable in terms of relationships between variables, and where such causal tendencies can be plausibly expected, to identify, measure, and explain them. **INDEPENDENT VARIABLES** are causes, and **DEPENDENT VARIABLES** are effects. The behaviourist investigates voting behaviour (dependent variable) by looking at the relationships between individuals' activity (voting) and their income, or education, or parents' party affiliation, etc. (independent variables). The comparativist explores the length of time between elections (dependent variable) in various democracies by looking for patterns or correlations with the type of constitution, or party system, or electoral system, etc. (independent variables). The ability to find such correlations or relationships between variables makes political inquiry scientific;

that these correlations are better described as tendencies than laws underlines an important difference between social sciences like politics or sociology, and natural sciences like physics or chemistry. In short, political scientists look for generalizations that explain more or less accurately regularities within the political world, and try to specify the conditions that make these generalizations more or less true.

The philosophical versus scientific distinction is one way of explaining the diversity of approaches to political inquiry (and students should not conclude that one must necessarily choose between these; one can be philosophical *and* scientific). Another basis for divergence (within either the normative or the empirical camp) is differing perspectives about what constitutes the most basic unit of analysis. What is our starting point? What is the most fundamental level on which we should focus? There are many possible answers to this question, and we will discuss briefly only a few of the most influential approaches political scientists have taken.

2.4
UNITS OF ANALYSIS: INDIVIDUAL, GROUP, OR CLASS?

Atomism (politics is about the activity of individuals)

An extremely popular and durable approach to studying politics has been to treat the individual as the fundamental unit; in fact there have been several different approaches based on the individual as a political atom. Classical liberalism, in both its political and economic dimensions, began with and proceeded on the basis of individuals as rational, self-interested actors seeking to maximize their position (economic or political) within society. We will have more to say about liberalism as a philosophy and ideology in Section II, but one interesting application of economic liberalism to the political sphere has been the development of **PUBLIC CHOICE** theory. Public choice theory combines the economic liberal assumption of the individual as a rational, self-interested maximizer with insights from game theory to explain how different types of political actors seek to improve their position within various institutional settings, by bargaining and trading with the various resources at their disposal. Citizens who desire particular public policies offer to (or withhold from) politicians the resources they control (votes, campaign contributions, civil obedience) in return

THE RESEARCH PROCESS

Insofar as empirical research attempts to uncover relationships between variables, the research process involves several components and stages. We begin with **theory**, which states our beliefs and current knowledge about the phenomena in which we are interested by means of a concise, logical organization of concepts. On the basis of our theory we generate **propositions**, conditional statements predicting relationships between our concepts (or variables); for example: political participation should be higher in countries where non-voting is penalized. Propositions, in turn, lead to **hypotheses**, which are propositions more concretely stated as guesses about the correlations we will find between variables; e.g. as income and level of education increase, the rate of political participation will rise. The next challenge is to **operationalize** the hypothesis; how will we measure income, how define political participation? These are practical questions of utmost importance if we are to generate reliable findings. **Research design** indicates the process of deciding what operations will best test our hypotheses and deliver observations for analysis; this may involve survey of opinions, a search of databases, a newspaper content analysis, and so on. Performing these operations then will enable us to record our **observations** or **data**, which in turn tell us little or nothing without further **analysis**, which is how we identify the relationships between variables revealed by our data. To the degree that our hypotheses have been confirmed or refuted, we now engage in reflection about what this reveals about our propositions and theory. Our research is successful if it allows us to refine our theory (improve our current knowledge about phenomena), and this in turn should allow us to generate new propositions and hypotheses as the basis for further research.

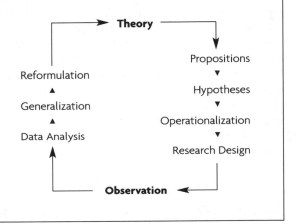

FIGURE 2.3

for their desired policies. Bureaucrats who seek increases in programs and program dollars (which elected politicians control), bargain with the resources they control, such as information and expertise (which elected politicians need). Politicians want favourable publicity; journalists want inside stories or advance notice of events: the possibility of a mutually beneficial exchange is clear.

Not all individualist approaches to politics stress the competitive, acquisitive dimensions of human nature. An influential treatment of public policy in Canada has been Ron Manzer's application of Abraham Maslow's categories of human need to a discussion of political goods (see Figure 2.4). (This is also a good example of the interdisciplinary possibilities of social science; Maslow's field was not politics but psychology.) Maslow argued that our needs (which are properties of our being as an individual) can be understood as hierarchically organized. It is only as each level of needs is satisfied that we are able to move successfully to the next level. If our basic physiological needs for food and shelter are not adequately satisfied, we will remain focused upon their attainment, and thus be unable or unlikely to progress to a proper attention to our safety or belongingness needs. At Maslow's highest level are self-actualizers, who seem to realize an ideal character of autonomous individuality (Maslow believed that, in fact, only a small proportion of us are capable of attaining this level). Manzer has defined a political good as "a condition we have some reason to regard as agreeable, beneficial, commendable, right, proper, or morally excellent," and that "represents a public virtue realizable at least in part through collective action" (1974: 8). In other words, what is good here is grounded in our nature as individuals, but requires our collective or co-operative activity for realization; we cannot provide these goods for ourselves but depend, to at least some degree, upon the resources of the community (or the state). In a relatively brief space Manzer presents a convincing association of each of Maslow's needs categories with a traditional political good, and in doing so generates (in his own words) "a useful framework for analyzing the purposes and assessing the results of the political arrangements in a community" (ibid., 7). Neither Maslow's theory of needs nor Manzer's discussion of political goods is unproblematic, but together they provide a fruitful starting point for an evaluation and comparison of political systems and their outputs.

MASLOW'S CATEGORIES OF NEEDS	MANZER'S POLITICAL GOODS
self-actualization	liberty
▲	
esteem	equality
▲	
belongingness	fraternity
▲	
safety	security
▲	
physiological	welfare

FIGURE 2.4

Class Analysis (politics is about the class struggle)

One criticism of atomism is that it is too abstract, that it assumes an equality between individuals that is belied by the very real structures within society that determine advantage and opportunity. Central among these structures is **CLASS**, the existence of *hierarchical stratification that implies differential access to scarce goods.* For some, then, class is the fundamental unit of analysis, because they believe that most often it is class that determines individuals' outcomes, not individuals who determine class. The most significant proponent of class analysis was Karl Marx, but one does not have to be a Marxist or seek the overthrow of the class structure to see class as a central variable. We will have more to say about class and about Marx in Chapter Five, and about classes in Chapter Sixteen.

Pluralism (politics is about the competition of groups)

A third position argues for neither individuals nor classes, but something intermediate: the group as the fundamental unit of analysis. Atomism may be too abstract, but the class model is guilty of abstraction in its own way, and certainly oversimplifies social reality (or so the pluralist argues). Individuals tend to act neither alone, nor as class-conscious workers or capitalists, but as members of any number of different, shifting groups. Some of these will be very much concerned with securing power and influence; some will not. But the point is that power will not be concentrated in the hands of one class, nor dispersed equally among all individuals. Which groups are privileged in terms of getting their way will depend on any number of factors and circumstances. Some individuals may belong to many (even competing or conflicting) groups, some may have little involvement at all, but it is only through their association with the organization, expertise, and information of the group that individuals have influence in society. Or so the pluralist argues. We will have more to say about pluralism and organized groups in Chapter Fourteen.

A couple of general observations are in order. These different perspectives on the fundamental unit of political analysis do not reject the units of their rivals: pluralists do not deny the existence of class, or of individuals apart from groups, and Marxists do not dispute the reality of individuals or groups. In each case the argument is simply that these other units are less significant, or are not at all significant in the final analysis. It is also interesting that while the dispute seems to be about the proper orientation of empirical research, it also reflects normative judgements. For the pluralist is not simply saying that it is a fruitful research strategy to focus on groups, but also that groups *should* be paramount. Similarly, it would be unthinkable for a Marxist to say, "Yes, ideally politics should be about the class struggle, but in contemporary society it makes more sense to explore the competition of groups for influence." The way we see the world is very often closely related to the way we think the world should be.

What are the implications of different approaches to the discipline? Must students choose one or another, and if so, what should guide their choice? I have opted for methodological **ECLECTICISM** on the view that there is something to be said for each of the methods (and others not considered to this point). Alternative methods persist for studying politics because each focuses on a different portion of the political world; each is valid but partial. In certain respects and situations, the focus should be on individuals; in other cases or for other questions, class, or group, or gender may well be more relevant.

The diversity of approaches to the study of politics also reflects the interdisciplinary nature of social science. In other words, the concepts and methods of any one discipline (such as economics, anthropology, psychology, or sociology) may be applied in another discipline (such as politics) to generate new insights. Classical economics is concerned with the activities of individuals in the market system. Political economy approaches to economics and sociology are more likely to focus on class. Psychology tends to begin with the conscious and unconscious formations of the individual mind; anthropology investigates small social wholes like the band or tribe. Each of these fields of study borrows and learns from the others. In the next section, for example, we will take a brief field trip into the realm of political anthropology.

The challenge is to put all the pieces together, drawing the insights from each methodological stream into one coherent whole. While this is not a task for the novice, it also suggests the virtue of remaining open to the possible contribution of each sub-field or sub-discipline to our knowledge of the political world. The closing of doors that specialization requires is best left to the graduate student or to post-graduate research.

Our final example illustrating the methodological diversity possible in studying politics is drawn from the field of political anthropology. Here the fundamental unit of analysis is the social whole, the society or community as an organic body, rather than its parts, as implied when the unit of analysis is the class, the group, or the individual. Anthropology is traditionally concerned with the investigation of societies today designated as pre-industrial, or pre-technological—basically societies at a level of development where stratification and differentiation are at least initially not present or remain less important.

Evidence from anthropology suggests that the less complex a society, or more precisely, the smaller and more cohesive the community, the less politics has to do with government, or with what we recognize as "the state." Anthropologists employ a typology to classify these pre-industrial political systems and, following Elman Service, typically use a scheme that differentiates

2.5
POLITICS AS
ANTHROPOLOGY

PRE-INDUSTRIAL SOCIETIES

BAND A small group of related people occupying a single region.

TRIBE A group of bands occupying a specific region, that speak a common language, share a common culture, and are integrated by some unifying factor.

CHIEFDOM A ranked society in which every member has a position in the hierarchy.

STATE In anthropology, a centralized political system with the power to coerce.
— Haviland, 1991: 530-37

FIGURE 2.5

among bands, tribes, chiefdoms, and states. Bands and tribes are regarded as uncentralized, egalitarian societies, while chiefdoms and states are centralized, inegalitarian societies (see Figure 2.5). We need to explore these distinctions more closely.

Bands are the smallest type of society, numbering usually less than two hundred individuals. They are characterized by a lack of specialization; the only division of labour is likely to be made on the basis of gender. Otherwise, the tasks of survival (e.g., hunting or locating water) are carried out collectively by band members. Typically, these hunting and gathering (foraging) societies have established a more or less stable equilibrium with their environment. Noteworthy is the nature of their politics. As Lewellen notes: "decision-making is usually a group enterprise and access to leadership positions is equally open to all males within a certain age range. Leadership, which temporarily shifts according to the situation, is based on the personal attributes of the individual and lacks any coercive power" (1992: 28). This last point is crucial: since there is no coercive power (i.e., no means of forcing individuals through physical punishment), all decisions must ultimately reflect a consensus. An individual who refuses to accept the consensus will face expulsion from the community, and insofar as survival requires a collective effort, exile carries with it the threat of death. More importantly, though, because individuals in such societies will not be able to conceive of life without or outside the community, they will be unlikely to refuse to accept its ways. Moreover, a common culture will reinforce the cohesion of the society: "the unity of the wider group is ... based on custom, tradition, and common values and symbols" (ibid., 27). The band provides a clear example of the homogenous, shared life that we indicate with the term community. Here we see in actual case the truth of Laver's point that where community is strong, government is superfluous. Decisions are the result of a consensus of the group, a consensus which may be preceded by considerable debate, or even conflict, but a consensus which the group must ultimately reach if it is to get on with the necessary tasks of survival. There is no need for a government separate from the group as a whole (nor are there resources to sustain one), and because authority is not permanently placed in the hands of one or a few, all members are generally equal in power or status. For this reason, bands are characterized as egalitarian (meaning marked by equality, an absence of strata or classes) and uncentralized (authority or power is diffused among the group).

54

The **TRIBE** is a society in which for practical reasons (such as defence against other people) bands are united into a larger group by means such as kinship. Tribal kinship systems vary tremendously, and are based not only on true consanguinity (blood relationships and descent from common ancestors) and affinity (relationships to a spouse's blood relatives) but also on hypothetical or even mythological consanguinity. For example, among tribes as diverse as the Haida of British Columbia or the Shona of Zimbabwe, one is related to all those in the clan with the same animal symbol (totem). Commonly, tribal peoples are agriculturalists, and the tribe coordinates or regulates a much larger population than the band. Central to both bands and tribes is the *dispersion of power and authority* throughout the community; the headman position, where it exists, often fulfils merely formal functions, perhaps as a symbolic focus for tribal unity, rather than operating as a government. Kottak notes that band leaders "are first among equals ... [and] have no means of enforcing their decisions," a feature that remains essentially true of tribes also (1991: 103, 105). Whatever authority the village or tribal leader has is a product of personal traits, and thus is not institutionalized. This means that such societies possess little means of enforcing decisions that do not have the common consent of community members. As we noted abstractly above concerning communities, we find empirically in bands and tribes that there is often little to distinguish politics from the general life of the community.

Whatever power we find in bands and tribes is temporary, and authority is generally dispersed throughout the community/ society. With **CHIEFDOMS** and **STATES**, power becomes a permanent feature of the social structure, through the centralization of authority in the hands of one or a few individuals, and through its institutionalization in political offices. Kottak defines an **OFFICE** as "a permanent position which must be refilled when it is vacated by death or retirement" (1991: 125). Power and/or authority is now a property of a position, independent of whoever holds that position. It is here that we can speak for the first time about the existence of government. A question that intrigues anthropologists is why peoples exchange egalitarian, uncentralized social forms for the centralized, inegalitarian chiefdom and state. While virtually all agree that there is an evolutionary process at work here, just what accounts for that evolution has received different explanations or emphasis. It is clear, though, that political centralization or specialization accompanies or is required by a variety of other social changes:

EGALITARIAN AND HIERARCHICAL SOCIETIES

	DECENTRALIZED EGALITARIAN		CENTRALIZED HIERARCHICAL	
Type	Band	Tribe	Chiefdom	State
Mode of Subsistence	foraging		agriculturalist	
Means of Regulation	consensus	persuasion	redistribution	coercion
Political Office	informal		initial specialization	permanent bureaucracy
Social Strata	none		rank differentiation	class/caste stratification
Economic Distribution	reciprocity		redistribution	market exchange
Population	⟶ increasing size and density ⟶			

FIGURE 2.6

- greater population density
- stratification by rank or class
- new productive technology
- specialized social and occupational roles
- economics based on centralized redistribution.

In other words, where the state emerges, society has become larger, inequality has become a regular feature of the social structure, a division of labour has been employed, and the tasks of production have become more individual and specialized. Redistribution of products reflects these changes, and can serve a variety of purposes—from stimulating production, to making scarce products available to all, to guarding against famine. This redistributive function, missing from regulation in earlier social forms, is one reason for the centralization of political authority in chiefdoms and states, but there is also a crucial difference in how each of these societies uses redistribution.

The chiefdom seems to be a transitional stage on the route from tribes to states, and a close look at the chiefdom demonstrates just how significant a transition it is. In chiefdoms, leadership (which can now be identified as the office of chief) is usually vested in an individual, and is typically hereditary. The power of the chief comes from control of economic resources such as land or goods, or from leadership of a military force.

Normally, though, enforcement of decisions is dependent on the ability of the chief to acquire loyalty through granting goods and benefits to individuals. The egalitarian character of earlier societies is compromised not only by the concentration of public authority, but also by a system of ranking, generally on the basis of kinship or lineage: "Every individual is ranked according to membership in a descent group: those closer to the chief's lineage will be higher on the scale and receive the deference of all those below" (Lewellen, 1992: 37). While the equality of the tribe or band has been eroded, there is as yet no sharp distinction between elites and non-elites in the chiefdom. While this inequality is manifested in a differential access to resources, as Kottak points out, "even the lowest-ranking person in a chiefdom was still the chief's relative. In such a kin-based context, everyone, even a chief, had to share with his or her relatives" (1991: 126).

In the move from tribe to chiefdom, decision-making power and the authority that enforces decisions cease to be exercised by the community as a whole, and are placed instead in the hands of one or a few. In this society the offices of government appear to be the personal property of those who in fact occupy them. The further transition to the state brings a **DEPERSONALIZATION** of this power, and an increase in the coercive resources that enforce decisions. Whereas the chief's ability to regulate was largely confined to withholding or bestowing valued goods upon citizens, the state is characterized by its ability to apply physical sanctions against those who do not obey decisions. This in turn requires the establishment of institutions or a bureaucracy to carry out these sanctions.

The first states appear to have emerged about 5,500 years ago, and this development involved an exchange of kinship networks for a "permanent administrative bureaucracy" (Lewellen, 1992: 47). With this sort of consideration in mind, Robert Carneiro (1970: 733) defines the state as follows: "an autonomous political unit encompassing many communities within its territory, having a centralized government with the power to collect taxes, draft men for work or war, and decree and enforce laws." These early, pre-industrial states are sometimes called **ARCHAIC** to distinguish them from modern industrial polities.

Three points should be made here. First, the existence of permanent institutions of government and the permanent staffing of these by individuals changes the nature of redistribution. In earlier chiefdoms, or tribal "big man" systems, what was collected from the people was largely returned to the people. By contrast, much of what the state collects may be kept to maintain the state.

KEY TERMS

analysis
anthropology
archaic
atomism
bands
behaviouralism
causal tendencies
chiefdoms
class
correlations
dependent variables
depersonalization
description
eclecticism
empirical
explanation
generalization
goods
groups
hypotheses
independent variables
individual
inputs
kinship
liberal democracy
needs
normative
observation
office
operationalize
outputs
philosophy
pluralism
propositions
public choice theory
research design
social science
states
systems theory
tribes
"value-free" inquiry

Second, the stratification of society increases as we move from chiefdom to state; kinship is replaced by social strata based on differential access to wealth, power, and social status. In short, the structures of inequality broaden and stiffen.

Third, increased social complexity necessitates a depersonalization of decision-making: "Because of the vast range of individual and class interests within a state, pressures and conflicts unknown in less complex societies necessitate some sort of rule of impersonal law, backed by physical sanctions, for the ongoing maintenance of the system" (Lewellen, 1992: 40-41). Haviland (1991: 544) confirms that this is a move from internalized controls ("beliefs ... so thoroughly ingrained that each person becomes personally responsible for his or her own good conduct") to sanctions or externalized controls, of which a prime example is law: "a social norm, the neglect or infraction of which is regularly met, in threat or in fact, by the application of physical force on the part of an individual or group possessing the socially recognized privilege of doing so." The authority that governs social life has been depersonalized, and there is a very good reason for this: social life itself has become depersonalized. The emergence of archaic states is in part a signal that societies have reached a stage where they can no longer be regulated solely by the mechanisms of community. The stratification and centralization that accompany the state are in turn evidence that what is held in common has diminished.

The state represents a real revolution in terms of social organization, a revolution that occurred independently in at least six different places: in Mesopotamia, Egypt, India, China, Peru, and Mexico. Theories explaining the emergence of the state vary from single-factor explanations such as Wittfogel's notion that states emerged to build, maintain, and regulate irrigation systems (1957), to multivariate explanations such as Carneiro's theory that the state originates as the product of environmental circumscription, population increase, and warfare (1970). We should keep in mind Kottak's observation that "people didn't choose but were *forced* to accept state organization" (1991: 133). After all, one might argue that in the earlier social forms, life was richer in terms of freedom, equality, and personal attachments. Nonetheless, over what may have been considerable periods of time the state emerged to deal with problems posed by population growth, the persistent encounter with other peoples, and increasing economic and technological complexity. Our intention has been to review various types of society that have organized human life: the most "advanced" in evolutionary terms, and the one which has come to predominate in the last two millennia, is the state. Although our concern during much of what follows will be with a specific kind of state, the modern **LIBERAL DEMOCRACY**, there are several general insights we can take from the anthropological record:

As societies become more complex, differentiated, populous, and technologically advanced, their political organizations become centralized, more divorced from other social roles and occupations, and correspondingly, more autonomous in their justifications.

As societies develop from band to state, they become *less* egalitarian and *less* participatory. That is to say, as population density increases, and as pressure on existing resources increases, political centralization also increases, and by the same token, popular input and control over decisions decrease.

As societies become more complex, the role of community (that is, the *common life* which individuals share and in which they participate) in social organization is diminished, and that of the state (or government) increases.

We began Chapter One with the observation that politics is in part inevitable because our lives are always intersecting with those of others. The anthropological record indicates that, as these intersections multiply and become more varied, the business of regulating and adjudicating them becomes increasingly specialized. As we move from band to state, and politics becomes differentiated from the rest of social life, we find that regulation has less to do with personal authority and more to do with impersonal power. This in turn gives rise to questions about justification, or what we described above as the problem of obligation.

The distinction between power and authority made in Chapter One is readily illustrated by the anthropological evidence presented above. The band is characterized by an absence of power and a dispersion of authority; that is, there are no institutional means by which some individuals force their will upon others; decisions reflect a necessary social consensus and in the end normally obtain the compliance of everyone. What distinguishes the state, at the other end of the evolutionary spectrum, is the creation of the institutional means by which individuals can be physically forced to perform or refrain from certain actions. Here there is power, and the state is often defined

2.6 AUTHORITY AND POWER REVISITED

REFERENCES AND SUGGESTED READING

Carneiro, R.L. 1970. "A Theory of the Origin of the State," *Science* 69: 733-38.

Dahl, Robert A. 1971. *Polyarchy: Participation and Opposition.* New Haven: Yale University Press.

——. 1991. *Modern Political Analysis*, 5th ed. Englewood Cliffs, NJ: Prentice Hall.

Easton, David. 1965. *A Systems Analysis of Political Life.* Chicago: University of Chicago Press.

——. 1971. *The Political System.* New York: Alfred Knopf.

Gellner, Ernest. 1985. *Relativism and the Social Sciences.* Cambridge: Cambridge University Press.

Hague, Rod, et al. 1992. *Comparative government. An Introduction*, 3rd ed. London: Macmillan.

Harris, Marvin. 1979. *Cultural Materialism: The Struggle for a Science of Culture.* New York: Random House.

Haviland, William A. 1991. *Anthropology*, 6th ed. Orlando, FL: Holt, Rinehart and Winston.

Kottak, Conrad Phillip. 1991. *Cultural Anthropology*, 5th ed. New York: McGraw-Hill.

Lasswell, Harold D. 1960. *Psychopathology and Politics.* New York: Viking Press.

as that which has a monopoly on legitimate coercion. This last term—"legitimate coercion"—may seem curious, because it suggests a mixture of both authority and power, but we argued above that the politics of any society which is more complex than bands or tribes is characterized by a mixture of authority and power. If the movement from band to state is the movement from dispersed authority to institutionalized power, then a central problem for states is how to minimize the power they must employ and maximize their authority among the population they administer.

We can also compare Weber's categories of legitimacy with the anthropological record. The type of authority prevailing most often in bands and tribes appears to be traditional, based on persisting customs and norms handed down from generation to generation. While it is not impossible for other forms of society to be governed by traditional authority, we expect bands and tribes to be particularly so characterized, given our observations of the nature of communities. As structures where individuals share a common set of values, beliefs, and practices, communities are often traditional. The life that is common to the community is transmitted across generations, and the conservative character of communities reinforces existing ways by appealing to the shared history and traditions of the people. The more a society is characterized by the specific features we have identified by the term community, the more likely it is that authority will rest on traditional legitimacy. Where we move to chiefdoms—societies where authority is concentrated in the hands of one individual—we will expect traditional authority to be supplemented, if not replaced, by appeals to charismatic obligation. That is to say, those who rule will claim to possess unique gifts that entitle them to their position. Finally, the depersonalization of power that accompanies the move to the state will be accompanied by the attempt to justify authority on the basis of the instruments used (i.e., the law) and the rules either governing their exercise or restraining those who exercise them (such as rules of succession in hereditary monarchies). Just as we characterize the evolution from band to state as a political response to increasingly complex societies, so too in the move from traditional to charismatic to legal-rational authority can we observe a corresponding shift in the grounds that confer legitimacy upon the government of society. We will return to this theme in the next chapter when we explore the historical underpinnings of liberal democracy.

In this chapter where we have had much to say about methods and approaches, it may be appropriate to remind students that the study of politics and the pursuit of politics are two different matters. University courses in political science are not where one learns how to become a politician, or how to win an election, or how to wield power or authority. The student whose interest in politics is *immediately* practical—wanting to *be* a politician or political strategist—is best directed to become politically active: to join a party, to work in a political campaign, to make political friends, allies, or contacts, and gain the experience that only comes from doing. There is no denying that the study of politics could be beneficial to someone seeking a political career. But this study will not by itself lead to such a career, nor will the desire to hold political office give one the aptitude for studying politics. The difference is that the study of politics should lead to an *understanding* of political institutions, processes, and behaviour, without providing a *training* in the specific activities that characterize the elected politician or the government official. Understanding something requires in some measure a degree of detachment from it. As political scientists we are observers or spectators, but as political partisans or candidates we are participants. It may well be that the perspective of the participant is important for our understanding of political activity, but it is also true that the interest the participant has in the outcome of political activity may blind him or her to important facts or considerations. As political scientists we often wish to adopt or acquire the perspective of the participant without actually becoming political actors whose view may be clouded by their own interests.

It is also true that this distinction is more easily made than maintained. The study (and teaching) of politics is in many ways itself a political activity, one that may have or seek to have some impact on the way power and authority are ultimately exercised. To put it another way, in theory, the study of politics is "disinterested" and political activity is "interested"; in practice, the study of politics often turns out to be "interested," too. Presumably, we engage in political activity to change the world in ways beneficial to ourselves or others, or to prevent others from changing the world in ways detrimental to ourselves or to others. In this way we have an "interest" in outcomes that change or maintain the status quo, and, insofar as each of us is likely to have a set of such interests, we are also likely to bring them to our study of politics.

2.7
POLITICS AND THE STUDY OF POLITICS

Lewellen, Ted C. 1992. *Political Anthropology: An Introduction*, 2nd ed. South Hadley, Mass.: Bergin & Garvey.

Lizot, Jacques. 1985. *Tales of the Yanomami*. Cambridge: Cambridge University Press.

Manzer, Ronald. 1974. *Canada: A Socio-Political Report*. Toronto: McGraw-Hill Ryerson.

Miliband, Ralph. 1973. *The State in Capitalist Society*. London: Quartet.

Parenti, Michael. 1978. *Power and the Powerless*. New York: St. Martin's Press.

Raphael, D.D. 1976. *Problems of Political Philosophy*, rev. ed. London: Macmillan.

Wittfogel, Karl. 1957. *Oriental Despotism: A Comparative Study of Total Power*. New Haven: Yale University Press.

Wiarda, Howard J. 1993. *Introduction to Comparative Politics*. Belmont, Calif.: Wadsworth.

The dilemma, then, is that the study of politics invites us to adopt the "impartial" standpoint of the spectator, while the practice of politics and our situation as social actors make inevitable reference to our interested characters. The challenge is to fashion a proper compromise between these two elements. One approach is to attempt the pursuit of a disinterested political discourse *to the degree this is possible*, recognizing in the attempt that there are limits to its feasibility. On the other hand, some discard the notion of disinterested analysis and simply pursue a frankly interested politics, in keeping with Karl Marx's dictum that "The philosophers have only *interpreted* the world, in various ways; the point, however, is to *change* it." The reply to Marx may well be that in order to change the world, one needs to understand it, and the goal of disinterested analysis is to minimize any distortion that our interested perspective provides to our view of what the world is. The counter-argument is that there is simply no disinterested perspective from which we can identify what the world is. Against this, in turn, one might observe the difficulty of adequately identifying our interest(s) in the absence of a realistic assessment of the world in which our interest(s) are situated. Like many debates in political science, this one is endless, but worth revisiting.

SOMETHING TO CONSIDER

Given the considerable difference between *the study* of politics and *engaging in political activity*, or following political events in the news, what are the pros and cons of including political education in the curriculum of all citizens?

Just how much political knowledge do citizens require to make informed decisions within a democracy?

---

3 the emergence of liberal democracy

Beliefs about what we may learn from history are often narrowly based on the notion that studying history will help us to avoid the repetition of past mistakes. We may benefit from our reflection on our past, though, by arriving at a clearer understanding of who and what we are. Individuals, social wholes, institutions, ideas, and processes all are outcomes of behaviour, actions, and circumstances; this seemingly obvious truth is too easily ignored or overlooked. In political science, much of what we study has been handed down from previous generations or eras, is the product of old wars or revolutions, or reflects bygone values or attitudes. To understand the history of something is not to justify it, but to explain it to ourselves better. This is as true of that institutional complex, the state, as it is of anything else. This chapter will discuss the emergence and development of the state, culminating in the modern state that is the focus of this text.

J.M. Roberts (1980) has argued that the dominant theme of human history in the last two thousand years has been the rise and fall of world domination by Western Europe. Although much of the history since World War II signals the relative decline of Western Europe, it is still true that political models and principles produced by European culture provide standards for most nations outside of the Islamic world. The point is not to suggest the superiority of European culture, but simply to note its historical dominance and the political legacy of that dominance; political history *has been* Eurocentric in some important ways that we cannot ignore without turning our backs on history.

European political history may be divided into three broadly defined periods—**CLASSICAL ANTIQUITY**, **MEDIEVAL SOCIETY**, and **LIBERAL MODERNITY** (see Figure 3.1)—and ultimately it is

3.1 INTRODUCTION

3.1   Introduction
3.2   Classical Antiquity
3.3   Feudal Society
3.4   The Reformation
3.5   The Enlightenment
3.6   The Market Economy
3.7   The Liberal Revolution
3.8   Liberal Democracy

63

WESTERN EUROPEAN POLITICAL HISTORY

	CLASSICAL ANTIQUITY 400 BC – 400 AD	MEDIEVAL AGE 400 – 1400	MODERNITY 1400 – ?
Form of Government	polis to empire	feudal fiefdom to nation state (absolute monarchy)	constitutional monarchy to representative government to liberal democracy
Central Moral-Political Concepts	virtue citizenship	natural law divine right	popular sovereignty individual rights
Economic Modes	slavery military agricultural	agrarian military commercial	commercial industrial market activity
Religion	pagan	Catholic Christianity	from Christian pluralism to secularism
Intellectual Approach	philosophical	scholastic	scientific

FIGURE 3.1

the passage from the second to the last of these that most interests us here. Contemporary Canadians are beneficiaries of a revolution that occurred for the most part between three and five hundred years ago. (With minor qualification, the same is true of the citizens of Great Britain, the United States, France, Germany, the Netherlands, Belgium, Switzerland, Austria, Italy, Norway, Sweden, Iceland, Denmark, New Zealand, Australia, and many other countries.) This revolution was the transformation from a medieval community to a liberal society, a multi-faceted transformation—economic, cultural, religious, scientific, even psychological. The *political* nature of that revolution is our primary concern here, but its significance may be easier to appreciate if we consider the periods that preceded this time of transformation.

3.2 CLASSICAL ANTIQUITY

Just as students a hundred years ago would have encountered the study of politics as a branch of moral philosophy, so too at that time an education without mastery of Greek or Latin would have been regarded as deficient. Ancient Greece and Rome were regarded as the epitome of classical civilization, although neither is one of the six sites where the state as a form of political organization emerged independently. Certainly European culture (the arts and sciences) flourished in these two civilizations to a degree

64

not seen in Europe for centuries after their demise, and if we often overlook the accomplishments of contemporaneous civilizations in Egypt or China or India while celebrating the achievements of Athens or Rome, it is in part out of ignorance, and in part because of the overwhelming impact of these latter on subsequent European history and culture, and thus on the political tradition we inhabit in the West. Much of our political vocabulary has its roots here, from terms like democracy, monarchy, dictatorship, republic, or citizen, to institutions like a Senate or Council, to the very word "politics" itself. Whatever the field, knowledge is almost always generated within a tradition, where meanings, methods, and even the very questions asked are transmitted across generations. It is a commonplace observation that all philosophy is merely footnotes to Plato; certainly most political discourse prior to the nineteenth century was heavily influenced by the ancient texts of Plato, Aristotle, Cicero, Seneca, and others. It is probably in the field of political philosophy, in the ways we think about politics and about humans as political animals, where the influence of classical antiquity remains strongest today. We will see some of this influence in Chapter Four on political philosophy, and in the discussion of democracy in Chapter Eleven. For now, two other points about classical antiquity are worth noting.

One is the absence of what we would recognize today as the nation-state. Politics in this period was either local or (relatively) global: the political unit was either the city-state like Athens or Sparta, or an empire, like that assembled by Alexander the Great or by Caesar Augustus. In the former case, it was possible for politics to be highly participatory, engaging the energies and attention (at least at times) of a considerable portion of the population. As was implicit in the anthropological record of the previous chapter, a participatory politics quickly runs into a limit of size; once the community has become too large, either in territory, or population, this kind of politics is no longer practical. In the empire, on the other hand, politics was not participatory (except in a limited sense, for limited periods, in the capital), but military. The organization, extent, and skill of Rome's armies kept Rome together, just as military defeat at the hands of the Goths and Vandals brought the empire to an end. Interestingly, what was missing in either case—city-state or empire—was an adequate professional bureaucracy (which, of course, is an advantage Chinese dynasties had over their European counterparts). Without it, the city-state could not expand beyond a certain size, except militarily. Empires could grow so enormous because they were primarily about military security, not about providing public or political goods to their enormous populations. Nation-states would not emerge in Western Europe until the end of the feudal period.

The other point of interest is the sheer diversity of political organizations and types of government in this period. Most of the terms we use to describe different forms or types of government have come to us from the classical period, and a primary theme in much political thought of that time is "what is the best form of state?" It is not just that there were, for example, so many Greek city-states that this inevitably entailed diversity, but that also within each **POLIS** there was often considerable upheaval as one form of government was replaced by another, whether peaceably or after violence. Not surprisingly, a big issue in this time was the question of stability, and closely related to this were more philosophical questions about legitimacy and obligation.

3.3
FEUDAL SOCIETY

The end of the Roman Empire (and the beginning of the medieval period) was brought about by the migration of several peoples from Eastern Europe and Central Asia. Nomadic warrior societies were pushed westward by other peoples behind them; these tribes eventually defeated the armies of an aging, decaying empire. Much of the politics and society of the medieval period reflects an uneasy marriage of tribal customs and traditional ways with imperial remnants, such as Roman law, and the Catholic Church. Pagan tribes were eventually converted to Christianity, while tribal customs and rules were incorporated into codified laws. The political product was something identified as **FEUDAL SOCIETY** or **FEUDALISM**.

Employing the anthropological categories presented earlier, we can describe feudal society as a product of the encounter of tribal chiefdoms with the remnants of the highly developed Roman state. In feudal society, authority was fragmented—a characteristic that marked the medieval period until late in its development. Tribes united for military purposes under a powerful chieftain or king would become dispersed upon settlement after victory. Authority would then be exercised by local nobles, whose position, initially at least, reflected military rank or prowess. Although there were attempts to reunite Western Europe by reconstituting the Roman Empire—most successfully under Charlemagne—it would be accurate to say that a medieval emperor was at most a "chief of chiefs" rather than someone who personally governed the "empire." This last point is important: medieval authority, reflecting its tribal roots, was largely personal.

The personal nature of authority in the medieval period is indicated by the dominance of traditional justifications. (Hereditary monarchy, a product of this period, is a classic example of the selection of leaders based on custom, tradition, and adherence to "accepted ways.") At the same time, there was considerable effort by leaders to secure claims to charismatic authority: the "divine right of kings" is a theory that claims leaders are anointed and justified by God in their exercise of power. The religious unification of Europe under Catholic Christianity meant that rulers were not only claiming justification under the same God, but that medieval politics often focused on the relationship between the state and the church, or between secular and ecclesiastical authority. Feudal society was subject to a dual authority—that of the secular state, and that of the Church. A central question at any time and often a primary source of conflict was the issue of the relationship between Church and state. For the most part, weak, fragmented political power was complemented by a universal Church exercising considerable authority in a variety of contexts. This contrast reflects another: governments were weak and fragmented because they ultimately rested more upon power than authority, but the physical ability of rulers to exercise power was limited by various factors, principally the absence of resources and the difficulty of transporting them quickly. The influence of the Church on the other hand reflected a universal authority grounded in a common religious creed, but often hampered by an absence of power. In this situation, rulers sought favour from the Church in order to enhance their legitimacy, while the Church often required the power of the local state in order to enforce authoritative decisions or policies. The desire of either church or state to have the upper hand or final word set the stage for many of the conflicts of medieval politics.

Feudal society was a collection of communities, very alike in certain respects, vastly different in others. Most individuals were peasants, engaged in subsistence agriculture and the performance of obligations to lord and to Church. In return, peasants received protection from the lord against assault or invasion, and hope for salvation through the mediation of the Church. These reciprocal obligations were an essential feature of feudal society, and the source of its own justification; while the preponderance of these obligations fell on the peasantry, their justification was held to be the common good of the community, for which the feudal lord was ultimately responsible. The mutual obligations between nobility and peasant mirrored the relationships between different levels of nobility; what the peasant owed to his local lord, the local lord owed to the duke or prince, who in turn was obliged to the king or emperor. Medieval society presented an **ORGANIC HIER-ARCHY**, hierarchical because of a structure of unequal resources and power, but organic in that the various components were linked by reciprocal obligations and duties. Power and authority also reflected this organic hierarchy. An emperor's power and authority would depend on his ability to coerce or influence the princes and kings, and would thus depend on their ability to coerce or influence the lesser nobility, and thus ultimately on their control of the peasantry—the final source of labour and production. Much of the medieval period is marked by struggles among the nobility to establish their positions within this hierarchy of claims and obligations, struggles usually settled by battle. Similarly, the laws promulgated by a king would extend only so far as his ability to enforce them, or as far as the willingness of his vassals to enforce them on his behalf. These vassals, in turn, would make and enforce their own laws to the extent of their ability. While in theory law might announce common standards for a kingdom, in practice, law would be as fragmented as political power, and on a local level reflect the traditional practices and customs of the community.

This was also a very rigid society, that is, one not characterized by social mobility. Social position, high or low, was inherited, and with social position came a set of obligations and rights specific to that rank or occupation. Feudal society represented and reinforced a web of connections between entrenched social positions. This was a durable form of living, lasting for centuries, yet accommodating development and change within. The rigidity and durability of feudal society also meant that when powerful forces of social change arose in the fifteenth and sixteenth centuries, they could not be reconciled with the structure of that society, but required a social and political revolution ushering in a radically different form of life.

Certainly it is possible to overstate the static, conservative character of feudal society, just as the generations who once thought of the medieval period as the Dark Ages tended to forget that the darkness was our own ignorance of what transpired during that time, not the character of life in those days. As historical scholarship has improved our knowledge of this time we recognize its rich cultural life—of which the Renaissance was the highest statement—and the often considerable social and political changes that transpired. Foremost among the latter was the development of **NATION-STATES** out of the plethora of feudal principalities, dukedoms, and baronetcies. This required a development and strengthening of real power in the hands of monarchs—"real" meaning the ability of monarchs to enforce their claims actually to rule in the face of challenges from subordinates or external rivals. As one might expect, the development of the nation-state and of absolute monarchy were often coincident, and were often accompanied by a corresponding decline in the power or influence of the lesser nobility. Needless to say, the aristocracy did not always submit to these changes willingly or without struggle, and the ability of monarchs to consolidate and make real their claim to rule varied from state to state. Germany and Italy, for example, were among the last of the large European nations to be effectively united into kingdoms (the first form of the modern European nation-state), something which continued to influence their politics well into this century.

The medieval period ended when various forces of social change (including the desire or need for the nation-state) became strong enough to dissolve the bonds that had held together the feudal structure. Sometimes change was gradual, and sometimes there were explosive developments; feudal society dissolved in nations at different times. For example, the transformation that was relatively gradual and complete in Britain by the end of the seventeenth century, exploded violently in France in 1789, was not complete in Germany until well into the nineteenth century, and came to Russia early in the twentieth century. Generally speaking, though, it is possible to identify three developments that were instrumental in the dissolution of feudal society and the emergence of its successor, liberal modernity: the Reformation, the Enlightenment, and the rise of the market economy. All three still exert considerable influence on contemporary Western culture.

The **REFORMATION** refers to the breakdown of the religious (and often cultural) dominance of the Catholic Church. It is usually dated from Martin Luther's rebellion in 1517, but this was only the first in a series of reactions against the practices and

3.4
THE REFORMATION

theology of the Roman Church. These rebellions established various Protestant sects, and in doing so produced widespread social unrest, including war between and within states. *Politically,* what matters is that the Reformation corroded the bonds of feudal society. The rise of Protestantism in the sixteenth, seventeenth, and eighteenth centuries shattered the unity of the religious life of Western Europe, and in doing so undermined the authority of one of its central institutions, the Catholic Church. Rulers who converted to one of the Protestant religions found this a useful way of establishing their own independence from the Church at Rome, and of shaping laws and practices free of ecclesiastical influence. Rulers of either confession found religion a useful pretence, or the basis of a duty, to go to war against rulers of the opposite conviction. But most immediately, for the ordinary individual, the establishment of reformed Christianity (which failed to become established in some nations, e.g., France, Spain, Italy) brought an increased measure of individual freedom; liberation from the authoritative obligations and duties imposed by the Catholic Church, and an increased emphasis on individual conscience and self-direction.

This last point concerning the impact of the Reformation on individuals should not be taken too far. There was an important theological difference between the Reformed churches and Roman Catholicism concerning the role to be played by the Church in the salvation of individuals; for Catholicism, the individual comes to God through the sacraments of the Church (hence the significance of being "excommunicated"), whereas Protestant theology stresses a more direct relationship between the individual and God—the institutional church on this latter view is important, but ultimately not essential. Notwithstanding this, the demands of a Reformed Church upon its members could often be just as severe or unbending as any Catholic doctrine (and for some Protestant sects, much more so). We should also note that the end of the Roman Church's monopoly on European Christianity did not immediately bring religious pluralism. In many cases the established (Catholic) church was simply replaced with another established (Protestant) church, as in England and the Scandinavian countries. For a considerable period of time, to be a Protestant in an officially Catholic country or a Catholic in an officially Protestant country was to guarantee discrimination, to invite persecution, or to risk death. From the perspective of our religiously pluralistic, (usually) tolerant society it is easy to forget or overlook just how questions of creed (i.e., theological belief) were burning political issues responsible for wars, civil war, and revolution.

Ｉf the Reformation was a revolution against the traditional (Catholic) Church, the **ENLIGHTENMENT** was a revolution against traditional philosophy and science, a movement that sought to understand the world and humanity on a new, more rational basis. Medieval philosophy and its accounts of natural scientific phenomena were marked by what is called Scholasticism. What this means is that education in the medieval period was provided, almost without exception, by men of the Church teaching in schools where the priesthood and nobility received their education. Moreover, and not surprisingly, medieval thought was concerned to give an account of the world that was consistent with Catholic theology. Given the Biblical account of creation, for example, the Church maintained that the earth was the centre of the universe, a teaching challenged by the Polish astronomer Nikolas Copernicus, whose observations led him to suggest that the planetary bodies revolved around the sun. Galileo, an Italian astronomer, conducted observations with a telescope, providing evidence to confirm Copernicus's theory. Under extreme pressure from the Church, Galileo was forced to recant his own findings.

It should not surprise us, perhaps, that the Enlightenment—a new, non-theological way of thinking—followed on the heels of the Reformation. But the Enlightenment was by no means confined to Protestant thinkers. Indeed, the Enlightenment flourished not only because the Church's influence waned, but also because the new explanations of the world could be applied practically, and be demonstrated as superior to traditional accounts. New ways of understanding led to new ways of doing, and where human practice confirmed these revelations, theology had to give way. The term "Enlightenment" covers several, often opposing approaches to understanding the world—e.g., idealism, empiricism, rationalism, utilitarianism, materialism. These approaches nonetheless had two particular themes in common. One was a "scientific" approach to understanding the world. Science bases explanation upon experience, in particular on the critically controlled experience that results from the development of an experimental methodology; indeed, critical reflection on experience was perhaps the kernel at the heart of the Enlightenment.

3.5
THE ENLIGHTENMENT

Second, and an offshoot of this emphasis on examination of experience, was the **SCEPTICISM** of the Enlightenment. By this, we mean the disposition to take nothing for granted, to question, probe, and challenge existing ways of thought in order to uncover and eliminate error, weakness, or inconsistency. All traditional theories or explanations, whether scientific, religious, political, or moral, were open to challenge—and in fact *were* challenged. The Enlightenment has been called the "Age of Reason," and this emphasis on the capacities of human rationality informs both the adoption of scientific methodology and the sceptical approach to all received doctrines. The fundamental premise of all Enlightenment thought is that human experience, whether in the natural world or in social life, is accessible to human reason and explicable in rational terms.

The Enlightenment had a profound impact on feudal society because it challenged all existing ways of living and the justifications offered for them. In the face of reason, one cannot justify political institutions by simply saying "that's the way it's always been"; the arrangements of society, like all others, are open to inspection on the grounds of their rationality. Understanding life rationally also carries with it the imperative to organize and conduct life rationally; in the context of traditional institutions this often had revolutionary implications. Many of our key political ideas—liberty, equality, popular sovereignty, the rule of law, rights, etc.—are products of the critical reflection on political experience conducted by Enlightenment thinkers. More immediately, the Enlightenment proposed that each individual has in his and her reason a capacity for reflecting on the world, for judging that world, and ultimately for changing it.

**3.6
THE MARKET
ECONOMY**

The Reformation and the Enlightenment were revolutions in the way in which humans thought and believed, revolutions that also had great impact on what people did and how they did it. By contrast, the growth of the market economy was a revolution in the organization of practical life that also transformed human culture. By a "market" we mean the exchange of goods, services, and labour in transactions between individuals. A market economy exists when economic activity is undertaken for the purpose of exchange in the market. Thus we can observe that feudal society had market activity—individual transactions of labour, goods, and services—but was not a market economy because most economic activity was for the purposes of immediate consumption or authoritative transfer (e.g., taxes to the landlord, or tithes to the church) rather than exchange. Feudal peasants engaged in market activity only on a limited basis, and only after other ends such as immediate consumption and the payment of feudal obligations had been met. (By contrast, imagine growing most of your own food, making your own cloth for garments, cutting or gathering wood for your fuel, etc.—these are examples of immediate consumption.) Markets need buyers as well as sellers, and feudal peasants generally had little or nothing to spend or trade in the marketplace. The consuming class consisted of the nobility and those wage labourers in the employ of the nobility, together a very small proportion of the population. Market activity in feudal society took place largely in towns or when travelling merchants came to the feudal manor/castle, and was limited principally to basic necessities that required craftsmanship (tools, utensils), or luxury articles imported from other places. Thus, markets existed throughout the feudal period, but were not the central focus of economic activity or production. About the sixteenth century, this began to change; a market economy could not develop without the erosion of feudal relations, and as the market economy grew, it in turn eroded what remained of feudal society.

A market economy has two fundamental requirements which feudal society could not fully meet: that economic production be undertaken for the purpose of exchange in the market, and that individuals obtain the goods they consume through purchases in the market. It was necessary, then, to transform the rural, self-sufficient production of feudal society into a predominantly urban market-oriented production. Ideally, even agricultural production would be reorganized on capitalist rather than traditional lines (farmers would own their own land and grow foodstuffs or livestock for sale rather than for immediate consumption). An emerging market thus challenged the very basis of feudal society—the relationship between lord and peasant. As the extent of market activity grew, it required the transformation or elimination of feudal institutions, practices, and structures. For example, production for the marketplace requires the ability to hire labourers to produce goods or commodities. To develop a market in labour requires displacing peasants from subsistence agriculture and paying them a wage for engaging their labour in some other form of production; to displace peasants from the land requires freeing them from feudal obligations to the lord and Church. As with the

Reformation and the Enlightenment, the growth of a market economy meant dissolving the bonds that held together feudal society and thus tied individuals to their place within this organic, traditional society.

As may now seem obvious, the Reformation, the Enlightenment, and the emergence of the market economy were not wholly separate events, but mutually reinforcing. It is difficult to imagine the growth of the market occurring as rapidly as it did without the social and cultural changes brought about by the other two revolutions. For example, in contrast to the emphasis placed by the Catholic Church upon the virtues of poverty and the potential sinfulness of riches, several variants of reformed Christianity regarded the accumulation of worldly goods as a sign of one's upright character. The development and expansion of the market required a moral revolution through which it could be seen as proper for ordinary individuals (non-nobles) to be concerned with the acquisition of wealth; the Reformation helped to accomplish this revolution. Likewise, the diminution of the power of the Church, generally a conservative institution, generally weakened resistance to social change. The Enlightenment was also of great practical importance to the economic transformation of Europe. The market economy could not have become so dominant without the development of processes of manufacture and the reorganization of social labour around production for the market. The practical side-effect of the new scientific rationalism of the Enlightenment was an explosion of technology, tangible in the inventions that sparked the **INDUSTRIAL REVOLUTION**. Science not only provided new ways of transforming raw materials and new kinds of goods, but a way of problem-solving that allowed for continual innovation, invention, and improvement on existing designs. Not coincidentally, those whose interests were served by the changes being brought about in society found in Enlightenment philosophy the concepts and arguments with which to justify the new, and undermine the traditional. The rising middle class (neither peasantry nor aristocracy, but business owners, land-owning entrepreneurs, etc.) created by the emerging market, was often quick to embrace the Reformation and the Enlightenment, recognizing in them ammunition for an assault on traditional privilege and rigid political structures.

I alluded above to a great transformation in Western Europe, an event or process to which most Western nations owe their political institutions and the central concepts of their political culture. This is the **LIBERAL REVOLUTION**, which marks the passage from medieval society to what we recognize as modernity. More specifically, we have seen that feudal society was eroded by tremendous social transformations, chief among them the Reformation, the Enlightenment, and the market economy. In place of an organic, hierarchical, traditional society these phenomena created an increasingly individualistic, fluid, pluralistic society in which reason and science replaced custom and divine intention as central standards by which policy and institutions could be evaluated. In contrast to a rigid order of entrenched social positions, the new society was premised on the liberation of individuals from arbitrary, traditional, involuntary bonds, and on the replacement of these with relationships of rational self-interest. Not surprisingly, this new society was not one to which feudal political institutions could be accommodated. Material pressures demanded new institutions, and the cultural changes we have examined undermined the traditional justifications of medieval authority. The liberal revolution is the political counterpart of the social transformations brought about by the Reformation, the Enlightenment, and a market economy. In addition to new ways of organizing religious life, new approaches to understanding the human and natural world, and new ways of organizing economic production, Western Europe undertook to reorganize its political life, to establish new institutions and structures of authority, and to justify them in ways consistent with the social changes that had taken place, and that were continuing to be at work. This new political order, in brief, is the product of what we are calling the liberal revolution.

We may use the term **REVOLUTION** in at least two senses. One indicates a radical (i.e., comprehensive) change or set of changes. Another describes a sudden event that brings about radical change. The liberal revolution should be understood in the former sense, because the radical change Europe underwent did not necessarily occur suddenly or violently, and sometimes took place gradually and (relatively) peacefully. Revolution in the second sense (a sudden series of events bringing radical change), is often the result of the failure to accommodate political institutions to a changing society or set of social values. The **FRENCH REVOLUTION** of 1789, perhaps the most striking example of a revolution in this dramatic sense, can be seen as such an eruption

**3.7
THE LIBERAL
REVOLUTION**

created by an intolerable tension between the old political order and the new social forces created by economic and cultural change. These most drastic revolutions are often the least surprising, because the need for change or the desire for change is so clearly evident to so many. What the English call the Glorious or **WHIG REVOLUTION** of 1688 was simply one of several dramatic changes in English life over the course of a century or more. In fact, the Whig revolution was only dramatic in that it replaced the ruling Stuart dynasty with a monarchic family (William and Mary of Orange) willing to acknowledge parliamentary supremacy (see Chapter Fourteen). This relatively bloodless transformation had very little immediate effect on the ordinary citizen because in many if not most respects England had already been transformed from feudal society into something else. In fact, we might go further and suggest that revolutions that are accomplished gradually, without violent disruption to a society and its citizens, are more likely to succeed in the long run.

Students might observe that neither Canada nor the United States has undergone a liberal revolution. The original British North American colonies were largely populated with immigrants from Britain who espoused modern values, concepts, and liberal institutions. The War of Independence arose from a conflict between relatively liberal colonies and an imperial administration under George III exercising an absolute authority towards the colonies. In fact, many Whig politicians in Britain supported the colonial cause. The **AMERICAN REVOLUTION** was the revolt of a society more modern and liberal against the remnants of medieval authority exercised by the monarch. As future monarchs left colonial policy to Parliament, liberal self-government came to colonies such as Canada and Australia peacefully and gradually. In the colony of Quebec, which had been settled along quasi-feudal lines by the French, the British actually reinforced existing structures of authority—the Church and the seigneurs—with the Quebec Act (1774). The so-called Quiet Revolution of the 1960s in Quebec may in some respects be seen as the belated arrival of the liberal revolution for this francophone society. In this case modern liberal political structures existed, but social and cultural changes suppressed by established interests finally were unleashed.

In short, the liberal revolution is the political restructuring that accompanies a transformation from a traditional, agrarian, organic society to a rational, market-oriented, pluralist society. It is a stage through which various societies have passed at different times, depending upon their history, culture, and prevailing conditions. It is by no means obvious that every society *must* undergo such a transformation, but it is common to all so-called "Western" nations. Such a transformation is behind the development of modern notions of legal-rational authority, and such central normative concepts as justice and democracy. It also has informed the understanding of state and government indicated above. The liberal revolution stands in the background of the constitutional systems or governmental institutions we examine in Section III, and indeed is presupposed by our discussion of the modern state throughout this book.

3.8
LIBERAL DEMOCRACY

The liberal revolution created a new form or style of government, in some cases dramatically redesigning the institutions of state (as in France), in other cases changing the rules and conventions that determine how existing institutions function (as in England). In the former instance, government by a monarch and noble-born aristocracy was rejected for a **REPUBLICAN** form of government, a republic being a nation of citizens equal in political rank and status (at least in theory, if not practice). In the latter case, the monarchy was retained, but its power diminished (as it would continue to be reduced). In either instance, the common theme is the **DEPERSONALIZATION** of authority and power. No longer was the power of the state to be seen (as it was in feudal times) as a possession or right of the individuals (or families) wielding it, but rather as something exercised on behalf of "the people." The essentially "liberal" idea at the core of the liberal revolution was that *the power and authority of government exist for the sake of the interests of the individuals governed* (an idea explored more systematically in Section II). The "rule of men" was to be replaced with the "rule of law" (see also Chapter Seventeen). Reflecting its connection with the Enlightenment, the liberal revolution was about replacing arbitrary, unpredictable, personal power with rational, predictable, impersonal authority. One device for realizing these possibilities is a constitution, and as important or more so, is the commitment to **CONSTITUTIONALISM**: an acceptance that the constitution places limits on the way power or authority can be exercised within the state. This distinction is not academic; there have been many examples of states whose constitutions the political authorities have simply suspended or set aside whenever it became expedient to do so. Liberal constitutions are designed to protect individual citizens from the possibility of an arbitrary, absolute authority by placing roadblocks in the way of the emergence of such a power. The nature of these roadblocks, typically achieved through institutional relationships such as those imbedded in responsible government (parliamentary systems), or checks and balances (the American constitution), or judicial independence, or entrenched individual rights, will be examined in greater detail below (see especially Section III).

It is worth stressing, though, that the liberal revolution was not initially democratic. The modern state of Western Europe and its colonies was liberal first, and only later democratic, and when it became democratic, this was usually through a series of gradual, cautious expansions of the class of those with political standing. With the exception of the United States, a typical pattern for Western democracies was an evolution from responsible government to representative government to liberal democracy. What we would today recognize as democracy did not come about in the first group of liberal societies until the very close of the nineteenth century and the first two decades of the twentieth. Another "wave of democratization," as S. Huntington has described it, occurred after the end of World War II, again in liberal industrial societies. A third wave began in 1974, and the nature of the historical ebbs and flows will be discussed in greater detail in Chapter Eleven. The significance to note here is that liberal democracy has been the product of considerable development within the liberal nation-states that resulted from the demise of feudal society, a development that took a long time to produce democracy. This is one point of considerable difference between the beginning of liberal modernity in the late seventeenth century and where we stand at the end of the twentieth century; today the liberal states are (more or less) democratic. There have been several other equally or more important developments.

One has been the continued growth and development of market society, which began in trade, grew exponentially with the development of manufacturing as a result of the Industrial Revolution (itself a practical offshoot of the Enlightenment), and has been periodically renewed by the emergence of new technologies. In the twentieth century, and particularly in the post-war period, market society in the industrialized West has become a mass consumer society, by which we mean that an increasing proportion of production and consumption involves items that cannot be considered basic necessities of life. It is still possible at this time to note that only seventy-five years ago the mass entertainment industry as we know it today did not exist. In part a consumer society has been accomplished through the continuous exploitation of the possibilities afforded by science and technology; in part it has been a fruit of the historical exploitation of peoples, domestically, but especially abroad in the age of imperialism that has continued in one form or another since the nineteenth century.[1] It has also meant the creation of a large middle class of professionals and skilled workers that did not exist at the beginning of the modern period.

The development of the post-industrial societies of the West also reflects and has reinforced changes in the nature of **CIVIL SOCIETY**. As discussed earlier, the three primary institutions of civil society have been the family, the church, and the market economy. It is clear that in the past hundred years or so the role of the first two has been radically changed or has declined significantly, while the third may no longer qualify (if it ever did) as standing sufficiently outside the scope of governmental activity. In the twentieth century a new institution of civil society has emerged that continues to grow in its influence, with significant political implications—the mass media. Aptly dubbed the "fourth estate," this institution will be examined in greater depth in Chapter Six. For now, we would point out that the changes we have been discussing—the rise of democracy, the growth of an affluent middle class, and the changing nature of civil society— have all contributed to the growth and (more recent) decline of the modern state.

The contemporary liberal democratic state, then, has its roots in the liberal revolution described above, but it is also very much the product of developments in more recent decades. Within the framework of liberal-democratic institutions and values, the twentieth century state has expanded so much in its scope, its organization, and its complexity that our political vocabulary, rooted in eighteenth- and nineteenth-century models, sometimes fails to capture adequately the nature of modern government. At the same time, questions that were debated during the expansion of government earlier in this century continue to challenge citizens and policy-makers alike. Specifically, reform in Eastern Europe and the former Soviet Union, ideological change in the West, economic globalization, levels of governmental indebtedness, and emerging social and environmental issues have breathed new life into an old and enduring debate: what is the proper role of the state?

The state's assumption of new responsibilities (or, what is sometimes more relevant today, its retreat from certain activities)

1. In fact, imperialism is much older than the nineteenth century; one need only think about the Spanish, Portuguese, French, and British conquest of the "New World" from the sixteenth century onward, or the development of the slave trade. In the nineteenth century, though, European countries divided up Africa among themselves and exploited its lands and peoples as cheap sources of labour and materials. Today, multinational corporations continue to shift production to cheaper labour markets in developing nations, and Western institutions like the World Bank and the International Monetary Fund finance projects and approve loans on the basis of criteria that often seem more consistent with the interests of the developed world creditors than those of the developing world clients.

does not occur without considerable debate or opposition. Very different conceptions exist about the proper role or functions of the state, and often quite distinct interests are represented by positions taken on these issues. In part, then, the nature of the state is a product of ideology, and the level of state activity at any point in time may reflect an ideological consensus, a balance of ideological forces, or the temporary dominance of one viewpoint over others. The ideological landscape within contemporary liberal democracies is our concern in Chapter Five. Underlying ideological positions are often perceptions of interest, people's conception of their own needs and wants as experienced from a particular social position. It is generally on the basis of such perceptions of interest that people turn to the state for action, or conversely, object to governmental policy. It is particularly important to ask who the state serves or represents given that modern societies are typically fragmented in terms of classes, or interests, or ethno-linguistic identities (in short, in terms of all the particular communities or groups that may exist within the larger polity, and which complicate the relationship between state and society).

While it may be fine in theory to say that the state should represent everyone or all groups, this may in practice be neither possible nor desirable. Who is represented by the state? This will depend in large measure on the nature of the political process (the means by which individuals' policy preferences are transmitted from the public to the government—see Section IV). In any polity there are crucial questions about the adequacy of the political process to the interests of the citizens generally, or for particular groups or interests within the polity. To assume that the actions of government reflect a consensus concerning the role of the state in society is to assume (unwisely) that the political process gives all interests and parties a political voice equal to their social strength. For any number of reasons this is not likely to be the case, as we will see below.

While much of the remainder of our discussion will focus on liberal democracy as the system that categorizes the political systems of Western Europe, North America, and most of the rest of the world's economically developed nation-states, it is worth noting that no two liberal democracies are exactly alike. Each reflects the way certain ideas and principles have been refracted by the history of the given society, and each is rooted in the political culture of the historical community involved. Liberal democracies are products of a process of development, one by no means finished or exhausted. The liberal notions of justice and democracy prominent today are far from identical to those that first emerged some three hundred years or more ago. Considering the changes liberal democracies have undergone, is there a point at which they are better described as something else? It is also possible to ask about the directions in which liberal democracy could or should evolve. The implication here is that today's liberal democracies were only able to become democratic after they developed the institutions and civic habits of a liberal society. The establishment of the rule of law, of constitutionalism, of the peaceful change of one government for another through elections, of individual rights, as well as the replacement of patronage with a professional public service, required not just the creation and consolidation of institutions like parliament, the courts, and government bureaucracies, but also the development and popularization of the attitudes and values that inform and support them. This in turn was aided by the spread of literacy, of general education, of urbanization, and by the development of means of mass communication. Many of these developments took a long time to happen, and happened long ago. It is often easy for those of us raised within liberal democracies to take them for granted.

In the past few decades an unprecedented number of countries have adopted the formal machinery of democracy. A great question for comparative politics will be whether or not there is a necessary connection between democracy and the development of a liberal society, using "liberal" in the senses we have been discussing. If this connection is crucial, then many new democracies will have much work to do before they can be secure, for they have adopted democratic institutions without having nurtured the liberal civic traditions and values noted above. This may be one (and by no means the complete) explanation for the populist dictatorships that have emerged, for example, under Fujimori in Peru and Chavez in Venezuela. The Turkish military still threatens to intervene whenever the rise of Islamic parties poses a threat (however real or imagined) to the secular state founded by Attaturk. If the connection between liberalism and democracy is only accidental—and we will discuss this at greater length in Chapter Eleven—then the possibilities of political experience will turn out to be much broader than most Western political scientists have supposed.

KEY TERMS

American Revolution
Catholic Church
civil society
classical antiquity
constitutionalism
custom
depersonalization
divine right
the Enlightenment
feudalism
the "fourth estate"
French Revolution
imperialism
individualism
Industrial Revolution
liberal democracy
liberal modernity
liberal revolution
market economy
medieval society
nation-states
organic hierarchy
populist dictatorship
Protestantism
the Reformation
republicanism
revolution
scepticism
Scholasticism
science
Whig Revolution

**REFERENCES AND
SUGGESTED READING**

Barraclough, Geoffrey. 1967. *An Introduction to Contemporary History.* New York: Pelican.

Hill, Christopher. 1969. *Reformation to Industrial Revolution.* Harmondsworth, U.K.: Penguin.

Hobsbawm, E.J. 1969. *Industry and Empire.* Harmondsworth, U.K.: Penguin.

Keen, Maurice. 1969. *The Pelican History of Medieval Europe.* Harmondsworth, U.K.: Pelican.

Roberts, J.M. 1980. *The Pelican History of the World.* New York: Pelican.

Rudé, George. 1964. *Revolutionary Europe: 1783-1815.* Glasgow: Fontana.

Watkins, Frederick. 1957. *The Political Tradition of the West.* Cambridge, Mass.: Harvard University Press.

SOMETHING TO CONSIDER

Is it a Western prejudice or what some would call "Euro-centricism" to suggest that liberal democracy is the historical destination of all political communities?

IDEAS

Ideas matter in politics. We may wish to debate how much they matter, or in what way they play their role, but to deny them any significance would be to declare the futility of all political discourse. It would be pointless to study politics, to read or write political prose, or even to engage in political activity, if the notions that animate such practices were utterly spurious. It is possible to see how important ideas are by comparing the very different political possibilities that exist in various countries, whether the issue is capital punishment, or abortion, or freedom of the press, or regulation of the marketplace. What people believe about politics, about the state and society, about government and power and authority, about rights and equality and opportunity— all these beliefs make a difference to what happens in the real world. The very different experiences (at least up to the present) of Canada and the United States concerning regulating handgun ownership, or the success of European socialist parties put beside the relative failure of their North American counterparts, or the fragility of Italian coalitions compared with Switzerland's stable governments—each of these examples is testimony to the influence of patterns of belief that are, in each country, somewhat unique.

Ideas also exist at different levels of abstraction, and in a not unrelated fashion, are diffused among the population with varying density. In this section we will begin with the most abstract and specialized and move toward the most familiar and widespread, presenting in turn, political philosophy, political ideology, and political culture.

4 political philosophy

It is not usual to include political philosophy in an introduction to political science, the rationale being that it is a subject for the specialist, something that requires more attention than an introduction to the discipline can afford. The passage from Aristotle suggests disagreement with this reasoning: in his view we are not capable of participating properly in politics unless we have directed (at least part of) our attention to the questions of political philosophy. If politics has the normative character that we ascribed to it in Section I, then it is difficult not to agree, at least in part, with Aristotle. Experience suggests, however, that the proper study of political philosophy requires more attention than this text will permit. This chapter, then, is not a comprehensive treatment of political philosophy, but a short introduction designed for two purposes. One is to illuminate some of the philosophical background underlying the long tradition of political discourse, especially given that until relatively recently, most of that discourse took place within political philosophy. The other purpose is to acquaint students with some of the principal thinkers of the Western political tradition and with the questions they addressed; those wishing to study politics in greater depth may gain an inkling of their interest or disinterest in the philosophical path. A qualification is necessary, though: reading *about* political philosophy (e.g., this chapter) is in no way a substitute for reading political philosophy itself. Students are urged to consult primary texts themselves (see list A at the end of this chapter) or collections of material selected from primary texts (see list B). In addition to primary texts, there are comprehensive treatments of the history of political philosophy, where each thinker receives an insightful chapter (see list C).

4.1 THE NATURE OF POLITICAL PHILOSOPHY

"We have laid it down that the excellence of the full citizen who shares in the government is the same as that of the good man. We have also assumed that the man who begins by being a subject must ultimately share in the government. It follows on this that the legislator must labour to ensure that his citizens become good men. He must therefore know what institutions will produce this result, and what is the end or aim to which a good life is directed."
— Aristotle, *The Politics*, VII, xiv, 8

4.1 The Nature of Political Philosophy
4.2 Plato and Aristotle
4.3 Aquinas and Machiavelli
4.4 Hobbes and Locke
4.5 Rousseau and Burke
4.6 Marx and Mill
4.7 Conclusion

POLITICAL PHILOSOPHY IS …

"an effort devoted to gaining
wisdom about the nature of
human beings and politics."
— Leo Strauss, 1987

"a reflective discourse on the
meaning of the political."
— Sheldin Wolin, 1960

"a critical and creative activity in
which each generation participates
in a continuous tradition."
— Losco and Williams, 1992

FIGURE 4.1

Philosophy comes from two Greek words: *philos* "loving," and *sophia* "wisdom"; the philosopher is one who loves wisdom, and the political philosopher one who loves wisdom or seeks truth about the political world in particular (see Figure 4.1). Until the present century, most political philosophy was written by thinkers whose concerns were much broader than merely the political realm; what they said about politics was part of a larger whole, often part of a system that attempted to articulate the fundamentals of *all* knowledge (see Figure 4.2). This is one reason why the study of political philosophy can be so specialized—a particular author's position on government, or on political goods like justice or equality, cannot be separated from his or her beliefs about the fundamental substance of the universe, or about how we know the things we know. Nonetheless, thinkers as diverse as Aristotle and Marx have agreed that politics is ultimately (if not essentially) practical, and however abstract or esoteric the questions political philosophy addresses, they must ultimately connect with how humans live their lives within (or in contest with) the structures of authority and power of the communities and societies they inhabit.

Traditional questions of political philosophy include the following:

- What is the good life for humans?
- Who should rule? What is the best form of government?
- Is there a law higher than or prior to the civil law (that made by political officials) to which we are primarily obliged?
- What is justice? What is right? What is liberty?

Take, for example, the first of these questions: "What is the good life for humans?" Note how this differs from asking "What do humans like to do?" or "What makes humans happy?" To say the good life consists in *being happy* is one way to answer the original query, but so too is *being virtuous* or *being victorious in combat*. (And the degree to which "being happy" seems more sensible or normal than the other responses reflects the philosophic tastes of our own place and time.) We can disagree then, about the answers to our question "What is the good life for humans?," or we might agree that the human good is happiness, but then disagree about the nature of happiness: Is it pleasure, or well-being?

On the other hand, why should we assume that there is just *one* human good (which, mind you, is not the same as claiming that there is only one human desire or pleasure)? Are we making

ELEMENTS OF PHILOSOPHY

METAPHYSICS (OR ONTOLOGY) concerns fundamental questions about the nature of reality as a whole rather than considered in its particulars: e.g., idealism says that the fundamental reality is ideal; materialism argues that it is sensuous matter.

EPISTEMOLOGY addresses fundamental questions about our knowledge: What can we know? How do we know what we know? What is the certainty of our knowledge?

LOGIC presents rules and arguments about the rules and arguments of reasoning, that is, the way we draw conclusions. Many errors in philosophy (and elsewhere) are the result of inattention to the niceties of logic.

ETHICS explores the fundamental questions concerning our duties to one another (and, in some cases, whether our duties to one another are related to our duties to a higher being).

AESTHETICS articulates theories about the nature of beauty, of form, style, and taste.

As noted, in many cases, thinkers have addressed all or several of these subfields in philosophy (and others) *systematically*, meaning that they are linked as parts of a larger whole. What the thinker has to say in the field of ethics or epistemology, for example, may be ultimately connected to his or her metaphysical position. Belief in the existence of a god or gods may have different implications for ethical life than agnostic or atheistic beliefs. Thoroughgoing materialists, as a rule, are more likely to be agnostics or atheists than idealists, but not all idealists are theists (e.g., believers in a God transcendent to the world and humanity). One of the last great systematic thinkers, Georg Wilhelm Friedrich Hegel (1770-1831), believed he had summed up the substance of the entire universe (including God) in his system, which he presented in published texts and university lectures.

Following Stace (1955), the major elements of that system were as follows:

FIGURE 4.2

certain assumptions or demonstrating particular beliefs about human nature? That there is, for example, one universal human nature that each of us exemplifies? It is quite common for philosophers to base their prescriptions for what humans ought to be, or do, or become, on claims about what humans *are*; it is just as common for philosophers to disagree on the fundamentals of human nature. Are humans, for example, fundamentally spiritual—that is, essentially souls (temporarily?) at home in a body, or are they thoroughly material, sensuous beings? Are we by nature lazy or creative, consumers or participants, passive or active? A much stronger philosophical case for democracy can be made if we are by nature active, creative participants rather than lazy, passive consumers, but then this way of arguing seems to suppose that our natures are fixed, or "given," rather than something constructed, that our way of being is static and never dynamic. These and countless other questions are the stuff of political philosophy, which can be summarized as *critical, systematic argument about the ends (purposes) of human life, and about how our society or community should be ordered so that citizens can best attain those ends.*

If political philosophy addresses such questions, it does not do so in a vacuum, but rather within a context that presents at least two relevant dimensions. One is the context of space and time provided by sociology and history. Political philosophers cannot help but think and work within the context of the particular society in which they live; there are many different types of society, and each society has its own history. To illustrate, consider the suggestion made above, that we could respond to the question "what is the good life for humans?" with the answer: "to be victorious in combat." To contemporary North Americans, that might seem a strange answer, but not so to Greeks of Homeric times, because theirs was a society in which the skills or virtues of the warrior were valued. In other warrior cultures or societies one might expect similar virtues or values (one warrior society many students understand is that of the fictitious Klingons of *Star Trek* fame, for whom the only honourable death is to fall in combat). To return to the Greeks, though, we find that by the time of Plato and Aristotle (4th century BCE) other virtues had displaced the warrior ethic, in part if not principally because the nature of Greek society had changed. In Chapter Three we noted the significant social transformation that was the end of feudalism and the beginning of liberal modernity; we find correspondingly (and it would be odd if we didn't) that the political philosophy of early modernity is strikingly different from that of medieval society, in the questions it considers, the mode of argument it uses, and the conclusions it reaches.

The other context we should note is one that manages to transcend the particular historical and sociological contexts of the first dimension, allowing political philosophy to partake of a longer, deeper tradition. If this were not the case, none of us today could be Aristotelians, or Marxists, or Adam Smith liberals (see Chapter Five); but indeed, examples of each can still be found. In practice, the philosopher is not a solitary figure who thinks and writes, but someone engaged in critical, rational

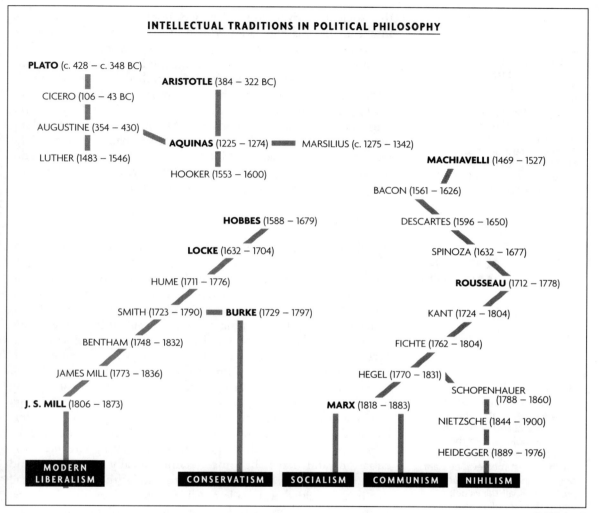

FIGURE 4.3

dialogue with the body of thought that has come before. Almost any decent work of philosophy is a response to, or refutation of, or commentary on, or synthesis of, the work or works of other philosophers, many if not most of whom will be long dead (hence the oft-quoted observation that all political philosophy is merely footnotes to Plato). In this way philosophy reaches across generations, types of society, and periods of local history to become a larger tradition or, more accurately, a set of (often competing) traditions within which individual philosophers are situated (see Figure 4.3). Of the two contexts we have identified,

1. One by-product of the existence of philosophic traditions transcending the boundaries of space and time is the habit of speaking of philosophers and their works in the present tense: "Hobbes states that the Sovereign must be absolute ..." or "Marx argues that the proletariat is not automatically conscious of itself as a class."

the socio-historical and what we might call the textual or intellectual, it is the latter which has most often been more evident to philosophers themselves as they work, and which is often most explicit in their work. This is another reason why political philosophy is most fruitfully studied in some depth; to understand fully any one thinker requires familiarity with the intellectual tradition within which he or she is working and the thinkers he or she is addressing in his or her work (something which may at times be implicit rather than explicit).[1] The remainder of this chapter is intended, then, to whet the appetite of students for studying political philosophy, by providing just a little background to five pairs of important thinkers.

4.2
PLATO AND
ARISTOTLE

2. Slavery is slavery, but Greek slaves in classical antiquity could enjoy a considerable amount of freedom and authority *within* the households where they were kept, and were probably better off than most medieval peasants or early nineteenth-century proletarians, all things being equal. The fact of slavery was *not* an issue during the time of Plato or Aristotle; as an institution of civil society it was taken for granted.

The stature that Plato and Aristotle continue to hold within philosophy not only says something about the remarkable quality of these two intellects, but also about the society that could produce them. Both were active in fourth-century Athens, the leading **POLIS** of the Greek city-states, and the particular problems and challenges of governing such political entitities preoccupy Plato and Aristotle in their political writings. The *poleii* of this period were agrarian, pre-industrial societies, dependent for economic life on the continued exploitation of a large class of slaves, many of whom were foreigners captured in war.[2] These societies were primitive by our standards in terms of technology and practical science, but extremely advanced in terms of intellectual disciplines like philosophy and the cultivation of the arts. (Critics of modernity often argue that we have simply reversed the equation and have become technologically proficient and culturally impoverished.) As noted previously, the relatively small size of these city-states made possible quite a diversity of political arrangements within Greek experience, many of which were extremely unstable. Hence, who should rule, and how they should rule, were central questions of political philosophy in this period.

Athens was, during the time of Plato and Aristotle (and indeed from the sixth century BCE until its destruction by the Romans in the first century), a democracy in which the most important decisions were made by a body of all the citizens (the Assembly), or rather, of all those who chose to attend the business of the Assembly. A Council of Five Hundred, chosen by lot from the body of citizens, set the agenda for the Assembly. While the tradition of democracy, including the word itself, dates from this period of classical Athens, neither Plato nor Aristotle was a demo-crat, although Aristotle's objections to democracy were less cate-gorical than Plato's. We do well to keep in mind, though, that democracy in Athens meant not the modern practice of electing representatives, but actual government by the body of citizens (which, since it did not include slaves, women, children, or for-eigners, amounted to perhaps 20 per cent of the population).

One of the most striking features of Plato's philosophy is that it is presented in the form of dialogues (conversations) between young Athenian noblemen, at the centre of whom (and representing Plato's own position) is the philosopher Socrates. In most of the dialogues (there are about twenty-seven) Socrates challenges the common-sense beliefs or opinions of his companions concerning the nature of various virtues, and other philosophic questions; he does this by rigorous questioning (the Socratic method) that leads the speakers into contradictions that reveal the flaws of their initial positions. In each case, Socrates tries to move the entire company from opinion, which is uncritical and conventional, to knowledge, which should be critical and disclose the true nature of things.[3]

Plato was an idealist: he believed that the true nature of the universe is ideal, or even intellectual; behind the constant flux of empirical events and material appearances lies an enduring reality that can be approached only through thought. This is the world of the Forms, which for Plato are the fundamental nature of the universe, persisting behind or beyond the world as it appears. Just as our common sense can easily become preoccupied with the world of appearance, or the material of the senses, so, conversely, does knowledge require the critical ability to achieve clarity with concepts and proceed to intellectual apprehension of the Forms (or Ideas). All idealism, one of the strongest currents in the philo-sophic tradition, has its roots in Plato's metaphysics.

In Plato's most famous political work, *The Republic*, the principal topic is the nature of justice, or the matter of *how* the people are to be ruled. After demonstrating the weakness of cur-rent, conventional understandings of justice, Socrates presents his own (i.e., Plato's) understanding of justice by way of an analogy that is truly representative of the nature of Plato's politics and phi-losophy. Socrates convinces his listeners that the human soul has three parts: a rational part, a spirited or courageous part, and an appetitive (irrational) part. Justice in the soul consists of each part performing its own function, which means, among other things, that the rational part will dominate or rule the appetitive part

3. This view of knowledge and philosophy is very much out of fashion in many circles of contemporary philosophy.

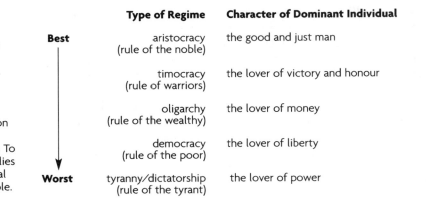

TYPES OF REGIME

PLATO

In *The Republic*, five types of regime are presented, differentiated on the basis of the type of character that predominates in each. Starting with the ideal regime, aristocracy, each successive regime is presented as a degeneration from the one preceding, a series that ends in tyranny. To a certain degree Plato implies that this descent from ideal to worst regime is inevitable.

	Type of Regime	Character of Dominant Individual
Best	aristocracy (rule of the noble)	the good and just man
	timocracy (rule of warriors)	the lover of victory and honour
	oligarchy (rule of the wealthy)	the lover of money
	democracy (rule of the poor)	the lover of liberty
Worst	tyranny/dictatorship (rule of the tyrant)	the lover of power

FIGURE 4.4

4. In most later treatments of human nature, the tripartite soul of Plato is simplified to a dualism of mind versus body.

5. The city depicted in *The Republic* seems so unlikely to some commentators that they have concluded that Plato actually intended the book as an argument *against* political idealism.

(mind over body, intellect over senses), and will do this with the aid of the spirited part.[4]

Justice in the *ideal* city will parallel justice in the soul, for the city will have three classes corresponding to the three parts of the soul. The rational part of the city will be the class of Guardians, whose business it is to deliberate about the city as a whole. Assisting them will be a class of Auxiliaries, courageous warriors who will preserve the city from external foes and internal dissension. The largest part of the city will be the body of citizens (the Artisans) who are concerned with the mundane business of acquiring wealth. Justice in the city will consist in each class performing the function for which its nature has fitted it: the Guardians ought to rule, the Artisans ought to make money, and not vice-versa. It is also Plato's belief that individuals are *by nature* determined for one class or another. Much of *The Republic* is concerned with the education and training that the small elite class of Guardians is to receive, and with the nature of their living. Since they are to put the good of the city first, their own desires are least important, and for this reason *for this class* Plato recommends a primitive communism (no private property, nor, for that matter, monogamous marriage). From the class of Guardians will come philosophers (or a philosopher) fit to rule, but interestingly, since philosophers will love knowledge and wish to spend their time in contemplation of the Forms, philosopher-kings will have to be forced to rule.[5]

Perhaps it is a little clearer now why Plato was not a democrat. In the first place, he did not have the belief in fundamental human equality which democracy, at least on one level, presup-

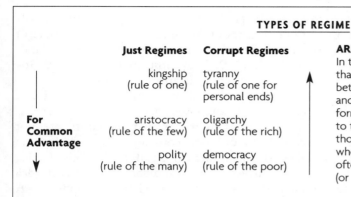

<u>**TYPES OF REGIME**</u>

	Just Regimes	**Corrupt Regimes**	
	kingship (rule of one)	tyranny (rule of one for personal ends)	
For Common Advantage	aristocracy (rule of the few)	oligarchy (rule of the rich)	
	polity (rule of the many)	democracy (rule of the poor)	

ARISTOTLE
In the *Politics*, Aristotle articulated the distinction that became most common through the centuries, between the Rule of One, the Rule of the Few, and the Rule of the Many. Each of these has a just form and a corrupt form, just being those directed to the common advantage, and corrupt being those in which rule is for the advantage of those who rule. In later times, this sixfold typology was often shortened to simply monarchy, aristocracy (or oligarchy), and democracy.

FIGURE 4.4 CONTINUED

poses. To Plato, we have different natures, which means that most of us are suited by neither aptitude nor inclination for making intelligent political decisions. We are better fitted perhaps for combat, or for acquiring wealth, and these are what we should do, leaving the business of governing to those whose natures are so gifted. Given the diversity of types of state present in classical Greece, most political thinkers offered a means of classifying different regimes, and Plato was no exception. In his fivefold schema, each state corresponding to the dominance of a particular type of individual, democracy is second from the bottom (see Figure 4.4). Whether or not we agree with Plato on this, we should acknowledge one fundamental sense in which Plato stands at the root of all Western political philosophy: his notion that ruling is something done for the benefit of those who are ruled, not for the interest(s) of the rulers. Interestingly, the only way Plato saw to achieve this was to have the wise rule; in other words, the emphasis is on achieving rulers with the *best character*. Character is innate, that is, part of one's given nature, but it is also as such merely a potential or possibility not realized without the proper nurture or education. One of Plato's lasting achievements was his Academy, founded with a view to providing young Athenian nobles with the education that would develop the character to enable them to rule. This school lasted for several centuries.

A student in Plato's academy, and later one of its teachers, Aristotle demonstrated a more empirical cast of mind than his mentor. Some interpreters stress the continuities between Aristotle and Plato, others the differences; we will look at some of the significant differences. Sinclair (1959: 210-11) contrasts Aristotle—"a middle-class professional man, a husband and a father, scientific observer and practical administrator"—with Plato—"the Athenian aristocrat, mystic, ascetic, [and] puritan"—and points out the following non-Platonic features of Aristotle's politics: "the value of family life, the pursuit of health and happiness, property, [and] respect for public opinion." Perhaps most important, for Aristotle, politics is in a very real sense the art of the possible.

Like Plato, Aristotle believed in Forms, but believed that they are immanent, that is to say, inseparable from the matter that is common to particulars. This means that the forms are not something inaccessible to ordinary consciousness, and that the realm of appearance (the phenomenal) *is* real for Aristotle. Hence there is not the same dualism or radical dichotomy between idea and matter, mind and senses, found in Plato's metaphysics. A central notion in Aristotle's thought is the idea that everything has a **TELOS**, an end or purpose or goal to which it strives or is destined or develops. This *telos* is contained in the essence of the object; to explain an object then requires identifying its kind or species, which allows us to understand its essence, and hence the *telos* or end it serves. One result of this teleology is a more universal or implicitly egalitarian view of humanity; whatever the differences in our nature, as human beings we share a common *telos*. Thus Aristotle can state—something it is difficult to imagine Plato uttering—at the beginning of his *Metaphysics*: "All men by nature desire to know." Like Plato, Aristotle does not question slavery as natural, does believe in a natural distinction between women and men, and thus accepts hierarchy and patriarchy, but he nonetheless presents us with only one human nature, of which there is by nature an inferior or superior manifestation in particular individuals.

In both the *Ethics* and *Politics*, Aristotle is concerned with how humans realize the telos that is uniquely theirs as humans. He draws here upon a distinction (missing in Plato) between theoretical and practical reason. Theoretical reason is appropriate for the study of nature; it uncovers necessary and universal laws that constitute knowledge or science. Practical reason is appropriate for human affairs, is situational or contextual, and produces wisdom or judgement. This view of the reasoning we bring to politics as something fallible and gained only through experience is one students may understand but not appreciate, since it implies that wisdom comes as much as a product of age as of intelligence. Our *telos*, Aristotle argues, is to seek *eudaemonia*, which is often translated as happiness, but is perhaps more accurately presented by the term "well-being." Well-being turns out to be living a life in accordance with virtue, which can mean the pursuit of intellectual excellence, or acting on our desires in a rational way. In either case, realizing our *telos* does not simply happen, but must be cultivated, requires education, and this in turn rests on the foundation of good laws. In this way, Aristotle's ethics leads to his politics, and conversely, the purpose of political life is to present the opportunity for us to realize our *telos*—to live a virtuous life. We cannot be moral beings in a corrupt city or *polis*. Like Plato, Aristotle places little importance on the pursuit of wealth, and none on the pursuit of wealth for its own sake. Properly understood, money or wealth is simply the means that provides us with the leisure to take part in civic life, to cultivate our sense of virtue, and to develop and exercise wise judgement. The primary purpose of the state is educative, and we cannot benefit from this education unless we participate in the politics of the state.

The concept of citizenship is thus very central to Aristotle, as indicated by the quotation with which this chapter began. To be a citizen, or more exactly, to be a good citizen, is necessary to fulfil the *telos* of being human, but here is the problem: not all can be citizens. To be a citizen is to have the right to share in judicial or deliberative office [III, iv, 1] and Aristotle accepts, first, that certain classes of people (e.g., slaves, women, foreigners) will never possess citizenship, and second, that who does qualify as a citizen will vary from constitution to constitution (that is, according to the type of government).[6] Whatever the type of constitution, the citizen will be someone engaged in ruling *and* being ruled, and Aristotle defines the excellence of the good citizen as "consisting in 'a knowledge of rule over free men from both points of view'" [III, iv, 15].

6. One of Aristotle's preparations for his *Politics* was a study of 158 Greek constitutions.

Like Plato, Aristotle believes that political authority is properly exercised when it is directed to the common good. Hence, any regime that is directed to the common advantage is just, and any that pursues a partial interest is corrupt, regardless in either case of who rules (see Figure 4.4). It is interesting to note how Aristotle's discussion of types of rule differs from Plato's, and Aristotle is much less categorical about which is the best regime. On the one hand, being more pragmatic, Aristotle distinguishes between the best regime (i.e., the ideal), the best possible regime, and the most likely regime. He also seems prepared to accept that what kind of regime works best will depend on circumstances and social conditions, which will vary from *polis* to *polis*. Unlike Plato, though, Aristotle is inclined to the view that many heads are better than one (or a few): "Each individual may indeed, be a worse judge than the experts; but all, when they meet together, are either better than experts or at any rate no worse" [III, xi, 14].

Finally, regardless of the type of regime, an enduring issue in political philosophy to which Aristotle makes significant contribution is the issue of the sovereignty of law: should we be governed by the wisdom of wise rulers, or by the impartial neutrality of laws? As we shall see below, the answer of modernity has been to institutionalize the principle of the rule of law, but as Aristotle notes, with the impartiality or neutrality of law comes inflexibility, an inability to account for differences in circumstance or application. Ultimately Aristotle argues that the rule of law is to be preferred, and where there are matters that law cannot deal with adequately, these are best decided by many individuals rather than one (or a few). As to how we know which matters fall in the latter category, Aristotle is less clear.

Common to both these great thinkers, Plato and Aristotle, is the quest for a politics where rule is wise, virtuous, and directed to the advantage of all.[7] For both, development of the character of those who rule is crucial and education is central. For Plato this is a very special education for those with the nature that equips them for philosophy (which equals science). For Aristotle, the education of those who rule is more practical, and more gained through experience than training or reflection, although these too are important. For each thinker, law is important, but whereas for Plato this is ultimately the eternal law of the Forms which transcends any particular *polis*, Aristotle is more concerned with the actual laws of constitutions, which may be just or corrupt. While there is much that is passé in the thought of each (especially their unquestioning acceptance of slavery and patriarchy), each also has much to say to us today, as indeed they have spoken to countless generations in the past two millennia.

7. For the classical thinkers, these qualities—wise, virtuous, and directed to the advantage of all—were one and the same thing; it is not clear that they are necessarily so regarded today.

**4.3
AQUINAS AND
MACHIAVELLI**

The distance between Aristotle and Thomas Aquinas is some sixteen centuries, and Niccolo Machiavelli follows Aquinas by another two hundred and fifty years. Such a leap on our part implies that nothing much was happening in political philosophy for a very long period of time. This, of course, is not true. We have skipped over a variety of schools of early Greek philosophy such as the Sceptics and Stoics, the thinkers of Ancient Rome such as Cicero and Tacitus, and the philosopher who sought at the time of the fall of the Roman Empire to join Christian theology to the political thought of Cicero and Plato: Augustine of Hippo. On the other hand, relatively speaking, not much did happen in the political philosophy of Western Europe in the first millennium of the Christian era, perhaps primarily because not much was happening in the static world of feudalism, but also in part because centres of learning had been destroyed and intellectual cultures diluted with the invasion of Western Europe by warrior societies from the East.

Aquinas deserves to be highlighted here, because he is the greatest of the medieval philosophers, and his philosophy is representative of several interesting characteristics. In the first place, Aquinas illustrates the degree to which philosophy is a dialogue with thinkers from the past, and in this way becomes situated within a **TRADITION**. Looking back, Aquinas synthesized Aristotelian philosophy with the Christian theology of Augustine. When we recall that Augustine himself was heavily indebted to Cicero (and through Cicero to Plato) for his political thought, we can appreciate the degree to which the entire European philosophic tradition to date was present in Aquinas's system. Looking forward, we find that pronouncements of various popes at the end of the last century and the beginning of this one enshrined Aquinas's philosophy as the official doctrine of the Roman Catholic Church, a body of thought with which all teachers of "mental philosophy and theology" are expected in principle to agree. Recently, Alasdair MacIntyre, an influential contemporary philosopher, has argued the continued superiority of the Thomist approach to moral inquiry. This makes for a long philosophic tradition indeed!

Aquinas also epitomizes the character of medieval thought, and in doing so demonstrates the way thought reflects the socio-historical context of its generation. As noted earlier, politics in the medieval period was dominated by the relationship, often fractious, between the halves of a dual authority comprising Church and state. Not surprisingly, medieval political thought is largely concerned with the relationships between secular and ecclesiastical (i.e., Church) authority, and with the relationship between philosophy and Church teachings (theology). In Aquinas's time, universities were first emerging as schools of professional instruction in medicine, law, the arts, and the special training of monks and priests. The latter concern meant that universities were usually staffed by, and run under the supervision of, the Church, which was throughout the medieval period the main source and support of intellectual and cultural life. As a consequence, it was expected that this intellectual and cultural life, and hence what was taught in universities, would be consistent with the Church's teachings. Eventually, thinkers like Aquinas, whose teachings received official Church approval and were the basis of university curricula, became known as Scholastics, and medieval philosophy was called Scholasticism. In the medieval view, philosophy was the handmaid of theology (and this is what Scholasticism came to represent to later, post-Enlightenment thinkers).

The intellectual and practical puzzle of medieval politics, then, was to reconcile the authority of kings with the authority of the church, to sort out the relationship of the sacred and secular spheres. There are two important differences between medieval and classical philosophy which are the result of Christianity's presence. One is the devaluation of political life in light of the Christian belief in eternal life as an ultimately otherworldly destination. If this finite life of our bodies is not the only or final condition we will endure, then it is surely not as important, nor then is political life our highest calling or activity, as Aristotle might have argued. Augustine had argued that we can be citizens of two worlds: the worldly *polis* of men, or the heavenly city of God. For the believer, secular purposes, punishments, and rewards must be seen as secondary to those of the world to come, represented by sacred authority (e.g., the Bible, the Church) and authorities (e.g., priests, bishops, popes). The second large difference Christianity makes is its focus towards a universal kingdom that includes all believers, regardless of nation or state or status. The centrality of the *polis*, the ultimate identification of authority with the community that was central to Greek political thought, is no longer acceptable. In part this is a remnant of the Roman empire and its successful embrace of so much of Western Europe, but it is also, and perhaps principally, the product of the message of the Christian religion, preaching one universal community of humans with God through Christ. In central and interesting ways, then, for medieval thinkers like Aquinas, humans are no longer seen to be political animals in the way that Aristotle had argued or understood.

Lastly, we should note the important political concept medieval philosophy bequeathed to subsequent generations: the notion of **NATURAL LAW**. Most students are familiar with the generalizations that science has enabled us to identify as "laws of nature" such as the second law of thermodynamics, or the law of gravity; these generalizations describe regularities in the relationships among natural phenomena. The natural law medieval thinkers like Aquinas discussed was conceived to be just as real as the laws of nature with which we are familiar today, but applicable to the moral and political realms. It is part of the way in which God has structured the universe, and as creatures with reason we are especially capable of knowing the natural law, and are thus obliged to follow it. As Fortin (1972: 264-65) put it:

> Precisely because he is endowed with reason man participates more perfectly than all other natural beings in the order of divine providence. Through the knowledge that he has of his end and of the natural inclinations that reveal its existence, he is immediately aware of the general principles that govern his conduct. As dictates of practical reason these principles constitute a 'law,' promulgated by nature itself, which enables him to discriminate between right and wrong and serves as the infallible criterium of the goodness or badness of his actions…. Since they are considered to be laws in the strict and proper sense of the term, the moral principles in question take on a compulsory character they did not have for Aristotle and the philosophic tradition generally. For the natural law … thus clearly presupposes both the personal immortality of the human soul and the existence of an all-knowing and all-powerful God who rules the world with wisdom and equity and in whose eyes all individual human actions are either meritorious or deserving of punishment.

Admittedly, the notion of natural law as the Scholastics understood it is rather foreign to contemporary students, and something they may not need to understand in order to make sense of the political institutions and practices of today's world. Nonetheless, it was a dominant way of conceptualizing politics for many centuries, and certainly the early liberal political philosophers who *have* exerted considerable influence on our political culture began by using or rejecting the language of natural law.

If Aquinas (like Aristotle) conceived politics as morality, but (unlike Aristotle) as a specifically Christian ethics, Machiavelli is famous (or infamous) for identifying politics with immorality through his doctrine that the end justifies the means. He is regarded by many as the first truly modern political thinker, but he may with some justice also be seen as clearly linked to the classical political thinkers through his connection with the Italian Renaissance and his attraction to the civic republicanism of ancient Rome. What gained for Machiavelli his reputation was his rejection of divine (and hence natural) law, *and* of the classical notion that political rule is ethical activity. In this way he seems to reject both medieval Christianity and classical Platonic or Aristotelian civic virtue. The goods which Machiavelli recognizes are power, greatness, and fame, and *virtu* represents the qualities that contribute to attaining these goods. Unlike previous thinkers Machiavelli seems prepared to view political power as an end in itself, and this seems at odds with the view—common to both the ancients and the moderns—that political power is to be exercised on behalf of the common or collective advantage, not for the purposes of rulers. On the other hand, the end which Machiavelli most consistently seems concerned to promote is the creation, nourishment, and expansion of the nation-state, ideally conceived as a republic. When Machiavelli condones what are clearly unethical or immoral acts by rulers, this is always because the effect is to stabilize, strengthen, or expand the state, not because it brings personal gain or pleasure to the rulers. This concern for the welfare of the state makes him, like the nation-state itself, particularly modern, and the last chapter of his work *The Prince* is one of the first great statements of nationalism.

What clearly differentiates Machiavelli from most, if not all, of his predecessors is that his entire attention is focused on the realm of the possible; depending on one's perspective, he is a pessimist or a realist where human nature is concerned and does not hold that wisdom, virtue, and good government are necessarily connected. It may be difficult for us to comprehend today, but in classical times, and in much of medieval time, it was difficult to conceive of a conflict between being rational and being virtuous. To be rational, for Plato and Aristotle, is to be morally good, and vice-versa; one cannot freely choose evil and be considered rational. By Machiavelli's time, and clearly in his thought, this equation of goodness and reason has been broken; the wise man may well choose to do what is immoral or unethical for the sake of some good defined in non-moral terms (like the good of the state or empire). This view of reason as **INSTRUMENTAL** (it may serve any number of purposes, good, evil, or indifferent), whether we like it or not, has been very much part and parcel of the modern world. One factor contributing to the dissolution of the identity of reason and virtue is the increasing diversity of perspectives on what is good, or virtuous, or right. And out of this diversity, in part, comes the modern reliance on institutions and rules rather than good character to be the guarantee of good government. To the degree that Machiavelli remains focused on the character and judgement of rulers, to the degree, that is to say, that he is concerned with greatness, he remains typical of late medieval thought and the age of kings.

Thomas Hobbes has been described as the greatest of all English political thinkers, and there are very few ideas in liberal thought that do not stem from Hobbes, or from critics of Hobbes, the first and perhaps the greatest of whom was John Locke. Together, Hobbes and Locke first put into conceptual form the character of modern society and the liberal government that seems necessarily (to liberals) to accompany it. To the degree that liberalism has been the dominant ideology of the modern period, and because we discuss ideology at greater length in the next chapter, the emphasis here will be less on the substance of Hobbes's and Locke's philosophies, and more on the significance of each for liberalism.

4.4 HOBBES AND LOCKE

The political event most crucial for Hobbes was the struggle between monarch and parliament that shaped English politics in the 1600s and led to the Civil War, Cromwell's Commonwealth, the Restoration of the Stuart monarchy, and finally to the Glorious (or Whig) Revolution of 1688. This series of events marks England's adjustment from a feudal, traditional society to a modern, legal-rational polity—England's experience of the "liberal revolution" referred to earlier. Not only was Hobbes aware of the social transformation his society was undergoing, but he seems also to have understood and welcomed it. Having opted for the new market-driven, Protestant, rational society, Hobbes intends to provide a political theory for the new age. It is his insight into the nature of post-feudal society that makes him so "modern," so "radical" for his own time, and so enduring for us today. Of course, he argued in the language of his day, addressing those shaped by or attempting to defend feudal doctrines and practice— for this reason he can seem archaic and "dated" to contemporary students. There is also a strongly conservative dimension to Hobbes, expressed in his fear of conflict, his concern for order and stability, and in the paternalism in his theory of government.

Hobbes begins not with the community, but with the **INDIVIDUAL**. Individuals, for Hobbes, are logically prior to any group or collective formation, and this in part is what is meant by describing Hobbes's theory as atomistic. Hobbes believes that individuals are fundamentally bodies in motion, guided by their passions, the strongest of which is the fear of death. Two consequences follow from Hobbes's account of appetitive man. First, human reason is instrumental: it exists and operates to serve the passions in obtaining their object (pleasure or the avoidance of pain). Reason thus has no "higher" status, and provides no independent course of action for us to follow: all voluntary actions and inclinations we have are concerned with "securing a contented life" (*Leviathan*, ch. XI).

Second, society is artificial: "All society therefore is either for gain, or for glory; that is, not so much for love of our fellows, as for the love of ourselves" (*De Cive*, ch. I). Others are of value to us only instrumentally, that is, as means to our ends, and they have no intrinsic value in and of themselves. We value others for the power they have, and Hobbes defines power as a present means to some future end.

Because fear of death is our strongest passion, we desire satisfaction not only now, but also in all future instances. Therefore, we desire power (a present means to a future end), and Hobbes proposes that "a general inclination of all mankind" is "a perpetual and restless desire of power after power, that ceases only in Death" (*Leviathan*, ch. XI). A modest or moderate power is not enough, Hobbes notes, because we can never be certain it is enough. Men compete with each other for particular powers such as wealth, status, and authority. This competition in turn leads to war, because the most effective victory over one's opponents is that which causes their death. Thus Hobbes's basic and initial propositions about human nature place each individual in conflict with every other individual. You are my enemy because you want the same things I want, and presumably both of us cannot have or enjoy them.

For Hobbes, the **STATE OF NATURE** is a hypothetical condition, a statement of what *would* be the case *if* we were to remove all social and political authority. From the equality of our appetitive natures, Hobbes concludes that each person is the enemy of every other. The best defence in such conditions is a good offence: "there is no way for any man to secure himself, so reasonable as anticipation; that is, by force, or wiles, to master the persons of all men he can, so long, till he see no other power great enough to endanger him: And this is no more than his own conservation requires, and is generally avowed" (*Leviathan*, ch. XIII).

In other words, each individual, in order to preserve himself from defeat, must kill all others. Therefore, the state of nature turns out to be a state of war, "and such a war, as is of every man against every man."

This Hobbesian conception of the state of nature as a state of war is one of the most powerful images of political thought: an anarchy of the worst kind, a condition of violent stagnation that recommends itself to no one. At the same time we should note that this condition is the product of a rational strategy undertaken in the absence of government, given the nature of human passions. The individuals in this state of nature are acting rationally on the basis of their appetites, and Hobbes tells us that their actions are not sinful or evil or unjust. Good and evil, justice and injustice, right and wrong can exist only when there is a commonly agreed upon standard and a power to enforce it. Neither of these conditions exists in the state of nature.

Having established, then, that without authority men are in a horrible state of war, *and* that their natures prevent them from escaping this condition, Hobbes offers an apparent solution. This is an agreement, of every man with every other man, to be ruled by a common power (a Sovereign) who "shall act, or cause to be acted, in those things which concern the common peace and safety" (*Leviathan*, ch. XVII). This is the great Covenant (an agreement binding the parties to future compliance) by which civil society is created, and by which individuals escape the state of war. Each individual surrenders his right to do whatever is necessary to defend himself from others, and agrees to the protection provided by a Sovereign, who is thereby empowered to make laws and enforce them. We might note that Hobbes does not say that individuals in the state of nature actually could make such a covenant—his own description of their nature suggests they couldn't—but rather that if they were to escape the state of nature, this is what would be required of them.

The notion that political society is something to which individuals agree, and which they collectively construct or implement in order to protect or further their self-interest, clearly signals the way in which society is instrumental and artificial for thinkers like Hobbes. A central proposition of such theories is the notion that the purpose of government is the security and well-being of the individuals governed. Thus, Hobbes is justifying the state on the basis of its contribution to individual welfare. He is not saying that the state provides individuals' welfare, but rather that the state provides a framework of stability and security (through laws) in which individuals may pursue their own ends. Individuals are no less self-interested and driven by their passions or appetites in civil society than in the state of nature. What has changed is that the law enforced by the Sovereign protects individuals from the actions that others might take on the basis of their self-interest.

For Hobbes it does not matter how governments come into being: their nature, their purpose, and their justification are the same. Because humans are the way they are, a Sovereign power is necessary to keep peace. Therefore, all Sovereigns are justified in exercising power. Without a Sovereign to keep the peace by enforcing law, men would return to the state of nature, which is a state of war. The surest sign of this, Hobbes suggests, is the destruction brought by civil wars, where authority is in dispute. For Hobbes, then, all government is legitimate. But because government is justified on the basis of individual self-interest, the ends or purposes of government are public, not private. All governments will properly be concerned with providing for the welfare of their citizens.

Hobbes's hypothetical devices of a state of nature and of a covenant that establishes civil society are intended and designed to establish two points. One, for citizens, is the necessity of an absolute, unlimited Sovereign to enforce the laws necessary for stability and security. The second, for rulers, is to stress that the justifications and purposes of government are ultimately the contribution that government makes to the individual pursuit of self-interest. To make the Sovereign anything less than absolute is to invite conflict over power, and among other things, this would weaken the ability of the Sovereign to enforce the law. A Sovereign less effective in enforcing the law would be unable to adequately protect citizens from each other, and they would eventually revert to the state of nature.

Hobbes's arguments for an absolute Sovereign are quite independent of his treatment of another question: What form shall the state take? To this Hobbes has two answers. The first is that it does not matter what kind of government there is, as long as it has a monopoly of power, and it is unlimited in its authority. Secondly, Hobbes believes that democracy is not possible in practice, and that monarchy is preferable to aristocracy. This means that while he considers it possible for the Sovereign to be one man, or an assembly of men, his preference is for the former. It is his belief that an assembly of men would suffer from internal conflict, largely because the members would be concerned as much or more with their own personal well-being than with that of the

Commonwealth. It is worth remembering the contemporary context, though; all governments in Hobbes's day were absolute and unlimited in their exercise of power and authority. There was nothing "new" or "radical" in his suggestion that government must be absolute.

One reason we may reject Hobbes's insistence on an absolute Sovereign is the value we place on liberty, a condition to which the notion of an absolute Sovereign seems totally opposed. We ought, then, to consider Hobbes's treatment of liberty, especially since we have identified him as a great *liberal* thinker. He defines **LIBERTY** as "the absence of external impediments" (*Leviathan,* Ch. XIV), in which light it appears that the state of nature is a condition of absolute (unhindered) liberty (since there is no authority). In the civil state accomplished by the Commonwealth, the impediments to liberty are provided by Civil Laws, that is, the laws made and enforced by the Sovereign. The establishment of government thus entails an agreement by the subjects that their liberty will be limited by the Sovereign, and these limits are established by the laws the Sovereign makes. It should be stressed that liberty is not confined by authority. If this were the case, then the establishment of an absolute Sovereign would also amount to the absence of citizen liberty. It is *law* that limits liberty, and therefore how much or how little liberty citizens enjoy will depend on the nature of the law made by the Sovereign. Hence Hobbes's famous formulation, that the liberty of citizens consists in "the silence of the Law." While Hobbes insists upon an absolute Sovereign, he also believes the Sovereign will permit subjects an extensive sphere of personal liberty, and this is done by the making of "good laws," defined as those which are "needful, for the good of the people, and withall perspicuous" (*Leviathan,* ch. XXX).

There are two important points here. The first is that authority is not a personal possession of those who exercise it, but something justified on the basis of the interests of those governed. The state exists and is justified solely for public and not private purposes. Second, the role of the state is to provide, through a framework of law, an environment of stability and security in which individuals continue to pursue the self-interest that lies at the core of their nature. The individuals Hobbes described in the state of nature are the same ones who inhabit civil society: self-interested, appetitive, desiring power after power, competitive, and however rational, subject to the strength of their passions. The institution of government does not seek to change men, but rather to provide the conditions within which their natures can coexist peacefully and prosper. It does so through the framework of law, and the power that enforces this law, in Hobbes's view, must have no rivals, no limits, and no external authority to which it answers.

Any evaluation of Hobbes's political theory must give due consideration to the context within which he was writing. On the divide, as it were, between feudal society and modern market society, Hobbes gives us a vision of government for the newly emerging society, while still reflecting many of the assumptions and maintaining many of the formulations of the old. He is a radical conservative, a liberal monarchist, a modern thinker at work in an as yet unmodern world. We should not evaluate Hobbes's work as the last word in modern liberal thought, but rather as its initial systematic statement; there is much in Hobbes that survives in later philosophies, as well as much that is discarded.

Locke, curiously enough, is much more traditional than Hobbes when it comes to human nature, morality, and our relationship to society, but much more modern when it comes to confidence in institutions. In important ways, Locke has more confidence than Hobbes in our ability to use our reason and, recognizing the law of nature, to regulate our passions and live together morally. For this reason Locke imagines that we could live peaceably, sociably, in a state of nature without government, but with property, money, and other features of social existence. Indeed, it is conflicts over property that, in Locke's view, form the greatest impediment to our peaceful existence in the state of nature, and it is for the protection of property (which, we should note, Locke defines as "life, liberty, and possessions") that we abandon the state of nature and create a political society.

Like Hobbes, then, Locke puts a social contract at the beginning of **CIVIL SOCIETY**—a mutual agreement among those who wish security and stability. Unlike Hobbes, though, Locke writes as if the social contract is not hypothetical but a real, historical event, and unlike Hobbes he conceives this to be a contract *between* the Sovereign and the subjects. Therefore, the origin of government is the *consent of the governed*, which constitutes a genuine notion of **POPULAR SOVEREIGNTY**. Locke even argues that the people have a right to revolution if the Sovereign becomes a tyrant or abuses the terms of the social contract. This also means that Locke is willing, unlike Hobbes, to place limits on the authority of the Sovereign. The unanimity of all participants in

Hobbes's imaginary covenant is replaced by the more practical principle of *majority rule* in Locke's version.

Perhaps the most important revision Locke makes is the notion that the Sovereign power can be divided; indeed it *must* be divided, the executive and the legislative powers placed in different hands. This presents a clear expression of and argument for the doctrine of the *separation of powers* that was to be so influential among designers of liberal constitutions. Contrary to Hobbes's preference for monarchy, Locke argues that the legislative power should be in the hands of an assembly, a body of men who together make the law, but are also at the same time subject to it. Locke insists that the legislative power is the supreme power, in part because he also insists that the people have a right to alter the legislature when it acts contrary to the trust placed in it. By making a series of important modifications to the arguments that Hobbes had advanced, Locke presents a picture of government much more familiar to us than Hobbes's absolute Sovereign. We should be clear that Locke was no more a democrat than Hobbes, but he did articulate the principles of popular sovereignty and of representative government. He simply assumed, as did most thinkers of his day, that the class of citizens who might vote and sit in the legislature would be limited to males who held a significant amount of property.

Hobbes had written within the context of the English Civil War, a struggle—complicated by religious issues—between the monarchy and those defending Parliament. In 1688 the Glorious Revolution installed William and Mary of Orange on the English throne and guaranteed a Protestant succession. More importantly, the new monarchs agreed to conditions that eventually resulted in the supremacy of Parliament and led to an increasing diminution of the active role of the monarch in political affairs. We now know that Locke's *Second Treatise on Government* was written in anticipation of the Glorious Revolution, and the outcome—a limited government of the propertied class represented in an assembly, subject to majority rule; executive power in the monarch, subordinate to the legislative power—corresponds rather well to the basic outlines of Locke's theory.

**4.5
ROUSSEAU AND BURKE**

Jean-Jacques Rousseau and Edmund Burke are two critical voices within the liberal tradition, opposing each other from opposite sides of the French Revolution. In their thought the emphasis turns to the relationship of liberty to **EQUALITY**, or in Burke's case, to **INEQUALITY**.

Writing in pre-revolutionary France, Rousseau was a critic of absolute monarchy and of the social, economic, and political inequality of the late feudal and early modern periods. Interestingly, while there is in the liberal celebration of the individual a potentially powerful current of egalitarianism (promoting equality), liberalism has succeeded as a political ideology in part because it has been blind to, or been able to turn a blind eye to, certain economic, political, and social inequalities. Rousseau stands out for his uncompromising egalitarianism, which has an elegantly liberal basis: we cannot be free if we are not equal. For Rousseau, liberty is not the absence of law, but rather the absence of dependence upon another or others. Freedom is independence. Whatever else they may be, social and economic inequalities outline relationships in which some are dependent on others, and unevenly so. The dominance of the wealthy master over the dependent servant gives the former a liberty denied to the latter—an idea that worked its way through German thought via Hegel to Marx (see next section). Rousseau, though, was not an early socialist: his ideal society is pre-industrial and his hero is the independent farmer/artisan, self-sufficient in his own labour on the land and the materials it supplies him.

In the earlier of the two political works for which he is best known, the *Discourse on the Origin of Inequality*, Rousseau presents a state of nature almost diametrically opposed to Hobbes's. Here primitive man (as Nature formed him) roams the forest, all wants readily supplied because his needs are as yet very simple. This is the famous "noble savage," living at peace with all other creatures, if yet somewhat indifferent to them. All humans are equal; all are free. The differences between individuals do not yet make a difference.

Development beyond this initial condition is initially a blessing, but contains within it the seeds of a subsequent fall. At first, solitary man becomes social, living in community with others and enjoying the benefits of collective effort and company, without surrendering the independence of the one who works for himself. It is in society, though, that humans begin to compare themselves with others, and in society that social, economic, and political distinctions and inequality eventually arise. Nonetheless, as long as humans are socially united but remain economically independent of one another, they are, in Rousseau's view, in the best of all possible worlds. The central moment where this all begins to unravel is the introduction of private **PROPERTY**, conceived of as ownership of land. Private property relations lead to a division of labour, to exchange, to profit, exploitation, and inequality. What begins as a relatively equal distribution becomes increasingly—and for Rousseau inevitably—an unequal concentration in the hands of a few. Now the natural differences between humans are able to contribute to differences that are lasting and can be passed from one generation to the next.

In this *Discourse* Rousseau follows Locke in seeing political society as something created by those with property wishing to protect it from those without. The degree of political inequality will be initially a direct function of the degree of economic inequality at the time government is instituted. As economic inequality increases over time, so too will political inequality, until a situation is reached of complete despotic rule of one individual over the rest (Rousseau's view of absolute monarchy). As this all too brief sketch implies, Rousseau is a fatalist; he believes not in inevitable progress, but in inevitable decline, a position which certainly set him apart from most thinkers of his day.

Rousseau's fatalism is also present, although less pronounced, in his most famous work, *The Social Contract*. This book presents Rousseau's answer to one fundamental question: "What conditions must be satisfied for government to be legitimate?" Speaking hypothetically, Rousseau does not criticize any particular state (although in effect he condemns them all). Starting from rather liberal premises, Rousseau reaches different conclusions from the liberal thinkers we introduced in the previous section. Like Hobbes, Rousseau begins with the notion that individuals are by nature free and equal. To be legitimate, any political society must be voluntary, not forced. In agreeing to political community we surrender our natural liberty to the community in exchange for civil liberty. Our bond with others is "a form of association which will defend the person and goods of each member with the collective force of all, and under which each individual, while uniting himself with the others, obeys no one but himself, and remains as free as before" (Bk. I, ch. 6). A very important point here is Rousseau's definition of liberty, seen not as Hobbes did, in "the silence of the law," but in "obedience to a law we give to ourselves." The absence of law is merely licence; we are free when we are self-regulating, self-determining beings.

In Rousseau's legitimate political community we will be collectively self-governing by virtue of our participation in what he calls the "general will": "Each one of us puts into the community his person and all his power under the supreme direction of the general will; and as a body, we incorporate every member as an indivisible part of the whole" (Bk. I, ch. 6). What this amounts to in simple terms is a fully democratic body politic, in which all the citizens take part collectively in making the laws by which they are governed as individuals. To paraphrase Rousseau, the Sovereign is all the people, and never anything less than all the people. In other words, Rousseau identifies legitimate government with full popular sovereignty, realized through the democratic participation of the people as legislators.

Obviously, Rousseau's vision of the citizen body legislating draws upon his knowledge of the constitutions of ancient Greece. Like the ancients he also believed that laws should be relatively simple and not require great adjustment or supplementation; while the people would be Sovereign, the Sovereign would not be extremely busy. As for administering the law, or applying it to particular cases, this is what Rousseau called "government" (what he also called and we will identify below in Chapter Seven as the "executive function"), and he expected that this would be carried out by a much smaller group of deputies acting on instructions from the Sovereign and continually accountable to the Sovereign.

There is much more that is interesting and much that is controversial in Rousseau's *Social Contract*. Exactly what he understood the general will to be; whether or not his political theory justifies totalitarian rule; the reasons why he believed any political community, however wisely constructed, will nonetheless become corrupted and degenerate; the role of the legislator, of civil religion—all these are beyond our scope here, but they make a careful reading of the *Social Contract* worthwhile. What ought to be stressed is Rousseau's vision of legitimate government as a fully democratic state, and one not only founded on initial conditions of equality and freedom, but ultimately surviving only so long as it is able to maintain some semblance of these conditions. Rousseau's understanding of the relationship between liberty and equality, and of the collective participation of citizens in a common good (i.e., the general will), makes him a powerful source of the communitarian tradition that has developed within modern democratic thought. As with many thinkers, with Rousseau it is the broad outlines and powerful principles of his thought more than the details of his politics that have inspired others.

Among those who drew upon Rousseau's political thought were many important figures behind the French Revolution of 1789; the revolutionary slogan "liberty, equality, fraternity" certainly seems Rousseauian in spirit, if not in words. While there is a strong case to argue that Rousseau (who died in 1778) was wary of revolutions in general and would have disapproved of much of what the French Revolution embodied, it remains nonetheless true that for many the events of 1789 and the political thought of Rousseau were necessarily linked. One who certainly seemed to think so was Edmund Burke, the English thinker and statesman.

Burke's writings and speeches often seem to be the fount from which all modern conservatism flows. Although Burke sat in the English Parliament as a Whig for almost thirty years, he was both an aristocratic and a situational conservative. The key to Burke's apparent inconsistency (he could support the American Revolution and condemn the French Revolution) is the gradual way in which England became liberal, so that parliamentary, representative government coexisted with a traditional monarchy, landed aristocracy, and the absence of democracy. Burke supported *all* the fundamental institutions of his England. His most famous work is the *Reflections on the Revolution in France* (1790), written before, but anticipating those darkest periods of the upheaval that became known as The Terror. Here he lamented that "the age of chivalry is gone. That of sophisters, economists, and calculators has succeeded, and the glory of Europe is extinguished forever." In contrast to the revolutionary spirit, Burke preached a loyalty to traditional institutions:

> We know that we have made no discoveries, and we think that no discoveries are to be made, in morality, nor many in the great principles of government, nor in the ideas of liberty, which were understood long before we were born, altogether as well as they will be after the grave has heaped its mould upon our presumption and the silent tomb shall have imposed its law on our pert loquacity.... We fear God; we look up with awe to kings, with affection to parliaments, with duty to magistrates, with reverence to priests, and with respect to nobility ... instead of casting away all our old prejudices, we cherish them to a very considerable degree, and ... the longer they have lasted and the

more generally they have prevailed, the more we cherish them. (*Reflections*)

In addition to praising traditionalism, Burke's conservatism also celebrates the virtue of a natural aristocracy. Burke believed in the hierarchical ordering of society, and that the privileged orders, namely the nobility and the clergy, were what give to society its civilization and refinement:

> Nothing is more certain than that our manners, our civilization, and all the good things which are connected with manners and with civilization have, in this European world of ours, depended for ages upon two principles ... I mean the spirit of a gentleman and the spirit of religion. The nobility and the clergy, the one by profession, the other by patronage, kept learning in existence, even in the midst of arms and confusions, and whilst governments were rather in their causes than formed. Learning paid back what it received to nobility and to priesthood, and paid it with usury, by enlarging their ideas and by furnishing their minds. (*Reflections*)

Last, but not least, we remember Burke for his defence of the autonomy of representatives from their constituents, expressed in a speech still quoted today by MPs wishing to justify taking a position they know to be contrary to the opinions of their electorate. We will consider Burke's arguments for this autonomy in our chapter on democracy. Interestingly, this is an issue on which Burke and Rousseau stand at completely opposite poles, Rousseau arguing that any representatives could only be deputies, mere agents carrying out the instructions of the people to whom they remain ever accountable. Rousseau says on this that "The English people believes itself to be free; ... it is only free during the election of Members of Parliament; as soon as the Members are elected the people is enslaved; it is nothing" (*Social Contract*, III, 15).

Karl Marx is undoubtedly the most influential figure in all of political ideology. His thought drew upon and extended three currents in the history of ideas. The one most obvious is his transformation of the socialist and communist ideas of the early nineteenth century into something based less on utopian ethical theories and more on a social scientific appreciation of economic and political forces. Socialism has been dominated by Marxism (either directly, or in opposition to it), and both liberalism and conservatism have been shaped by their struggles against Marxism. We will examine socialism and Marx's contribution to it in Chapter Five.

Second, most of Marx's life was devoted to the study, analysis, and critique of capitalist economic theory and practice. In this effort he was part of the political economy tradition established by liberal thinkers such as Adam Smith, David Ricardo, and James Mill. One does not have to be a socialist to recognize the strength of Marx's critique of capitalism and the responses it has (in part) generated. We will examine this critique in greater detail in Chapter Seventeen.

The other major dimension of Marx's thought, and in fact, his original occupation, was as one of a group of philosophers known as the Young Hegelians—left-wing disciples of Hegel, the Prussian idealist and conservative. Marx turned Hegel's idealism upside-down, but retained certain features of Hegel's idiosyncratic logic, the result being what Marx called historical materialism, and that Engels and Lenin would later develop as dialectical materialism. More intriguing, though, was Marx's exploration of some other themes in Hegel's thought, which led him to the notion of "alienation." Marx argues that it is our nature to be active, creative beings, expressing ourselves in and through the products of our labour—i.e., our activity with the materials of nature. We are alienated from our essence or nature when the conditions of our labouring activity are perverted. In his early writings Marx rejects capitalism because the wage-labour relation is alienating. That is, once we sell our labour power for a wage to an employer our labouring activity is no longer freely creative: the products of our activity are no longer ours, the activity itself is now under the direction of another, and our relations to others are now mediated by impersonal things. In this way, Marx rejects capitalism less for its inequality, and more for the assault on our freedom that this inequality entails. It is possible to extend Marx's critique from the division of labour and wage relations to the effects of technology and a culture of entertainment on our

4.6
MARX AND MILL

potential and actual development as freely creating agents. Just as much has been done in the world in the name of Marx that bears no relation to anything he ever wrote, so too does his influence on any number of intellectual disciplines remain strong, quite irrespective of the future success or failure of socialist political movements.

Both Marx and his contemporary, John Stuart Mill, demonstrated key elements of nineteenth-century thinking in their work, in particular the recognition of human development, both individually and collectively as peoples or even as a "species." Human nature is not a static given, but a potential to be developed, or a possibility to be realized, and politics can be about providing the opportunities for the fullest flowering of human individuality, or about removing the obstacles to this unfolding of human nature's richness. On this point, despite a host of differences, Marx and Mill were in essential agreement. If Marx is the giant of nineteenth-century socialism, whose thought has inspired generations of left-wing critics of capitalism in the last two centuries, Mill has played a similar role for liberalism, and particularly for the reformist liberalism we will identify more clearly in Chapter Five. Mill may in fact have been one of the last great polymaths (an expert in several fields), something demonstrated by the number of his contributions of note to political science.

Of least interest to students today, perhaps, is Mill's contribution to political methodology in his *Logic*, where he distinguishes four "methods of experimental inquiry," work that remained influential well into this century. Also, Mill was yet another in the line of British political economists, one who came at the end of his life to a tentative endorsement of democratic (but not revolutionary) socialism. His socialism remained grounded in liberal principles, and for this reason he continues to attract the attention of those interested in developing a liberal social democracy. A third area in which Mill was active was the advocacy of women's rights; he advocated a "perfect equality" between the sexes in his work *The Subjection of Women* (1869), and as a member of Parliament he introduced legislation to give women the right to vote, although it would be another fifty years before the British Parliament so moved. Mill's arguments on this matter were typical of his thought: the subjection that women endure in marriage and in society is an impediment to their liberty, which not only limits them from developing their full potential, but in doing so impedes the full perfection of *both* sexes.

Mill provided perhaps the most attractive presentation of **UTILITARIANISM**, a stream of liberalism based on a hedonistic (pleasure-seeking) psychology, rather than arguments from an imagined or hypothetical state of nature. The idea that each of us seeks to maximize our pleasure and minimize our pains was very central to Hobbes, but utilitarians turned this into an ethical and political theory, and looked to maximize social, rather than merely individual utility. The first famous utilitarian was Jeremy Bentham, who formulated the principle of the "greatest happiness of the greatest number" as the maxim on which all rational government should rest. Although simple, and intuitively attractive, there are difficulties with realizing this idea consistently, particularly in the notion that we can assign values to pleasures or pains, or that we should treat all pleasures as equally deserving of consideration, or that only the consequences of actions and not the intentions or motivations are what matter. A friend and disciple of Bentham was James Mill, whose son, John Stuart, was a pupil of both. The younger Mill's contribution to utilitarianism was to argue for a qualitative difference between pleasures, and hence for a maximization of those higher pleasures that are the product of civilization and the better realization of our human potential. Mill was a "rule utilitarian," meaning that he believed not that each act should be considered in terms of its contribution to the greatest happiness of the greatest number, but that the moral rules of society are derived on the strength of their tendency to produce the greatest happiness of the greatest number.

There is a certain logic in the utilitarian concern for the greatest happiness of the greatest number that leads in the direction of democracy. James Mill had concluded that the self-interest that drives us to seek pleasure and avoid pain makes it necessary for our security that we have a share in government, or else be abused by those who do have such a share: "Whenever the powers of government are placed in any hands other than those of the community—whether those of one man, of a few, or of several—those principles of human nature which imply that government is at all necessary imply that those persons will make use of them to defeat the very end for which government exists" (*Essay on Government*). Concluding that it would not be practical for the people to exercise the authority of the state directly, James Mill advocated representative government chosen by the people. Then, recognizing how radical a proposal this was, he considered if it would be possible to have this government chosen by

KEY TERMS

aesthetics
citizenship
civil society
consent
epistemology
equality
ethics
historical materialism
idealism
individualism
inequality
instrumentalism
liberty
logic
materialism
metaphysics (ontology)
natural law
polis
popular sovereignty
property
regimes
social contract
state of nature
telos
tradition
utilitarianism

**REFERENCES AND
SUGGESTED READING**

**A. Primary Texts in
Political Philosophy**

PLATO
Selected Dialogues (especially *The
Apology, Crito*)
The Republic

ARISTOTLE:
The Politics
The Nichomachean Ethics

AQUINAS
Summa Theologiae (selections)

MACHIAVELLI
The Prince
The Discourses

HOBBES
Leviathan

LOCKE
The Two Treatises on Government

ROUSSEAU
*Discourse on the Origin of
Inequality*
The Social Contract

MARX
The German Ideology
Manifesto of the Communist Party
Critique of the Gotha Programme

JOHN STUART MILL
Utilitarianism
*Considerations on Representative
Government*
On Liberty

anything less than all the people. By a dubious set of arguments, James Mill reduced the electorate necessary for good government to the richest one-third of males over the age of forty. Even his friend Bentham, who had by the end of his life become a democrat, found James Mill's arguments ridiculous, but in many circles the criticism was that Mill's proposals went too far and would have given too much power to the wrong sort of people.

At any rate, the topic of representative government was one to which the younger Mill eventually turned, publishing a work on the subject in 1861. Typically, while the older utilitarians had justified democracy as a means of protecting the people from the abuse of power, J.S. Mill recommended representative government as a means of involving the public in political life, and of thereby educating them to nobler purposes: "the most important point of excellence which any form of government can possess is to promote the virtue and intelligence of the people themselves" (*Considerations on Representative Government*). If this seems rather Aristotelian, then so too might Mill's proposal that those with education should be given more votes than those without, and skilled labourers more votes than unskilled, etc. Like the classical thinkers, Mill believed that government should be placed in the hands of the wisest; unlike them, though, he thought that all have the potential to become wise, and in an ideally constituted society, all would become so.

There are several dimensions of Mill's thought, such as the differential voting for those with "higher intelligence," or the utilitarian pursuit of the "higher" pleasures, which seem elitist. This may also seem to be the case with his concern in the essay *On Liberty* with the possibility of a "tyranny of the majority" and the dangers of "collective mediocrity." In every case, however, Mill is concerned with the promotion of what is finest in human nature and with opposing any obstacles to the development of the potential that is in each one. As a liberal, Mill believed that the best in human nature is promoted by encouraging the greatest possible room for individuality, the largest grant of individual liberty that is consistent with the happiness principle that utilitarianism enjoins. Accordingly, Mill's most famous work is the essay *On Liberty*, the classical defence of liberty of thought, expression, and individuality (or what we might today call "lifestyle"). In this work, Mill articulates the famous (if philosophically controversial) principle that "the sole end for which mankind are warranted, individually or collectively, in interfering with the liberty of action of any of their number is self-protection....The only part of the conduct of any one, for which he is amenable to society, is that which concerns others. In the part which merely concerns himself, his independence is, of right, absolute. Over himself, over his own body and mind, the individual is sovereign" (*On Liberty*).

Mill's arguments in this work have provided inspiration to liberals of every generation since, and are often quoted (or misquoted) in whole or part to justify any number of liberal positions. What is sometimes forgotten is that Mill's greatest concern in this essay is not with government, or with the laws enforced by the state, but rather with the power of public opinion. It is the pressures of mass society for conformity that stifle individuality and creativity, that impede the full development of human nature(s). In an age of media-informed consumerism and globalization, one wonders what Mill might conclude today. It is also interesting that Mill did not base his arguments for individual liberty on claims about rights, but instead on the consequences of this liberty for the collective well-being of humanity: "utility in the largest sense, grounded on the permanent interests of a man as a progressive being" (*On Liberty*). These phrases crystallize the concern that seems to have inspired Mill in all his investigations and conclusions.

There are two reasons for ending our tour of political philosophy at this point. One is that as we move from the nineteenth into the twentieth century, political philosophy becomes increasingly less accessible to the educated layperson and more something that requires specialized training and background in philosophy to understand. While this is not universally so, it has become true of large areas of philosophy, especially those drawing upon thinkers from continental Europe, and in particular in the second half of this century. Political philosophy today is very often less about the traditional objects of politics—institutions of government, political processes, etc.—and more about ontology, or theories of meaning, or linguistic analysis. The second reason for turning from philosophy at this point is that political thought, up to and including much of the nineteenth century, was largely the work of a few thinkers who participated in a philosophic tradition. With the nineteenth century came the development of modern urban societies, of newspapers, the beginnings of mass culture, of political parties, trade unions, public libraries, and lecture circuits. In short, political ideas began to be popularized

B. Collections of Political Philosophy

Ebenstein, William, and Alan O. Ebenstein, eds. 1992. *Introduction to Political Thinkers*. New York: Harcourt Brace Jovanovich.

Losco, Joseph, and Leonard Williams, eds. 1992. *Political Theory: Classical Writings, Contemporary Views*. New York: St. Martin's Press.

Porter, Jene M., ed. 1989 *Classical Political Philosophy*. Englewood Cliffs, NJ: Prentice Hall.

4.7 CONCLUSION

C. Histories of Political Philosophy

Plamanetz, John. 1963. *Man and Society*. London: Longmans.

Sabine, George. 1950 [1937]. *A History of Political Theory*, rev. ed. New York: Henry Holt.

Strauss, Leo, and Joseph Cropsey. 1987. *History of Political Philosophy*, 3rd ed. Chicago: University of Chicago Press.

D. Other

Bowle, John. 1961. *Western Political Thought*. London: Methuen.

Halévy, Elie. 1972. *The Growth of Philosophical Radicalism*. London: Faber & Faber.

Held, David, ed. 1991. *Political Theory Today*. Oxford: Polity.

Horowitz, Asher, and Gad Horowitz. 1988. *"Everywhere They Are In Chains": Political Theory from Rousseau to Marx*. Scarborough, Ont.: Nelson.

Irwin, Terence. 1989. *Classical Thought*. Oxford: Oxford University Press.

MacIntyre, Alasdair. 1984. *After Virtue*, 2nd ed. Notre Dame, Ind.: University of Notre Dame Press.

Sinclair, T.A. 1959. *A History of Greek Political Thought*. London: Routledge & Kegan Paul.

Stace, William. 1955. *The Philosophy of Hegel*. New York: Dover.

Wolin, Sheldon. 1960. *Politics and Vsion*. Boston: Little, Brown.

and to be expressed in forms that, while grounded in the ideas of political philosophers, were no longer confined to either philosophers or a narrow circle of educated political actors. Beginning in earnest in the nineteenth century, and continuing into the twentieth, was the age of **IDEOLOGY**.

SOMETHING TO CONSIDER

Is there any value, for today's citizens, in being acquainted with the basic ideas of political philosophy? Whatever your answer, does this say more about political philosophy or about today's political practice?

---

5 ideology

Few among us will become political philosophers, but many will come to adhere to an ideology, or more likely, come to hold beliefs of an ideological character. Terms like "liberal," "conservative," "radical," "progressive," "reformist," and "populist" are commonly used to describe the positions staked out by political actors and their supporters and allies. Like many political science terms, "ideology" is employed in different ways. Here ideology will be defined as *a more or less consistent set of beliefs about the nature of the society in which individuals live and about the proper role of the state in establishing or maintaining that society* (see also Figure 1.1). It may be useful to compare ideology with political philosophy, which we discussed in the previous chapter.

Like philosophy, ideology is *systematic*: beliefs about one topic are related to beliefs about another, different subject. For example, beliefs about the nature (real or ideal) of society may be connected somehow to beliefs about the role(s) of the state in society, which in turn informs beliefs about a particular policy such as child care or tax cuts or gun control. It is sometimes useful to think of ideologies as sets of answers to questions that range from the very general and abstract to the concrete and particular. Also, like political philosophies, ideologies are *normative*. They are beliefs about how the world *ought* to be. A related dimension of ideology, but not necessarily of philosophy, is that it orients action or requires change in the world, following up on the normative beliefs contained in ideology. Ideologies typically offer or inform a program of action that seeks to transform the world from the way it is into what (for the ideology) is its ideal shape. (Conversely, the ideology may seek to protect a valued way of life from change.) The capacity of ideologies to guide or even incite polit-

5.1
IDEOLOGY DEFINED

5.1   Ideology Defined
5.2   Classic Liberalism
5.3   Traditional Conservatism
5.4   Socialism
5.5   Shifting Contexts
5.6   Reform Liberalism
5.7   Liberal Conservatism
5.8   Socialism: Communism and
      Social Democracy
5.9   Beyond the Consensus
      5.9.1   Anarchism
      5.9.2   Populism
      5.9.3   Feminism
      5.9.4   Environmentalism
      5.9.5   Nationalism
5.10 Beyond Ideology?

MARX'S VIEW OF IDEOLOGY

"The ideas of the ruling class are in every epoch the ruling ideas: i.e., the class which is the ruling *material* force of society is at the same time its ruling *intellectual* force. The class which has the means of material production at its disposal, consequently also controls the means of mental production, so that the ideas of those who lack the means of mental production are on the whole subject to it....

If now in considering the course of history we detach the ideas of the ruling class from the ruling class itself and attribute to them an independent existence, if we confine ourselves to saying that these or those ideas were dominant at a given time, without bothering ourselves about the conditions of production and the producers of these ideas, if we thus ignore the individuals and world conditions which are the source of the ideas, then we can say, for instance, that during the time the aristocracy was dominant, the concepts honour, loyalty, etc., were dominant, during the dominance of the bourgeoisie the concepts freedom, equality, etc. The ruling class itself on the whole imagines this to be so. This conception of history, which is common to all historians, particularly since the eighteenth century, will necessarily come up against the phenomenon that ever more abstract ideas hold sway, i.e., ideas which increasingly take on the form of universality. For each new class which puts itself in the place of one ruling before it is compelled, merely in order to carry through its aim, to present its interest as the common interest of all the members of society, that is, expressed in ideal form: it has to give its ideas the form of universality, and present them as the only rational, universally valid ones."
— *The German Ideology*, MECW, 1976: V, 59-60

ical activity is one principal feature that makes them interesting to social scientists.

In addition to promoting a specific view of how the world should be, an ideology very often presupposes definite notions about what the world *is*, or employs unique concepts to explain or make sense of the world of experience. For example, both radical feminism and Marxism seek to eradicate inequality from the world, but each identifies inequality differently, and the equality each seeks to establish is distinct (although not necessarily incompatible). The primary concept Marxists have used to describe and explain the social relations of society is that of **CLASS**. For radical feminists, the structure of social reality is provided not primarily by class but by **PATRIARCHY**, the historical subjugation of women by men through socially constituted gender relations. Feminists do not deny the existence of the economic or material relations indicated by the term "class" but argue that these are not the *essential* relationships. The point of this example, then, is that ideologies can operate as different ways of seeing and understanding the social world(s) we inhabit, and this, too, is similar to the way philosophy can shape our perceptions.

Karl Marx argued that the ruling ideology in any society will be that which protects and reflects the interests of the dominant economic class (*even though* it may not be presented or understood by its adherents in such terms). Two of Marx's ideas on this subject have been adapted by others who might agree with him on little else: one is the (often hidden) connection of ideas with interests; the other the notion that ideologies are partial views of social and political reality, and in this partiality or bias are incomplete or even untrue. Of course, it is not necessary for ideas to be true to be powerful or to regulate activity.

Ideologies differ from political philosophy in several ways. First, and perhaps most obviously, they are simpler, proceeding at a less sophisticated level of abstraction. Second, and related to the first, they are more popular and more accessible to a broader public than is philosophy. Finally, ideologies can be described as "political philosophies geared for action": they are thus primarily about changing the world (or preserving it from change). The philosopher continues to ask about what the political world is and how it should be; the ideologue has definite answers to these questions and seeks to put them into practice.

The implication here is that ideologies are fundamentally critical in their orientation: while this is often true, it is not universally so. Many ideologies are basically critical of the existing social and political arrangements (the **STATUS QUO**) and present programs for radical change. But ideologies may also justify a status quo and present a program that resists fundamental reform. When an **IDEOLOGICAL CONSENSUS** emerges in a society, ideology may be much less about creating social change or transformation than about presenting competing solutions to problems or managing change brought about by other circumstances.

One last general observation is that ideology, even more than philosophy, is determined by **CONTEXTS**. Because ideology is oriented to political action, it is sensitive to the actual politics of particular societies, and in this way is reactive to the specific contexts of place and time. We must pay particular attention to the way ideology reacts to specific circumstances to explain why conservatives in such countries as Britain and the United States want government to give greater freedom to market forces, while conservatives in Eastern Europe resist reforms that would do just that. Or to understand why contemporary conservatives are often difficult to distinguish from early nineteenth-century liberals. Comparative politics teaches us that within any given society an ideology or two will dominate, a couple of others may compete, and the rest are absent or so marginal as to elude the acquaintance of most citizens. Differences in public support for gun control in the United States and Canada, or the contrast between the success of socialism in Europe and its absence in the United States, reflect the fact that the ideological landscape in each of these settings is distinct. The success in the United States of liberal conservatism with its distrust of the state is no doubt in part rooted in the birth of that country through revolution against a perceived tyrannical power. The viability of tory and socialist parties in Europe in the past has probably owed something to the clarity with which class is perceived in formerly feudal societies. Each case deserves to be considered on its own merits.

Similarly, the meaning of "liberal" changed in the United States after the Depression and the Roosevelt New Deal, and seems to mean something quite different today than it did 25 years ago. How will ideologies that sustained themselves in the context of the Cold War redefine themselves in its absence? It is as much because of shifting temporal contexts as anything else that the meanings of liberalism, conservatism, and even socialism have been impermanent. For this reason it is useful to approach ideologies as having undergone changes that allow us to speak of different "generations." In turning to specific ideologies we will examine the context in which the ideology arose and by which it was defined, as well as the ways in which successive changes in context have transformed ideological perspectives.

5.2 CLASSIC LIBERALISM

Liberalism is the first modern ideology and still remains the dominant ideology of the contemporary age. The context in which liberalism was born was one of reaction to the feudal structures of medieval society. From the mid-seventeenth to the early nineteenth centuries, liberalism received systematic articulation and refinement by a series of philosophers and political activists.

The reaction against the organic, hierarchical structure of feudal society is seen clearly in three characteristics of liberalism:

a) a focus that gives primary value to the individual;

b) the view that society is an artificial construct; and

c) a belief in the rational, instrumental character of political institutions, which liberals justify on the basis of their contribution to the self-interest of individuals.

JOHN LOCKE

"[W]e must consider what state all men are naturally in, and that is, a *state of perfect freedom* to order their actions and dispose of their possessions, and persons as they think fit, within the bounds of the law of nature, without asking leave, or depending upon the will of any other man.

A *state* also *of equality*, wherein all the power and jurisdiction is reciprocal, no one having more than another ..."

— *Second Treatise*, 4

If medieval society embodied the dominance of social structure over individuals, then liberalism is the political philosophy of **INDIVIDUALISM**; political community is somewhat artificial, something we establish from our position as individuals in order to improve our personal well-being. Correspondingly, social structures or institutions are reasonable instruments (i.e., means we devise with our reason) that ought to maximize the well-being of individuals. Liberal thinkers have differed in identifying the character of well-being (security, pleasure, self-determination), but they have agreed that political society ought to secure this individual well-being. The verb "secure" is important here, for early liberals believed the state should provide a framework of laws and order within which individuals could safely pursue their own interests. They did not believe that the state should actually provide the tangible means of well-being to individuals. Early liberal thought, then, is not only about self-interest, but also about self-reliance and self-regulation.

Liberalism is the ideology not only of individualism, but also of freedom or liberty. Liberals believe that we are free by nature, but surrender some of our liberty to live in society with others, a surrender made in exchange for some other good, like security.

("By nature," liberals believe, we are also equal, but this receives less emphasis.) Liberals see government as a necessary evil and seek to restrict the extent of limitations on personal liberty. Increasingly, this liberty has come to be expressed or defined through appeal to individual **RIGHTS**, which are claims sometimes made against other citizens, but also and most importantly against the state. Government exists—at least in theory—to serve the interests of *all* individuals. To ensure this, liberals argue for limits on the state, such as removing certain subjects from the compass of state authority (as in the device of rights), or giving greater control over government to the individuals whom government is supposed to serve (as through democracy). Either path embodies the notion of **CONSTITUTIONALISM**, and this in turn implies **POPULAR SOVEREIGNTY**.

Constitutionalism means that there are established, understood rules concerning the exercise of power and authority and that those who exercise power and authority respect these rules. In practice this means a set of limits or restraints on the scope of governmental authority or power, and the rules that provide this restraint embody a constitution, the most fundamental law of a polity. Clearly, constitutionalism is liberalism's response to the arbitrary, personal nature of absolute power as it developed at the end of the feudal period.

Popular sovereignty is the notion that the authority or power of the state is traced ultimately to the people who are governed within that state. Authority is entrusted to elites by the people and is to be exercised for the people's interest. Early liberals were somewhat uneasy about democracy and looked for other constitutional means of keeping rulers in check. In Britain, liberals (called Whigs) pushed for **RESPONSIBLE GOVERNMENT**, and the so-called Glorious (or Whig) Revolution of 1688 led to a system of responsible government that has been the model for most of the world's parliamentary constitutions. Responsible government means that the political executive is not able to act without the support of a majority in the legislature (i.e., the chamber of representatives). A different path to the same goal was the advocacy of **MIXED GOVERNMENT**, of a **SEPARATION OF POWERS**, as embodied in the American Constitution. Through history, mixed government had meant tempering government by one (monarchy) with government by the few (aristocracy) and by the many (democracy). This was the model for the American Constitution of a President, Supreme Court, and Congress, with

JOHN LOCKE

"Men being, as has been said, by Nature, all free, equal and independent, no one can be put out of this estate, and subjected to the political power of another, without his own *Consent*. The only way whereby any one divests himself of his natural liberty, and *puts on the bonds of civil society* is by agreeing with other Men to join and unite into a community, for their comfortable, safe, and peaceable living one amongst another, in a secure enjoyment of their properties, and a greater security against any that are not of it.... When any number of men have so *consented to make one community* or government, they are thereby presently incorporated, and make *one body politic*, wherein the *majority* have a right to act and conclude the rest."

— *Second Treatise*, 95

"And thus that, which begins and actually *constitutes any political society*, is nothing but the consent of any number of freemen capable of a majority to unite and incorporate into such a society. And this is that, and that only, which did, or could give *beginning* to any *lawful government* in the world."

— *Second Treatise*, 99

THOMAS JEFFERSON

"We hold these truths to be self-evident: that all men are created equal; that they are endowed by their Creator with inherent and inalienable rights; that among these are life, liberty, and the pursuit of happiness; that to secure these rights, governments are instituted among men, deriving their just powers from the consent of the governed; that whenever any form of government becomes destructive of these ends, it is the right of the people to alter or to abolish it, and to institute new government, laying its foundation on such principles, and organizing its power in such form, as to them shall seem most likely to effect their safety and happiness."
— from *The Declaration of Independence*

JAMES MILL

"For though the people, who cannot exercise the powers of government themselves, must entrust them to some one individual or set of individuals, and such individuals will infallibly have the strongest motives to make a bad use of them, it is possible that checks may be found sufficient to prevent them.... It is sufficiently conformable to the established and fashionable opinions to say that upon the right constitution of checks all goodness of government depends."
— *Essay on Government*, VI

an equilibrium of power and authority maintained by a system of checks and balances.

Whether they advocated responsible government or separate branches of government kept honest through checks and balances, liberals tended to agree on the necessity of representative government. This means that an important part of the state (and for some liberals the supreme part), the legislature, would be composed of representatives of the people. We will find that many early liberals had a very narrow view of who should be entitled to sit in the legislature or vote for such representatives, but it was not a large step to move, as liberals eventually did, from supporting representative government to advocating representative democracy as the surest means of preserving citizens' liberty.

As important to the early liberals as political liberty was economic liberty, or **MARKET AUTONOMY**, meaning that the state leaves unregulated the private economic transactions of individuals. Again, this clearly contrasts with the feudal economy, which was heavily controlled by both church and state, and which entailed a variety of authoritative transfers of resources from citizens to state and church. The classic liberal statement on economic matters has been considered the **LAISSEZ-FAIRE** doctrine of minimal government activity in the marketplace. (The emphasis on *laissez-faire* within the minimal state sometimes obscures the fact that market society did not "just happen," but required a variety of supportive policies and activities to be undertaken by the state, e.g., rules governing exchange, enforcement of contracts, stable currency, etc. In its early days, liberalism was as much about creating the conditions for a market society to flourish as it was about letting the market do its own thing.)

After political and economic liberty, liberalism came to argue for **SOCIAL** or **MORAL LIBERTY**. The most famous statement of this strain of liberalism remains John Stuart Mill's essay *On Liberty*, which is about freedom of opinion, belief, and lifestyle. These concerns are consistent with an ideology of individualism; if individual well-being requires political and economic liberty, why not also social or moral liberty? In asking such questions, however, J.S. Mill went further than many previous liberals had been prepared to go. Since Mill's time liberals typically have been tolerant of moral and religious difference or plurality.

A final point to note is the importance of *reason* in liberalism, which espouses a *rational* individualism. Here the contrast is with the traditional character of feudal society, and we need simply recall liberalism's roots in that rationalist revolution known as the

Enlightenment. The concern for representative, limited govern-ment is a belief that individuals can be protected from arbitrary, irrational authority through rational, predictable government; the market can be seen as a rational alternative to medieval rules and regulations; and liberal ethical theory looks to rational principle rather than traditional justification. In all these ways liberalism supposes that government, politics, and social life generally can be ordered by human reason in ways that will make individuals better off than they might otherwise be.

In short, the liberal perspective is that the world consists of rational, self-interested *individuals*, who are essentially prior to political society and, by nature, exist free and equal. The ideal for which liberalism strives is the preservation and enhancement of individual *liberty* within a system of enforceable rights under a government committed to the rule of law. Within such a frame-work, individuals will be able to cultivate their own particular good with security and at peace with others. The program of liberalism, at least initially, was to secure its ideal through *reform* of traditional institutions or their actual replacement with rationally designed instruments of accountable, *limited government*.

Conservatism seems the opposite of liberalism, its natural reverse as day is to night or winter is to summer. But it is sometimes possible for liberals to be conservative, or for conservatives really to be liberals. In the early 1990s in Russia, for example, "liberals" led by Boris Yeltsin pressed for the kind of economic system favoured by North American "conservatives," though similar to the economic vision of "liberals" in early nineteenth-century Britain. This sort of contradiction begins to dissolve if we realize that conservatism is even more bound to the contexts of place and time than are other ideologies. Conservatism might be understood initially as a *disposition* to preserve what exists, to resist change, or to support the traditional ways of a community or society. The content of conservatism will thus depend on what already exists, what is traditional or prevalent in the community. (Those who would go further by bringing back what is going or gone may be termed *radical conservatives* or, more pejoratively, *reactionaries*.) In a society where liberal values have become well established or entrenched, conservatism in fact may seek to preserve liberalism from reform or radical change; in an authoritarian dictatorship, conservatism may support clearly

5.3 TRADITIONAL CONSERVATISM

JOHN STUART MILL

"Protection, therefore, against the tyranny of the magistrate is not enough: there needs protection against the tyranny of the prevailing opinion and feeling; against the tendency of society to impose, by other means than civil penalties, its own ideas and practices as rules of conduct on those who dissent from them ...

The object of this Essay is to assert one very simple principle ... that the sole end for which mankind are warranted, individually or collectively, in interfering with the liberty of action of any of their number, is self-protection.... The only part of the conduct of any one, for which he is amenable to society, is that which concerns others. In the part which merely concerns himself, his independence is, of right, absolute. Over himself, over his own body and mind, the individual is sovereign....

This then, is the appropriate region of human liberty. It comprises, first, the inward domain of consciousness; demanding liberty of conscience in the most comprehensive sense; liberty of thought and feeling; absolute freedom of opinion and sentiment on all subjects, practical or speculative, scientific, moral, or theological.... Secondly, the principle requires liberty of tastes and pursuits; of framing the plan of our life to suit our own character; of doing as we like, subject to such consequences as may follow: without impediment from our fellow-creatures, so long as what we do does not harm them, even though they should think our conduct foolish, perverse, or wrong. Thirdly, from this liberty of each individual, follows the liberty, within the same limits, of combination among individuals; freedom to unite, for any purpose not involving harm to others: the persons combining supposed to be of full age, and not forced or deceived." — *On Liberty*, I

illiberal ideas. The original conservatives who sought to preserve the traditional institutions and values of aristocratic society in the face of the liberal revolution need to be distinguished from those conservatives with whom we are familiar today. These initial conservatives can be identified by their British name, tories, a term also sometimes used by liberals to describe their opponents in the early days of the American republic.

If, generally speaking, liberalism is the ideology of the individual, conservatism is an ideology of the community, and toryism the ideology of an idealized **HIERARCHICAL** community resembling late feudal society. In contrast to liberals, tories see the organic, hierarchical organization of society as natural; indeed, an organized society or community is natural in the same way that family is. Tories value whatever contributes to the coherence, cohesion, and continuance of this community: its traditions, conventions, time-honoured institutions, structures, and practices. The conservative views these institutions (such as monarchy, the church) or practices (traditional morality, deference to authority, performance of duty) as inseparable from a way of life handed down by history; the primary task of the state is to preserve the integrity of the community, which includes such institutions, practices, and values. In contrast to the abstract, often ahistorical character of liberalism, conservatism (especially the tory variety) venerates history and custom.

TORYISM takes the position that individuals are necessarily (as history and experience demonstrate) unequal by nature. It is, therefore, not surprising if individuals are ordered and structured in society; on this view the hierarchical organization of society simply reflects the reality of different individual capacities, and is essential to the community's survival. Thus the aristocracy of feudal society is a natural governing class that has emerged through history on the basis of its superior endowments. Central to this vision is the recognition that such a natural inequality establishes mutual obligations between the superior and the inferior. The aristocracy holds a privileged position at the head of society, but it also has responsibility for the welfare of the less fortunate; it is privileged in its possession of political power, but also obliged to exercise that power responsibly in the general interest. It is essential that *each* individual, regardless of rank or station, perform the duties and responsibilities associated with that situation. This is because each individual, from monarch to slave, is part of a larger whole *and* serves a larger or nobler purpose. Thus, in contrast to the liberal emphasis on freedom or liberty,

126

toryism stresses order, stability, adherence to duty. **PRIVILEGE** is necessary and right.

There is an ambivalence to the tory stance regarding power and authority. On the one hand, strong authority is necessary to sustain the organic structure of the community. On the other hand, inasmuch as the community is preserved through custom, convention, and tradition, ideally the active scope or role for government is quite small. Thus, tories favour a strong but relatively inactive state (besides, a state too busy will inevitably bring about unnecessary change). They are comfortable with the absolute state if its authority is exercised by the right people: tories are fond of traditional institutions, such as hereditary monarchy, and of legislative assemblies so long as they are aristocratic or controlled by the privileged classes. It is when government becomes more democratic or representative of the non-privileged classes that tories become more supportive of the limited state. These conservatives are fonder of constitutionalism than of democracy. The ultimate source of authority for tories often is transcendent, such as God, or the "natural order," in contrast to the popular authority that grounds liberalism.

The foundation of the traditional aristocracy was the feudal relation between landlord and tenant. The secure identification of an individual with a place, a particular occupation, a clearly recognized set of duties and obligations, and a sound knowledge of one's inferiors and superiors: all this was challenged by market society. Small wonder that tories first resisted its triumph. In many cases, though, members of the landed aristocracy realized that there was no incompatibility between an aristocracy of birth and an aristocracy of wealth, and that wealth grounded in land could be supplemented with wealth gained in commerce and manufacture. Toryism eventually made its peace with the market economy, but in doing so, the conservatism it represented started down the road to liberalism. Tory antipathy to markets survives in the insistence sometimes found in conservatism that markets serve the good of the community, an insistence that is more in tune with economic nationalism than with *laissez-faire*.

One of the strongest elements of toryism is its support of traditional values: religious, moral, and social. The religious and moral beliefs and practices of a society are regarded as part and parcel of its necessary structure; to challenge or reject them is to challenge the value or integrity of the community itself. Tories, then, will generally be closely allied with the Church (particularly if it is an officially sanctioned or established church) and, above all,

CONSERVATISM AS DISPOSITION: MICHAEL OAKESHOTT

"To be a conservative is to be disposed to think and behave in certain manners; it is to prefer certain kinds of conduct and certain conditions of human circumstances to others; it is to be disposed to make certain kinds of choices....

To be conservative, then, is to prefer the familiar to the unknown, to prefer the tried to the untried, fact to mystery, the actual to the possible, the limited to the unbounded, the near to the distant, the sufficient to the superabundant, the convenient to the perfect, present laughter to utopian bliss. Familiar relationships and loyalties will be preferred to the allure of more profitable attachments; to acquire and to enlarge will be less important than to keep, to cultivate and to enjoy; the grief of loss will be more acute than the excitement of novelty or promise. It is to be equal to one's own fortune, to live at the level of one's own means, to be content with the want of greater perfection which belongs alike to oneself and one's circumstances."

— "On Being Conservative"

THE ORGANIC CONCEPTION OF SOCIETY: EDMUND BURKE

"Nothing is more certain than that our manners, our civilization, and all the good things which are connected with manners and with civilization have, in this European world of ours, depended for ages upon two principles ... I mean the spirit of a gentleman and the spirit of religion. The nobility and the clergy, the one by profession, the other by patronage, kept learning in existence, even in the midst of arms and confusions, and whilst governments were rather in their causes than formed. Learning paid back what it received to nobility and to priesthood, and paid it with usury, by enlarging their ideas and by furnishing their minds."

— *Reflections on the Revolution in France*

convinced of the importance of religion. Traditional moral values and practices will also be central to these conservatives, not simply as individual beliefs but as matters of public morality. Unlike the liberal, who may well share with the tory many beliefs about right and wrong but who is willing to let individuals decide for themselves, the tory is not usually so tolerant, advocating an active enforcement of moral standards. If public opinion and censure are not enough to do this, then the state should be employed to uphold what is right. Tolerance is not generally a central feature of toryism.

Finally, just as liberalism stresses **RATIONALISM**, toryism justifies itself on the basis of **TRADITION**. What has been handed down from generation to generation through history is regarded as right or worth preserving simply because it has withstood "the test of time." It is a temptation (to which liberals often succumb) to see this traditionalism as simply the irrational veneration of history, but it may sometimes be a justifiably cautious attitude towards the powers of reason. The liberal is confident that we can design institutions and programs to change the world in ways that will solve our problems; the conservative is not so sure. What "passing the test of time" may mean is methods or practices that have succeeded, have worked, whatever their limitations. The conservative is reluctant to throw these away for something new and unproven.

5.4 SOCIALISM

If toryism was a reaction against liberalism on behalf of a vanishing status quo, socialism was a reaction against the world created by successful liberalism. Some early socialists, it is true, were reacting with liberals against aristocratic society, but the most significant socialist thinkers were motivated by a distaste for liberal society, particularly for the consequences of the market economy so central to the liberal vision. Socialism was *the* ideology of the nineteenth century, gaining significance after the effects of the Industrial Revolution had become obvious and after the liberal revolution had succeeded in dissolving feudal society in most of Europe.

A noteworthy distinction was made by Karl Marx, who contrasted his own "scientific" socialism to the "utopian" socialism of previous (and contemporary) thinkers, such as Owen, Saint-Simon, Fourier, and Proudhon. The fundamental difference is that so-called "utopian" socialists believed that socialism would be achieved by a moral revolution, a transformation in what people believed and acted on; the "scientific" socialism of Marx and Engels saw socialism as the eventual outcome of material factors, the product of economic and social transformations embedded within the nature of capitalist society. In this latter view, the revolution would depend on "objective" conditions, not the good intentions of individuals.

Like liberals and contrary to tories, socialists begin with the proposition that humans are fundamentally equal; unlike liberals and in agreement with tories, socialists see humans as having an essentially social or communal nature. Socialists oppose the inegalitarian beliefs of tories and the individualism of liberals. Socialists also disagree with liberals about the nature of equality or inequality present in society and about what is acceptable or not. Liberals oppose the inherited or traditional inequalities of the hierarchical feudal condition; they are concerned to ensure that neither laws nor regulations deny individuals the same chances or opportunity to achieve their goals, protect their self-interest, or obtain well-being. Inequalities that result from differences in individual effort, or from how individuals exploit the equal opportunity provided them, are not problematic to most liberals and are quite acceptable or "natural" to many. Early liberals also accepted a wide range of existing structural inequalities: in asserting that all had "equal opportunity" these liberals were blind to those disadvantages of poverty, social class, and gender under which most of the population laboured. To the socialist, the inequalities to which the liberal did not object simply were unacceptable. There can be no equality of opportunity in a class-ridden society, and individuals everywhere owe their outcomes as much to chance, inheritance, unequal opportunities, and structural factors as to individual effort.

In practice, the socialist argues, the market is partial to those with resources and rewards classes of individuals privileged in terms of such assets as capital, information, or education. The social science of the socialist is concerned with how individuals are privileged or disabled by their position within the social structure, a structure seen largely in economic or political-economic terms. What matters about individuals is their social relations, and, following Marx, the socialist sees these as class relations.

From the socialist perspective, the liberal revolution managed to replace an aristocracy of birth with an aristocracy of wealth. A privileged elite founded on aristocratic tradition and birth-lines gave way to a privileged elite founded on economic

CONSERVATISM AND RELIGION: G.W.F. HEGEL

"[T]he world is not abandoned to chance and external accident but controlled by *Providence*.... The truth that a Providence, that is to say, a divine Providence, presides over the events of the world corresponds to our principle; for divine Providence is wisdom endowed with infinite power which realizes its own aim, that is, the absolute, rational, final purpose of the world."
— *Reason in History*, 14-15

CAUTIOUS ATTITUDE TOWARDS CHANGE: MICHAEL OAKESHOTT

"What others plausibly identify as timidity, he recognizes in himself as rational prudence; what others interpret as inactivity, he recognizes as a disposition to enjoy rather than to exploit. He is cautious, and he is disposed to indicate his assent or dissent, not in absolute, but in graduated terms. He eyes the situation in terms of its propensity to disrupt the familiarity of the features of his world."
— "On Being Conservative"

CLASS ANTAGONISMS: KARL MARX AND FRIEDRICH ENGELS

"The history of all hitherto existing society is the history of class struggles.

Freedom and slave, patrician and plebeian, lord and serf, guild-master and journeyman, in a word, oppressor and oppressed, stood in constant opposition to one another, carried on an uninter-rupted, now hidden, now open fight, a fight that each time ended, either in a revolutionary reconsti-tution of society at large, or in the common ruin of the contending classes....

The modern bourgeois society that has sprouted from the ruins of feudal society has not done away with class antagonisms. It has but established new classes, new conditions of oppression, new forms of struggle in place of the old ones.

Our epoch, the epoch of the bourgeoisie, possesses, however, this distinctive feature: It has simplified the class antagonisms. Society as a whole is more and more splitting up into two great hostile camps, into two great classes directly facing each other, bourgeoisie and proletariat."
— from the *Manifesto of the Communist Party*

power. Even worse, the reciprocal obligations that bound feudal lord to peasant and were at least a meagre compensation for the structural inequality of medieval society, also vanished; the liberal allows such obligations to lapse in the belief that individuals are authors of their own fate.

While socialism is concerned ultimately with creating a society in which all individuals truly are equal, its concern in the present world is to eliminate what it sees as exploitation or subjugation of the least privileged classes in society. In seeking to do so, it gains little affection from those most advantageously positioned in society. Ideally, then, for the socialist the state is an instrument to be used on behalf of the exploited or under-privileged classes against the advantaged classes. Like the tory, but for different reasons, the socialist believes in a strong state, not the limited, minimal state of classic liberalism. The socialist tends to be wary of rights because they are more effectively employed by those with resources than by those without, often to thwart the fundamental social change socialists believe is necessary. Unlike tories, though, who are concerned that a strong state be in the right hands, socialists are (in theory at least) strong supporters of democracy; instead of rights that an elite minority can use to prevent the state from acting, socialists favour a strong state controlled by the majority. After all (the socialist reasons), those less advantaged are usually the majority rather than the minority. At the same time, successful social and political transformation should diminish the need for state activity. Socialists are in theory even more radically disposed towards democracy than are liberals, with important exceptions that we will note below.

The most important task of the state, for socialists, is to reg-ulate, to reform, even to replace the private property market economy of liberalism because of the inequality or alienation it creates. It is precisely the economic liberty or market autonomy, which the liberal values, that the socialist says is responsible for the inequality of capitalist society and for the consequent absence of genuine freedom for all those underprivileged in that society. In the place of private property, the socialist argues for collective or public ownership of the means of production, distribution, and exchange employed by capitalism (i.e., industry, transportation, financial institutions, etc.). In the place of market autonomy and the (mal)distribution it creates, the socialist calls for central plan-ning and redistribution on rational, egalitarian principles. These are the most contentious parts of the socialist position. Within socialism, considerable difference arose about the degree of emphasis that should be put on collective ownership and about those forms of democracy associated with liberal individualism. These and other differences lie behind the distinctions between **COMMUNISTS** or **MARXISTS**, after the nineteenth-century German philosopher Karl Marx, and socialists of a less radical variety, committed to at least some elements of liberal democracy, who called themselves **DEMOCRATIC SOCIALISTS**.

So far we have discussed ideologies in their initial formation, as they were shaped in contexts far removed from our historical present and, therefore, distant from the everyday experience of contemporary readers. It may well seem strange to talk of a liberalism that does not embrace democracy, or of a conservatism that is suspicious of capitalism, but that is how matters once stood. Many features of our own society, such as a general public education, the absence of child labour, a minimum wage, and formal equality between the sexes, were radical ideas that 150 years ago *only* socialists espoused. As matters change, ideology changes, too.

It might be useful today to understand liberalism and socialism as each being the source of a family of ideologies with certain fundamental principles in common, but divided over other, sometimes crucial points. Our frame of reference is the last two centuries, or roughly from 1789 (the French Revolution) to the contemporary age. In that time, one ideological current, toryism, has largely evaporated, or to the extent that it has survived has been absorbed within liberalism. There are some who also believe that socialism is a spent ideological current, and the most obvious reason for thinking so is the collapse of communist regimes in the former Soviet Union and Eastern Europe. On the other hand, socialism and communism diverged long ago, and socialist parties are part of the government or form the main opposition in almost all countries of Europe today, as well as in Japan, Australia, and New Zealand. Tony Blair's Labour Party in Britain, Gerhard Schroeder's Social Democratic Party in Germany and Lionel Jospin's Socialists in France at the end of the 1990s are representative of the evolution of a new, pragmatic socialism, about which we will say more below.

Ideologies fall out of fashion when their vision no longer appeals or when their perspective no longer makes sense of individuals' social and political realities. Contexts change, and an ideology that remains static risks being left behind. Liberal

**5.5
SHIFTING CONTEXTS**

A MANIFESTO OF COMMUNITY AND EQUALITY: FRANCOIS BABEUF

"1. Nature has given every man an equal right to the enjoyment of all its goods.

2. The purpose of society is to defend this equality ... and to increase, through universal cooperation, the common enjoyment of the goods of nature.

3. Nature has imposed upon everyone the obligation to work; no one has ever shirked this duty without having thereby committed a crime.

4. All work and the enjoyment of its fruits must be in common.

5. Oppression exists when one person exhausts himself through toil and still lacks everything, while another swims in abundance without doing any work at all.

6. No one has ever appropriated the fruits of the earth or of industry exclusively for himself without having thereby committed a crime.

7. In a true society, there must be neither rich nor poor.

8. No one may, by accumulation of all the available means of education, deprive another of the instruction necessary for his well-being: instruction must be common to all...."

— From the doctrine of Babeuf

successes have challenged conservatism and socialism, while liberal failures have energized these rival systems and given liberals cause for self-reflection. In the background of these ideologies in their current form are also several ideas that gained special prominence in the nineteenth century.

One of these is the notion of human **PERFECTIBILITY**, the idea that humanity is capable of a progressive development from a primitive or imperfect state of being to an increasingly refined and elevated condition. Human nature, on this view, is not the same in all times and places, but something of a work in progress (this was the century, after all, that discovered "evolution"). Both liberalism and socialism share, in their own way, in the belief in human progress. Conservatives, on the other hand, are more sceptical, doubting that all change is necessarily for the better, and certainly dubious that all (or any) individuals have a perfectible nature.

The nineteenth century also was the century of social science, giving birth to anthropology, sociology, psychology, economics, and political science as professional disciplines. A by-product of this academic specialization was the increasing perception that individuals are very much the product of social institutions, such as educational systems, economic and social class, kinship systems, and family structures. This had enormous significance for socialism, but was accorded relevance by conservatives and liberals only grudgingly, if at all. Opposing the socialist notion that humans are socially determined in their destiny, conservatives argue that they are determined by nature (or by "their nature"), and liberals insist that nature and environment aside, individuals are self-made, or at least are capable of making their own destiny.

Enlightenment rationalism abstracted from both time and place, tending to treat all individuals, regardless of nationality or culture, as members of a common humanity. Both liberalism and socialism drew on this idea, but the nineteenth century was also the time when nationalism exploded in much of the world as the awareness, promotion, and celebration of an exclusive particular identity. There is often a strongly conservative element in the nationalist disposition, but as a sense of identity, nationalism cuts across, or perhaps precedes, ideological divisions, as liberal and socialist cosmopolitanists have found often to their chagrin.

132

In the last century and a half, liberalism has been significantly transformed. The short explanation is that liberalism reacted to its own successes and shortcomings. It responded to the competition provided by socialism, to the demise of feudal society and with it (by and large) toryism, and to the pressures of a democratic political process that liberalism itself had helped to democratize. The vision of liberalism did not alter fundamentally: liberals continued (and continue) to seek a society in which individual well-being is maximized through the enlightened pursuit of self-interest within a progressively broadening and secure sphere of individual liberty. Over time, though, the breadth and scope of liberals' concerns have altered.

On the one hand, with each success in securing individual liberty, liberalism has not halted but moved on to fresh concerns. A modern liberal's concerns with racial and gender equality, with rights for gays and lesbians, for the continued absence of prayer in schools, and for the public provision of goods, such as education and health care, would have struck early liberals as radical, perhaps outrageous, demands. Nonetheless, what the modern liberal demands is grounded on the same principles with which the classic liberal demanded representative government, the protection of property, and religious freedom. At the same time, as liberals succeeded in implementing their political and economic agenda, they often came to the recognition that their liberal vision was as yet incompletely realized. Representative, liberal government and a thriving market economy did not suffice to ensure liberty and well-being for all. This recognition led to two strategies: the reform of political and economic institutions and the reform of traditional social institutions as they touched upon issues such as education, the status of women and children, sexuality, and other areas of social and personal liberty. Like others, we will call these modern (twentieth-century) liberals "reform liberals," in contrast to the "classic liberals" of the eighteenth and early nineteenth centuries.

When the status quo was the rigid, relatively authoritarian structures of feudal society, liberalism tended to emphasize the negative role of the state in restricting individual freedom. While liberals recognized that some restriction of the ability of individuals to act is necessary for social peace and security, they sought to minimize these restrictions, especially where they were fetters on economic and social progress. By the nineteenth century, in many nations, liberalism had become the new status quo, and yet many individuals were not appreciably better off or more

5.6
REFORM LIBERALISM

THE RULE OF THE BOURGEOISIE: KARL MARX AND FRIEDRICH ENGELS

"Each step in the development of the bourgeoisie was accompanied by a corresponding political advance of that class ... the bourgeoisie has at last, since the establishment of modern industry and of the world market, conquered for itself, in the modern representative state, exclusive political sway. The executive of the modern state is but a committee for managing the common affairs of the whole bourgeoisie."

— from the *Manifesto of the Communist Party*

133

JOHN DEWEY

"The history of social reforms in the nineteenth century is almost one with the history of liberal social thought. It is not, then, from ingratitude that I shall emphasize its defects, for recognition of them is essential to an intelligent statement of the elements of liberal philosophy for the present and any nearby future. The fundamental defect was lack of perception of historic relativity. This lack is expressed in the conception of the individual as something given, complete in itself, and of liberty as a ready-made possession of the individual, only needing the removal of external restrictions in order to manifest itself.

... an individual is nothing fixed, given ready-made. It is something achieved, and achieved not in isolation, but with the aid and support of conditions, cultural and physical, including in `cultural' economic, legal, and political institutions as well as science and art. Liberalism knows that social conditions may restrict, distort, and almost prevent the development of individuality. It therefore takes an active interest in the working of social institutions that have a bearing, positive or negative, upon the growth of individuals who shall be rugged in fact and not merely in abstract theory. It is as much interested in the positive construction of favourable institutions, legal, political, and economic, as it is in the work of removing abuses and overt oppressions.... The two things essential, then, to thorough-going social liberalism are, first, realistic study of existing conditions in their movement, and, secondly, leading ideas, in the form of policies for dealing with these conditions in the interest of development of increased individuality and liberty."
— "The Future of Liberalism," 1935

free than they would have been in medieval society. In the immediate aftermath of the Industrial Revolution, many of those in the lowest strata of society clearly were worse off. While the liberal revolution had brought political and economic liberty, it had not brought these freedoms, or their benefits, to all. This had two consequences for liberalism.

One was the recognition that the state (or government) is not the only institution (more correctly, set of institutions) that restricts the freedom of individuals. The institutions of civil society—the capitalist economy, the family, and social norms and attitudes—also can restrict individual liberty. As John Stuart Mill argued in *On Liberty*, and as we may often find true still today, personal liberty has as much or more to fear from public opinion and its pressures for conformity as from the activities of the state. Second, it is possible to see liberty not only in the negative sense of an absence of restrictions, but in the positive sense of an ability to do this or that. For example, it may be legally possible for anyone to acquire property, but if the economic system does not provide real opportunity for those born in poverty to acquire property and escape that condition, are they any more free than if they were legally barred from ownership?

In the nineteenth century, some liberals came to see that individuals are denied freedom in the positive sense by the laws and institutions of a purportedly liberal society. At the same time, liberals increasingly accepted the notion of progressive humanity, and with it the imperative to remove restrictions or impediments to that progress. The result of these developments was a shift in liberalism from emphasizing the need for greater freedom from the state to an emphasis on the need for greater equality in the enjoyment of liberty.

To enhance a positive enjoyment of liberty, to promote equality of opportunity, and to reform any number of institutions that diminish individual freedom, liberalism changed its posture towards the state. Liberals came to believe that the state in a liberal society can function to preserve and enhance liberty, to reform the institutions of civil society, and to provide opportunity for those disadvantaged by their ascribed social position. From the stance of *laissez-faire* and the minimal state, liberals moved to acceptance of an activist state, a government much larger than what liberalism originally envisaged. In short, a variety of problems associated with continued inequality and the lack of freedom provided the incentive for the reform of liberalism, a reform that took three main directions:

1) the incorporation of political democracy;
2) an expansion of rights claims by individuals; and
3) the abandonment of *laissez-faire* political economy.

One of the earliest and most significant revisions of liberalism was an incorporation of political democracy. Early liberal thinkers, such as Locke, had advocated representative government but had expected that the representatives would be drawn from and selected by the property-owning classes. The Industrial Revolution had created a large class of urban workers who, owning no property, had no political rights. It was this class (by and large) that socialism claimed to represent and to whom it appealed for support. Partly for reasons of principle and partly for the pragmatic purpose of heading off the socialists, liberals came to support extending the franchise (the right to vote), first to male members of the working class, and, much later, to women of all social classes.

A second dimension of liberal reform was an expansion of rights claims on behalf of individuals. **RIGHTS** may be understood as *entitlements individuals claim from the state or other individuals*. Entitlements may be moral or legal; in the latter case the state is legally obliged to respect or enforce entitlements. Although it is not always the case, rights are often about protections for something individuals value (like their lives, freedoms, properties, etc.). The extension of entitlements to individuals previously unprotected from the state or other individuals is a significant (and ongoing) development within liberalism. The extension of legal and political rights to women in the first decades of this century, the civil rights movement in the United States in the 1960s, and the addition of the Charter of Rights and Freedoms to the Canadian constitution in 1982 offer clear examples of reform liberalism in practice.

The third and perhaps most significant area of liberal reform was the abandonment of *laissez-faire* political economy and participation in the development of the twentieth-century welfare state. Advocates of the market economy, such as Adam Smith, firmly believed that if competition and market mechanisms were allowed to work unfettered by government regulation, the condition of the working class would be improved; over the long term wages would rise, prices would fall, and all would become wealthier. Similarly, liberal economists could argue that the tremendous economic growth created by capitalism more than compensated for any inequality by providing better than any other system might for

LIBERALISM AND DEMOCRACY: JOHN DEWEY

"The foundation of democracy is faith in the capacities of human nature; faith in human intelligence and in the power of pooled and cooperative experience. It is not belief that these things are complete but that if given a show they will grow and be able to generate progressively the knowledge and wisdom needed to guide collective action. Every autocratic and authoritarian scheme of social action rests on a belief that the needed intelligence is confined to a superior few, who because of inherent natural gifts are endowed with the ability and the right to control the conduct of others; laying down principles and rules and directing the ways in which they are carried out."
— "Democracy and Educational Administration," 1937

those at the bottom of the economy. In practice, though, the liberal economy did not work as beneficially for the labouring classes or the unemployed as theory promised. Socialism claimed to offer a political economy that could improve the conditions of the least advantaged, employing the productive capacity of market society without reproducing its attendant inequality.

Abandoning the minimal state, reformist liberals looked to an activist state to overcome the weaknesses of *laissez-faire*, to moderate the inequalities and inequities of the market economy, and to act positively to enhance the actual liberty of all in society, but particularly of those currently disadvantaged by the existing social arrangements. A wide variety of tools was developed and employed by liberals in power, including increasing regulation of economic life, actual intervention in the economy, and progressive application of levers of economic management, all culminating in the twentieth-century welfare state. Despite the scope and extent of these departures from *laissez-faire*, this reformed liberalism remained committed to the market and to private property. For this reason, despite what its critics have sometimes alleged, the activist state of reformed liberalism falls far short of the interventionist state of socialism. In this regard, too, it is notable that the liberal welfare state has usually been much less comprehensive and extensive than the welfare state constructed by social democrats or socialists (see below).

5.7 LIBERAL CONSERVATISM

The point has been made already that the content of conservatism is to a great degree dependent on the context: what is it that conservatives wish to "conserve"? If conservatism is a defence of the status quo against the efforts of those who would implement serious reform or change, then there can be as many different conservatisms as there are status quos. If, then, at some time in the eighteenth and nineteenth centuries in most of Europe and many of its present or former colonies, liberalism became the status quo as represented by the dominant political and economic institutions, *conservatism in such liberal societies should have a markedly liberal character.*

At the same time, in describing tory conservatism, we encountered several ideas capable of surviving the demise of any fondness for feudalism. These were notions such as natural inequality, the importance of religion, the value of traditional morality, and a pessimism about human nature (what the conservative might claim is simply a "realism" about people). None of these is incompatible with the primary institutions of liberal society, in particular a constitutional, limited government and a private property market economy. In almost every case, modern conservatism in liberal societies has turned out to be a mixture of (traditional) conservatism and liberalism. What makes this quite easily confusing is the variety of ways in which liberalism and conservatism may be combined. At the very least, all conservatives in modern liberal societies partake in the liberal consensus that accords legitimacy to a private property market economy, the basic institutions of constitutional representative government, and the rule of law. This consensus is so complete in some societies (like the United States) that it is no longer recognized by many people as specifically "liberal." What distinguishes conservatives from one another is how much of this liberal consensus they have come to share, and on the other hand, what they reject in the liberal catalogue of values.

Consider, in the first instance, classic liberals who objected to the changes brought about by reform liberalism. Wishing to preserve the status quo in the face of reform, these are **CONSERVATIVE LIBERALS**. They support a *laissez-faire* economy and the associated notion of the minimal state. They support representative government, are wary of extending popular democracy too far, and probably regard the American Bill of Rights (1789) as a code needing no expansion or supplementation. The moral values of the nineteenth century, stressing the virtues of the Christian family, would sit comfortably with them. Over time, these conservative liberals have come to be called conservatives, just as reform liberals have become simply liberals. In fact, some of the most eloquent spokesmen of conservatism have been conservative liberals, such as Edmund Burke (who was a Whig and not a Tory) and Michael Oakeshott.

A very similar position can be reached from a different angle. Imagine that as liberal political and economic institutions are entrenched, tories become reconciled to them, but do not abandon their own beliefs about human nature, order and stability, change, and natural inequality. Since the liberal institutions they come to accept are the as yet unreformed institutions of classic liberalism—*laissez-faire* and limited representative government—there is very little to distinguish these **LIBERAL CONSERVATIVES** (conservatives who adopt liberal institutions) from the conservative liberals (liberals with a conservative disposition). Yet the picture is more complicated than this.

EQUALITY OF OPPORTUNITY: JOHN DEWEY

"Belief in equality is an element of the democratic credo. It is not, however, belief in equality of natural endowments. Those who proclaimed the idea of equality did not suppose they were enunciating a psychological doctrine, but a legal and political one. All individuals are entitled to equality of treatment by law and in its administration. Each one is affected equally in quality if not in quantity by the institutions under which he lives and has an equal right to express his judgment, although the weight of his judgment may not be equal in amount when it enters into the pooled result to that of others. In short, each one is equally an individual and entitled to equal opportunity of development of his own capacities, be they large or small in range. Moreover, each has needs of his own, as significant to him as those of others are to them. The very fact of natural and psychological inequality is all the more reason for establishment by law of equality of opportunity, since otherwise the former becomes a means of oppression of the less gifted."

— "Democracy and Educational Administration," 1937

THE NEO-CONSERVATIVE AS ECONOMIC LIBERAL: KEITH JOSEPH (A FORMER SECRETARY OF STATE UNDER MARGARET THATCHER)

"I would explain that, if allowed to, the market will provide a constantly rising set of minimum standards including rising minimum standards of income. I would explain that there is now very little, if any, primary poverty in this country that is, households with too little income, if reasonably managed, to pay for sufficient necessities, as currently conceived. Some special groups, such as widows and disabled, have too little income in general for their special needs. But though there is little, if any, primary poverty, there is in this country a substantial amount of secondary poverty: discomfort, shortage and squalor. It exists in homes where there is an inability to put what money there is to good use. The fact is that whether among the elderly or among two-parent or one-parent families there are copers and non-copers. No one knows how in a free society to teach every non-coper how to cope. What is known is that in many cases extra money does not end squalor.... The fact is that it is only from the increasing efficiency of the free enterprise system that higher wages can be paid out of which the tax base will rise, thus supporting both higher earnings for those at work and more benefits for those who are dependent."

— *Stranded on the Middle Ground: Reflections on Circumstances and Politics,* 1976

Two further variations on the conservative theme may seem odd or curious to many North Americans. Over time, most if not all tories made their peace with the economic side of liberalism, accepting and adapting to the modern, industrial market economy. The critical issue here is which dimensions of their tory conservatism did they bring with their new allegiance to liberal economics? One of the features distinguishing tories from liberals was their belief in natural inequality. The inequality associated with a market economy would pose no problem to tories adapting to liberal institutions. For a supposed "natural" aristocracy based on family and social class, the market economy substitutes an aristocracy based on wealth and economic class.

Aristocratic conservatives, though, also possessed a belief in organic community that complemented their belief in natural inequality. If the least advantaged somehow have "inferior" natures, then this is the lot that nature has given them and not something attributable to their own failures or lack of effort. So, too, by this logic, the "superior" individuals of noble character are not self-made, but naturally endowed with the abilities, temperament, intellect, or whatever it is that makes them "superior." In an organic conception of society, those naturally superior have an obligation towards their inferiors: to educate them, to present to them an example of proper conduct, and where possible to provide for those unable to provide for themselves. Tories who bring this sense of *noblesse oblige* to their adoption of liberal institutions will have a basis for agreeing to some of the measures brought in by reform liberalism, in particular, those features of the welfare state designed to provide social relief to the least advantaged in society. It is important to understand the difference here: reform liberals reform the market economy to enhance equality of opportunity for individuals; market tories (as we might call them) reform the market economy because they employ a collectivist (albeit inegalitarian) understanding of market society.

Similar to market toryism is European **CHRISTIAN DEMOCRACY**. Recall that feudal society involved a close but fractious relationship between the state and the Roman Church. Liberalism, influenced by the rationalist Enlightenment and by Protestantism, argued for a separation of church and state. Free thinkers, dissenters, and non-believers were usually liberals. Particularly in those countries that remained predominantly Roman Catholic, liberalism was seen to be the enemy of religion and the Church and was opposed to any official position for the Church in civic life. Moreover, many Church adherents identified liberalism and

its modern ways with materialism, urbanization, and secularization, features believed to undermine the faith and the institutions
in which it is most at home: the family and the local community.
Christian Democratic parties were formed to oppose liberal parties and defend the Church and its values.[1] Not surprisingly,
Christian democratic ideology has tended to support traditional
Church positions on social and moral matters: opposition to abortion, civil divorce, and contraception; support for the traditional
family; and deference to legitimate public authorities. The major
difference between European Christian Democrats and secular
conservatives has tended to concern the role of the state in the
economy. Whereas Europe's secular conservatives (like American
conservatives) are usually economic liberals advocating a minimal
state, Christian democracy has believed that economics should
take second place to social concerns and, for this reason, has in the
past supported state policies to protect or give relief to the poor
or working classes, even when this has constituted what liberals
would call "interference" in the marketplace. Interestingly, Pope
Leo XIII wrote in his encyclical *Rerum Novarum* (1891) that "the
public administration must duly and solicitously provide for the
welfare and comfort of the working classes; otherwise that law of
justice will be violated which ordains that each man shall have his
due." The advanced welfare states of Western Europe have often
been the product of a consensus (or compromise) between social
democracy on the left and Christian democracy on the right.

While Christian democracy may be foreign to North
American students, the association of religious adherence and
conservatism will not be. In almost any culture, in normal circumstances, adherence to the dominant religion will be somewhat
conservative, preserving traditional values and ways of life. The
degree to which a society or its politics have been secularized will
have a bearing on the link between religion and politics. The
RELIGIOUS RIGHT in the United States (and less so in Canada)
would alter a long-standing relationship of official religious
neutrality. Like other conservatives, the religious right supports
traditional moral values, grounded here in a fundamentalist
reading of Christian scripture. These conservatives would like to
see prayer in schools, believe in a strong law-and-order state
(including capital punishment), and generally oppose abortion,
feminism, rights for gays and lesbians, sex education in schools,
and whatever else they identify with "secular humanism," a
generic label assigning responsibility for the ills of modern
society.[2] What takes these conservatives further than others who

1. Although Christian Democratic
parties are Protestant in
Scandinavia, and the large German
party appeals to both Protestants
and Catholics, most Christian
Democratic movements have
succeeded in predominantly
Catholic nations. As Mény (1993:
66) points out, however, in
countries where *all* parties profess
allegiance to the Catholic Church,
such as Ireland and Spain, Christian
democracy does not exist.

2. In 1999, the state school board
in Kansas voted to remove
evolution from the required
state curriculum.

might share part or all of the same concerns is their determination to use the state to further their religious agenda or to dismantle the laws that contradict it.

In the modern Western world, then, all conservatives are marked by a belief in the private property market economy and by and large agree on a *laissez-faire*, minimal state approach to this economy. As the twenty-first century begins, they are concerned to reduce the size and scale of government operations and eliminate government deficits. In this sense, they are all fiscal conservatives. The one exception to this is that sort of conservatism, mainly European Christian Democracy, that continues to value social welfare just enough to justify government regulation of, or activity in, the market.

Conservatism in Western societies comes in any number of flavours today, although increasingly common to all versions is a belief in "fiscal responsibility," a general adherence to economic liberalism, and a strong commitment to moral principles, usually (but not always) of a traditional character and usually (but not always) linked to Christianity.

5.8 SOCIALISM: COMMUNISM AND SOCIAL DEMOCRACY

At the beginning of the twentieth century, Vladimir Lenin (the most influential socialist after Karl Marx) published a small book entitled *What Is To Be Done* (1902), arguing the path socialist theory and practice should take. Now, at the beginning of a new century, the question more likely to be raised is whether or not socialism is dead. Writing at the end of his life, the American socialist Michael Harrington (1989: 1-2) observed of the world's successful democratic socialist parties that "none of them has a precise sense of what socialism means, even if they have often proved to be more humane and efficient trustees of capitalism than the capitalists themselves." At the beginning of the twentieth century socialism splintered over the question of means, over *how* capitalism was to be transformed into socialism; today the biggest question for socialists is *what* they would transform capitalism into.

At the time Lenin wrote, all socialists agreed that capitalism required a radical, thorough transformation, but they disagreed about whether this could be achieved gradually through reform or required sudden, drastic revolution. If the latter, would this be a violent or non-violent revolution? And further, who should carry it out? Is socialist society necessarily the product of popular political action by the working class, or is revolution brought about by an informed, dedicated elite?

Karl Marx had suggested that the revolution would occur in the most developed capitalist societies where the working class would become conscious of its exploitation and, acquiring revolutionary consciousness, would act to overthrow capitalist institutions, both economic and political. This would be a two-stage process: a political revolution by the working class to take control of the state, and a social revolution to eliminate capitalist relations of production, thus creating a classless society. Until the social revolution had been completed, the state would remain a strong instrument of the working classes. Marx called this period the "dictatorship of the proletariat," and identified this stage as "socialism." Once the work of eliminating capitalist vestiges was complete, the state could "wither away," and only then would society have reached the stage of "communism." At the time of Marx's death in 1883, the proletarian revolution had not occurred anywhere.

In 1899, Eduard Bernstein published *Evolutionary Socialism,* in which he observed that capitalism was not on the verge of collapse, nor was the condition of workers continuing to deteriorate. Marx had failed to appreciate the possibilities of democratic reform within the capitalist state and the fact that the state could be an instrument of regulation, reform, and redistribution and thus a means to improve the condition of the working classes. Hence, Bernstein argued for a gradual transition to socialism through reform *within* the capitalist, democratic state: what he called "evolutionary" socialism. Opposing Bernstein and supporting Marxist orthodoxy was Karl Kautsky, but over the long haul, Bernstein's revisionism won out among the socialist parties of the Second International. From this point on, socialism represented a democratic, piecemeal approach to reforming and replacing capitalism.

Lenin rejected the evolutionary path to socialism, arguing that at best workers in capitalist society can develop only a trade union mentality and not the revolutionary consciousness necessary to promote and carry through radical change. The revolution of the working class would require the dynamic leadership of a committed core of revolutionaries, intellectuals grounded in Marxist theory, who would engage in agitation and propaganda. This would be what Lenin called a "vanguard," who would act and decide on behalf of the working class (the **PROLETARIAT**). The vanguard would be a party rigorously organized, selective about

A CONSERVATIVE REFLECTS ON DEMOCRACY: DAVID FRUM

"In a democratic culture, feeling yourself separate from the people is distressing, even frightening: Can there be a stronger temptation than the desire to please the crowd, to say only what it wants to hear? Conservatives are fighting harder against gays in the military than against the Clinton health plan because they know that on the former issue the crowd will be with them and fear that on the latter, the crowd will not....

The early 1990s are in some ways more conducive to conservatism than the 1980s were.... Far more than in the 1980s, governors and mayors face voters who profess to prefer budget cuts to tax increases. But those same voters continue to expect lavishly equipped suburban high schools, subsidized tuition at state colleges, toll-free highways, and environmental improvements at others' expense. What could be more tempting to a politician than to teach voters to blame taxes and regulations not on the requirements of the middle class but on the inordinate demands of the poor? What could be more politically reckless than to attack bloated education, highway, and farm budgets, which largely benefit the middle class? Unfortunately, the refusal to take that apparently reckless course dooms all other conservative hopes to futility ... conservative intellectuals should learn to care a little less about the electoral prospects of the Republican Party, indulge less in policy cleverness and ethnic demagoguery, and do what intellectuals of all descriptions are obliged to do: practice honesty and pay the price."

— *Dead Right,* 1994

THE REVOLUTION: VLADIMIR LENIN

"... the theory of Marx and Engels of the inevitability of a violent revolution refers to the bourgeois state. The latter cannot be superseded by the proletarian state (the dictatorship of the proletariat) through the process of `withering away,' but, as a general rule, only through a violent revolution.... The necessity of systematically imbuing the masses with this and precisely this view of violent revolution lies at the root of the entire theory of Marx and Engels.... The supersession of the bourgeois state by the proletarian state is impossible without a violent revolution. The abolition of the proletarian state, i.e., of the state in general, is impossible except through the process of `withering away'."
— *State and Revolution*, 1917

membership, and run on the principle of so-called "democratic centralism." When Russia experienced a liberal revolution in 1917, the vanguard party of Bolsheviks under Lenin and Trotsky eventually seized power. In 1919, the Third International (Comintern) was formed, an association of communist parties worldwide, dedicated to promoting and defending the proletarian revolution internationally (in effect, a network of parties faithful to and consistent with the communist ideology of the Soviet party).

Since early in the twentieth century, then, it has been possible to distinguish clearly between socialism and communism. Socialism is democratic, reformist, and peaceful; communism is authoritarian, revolutionary, and, if necessary, committed to violent struggle. These differences are significant and underpin others. Communism is authoritarian in two important senses: it involves an anti-democratic concentration of power and a commitment to a total employment of the state on behalf of the revolution's ends. In the former case the vanguard party is not simply an elite acting on behalf of the proletariat; it is the *only* party permitted to exist, to organize, to solicit public support, and most importantly, to gain office. The distinction between party and government is completely obscured, if it can be said to exist at all in any meaningful sense. No opposition to the communist party or its positions is tolerated or regarded as legitimate. By contrast, democratic socialism accepts the legitimacy of opposition, the inevitability of plurality within contemporary society, and the challenge of competing for public support within electoral democracy. The state and government are and remain separate from the party, even if it succeeds in winning elections.

Second, the communist party's monopoly on power goes hand in hand with a commitment to the total employment of the power of the state on behalf of the ends defined by communism. This complete exercise of the power of the state is often described as **TOTALITARIANISM**. There is no sphere of society in which the state is not seen to have a legitimate interest. The distinction between private and public, so central to liberal thought, is erased on the basis that it is bogus, and a barrier to the eradication of liberal capitalism. By contrast, in its commitment to peaceful, piecemeal reform, democratic socialism accepts implicitly, if not explicitly, that there is a boundary between the public and the private, even if it might redraw or shift this line.

It is important to note that the denial of democracy and the totalitarian exercise of authority by the state under communism were usually justified as short-term expedients necessary to consolidate the revolution. The political monopoly of the communist party was deemed necessary to prevent the disruption of the social transformation, either by those insufficiently grounded in socialist thought to understand what must be done or by those remaining committed to bourgeois society (i.e., the owning classes). Once such opposition ceased to exist, the state would wither away and the communist party would be inclusive of all. In practice the monopoly of power was never relaxed in those countries that were communist until they ceased to be communist. Instead of transforming the economy and perfecting the economic management implicit in the concept of a socialist mode of production, communist governments spent much of their energy coping with resistance to their programs and policies. The government that was to accomplish so much for "the people" often became the enemy of the people.

The fundamental distinction between socialism and communism was originally rooted in differences over democracy and about a revolutionary or reformist strategy of change. Both believed in the replacement of a private property market economy with a socialized (**COLLECTIVE** or **PUBLIC OWNERSHIP**) economy under the direction of the state. Over time, though, socialism has also increasingly accepted the private ownership of property. Democratic socialism has long ceased to call for the total collectivization of property in the hands of the state, or otherwise. Various elected socialist governments (e.g., in France, Britain) have nationalized private corporations in areas like coal-mining and steel production without attempting to replace the market as the primary means of allocation of resources and without having any designs on private property at large. Such partial nationalization has been the extreme edge of democratic socialism in recent decades and a policy increasingly unlikely to be employed, even by parties that have done so in the past. Socialists continue to worry about the influence and power of corporate property and, by the same token, are supportive of genuine collective ventures such as co-operatives or worker-owned businesses, but they are no longer committed to eliminating private corporations or to restructuring the entire economy on an alternative basis.

The retreat of socialism from radical positions to accommodation with private property and the market means that it is increasingly difficult to distinguish socialism from social democracy. (This may seem an extremely fine distinction to North Americans, but in several European countries socialist and social democratic movements have existed quite distinct from

EVOLUTIONARY SOCIALISM: EDUARD BERNSTEIN

"... No-one has questioned the necessity for the working classes to gain the control of government. The point at issue is between the theory of a social cataclysm and the question whether with the given social development in Germany and the present advanced state of its working classes in the towns and country, a sudden catastrophe would be desirable in the interest of the social democracy. I have denied it and deny it again, because in my judgment a greater security for lasting success lies in a steady advance than in the possibilities offered by a catastrophic crash.... Whether the legislative or the revolutionary method is the more promising depends entirely on the nature of the measures and on their relation to different classes and customs of the people. In general, one may say here that the revolutionary way (always in the sense of revolution by violence) does quicker work as far as it deals with removal of obstacles which a privileged minority places in the path of social progress: that its strength lies on its negative side. Constitutional legislation works more slowly in this respect as a rule. Its path is usually that of compromise, not the prohibition, but the buying out of acquired rights. But it is stronger than the revolution scheme where prejudice and the limited horizon of the great mass of the people appear as hindrances to social progress, and it offers greater advantages where it is a question of the creation of permanent economic arrangements capable of lasting; in other words, it is best adapted to positive social-political work."

— *Evolutionary Socialism*, 1899

DEMOCRATIC SOCIALISM

The Frankfurt Declaration (produced at the 1951 meeting of the Socialist International, as summarized by Laidler):

"1. Socialism does not require a rigidly uniform approach. Socialists are flexible about means but strive for the same goals social justice, freedom, and world peace.

2. Socialism must be democratic and democracy can be realized only through socialism.

3. Socialism seeks the replacement of capitalism by a system based on a fair distribution of income and property.

4. The immediate aims of socialism are full employment, higher productivity, and social security.

5. Public ownership may include nationalization, creation of new public enterprises, or producers' and consumers' cooperatives.

6. Economic decision making should be decentralized whenever this is compatible with socialist planning.

7. Trade unions and cooperatives are necessary elements of democratic socialism.

8. Socialism seeks to abolish legal, political, and economic discrimination based on sex, regionalism, or racial and ethnic groupings."
— *History of Socialism*, 863-64

each other.) Social democracy differs from socialism in two primary ways. First, it sees itself (as does liberalism) as a movement that cuts across class lines, appealing to the interests of all in society, in the name of social justice or fairness. In this respect, social democracy rejects the class-based politics of Marxism; it has often been inspired by and appealed to notions of fraternal equality. Second, social democracy tended to rely more on regulation and redistribution when socialism was pressing for nationalization or alternatives to the market economy. In other words, social democrats were less concerned with transforming capitalism than with adjusting or compensating for its outcomes. The culmination of social democracy is the fully developed welfare state, and the epitome of this has been the egalitarian society constructed and presided over by the Swedish Social Democratic Party.

As socialism has in practice moved closer to the positions of social democracy, the contrasts made here may seem like differences in emphasis rather than in kind. Indeed, as we move from communism to socialism to social democracy, we come to a point at which we approach reform liberalism. Nevertheless, the telling distinction here is the perception of the fundamental relationship of the individual to society and to other individuals. What marks the communist, socialist, and social democrat as different from liberals, however reformed or progressive these liberals may be, is a primary emphasis on the whole and on the collective basis of individual experience.

In the last two decades, the survival and success of leftist parties has seemed to require a shuffle to the right. Parties that were once socialist in name or platform have become social democratic in practice, and in some notable cases seem to be barely left-of-centre liberal in what remains of their ideology. Tony Blair's "New Labour" government in Britain is perhaps the most famous contemporary example of this, imitated by others such as Germany's Social Democrats under Gerhard Schroeder. The traditional tools of socialist government—public ownership, generous social programs, vigilant regulation of the marketplace—have been set aside, at least temporarily, for balanced budgets, deregulation, reform of social assistance, and tax cuts. Critics on the left argue that these parties have sold out to the conservative liberal agenda of the marketplace, and that all these parties can claim for themselves is to implement the downsizing and dismantling of the welfare state in a gentler fashion than their conservative rivals had done (or would do).

144

Another way of looking at things is to suggest that the ideology of social democracy has not changed, but rather social democratic parties have abandoned their ideology to achieve electoral success. The socialist parties that remain closest to traditional socialist ideology can be found today in the formerly Communist states of Eastern Europe. Interestingly, in Germany today, socialists unhappy with the drift of the Social Democratic Party to the right have the option of supporting the more orthodox Party of Democratic Socialism that emerged in what was East Germany after the collapse of communism there.

Stepping back and looking at the larger landscape reveals that in the past two centuries the ideological horizon has become narrower and less clearly defined. The common element eroding these distinctions is the pervasive success of liberalism, a success confirmed (not refuted!) by the fact that few of those who are liberals call themselves such today. Liberalism's rivals on both the right and left have accommodated themselves to liberal society to a large, if still varying, degree. Within the ideologies of the Western world, then, there has been considerable convergence, which expresses itself as a consensus of values, *within which it is still possible for there to be quite polarized and passionate differences*, usually about which policies and programs best reflect or realize those values.

So far our focus has been on the mainstream ideologies (or families of ideologies) that seem to have fashioned a rough consensus about the central institutions of contemporary liberal democracy. Conservatism, liberalism, and socialism do not manage, though, to cover all the ideological bases. In this section we will consider briefly (and sometimes too briefly) some other "isms," some of which challenge from within the consensus just noted and some that stand outside (if not in direct opposition to) that consensus.

**5.9
BEYOND THE
CONSENSUS**

5.9.1 Anarchism

Although anarchism (from the Greek *an* "without" and *archon* "a ruler") is a system of thought organized around the idea that humankind can (and ought to) live without a government organized through the complex of institutions we recognize as the state, there are reasons why it is hard to imagine anarchism arising any-where but in the context of liberal society and its institutions.

We have observed that modern states seek to rule through the exercise of authority (which implies consent) rather than power (which involves coercion or force). Still, those states that have secured legitimacy continue to be recognized as the sole institutions, in their societies, that can legitimately employ force. What the anarchist seeks is not necessarily the absence of author-ity but the elimination of force or coercion from public life. Early liberals conceived of a "state of nature," a condition of human life without government. Suppose that it were possible to remain in the state of nature, to have a peaceable social existence without the creation of a state. Anarchists such as William Godwin (1756-1836) and Peter Kropotkin (1842-1912) seem to have been inspired by such notions of natural liberty. Another source of inspiration for anarchism was the discovery by Europeans of soci-eties elsewhere (e.g., in the New World) that flourished without evident (at least to Europeans) political institutions or govern-ment. Such anthropological evidence seemed to confirm the human ability to live peaceably without a coercive state. Ironical-ly, the last current that feeds anarchist thought is the modern notion of progress. Once humans have developed and organized their material and social lives and learned to balance the conquest of scarcity with proper respect for the imperatives of nature, the state may be seen to be superfluous. Modern technology and sci-ence become instruments that supposedly offer the possibility of realizing the anarchist vision; some anarchists have taken literally Marx's notion that in a socialist future the state might indeed "wither away," its tasks accomplished, with future social manage-ment entrusted to voluntary co-operation.

In common usage, the word "anarchy" is often a synonym for "chaos," a condition of disorder, confusion, and even destruc-tion. This set of images is wholly inappropriate to the anarchist vision. The anarchist seeks to eliminate coercion, but not order. The power of the state is to be replaced by the authority of the community, and that authority is to be largely, if not entirely, the unforced, shared decision-making of voluntary co-operation. This presupposes some sense of common identity and some common sense of good, a mutual respect and courtesy, and either a com-mon set of purposes or a willingness to tolerate diverse ends. In other words, it is a vision of a moral community functioning so well that it does not need to establish a formal political commu-nity. Most anarchists subscribe to some form of communitarian or collectivist thinking. What separates them from other collectivists, such as socialists, is their insistence that the community must always rest on the voluntary consent of all its members. There is no instance, and indeed no means, whereby some portion of the community can force some other portion to follow its decision.

An almost diametrically opposed strain of anarchist thought is intensely individualist. Thinkers like the German Max Stirner (1806-1856) and the American Benjamin Tucker (1854-1939) denounced the state and its structures of power and authority with the sole purpose of expanding the freedom of the individual, to remove obstacles to *whatever* conduct individuals might choose to engage in. Such thinkers provide the most extreme examples of *libertarianism*, a brand of political thought that opposes almost any activity or regulation by the state; the libertarian supports the most minimal of minimal states. By the same token, the libertarian finds the moral authority that organizes collectivist anarchism no better than the coercion of the state. For individualist anarchists the fundamental human relation is a contract, a voluntary agreement between two parties.

Anarchism has not been a dominant ideology, and given the tremendous expansion of the state in the twentieth century, it becomes increasingly difficult to imagine a stateless society, particularly with the complexity and size of contemporary societies. For collectivist anarchism to be a possibility, communities need to be small and homogeneous; presently, however, societies are becoming larger and more pluralist. The prospects seem better in this respect for individualist anarchism, but the challenge is not only to convince the majority of people that they would be better off without a state, but also to demonstrate over the long term that this is actually the case. Short of the elimination of the state, libertarians lobby for the rollback of legislation and regulations that confine individual liberty, a liberty defined in classically liberal terms as the absence of legal restraint.

5.9.2 Populism

Unlike anarchism, but like nationalism, populism is more of a disposition than a complete ideology. It is a current within political movements and generally complements another ideological agenda. Populism is an anti-elitist celebration of the wisdom of ordinary citizens. Peter Wiles (1969: 166) has suggested that populism is "any creed or movement based on the following

LIBERTARIAN ANARCHISM: SEBASTIEN FAURE

"There is not, and there cannot be, a libertarian Creed or Catechism. That which exists and constitutes what one might call the anarchist doctrine is a cluster of general principles, fundamental conceptions and practical applications regarding which a consensus has been established among individuals whose thought is inimical to Authority and who struggle, collectively or in isolation, against all disciplines and constraints, whether political, economic, intellectual or moral. At the same time, there may be and indeed there are many varieties of anarchist, yet all have a common characteristic that separates them from the rest of humankind. This uniting point is the negation of the principle of Authority in social organizations and the hatred of all constraints that originate in institutions founded on this principle. Thus, whoever denies Authority and fights against it is an Anarchist."
— *Encyclopedie anarchiste*, no date

POPULISM: PETER WILES

"To me, populism is any creed or movement based on the following major premise: virtue resides in the simple people, who are the overwhelming majority, and in their collective traditions....
The following things, then, tend to follow from the major premise.

1. Populism is moralistic rather than programmatic....

2. This means that unusually much is demanded of leaders in respect of their dress, manner and way of life....

3. Populism is in each case loosely organized and ill-disciplined: a movement rather than a party.

4. Its ideology is loose, and attempts to define it exactly arouse derision and hostility.

5. Populism is anti-intellectual. Even its intellectuals try to be anti-intellectual.

6. Populism is strongly opposed to the Establishment.... It arises precisely when a large group, becoming self-conscious, feels alienated from the centres of power...."

— A Syndrome, Not a Doctrine, 1969

major premise: *virtue resides in the simple people, who are the overwhelming majority, and in their collective traditions.*" In the United States, populism was originally a movement of disaffected farmers who formed the Populist or People's Party of the 1890s. An agrarian basis has been common to many populist movements, which have championed the virtue of the independent farmer and fought against opposing interests represented by banks, railroads, and urban capitalists.

More generally, populism survives—and is capable of being tapped—as a resentment of privileged elites, or of their clients, identified as "special interests." In its celebration of "ordinary people" and their values, populism opposes change introduced on behalf of new groups or newly empowered interests in society. In part, populism often reflects an alienation produced by social transformation and modernization. Parties of protest not only draw upon, but often fuel popular resentments as a source of their strength. "Special interests" is a handy term for those who have (or it is imagined have) captured the attention and concern of politicians, thereby excluding the voice or interests of the "silent majority." In extreme forms, populism draws on conspiracy theories of how public policy is made by or in the service of a small elite.

To many, populism seems very much in the democratic mould, and modern populists have often been strong advocates of using or introducing instruments of direct democracy, such as referendums, initiatives, and the process of recall of elected representatives. Nonetheless, there are three qualifications to keep in mind. First, populism is often employed by one set of elites against another; individuals who have much to gain by exploiting public discontent are often the loudest supporters of "the people," but have no intention of giving the people control of public affairs. Second, populism rails against political elites but rarely against other elites, such as business leaders. Lastly, populism often champions an uninformed public opinion (this is the anti-intellectual strain in populism), and to the degree that this is so it risks elevating ignorance at the expense of informed, rational judgement.

Populism remains a potential political force today because of the ability of modern society to alienate so many different interests. The middle class has become a fertile ground for populist appeals as modern states have shifted much of the tax burden of the welfare state onto middle-class constituents. Blue-collar skilled labour and white-collar managers displaced by "restructuring" or the export of production to the developing world represent other possible constituencies for populism. Those traditionally privileged groups in society that feel threatened by progressive social programs and hiring practices designed to empower historically disadvantaged groups constitute yet another base for populism (e.g., the backlash against "political correctness"). The success of Ross Perot in the 1992 presidential campaign in the United States, the rise of the Reform Party in Canada in the 1990s, and the surge of support for far-right (anti-immigrant) parties in Europe in the past decade are all examples of the continuing capacity of political actors to capitalize on populist appeals. This is not to suggest that Ross Perot, the Canadian Reform (now Canadian Alliance) Party, and European far-right politicians are interchangeable, but rather that populism takes many forms and succeeds in many different contexts.

5.9.3   Feminism

Unlike populism, feminism makes a strong claim to be considered a full-fledged ideology in that it has a vision, a perspective, and a program. On the other hand, it can be misleading to speak of "feminism" when there are so many feminisms. No more than we would be willing to equate social democracy and communism should we be willing to treat the various schools of feminist thought as one and the same. In some cases, these varieties of feminism are the feminization of ideologies with which we are already familiar: hence liberal feminism, Marxist feminism, social democratic feminism, etc. Other currents, particularly radical and postmodern feminism, appear to reject any accommodation with ideologies from the past. The approach here will be to outline what all these feminisms share to the degree that they have a common vision and perspective.

Like socialism, feminism is in some senses easiest to approach through its perspective, its particular diagnosis of the status quo. Feminists see contemporary social relations as expressions of patriarchy, a structure of domination of women by men. The primary goal of feminism is to create gender equality, and thus to dismantle patriarchy. Susan Moller Okin defines gender as "social institutionalizations of sexual difference," and notes that much of this sexual difference is not immutably biological but "socially constructed" (Held, 1991: 67). Feminists work to overturn these social institutionalizations and social constructions of sexual difference that have come at women's expense, seeking to create a world of structural equality in which women, as women, have full autonomy. Achieving these goals requires action on a variety of

PATRIARCHY: KATE MILLET

"... our society, like all other historical civilizations, is a patriarchy. The fact is evident at once if one recalls that the military, industry, technology, universities, science, political office, and finance in short, every avenue of power within the society, including the coercive force of the police is entirely in male hands. As the essence of politics is power, such realization cannot fail to carry impact. What lingers of super-natural authority, the Deity, `His' ministry, together with the ethics and values, the philosophy and art of our culture its very civilization as T.S. Eliot once observed, is of male manufacture.

If one takes patriarchal government to be the institution whereby that half of the populace which is female is controlled by that half which is male, the principles of patriarchy appear to be two fold: male shall dominate female, elder male shall dominate younger."

— *Sexual Politics,* 1970

policy issues such as pay equity, reproductive choice, and child-care. One of the distinguishing marks of feminism has been its insistence on examining the dynamics of power within what is often regarded by "mainstream" political science as the private sphere—that is, the relations within families and marriage, and the sexual relations between individuals. This focus is captured in the phrase "the personal is the political," which rejects the more orthodox dichotomy of private/public.

As with other ideologies, feminism's adherents differ in the intensity of their involvement (that is, the degree to which their perspective is wholly feminist). Just as there are radical and not-so-radical socialists or conservatives, there are radical feminists and not-so-radical feminists. First-wave feminism sought to increase opportunities for women within the existing structures and processes of capitalist, liberal (patriarchal) society without challenging their legitimacy. Important strides were made in terms of gaining for women rights that were previously lacking or inadequately enforced, but many felt this was insufficient. Second-wave feminists go further and challenge the very structures by which gender inequality has been reinforced and perpetuated. Second-wave feminism, then, in many ways and certainly for its more radical adherents, is a revolutionary perspective that calls for a fundamentally different kind of society and social relations.

One effect of feminism on the narrowly defined political realm has been a marked increase in the number of women in politics over the past generation. In some respects this has been even more noticeable in the number holding high political office. Nonetheless, women remain badly under-represented in politics, even in the most "advanced" democracies. In addition, there have been few signs of a "feminization" of the political process. It was once predicted that the rise of women to positions of power would be accompanied by a shift to a less confrontational, adversarial, and partisan politics, that there would be a more constructive opposition of viewpoints. As yet such a change has not been evident.

Increasing numbers of women (and men) have embraced principles and goals of feminism, although it is fair to speculate about how many, outside the academic and intellectual communities, have progressed from "first-wave" to "second-wave" feminism. Moreover, feminism, like nationalism or populism, has found its home within many ideologies; only those that remain unabashedly traditionalist on moral and social questions are impervious to feminism.

5.9.4   Environmentalism

In 1962 Rachel Carson published *Silent Spring*, which documented in a powerful way the effect on the environment of pesticides, herbicides, and other man-made chemicals—indeed, many date the beginning of the environmental movement to the public awareness created by this book. **ECOLOGY** (the science) supplies the perspective, the way of seeing the world, that informs **ENVIRONMENTALISM** (the political movement, such as "Green" politics).

The ecological perspective is one of interdependence, looking at humanity and nature through a systems approach that examines how species and their environment move in and out of balance with each other. Ecologists point out the ways that human activity in the world upsets the balance between creatures and their environment by destroying habitats, polluting the environment, using up non-renewable resources, transforming the climate, crowding out other species by overpopulating the planet, etc. As humanity progressively makes the world a less hospitable place for life, which in its diversity is steadily diminishing, the quality of life lived by humans is also diminished. Ultimately, as the ecological perspective reminds us, there is a finite limit on the ability of the planet to sustain life. The human population and its consumption of resources cannot grow *ad infinitum*.

The concern of environmentalism, informed by this ecological perspective, is to slow down and eventually reverse the trend of an ever-increasing human consumption of resources and human domination and degradation of "the environment." Certainly one obvious issue is the question of uneven economic development and the desire of many of the world's nations to "catch up" to the standard of living of advanced industrial societies, a process that would involve a tremendous acceleration in the consumption of resources and the production of associated wastes. Interestingly, though, its long-term effect might be to stabilize population, since there seems to be a strong inverse relationship between birth rate and standard of living. (For an environmentalist, the measure of "standard of living" in terms of output, or consumption, or purchasing power, is a symptom of the skewed perspectives of industrial societies.) Much attention in recent years has focused on the notion of "sustainable development," a term implying a modernization and enrichment of life that is neutral in its effects on the environment, or, as defined by the World Commission on Environment and Development

THE "CONQUEST" OF NATURE:
FRITZ SCHUMACHER

"One of the most fateful errors of our age is the belief that 'the problem of production' has been solved. Not only is this belief firmly held by people remote from production and therefore professionally unacquainted with the facts it is held by virtually all the experts, the captains of industry, the economic managers in the governments of the world, the academic and not-so-academic economists, not to mention the economic journalists. They may disagree on many things but they all agree that the problem of production has been solved: that mankind has at last come of age. For in the rich countries, they say, the most important task now is 'education for leisure' and, for the poor countries, the 'transfer of technology.' ...

The arising of this error, so egregious and so firmly rooted, is closely connected with the philosophical, not to say religious changes during the last three or four centuries in man's attitude to nature.... Modern man does not experience himself as a part of nature but as an outside force destined to dominate and conquer it. He even talks of a battle with nature, forgetting that, if he won the battle, he would find himself on the losing side. Until quite recently, the battle seemed to go well enough to give him the illusion of unlimited powers, but not so well as to bring the possibility of total victory into view. This has now come into view, and many people, albeit only a minority, are beginning to realize what this means for the continued existence of humanity."
— *Small is Beautiful*, 1974

(WCED, 1987), "development that meets the needs of the present without compromising the ability of future generations to meet their own needs."

As this indicates, environmentalism challenges the very economic and political-economic assumptions that have been central to the ideologies of the modern world; conservatism, liberalism, and socialism alike have accepted the desirability of economic growth and development without limits. According to dominant schools of economic thought, and to most economic policy-makers, the economy is "working" only when it is growing. Environmentalism is thus seen to be post-industrialist and post-materialist; a popular slogan among Greens has been "neither right nor left nor in the centre," indicating their distinction from all established parties.

The program of environmentalism is diverse, comprehensive, and still very much contested. All agree on the need to reduce, if not somehow eliminate, the production and eventual release of toxic substances into the environment. How this should be done is a question of competing strategies: while some look for non-toxic alternatives, some stress eliminating the need for such substances at all. Some will be concerned with the regulatory mechanisms in place (or not), while others will urge using market mechanisms to provide incentives for polluters rather than legal sanctions as disincentives. An issue of some debate is whether it is more appropriate to develop new ecologically sound technologies, such as alternative energy sources (wind, solar panels, etc.), or to work to change the structure of societies and, accordingly, human consumption habits. All environmentalists wish to stop new development that is harmful to the environment; all wish to clean up or eliminate those activities currently harming the environment. The question for many is: Is this enough? Or does sustaining the planet that sustains us require us to change our lives more drastically? Must humans eventually consider a process of deindustrialization?

A final area of considerable debate and disagreement within environmentalism and among Greens concerns the political strategy of the movement/party. Should Greens be active as a political party, thus giving legitimacy to the very system that sustains a materialist, unsustainable development? Or should they concentrate on getting their message across to the general public? It can be argued that Green parties and environmental interest groups have had considerable success on the front of public education. The surest proof of this is the tendency of *all* political parties today to at least make the right noises about their concern for environmental issues, even if their policies don't always demonstrate this.

5.9.5 Nationalism

It may be useful to think of nationalism in liberal democracies as a (usually) subordinate element within the broader ideologies of conservatism, liberalism, and socialism. (By contrast, in authoritarian regimes, nationalism can become *the* dominant element in the ideology of the state.)

By nationalism we may mean several things, but behind them all stands the idea of "the nation," a term indicating (as discussed in Chapter One) a common identity and purpose that unites people for political purposes. A nation exists where a people share a common language, culture, religion, set of customs, and an understanding of their collective history as a people. Nation-states as we understand them today only emerged in Western Europe at the end of the feudal period as the patchwork system of feudal kingdoms, duchies, and principalities was forged into larger territorial units under the developing authority of absolute monarchs. The work of creating among citizens an identity corresponding to these larger political units was something accomplished after the demise of feudal society and owes much to the first- and second-generation ideologies we have discussed and to the institutions and practices they have established and sustained. The notion of a national identity depends to a large degree on the development of means of communication and travel and on the standardization of laws and institutions. Each of these serves to break down the differences that define local communities and provide them with their own unique identity. Nationalism, then, is the political dispositions that promote and maintain the interests of "the nation," so understood. There are three general forms in which we might encounter nationalism.

The first sense of nationalism is *the goal of achieving political autonomy or independence for a people* (that is, for the "nation"). Typically, this nationalism is a movement by a specific people within a larger society for self-determination, which may be seen to require the separation of a territorial unit inhabited by the "nation," the departure of a ruling colonial power, or, less drastically, the granting of various measures of political autonomy. The nationalism of self-determination seeks greater autonomy (e.g.

KEY TERMS

anarchism
Christian democracy
class
collective ownership
communism
conservatism
constitutionalism
context
democracy
democratic socialism
dogmatic
ecology
environmentalism
feminism
hierarchy
ideology
individualism
laissez-faire
liberalism
libertarian
market autonomy
Marxism
minimal state
mixed government
nationalism
national preference
nation-building
patriarchy
perfectibility
popular sovereignty
populism
privilege
proletariat
rationalism
reform
religious right
representative government
responsible government
revolution
rights
self-determination
separation of powers
social democracy
social or moral liberty
socialism
status quo
tolerance
toryism
totalitarianism
vanguard
welfare state

REFERENCES AND SUGGESTED READING

[Publishing information is not provided for texts in political thought that are either out of print or widely available in contemporary editions.]

Avineri, Shlomo. 1968. *The Social and Political Thought of Karl Marx*. Cambridge: Cambridge University Press.

Bakunin, Mikhail. 1873. *Statehood and Anarchy*.

Bell, Daniel. 1960. *The End of Ideology*. New York: Free Press.

Bell, Daniel, and Irving Kristol. eds. 1981. *The Crisis in Economic Theory*. New York: Basic Books.

Berlin, Isaiah. 1969. *Four Essays on Liberty*. Oxford: Oxford University Press.

Bookchin, Murray. 1980. *Toward an Ecological Society*. Montreal: Black Rose Books.

Buckley, William F., ed. 1970. *Did You Ever See Dream Walking? American Conservative Thought in the Twentieth Century*. Indianapolis: Bobbs-Merrill.

Carson, Rachel. 1962. *Silent Spring*. London: Hamish Hamilton.

Cunningham, Frank. 1987. *Democratic Theory and Socialism*. Cambridge: Cambridge University Press.

Dewey, John. 1935. *Liberalism and Social Action*. New York: G.B. Putnam's Sons.

Dobson, Andrew, ed. 1991. *The Green Reader*. London: André Deutsch.

state-building) for a people whose common identity marks them as a "nation" (which may itself be contested). This is the nationalism that inspired revolutions (or national liberation movements) within territories in the developing world that were ruled as colonies by European powers. It is also the nationalism that motivates action for self-determination by a people not successfully integrated into the larger identity of a nation-state, a people who usually constitute a cohesive minority within that state. The desire of a significant portion of the Québécois in Canada or of the Basque and Catalan peoples in Spain for political autonomy are contemporary examples. Finally, the desire for self-determination is the nationalism that feeds the dreams of peoples without a state to establish one; e.g., the creation of Israel and the Kurds' desire for their own homeland.

A second sense of nationalism has the goal of creating, fostering, or sustaining a common identity among the citizens of a political state. In many cases this is an attempt to unite those who otherwise do not see themselves as sharing a common identity (an exercise often called nation-building). This is the nationalism that lay behind the creation of modern nation-states out of smaller communities and societies. That nations are often so constructed is more obvious perhaps to citizens of newer nations like the United States, Canada, and Australia, where peoples of various backgrounds and experiences share a nation-state. In the case of Canada, at least, the question of national identity (i.e., what it means to be a Canadian) is very much still in debate. On the other hand, the disintegration of what once was Yugoslavia, the divorce of the Czech Republic and Slovakia, and the falling apart of the former Soviet Union all indicate how the nationalism of nation-building can sometimes fail to overcome and supplant the more particular identities of ethnic and linguistic communities that maintain their integrity within the larger nation-state. In the absence of integration into a large whole, it is perhaps inevitable that such communities look for a degree of self-determination. The failure to create a common Yugoslavian identity is reflected in the desire of national groups such as Albanians, Croats, Serbs, Bosnians, and Slovenians to obtain and preserve their own geopolitical autonomy—and in the willingness of some of these to engage in brutal warfare and widespread civilian destruction for that purpose.

The third sense we may attach to nationalism is an emphasis on the integrity or priority of the nation-state. This is a rather vague description that covers a variety of stances opposing something we might with similar vagueness call internationalism. The tendency in foreign policy, for example, to act unilaterally rather than in concert with other nations or through supranational organizations such as the United Nations is one such expression; isolationism, in which a country withdraws from activity in the international arena, is another. (The United States exhibited both of these tendencies at various times during the twentieth century.) Free traders are economic internationalists; their counterparts are economic nationalists, who may advocate protectionism or national standards with respect to employment or environmental policies, or restrictions on foreign investment. In Canada the protection of cultural industries and the general concern to prevent cultural assimilation by the United States comprise a familiar example of nationalism in this last, and perhaps most politically benign, sense.

Each of these senses of nationalism—**SELF-DETERMINATION, NATION-BUILDING, NATIONAL PREFERENCE**—is compatible with the mainstream ideologies we have discussed. One could be a conservative nationalist, or a liberal nationalist, or a conservative internationalist, or a socialist who is nationalist on economic issues and internationalist on foreign policy, and so on. At the same time, there are certain affinities or tendencies for specific ideologies to be nationalist or internationalist. Liberalism, because it celebrates the individual and not the group, very often favours internationalism and is suspicious of nationalism (which it rightly associates with conservatism). Communism or radical socialism is also internationalist, since it ultimately promotes solidarity with humanity as a whole, or at least among the working classes worldwide. On this basis one might regard socialism and social democracy as more susceptible to nationalism than is communism. On the other hand, communist regimes have often been totalitarian authoritarian states, highly motivated to tap into nationalism whenever it has suited their purposes. Ultimately, all ideologies have demonstrated an ability to accommodate nationalism, depending on the circumstances and the context.

Dworkin, Andrea. 1976. *Our Blood: Prophecies and Discourses on Sexual Politics*. New York: Harper & Row.

Eccleshall, Robert, Vincent Geoghegan, Richard Jay, and Rick Wilford. 1984. *Political Ideologies: An Introduction*. London: Hutchinson.

Eisenstein, Zillah. 1981. *The Radical Future of Liberal Feminism*. New York: Longman.

Fried, Albert, and Ronald Sanders, eds. 1964. *Socialist Thought: A Documentary History*. Garden City, NY: Anchor Books.

Friedan, Betty. 1963. *The Feminine Mystique*. New York: W.W. Norton.

Gutman, Amy. 1980. *Liberal Equality*. Cambridge: Cambridge University Press.

Harrington, Michael. 1989. *Socialism*. New York: Penguin Books.

Hayek, Friedrich A. 1957. *The Road to Serfdom*. Chicago: University of Chicago Press.

Held, David. 1991. *Political Theory Today*. Stanford, CA: Stanford University Press.

Jagger, Alison M. 1983. *Feminist Politics and Human Nature*. Totawa, NJ: Rowman & Allanheld.

As indicated earlier, ideology is often viewed unfavourably; to be called an *ideologue* is rarely a compliment. The supposedly negative features are that ideology is simplistic and one-sided, dogmatic, biased, and emotional. There is enough truth to each of these claims to merit a closer examination. We have noted that ideology is simpler than philosophy, and this is something that

5.10
BEYOND IDEOLOGY?

Kolakowski, Leszek. 1978. *Main Currents of Marxism: The Founders.* Oxford: Oxford University Press.

Kristol, Irving. 1983. *Reflections of a Neoconservative.* New York: Basic Books.

Kropotkin, Peter. 1886. *Law and Authority.*

Lenin, V.I. 1902. *What Is To Be Done?*

MacIntyre, Alasdair. 1978. *Against the Self-Images of the Age.* Notre Dame, Ind.: University of Notre Dame Press.

Mannheim, Karl. 1936. *Ideology and Utopia: An Introduction to the Sociology of Knowledge.* London: Routledge & Kegan Paul.

McLellan, David. 1983. *Marxism after Marx.* London: Macmillan.

Mény, Yves. 1993. *Government and Politics in Western Europe.* Oxford: Oxford University Press.

Mill, James. 1820. *On Government.*

Mill, John Stuart. 1859. *On Liberty.*

Millet, Kate. 1970. *Sexual Politics.* Garden City, NY: Doubleday.

Minogue, Kenneth. 1963. *The Liberal Mind.* New York: Vintage Books.

Nozick, Robert. 1974. *Anarchy, State, and Utopia.* New York: Basic Books.

Oakeshott, Michael. 1962. *Rationalism in Politics.* London: Methuen.

Pateman, Carole. 1978. *The Relevance of Liberalism.* Boulder, Colo.: Westview Press.

makes it accessible to the public. It is not a great leap to go from "simpler" to "simplistic," to the claim that the world is more complex than the picture ideology typically presents, a picture that for that reason is inadequate. This view of ideology as one-sided is related to the particular perspective often unique to an ideology. The example drawn earlier concerning Marxism and class, on the one hand, and feminism and patriarchy, on the other, suggests that there may often be validity to the characterization of ideology as one-sided. *Both* class and patriarchy may be features of contemporary social relations, but to take either by itself as the whole or dominant truth *is* one-sided. It may be that part of the price ideology pays to be popular or accessible is to remain one-sided or at times simplistic. Is this too large a price to pay?

To call ideology **DOGMATIC** is to say that its adherents insist on the truth of their belief system come what may and will admit no exceptions, accept no challenges, and rethink no principles. This, of course, is an observation that speaks more about those who believe in an ideology and about the way they believe than about ideology itself. To adhere uncritically to an ideology may not be uncommon, but neither is it something necessarily intrinsic to ideology. To identify ideologies as biased is significant only if, by comparison, there is an "unbiased" way of thinking that is somehow more "objective" than ideology. With the demise of the myth of "value-free" inquiry years ago, it is not clear what that more objective way might be. Ideologies are no more or less biased than philosophies, theories, or any other systematic bodies of beliefs or ways of thinking. Ideologies *are* partial in the sense identified above in that they entail a specific way of seeing, but that is as much their strength as their weakness. Finally, the claim that ideologies are emotional is like the claim that they are dogmatic; it is a claim about those who hold an ideology and about how it excites them. Ideologies often make emotional appeals on the strength of the symbols and slogans they employ, and one of the strengths of ideology may well be that as a simplified system it is capable of appealing to affect rather than to intellect. Nevertheless, there is no reason to assert that this is the only appeal of ideology, or even necessarily its strongest appeal.

Criticisms of ideology come down to one point, which is well taken: ideology can become a substitute for independent thinking, for analysis, and for reflection. The individual attaches herself to a belief system and thereafter allows her judgement to be determined more or less automatically by the prescriptions of the ideology. Like all uncritical forms of thought, ideology employed in such a manner is deserving of disdain. However, nothing in the nature of ideology requires it to be employed uncritically or dogmatically. At stake here may well be the manner by which we come to have an ideology. Do we adopt it ready-made and complete as others have fashioned it, or do we construct for ourselves an ideology out of the numerous options available? Is our ideology a passive product of our socialization, a by-product of our experience, or the active result of questioning, debating, and subjecting our own answers to challenge? Do these distinctions matter at all, or is it just a question of whether we think with our ideology, or let our ideology think for us?

Again, it is possible to distinguish between the aspects of ideology identified above. The greatest danger of an uncritical use of ideology attends its perspective, the particular way of seeing the world unique to an ideology; if we let an ideology become a substitute for thinking hard about the world, then the very partial character of the ideology, its tendency to be one-sided, becomes our prison, albeit one of our own making. There is an argument to be made that most successful ideologies survive because there is an element of truth in the partial picture of the world they present. The danger of ideology is to present this important partial truth as the whole truth, thereby keeping other truths from our attention and our concern. The challenge is to make one's way critically among these ideological visions, perspectives, and programs, to arrive through discourse and inquiry at some conclusions about their relative merits and weaknesses. If we do not have ideology, then what? Moving in the direction of a *more* systematic, consistent, multi-perspective way of thinking about politics brings us to political philosophy (although as noted, where the line is crossed from ideology to philosophy, or vice versa, is not clear). In some utopias, perhaps all citizens can be philosophers, but this is simply not a possibility in our own society, whatever might be the merits of such a state of affairs. In the opposite direction we move towards what might at its best be called an expedient approach to politics and what is at worst a wholly unprincipled, often inconsistent thinking about politics. Expedience can well avoid some of the pitfalls we have identified as possible companions of ideology, but it can also mean losing two of the central virtues of ideology.

First, ideology is principled; fundamental propositions about what is right or wrong in the social and political realm run through an ideology and structure it. This means that its adherents are also guided by such propositions, and the consequence of this

Phillips, Anne. 1991. *Engendering Democracy*. Oxford: Polity Press.

Sandel, Michael, ed. 1984. *Liberalism and Its Critics*. New York: New York University Press.

Sargent, Lyman Tower. 1987. *Contemporary Political Ideologies*, 7th ed. Chicago: Dorsey Press.

Schumacher, E.F. 1974. *Small is Beautiful*. London: Random Century.

Skidmore, Max J. 1989. *Ideologies: Politics in Action*. New York: Harcourt Brace Jovanovich.

Smith, Adam. 1776. *The Wealth of Nations*.

Stirner, Max. 1845. *The Ego and His Own*.

Sunstein, Cass R., ed. 1982. *Feminism and Political Theory*. Chicago: University of Chicago Press.

Taylor, Charles. 1991. *The Malaise of Modernity*. Concord, Ont.: House of Anansi.

Wiles, Peter. 1969. *Populism*. London: Weidenfeld and Nicolson.

Woodcock, George, ed. 1977. *The Anarchist Reader*. London: Fontana.

World Commission on Environmental Development (WCED). 1987. *Our Common Future*, New York: Oxford University Press.

is that their political judgements and activity are not simply the product of the most narrowly defined or circumstantially constrained calculations of self-interest. In this way political judgements gain some measure of objectivity, and in this way they become subjects for public debate, challenge, and rethinking. These latter activities, of course, are at the heart of any meaningful democracy. Second, and not entirely unconnected, ideology is goal-directed, animated by a vision of what is the best world, the best of all possible worlds, or the best we can make of this world. Political judgements informed by ideology, then, are oriented towards making the world in some way a better place (or preserving it from forces that would make it worse). Here, too, politics becomes more than simply reacting to circumstances or accepting the world as it is and surviving in it; instead of being the passive product of social and technological forces, ideology expresses our desire to shape our world, to engage in the kind of purposive action that is essentially human.

Ideology that is employed and acquired critically, in a manner that remains open to debate and challenge, has an important role to play in the real world of political citizenship. The catch, and there always is a catch, is to appropriate the good points about ideology—its systematic, principled, goal-directed approach to politics—while avoiding its pitfalls: its one-sidedness, and the temptation it can bring with it to cease thinking for oneself.

SOMETHING TO CONSIDER

Given the appropriation of "liberal" positions by conservatives and socialists alike, is it safe to assume that Western democracies have arrived at an "end of ideology"?

What are the fundamental issues over which ideological differences might emerge in the future?

6 political culture

If political philosophy is the domain of philosophers and ideology the territory of political activists and partisans, then political culture is the world of all of us, regardless of our political education or our degree of political interest. Every society possesses a **POLITICAL CULTURE** (and often, political subcultures) —this broad term encompasses many elements concerning the intellectual dispositions (beliefs, attitudes, values) that people have about politics. A political culture is an aggregate like "the public" or "society"; it indicates a collection of the ideas of the individuals who comprise a community. For this reason it is something independent of the ideas of any *particular* individual. Each of us reflects, more or less, the political culture of the society we inhabit or have been raised in, and the "more or less," as well as the ways in which we acquire political culture, can be particularly challenging to measure and demonstrate. Social scientists study political culture because they believe that what people think about the political world shapes their behaviour, their consent, or their level of tolerance. It is often suggested that political culture defines the boundaries of political activity within a polity and in this way limits the realm of political possibility. Within any given society certain policies are seen to be legitimate, others not; political debate, competition for authority, and the actual implementation of policy will generally occur within the boundaries of acceptability defined by the political culture. Many Americans view with suspicion the kind of government-funded and administered health care that Canadians take for granted or cherish. Australians tend to espouse an egalitarianism that scorns the deference to authority for which Canadians, at least in the past, have been noted.

6.1 DEFINITION

6.1 Definition
6.2 Beliefs, Attitudes, Values
6.3 Mass Culture and Socialization
6.4 Mass Media
6.5 The Politics of Public Opinion
6.6 Conclusion

159

Let us begin by regarding a political culture as *the collective political consciousness of a polity* and then deconstruct this a little. First, consider the ways in which political culture is collective and not individual. As noted above, individuals reflect a political culture more or less, and this is for at least a couple of reasons. One is the size and complexity of modern societies, which are no longer homogeneous communities. In a small, completely homogeneous community, i.e., where all have the same beliefs about politics, religion, ethics, etc., it might be reasonable to expect each mature individual to reflect quite accurately the political culture of the community, because in such a society each individual is a miniature copy of the whole (this is akin to what Durkheim called "mechanical solidarity"). The pluralism of modern society, then, is one reason that the whole remains greater than the sum of its parts. The fluidity of modern society is another; that is, people do not spend their lives in one locale, but often come and go many times in a life, great distances and small, and in doing so partake of many different cultures in different degrees.

There are also the effects of the increasing pace of social and technological change. In political terms, for example, the television age is less than 50 years old, which means that there are people whose beliefs about politics are still influenced, if not shaped, by their experience of a political world before the dominance of mass media. For those under the age of 30, though, political knowledge and attitudes may be based principally, if not entirely, on television news and political coverage. People's political dispositions and normative beliefs are often nostalgic, that is, influenced by how they remember circumstances at an earlier stage in their lives. Two or three centuries ago, an individual's way of life and experiences might not have been very different from those of his or her parents or grandparents; today no two decades are alike, and siblings born a half-dozen years apart may seem to have grown up in different worlds. All of these considerations should clarify why we note that the beliefs, attitudes, or values of any particular individual tell us nothing about the political culture in general. We have to aggregate or collect the totality of beliefs present in the population to get a picture of the culture and hence of its effect on the world of political action. Moreover, only individuals have beliefs, values, attitudes, etc.—there is no sense to phrases like "society believes that ..." or "Canada values ..."; the collective shape of our beliefs, attitudes, and values is very different from any particular individual's perspective.

Political culture is thought about political objects, and if this seems rather obvious, it is important to realize the diversity of objects that are political, a point clarified somewhat by talking about the kinds of attitude involved—each kind of attitude corresponds to certain kinds of object. More problematic is the description of political culture as "consciousness," for what do we make of the subconscious or unconscious, or what is implicitly conscious but has yet to be stated? If a researcher enters the classroom and asks first-year university students to respond to questions about foreign policy issues, what is being measured here? These students may have never considered the question, "Which is the greatest threat to world peace: abject poverty or religious fundamentalism?" Is any response recorded actually measuring the student's attitude, or is the exercise actually *creating* attitudes that didn't previously exist? This is not a trivial point, because this *is* the way political culture is often measured: through survey research. It is also the way that public opinion polling operates, and we will need to consider the possibility that public opinion is not measured, but is rather *constructed* by those who purport to be measuring it. The easiest way to avoid the question of consciousness would be to describe political culture instead as the way we learn to think about political objects; in this way we could see the answer to the question about the greatest threat to world peace as being shaped by the political culture, whether or not it was a newly minted opinion. The difficulty is that this formulation—the way we learn to think about politics—tends to focus again on individuals rather than on the collective product of individuals' consciousness.

It is not accidental that we keep referring to "beliefs," "attitudes," and "values," for while these terms may seem interchangeable, they can be used to refer to three distinct kinds of idea that we have about politics.[1] And, as we noted above, each kind of idea refers to different categories of political object.

Beliefs can be understood as our **COGNITIVE** ideas: these contain our knowledge about the political world, and obviously will depend very much on our education about politics, whether formal or informal. Periodically we are informed that a low percentage of Canadians can name their MP or identify more than a handful of cabinet ministers in the current government, or that large numbers of Canadians remain unclear about just what

6.2 BELIEFS, ATTITUDES, VALUES

1. The initial distinction between cognitive, affective, and evaluative ideas in the political culture was made by Gabriel Almond and Sidney Verba in *The Civic Culture* (1965).

Parliament does or about the division of powers between provincial or federal governments. Given the low importance attached to political education in the public school system and the tendency of mass media to describe events rather than explain them, low levels of political knowledge in the population should not surprise us. This can be seen, though, as an impediment to democracy, or alternatively, as the sign that not much is expected of citizens in our system; people inform themselves only when they have pressing reasons to do so.

"Attitudes" is a term we can use to describe those ideas laden with **AFFECT**: our dispositions for or against particular political objects. For example, one attitude social scientists measure is *support*, and David Easton (1965) has identified three foci of political support: (a) the community, (b) the regime (what we have called the state), and (c) the authorities (the government). These are useful and important distinctions. One strength of democracy is that it allows citizens to oppose the government (or governing party) while still supporting the state (the institutional system). On the other hand, sovereigntists in Quebec clearly support a different community than do federalists in that province or in the rest of Canada. In federal countries like Canada and the U.S. there may be important differences in levels of support for any of these three foci, divided yet again between national and provincial or state levels.

Two other attitudes commonly measured are **TRUST** and **EFFICACY**, which might, like support, be directed to the state (especially efficacy) and/or the government (especially trust). Trust is fairly straightforward, but efficacy may be less familiar. Simply put, efficacy measures the degree to which an individual feels that his or her participation or activity is worthwhile or meaningful or "makes a difference." Those who feel politicians never listen to the people, or that their vote makes no difference, are clearly low in efficacy. David Elkins and Richard Simeon (1965) have combined measures of trust and efficacy to come up with four categories of citizens, as shown in Figure 6.1.

These categories are not idle labels, but imply an orientation to the political system that may well have consequences for political participation. Those who are high in efficacy are likely to be willing participants, but whether their participation is supportive or critical will depend on their levels of trust. Those who are less likely to participate will be divided between those who simply trust officials to do what is right (the deferentials) and those who believe they will always be short-changed by those in authority

Efficacy

		HIGH	LOW
Trust	**HIGH**	Suppoters	Deferentials
	LOW	Critics	Disaffecteds

FIGURE 6.1 (FROM ELKINS AND SIMEON, 1965)

(the disaffecteds). The actual proportions of the population that fall into these categories will tell us something about the health of the particular polity (as will measures of support). From a democratic perspective, it would be ideal to have the largest number of citizens measuring high in efficacy, whether supporters or critics. From the perspective of stability (or from the standpoint of those in power), it is ideal to have the largest proportion measuring high in trust, whether supporters or deferentials. Combining both, the obvious ideal measure is to have a high percentage of supporters, while the least healthy polity is one with large numbers of disaffecteds. The clear possibility exists that those who are disaffected (or disillusioned) will "drop out" of the political process, ceasing to participate, and the danger is that instead of mere apathy (the withdrawal of support) their disaffection could lead to opposition to the regime. None of this is good for the "legitimacy" of the state, and in cases where a significant class of dissidents has been created, the legitimacy of the regime is challenged.

It is striking that social scientists and public opinion pollsters alike have found very little good news in North America, particularly in the 1990s, insofar as support, trust, and efficacy are concerned. This is particularly true of public attitudes towards politicians, who now very often compete with lawyers for last place on the list of esteemed professions. In many cases, being a career politician or a political insider is now seen to be a liability for political candidates. In the 1994 national (congressional) election in the United States, only 38 per cent of eligible voters bothered to cast a ballot, and the 1996 presidential election recorded the support of less than half the registered electorate. All of this serves as evidence that something is not well with the political culture of North American democracies, or with a political process that citizens seem increasingly dissatisfied with. The list of possible causes or suspects—the mass media, flaws in the institutional machinery, the professionalization of politics, the politicians themselves, or the unreasonable demands of citizens—is lengthy.

163

The term "values" is employed to designate **EVALUATIVE** or normative ideas about the political world. We already have considered such ideas in our discussions of political philosophy and ideology, both of which occupy a large place in the political culture of almost any polity. In most political cultures, as well, certain evaluative ideas or norms cut across the differences of ideology, and are too widespread to be the particular domain of philosophers. A commitment to democracy is one such idea, and one we expect to hold a central place in the political culture of democratic polities. The level of this commitment can vary considerably, though, as can the understanding of what is being supported or demanded by such a value. If, as Rand Dyck (1996: 284) suggests, Canadian notions of democracy stress the idea of *majority rule*, it is the case that in many European countries democracy means *consensus,* a more demanding standard. None-theless, in Western democracies we expect to find conservatives, liberals, and socialists all stressing their democratic credentials.

Central political values like democracy, or certain norms of justice, can provide an interesting basis for comparison between political cultures; many political scientists (most famously Seymour Martin Lipset) have contrasted the political cultures of Canada and the United States by comparing key political values supposed to be dominant in each. Canadians are said in the past to have demonstrated much greater *deference to authority* than Americans, meaning that they have more willingly accepted the necessity of hierarchy and authority and have been willing to obey their "superiors."[2] It is possible to construct any number of axes with opposing value terms at either pole of each axis. The political culture of any polity could, in theory, be located at a point on the axis and compared with other cultures. One such axis might put egalitarianism at one end and elitism at the other. Most observers would probably put Australia, for example, towards the egalitarian end, meaning not that Australia is in fact a country more equal than others (although it may be), but rather that egalitarianism is highly valued in its political culture. The United States has traditionally been believed to value egalitarianism highly (although not as highly as liberty or enterprise), but the U.S. is one of the developed world's most inegalitarian countries. Another axis might oppose "tolerance of diversity" to "pressure for conformity," while another might oppose "individualism" to "collectivism." There are numerous possibilities here.

2. Neil Nevitte's *The Decline of Deference* (1996) suggests that Canadian political values are changing, not so much as a result of American cultural imperialism, but as a product of changes that affect post-industrial societies generally.

Each of the ideas discussed in the previous section—beliefs, attitudes, and values—can be measured directly by asking individuals to respond to questions (and, of course, by aggregating the results), or indirectly by analysing political speeches, party platforms, newspaper editorials, and even the literature and songs of a people. What all this obscures is how modern the notion of such a measurable political culture is. Two hundred years ago, in most modern polities, *a* political culture that could be found among "the people" did not exist. The kind of political culture we have been describing in this chapter presupposes the development of a mass society that overcomes differences of space, class, education, etc., to create a set of shared understandings or of contexts for dispute. This may be easier to see by thinking about some of the things that had to happen for a mass culture to emerge.

Let us begin with the creation of nation-states at the end of the feudal period, as discussed earlier. This wasn't simply the consolidation of territory and people under one ruler but under one set of common rules, displacing local customs and traditions with the uniformity of law. Over time this also meant standardization of other aspects of social life, such as language, forging both a common pronunciation and spelling out of a variety of local variations or dialects. The invention and development of printing was of incalculable significance, especially once education ceased to be the privilege of the wealthy. General education (accompanied by general literacy) was to a certain degree more practical, and perhaps necessary, once humans began to live in cities and towns rather than scattered through the countryside. Urbanization erodes a great deal of the distinctiveness of locality, especially as cities, the sites of the development and application of technologies of every kind, become more and more alike over time. As railroads, then the automobile, and finally the airplane made travel a commonplace rather than an adventure, differences in lifestyle were further erased by the ease with which *ideas* and *information* could also travel. Undoubtedly the most significant contribution to the development of mass culture, though, has been the emergence of electric and electronic means of communication. The telegraph, telephone, radio, television, cable and satellite communications, and now the personal computer have not only given each of us windows on the wider world, but have made what each of us sees through the windows more and more alike. Finally, we may add the growth of the multinational corporation and the globalization of the marketplace to note the continued homogenization of mass culture to a degree that may soon begin to

**6.3
MASS CULTURE AND
SOCIALIZATION**

erode (if it has not already done so) the distinctiveness of national cultures.

Interestingly, the growth of a mass culture has paralleled the growth of a political public; at the end of the feudal period and during the first centuries of the modern era, the political class (those with political rights and political influence) comprised a relatively small elite within society. With the creation and development of mass society and of the mass culture that accompanies it, the pressure for representation of the broader public in the political system mounts. The creation of a political class that, in theory at least, includes adults of all classes and gender (in other words, *democracy*), was in most cases a belated response to changing social realities. On the other hand, we should also consider that many new nation-states, often artificially put together by colonial administrators, have yet to complete the transition to a mass society, a transition that is readily taken for granted in developed countries because most of the transformations took place in previous generations. These newer nations have yet to develop a national identity transcending region, or tribe, have yet to forge a common political culture or strong institutions of civil society. Not surprisingly, political instability is not uncommon.

In short, there are various means by which humans have shrunk the differences of space and time that lead to differences in experience, ways of life, and ultimately of ideas and understandings—of culture. Some barriers between different cultures are less permeable than others: language, for example, which has always been closely linked to culture, religious differences, or collective historical memories, but these, too, are probably less impenetrable than ever. As the forces shaping culture have changed with modernization and the growth of technology, so, too, have the ways by which culture is transmitted from one generation to another, what is generally called **SOCIALIZATION**.

Socialization refers to the processes by which individuals acquire the values and beliefs of their society or community. Our political dispositions are not innate (we are not born "democrats" or "conservatives" or "feminists"), but are learned or acquired at various stages of our experience of the world. Socialization is a means by which political culture is transmitted to new generations of citizens, and unless there is a conscious effort to do otherwise, the process is generally conservative—reinforcing the status quo, the values and norms currently popular or dominant in society— in part because socialization is usually a by-product of other activities. Although not everyone would agree, it is possible to view socialization and education as different processes. Education is a deliberate attempt, on the part of others or of ourselves, to impart or gain knowledge or skills or to refine talents and aptitudes. Taking or teaching a political science course is education, not socialization. Starting the school day with the national anthem, or pledging allegiance to the flag (as in the U.S.), and passing by a large picture of the Queen in the school hallway each day (as in many Canadian schools) are examples of experiences that socialize, by generating attitudes or habits of mind.

Most discussions of socialization make two observations, one about *agents*, one about the *stages* or timing of socialization. For example, typical agents of socialization are parents, teachers, and peers, and this should not surprise us, since these are the people with whom we have primary contact. Repeating the point made above, these agents do not (or do not normally) deliberately strive to socialize us, but end up participating in our socialization by teaching us, playing with us, nurturing us, etc. The degree to which socialization is regarded as involving an unconscious accumulation of dispositions and habits on our part is also indicated by all the discussion of how we are socialized most in our early years and, like the proverbial old dog, become increasingly unwilling to learn new tricks as we grow older.

Discussion of the agents of socialization tends to emphasize the personal dimension, or how we are shaped by our interaction with other individuals. But it is also the case that we are socialized by institutions or by individuals in their institutional capacity. The influence of our parents is profoundly personal, but at the same time it reflects the role of the institution we call the family. As the structure of the family changes and diversifies we can expect increasing speculation and research into the subsequent effects on the socialization of children. Teachers, too, are agents of socialization because of the institutionalization of education in our society. Once upon a time in most Western societies (and in parts of some of them still today) the Church was an important agent of socialization. In recent decades a new agency—the television set—has risen to prominence, in part because television has taken over to some degree (and in some cases quite a large degree) the roles of parent, best friend, teacher, and even pastor. Again, television programs generally do not aim to socialize young viewers, but to inform or, more usually, to entertain them. Still, it is in the process of informing or entertaining that they socialize by helping to reinforce or transmit values, beliefs, or attitudes prevalent in our culture. If, for example, in all television programs, women are

167

3. See *The George Gerbner Study Guide*, an excellent online resource, at http://www.mediaed.org/guides/gerbner/gssgtoc.html.

portrayed as stay-at-home mothers, then this may well transmit or reinforce the attitude that a woman's primary vocation is to find a husband and have children. This is one reason for the concern about stereotypes in the media: they tend to reinforce the attitudes responsible for such stereotypes. This is what Dr. George Gerbner has called "casting and fate."[3] As increasing numbers of young citizens are linked by personal computers through the Internet, we may see the emergence of yet another agency of socialization.

Socialization matters because it is the way a political culture is passed on from one generation to another, a transmission that is in all likelihood always somewhat imperfect or incomplete. Despite the disposition socialization has towards reproducing the status quo, each new generation will undoubtedly also have its own perspective. To the degree that we are socialized early and become less susceptible to influence or unlikely to change our fundamental dispositions later, socialization warns us that there are limits to what is politically possible or what we can expect particular publics to support or accept.

To offer an extended example, we have noted the presence in political cultures of advanced industrial societies of the "value" attached to democracy. This usually does not mean the kind of direct democracy practised in ancient Athens, or the participatory legislature that Rousseau spoke of in *The Social Contract*—our societies are too large and the tasks of governing too specialized and continuous for much "government by the people." Not surprisingly, we are socialized not to demand or expect too much of a say in how we are governed. The institutional limitations to democracy are buttressed by cultural messages transmitted from generation to generation. The belief in democracy that is central to our political culture is at the same time a limited belief in democracy, just as the democracy of our institutions entails a limited public participation. Hand in hand with the belief in the legitimacy of democracy often goes the age-old suspicion of "the public" or of its competence to judge how authority and power should be exercised. The phrase "too much democracy is dangerous" seems to capture this ambivalence: democracy is good, but it must be kept within limits, not taken too far.

The socialization process in representative democracies often reflects and reinforces this ambivalence towards democracy. Consider the amount of democratic decision-making that citizens are likely to encounter in non-governmental organizations or institutions. Most areas of individual life—family, school, church, workplace—are dominated by authority structures of a non-democratic nature. When we consider that primarily within such settings citizens are socialized, it should not surprise us that many citizens are ambivalent about democracy, nor that non-democratic or authoritarian attitudes are not infrequently encountered within a nominally democratic political culture.

For many of us living today, the history of the world beyond us has footage, a set of remembered television images on file somewhere in our minds—the film of Jack Ruby shooting Lee Harvey Oswald, astronauts golfing on the moon, Parti Québécois leader René Lévesque conceding defeat in the 1980 referendum before a packed arena of supporters, crowds milling back and forth at the Brandenburg gate as the Berlin Wall came down, masked Mohawk Warriors confronting the armed forces of the state during the Oka crisis, President Bill Clinton apologizing to the American people, and so on. So, too, for most of us, our perceptions and attitudes (if not our knowledge and understanding) of political figures and institutions are mediated by images relayed by television or headlines in newspapers (although more likely the former than the latter). One of the most important contributions to the mass culture described in the last section, and certainly what shapes it most today, is the mass communications technologies or media developed in this century. We are living today in the Television Age of politics, and it is noteworthy that we are just beginning to grasp the significance of this; it is easy to overlook the fact that the Television Age in the U.S. is only 40 years old (at the time of writing) if dated from the Kennedy-Nixon debate of 1960, and in Canada 32 years old if inaugurated by the Trudeaumania campaign of 1968. It is easy to overlook because of the extent to which television today dominates not just the *coverage* of politics (even shaping the way that newspapers present the news), but the way politics is *practised*—from the domination of election campaigns, to the centrality of the scheduled or unscheduled news conference, to the presentation of parliamentary business on a specialty cable channel. Does this matter?

Representative democracy rests in part on an ongoing relationship between the people and the political elites they elect. Crucial to this relationship is the information available to the public about their representatives, through media such as newspapers, radio, and television. When accountability is provided for by the granting or withholding of support at election

6.4
MASS MEDIA

time, an informed vote requires information about the performance (past, present, and promised in the future) of candidates. Citizens can evaluate their government solely on the basis of the information accessible to them; their interest is obviously in having the most thorough and penetrating information brought to their attention.

The reason it *does* matter how media such as television deliver the news, then, is that in a mass political culture, especially a democratic one, citizens require information about what the state, government, and politicians are or are not doing. The only means of delivering this information regularly and reliably to the general public are the resources of the mass media. Most citizens cannot inform themselves directly, and other possible sources—academic studies, government documents, private consultants—have too many limitations, ranging from bias to lack of timeliness to being prepared for a specialist public. The media, in short, play a public role, and are a key institution of civil society in any liberal democracy. To play this public role the media must be free from government censorship or other influence—what is normally meant by a "free press." Media firms are clearly aware of their public role, for they protest loudly whenever they fear that their liberty or privileges are threatened.

Ever since the first newspapers came into being, the preponderance of news delivery has been through private companies, and having private organizations perform a public function presents several interesting situations. One underlying issue here is the matter of accountability. Public institutions (or those who run them) must ultimately answer to the people, either directly or through their elected representatives; private organizations must answer only to those who own them: the shareholders, who may be few or many. It is possible to regulate private corporations to force their compliance with certain public objectives, but the difficulty with regulating the press beyond a certain point is the possibility that governments might use the excuse of "public objectives" to exert political influence or even censorship of unfavourable publicity. Ultimately, the public requires not regulated but "responsible" journalism, which means the onus is on a self-regulated media. Insofar as the media are concerned to fulfil the public role of providing citizens with the best available information in an accessible and timely fashion, this is not problematic, but there are pressures inherent in the private ownership of media firms, and in the nature of the medium itself, which get in the way of this public responsibility.

By definition almost, private companies exist for the purpose of making a profit; those that do not generate a surplus for their owners will not be around long—unless their owners have very deep pockets and some reason for wanting to lose money. It is true that some media firms, particularly in the Newspaper Age, were run not primarily for profit but to get a particular point of view before the public, to advance the interests of a particular party, or on the basis of some philanthropic patronage. These kinds of operation are increasingly rare and occupy a minuscule share of the media market. Like almost everything else today, presenting the news is a business, and as a business it is expected to pay dividends to its shareholders. This raises the possibility that where there is a conflict between performing the public role (practising responsible journalism that presents the public with critical, quality information) and realizing the private end (maximizing profits), shareholders will expect or want the latter to predominate. This is not to suggest that presenting quality information through responsible journalism cannot be profitable, but rather that there is no guarantee that it will be, and perhaps in today's mass society there is less likelihood it will be.

This is because modern media companies are primarily concerned with two activities other than presenting the news that citizens need: selling advertising and providing **ENTERTAINMENT**, and the two are obviously linked. Media firms—newspapers, radio, and television alike—depend on the sale of advertising for the largest share of their revenue. Naturally, this creates pressures to provide whatever is most attractive to advertisers. For their part, advertisers will turn to those newspapers or TV stations that attract the most readers or viewers (or those most likely to buy the advertiser's service or product). If entertainment attracts a larger readership or audience than does quality political journalism, or if sensational, superficial political journalism attracts more attention than serious, nuanced analysis, it is not hard to see how the need to stay profitable influences media products.[4] Thus, most modern metropolitan newspapers are no longer only (or even primarily) about the presentation of news, but are multi-dimensional publications that entertain readers in any number of ways. Television, of course, is primarily about entertainment. Neil Postman (1985), among others, has written about how the entertainment imperative also extends to the way that newspapers and television gather and present the news.

At least three kinds of exceptions exist to this hijacking of the serious public role of the mass media by the more profitable

4. An interesting phenomenon of the 1990s has been the increasing gap between the reality of violent crime (which has been decreasing) and the public perception of crime (that it is increasing or static). One possible explanation would be the sensational treatment that all crime receives in the media. As the famous journalistic adage goes: "If it bleeds, it leads." But of course the presentation of crime is not just through media news coverage but also forms a central element in much contemporary dramatic programming.

imperatives of entertainment, but like many exceptions they only prove the rule. One is the rare private media firm that caters to a market of serious information-seekers, people willing to pay for quality, responsible journalism presented as the only (or main) fare. This is particularly true of journals and magazines that can survive on grants, endowments, and subscriptions and hence eschew advertising revenue. Or, such publications can offer to advertisers a particular type of reader who suits the demographic profile that marketing research has identified as a potential buyer or client. Canada's self-styled "National Newspaper," the *Globe and Mail*, has a more traditional news journalism focus than its competitors in part because it caters to the business, political, and academic elite who demand quality newsgathering and serious analysis and commentary. It is able to do so by selling its advertising space to sponsors who wish in turn to sell their product to this presumably higher-income clientele. Such a paper, however influential and respected, remains outside the mainstream of popular culture; it is not read by many in the middle or working class.

A second potential source of uncompromised journalism is public broadcasting, where radio and television are owned by the state, usually through an arm's-length arrangement like a Crown corporation (Canada's CBC, Britain's BBC, etc.). Because funding comes from the state, such broadcasters are also released from the imperatives of pleasing advertisers and appealing to the markets that advertisers want. Here, too, though, there are problems. If these networks succeed in attracting an audience of significant proportions, they do so often by offering a form of entertainment that is different from or superior to that of the commercial networks. The serious documentaries and news affairs programming they present are usually among their least-watched shows, meaning that, again, serious journalism remains on the margins of popular culture. In recent decades, governments have been less willing to fund public broadcasting, which forces the networks to rely on popular subscriptions or fund-raising or to turn to advertising as a principal revenue source. Once this happens, the same imperatives that determine the content of commercial television become the norm. The great expansion of "specialty" channels offers a third possibility, but here, also, there seems to be a trade-off between ratings and seriousness of content. The more entertaining and visually focused—like—CNN or Headline News or even NewsWorld—the larger the ratings; the more political and serious—C-Span or CPAC—the smaller and more specialized the audience.

We have been discussing how the need for profitability of privately owned media firms leads them to present all manner of content, most or much of which has little to do with the public function of informing citizens for democratic judgement and participation. There are really two sets of issues here: one is the role of private ownership and profitability, which affects all types of media; the second is the nature of the particular medium itself and how this shapes the messages it delivers, and here the principal concern of most critics is with the limitations of television as a medium (privately *or* publicly owned).

The way in which concern with profitability shapes how media firms operate is accentuated by the increasing **CONCENTRATION** of ownership within the media world and the integration of media firms into larger corporate entities. In the second half of this century, the independent newspaper and the non-affiliated television station have become increasingly rare; newspaper chains and media companies owning strings of stations are now the norm.[5] The next stage of concentration is when different branches of the media world are integrated in one corporate entity. Thus the same company may own a television network, a movie company, publishing interests, and recording companies. Cable distribution companies own specialty channels and operate cellular phone networks. The final stage is when these media conglomerates are themselves part of larger corporations that include such non-media concerns as brewing, manufacturing, and financial services.

The increasing degree of corporate ownership and concentration raises several issues. First, it ensures that profitability will be a fundamental concern, if not *the* consideration before which all else must give way. It also means that the individuals who run media firms may themselves have no media background or experience, but impressive credentials in achieving management objectives. Second, chain ownership and corporate concentration have tended to reduce the diversity of views put before the public in two ways. One, particularly in the newspaper world, has been the elimination of competition; few communities have more than one paper, and in many parts of Canada all papers in a region or province are owned by the same corporation. The other way, even where there is competition, as may be more likely in television or radio, is that it can work to make companies more alike rather than different, as they copy one another's successes and learn from one another's failures. Lots of studios make Hollywood movies, but that's the point: they *all* make Hollywood-style

5. The last independent newspaper in Canada's largest province, Ontario, was sold to one of the large chains in 1999.

173

movies. Opinion and information are areas where diversity rather than uniformity is what best suits the interests of the consumer. Finally, the degree of corporate ownership of media outlets raises questions of conflict of interest. One of the reasons a free press is central to liberal democracies is its ability to keep governments honest by shining the light of publicity on their misdeeds. But what happens when the government's actions are in the interests of the corporate sector that owns media firms, *or* contrary to those interests? In either case, can the public expect a full, objective, critical discussion of the issues in the media outlets controlled by these interests? The state is not the only source of power in contemporary society; in capitalist economies considerable power can be based on private wealth. Traditionally, the independent press has had as impressive a record in exposing abuses of private power as it has had in blowing the whistle on public figures. The concentration of media power in the hands of a few large corporations endangers the ability of the press to be an effective public watchdog.

Insofar as the media play an important role in setting or reinforcing the public agenda, any corporate bias (e.g., promoting tax cuts rather than government spending on public goods) is not only a threat to democracy (because it privileges one set of interests and shuts out others), but insidious, because it is presented as if it were wholly objective, neutral commentary.

An entirely separate source of issues surrounds not the ownership of media but the nature of the media itself, or more exactly of the medium by which information is transmitted. The concern of culture critics ever since Marshall McLuhan coined the phrase "the medium is the message" is that television, which has become the dominant medium, is unable (or unlikely) to present the kind of information that citizens need to evaluate properly their governments and representatives. One of the most compelling examinations of the limitations (or dangers) of television is Neil Postman's *Amusing Ourselves to Death: Public Discourse in an Age of Show Business* (1985). The point at the heart of Postman's analysis, and indeed of all criticisms of television, is that it is image-based. Images entertain, amuse, perhaps shock or amaze, but they do not easily permit (or encourage) debate, analysis, or thoughtful reflection. Postman argues that "embedded in the surrealistic frame of a television news show is a theory of anticommunication, featuring a type of discourse that abandons logic, reason, sequence, and rules of contradiction." He concludes that Americans are "the best entertained and quite likely the least well-informed people in the Western world" (1985: 105-06). The medium Postman opposes to television is, of course, the printed page of books, magazines, and perhaps newspapers. One of his arguments, though, is that the incoherence, triviality, and irrationality of television is leaking into other forms of communication such as newspapers and magazines, and that a public dependent on television for its information and culture will begin to think about the world in ways that mirror this medium: "How delighted would be all the kings, czars, and führers of the past (and commissars of the present) to know that censorship is not a necessity when all political discourse takes the form of a jest" (1985: 141).

Interestingly, an increasing body of evidence suggests that the public is finding the jest less and less amusing. The shallowness and anti-intellectual biases of television cannot, perhaps, always manage to amuse and entertain, particularly when coverage of what is supposed to be serious—elections, policy struggles, political crises—cannot be avoided. We noted earlier the increasing disillusion with, and distaste of the public for, politicians and public officials. This would not seem consistent with the thesis that all television does is entertain—and where else can we look to explain public attitudes towards political actors *but* television? The last media topic we will explore, albeit briefly, is the peculiar relationship of journalists and politicians in the Television Age: briefly, because, like many other aspects of the Television Age, the relationship of journalists and politicians is still evolving.

As Lance Bennett (among others) has pointed out, journalists and politicians exist in an uneasy symbiosis: each is dependent on the other for what they need. Political actors need (preferably favourable) publicity; journalists need (preferably topical) information. This creates the potential for mutual accommodation and co-operation in many ways. A journalist who asks embarrassing questions risks getting shut out of future stories or not recognized at the next press conference. The journalist who presents the politician in a favourable or sympathetic light may well receive some inside information or background somewhere down the road. A politician who has the qualities the particular medium is looking for—providing snappy quotes (print), being photogenic (television), having a pleasant, reassuring voice (radio)—is more likely to receive publicity than someone who is boringly verbose or physically "unattractive" or plagued with an overly nasal voice. Most meetings between press and politicians are not spontaneous events, but routine encounters that both plan for: the scheduled

6. The 'scrum', which refers to the situation such as when the politician is caught in the halls between her office and the legislative chamber, was once the epitome of a spontaneous exchange with journalists, in contrast to the "press conference." Nowadays, cabinet ministers' offices will issue a "media advisory" announcing when and where the minister will be available for such an exchange.

press conference, the so-called "scrum" in the corridors of Parliament,[6] the office interview, the campaign bus or plane, etc. It is, of course, in the interest of both parties to make these encounters appear more spontaneous than they in fact are, so that much of the co-operation between the two sets of actors is hidden from the innocent public. In the last couple of decades, though, much has changed in the relationship between politicians and journalists, and it has changed largely because of the realization of the importance of television.

From journalists, we witness increasingly the phenomenon associated with what has been called **JUDGEMENTAL JOURNAL-ISM**. This represents the response of journalists to the increasingly manipulative behaviour of politicians in the attempt to control the outcome of their encounter with the media. The political manipulation of the media in the Television Age is itself a product of the realization that politicians no longer control the content of the news. Each of these points needs a little further explanation.

Consider the fundamental character of political news in the Age of Print compared with political news in the Age of Television. In the former, the primary news takes the form of words. Politicians appear in the news through their statements (something that remains true or becomes even more true in radio). This means that politicians control the content of the news: whether delivering speeches, speaking from prepared texts, or responding to questions, they determine what will or will not be available for report. Journalists may choose to ignore these words, but without the words of politicians news on the printed page or over the airwaves of radio is either empty or just composed of journalists' opinions. Moreover—and this is easily overlooked—in pre-television times, the words politicians were speaking (and journalists recording) were being spoken *not* to journalists, but to other politicians (in Parliament, say) or to sections of the general public. This placed journalists in the role of supposedly neutral or objective observers or *reporters* to those sections of the public not present at these speeches. The ability of journalists to put their own "spin" on events was also limited by the fact that the spoken word is, or can be made to be, a matter of public record.

When the medium changes to television, which is image-based, all kinds of material *other* than the speaker's words and their meaning become capable of transmission. The tone of voice, the delivery of a speech, nervous habits, a perspiring brow, yawning or amused faces in the audience, the dress and physical appearance of the candidate, whether the speaker is using notes—these and

176

countless other aspects can now be shared with the wider public through television, and which of these is shared is no longer in the control of the politician but rather of the television camera operator, director, or producer. Television newscasts can edit footage to select the images to present, which may or may not be flattering to political actors, and these images, because they are images, "do not lie." They may be irrelevant to almost anything, but they can and do create impressions that may become relevant to everything. With the advent of television, control over the content of the news shifts, at least temporarily, to the journalists.

Over time, discerning politicians and their advisers realize what works and doesn't work on television. Political parties learn to judge what kinds of candidate attributes will or will not play well on television. In any number of ways, political actors seek in the Television Age (in a way they never needed to in the Print Age) to manage their encounter with journalists. This means trying to control the timing, the setting, and the nature of their interaction with the press. Attention is paid to the personal appearance of candidates in a way that was never quite done before; venues where politicians speak are scouted for how they will look on television, for the possible camera angles that will be used to portray the candidate; staged media events become the staple of election campaigns and sometimes of the "normal" non-election political day; "spin doctors" attempt to influence media interpretations and reactions. Political actors are no longer addressing words and, through them, ideas to (portions of) the public, but rather they pitch their message to the media in the hope that the images the media present to the public will be favourable. In other words, politicians and their support staff try to manipulate the medium of television.

This attempt by political actors to use television to their favour has tended to turn reporters (by experience a cynical lot) into "judgemental journalists." No longer content to be simply the conduit through which politicians send their message to the public, journalists have become self-conscious about their own role in the process and the role of their medium. An attendant irony is that while television has become the dominant medium, there are still large numbers of print journalists covering politics and trying to find something to say about a presentation that is geared for television. Bennett (1992: 23) reports that in the 1988 U.S. election campaign the average television "sound bite" was 9.2 seconds, down from 14 seconds in 1984. As he notes, "It is hard to discuss the meaning of any 9.2 second slice of a text, particularly when such slices are constructed to stand alone, rendering the rest of the text something like a serving utensil." Not surprisingly, print journalists have less and less to report on the issues, or what candidates are saying, because the issues are increasingly irrelevant, because the candidates have less and less of substance to say. The attention of journalists turns to the campaign itself, to reporting how the parties and candidates are trying to manipulate journalists and the public in their attempt to gain support. Bennett reports on a study of the 1988 U.S. election by Marjorie Harris that found that coverage in the print media from September to election day was devoted two-thirds of the time to discussing the parties' campaign strategy: "In short, the campaign became its own news. The media reflected on their own role as never before, resulting in redundancy, self-referential logic, and loss of context, which are the hallmarks of postmodern symbolics. The media couldn't get out of their own loop" (1992: 26). As journalists become increasingly disillusioned with the political efforts to manipulate their media, it is small wonder that political figures are increasingly despised by a public less and less interested in politics. The technology that seems to offer the greatest potential ever for getting information to the public has in fact spawned a medium that leaves citizens less well informed than ever, and by and large not a bit concerned about it. Worst of all, there seem to be very few practical ideas about how to make things any different.

6.5 THE POLITICS OF PUBLIC OPINION

We have examined how, in the course of their business, politicians seek to manage their encounters with journalists, or in less polite terms, seek to **MANIPULATE** the media. Yet the ultimate target of this activity is not journalists, but the wider public, the consumers of media. In an age where popular sovereignty has become a fundamental political value and where political legitimacy rests (in the long term if not the short term) on support from the public, political figures seek not merely to win elections, but if possible to remain high in public opinion in the times between such contests. Thus, political elites have an interest in an informed public, but a public that is *favourably* informed, and political actors use their resources to enhance their public image whenever and wherever possible. In part, this emphasis on sustained popularity rather than simply on the ability to win an election campaign is the product of the development and increasing presence of

---

QUESTIONS AND ANSWERS

OPEN-ENDED QUESTIONS

What do you think of the performance of the government?

What are the important issues you feel government should address?

Which political leader is performing the best?

ORDINAL QUESTIONS

On a scale where 1 is poor and 10 is excellent, rate the performance of the government.

Rank the following issues in terms of their immediate importance: the environment, the deficit, unemployment.

In terms of performance, rank these political leaders from best to worst. Jean Chrétien, Preston Manning, Jean Charest, Alexa McDonough.

CATEGORICAL QUESTIONS

The performance of the government is (a) good (b) bad (c) don't know.

Unemployment is more important than the deficit: (a) agree (b) disagree.

The performance of Prime Minister Chrétien has been (a) good (b) mediocre (c) bad (d) don't know.

FIGURE 6.2

public opinion polls. What we often overlook is that these polls are as much about the *construction* of public opinion as they are about its measurement.

Modern **POLLING** is a social science using refined techniques based on probability theory that enable investigators to obtain data from a relatively small sample of individuals and yet have a reasonable confidence that their findings are an accurate representation of the larger population. No one (to our knowledge, at least) challenges the probability theory on which scientific polling is based, nor do we need to dwell on the practical difficulties encountered (and there are many) in actually taking a poll. Several other characteristics, however, make poll results somewhat artificial, what we might better call "constructs" of public opinion.

First of all, the questions asked in an opinion survey are typically hypothetical, "what if …?" statements that involve no actual commitment or activity on the part of the respondent. A pollster might ask, "If there were an election today, which party would you vote for?" Is there any reason to believe that your answer today, when you know there is no election, would be the same as your actual vote today, if there were in fact an election? In other words, because you know the question is purely hypothetical, you know there is nothing at stake for you in your answer; you are, in fact, free to answer however you like because there are no real-world consequences for you.[7]

A second element, somewhat related to the first, is the very nature of *opinion*. A survey researcher simply wants your responses to her questions; very rarely will you be asked *why* you responded as you did, and never will you be asked for evidence or logic to support your answer. Polling, in this way, does not seek judgements or expertise, in part because it is not equipped to make such dis-

A: Do you agree with the following statement?

Taxes are an unwelcome intrusion of the state upon the property of the individual.

Agree
Disagree
Don't Know

B: Do you agree with the following statement?

Taxes are necessary to pay for public goods like education and health care.

Agree
Disagree
Don't Know

FIGURE 6.3

7. Anyone who has been polled by an opinion research firm may have had the experience of being asked not one, or a few, but indeed many questions. In my own experience, there is a point at which the questions become tiresome, and then another point at which one realizes it is not necessary to think deeply or reflect carefully about the answer—one can say whatever one likes! At this point the exercise can even become fun.

Scenario A:

1. Comparing your financial position today with what it was before the last election, do you find yourself (a) better off, (b) worse off, (c) about the same?

2. What was your opinion of the tax increases introduced by Prime Minister Smith: (a) in favour (b) opposed (c) no opinion?

3. Taxes are an unwelcome intrusion of the state upon the property of the individual: (a) agree (b) disagree (c) don't know.

4. Prime Minister Lois Smith is doing a good job: (a) agree (b) disagree (c) don't know.

Scenario B:

1. Rank the following issues in order of their importance to you: (a) unemployment (b) an aging population (c) the environment (d) health care costs

2. Taxes are necessary to pay for public goods like education and health care: (a) agree (b) disagree (c) don't know.

3. What is your opinion of Prime Minister Smith's government's increases in the taxes on gasoline and tobacco products: (a) agree (b) disagree (c) don't know.

4. Prime Minister Lois Smith is doing a good job: (a) agree (b) disagree (c) don't know.

FIGURE 6.4

tinctions, in part because those who do polls don't care. Polls are very egalitarian: everybody's opinion is equally valid. The argument here is not that some people's opinions are more valid, but rather that everyone's *considered judgement* is worth considerably more than their opinion. Again, the hypothetical or artificial character of the polling situation comes into play. When we make real decisions with consequences in the real world, we are more likely to consider evidence, possible outcomes, ethical considerations—in short, all the things that go into a judgement, but do not necessarily inform an opinion. Similarly, while it is one thing, in the abstract, to say that all people's opinions are equally valid, in practice we are likely to consult the individuals who, our experience teaches us, have the knowledge and experience to give us sound advice.

Third, public opinion polls can claim only to represent opinion at a given moment in time (or what amounts usually in practice to a period of several days during which the poll was conducted). A poll taken in the first week of June 1989 can speak only about what was believed or known by respondents during the first week of June 1989, for who can say that public opinion wasn't changed significantly by subsequent events, perhaps even moments after the poll was taken? For this reason, polls are often described as giving us "snapshots" of public opinion, and only the eagerness of news firms to report poll results obscures to us that they are invariably "old news."

Finally, perhaps the most important aspect of modern polling that makes it a "construction" of public opinion, is a complex set of issues dealing with the way that questions are worded and presented to respondents. Consider, for example, possible differences in the answers respondents are permitted. A *categorical* format permits only two (or perhaps three: "agree," "disagree," "don't know") responses; an *ordinal* format allows one to rank several choices or assign a number to indicate the degree of response; an *open-ended* format allows the respondent to reply in words of his or her own choosing (see Figure 6.2). Clearly, the open-ended format is the most informative in terms of the range and accuracy of responses that it permits; ordinal and categorical formats force respondents into choosing between respectively fewer options, and hence to select a response that may be a less than completely accurate statement of their position. On the other hand, pollsters want answers that are quantifiable and do not leave a great deal of room open to interpretation, and here categorical and ordinal formats are much superior to the open-ended question, which may in fact produce no two responses alike.

As important as the range of responses permitted (or not) is the wording of poll questions. Consider the two questions in Figure 6.3: are they equally viable ways of asking about taxes, or does the wording of each tend to favour one response over the other? Indeed, every student (and particularly any who have taken a multiple-choice examination, for opinion surveys are often just simplified multiple-choice questionnaires) knows how important the wording of a question can be, and that there may be no such thing as a neutral question. Complicating this further is the fact that a poll is a set of questions in which one question, seemingly innocuous on its own, takes on greater significance when viewed in light of what precedes and/or follows. Questionnaires may be designed to "set up" particular questions. Consider the two scenarios in Figure 6.4: neither of these is neutral, and each could be seen as an attempt to influence the final question, in the first case in a manner unfavourable to the Prime Minister, while in the second in a fashion favourable to the PM's approval rating. Admittedly, our examples are a little crude; if nothing else, pollsters would likely not put these questions one after the other, but intersperse them with others less obviously pointed than these.

The final point to consider in light of the preceding material is that most public opinion polls are conducted by private companies that sell their social scientific/survey research expertise to various clients. Chief among these are political parties, governments, interest groups, and media companies. With the possible exception of the latter, each of these clients commissions opinion surveys not so much because they want to know what public opinion is, but because they hope to use the results of public opinion surveys as ammunition in their efforts to secure (or block) specific public policies. To be more precise, they will commission polls with one eye on ascertaining the state of public opinion. If the results are (or can be interpreted in a way) favourable to their cause, they will publish or publicize the results in an effort to influence policy-makers or convert the unconverted, in either case with the argument that "public opinion" is on their side. Poll results that are less than favourable are unlikely to see the light of day, particularly when commissioned by private organizations. Governments use polls to get an idea what public reaction is likely to be to particular policies under consideration; it can be embarrassing when polls are made public showing opinion opposed to the policy direction of the government. On the other hand, governments that simply follow the path of least resistance are criticized for "governing by polls," and given what we have

KEY TERMS

affect
attitudes
beliefs
cognitive ideas
corporate concentration
efficacy
entertainment
evaluative ideas
information
judgemental journalism
manipulation
mass culture
mass media
opinion
political culture
polling
public opinion
socialization
trust
values

**REFERENCES AND
SUGGESTED READING**

Almond, Gabriel, and Sidney
Verba. 1965. *The Civic Culture*.
Boston: Little, Brown.

Bell, David V.J. 1992. *The Roots
of Disunity*, rev. ed. Toronto:
Oxford University Press.

Bennett, W. Lance. 1980. *Public
Opinion in American Politics*.
New York: Harcourt Brace
Jovanovich.

——. 1992. *The Governing Crisis:
Media, Manipulation, and
Marketing in American
Elections*. New York:
St. Martin's Press.

Dyck, Perry Rand. 1996. *Canadian
Politics: Critical Approaches*.
Scarborough, Ont.: Nelson.

Easton, David. 1965. *A Systems
Analysis of Political Life*. New
York: Wiley.

been discussing, rightly so, for not only is the measurement of public opinion a hypothetical, undiscriminating "snapshot," it is also constructed at least in part through the ingenuity of survey designers. Given the myriad ways one can ask questions, limit the possibilities of answers, choose not to ask other questions, create moods, or influence attitudes by careful wording of questions and intelligent sequencing and juxtaposition of questions, the business of the pollster is not about finding "the truth"; there are any number of "truths" to be uncovered by the pollster's art, or, more accurately, science. Given that polling companies serve a paying clientele, it would seem desirable that, wherever possible, the "truth" the poll reveals be the "truth" the client was looking for.

These observations about polling are not meant cynically or pejoratively, but simply reflect the observation that the principal *raison d'être* of polling is not investigative (to uncover previously obscure truths), but *rhetorical*: to convince, persuade, or otherwise motivate someone or something. The notion that polls are somehow objective, disinterested, neutral measures of public opinion is a myth born out of a failure to understand how polls are constructed and the purposes for which they are designed, and this myth is maintained by pollsters, who wish to capitalize on the added influence that this supposed objectivity gives to their results.

6.6
CONCLUSION

The twentieth century witnessed the creation and sophistication of a mass culture in developed societies and, consistent with the expansion of the political class to include all adults, the development of a mass *political* culture. These transformations have relied on the successive emergence of communications media that served to shrink the worlds of place and time, and these media have come to be less and less about merely the transmission of information, and increasingly about entertainment and diversion. Just as citizens have come increasingly to rely on mass media (and among these, to rely predominantly on television) to inform them about the political world, politicians have become increasingly dependent on the media to put them in touch with an ever-increasing electorate. This, in turn, is symptomatic of a more general dependence of contemporary politicians on social scientific expertise to manage their encounter with the public. The use of public opinion polling, sophisticated marketing techniques, advertising expertise, controlled access to the media, professional image consultants, and public relations experts is now standard practice in attempting to maintain a favourable public image. It is not cynicism to regard these attempts at managing the public perception of the political world as manipulative. To the extent that these attempts at manipulation succeed, they make a sham of whatever democratic process exists. To the extent that they fail (and it is remarkable, given the expertise and effort behind them, how often they fail) they undermine democracy by alienating the public from the political realm (see also Chapter Eleven).

SOMETHING TO CONSIDER

Do the institutions of mass culture adequately prepare citizens for informed political action?

If yes, how is this measured?

If no, how might this preparation (i.e., acquiring a sufficient level of knowledge) be brought about?

Elkins, David, and Richard Simeon. 1965. *Small Worlds: Provinces and Parties in Canadian Political Life*. Toronto: Methuen.

Herman, Edward, and Noam Chomsky. 1988. *Manufacturing Consent: The Political Economy of the Mass Media*. New York: Pantheon Books.

Nevitte, Neil. 1996. *The Decline of Deference*. Peterborough, Ont.: Broadview Press.

Nevitte, Neil, and Roger Gibbins. 1990. *New Elites in Old States: Ideologies in the Anglo-American Democracies*. Toronto: Oxford University Press.

Parenti, Michael. 1992. *Make-Believe Media: The Politics of Entertainment*. New York: St. Martin's Press.

Postman, Neil. 1985. *Amusing Ourselves to Death: Public Discourse in the Age of Show Business*. New York: Penguin.

Taras, David. 1990. *The Newsmakers*. Scarborough, Ont.: Nelson.

INSTITUTIONS

Our distinction between the government and the state has come down (in large part) to the difference between people and institutions, and it is to the latter that we turn in this section. The ideas discussed in the previous section are actualized or become manifest in the form of institutions. Institutions are patterns of behaviour that become regularized and rule-governed, fulfilling particular functions within a society or political system.

Every human community or society has institutions, without which it would function very differently or perhaps not function at all. A large number of social institutions, such as the institutions of civil society (the family, the church, the corporation), are not primarily or fundamentally political. Our interest here is in the institutional forms that our ideas of justice and popular sovereignty have taken in the modern world, and in the considerable variation on some recognizable themes found in the world's stable democracies.

7 the state: functions, institutions, systems, constitutions

We have seen that as societies attain a sufficient size and complexity, they develop the permanent bureaucratic structure we associate with the state. The liberal democratic version of the state is in part a by-product of the depersonalization of power and authority that reflects dissatisfaction with late feudal forms of government such as absolute monarchy. Depersonalizing government means relying upon institutions and processes (i.e., rule-governed procedures) rather than the arbitrary decisions of individuals. We need to recall that one of the purposes—if not *the* purpose—of government is to provide order and stability, a certain coherence and predictability to the interactions of members of a society. As these societies continue to expand and become more diverse, mobile, and technologically driven, the ordering activity of government *necessarily* relies increasingly on institutions and processes, or on increasingly sophisticated institutions and processes. In short, as society (and life within society) becomes more complicated, so, too, must government (or, in its place, the institutions of civil society).

Within the wide diversity of states and the multiplicity of constitutions that define them, a few basic functions are common; indeed, it is arguable that such functions must be performed in some way in any political society. It is important to keep distinct the **FUNCTIONS** that governments perform from the **INSTITUTIONS** that perform these functions, and both of these distinct from the type of **SYSTEM** or **CONSTITUTION** that arranges the institutions and their relationships.

7.1 INTRODUCTION

7.1   Introduction
7.2   Functions of the State
7.3   Institutions
    7.3.1   Legislatures
    7.3.2   Executives
    7.3.3   Judiciaries
7.4   Systems
    7.4.1   Concentrated powers (parliamentary)
    7.4.2   Separated powers (the U.S.)
    7.4.3   Comparing systems
7.5   Constitutions and Constitutionalism

**7.2
FUNCTIONS
OF THE STATE**

The classic threefold distinction we will begin with revolves around three different aspects of one inescapable fact: governments *decide*—this is what it means to have power, to be authoritative. In all collective enterprises, short of achieving unanimity, someone or some group must decide for the rest *and* do so in such a way that the rest acknowledge their right to do so. Thus, the most basic function of the state is one of decision-making. Because authority is now generally exercised through the impersonal instrument of law, the **DECISION-MAKING** function is often called the **LEGISLATIVE** function, "legislating" being the business of making laws. We should recognize, though, that the decisions made by government may be quite different from law. On the one hand, whereas laws are rules that apply more or less universally and continually, some decisions (e.g., to appoint an ambassador, to declare a national disaster, or to recognize a citizen's outstanding bravery) may be one-time and quite particular. On the other hand, while laws are generally statements about what may or may not be done, or about what must or must not be done (i.e., they "permit" or "prohibit," "prescribe" or "proscribe"), many authoritative decisions are about conferring benefits (like pensions) or providing public goods (like education or health care), or encouraging economic activity (through subsidies, loans, or setting interest rates, etc.). Most of us meet government more often through these kinds of programs than by encountering "the law." In this sense, the decision-making function is broader than law, and is better captured by the term "policy-making." Policy, in turn, can be defined broadly as *any course of action or inaction that government deliberately chooses to take.*

In any organized society, decisions—whether particular rules or programmatic—must be made in an authoritative way. Institutions, processes, and the systems that organize both will determine at least three things:

1. *who* will make these decisions;
2. *how* these decisions will be made;
3. *what* decisions can or cannot in fact be made.

These three variables, the "who," "how," and "what" of decision-making, will vary considerably from polity to polity, or even more so, from one type of political system to another. As might be equally obvious, these same variables will also apply to other functions of the state.

To make a decision is one thing; to implement it or carry it out is another matter altogether. It is probably safe to say that most of us are better at making decisions than at realizing them, and most of us would rather make decisions ("make it so!") than implement them, given the choice. Nonetheless, if decisions are not somehow put into effect, they become meaningless. Just as the kinds of decision governments make can vary, so, too, will **IMPLE-MENTATION** of these decisions. In the case of a law, it may mean enforcing sanctions or penalties against those who do not obey; with a policy or broad program it may involve the delivery of services, or the payment of funds, or the maintenance of physical plant. In either case, a complex organization of resources, human and otherwise, is required to carry out what was intended in the authoritative decision. This function is typically called the **EXECUTIVE** or administrative function of the state. By and large this is entrusted to the permanent **BUREAUCRACY** that characterizes the state as a form of social organization. Modern government consists (to a large degree) of many bureaucracies, organized to deliver programs, enforce laws, or administer regulations. Collectively, these various government departments that implement decisions are sometimes called "the bureaucracy."

Finally, wherever authoritative decisions are made and implemented, there will be disputes, and the kinds of disagreement will be as various as the decisions and their implementation. Consider the "who," "how," and "what" of decision-making again—each of these is a possible source of dispute. Was the decision made by the person or body authorized to make such decisions? Was the decision made according to the procedural rules set out for decision-makers? Was the decision one that can in fact be made by decision-makers? Someone or some body must have the responsibility for answering these questions or settling these disputes—if not, the legitimacy of the state could be undermined. This function of **ADJUDICATION** or dispute settlement has commonly been called the **JUDICIAL** function.

Judgement of disputes concerning the authoritative decisions of the state usually falls into one of two very broad categories: disputes about the decision itself (as the examples in the previous paragraph illustrate), or disputes about the implementation of the decision. Roughly (and only roughly), this corresponds to a distinction between matters of law and matters of fact. Most criminal and many civil cases, for example, are of the latter kind: what must be judged is the guilt, innocence, or liability of the accused party; the law itself is not at issue. In most constitutional cases, by

FUNCTIONS OF THE STATE

Kottak (1991: 129)

(Found in all states:)
1. Population control: fixing of boundaries, establishment of citizenship categories, census taking.
2. Judiciary: laws, legal procedure, and judges.
3. Enforcement: permanent military and police forces.
4. Fiscal: taxation.

Deutsch (1990: 24-25)

(May all be found in a single state, but not necessarily, and not in same priority:)
1. Pattern maintenance: to keep in power those who have power, wealthy those who have wealth.
2. Organizing for conquest.
3. Pursuit of wealth.
4. The welfare state.
5. The mobilization state.

Mann (1990: 69)

(Four most persistent types of state activities:)
1. The maintenance of internal order.
2. Military defence/aggression, directed against foreign foes.
3. The maintenance of communications infrastructures.
4. Economic redistribution.

FIGURE 7.1

contrast, what is in dispute is the law itself, its validity, or, in many cases, its meaning. Here judgement is primarily about *interpretation*. As with decision-making, so too for decision-adjudicating: there are variations with respect to who adjudicates, how they adjudicate, and what they may adjudicate.

If all societies require authoritative decisions and if, accordingly, making them is a primary function of *all* governments (or states), then it follows that these societies will also require decisions to be implemented and disputes about decisions to be settled—the executive and judicial functions will be as basic to government as the legislative function. Various political thinkers have ascribed other functions to the state, and in most cases what these indicate are more specific ends or goals that governments provide or seek to accomplish. These goals are in fact what governments use their decision-making and implementing power to accomplish. These particular goods or functions that constitute the business of the state will vary considerably according to the type of society, the level of technology, or the period in history. For example, we might say that it is a function of governments to ensure that citizens achieve an adequate level of education; 200 years ago few governments, if any, would have recognized such a task as their responsibility. On the other hand, defence of citizens and their possessions from aggression, internal or external, has been recognized as a purpose of the state probably for as long as there have been states (see also Figure 7.1).

**7.3
INSTITUTIONS**

Decision-making, implementation, and adjudication are common to all political communities that have a state. The alternative designation of these functions as the legislative, executive, and judicial functions indicates a relationship with the primary institutions responsible for performing these functions in the modern state:

FUNCTION	INSTITUTION
legislative	the legislature
executive (administrative)	the executive
judicial	the judiciary

Whether functions are named for institutions or vice versa is a moot point. Still, it is important to appreciate that this division is relatively modern, and that the correspondence of functions and institutions is not always as direct as may first appear.

Consider classical times. While the Greeks distinguished between democracy, aristocracy, and monarchy as types of constitutions or systems, common to all of them was the fact that whoever had the authority of the state had *all* of it: decision-making, implementation, and adjudication. Similarly, what made the absolute monarch of feudal times absolute was that in the final analysis he or she was decision-maker, implementer, and judge. He or she may not have actually exercised this authority in each particular case, choosing instead to delegate implementation or administration to trusted advisers or ministers, and to delegate judgement of disputes to magistrates. Delegation, though, is only a loan or impermanent transfer of power or authority, a loan or transfer that may be revoked at any time. The point is that the monarch could choose at any time, as he (or she) often did, to exercise all of these powers. Common to classical and feudal times, therefore, was a notion of unified sovereignty, located in one person or body of persons: this person or body retained the final word on all matters.

The alternate idea, which emerges with liberalism, is the notion of a separation of powers, which means placing the state's power to make decisions in a different set of hands from the state's power to implement decisions, and in a different set of hands from the state's power to judge disputes about decisions. In practice this has also meant placing the responsibility for each function not with a person or body of persons, but with an institution in which individuals exercise that responsibility. It is thus in the modern state that the institutions of the legislature, the executive, and the judiciary come into their own as distinct (but never wholly separate) institutions.

It is also true that however distinct and separate these institutions are (and the United States is usually regarded as the epitome of separated powers), it is rare for any one of them to have the sole responsibility for a function of government. At most, an institution has primary responsibility for the function but requires the approval or consent of another or other institutions of the state. To indicate this more clearly we need to discuss the actual organization of institutions within a system or type of government. But first some general comments about each institution are in order.

LEGISLATURES

BICAMERAL			UNICAMERAL
BRITAIN [Parliament] House of Lords House of Commons	**CANADA** [Parliament] Senate House of Commons	**AUSTRALIA** [Parliament] Senate House of Representatives	**SWEDEN** Riksdag
			NORWAY Storting
UNITED STATES [Congress] Senate House of Representatives	**JAPAN** [Diet] House of Councillors House of Representatives	**GERMANY** Bundesrat Bundestag	**NEW ZEALAND** House of Representatives
FRANCE Senate National Assembly	**ITALY** Senate Chamber of Deputies	**SWITZERLAND** Council of States National Council	**ISRAEL** Knesset
NETHERLANDS First Chamber Second Chamber			**DENMARK** Folketing

FIGURE 7.2

7.3.1 Legislatures

A legislature may be described as a body of individuals organized for the purpose of legislating, i.e., to make the laws that will be binding on the community. The history of legislatures is interesting and significant. In medieval times, monarchs who wished to mobilize the public to some great purpose (going to war, mounting a Crusade, etc.) would periodically summon representatives of the various classes or "estates" to an assembly, where they would be expected to give their approval to the business the monarch set before them. The usual classes or estates summoned were members of the Church, of the aristocracy, and representatives of the townsfolk and free peasantry. Two points are worth noting. One is that the original purpose of such assemblies was to give approval (and thus legitimacy) to decisions already made by the monarch, but that required public compliance in order to be implemented successfully. One of the changes that accompanies the end of feudalism and the beginning of liberal government is the insistence by legislatures upon taking a more direct hand (if not primary responsibility) for making decisions. The second point of significance is that from their earliest beginnings, legislatures were representative, although not democratic. In practice, then, a legislature is an assembly of representatives entrusted with the authority to legislate, and organized for that purpose. The democratization of representative assemblies is something we will discuss in Chapter Eleven.

It is also for historical reasons, generally, that many legislatures actually consist of two chambers or "houses" of representatives. As noted, the summoning of the estates meant assembling the representatives of different classes, who could hardly be expected to sit and deliberate together. Hence the distinction in the British legislature between the (House of) Lords, for bishops and nobles, and the (House of) Commons, for commoners (townsfolk and free peasants), a distinction that persists today. In most cases, though, the reason today for continuing to have two chambers, or a **BICAMERAL** legislature, is to embody different principles of representation, particularly in federal countries (see Chapter Ten). Thus in the United States, the House of Representatives is based on the principle of **REPRESENTATION BY POPULATION** (see Chapter Eleven), while the Senate is based on the principle of equal representation of the states. Names of some legislatures, bicameral (two houses) and unicameral (one chamber), are listed in Figure 7.2.

7.3.2 Executives

Executives are the highest-ranking individuals in organizations; this is as true of businesses, or universities, or charities, as it is of nation-states. Modern executive offices within the state are a result of the successive limitation, formalization, or replacement with a civilian counterpart of the traditional office of monarch. As noted, absolute monarchs were both makers and administrators of the law; a key accomplishment of the liberal revolution was to give real legislative power to legislatures or parliaments. This has meant that political executives in the modern period have been concerned primarily with what we have identified as the executive (or administrative) function: overseeing the administration or execution of authoritative decisions. This is the day-to-day functioning of government, or what might be called the ongoing activity of governing, and as the size and level of government activity has expanded so enormously in the past two centuries, so has the scope of the administrative side of the state grown in significance, especially given that this includes all of the vast bureaucracies involved in delivering government programs and other public goods.

	EXECUTIVES	
UNLIMITED STATES	**CONSTITUTIONAL STATES**	
Authoritarian Ruler	**SINGLE (UNIFIED) EXECUTIVE**	
Absolute Monarch	**Strong President**	United States
	DUAL EXECUTIVE	
	Constitutional Monarchy Head of State: Monarch (formal) Head of Government: Prime Minister (political)	Australia, Belgium, Canada, Denmark, Japan, Luxembourg, Netherlands, New Zealand, Norway, Spain, Sweden, United Kingdom

	Republic (1)
	Head of State:
	  Weak President (formal)
	Head of Government:
	  Strong Prime Minister (political)
		Austria, Germany, Greece, Iceland,
		Ireland, Israel, Italy, Portugal

	Republic (2)
	Head of State:
	  Strong President (political)
	Head of Government:
	  Prime Minister (political)
		France, Poland, Russia

FIGURE 7.3

Before we examine the different forms that the modern executive takes, it is necessary to explain a simple but crucial distinction between **FORMAL** and **DISCRETIONARY** power or authority. Formal authority is governed by rules, is procedural, and is often exercised in the name of the organization or body by an individual who is its representative. One should not conclude that because formal authority excludes individual discretion or decision that it is unimportant; rather, formality attaches a legitimacy to decisions and this allows others to recognize their validity. For example, when a student graduates from university, his or her diploma is signed by the university president (or equivalent official), and without this signature it would not be a valid diploma. The signature is a formality, though, in that the university president does not personally decide whether or not to sign each student's diploma. Instead, as long as certain rules and procedures have been satisfied (the student has a passing grade in a sufficient number and mix of courses, all outstanding fees have been paid, etc.), the signature of the university president is automatic, and informs one and all that this student has satisfied the requirements of the university degree. At the level of the nation-state, the **HEAD OF STATE** is the executive whose task it is to perform formal functions on behalf of the state, as well as ceremonial duties, which likewise do not involve great matters of decision-making but satisfy certain international and domestic requirements of etiquette. Whether the head of state carries out *only* formal and ceremonial functions will depend on the constitution of the state concerned, but where this is so, the head of state may be referred to as a *formal executive*.

Obviously, not all power, and not all executive acts, are formal. A considerable range of executive decisions involves actual discretion or judgement on the part of those who make them. The fact that there are no rules or procedures that executives must follow in these cases is the reason we call this kind of decision-making *discretionary* power or authority, although it is probably just what we normally think of as what power and authority involve—making decisions. As just one example that anticipates our discussion of constitutional systems below, consider the difference between law-making in Canada and the United States. In both these countries, as in many democracies, a bill that passes the legislature goes to the executive for approval. In Canada, this is a mere formality: the Governor-General, as a head of state whose role is largely (although not completely) formal, has no choice but to "give assent" to the bill and thus make it law (see Figure 7.4). In the United States, by contrast, the President (who is head of state, but is not a merely formal executive) has several choices, including the option of vetoing (cancelling or negating) the legislation; this is discretionary power that a merely formal executive lacks.

As noted above, modern executives can be explained as various transformations of traditional monarchy. In **CONSTITUTIONAL MONARCHIES** (which are all parliamentary systems, like Canada, Britain, Belgium, Sweden, and others), the role of the monarch has been limited and formalized; what discretionary executive power remains is transferred to a **POLITICAL EXECUTIVE**. This means, first, that unlike the monarch, who usually achieves office by birth and rules of hereditary succession, the political executive is designated by the operations of the political process, which in liberal states is representative and democratic. It also means that these countries have a **DUAL EXECUTIVE**, consisting of a formal executive (the monarch) and a political executive (usually a prime minister and cabinet).

GOVERNORS-GENERAL

Before 1867, Canada was a set of British colonies, and each colony was headed by a Governor, who acted as the representative of both the monarch *and* of the British government of the day, thus acting on instructions from the Colonial Secretary. When Canada became a self-governing Dominion, this was (as in Australia, New Zealand, and other former British colonies) a peaceful transition; the monarch remained the head of state, and the Governor-General (reflecting the amalgamation of colonies into one Dominion) continued to function as a mainly formal executive representing the monarch and the imperial (British) government. Since 1931, Governors-General in the Dominions have no longer represented the British government in any capacity, but serve as representatives of the monarch (i.e., the King or Queen *of Canada*) in his or her absence from the Dominion. Reflecting this, in Canada, since 1926, the Governor-General has been appointed by the monarch on the advice of the Canadian Prime Minister (advice that is always taken). Canada is thus a constitutional monarchy, with the Queen as head of state, this office of a formal executive being exercised by the Governor-General in her absence.

FIGURE 7.4

The historical assumption underlying traditional monarchy (and aristocracy) was that of a natural hierarchy of superior and inferior natures, natures that are at least in part inherited. The Enlightenment liberal view, by contrast, is that all humans are in essence of one common nature, equally deserving of rights and respect. The political community corresponding to this view cannot accept any "natural hierarchy," but is an association of free and equal citizens; a government of free citizens is called a **REPUBLIC**. The logically simplest path to a republic would be to replace the monarchy with a civilian office whose occupant—i.e., a president—was chosen by the citizen body. Traditional institutions like monarchy, though, are often deeply imbedded in the political culture and life of a country, so that not only does the monarch resist being deposed, but the monarchy also commands fierce loyalty from considerable portions of the public. In practice, then, to replace a monarch with a presidency has often been difficult, requiring revolution, or conquest and reorganization by a foreign power, or a military coup. Normally, a president will embody the role of head of state and carry out the formal and ceremonial executive functions. In systems with a single executive (like the U.S.), the president will also have responsibilities of a discretionary or political nature. The extent of these will depend, though, on the relationship of the presidency to other institutions like the legislature, and thus depend on the nature of the constitutional system. For the moment, we can consider the president to be the civilian equivalent of a monarch, the extent of his or her power dependent on the place of the presidency within the constitution (see also Figure 7.3, and Chapter Eight).

In democracies, the president will be accountable to the people, directly or indirectly. Not all republics are democratic, though, and when authoritarian rulers take the title of president the civilian equivalence of absolute monarchy is achieved. In either case, democratic or authoritarian, we have so far been considering a strong president, i.e., a unified or single executive. In countries where the monarch's role was diminished and formalized, there emerged a political executive exercising the bulk of discretionary power. This was the experience of parliamentary systems (to be discussed in greater detail below), where the executive, strictly speaking, is a collective body—the cabinet. At the head of the cabinet, and thus the head of government in these countries, is a prime minister. The dual executive in parliamentary systems was initially in most cases a pairing of monarch and prime minister. In some parliamentary countries the monarchy has been replaced with a civilian head of state, normally designated as president. Here then is a dual executive of a president who is head of state (a mainly formal office) and a prime minister who is **HEAD OF GOVERNMENT** (wielding discretionary power as chair or head of cabinet). As a generalization, presidency as sole executive is strong; presidency as head of state within a dual executive (e.g., in parliamentary systems) is weak. For reasons that will be clearer when we have examined the differences between systems with fused powers (parliamentary) and separated powers (presidential), the most "powerful" executive office in democratic or constitutional regimes is that of prime minister in a parliamentary system.

7.3.3   Judiciaries

The third institution of the state—the judiciary—is in normal cases part of the state, but not part of politics. By judiciary is meant magistrates or judges and the courts over which they preside. The task of the courts and their officers is the administration of justice, or what we have described as adjudicating disputes about authoritative decisions. A central principle of modern liberal justice (perhaps *the* principle) is the rule of law (see also Chapter Sixteen), which can be summarized as *the requirement that all citizens, rulers and ruled alike, obey known, impartial rules.* In short, no one is above the law, including the highest political officials. For this to be true, and for the law to be impartial, the ideal of **JUDICIAL INDEPENDENCE** must be met. This means that officers of the court, and judges particularly, must be free from political interference, that is, remain free from being influenced by those in positions of authority or power (see Figure 7.5). To the degree that judicial independence is realized in modern democracies, the ordinary business of the courts is a legal, not political, matter.

Two activities of the courts do have unquestionably political significance. One is the interpretation of law; the other is hearing constitutional cases. In applying laws to particular cases, judges are always engaged in interpretation of the law, i.e., clarifying the meaning of the words in the statute, and their relevance to the case at hand. This has political significance when the interpretation that judges give of a law has unexpected consequences, especially when these are contrary to the intention(s) of lawmakers. Law is an instrument that politicians use to make

JUDICIAL INDEPENDENCE

Theodore Becker (1970: 144) has defined judicial independence as: (a) the degree to which judges believe they can decide and do decide consistent with their own personal attitudes, values, and conceptions of judicial role (in their interpretation of the law), (b) in opposition to what others, who have or are believed to have political or judicial power, think about or desire in like matters, and (c) particularly when a decision adverse to the beliefs or desires of those with political or judicial power may bring some retribution on the judges personally or on the power of the courts.

In practical terms, this means that judges must have an adequate salary that is secure from interference by political actors; that their term of office must also be secure, with removal prior to the end of term occurring only for "just cause"; and that the appointment process is free of political pressure or influence.

FIGURE 7.5

policy; if the courts interpret law differently from what legislators intended, then judges are making policy—whether they intend to or not. Whether political actors can restore the original policy by making a new, differently worded law depends on a number of legal and political factors.

The most intentionally political role of the courts is to uphold the constitution, the framework of basic law that defines relationships between rulers, institutions, and citizens. If governments are to be limited in their activities by a set of rules such as a constitution provides, then there must be a forum where challenges to actions of the state or government can be heard and authoritative judgements delivered. While many question the need for the courts to make policy, few challenge the legitimacy of the constitutional role of this institution. The scope of this role depends on the nature of the constitution and on the organization of the courts.

In most countries, courts are organized hierarchically, in a pyramid that culminates in a high court from which there is no further legal appeal. The rulings of this court are binding on all lower courts and this ensures some uniformity to the application and interpretation of the law and, to the degree that uniformity imparts fairness, delivers justice. The high or supreme court is often the final court of appeal for all criminal and civil cases heard at lower levels of the court system. In many countries it also hears constitutional challenges, but in some cases there is a special constitutional court that deals only with this type of case (e.g., in Austria, Germany, Italy, Portugal, Spain, France, and most countries of Eastern Europe).

As noted, the actual role of the courts in respect to constitutional matters will depend on several variables. In most cases, the courts will be able to rule on whether government bodies or office-holders have exceeded the authority the constitution allots them. An important but more specialized function is disputes between levels of government, a central question in countries with a federal constitution (see Chapter Ten). Perhaps the most important variable is whether the courts are empowered to perform **JUDICIAL REVIEW**, that is, whether the courts are able to rule on the validity of laws passed by the legislature. The possibility of judicial review (see Figure 7.6) is enhanced by the inclusion in the constitution of a code or charter of citizens' rights, because this provides a set of standards that the courts can use to evaluate legislation, but there are several other variables involved in judicial review.

JUDICIAL REVIEW

Democracies with judicial review:
Australia, Austria, Canada, Denmark, France, Germany, Iceland, Ireland, Italy, Japan, Norway, Sweden, United States

Democracies without judicial review:
Belgium, Finland, Israel, Luxembourg, Netherlands, New Zealand, Switzerland, United Kingdom

[from Lijphart, 1984: 193]

FIGURE 7.6

"Concrete" review, for example, refers to consideration of a law resulting from an actual case tried under that law. Usually this means that the defendant charged under the law chooses to challenge the constitutional validity of the law. In the United States, appeal of an actual case to the **SUPREME COURT** is the only way judicial review by this body can happen. In Canada, the device of **REFERENCE** makes it possible for governments to use the courts to rule on the constitutionality of a bill or law in the absence of an actual case. (Ironically, one reason for doing so is to avoid anticipated court challenges that may bog down application or enforcement of the law.)

Reference is an example of what is called "abstract" review, that is, review in the absence of a case. In some countries only abstract review is possible; in some countries there is a time limit to the possibility of abstract review after the passage of a bill; and in some countries review *must* take place before a bill actually becomes law. In France, for example, the Constitutional Council may not overturn a bill once the President has signed it into law, so bills are referred to this special court after passage by the legislature and before presidential assent. Where abstract review is possible, there are usually rules about who can make such a reference to the courts. In some countries, such as Sweden, judicial review is constitutionally possible, but rarely happens; in the Netherlands, by contrast, judicial review is constitutionally prohibited.

7.4 SYSTEMS

As the discussion of institutions makes clear, it is difficult to separate legislatures and executives from the types of political system in which they are found. The political (or constitutional) system (or type) indicates two things: (1) the relationship between the institutions just discussed—legislatures, executives and judiciaries; and (2) how responsibility for the functions of the state is allocated among these institutions. Fortunately, there is less variety than one might think among the world's democracies. We will outline some of the principles that distinguish the principal varieties, and then in the subsequent two chapters explore these types in greater detail.

One basis of distinction has been the relationship of the institutions of state, or as Lipson (1990) puts it, between concentrated and dispersed powers of government. The parliamentary system of Great Britain epitomizes the former; the presidential system of the U.S. exemplifies the latter. Accordingly, some also refer to this distinction as one between parliamentary and presidential systems. The difficulty with this is that the stable, successful democracies *other* than the United States that have strong presidents are more likely to resemble parliamentary systems. For this reason it is perhaps best to remain with concentrated vs. dispersed powers (or fused vs. separated), and suggest why the concentration of powers offered by parliamentary systems has proven more durable and attractive, even if, in some cases, it has been supplemented by a strong presidency.

7.4.1   Concentrated powers (parliamentary systems)

The British Parliament at Westminster has been called the mother of all parliaments, and indeed most parliamentary constitutions offer variations on the basic arrangements put in place by the Whig Revolution of 1688, itself the product of struggles predating the English Civil War of 1642. The word "revolution" implies a turning around, and just such a reversal occurred in the respective roles of the monarch and the legislature. Prior to 1688, the monarch made decisions (acted) and expected the legislature (particularly the House of Commons) to give formal approval (ratification) to these executive acts. Since 1688, the reverse has become true: the legislature acts and the monarch gives the formal approval (assent) that legitimizes these actions.

Figure 7.7 is misleading in two respects. In the first place the shift presented should be understood as one of *relative* influence in government; the British system is one of **PARLIAMENTARY SUPREMACY**, not legislative supremacy. Under the British constitution neither the monarch nor the legislature can act alone (legislative supremacy implies the latter); they must act together.

Within this whole that is Parliament, the revolution of 1688 reversed the priority of the players; the play goes on with the same actors, but they have been required to exchange roles. The second respect in which the characterization is inaccurate is that it leaves out the **CABINET** (and **PRIME MINISTER**) and thus implies more power for the legislative chamber called the House of Commons than is actually the case. As we will see, the cabinet actually exercises discretionary power within parliamentary systems and is, in effect, the government of the day. This cabinet, though, is linked to the legislature in two important ways that require consideration. First, though, we should explain the origin of cabinet government.

BEFORE 1688

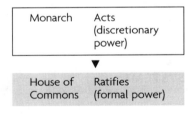

FIGURE 7.7

While absolute monarchs were ultimately responsible for all activities of the state—as Louis XIV said, "*L'Etat c'est moi*" (I am the state)—they normally delegated much of the actual labour to trusted advisers. Over time, assistance to the monarch was recognized in a set of offices, each with its own title and particular set of functions (looking after the treasury, or the King's cavalry, or granting licences to trade, etc.). Individually, those holding such offices had a title like Minister or Secretary, and collectively they met as advisers to the monarch (in England this body was known as the Privy Council). Originally, the monarch appointed his or her ministers from the ranks of the aristocracy, choosing favourites and dismissing them once they fell out of favour. This is the origin of the cabinet: a body of officials individually responsible for administering a portion of the state bureaucracy and collectively forming the "government" of the day. As a body performing the executive function of the state, the cabinet is a **COLLECTIVE EXECUTIVE**.

The cabinet arose, then, as a body of advisers serving the monarch, with a limited relationship to the legislature. In England, after 1688, this changed in two ways. It was necessary for the monarch to choose ministers from the more powerful chamber of the legislature; this, a result of social, economic, and political changes, was no longer the House of Lords (representing the aristocracy), but the House of Commons (representing the propertied interests of an emerging market society). In other words, those who were actually carrying out the executive function (and functioning as a collective executive) were also to be legislators drawn primarily from the lower chamber of the legislature. This dual membership of cabinet members in both the executive and the legislature is called a **FUSION OF POWERS**, and is common to almost all parliamentary systems.

The second change brought about by 1688 was the requirement that the cabinet (or Ministry, or Privy Council) have the continued support of the most powerful chamber of the legislature—the House of Commons. This is known as "maintaining the **CONFIDENCE**" of the legislature, and in bicameral parliaments the lower or popularly representative chamber is the confidence chamber (the one that matters). Maintaining confidence means being able to sustain the support of a majority of legislators present in the chamber on all important votes concerning government policy or expenditure. This requirement that the executive (the cabinet) have the support or confidence of the legislature (the lower chamber) is the principle of **RESPONSIBLE GOVERNMENT**,

THE PARLIAMENTARY SYSTEM

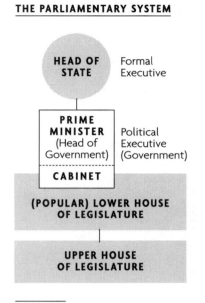

FIGURE 7.8

and it is *the* most important feature that distinguishes parliamentary government from all others. It is a principle intended to keep the executive accountable to the legislature, and in English politics means that instead of pleasing the monarch, the cabinet must be ultimately pleasing to the House of Commons. Any cabinet that fails to maintain the confidence of the legislature is expected to resign and be replaced by another that is able to command such a majority.

Both the fusion of powers and responsible government in Britain (and many other countries) are **CONVENTIONS**. A convention is an unwritten rule that is nonetheless binding because all parties agree to it (and the reason they agree to it is usually because it works, or works best). In the case of responsible government, the convention that a government failing to win majority support in the legislature must resign has a clearly practical basis. If the cabinet cannot gain the support of a majority, it cannot get its policies or its expenditures passed, and if it cannot make policy or spend money, it cannot govern.

Linking the political executive—the cabinet—to the legislature by means of responsible government and the fusion of powers has had (at least) two other consequences of note. One is the emergence of the prime minister at the top of the political executive, so much so that as head of government the prime minister is the most powerful individual in a parliamentary democracy. One popular account has it that the office of prime minister came to prominence in England in the eighteenth century when German-speaking English kings stopped attending cabinet meetings because of their lack of facility with the English language. Historian Christopher Hill, however, notes that George I "stopped attending the Cabinet not because of any lack of linguistic ability but because he had so little authority there" (1969: 216). Since it was now necessary for the cabinet to maintain the support of the House of Commons, monarchs had to choose ministers who could command that support, individuals with great following and influence among the members of Parliament. Once installed in cabinet, these individuals would determine government policy. Should the King, for example, insist on policy contrary to the wishes of the cabinet, he would risk its resignation, the loss of the government, and setting himself at odds with the entire House of Commons. After the Civil War and the Revolution of 1688, English monarchs were reluctant to antagonize Parliament to such an extent. Since the eighteenth century in Britain, and now the norm in most parliamentary systems, the prime minister (as chair of cabinet and thus head of government) controls most of the discretionary executive authority of the state; given the fusion of powers that links the cabinet and prime minister to the House of Commons, he or she usually dominates (if not controls) the legislature's business.

The second development, which clinched the dominance of the prime minister and cabinet within the parliamentary system, was the emergence of strong (disciplined) parties. Most readers undoubtedly are fully aware of the central role of political parties within contemporary politics, and we will discuss the nature and functions of political parties in greater depth below; what may be less familiar is the fact that in the early days of representative, parliamentary government, there were no political parties. Individuals stood for parliamentary election on their own merits or reputations, neither representing nor being sponsored by some larger organization or association. Within the legislature, it is true, individuals did not act as complete "independents" but associated in factions or groups, which might be organized around an ideological disposition, a religious affiliation, personal influence and obligations, naked ambition, or resentment of another group currently in power. Selecting individuals to the cabinet would be in part a calculation of which factions' support they might bring or control and thus contribute to putting together a legislative majority (which responsible government requires).

Because the convention of responsible government requires the cabinet to maintain the support of a majority, this provides a great incentive for political leaders to organize their supporters and provide some greater measure of predictability and discipline to their legislative behaviour. In parliamentary systems the stakes are high, because failure to maintain a majority means losing office. Consequently, in the British parliamentary system strong parties (now the norm in parliamentary regimes) replaced loose factions. What makes parties strong is their ability to discipline members through rewards for loyal behaviour and sanctions for failure to support the party leadership. As parties have developed, they have come to dominate the political process of democratic states, so much so that being elected to Parliament as an "independent" is now a rather exceptional accomplishment. In many cases, the rules of parliamentary procedure have been revised or rewritten to reflect (or ensure) the reality that the primary actors within the system are parties, not individual members.

Strong parties provide structure and predictability to activity within Parliament. As organizations that provide means for leaders to discipline members, parliamentary parties are hierarchi-

The link between strong parties and responsible government is demonstrated in Canada by the fact that Canada's first political party (the Liberal Conservative Party, today's Progressive Conservative party) dates from 1854, only six years after responsible government was first brought to reality in the colony of Canada.

RESPONSIBLE GOVERNMENT AND PARTIES (II)

The division of Parliament (in Britain, Canada, and some other former British colonies) into a government side and an opposition side and the designation of the leader of the largest party not in government as the Leader of Her (His) Majesty's Loyal Opposition are carry-overs from the time before disciplined parties. Members of the House would simply declare themselves for or against the government of the day and take their seats on the appropriate side of the chamber.

FIGURE 7.9

cal and (largely) run from the top down. To some degree, then, although **PARTY DISCIPLINE** is a product of the conditions created by responsible government, it also tends to undermine responsible government as a means by which the legislature keeps the executive accountable. This is so because party discipline means that party leaders in the cabinet have firm control over the votes of their members in the legislature. The executive dominance described above is thus confirmed and strengthened with the development of strong, disciplined parties. Ultimately, the executive answers not to the legislature, but to the electorate.

This last point is important. Parliamentary government is strong government. The executive is normally a relatively cohesive, collective body that controls both the executive and legislature, and it maintains this control through the mechanisms of party discipline. Because of its strength and strategic location within the political system, the cabinet government of a parliamentary system controls not only the legislative process, but also, and more importantly, the making and implementation of public policy. A prime minister in such a system can wield as much or more power than any absolute monarch ever enjoyed. One safeguard against the abuse of this power is the ability to appeal to the courts for any violation of the constitution. In many countries, though, there is no judicial review, as we have noted, so constitutional challenges are limited. (In Britain, not only is there no judicial review, there is no "written" constitution, which is why we have had very little to say about the courts in discussing British parliamentary evolution.) The other, and in the final analysis the most important, check against the abuse of power within parliamentary regimes is the power of public opinion, expressed most decisively (although not solely) at election time. This is why democracy requires not only free elections, but also a free press, a sufficiently organized political opposition, an educated citizenry, and as full an access as possible to information about policy decisions.

7.4.2   Separated powers (the U.S. system)

If the British system of parliamentary government was the product of a revolution against absolutist monarchy, the American system of separated powers was in part the result of revolution against the concentrated powers of the British Crown. "In part" because revolution in and of itself cannot explain the distrust of government that has been so imbedded in American political culture and the constitution (France, after all, has had several revolutions, and yet has one of the most activist states and political cultures in the democratic world). The framers of the American Constitution were also intrigued by the causes of the collapse of the ancient republic of Rome, and worried about the possible rise and dominance of factions within the body politic. They drew heavily on Locke's notion of a clear separation of the executive and legislative powers of the state, and on Montesquieu's ideas about mixed government. To some degree the revolution and the pre-revolutionary experience of the colonials only reinforced the antipathy to government that had brought many of them to the New World in the first place.

While the parliamentary system has evolved from very non-democratic origins (sovereignty embodied in the person of the monarch) to increasingly representative and democratic formations, the U.S. system begins with the liberal notion of popular sovereignty. The people entrust sovereignty to the institutions of the state by means of a constitution, which is their safeguard against abuses of power by those who exercise it. Although it is commonly observed that the framers of the Constitution were wary of government, it is clear that they were quite hard-headed about the people, too. As James Madison wrote in *Federalist Paper No. 51*:

> If men were angels, no government would be necessary. If angels were to govern men, neither external nor internal controls on government would be necessary. In framing a government which is to be administered by men over men, the great difficulty lies in this: you must first enable the government to control the governed; and in the next place oblige it to control itself. A dependence on the people is, no doubt, the primary control on the government; but experience has taught mankind the necessity of auxiliary precautions. (quoted in Landes, 1996: 113)

In fact, Madison displayed a particularly modern confidence in institutions, in the ability to secure justice through the clever design of institutions and procedures. In several respects it is the *Constitution* that is sovereign in the American system of government.

The most fundamental principle of the U.S. Constitution is a radical **SEPARATION OF POWERS**. This is accomplished by the creation of distinct "branches" of government and the restriction that no individual may serve or hold office in more than one of these branches at the same time. Thus, unlike the parliamentary convention where members of the cabinet also hold seats in the legislature, the American Constitution requires a member of Congress (the U.S. legislature) to resign his or her seat if appointed to the cabinet. In Britain, the highest court is technically the House of Lords (the upper chamber of the legislature), although its business is carried out in practice by nine Law Lords with the right to sit in the House of Lords. In the U.S., the Supreme Court constitutes a third branch of government, balancing the executive branch (President and cabinet) and the legislative branch (Congress: the Senate and House of Representatives).

The flip side of the separation of powers in the American Constitution is a set of **CHECKS AND BALANCES** designed to keep any one branch of government from gaining power at the expense of the others. This is one of the "auxiliary precautions" Madison referred to, and it is based on his premise that "Ambition must be made to counteract ambition" (*Federalist Paper No. 51*). The actual checks and balances are numerous, but their effect is that no branch of government can fully perform its function without at least the acquiescence of the other two. Thus, while each branch of government has primary responsibility for carrying out the function for which it is named, the other two branches also have a role with respect to that function. The legislature legislates (makes law), but as noted above, the President has the ability to veto legislation, and the Supreme Court by exercising judicial review can declare laws to be unconstitutional. By the same token, with a two-thirds vote in both Houses, Congress can overturn a presidential veto, and through a complex procedure involving the state legislatures, the Constitution can be amended. The President makes high-level appointments, from ambassadors and cabinet secretaries to Supreme Court justices, but the Senate of the legislature has the ability to hold hearings on these appointments and in some cases (e.g., Supreme Court appointments) to deny them. And these are just some of the checks and balances built into this constitutional system.

The third principle that explains this system is the notion of **MIXED GOVERNMENT**, the idea of combining elements of monarchy, aristocracy, and democracy in a constitution, an idea that can be traced back to Aristotle. The executive branch, centred on the President, represents the monarchic element and provides an example of a single unified executive fulfilling formal,

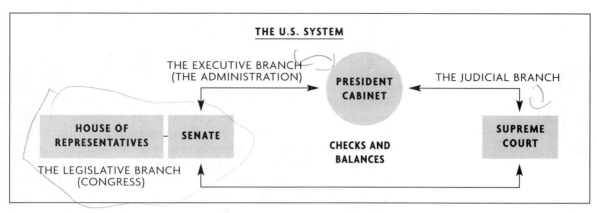

THE U.S. SYSTEM

THE EXECUTIVE BRANCH
(THE ADMINISTRATION)

**PRESIDENT
CABINET**

THE JUDICIAL BRANCH

**HOUSE OF
REPRESENTATIVES** - **SENATE**

**SUPREME
COURT**

**CHECKS AND
BALANCES**

THE LEGISLATIVE BRANCH
(CONGRESS)

FIGURE 7.10

ceremonial, and discretionary executive functions (including ultimate command of the American military). The Supreme Court, a panel of nine justices, represents the aristocratic element of government, although one can see the cabinet and the Senate as somewhat aristocratic in temper also. Finally, the democratic element is represented by Congress, in particular the House of Representatives, which is elected on the basis of **REPRESEN-TATION BY POPULATION** (the Senate represents the states, each with two senators).

In clear contrast to the parliamentary system, there is no responsible government in the U.S. system; indeed, one might say that there is no identifiable government here. It is possible to speak of the Reagan administration or the Clinton administration, but this refers only to the President, his cabinet, and White House officials, who have no control over the legislature. For a variety of reasons it may be rare for the American cabinet to meet collectively; by and large each secretary presides individually over a large administrative bureaucracy or set of bureaucracies. Those who make the laws and those who implement them are thus two separate sets of people. Not only might there be little co-operation between the executive and the legislature, there is also no group within the legislature that exercises clear control. In the first place, because there is no responsible government, American political parties have remained weak, relatively undisciplined bodies; the control of party leaders over their legislative members is tenuous at best. Second, unlike many legislatures, the American Congress has two strong chambers, which may often be working at cross-purposes.

In parliamentary systems, members of the legislature (or at least of the confidence chamber) and thus the members of the cabinet face the electorate at the same time; responsibility for policies—successful, unsuccessful, or lacking—is fairly easy to assign. In the United States Constitution, the terms of office are: the President, four years; congressional representatives, two years; and senators, six years, staggered one-third each two years. Combine these staggered terms with the absence of a unity between legislature and executive and the weakness of party discipline, and the ability to assign responsibility for what does or does not happen in American government is dubious. It is not impossible for President, Senate and House of Representatives to work together, but Madison's intention of setting "ambition against ambition" has worked well enough to ensure that this is as much the exception as the rule.

All of this combines to make the U.S. government, as Madison and the other constitution-framers intended, a weak government. This is sometimes obscured by the country's economic and military might, particularly as it is now also the world's third most populous nation-state. Nonetheless, relatively speaking, the separation of powers and corresponding checks and balances have put more obstacles in the way of government action than are present in parliamentary systems. This has meant that the enormous growth of the state in the twentieth century in advanced industrial societies was not nearly so large in the U.S. as in most parliamentary countries. While this no doubt has pleased those of a more libertarian frame of mind, it has been partially responsible for several troubling features of current American life—the most unequal distribution of wealth in the industrial world, continued racial inequalities and lack of opportunity, inner-city decay, a crumbling domestic infrastructure, one of the world's highest crime rates—and thwarts attempts by political actors to address these problems.

When the American executive and legislative branches are able to work together, they must still satisfy the review of their actions performed by the courts. The United States has one of the world's longest and busiest traditions of judicial review, dating back to the celebrated *Marbury vs. Madison* case of 1804. One reason for this is the inclusion in the American Constitution of a Bill of Rights, which provides a set of criteria the courts can apply to their review of legislation. Because the American Constitution reserves rights to citizens, on the one hand, and to the states, on the other, the ability of the federal government to act is constrained from the outset. In the 1930s, a conservative Supreme Court overturned legislation that was central to President Roosevelt's "New Deal" package of measures designed to combat the social and economic effects of the Depression. Roosevelt threatened to try to amend the Constitution in ways that would allow him to change the composition of the court. On the other hand, in the 1950s and 1960s, a liberal Supreme Court made landmark civil rights rulings that signalled the end of racial segregation and led directly to significant civil rights legislation in the Kennedy and Johnson years. Both examples illustrate the importance of the judiciary as a third branch of government in the U.S.

7.4.3   Comparing systems

The United States is the only industrial democracy with a separation of powers as we have described it above. Harmon Zeigler (1990: 108) listed Colombia, Costa Rica, Cyprus, the Dominican Republic, Ecuador, South Korea, and Venezuela as the other countries with a U.S.-style system. What he did not list were countries that once had a U.S.-style system but have since changed to a parliamentary constitution, or U.S.-style systems that have ceased, through military coup or otherwise, to be democratic. On the other hand, every industrial democracy except the U.S. has a parliamentary constitution, and all of the newly democratized countries of Eastern Europe and the former Soviet Union have incorporated the fundamental features of parliamentary government into their political systems. Insofar as nation-states have voted between these two systems by choosing one or the other, the overwhelming choice has been for parliamentary systems. Perhaps most tellingly, Zeigler reports that the American Committee on the Constitutional System, a prestigious bipartisan panel of individuals who had worked and served in government, concluded that the separation of powers "produces confrontation, indecision, and deadlock," and proposed serious changes to make the American political system "more like the British and other European parliamentary systems" (1990: 121).

Sartori (1994: 89) notes that of 18 countries outside the U.S. with U.S.-style systems, only three—Costa Rica (1949), Venezuela (1958), and Colombia (1974)—have been uninterruptedly democratic for more than 20 years, and concludes:

> Ironically, then, the belief that presidential systems are strong systems draws on the worst possible structural arrangements—a divided power defenseless against

divided government—and fails to realize that the American system works, or has worked, *in spite* of its constitution—hardly *thanks to* its constitution.

Parliamentary systems are more often chosen over the American separation-of-powers system because of the attraction of strong rather than weak government. Strong government does not necessarily entail large government, and conversely, a weak government may still produce a large state. What is meant by strong government is one that is able to make policy and implement it in response to problems in society that require (or for which the voters have demanded) a political solution. The relative unity, coherence, and discipline of the parliamentary system make it strong in this sense; the "confrontation, indecision, and deadlock" brought about by a separation of powers and system of checks and balances makes the world's largest democracy (apologies to India) one of its weakest. Those who adhere to the old maxim that "that which governs least, governs best" may not accept the need for strong government, although it may also be that they are confusing size and efficacy. Nonetheless, there are two considerations worth raising.

First, to the degree that government is a function of society, then (as suggested in Section I) as societies become more populous, technologically intensive, and in many other ways more complex, the need for government grows (and again, this is not saying that there is a need for *more* government). It seems difficult, at the beginning of the twenty-first century, to imagine how we will deal with the problems created by a doubling of the world's population and the continued drain and strain on the planet's ecosystems, including the effects of global warming, *without* the state playing an enormous part in their solution. Second, if weak governments are unable to solve societal problems, then it is worth considering the consequences upon those without other resources to fall back on. In a wealthy country like the U.S. it may be possible to get away with the side-effects of extreme inequality, sustained urban poverty and racism, and the absence of opportunity for significant minority populations within the whole, but in less well-off regimes the result of inadequate policy responses may well be civil unrest, violence, or even revolution. The weak government created by the framers of the American Constitution may have been right for the United States of 1787, and for many even today it still may seem to be the only possible framework for that country's politics. But as Hague, Harrop, and Breslin conclude, "the extensive dispersal of power which characterizes American politics is rarely seen as a good idea elsewhere" (1992: 318).

In the preceding sections the point has been made, among others, that England is a constitutional monarchy, and also that the English have no written constitution. On the other hand, in 1867, Walter Bagehot wrote a classic study entitled *The English Constitution*. The contradictions here are eliminated if we understand what Alan Cairns has called "the distinction between the constitution as an institution and the key statute that went into its formulation" (in Blair and McLeod, 1987: 5-6). When we talk about the "constitution" of some object, we are usually referring to how it is made or how its parts fit together or what makes it work; this is also true of political constitutions.

We might define a constitution as *a body of fundamental or basic rules* (indeed, the German constitution is called the Basic Law) *outlining the structures of power and authority and the relations between these, and between these and the people.* We do well to remember that as law, this written constitution is really a map or diagram purporting to outline the fundamental nature of the state as it exists and operates. What Bagehot called the "English Constitution" was not a written document, but rather the actual structure of the power and authority of the English state. On the other hand, when Americans talk about the Constitution, or Canadians about the Constitution Act (or sometimes older Canadians about the British North America Act), they are referring to a written document, a body of law that serves like a legal blueprint for the edifice of the state. This may be thought of as a distinction between the formal (written) constitution and the **MATERIAL CONSTITUTION** (the actual structure). Ideally, the formal describes the material. But just as a map becomes out of date when high seas wash away a coastline, or a dam floods a valley, so, too, can parts of the written constitution cease to describe the reality of the state; just as maps are redrawn to reflect a changing world, constitutions must change to match new political realities.

We might also consider that while all states have a constitution in the sense of a basic structure of power and authority, the idea that such a structure should be contained in and indeed be defined by a written document is a rather modern idea. It is another of those features we identify with the liberal revolution that overturned feudal absolutism, and is an application of the

7.5 CONSTITUTIONS AND CONSTITUTIONALISM

211

principle of the rule of law at the highest levels. Interestingly, a written constitution almost inevitably entails the notion of limited government. The English constitution of which Bagehot wrote is rather unique among modern democracies: it is (or is described as) "unwritten." In other words, there is no single document regarded as the English constitution, although several documents (the *Magna Carta*, the *Statute of Westminster*, etc.) have constitutional significance because they describe key relationships between institutions of the state or between the state and the people. It is no accident, then, that the British state is probably the most unlimited of modern democracies. As the second Earl of Pembroke once said, "A parliament can do any thing but make a man a woman, and a woman a man." There are important senses in which this remains true, particularly if the government has public opinion on its side.

To describe the idea that the state will be limited by a written constitution, we will use the term **CONSTITUTIONALISM**. Constitutionalism has several requirements. In addition to the rules defining what governments may or may not do (or how they may or may not do it), there must be a forum where disputes about the meaning of the constitution and whether or not it has been adhered to can be heard and decided. This, we have seen, is the function of a high or "supreme" or special constitutional court. It follows that there should also be a means of enforcing constitutional rules and rulings. In theory this would mean some other institution of the state, such as police or military, willing to employ force on behalf of the authority of the supreme or constitutional court. In normal practice, if ever, constitutions don't work this way. Constitutionalism requires, and rests on, a willingness of all political actors to abide by the constitutional rules of the polity, and where these are in dispute, to recognize the legitimacy of the body designated for deciding these disputes and to abide by its rulings. We might call this disposition on the part of political actors a constitutional ethic or norm; without it, constitutions will be merely symbolic documents. By analogy, when one agrees to play a game, one also agrees to abide by the rules of that game and accept the word of the duly constituted umpire if there are disputes about what is acceptable or not. You cannot, because a rule is contrary to your purposes, simply set it aside in the middle of the game. And yet, when a political leader who looks likely to lose an upcoming election "suspends" a constitution because of supposed "instability," that is all he has done. In such a case there is a constitution, but no constitutionalism. Ultimately, constitutionalism cannot be forced, or enforced, but must become such an integral part of the political culture that political actors cannot conceive of doing other than as the constitution permits. This is one reason why it is important that the body of constitutional rules remain in touch with the central values, beliefs, and aspirations of the population of the polity.

The English (or rather British) constitution discussed above provides a good illustration of the normative character of constitutionalism. As noted, there is no single written body of rules that can be identified as the British constitution, nor is there a supreme or constitutional court that can deliver rulings binding on Parliament. In a strictly *legal* sense, the government of Britain faces no limits upon its actions; it must only consider the *political* limits imposed by representative democracy. At the same time, numerous individual statutes, judicial rulings, and even unwritten rules define political relationships between institutions of state, and between the British state and the people, and these function as constitutional rules in the absence of a body to enforce them *because the relevant political actors accept them as constitutional.* The choice between having a written constitution and no ethic of constitutionalism (as in the former Soviet Union) and having an ethic of constitutionalism but no written constitution (as in Britain) is not a difficult one to make.

The preceding discussion points out that constitutional rules can take many forms. Most obvious are the written bodies of law identified as a constitution: the Constitution of the United States of America, Germany's Basic Law, Canada's Constitution Act. Sometimes these written constitutions are produced by legislatures, sometimes by a special assembly of delegates or representatives meeting for that purpose; whatever their origin they will (normally) be ratified by the legislatures of the political units involved and thus become part, the most basic part, of the law of the land. In almost all cases, what distinguishes these constitutional statutes from ordinary law, apart from their subject matter, is that they are more difficult to change. Normally the written constitution will contain rules about how it is to be altered, i.e., an **AMENDING PROCEDURE**. This will stipulate a higher level of consent than the simple majority usually required to make law, or the consent of more than one legislature or institution, or popular ratification through a referendum, or some combination of these. (See also the discussion of amending formulas in federal constitutions in Chapter Ten.) Amending procedures must meet

KEY TERMS

adjudication
amending procedure
bicameral
bureaucracy
cabinet
checks and balances
collective executive
common law
concentrated powers
confidence
constitution
constitutionalism
constitutional monarchy
convention
decision-making
discretionary power
dual executive
executive function
formal power
functions
fusion of powers
head of government
head of state
implementation
institutions
judiciary
judicial function
judicial independence
judicial review
legislative function
legislation
legislature
material constitution
mixed government
parliamentary supremacy
parliamentary system
party discipline
political executive
polity
precedent
president
prime minister
reference
representation by population
republic
responsible government
separation of powers
statutes
Supreme Court
systems

the challenge of being flexible enough to allow necessary change while remaining rigid enough to guide or limit rulers. At the very least, it is expected that constitutional laws will be more difficult to change than ordinary laws, and for this reason we usually describe constitutional provisions that are so protected from change as *entrenched*.

Constitutional matters may also be addressed, particularly in countries without a written constitutional document, in ordinary law, or what are called **STATUTES**. Change to such laws is achieved through the rules and constraints of the legislative process. If a simple legislative majority is necessary to make a statute, then a similar majority will suffice to change or cancel it. In such cases, constitutional rules are under the control of the legislature, and this puts limitations on the ability, and hence the willingness, of the courts to engage in judicial review on the basis of such statutes; legislatures unhappy with judicial rulings will simply change the rules.

A third kind of law is that made by judges in the Anglo-American legal tradition, what is known as **COMMON LAW**, articulated by magistrates through their verdicts and decisions. Sometimes called "judge-made law," common law builds on a tradition of previous cases by adhering to the rule of *stare decisis*, a commitment to abide by the example of previous decisions in similar cases, or what we commonly call **PRECEDENT**. The purpose of precedent is to avoid arbitrary decisions by treating common cases in a like manner, and in common-law countries (e.g., Britain, the U.S., Canada, Australia, New Zealand) it can also have constitutional significance: constitutional rulings and interpretations will, like criminal and civil cases, be argued on the basis of past decisions, where applicable. Decisions handed down by the high or supreme court will serve as precedents for future cases of a similar nature. Common law is more flexible than statutes, but it is also subordinate to the latter; once a matter has been treated in a statute it has been removed from the sphere of common law.

The last kind of constitutional rule is what is called a **CONVENTION**, which is best understood as an unwritten rule that nonetheless remains binding, although the force that binds here is that of tradition, or morality, or expedience, and not a legal force. Conventions are more central than might sometimes be supposed. The judicial rule of abiding by precedents noted above is conventional, and the requirements of responsible government and of the fusion of powers, both discussed above, are also only conventions. Because conventions are unwritten rules, they are the least enforceable, and the most dependent of constitutional rules upon the norm or ethic of constitutionalism for their force.

Of these four ways in which constitutional rules may be expressed—entrenched document, ordinary statute, common law, and convention—only the first two satisfy what is meant by a written constitution (i.e., formal constitution), but the material constitution of a state (i.e., constitution as institution) may be, and often is, expressed in a mixture of all four kinds of rules.

Last but not least, we should consider the content of constitutional rules. As the fundamental rules of the polity, the rules that govern rulers and ruling, constitutions do the following:

a) They define who exercises authority and/or the institutions and processes by which authority is exercised, and in either case, what kind of authority (or function of the state) is involved. Examples of this would include indicating that the chief executive is an elected president, or that legislation must receive the support of a majority in both houses of the legislature, or the maximum time permissible between elections, or rules concerning the qualifications for holding office, etc.

b) They outline the relationships between and the priority of the various primary institutions and offices (or branches) of the state. The various checks and balances of the American system would fall into this category, as would the fusion of powers of the parliamentary model, if constitutionalized. The relationship of the head of state to other fundamental institutions may be addressed here, or the relationship of a strong president to a prime minister in a system like that of France or Poland.

Both (a) and (b) cover the basic elements of systems or types of constitution, discussed above. In addition, constitutions may (but do not necessarily) do the following:

c) If applicable, they divide jurisdictions between levels of government and define other fundamental relationships between them. This is a necessary task in federal states, and we will discuss what this means at greater length in Chapter Ten.

REFERENCES AND SUGGESTED READING

Bagehot, Walter. 1872. *The English Constitution*. London: Oxford University Press.

Cairns, Alan C. 1970. "The Living Canadian Constitution," in R.S. Blair and J.T. McLeod, eds., *The Canadian Political Tradition* (Toronto: Methuen, 1987).

Deutsch, Karl Wolfgang. 1990. *Politics and Government*. Boston: Houghton-Mifflin.

Hague, Rod, et al. 1992. *Comparative Government. An Introduction*, 3rd ed. London: Macmillan.

Hill, Christopher. 1969. *The good old cause: the English Revolution of 1640-1660*. London: F. Cass.

Kottak, Conrad Phillip. 1991. *Cultural Anthropology*, 5th ed. New York: McGraw-Hill.

Landes, Ronald. 1996. *The Canadian Polity*, 4th ed. Scarborough, Ont.: Prentice Hall.

Lijphart, Arend. 1984. *Democracies: Patterns of Majoritarian and Consensus Government in Twenty-One Countries*. New Haven: Yale University Press.

——, ed. 1992. *Parliamentary versus Presidential Government*. Oxford: Oxford University Press.

Mahler, Gregory S. 1995. *Comparative Politics: An Institutional and Cross-National Approach*. Englewood Cliffs, NJ: Prentice Hall.

Mallory, J.R. 1971. *The Structure of Canadian Government*. Toronto: Macmillan.

Mann, Michael. 1990. *The Rise and Decline of the Nation State.* Oxford: Blackwell.

Sartori, Giovanni. 1994. *Comparative Constitutional Engineering.* New York: New York University Press.

Strong, C.F. 1963. *A History of Modern Political Constitutions.* New York: Capricorn Books.

Zeigler, Harmon. 1990. *The Political Community.* New York: Longman.

d) They establish the rights of citizens with respect to the state and indicate how they may seek redress for violation of these rights. The first 10 amendments to the U.S. Constitution comprise what is known as the *Bill of Rights*, and in 1982 amendments to the Canadian constitution included for the first time a *Charter of Rights and Freedoms*; these are examples of constitutional (or entrenched) rights codes, which protect citizens from certain uses or abuses of authority, or viewed another way, explicitly limit the state from certain exercises of authority. The likelihood and extent of judicial review is greatly enhanced by the presence of an entrenched rights code, and the significance of this for the political system will receive a closer look in Chapter Seventeen.

e) They indicate the conditions that must be satisfied to amend the constitution.

Not all constitutions will address all of these topics or give equal stress to them. The Canadian written constitution, for example, states in its preamble that this dominion is to have "a Constitution similar in Principle to that of the United Kingdom." In this respect, then, like the British constitution, the Canadian constitution is unwritten so far as much of the structure of government is concerned, many elements of this structure being defined by constitutional conventions. Canada's written constitution is much more concerned to address the federal dimensions of the system, and in 1982, citizens' rights and the amending procedures were important additions.

Regardless of their form, constitutions have a common function: to provide a fundamental definition of the structures and processes of authority.

SOMETHING TO CONSIDER

How might political life in Canada be different if Canada adopted a U.S.-style constitutional system?

How might political life in the U.S. be different if the U.S. adopted a system of responsible government?

How likely is it that either might ever take place?

8 parliamentary systems

The overwhelming majority of the world's successful democracies are parliamentary systems, whether one defines success in material terms or as the absence of authoritarian interruptions (military or civilian dictatorships). As noted in Chapter Seven, of the world's advanced industrial democracies, only the U.S. has a non-parliamentary constitution. Within the world of parliamentary democracy there is considerable variation, but this chapter will focus on one fundamental distinction, based on the electoral and party systems, between majoritarian and proportionate parliamentary systems. First, though, we will review the basic features of the parliamentary type of government.

At its most basic, the essence of parliamentary government is the relationship between the executive and the legislature, something expressed most succinctly as *responsible cabinet government achieved through a fusion of powers*. This means several things.

First, the government in power consists of a cabinet, which is a committee of individuals exercising executive power. Exercising executive power means in turn that each of these cabinet members (usually called ministers) is the executive or head of a government department or set of related departments. The area of responsibility of a cabinet minister is known as a portfolio. Second, the cabinet ministers are drawn from the ranks of the legislature, to which, as a body, they remain collectively responsible. (Exceptions to the parliamentary membership of cabinet ministers are Norway, the Netherlands, and Luxembourg, where cabinet ministers do not have a seat in the legislature, although they do participate in parliamentary debates.) While ministers answer individually to the legislature for their portfolios, collectively the cabinet must retain the support (confidence) of a

8.1   Introduction
8.2   Majoritarian vs. Proportionate Systems
8.3   Majority, Minority, and Coalition Government
8.4   Formation and Dissolution
8.5   The Head of State
8.6   The Prime Minister and Cabinet
8.7   Policy-Making: Executive Dominance

majority in the legislature. Failure to do so means the end of this particular cabinet and thus the defeat of the government. Although each minister has a particular portfolio, government policy for any and all portfolios is approved by the cabinet, and must have the public support of all members of cabinet. This is known as the principle of **CABINET SOLIDARITY** or of **COLLECTIVE RESPON-SIBILITY**, and indicates most clearly that this is a collective executive.

The head or chair of the cabinet is the prime minister, sometimes misleadingly described as a "first among equals," misleadingly because the prime minister is usually pre-eminent among ministers and in many parliamentary systems determines everything that matters about the cabinet, including its size, its membership, its structure, and its style of decision-making. As head of cabinet, the prime minister is thus both the head of government and the chief political executive in most parliamentary systems (examples where this is not true will be discussed in the next chapter). Parliamentary systems thus have a dual executive, for someone *other* than the prime minister will occupy the position of head of state, a formal executive with largely formal and ceremonial functions. Whatever the title of the head of state—king, queen, president, grand duke—it is the prime minister as head of government who exercises most of the authority of the state in a parliamentary system.

Finally, parliamentary government is about party politics. The fusion of powers and the requirements of responsible government provide an irresistible incentive for political parties to become highly structured, disciplined bodies. What we are largely talking about here is the behaviour of members of the party who sit in the legislature, or what is usually called the **PARLIAMENTARY PARTY** (or sometimes **CAUCUS**). Just as it is possible for parties to develop mechanisms or procedures for punishing disloyalty within the caucus, the parliamentary system provides many opportunities for parties to reward loyalty, chief among them participation in cabinet. Strong, unified parties and the competition between them are key ingredients to what happens in the legislature, in the cabinet, and in the relations between cabinet and legislature in normal parliamentary systems. Since the prime minister is also the head of his or her party, in addition to being head of government, he or she has a particularly central position within the parliamentary system. It is also here, though, with the relationship of the prime minister to the cabinet, of the cabinet to the legislature, and of cabinet, legislature, and prime minister to the political parties, that the distinction between majoritarian and proportionate systems becomes too important to ignore.

Because parties are so central to parliamentary systems, it makes a real difference to these systems how many parties are in the legislature, what their relative strength is, and how accurately their representation in the legislature mirrors their support in the electorate. In other words, a fundamental difference between parliamentary systems is the nature of their **PARTY SYSTEM**, and the party system is largely a function of (or associated with) the **ELECTORAL SYSTEM**.[1] (Both of these systems will be explained and discussed in greater detail in Chapter Thirteen, and students may wish to skip ahead and skim portions of that chapter before continuing here.)

In terms of electoral systems, we should distinguish between **PLURALITY** systems (sometimes called "majoritarian" systems), where the candidate with the most votes is declared the winner (as in Canada, the U.S., and Britain), and **PROPORTIONAL REPRESENTATION** systems, where candidates from parties are awarded seats on the basis of the vote for the party. The plurality system is sometimes called a "winner-take-all" system, because the margin of victory makes no difference to the outcome. If I finish with 9,999 votes and you have 10,000, you win the seat and I have nothing to show for second place. The same result happens if I finish with 1 vote and you have 19,999. The plurality system is not good at reflecting the amount of support that winners receive, and this is true not only on a riding-by-riding basis, but also as a whole when the results are aggregated for all ridings. As a general rule, and this becomes more likely the more parties there are contesting the election, *plurality systems overcompensate winners and penalize losers*.

For a variety of reasons (see Chapter Thirteen), the plurality system has two tendencies with which we are concerned here. One is to deliver a parliamentary majority to the winner of the election, i.e., to ensure that one party wins more seats in the legislature than all other parties combined. Given the tendency of plurality electoral systems to be associated with two-party systems this observation may seem trivial, but it is true also of countries such as Canada that have many electoral parties. The second tendency is that there is no necessary correspondence between a party's parliamentary strength and its electoral strength; as a

8.2
MAJORITARIAN VS. PROPORTIONATE SYSTEMS

1. In some cases, it is clear that the party system led to a proportionate electoral system being adopted, but this type of system reinforces a multi-party system and ensures a high degree of proportionality among parties.

1867

Party	% seats	% vote
Conservatives	60.0	50.1
Liberals	40.0	49.9

1997

Party	% seats	% vote
Liberals	51.5	38.5
Reform	19.9	19.4
Conservatives	6.6	18.8
Bloc Québécois	14.6	10.7
NDP	7.0	11.0

2000

Party	% seats	% vote
Liberals	57.1	40.8
Canadian Alliance (Reform)	21.9	25.5
Conservatives	4.0	12.2
Bloc Québécois	12.6	10.7
NDP	4.3	8.5

FIGURE 8.1

general rule winning parties will receive a higher share of seats in the legislature than their share of vote would warrant, and other parties will be correspondingly penalized by the system. In this way, the parliamentary majority of the winning party is often **MANUFACTURED**, meaning that the party won a majority of seats but received less than a majority of the vote. The tendencies associated with plurality systems here are even more likely when the number of parties increases. Figure 8.1 shows the results of Canada's first and most recent general elections. In 1867 the two parties competing split the vote almost evenly, but the ability of the system to reward the winner and penalize the loser ensured that the Conservatives received 60 per cent of the seats in the House of Commons with barely more than 50 per cent of the vote. The Conservatives "earned" their majority here, but it was exaggerated by the electoral system. In 2000, in a multi-party election, the Liberals won a parliamentary majority of 57.1 per cent of the seats, but it was clearly a "manufactured" majority as the total support for the party was only 40.8 per cent, a difference of 16.3 per cent (a larger disproportion than the 13 per cent of 1997). The serendipity of the system is illustrated by the fact that only one of the five parties (the NDP) received an increase or decrease in its share of seats that corresponded to the change in its share of the vote.

	Liberals	CA	PC	BQ	NDP
%v	+ 2.3	+ 6.1	− 6.6	0.0	− 2.5
%s	+ 5.6	+ 2.0	− 2.6	− 2.0	− 2.7

Again, for a variety of reasons, the situation of 1867 in Figure 8.1 is more typical of a plurality system than are the circumstances of 2000. The persistence of patterns like that of 2000 would in many cases lead to a call for electoral reform, for some form of proportional representation. If the primary feature of the plurality system is that it generates a clear winner, the chief aspect of a proportionate system is, as the name indicates, to apportion to each party seats in the legislature according to the share of vote received. *How* this happens will be explained in Chapter Thirteen. The close correspondence between share of parliamentary seats and share of electoral vote has two consequences of note for us here. One is the tendency to sustain a multi-party system, and the significance of this will be more apparent as we proceed. The other is the virtual impossibility of manufacturing a majority. Since the system does not over-reward or penalize parties, the only legislative majorities that result will be fully "'earned," that is, reflective of a majority of the votes cast by the electorate. The greater the number of electoral parties, the less the likelihood that one will command an absolute majority of support, and since proportionate systems sustain multi-party environments, legislative majorities for a single party are rare in these systems.

Hence, the distinction between majoritarian and proportionate parliamentary systems may be explained as follows:

Electoral System	Party System	Type of Parliamentary System
plurality +	two party =	majoritarian
proportionality +	multi-party =	proportionate

A majoritarian system is one in which the electoral and party system create a general tendency or normal expectation that following an election, one party will have control of a majority of seats in the legislature. A proportionate system is one in which the electoral and party system create the conditions whereby following an election, each party will have a share of seats corresponding to its share of vote, and for one party to control a majority of seats in the legislature will be the exception rather than the rule. A couple of clarifications are in order.

It should perhaps be emphasized that these are general tendencies, not absolute relations; for every generalization there are (or could conceivably be) exceptions. Not all plurality electoral systems produce two-party systems (as Canada clearly demonstrates), but on the other hand the persistence of a multi-party system in a plurality electoral system creates pressures for electoral reform. It is safe to say that plurality systems tend to reflect and sustain two-party environments, and that proportionate systems tend to reflect and sustain multi-party environments, but there are counter-examples to each generalization. Similarly, while it is not impossible for a party to win an absolute majority in a proportionate system with a multi-party environment, nor is there any guarantee that a plurality system will always produce a legislative majority for the winning party. What we are concerned with here is the usual or "normal" outcome of the system, because this will govern the expectations and calculations of the political actors and create the conventions and norms of institutional behaviour within these systems.

If the majority of the world's democracies are parliamentary, then we should also note that of the 22 parliamentary systems that have been continuously democratic since 1945, 15 (Germany, Italy, Sweden, Norway, Denmark, Finland, Iceland, the Nether-

2. The youth of these newly democratic regimes makes it premature to regard them as more than proto-democracies at this point in time.

3. Lijphart (1984) has made an influential distinction between "majoritarian" and "consensual" democracies based on nine variables, only some of which have reference to the parliamentary characteristics we are interested in here. Among other things Lijphart includes are characteristics linked to federalism and the degree of pluralism within the population of the polity.

lands, Belgium, Luxembourg, Ireland, Austria, Switzerland, Malta, and Israel) fit our classification as proportionate; three (the United Kingdom, Canada, and India) are majoritarian; and two (France and Australia) represent special cases in part because they have neither (single-member) plurality nor proportional representation electoral systems (see Lijphart, 1994: 2). Of these latter two, France has been more like proportionate systems and Australia more like majoritarian systems. Three European countries that became democratic in the mid-1970s—Greece, Portugal, and Spain—are also proportionate, as are most (if not all) of the newly created democracies of Eastern Europe and the former Soviet Union.[2] Finally, constitutional changes have meant that the most recent elections contested in Japan and New Zealand took place in a proportionate electoral system. The number (and share) of the world's majoritarian parliamentary systems seems to be declining, and may eventually become as anomalous as the American separation-of-powers constitutional model. However, as the division of countries above indicates, the majority of the world's English-speaking peoples live in non-proportionate systems (parliamentary or otherwise), so we will continue to contrast parliamentary government in majoritarian and proportionate systems in the remainder of this chapter.[3]

8.3 MAJORITY, MINORITY, AND COALITION GOVERNMENT

The first set of differences we can note concerns the nature of government in these two types of parliamentary system. If majoritarian systems tend to produce control of the legislature by one party through a majority that is often manufactured, then obviously the government (cabinet) in such systems will *normally* be drawn from the caucus of the winning (majority) party. This is what is known as a **MAJORITY GOVERNMENT**, and what should more precisely be called single-party majority government. In other words, the cabinet is drawn from one party, which happens also to have a majority of the seats in the legislature (or in the house of the legislature that serves as the confidence chamber). Given strong party discipline, the requirements of responsible government (i.e., that the cabinet retain the support of a legislative majority) are more or less automatically fulfilled, and one expects single-party majority governments to be very stable. Although majority government is possible under any legislative system currently in use, it is much more likely in countries with plurality electoral systems and less likely where there is proportional representation.

Suppose, though, that no one party wins a majority of seats in the legislature; who will govern? If the cabinet continues to be drawn from the members of one party in the legislature, this will constitute a **MINORITY GOVERNMENT**, so called because the government controls (through party discipline) the votes of only a minority of members of the legislature. One might expect that the party forming the government in this situation will be the largest of the parliamentary parties, but this is not necessarily the case, as we will see.

Meeting the requirements of responsible government will clearly be more of a challenge for minority governments; a legislative majority for the government will require the co-operation, active or passive, of at least one other party in the legislature. The general expectation might be, then, that minority governments will be less stable than single-party majority governments because the possibility at least exists for defeat of the government in the legislature. The stability of minority governments depends on some other factors, though, foremost being the type of parliamentary system, a point explained below.

The other possibility if no one party controls a legislative majority is to draw the cabinet from two or more parties that *between them* do control a majority of legislators. This is what is known as **COALITION GOVERNMENT**, which typically means a formal agreement between political parties indicating three things:

a) an agreement jointly to form a government;
b) a division of the cabinet seats between the parties and the allocation of specific portfolios, including that of prime minister;
c) an agreement about policies that the government will implement, or positions it will take on key issues.

Strictly speaking, this is what is known as an **EXECUTIVE COALITION**, because the members of the two or more parties share the posts of government (cabinet ministries). Normally, the division of seats in cabinet between the parties reflects their relative strength in the legislature; if party A contributes twice as many members to the joint legislative majority as party B, then we can expect party A also to hold twice as many seats in cabinet as party B. This norm of proportionality is followed quite faithfully in countries with coalition government. The allocation of port-

PARTIES

Political parties are organizations that serve several functions in the political system, and they are discussed in greater detail in Chapter Fourteen. A distinction is sometimes made between the parliamentary (or legislative) party, which consists of all elected members of a party, and the party-at-large, which also includes constituency officers and citizens who are members of the party. It is often said that after an election the party-at-large loses control of the parliamentary party, and this is particularly true if the parliamentary party is in government. Another distinction is between electoral parties, which are parties that contest elections by fielding candidates, and legislative parties, which are those parties that actually win seats in the legislature. When we talk about a country's party system, we are talking about the number and strength of the legislative parties. Obviously, the number of legislative parties cannot be greater than the number of electoral parties, but the reverse is often true. Officially, there were 19 electoral parties in the 1993 Canadian general election, which produced five legislative parties.

FIGURE 8.2

COALITIONS

EXECUTIVE COALITION
Where two or more parties formally agree to govern, dividing the cabinet posts between them, and (usually) agreeing on a joint policy platform (see also Figure 8.9).

LEGISLATIVE COALITION
Where two or more parties agree to vote together in the legislature but do not share the executive between them.

ELECTORAL COALITION
Where two (or more) parties agree to work together in an election, usually agreeing to provide mutual support, not to run candidates in the same constituencies, etc. Implicit in such electoral alliances is the possibility of working together in legislative or executive coalitions.

FIGURE 8.3

folios is less predictable, although there are certain affinities between party ideology and favourite cabinet ministries. These decisions, as well as the formal policy agreements, are the result of sometimes intense and protracted negotiations between the parties involved. Although it is possible for coalition governments to control less than a majority of seats in the legislature, this is very unusual, and coalition government is normally an example of multi-party majority government. Unless stated otherwise, this is what will be meant by the term "coalition government."

Executive coalitions are rare in Canadian parliamentary experience, the only instance at the federal level occurring at the end of World War I, when western Liberals supporting the war policies of the Borden government joined the Conservatives to form a "Union" government. Most recently, in the 1999 Saskatchewan election, the incumbent NDP government was returned with slightly less than half the seats. The Liberals, who won four seats, agreed to join the NDP in a coalition, with two Liberal MLAs going into cabinet and a third serving as Speaker of the Legislative Assembly. Interestingly, press reports suggested that the decision by the Saskatchewan Liberals to join in a coalition could "relegate it to long-term obscurity" (*National Post*, October 1, 1999). This perhaps reflects the assumption in Canada that parties are only relevant when they are capable of (and committed solely to) winning majorities, as opposed to the European view that participation in coalition government might very well be a significant way of providing meaningful representation for a party's supporters.

It is also possible in a parliament where no one party controls a majority for a single-party cabinet to govern with the support of another or other parties in the legislature. Where parties agree to support each other on legislative votes, we have a *legislative* coalition. Now, obviously, any single-party minority government that survives does so on the basis of legislative coalitions. This may be a formal agreement of mutual legislative support, it may be informal but ongoing because of ideological affinity, or it may be a series of shifting legislative alliances. In Ontario between 1985 and 1987 a minority Liberal government was kept in power by the support of the NDP, which had agreed not to defeat the government during a two-year period in return for certain policy concessions. This was a formal legislative coalition but not an executive coalition, as the NDP held no cabinet posts. The Swedish Social Democratic Party has governed successfully on many occasions with a single-party minority cabinet because it could count on the support of a small Communist Party that could

---

CONCEPTUALIZING GOVERNMENT

The political language we use reflects the political experience we have within one political system or another. In majoritarian systems, where the norm is for one party to gain a majority of seats in the legislature, therefore making the nomination of this party to govern virtually automatic, it is common to say that the party "won election to government" or "was elected government." Of course, neither of these phrases is strictly true, as is clearer when, as on rare occasion, no party wins a majority and the head of

state must decide which party leader to ask to try to form a government.

In proportionate systems, as in most of Europe, it is rare for one party to win a parliamentary majority. In such situations, it is much clearer that the government of the day is something decided *after* the election, the result of negotiations or arrangements made between the parties. Obviously, in these cases the parties' numerical strength in the legislature is one of the key variables, but only one. In these systems it is rarely meaningful to speak of a party "winning an election" or of a government being "elected."

FIGURE 8.4

---

not bring itself to vote with the government's right-wing opposition. In many European democracies, parties in the centre of the system have been able to provide effective minority government by crafting policies that were attractive to opponents on the left some of the time, to opponents on the right some of the time, but never offensive to both right and left together. This is an example of where the type of parliamentary system can make a big difference to the stability of minority governments.

Consider parliaments in countries where the norm is for the electoral system to produce a clear winner, a party controlling a majority of seats in the legislature. A situation where no one party controls a majority of legislators—the precondition of minority government—will be regarded as an abnormality, as an exception to the rule. The expectation will be that the next election will set things right by restoring a single-party majority. Minority government, when it occurs, will be regarded as an unusual or abnormal situation that will be put up with only until enough parties are willing to gamble that their positions will be improved by another election. This describes the position of minority government in most countries with plurality electoral systems, what we have called majoritarian parliamentary systems. (Since plurality electoral systems are more volatile—there is a greater likelihood of significant change in support for any one party from one election to another—than proportionate systems, the gamble that minority government will not simply be repeated is reasonable.)

In countries where the norm is for the electoral system to produce no clear winner, where no one party controls the legislature, the expectation will be that some sort of coalition will be formed. In some countries, the size or the strategic position of the largest party may make a minority government resting on

CHARACTERISTICS OF PARLIAMENTARY GOVERNMENTS

Type of Government	PARLIAMENTARY SYSTEM	
	Majoritarian	Proportionately
Single Party / Majority	normal	unusual
Single Party / Minority	occasional	common
Coalition	unusual	normal

FIGURE 8.5

legislative coalitions as attractive or feasible as forming an executive coalition. In countries with proportional representation electoral systems, with what we have called proportionate parliaments, minority government will be more likely, and will also more likely be regarded not as a temporary expedient but as a case of "normal politics." Figure 8.5 summarizes the characteristics of majority, minority, and coalition government in the two types of parliamentary system. As noted above, while it is possible for any of these types of government to be formed in either of the types of parliamentary system, there is in both systems a "normal" type of government and an "abnormal" type, abnormal because it works contrary to the tendencies of the electoral and party systems. In addition, while minority government may not be the norm, it is extremely common in proportionate systems. Coalition government in majoritarian systems is not simply abnormal, but usually happens only under extraordinary circumstances, such as the state of national emergency associated with war.

8.4 FORMATION AND DISSOLUTION

The distinctions we have been discussing have a bearing on two very fundamental aspects of parliamentary government: how it comes into being and how it is dissolved. In the constitution of every parliamentary country a government formation process is outlined, explicitly or implicitly. Contrary to popular perception, and to the way politics is reported in the media, parliamentary governments are not selected by the people but by the legislature. Elections in parliamentary countries return a set of representatives to the legislature; then the government formation process begins, and this can be simple or complex. Whether it is simple, complex, or in between, government formation in the parliamentary system involves variations on the following basic procedure:

a) the head of state invites someone from the legislature to form and head (as prime minister) a government;
b) the prime minister-designate presents a cabinet to the head of state and they are sworn in as ministers of the state or of the Crown, whatever is appropriate; and
c) the new cabinet government meets the legislature and receives its confidence (or does not).

In majoritarian systems, in the normal course of things, the government formation process is extremely simple: the leader of the party that won a majority of seats in the legislature is invited to form a government. Given strong party discipline, this party will control the legislature, and only a government from this party will receive the confidence of the legislature: there is no one else to ask. The same applies to those rare cases of a single-party majority being returned to the legislature in a proportionate system. If, on the other hand, in either system, no one party receives a majority of seats in the legislature, the process becomes more complicated, and the role of the head of state may be less of a formality. (It is noteworthy that in majoritarian systems, the rules and procedures of the government formation process are much less formal and more likely to be contained in conventions. One is tempted to attribute this to the expectation in these systems that there will be a majority returned to parliament and that there will be no need for rules to guide the process. On the other hand, most majoritarian systems are copies of the British parliamentary system, which has a largely conventional, unwritten constitution.)

When no party commands a majority, there are two logical choices of whom to invite to form the government: (a) the leader of the largest party in the legislature, and (b) the leader of the party that formed or led the previous government. In Canada, federal elections have returned a legislature without a majority party on eight occasions. In seven cases the largest party in the legislature formed a minority government, and of these three were the continuation in power of the party ruling before the election; only once (1925) did the second-place party form a minority government, in this case also being the party that had been in power before the election. It is possible though, that neither of these—the first-place party or the previously governing party—is the best choice.[4] This may be a matter of judgement for the head of state,

4. Consider the situation where there is a "pariah" party—one that no other party will co-operate with, like the situation of the Communists in post-war Italy. Even if this party finishes first, to invite it to form the government is futile because no other party will vote with it. Suppose also that the party that led the previous government has finished fourth in a five-party parliament. In this case the second-place party may be best placed to lead a government. In Canada, the Bloc Québécois would likely be treated as a "pariah" by the other parties in Parliament.

TERMINATION OF GOVERNMENT

1. Change in the party composition of the cabinet:

a) following internal dissension between coalition partners,
b) following defeat in the legislature, or
c) following constitutional intervention (executive dismissal—see discussion of France, next chapter).

2. A formal government resignation, which may come about for any of the reasons listed in (1) and lead to a new government, but not necessarily involve a change in the party composition of the cabinet.

3. A change in the Prime Minister:

a) through forced retirement (because of cabinet or party revolt),
b) through voluntary retirement, or
c) for health reasons.

4. An election, which may be "forced" by any of the preceding events, but which may also

a) be anticipated by a governing party choosing to maximize its electoral chances at a particular moment, or
b) be required because of constitutional limitations on the life of parliament, or because of fixed election dates.

FIGURE 8.6

it may be that there are established conventions about how this decision ought to be taken, or there may be explicit rules in the constitution that instruct the head of state on how to proceed. In European proportionate systems, the individual invited to form a government is often called a **FORMATEUR**. In Greece the constitution requires the head of state to invite first the leader of the largest party to act as *formateur*, and if this individual is unsuccessful in forming a government, then the leader of the second largest party, and so on in order. Where there is more discretion for the head of state and where the choices are less clear-cut there is a danger of the head of state being caught up in or appearing to be involved in the struggles of partisan politics, something heads of state are supposed to be "above." Accordingly, in some countries, the head of state will designate an *informateur*—a senior statesman or retired politician—whose role is to conduct informal inquiries and negotiations leading to the designation of a *formateur*.

Once a *formateur* has been designated, he or she must decide whether the conditions exist to govern as a single-party minority or whether it is more prudent to share power with another party or parties. There are advantages either way. A minority means not having to surrender portfolios or commit to a formal policy agreement, but it also means risking defeat in the legislature at any time and making policy compromises on issues to avoid this fate. Coalition government brings stability and predictability at the cost of sharing power and making policy compromises. The decision whether or not to seek partners will depend in the final analysis on the balance of circumstances and on the expectations generated by the parliamentary system. In majoritarian systems, because the absence of a majority is seen to be a temporary aberration, and because coalition is not common, leaders will likely prefer to govern as a minority, expecting to improve their fortunes through an election at the earliest convenient opportunity. In proportionate systems, where coalition is the norm, *formateurs* are likely to seek partners unless conditions for a long-term viable minority government are clearly present.

One important variation on the government formation process is the requirement of an **INVESTITURE VOTE**, which, we might note, is found only in proportionate systems. As we noted, once the government has been sworn in it meets the legislature, whose confidence it is required to maintain. Above all else this means being able to avoid or survive votes of non-confidence in the government. Where an investiture vote is constitutionally required (Belgium, Greece, Ireland, Israel, Italy, Portugal, Spain,

Sweden, and Switzerland), this means that the first order of business is for the legislature to express its confidence in the government. If this vote succeeds, the government survives and can begin to present its policies and legislation to the legislature. If the vote fails, the government is defeated and the process of finding an alternative must begin. The significance of an investiture vote is twofold. First, it means that the elected representatives of the people have an opportunity to accept or reject the government that emerges from backroom negotiations and bargaining. Second, it makes coalition more likely than minority government, because while a single-party minority might survive by brokering various legislative coalitions on a policy-by-policy basis, the investiture vote asks the legislature to evaluate the government as a whole, on the basis of all its policies, not any one in particular. The investiture vote is thus an institutional barrier to the formation of minority governments.

In countries where the investiture vote is required it constitutes the first legislative test of the government; it may also be the first opportunity for a government to die. Curiously, what constitutes the end of government is one of the areas of parliamentary theory on which there is considerable disagreement. Figure 8.6 lists (following Budge and Keman, 1990, and Laver and Schofield, 1990) four main causes of a termination of (or change in) government, and possible variations in underlying circumstances. Some authors (Lijphart, 1984) regard only a change in the party membership of cabinet—reason (1)—to indicate a change in government, so that a mere change in prime minister or an election that doesn't change the party or parties in power doesn't count. Laver and Schofield (1990) regard reasons (1) and (4) as valid terminations of government, but not (2) and (3) if they lead to no difference in the cabinet players. One reason this matters is that a perennial research question in parliamentary politics concerns which form of government is more stable: majority, coalition (in its various types), or minority? Obviously, the way one defines the termination of government will make a difference in the findings one generates on stability. This text will treat all four reasons as valid criteria for regarding a government as terminated.[5] As we have seen above, here, too, the kinds of government and the types of system make a difference to the end of governments. First, though, a couple of points need clarification and emphasis.

The end of a government means that it must be replaced by another. This means either that the new government will be drawn from the legislature as it stands, or that there will be an

5. Interestingly, the official practice in Canada is to regard a new Parliament to be formed by each general election, so that the 1997 election returned the 36th Parliament of Canada. In addition, a new Ministry is deemed to begin each time a new Prime Minister is initially sworn in with his/her cabinet and is regarded as lasting as long as this Prime Minister remains in office, no matter how many elections or changes in cabinet ministers there are. Changing the party composition by adding a partner or partners, as happened in 1917 with the creation of a wartime coalition cabinet, also creates a new Ministry. The current Chrétien Ministry is Canada's twenty-sixth Ministry; the longest serving was the eighth Ministry of Wilfrid Laurier, lasting from 1896 to 1911.

DEGREES OF CONFIDENCE

In addition to the cases of Switzerland and Germany, some other variations on the issue of legislative confidence (or non-confidence) are worth noting. First of all, in most of the majoritarian systems modelled on the British Parliament, the idea that a vote of non-confidence should be followed by the government's resignation is merely conventional, not a legally binding constitutional rule. In theory, governments could continue to try to govern following one or several such votes of non-confidence. In practice, though, if the legislature has truly lost confidence in the executive, continuing to govern will not be feasible, since it will not be possible for the government to gain approval for its legislation or its financial resolutions. In most other parliamentary systems, the requirement of resignation after defeat on a confidence vote has been constitutionalized. Here, too, there are variations. In Finland, the President is not required to accept the resignation of the government, but may do so (and, in practice, is unlikely not to do so.) In France and Sweden, defeat of the government requires the vote of an absolute majority in the legislature (that is, a majority of all legislators, not just a majority of those present at the time of voting. In Spain, a motion of non-confidence in the Prime Minister must specify his or her successor (Laver and Schofield, 1990).

FIGURE 8.7

election to return a new legislature and, out of it, a new government. When it is not possible to form a new government out of the existing party standings in the legislature, the head of state may agree to dissolve parliament—what is called **DISSOLUTION**—and issue a call for an election. As we will see, several variables are relevant here, and there are exceptions to every rule.

Moreover, there is *always* a government in power. The termination of a government (almost always) results in the presentation of a formal resignation of the government (or of the prime minister) to the head of state. Nonetheless, the government being terminated will in fact remain in power until another is instituted to take its place, and until this happens it will function as a **CARETAKER GOVERNMENT**. This means that the government will continue to administer existing policies and programs but will not introduce new policies or significant legislation. This latter point is only fitting, since the government has either lost the confidence of the legislature or voluntarily resigned it. If the existing government has collapsed completely (more likely in a coalition government than otherwise) it may not be able to continue even in a caretaker mode. Here the head of state may invite another party or coalition of parties to serve as a caretaker government until new elections or negotiations leading to a viable government can be held.

Consider a single-party majority government, which will most likely be found in a majoritarian system. A change in the party composition of the cabinet is unlikely to happen here *except* through defeat in an election. The odds of a single-party majority government losing the confidence of the legislature and being forced to resign are also slim. It is possible that a government with a very slim majority could become a minority through attrition (as happened at one point to the British Conservative government in the mid-1990s), and if the majority is razor-thin there is always the possibility of a miscalculation in the legislature and of being defeated if there should be more government members absent than opposition members. Still, these possibilities are exceptions, and the normal end of a single-party majority government comes when the government chooses it to or because it reaches the end of its term.

In some countries, election dates are fixed (e.g., in Germany and Norway every four years, in Sweden every three years) and the defeat or resignation of a government in the period between necessitates the installation of another government to finish out the time until the election is scheduled. In some other cases, election dates are fixed but there is a provision allowing the head of state to call early elections if there is no possibility of forming a viable government from the parties as currently situated in the legislature. If early dissolution of the legislature and elections are not constitutionally permitted, this is a case where a caretaker government may be necessary to serve the remainder of the period before mandated elections. To our knowledge, fixed electoral terms are only found in proportionate parliamentary systems.

In countries without fixed election dates, the term of government is *flexible* with a maximum time between elections established by the constitution. In most cases, this maximum term is four or five years.[6] Flexible terms of office characterize many parliamentary systems and certainly all those that have been described as majoritarian.

To repeat, then, majority governments (almost always found in majoritarian systems) usually end at the time of their own choosing, either serving the maximum time constitutionally permitted, or choosing to face the electorate sooner because they believe they are currently well placed to win the election. In Canadian politics, the norm for majority federal governments has been to seek a fresh mandate after four years; the closer governments get to their constitutional deadline before calling an election the more likely it is that they are unpopular with the public and are simply delaying an inevitable defeat. Paradoxically, while serving the longest term is a measure of government stability or durability, it can in fact mask political weakness. The point to note is that if a majority government resigns there is little choice but to call an election, since no other party or combination of parties in the legislature can govern successfully.

The other (fairly) common reason for government changes in majority situations is because of a change in prime minister. This is typically a voluntary retirement, usually coming near the end of a term of office, but as the caucus revolt that replaced Margaret Thatcher with John Major demonstrated, or the assassination of Swedish Prime Minister Olaf Palme, party revolt and death can remove incumbent prime ministers. In majoritarian systems with flexible terms, it is often expected that a prime minister sworn in without having faced the electorate as party leader will do so at the earliest possible opportunity and so "earn" his or her mandate.

Minority governments can end for the same reasons as majority governments, but are much more likely than these to be terminated by a defeat in the legislature, i.e., by a loss of confidence. With few exceptions, loss of a confidence motion means

6. The Canadian constitution is silent about the time between elections, but establishes that the maximum life of Parliament is five years "from the date fixed for the return of the writs of a general election," which means in practical terms that almost six years can elapse between elections in Canada. In times of war or insurrection the life of Parliament may be extended.

TYPES OF EXECUTIVE COALITION

Various theories of coalition formation exist, some based on the premise that coalitions are driven by the desire of their members for power, some based on the premise that political parties seek particular policy outcomes first and foremost, and some combining both elements. In any case, these theories compare the strengths and weaknesses of different types of executive coalitions.

MINIMAL WINNING COALITION

This is a coalition that has as many parties as are necessary to control a majority of the legislature, no more. In the example below, any combination of parties that adds up to no less than 251 members and that cannot lose a party and still have no less than 251 members is a minimal winning coalition: thus combinations AD, BD, ABC, and ABE are all minimal winning coalitions (there are other combinations, too), but BCD is not a minimal winning coalition because Party C's votes are not necessary to give control of a legislative majority.

MINIMUM WINNING COALITION

Depending on the number of parties and their relative strength there may be many minimal winning coalitions; the smallest of them is the minimum winning coalition. In our example this would be the government BD, with 265 legislators.

MINIMUM CONNECTED WINNING COALITION

We have ranged the parties ideologically below, and coalition theory expects a more stable government from partners closely aligned ideologically. Thus the minimum winning coalition BD joins two partners that are unconnected ideologically. In our example below there is only one minimal connected winning coalition: ABC, which is also therefore the minimum connected winning coalition.

SURPLUS MAJORITY COALITION

As we noted above, BCD is not a minimal winning coalition because Party C's votes could be lost without majority control of the legislature being compromised. Therefore Party C is an extra passenger. Surplus majority coalitions contain one or more surplus passengers. The government BD, which is a minimum winning coalition, may be made more stable by adding party C, which makes the government partners ideologically connected.

GRAND COALITION

When a surplus majority coalition contains all significant parties in the legislature, it is called a grand coalition, and this usually exists for reasons of national unity, or in response to a state of national crisis. Governments ABCDE or ABCD would be grand coalitions in our example.

EXAMPLE

Left		Centre		Right
Party A	**Party B**	**Party C**	**Party D**	**Party E**
135	**115**	**75**	**150**	**26**

[Total seats: 501 · Majority = 251]

FIGURE 8.8

the end of the government in parliamentary regimes. One exception is Switzerland, where the executive, having passed the investiture vote, is not subject to legislative votes of confidence. A partial exception is Germany, where the legislature can terminate the government only with a vote of **CONSTRUCTIVE NON-CONFIDENCE**, which means that in addition to rejecting the current executive, the legislators must have agreed on a successor in whom they have confidence (see Figure 8.7). Not surprisingly, Budge and Keman's study of 20 democracies between 1950 and 1983 found that defeat in the legislature was the most frequent cause of termination for minority governments, and of all types of

government, minority governments were most likely to be terminated by legislative defeat (see Figure 8.9).

Finally, in coalition government situations, a cause of
government termination arises that is not so likely in single-party
governments (majority or minority), namely, internal cabinet
dissension. As we have observed, cabinet government is a
collective executive and the failure of cabinet members to work
together and support a common policy platform signals an inability
to govern. While this is possible in single-party governments, but
not likely given the mechanisms of party discipline, it is very
possible once we have coalition (multi-party) governments.
Although coalitions involve a formal agreement about portfolios
and a policy platform, disagreements about either (let alone other
factors such as personality clashes between party leaders) may arise
during the life of a government. Failure to resolve these conflicts
may lead to the collapse of the coalition, or its defeat in the
legislature, and hence its resignation. The greater probability of
internal collapse in coalition governments is the primary reason
for their reputation for "instability," especially as compared with
single-party majority governments, and this is a key basis on which
majoritarian and proportionate systems have been compared and
evaluated. On this matter, a couple of observations are in order.

The stability of multi-party governments is itself highly
variable, depending on several factors. One area of continuing
interest and investigation is the kind of coalition formed, which
has to do with the number of parties involved in government and
their relationships to each other (ideology, relative strength) and
to the rest of the legislature (size of majority, etc.). Some of the
types of coalition are discussed in Figure 8.8, but otherwise this
remains a topic beyond our scope here. Second, coalition stability
depends greatly on the political culture, political practice, and
institutional rules of individual nation-states. Two of the countries
with the least stable coalitions—4th Republic France and Italy
since 1945—also have had unique features that account in large
part for their instability. One factor in Italy's instability has been
the fragmented party system and the attempt in the past to exclude
a large Communist Party from office at any cost. In more recent
years, with the demise of the Italian Communist Party and
electoral reform, Italy's government has been somewhat more
stable. Also, the practice of secret legislative votes weakens the
ability of party leaders to enforce discipline on their members. In
such countries as Switzerland and Germany, by contrast, coalition
governments have been as stable as single-party majorities

REASONS FOR TERMINATION, 1950-1983, IN PER CENT (NUMBER OF CASES)

| TYPE OF SYSTEM | ELECTION | | POLITICAL | | OTHER |
	Fixed	Anticipated	Government Dissention	Legislative Dissention	
Majoritarian (Australia, Britain, Canada, New Zealand)	44 (26)	24 (14)	5 (3)	8.5 (5)	18.5 (11) total cases = 59
Proportionate (Austria, Belgium, Denmark, Finland, France4, France5, Germany, Iceland, Ireland, Italy, Luxembourg Netherlands, Norway, Sweden)	27 (81)	11 (32)	30 (90)	15 (44)	17 (51) total cases = 298
Single-Party Majority	48 (44)	19 (17)	9 (8)	5.5 (5)	19 (17) total cases = 91
Coalition	27 (46)	8 (13)	35 (60)	13.5 (23)	17 (29) total cases = 171
Minority	20 (19)	16 (15)	16 (15)	25 (23)	23 (21) total cases = 93
Caretaker	2 (8)	24 (6)	36 (9)	4 (1)	4 (1) total cases = 25

(reprinted from Keman and Budge, 1990)

FIGURE 8.9

elsewhere. Collapse of a governing coalition is also one cause of government termination that need not lead to an election; it may be quite feasible to put together a fresh partnership of parties from the legislature as it stands. In fact, in many cases, the collapse of a coalition has led to a new government identical to the previous in its party composition, but with a new prime minister, or key portfolios shuffled or reconstituted on the basis of a newly negotiated policy platform. Behind the instability of coalition may stand a great deal of continuity.

The principal causes of government termination are shown in Figure 8.9, divided among the kinds of government and the types of parliamentary system. On the assumption that the resignation of the prime minister and constitutional intervention are causes of termination not related to the differences between type of system or type of government, these are collapsed into the category "other," and indeed, there seems to be little difference here between majoritarian and proportionate systems or among majority, coalition, and minority governments. The key differences have rather to do with governments terminating for electoral reasons and governments terminating for what Keman and Budge call "political" reasons. In general, the data show that governments in majoritarian systems are more likely to terminate because an election is required or is anticipated by the government, and less likely to terminate because of legislative defeat or internal cabinet conflict. Almost identical results are obtained for single-party majority governments, which is not surprising given that most of these will have occurred within majoritarian systems. Governments in proportionate systems are more likely to terminate for political reasons than for electoral reasons, and conflict between cabinet partners is the most frequent cause of termination; similar results show for coalition governments generally. Minority governments, by contrast, are more likely to be terminated by legislative defeat than are single-party majorities or coalitions.

In a parliamentary system, the head of state is a largely formal office, performing "a number of significant symbolic, procedural and diplomatic functions" (Gallagher et al., 1992: 14). As noted in the discussion of executives in Chapter Seven, in many cases the office of the head of state is a remnant of the traditional monarchy or has evolved from modifications of the same. Of the 19 parliamentary democracies of Western Europe, the head of state in seven is a monarch, and in Luxembourg a grand duke; in the remainder the head of state is a president. Of the 11 Western European presidents, six are elected directly by the people and five are elected by the people's representatives in the legislature. In three countries, the office of the head of state departs from the parliamentary norm in significant ways. In two countries (France and, to a lesser degree, Finland) the president exercises discretionary power in ways more like the strong president of the United States with its separation-of-powers constitution. We will discuss these strong presidencies, and Switzerland, which is a unique case, in Chapter Nine. In the remainder of the European parliamentary systems, heads of state perform functions as described by Gallagher et al. We should perhaps note that in Canada, Australia, and New Zealand, the active head of state is a governor-general who represents the sovereign—in each case the

8.5
THE HEAD OF STATE

PARLIAMENTARY HEADS OF STATE

A Monarchs
Belgium, Britain, Denmark, Luxembourg (Grand Duke), Netherlands, Norway, Spain, Sweden; exercised through a Governor-General: Australia, Canada, New Zealand.

B (Weak) Presidents
(a) directly elected: Austria, Iceland, Ireland, Portugal
(b) elected by legislature: Germany, Greece, Italy, Malta, Switzerland

C (Strong) Presidents
(all directly elected): France, Finland

FIGURE 8.10

British monarch. In most of the newly minted democracies of Eastern Europe and the former Soviet Union, the head of state is a president: in many cases the "weak" or non-political president one normally associates with a parliamentary system, but in several regimes (e.g., Poland, Russia, Ukraine, Belarus) the president has more formidable powers, thus combining parliamentary government with elements of strong presidentialism.

Beyond the symbolic and ceremonial roles of the head of state, this office serves two other political purposes. One has to do with the requirement that there always be a legal government in office; in most cases the most important political duty of the head of state is to see that this is so, whether this means an active role for the head of state in the government formation process or implementing constitutionally prescribed procedures.[7] In either case the head of state is supposed to serve as the representative of the whole people, "above" partisan politics and serving no particular interest or interests. Where heads of state manage to maintain the public respect for their office by observing these conventions of political neutrality, they are also in a position to act or intervene in times of constitutional crisis or deadlock and use their influence to ensure stability. A good example of this was the decisive role of King Juan Carlos of Spain in that country's transition from a dictatorship to a liberal democracy. As with other dimensions of parliamentary politics, so, too, may the role of the head of state be somewhat different in majoritarian and proportionate systems.

In the normal course of things in a majoritarian system, the head of state will have little decision-making to do. If the electoral system returns a single-party majority to the legislature, then the leader of that party will be invited to form a government. Should the prime minister of a majority government present his or her government's resignation to the head of state and/or ask for a dissolution of the legislature and a new election, there is no basis for the head of state to refuse. In other words, if there is a single-party majority, the birth of the government is automatic, and its termination is in the control of the prime minister. In either case, the head of state merely fulfils necessary procedural requirements. When there is no party with a legislative majority, or such a majority evaporates, the situation of the head of state may be quite different—subject, of course, to the constitutional rules alluded to earlier.

Consider the normal course of affairs in Canadian politics. On election night, as the results become clear, the press will

7. One exception is Sweden, which has transferred this role to the speaker of the legislature.

proclaim that party leader X has won the election and will become the new Prime Minister, just as it will report some four to five years later that Prime Minister X has called an election for eight weeks hence. In fact, in the former case, it will be the Governor-General who will ask party leader X to form a government, and four or five years down the road Prime Minister X will ask the Governor-General to dissolve Parliament and issue writs for an election on a specific date. Because X's party won and maintained a majority, the Governor-General's actions are prescribed, and so his or her role remains invisible to most of the general public. Suppose, however, that no party won a majority in the election. Now the Governor-General might have to decide whom to invite to form a government; in Canada there are no written constitutional rules on this matter, and conventions are not always clear about every contingency. What if two parties were tied in seats? What if the previously governing party finished second by only two or three seats—should its seniority give it the first crack at forming a government given that it only needs to convince three or four other legislators to support it? What if it finished second by a larger margin? When does the margin matter or not? These are questions a head of state might have to consider. The Governor-General has the obligation to do what is necessary to provide Canadians with a viable government. Uncertainty might not only attend the investiture of a government following an indecisive election, but also follow the defeat of a minority government. Two examples from Canadian politics illustrate the difficulty.

In 1926, the Liberal minority government led by Mackenzie King was embroiled in a scandal and on the verge of losing a vote of censure. To avoid this embarrassment, King asked the Governor-General, Lord Byng, to dissolve Parliament and call an election. When Byng refused this advice, King resigned his government (rather than the usual practice of offering his resignation), which left the country with no government. Byng immediately asked the Conservative Leader of the Opposition, Arthur Meighen, to form a government (incidentally, the Conservatives had won 116 seats in the 1925 election, to 99 for the Liberals). This government was in turn defeated in the House four days later. Lord Byng now had no choice but to dissolve Parliament and call an election. In the subsequent election campaign, King claimed that the Governor-General had been partial to the Conservatives and that this was British meddling in Canadian politics—the Governor-General was then appointed by the monarch;

8. Since 1952, with the appointment of Vincent Massey, Canada's Governors-General have been Canadian.

today this appointment is made "on the advice" of the Prime Minister.[8] The Liberals won a majority in the 1926 election.

In May 1985, under new leader Frank Miller, the Ontario Progressive Conservatives won 52 seats in a provincial election, to 48 for the Liberals and 25 for the NDP. As a minority government, the Conservatives met the legislature on June 4 and were defeated within a month. Premier Miller asked Lieutenant-Governor John Aird (the Queen's provincial representative) to dissolve the legislature and call a fresh election. Aird refused this advice, being well aware not only that the Liberals were prepared to govern, but also that the NDP would support them. This is one of the few cases in Canada's majoritarian system where change in party government has occurred without an election. The Peterson Liberal minority government lasted more than 26 months before winning a majority at the polls.

Because majority situations are the norm in Canada, the procedural role of the Governor-General and the Lieutenant-Governors is easily obscured, and the possibility that the head of state might be pivotal in the government formation process is not readily appreciated. By contrast, in proportionate systems where majorities are rare, the need for someone to oversee the government formation process, if not actually play a key role in it, is more obvious. This may also explain why, in many proportionate systems, the rules of government formation and the role of the head of state are explicitly or formally set out in the constitution.

8.6
THE PRIME MINISTER
AND CABINET

It should be clear by now that the central institution of the parliamentary system is the cabinet and that the central figure in the cabinet is the prime minister. Under the leadership of the prime minister, the cabinet makes policy, presents it (where necessary) in the form of legislation to parliament, and remains responsible for its implementation and administration by means of the agencies and departments of the state. The size, structure, and working styles of cabinet government vary from country to country, reflecting some of the differences in political culture, circumstances, and expectations that we have seen previously. At one extreme, the size and functioning is almost entirely at the discretion of the prime minister and will reflect his or her own style and philosophy of governing. At the other pole, the size of cabinet is fixed in the constitution (e.g., in Switzerland it is set at seven members). Comparative study of cabinets and cabinet government has produced a large and growing body of literature in recent years.

The size of cabinets seems to depend greatly on two factors: the size of the state and the size of the legislature. To take the latter first, the larger the legislature, the larger will be the group of supporters (whether from one party or several) on whom the government's life depends. It is obviously important to make sure a proper percentage of these supporters are rewarded for their loyalty with cabinet posts, parliamentary secretaryships, or other related positions of elevated status (and often pay). The smaller the cabinet (and related positions), the larger the body of potentially disgruntled "backbenchers."[9] All other things being equal, we will expect that the larger the legislature (or the larger the winning party's caucus) the larger the cabinet will be. Figure 8.12 indicates that the largest postwar cabinets have been in the countries with the largest legislatures: Italy, France, and Britain. In fact, the British keep the cabinet smaller than it might otherwise be by distinguishing between the Ministry, which includes all legislators sworn in as ministers of the Crown and thus exercising administrative responsibilities, and the cabinet, which is a special committee of senior ministers chaired by the Prime Minister.

The second factor that has had a large bearing on the size of cabinets has been the growth of the state, particularly in this century. An increase in the scope of government leads to new programs, new departments to implement and administer them, and thus to new ministries and **PORTFOLIOS**. One could argue that this is not an inevitable development, that ministers could double up, taking responsibility for more than one portfolio, or that (as in Britain) not all department heads or administrators (i.e., ministers) need be part of the cabinet. This is true, but it ignores the prestige that comes with cabinet status and the importance of this means of reward to prime ministers seeking to consolidate their hold on a parliamentary caucus. All things being equal, then, as the size of the state increases, we would expect the size of cabinet to grow also. Certainly the Canadian data reflect this (see Figure 8.12), and the corollary: that as the state shrinks, we should expect to see the size of cabinet decrease. As governments have become increasingly concerned about their operating deficits and accumulated debt, one response has been to reduce the size of government (or at least to halt or limit its expansion), and one way to do this (even if it is sometimes only a symbolic gesture) is to reduce the number of chairs around the cabinet table. In a comparatively short time, the size of the Canadian cabinet receded from 40

9. So-called because they sit on the back or rear seats in the House of Commons; cabinet ministers and the opposition critics sit on the front benches.

SIZE OF PARLIAMENTARY CABINETS (1945-1990)

Country	Average Size	Range of Size
Italy	24	15-32
France (5th)	22	15-36
Britain	21	16-33
Belgium	20	15-27
France (4th)	19	13-26
Germany	18	13-22
Sweden	18	14-21
Denmark	17	12-22
Norway	16	13-19
Ireland	15	12-17
Netherlands	14	10-18
Austria	13	11-16
Finland	13	7-18
Luxembourg	8	6-10

(from Steiner, 1995: 99)

FIGURE 8.11

PRIME MINISTERS AND THEIR CABINETS

Prime Minister	Years in Office	Size of Cabinets	Government Expenditure m$	Year
Macdonald	1867-73, 1878-91	13-14	13.7	1867
Mackenzie	1873-78	14	31.1	1875
Abbott	1891-92	13	40.2	1891
Thompson	1892-94	13	40.9	1893
Bowell	1894-96	14	42	1895
Tupper	1896	17	40.9	1896
Laurier	1896-1911	14	56	1900
Borden	1911-20	18-22	185	1913
Meighen	1920-21, 1926	16-17	321	1926
King	1921-26, 1926-30, 1935-48	15-20	4,412	1943
Bennett	1930-35	20	380	1933
St. Laurent	1948-57	20	2,370	1955
Diefenbaker	1957-63	21	6,746	1960
Pearson	1963-68	26	8,580	1965
Trudeau	1968-79, 1980-84	24-37	61,316	1980
Clark	1979-80	29	52,791	1979
Turner	1984	29	106,527	1984
Mulroney	1984-93	40	152,734	1990
Campbell	1993	25	160,700	1993
Chrétien	1993-	23-28		

FIGURE 8.12

10. In 1997, at the beginning of the Chrétien government's second term, the size of cabinet was 28 ministers, with 8 secretaries of state, for a total Ministry of 36.

members under Brian Mulroney to 23 under Jean Chrétien. The Chrétien government also took a leaf from the British book by creating eight parliamentary secretaries (not to be confused with ministers' parliamentary assistants) who serve essentially as junior ministers: while not part of the cabinet, they are designated part of the Ministry.[10] It is possible to argue that these parliamentary secretaries have really taken the place of ministers without portfolio, a fairly common device in the 1960s and 1970s before the size of government became a large issue. These ministers were not in charge of a government department, although they normally did have a particular responsibility, usually assisting one of the more heavily burdened senior ministers. There is little difference between today's parliamentary secretaries and yesterday's ministers without portfolio, except that the latter were in the cabinet while the former are not.

One additional factor that can contribute to the size of cabinets is representational concerns. In a country such as Canada, which is constitutionally federal and has a regionally fragmented political culture, the understanding has developed that each region will receive cabinet representation appropriate to that region's weight within Confederation. Given that the Prime Minister is confined to the representatives a region has elected (or must be willing to appoint senators to cabinet to represent a region with few or no elected MPs), requirements of regional representation can only add to the size of cabinet.

Closely related to the size of cabinets is their structure. Generally speaking, and as Canadian experience has seemed to confirm, the larger the cabinet, the more elaborate its structure. (It may well be that it is as much the other way around: the more structured the cabinet, the greater the incentive to appoint bodies to fill out the structure.) In the 30-year period from 1960 to 1990, as the Canadian cabinet grew larger, it also became increasingly structured by a system of committees assigned portions of the executive's administrative and policy-making duties. Most committees were involved either in co-ordinating activities or in advising the cabinet as a whole concerning certain substantive policy areas. Of particular interest in the period of large cabinets was the attempt to achieve greater efficiency through the creation of an **INNER CABINET** in one form or another. Obviously there is going to be a trade-off between cabinet size and the ease of decision-making: the larger the committee the more voices there are to be heard, the greater the potential difficulty of achieving consensus, and so on.

In the Trudeau era, which began in 1968, the central committee of cabinet was the Priorities and Planning Committee, which functioned as a *de facto* inner cabinet, controlling the government's agenda, overseeing the decisions reached in all other cabinet committees, and thus determining the directions, if not the details, of government policy. By contrast, the approach of Joe Clark, whose government lasted only nine months, was to reduce the size of cabinet and create a clearly designated inner cabinet (10 of 29 ministers). The Mulroney years continued with the large structured cabinets that had characterized the Trudeau period, in fact adding more committees and layers of committees to the system. Priorities and Planning remained at the hub, but something interesting happened here. Given the centrality of P&P, its status as an unofficial inner cabinet, it became *the* committee that mattered; it was not enough to be in the cabinet if one could not also sit on P&P. Even the principle of regional representation came to be applied to P&P as well as the cabinet as a whole. At one stage the Mulroney cabinet of 40 included 24 ministers on the P&P committee. In the second term of Mulroney's leadership, a new committee of seven ministers, called Operations, became the

MODELS OF CABINET DECISION-MAKING

EFFECTIVE POWER RESTS OUTSIDE THE EXECUTIVE

Bureaucratic Government:
The power to make public policy rests in this instance with the bureaucracy. In this case who is in the cabinet makes little or no difference to policy.

Legislative Government:
The legislature makes policy and the cabinet's role is simply that of implementation.

EFFECTIVE POWER RESTS WITH THE EXECUTIVE

Prime-Ministerial Government:
Policy-making takes place within a collective executive that is dominated by the Prime Minister.

Party Government:
The cabinet is subject to the parliamentary caucus, which can force policy options. Clearly this is most feasible in a single-party government.

Cabinet Government:
This is the classical counterpart of collective responsibility: a decision-making process that is also collective and is usually protected by conventions of confidentiality.

Ministerial Government:
In this model, one of autonomy within a collective executive, each minister has significant if not primary responsibility for policies that fall under his/her portfolio.

(adapted from Laver and Shepsle, 1994: 5-8)

FIGURE 8.13

gatekeeping, agenda-setting subcommittee of P&P—the inner cabinet of the inner cabinet, as it were. Mulroney's successor, Kim Campbell, whose tenure was only two months, reduced the entire cabinet to 25, and Jean Chrétien in 1993 brought in a cabinet of 23, but also with an extremely simplified structure, including only two substantive policy committees (economic policy and social policy). Although the Chrétien cabinet has since grown, the simplified committee structure has remained. On the other hand, in the province of Ontario, in 1999, a cabinet of 25 had a Priorities, Planning, and Communications Committee, a Management Board, a Statutory Business Committee, four policy sector committees, and two ad hoc specially mandated committees. What this indicates, more than anything, is that the structure of cabinets may be less a function of their size and more a product of the organizational styles and preferences of their leaders.

The point this chronicle should emphasize is the pre-eminence of the prime minister. Not only are ministers appointed by the prime minister, and continue to serve at his or her pleasure, but it is the prime minister who may determine the size and structure of cabinet, decisions that will depend very much on his or her philosophy and leadership style. The complete dominance of the cabinet by the prime minister is something we would expect more of single-party governments, majority or minority, than of coalition cabinets, where questions of size, structure, and functioning will be part of the negotiated agreement among coalition partners. As Laver and Shepsle point out, cabinet decision-making is also very much a question of how "individual cabinet ministers are constrained by key political institutions" (1994: 5). Figure 8.13 presents various models of cabinet decision-making they discuss.

8.7 POLICY-MAKING: EXECUTIVE DOMINANCE

Although there will be much more to say about policy-making in Chapter Fifteen, at this point a few remarks are in order concerning the role of the cabinet and prime minister in policy-making. To put it baldly, in parliamentary systems the cabinet monopolizes policy-making. Responsible government has been described as perhaps *the* distinguishing feature of parliamentary government, meaning specifically the requirement that the cabinet maintain the confidence of the legislature. Given the strength of party discipline in most countries, this confidence is virtually guaranteed for any party (or combination of parties) that controls a majority of the legislators in parliament. The result is that responsible government takes on a new meaning: the cabinet is "responsible" for everything. Deciding what government will do, or not do, when it will be done and how; drafting regulations or legislation and presenting the latter to parliament; overseeing the implementation and ongoing administration of policy: all of these are in the control of the cabinet, and that leaves very little. This is why parliamentary systems are usually described as having strong executives and weak legislatures, or to put it another way, as being systems characterized by *executive dominance*. This executive may be more or less stable, depending on the status of its majority, or the nature of the coalition that comprises it, but whatever the composition of the government, the relative centrality of the cabinet within the system remains. This dominance is emphasized if we consider the principal challenges to it.

Clearly, the solid foundation upon which modern cabinet government rests is strong party discipline, and those parliaments with unstable coalitions are often those in which, for one reason or another, this coherence is lacking. This is the exception rather than the rule, because there is every incentive for parties to develop mechanisms to enforce discipline and thereby enhance the odds of their own political survival (an undisciplined party risks alienating an electorate uncertain of what it stands for). The sanctions that party leaders employ will be a mixture of inducements and punishments. The control that the cabinet and, more usually, the prime minister have over appointments (to judicial office, commissions, boards, even second chambers of the legislature) means an abundance of rewards for loyal behaviour—quite apart from the hope of some day landing in cabinet or even the prime minister's office. The penalties for disloyalty can vary from exclusion from scarce positions of influence or additional remuneration, to exclusion from the party caucus (which, in those legislatures where the rules give privileges to parties, amounts to being silenced), to being dropped down or off the party's list of candidates for the next election.[11] The effect of these mechanisms of party discipline is to internalize any dissent and thus remove it from public view. This is one purpose of meetings of the party caucus (the parliamentary party); held behind closed doors, these meetings allow backbenchers to challenge the decisions of leaders, and in some cases have led to reversals of policy. More often than not, though, it appears that caucus functions to allow leaders to instruct backbenchers on what is expected of them: how they are to vote on issues, what the party's public position is on matters,

KEY TERMS

cabinet solidarity
caretaker government
caucus
coalition government
collective responsibility
constructive non-confidence
dissolution
electoral coalition
electoral parties
electoral system
executive coalition
executive dominance
formateur
government formation
grand coalition
head of state
inner cabinet
investiture vote
legislative parties
legislative coalition
majoritarian system
majority government
manufactured majority
minority government
parliamentary party
plurality
portfolio
proportional representation
proportionate system
termination

11. In Canada, for example, to run as a member of a particular party—and few independents ever succeed—one must have the consent of the party leader.

REFERENCES AND SUGGESTED READING

Budge, Ian, and Hans Keman. 1990. *Parties and Democracy*. Oxford: Oxford University Press.

Gallagher, Michael, et al. 1995. *Representative Government in Modern Europe*, 2nd ed. New York: McGraw-Hill.

Hogg, Peter. 1992. "Responsible Government," in R.S. Blair and J.T. McLeod, eds., *The Canadian Political Tradition*. (Toronto: Nelson).

Lane, Jan-Erik, and Svante O. Ersson. 1991. *Politics and Society in Western Europe*, 2nd ed. London: Sage.

Laver, Michael, and Norman Schofield. 1990. *Multiparty Government: The Politics of Coalition in Europe*. Oxford: Oxford University Press.

Laver, Michael, and Kenneth A. Shepsle. 1994. *Cabinet Ministers and Parliamentary Government*. Cambridge: Cambridge University Press.

———. 1996. *Making and Breaking Governments*. Cambridge: Cambridge University Press.

Lijphart, Arend. 1999. *Patterns of Democracy: Government Forms and Performance in Thirty-Six Countries*. New Haven: Yale University Press.

———. 1994. *Electoral Systems and Party Systems*. Oxford: Oxford University Press.

———. 1984. *Democracies*. New Haven: Yale University Press.

Mény, Yves. 1993. *Government and Politics in Western Europe*, 2nd ed. Oxford: Oxford University Press.

etc. Successful internal challenge of cabinet dominance is rare in parliamentary systems.

A second possible challenge to the dominance of the cabinet is the presence of a strong second chamber in those systems with *bicameral* legislatures. As we have seen, responsible government directs the attention of the cabinet to the popularly elected or "first" chamber of the legislature. It is also with respect to the behaviour of members in this chamber that party discipline will be most effective. In bicameral legislatures it is possible that the party (or coalition) controlling the first chamber (and the cabinet) does not have a majority in the second chamber or is less able to control party members in this chamber. Where this is so, the constitutional powers of the second chamber will make a clear difference to the dominance of the cabinet. If the second chamber has weak powers, the cabinet will not be seriously challenged by its dissent; if its powers are strong, the cabinet may well find here an effective opposition. Where the second chamber has the ability to veto or block legislation coming from the first chamber it will be in a position of potential challenger to the government. As Lijphart notes, this is enhanced by having the second chamber represent a different constituency or by having it (s)elected on a different basis from that of the first chamber. Of the world's democracies, he judges four to satisfy these twin conditions of *strong bicameralism*: Australia, Germany, Switzerland, and the United States. The latter, of course, is not parliamentary, and as we have noted and will explore further in Chapter Nine, Switzerland represents a rather exceptional case in several respects. In short, in most parliamentary democracies, the second chamber does not present an effective opposition to cabinet government.

A third possibility is the addition of a strong presidency to what is otherwise a system of responsible parliamentary government. This has been the experience in Western Europe of France (and, to a lesser extent, of Finland), and in Eastern Europe of several newer democracies, most notably Poland and Russia. These are exceptions to the parliamentary norm, and we will explore in the next chapter the reasons for creating a strong head of state in parliamentary systems. In most cases, though, this has not been to oppose an over-strong cabinet government, but to provide stability to weak multi-party systems.

In normal circumstances, then, parliamentary government means a relatively unhampered executive dominance over the legislature and a relatively coherent control by the cabinet of policy-making and implementation. This means that parliamentary government is, all else being equal, *strong* government, able—if it is willing—to put the power of the state behind the problem-solving it undertakes (not that this guarantees a solution). The ability of parliamentary government to act decisively and quickly is one of its advantages among democratic systems. This does *not* mean that parliamentary government is absolute; there are at least two other possible checks on the policy-making of cabinet government. One (albeit absent in many parliamentary constitutions) is the judicial review of legislation, as well as other constitutional judgements issued by the high courts concerning government actions. Where judicial review is possible, merely the possibility of its taking place may constrain governments from certain policies. Ultimately, though, the judgement that no cabinet government in a parliamentary democracy can escape is that of the people. Periodic, competitive elections offer citizens the opportunity to register their approval and disapproval of government policies and to replace one government with another. One could argue, in fact, that it is only on the premise that the political process delivers effective popular control over government that the powerful centralization of power in the hands of cabinet government can be justified. Where this premise is false, there is little that parliamentary government cannot do, and as in earlier days, citizens must rely on the wisdom and moral restraint of their rulers.

Sartori, Giovanni. 1994. *Comparative Constitutional Engineering.* New York: New York University Press.

Steiner, Jürg. 1995. *European Democracies*, 3rd ed. White Plains, NY: Longman.

SOMETHING TO CONSIDER

In 1999, Australians voted in a referendum to retain the monarchy, defeating a proposal for a republican head of state (and constitution). Is this a question that Canadians should consider?

If Canadians were to replace the monarch with a republican head of state, what powers should this president (or Governor-General) have?

Alternatively, would Canadians be better served by the kind of electoral system that would make coalition government more common?

9
presidentialism

L ijphart (1984) identifies presidentialism with a political (and not merely formal) executive that is not drawn from the legislature, and is not responsible to the legislature. This is in clear contrast to the parliamentary executive which normally is drawn from, and remains responsible to, the legislature. Sartori identifies a system as presidential "if, and only if, the head of state (president) i) results from popular election, ii) during his or her pre-established tenure cannot be discharged by a parliamentary vote, and iii) heads or otherwise directs the governments that he or she directs" (1994: 84). In democracies, a presidential executive is elected by the people, directly as in France or Finland, or indirectly as in the United States where the device of an electoral college is employed. Three variations in presidentialism will be discussed in this chapter. One, to which considerable reference was made in Chapter Seven, is the U.S. system of separated powers, where the entire executive has no standing in or responsibility to the legislature. Another case is where a strong head of state is added to what is otherwise a parliamentary system; here there is a president *and* a prime-minister. Contemporary France (which Sartori calls "semi-presidential") is the developed democracy that best exemplifies this kind of hybrid; many of the new democracies in Eastern Europe, such as Poland, Russia, and Ukraine, are newer examples. Finally, there is Switzerland, which Lijphart describes as a parliamentary-presidential hybrid; the executive is a seven-member cabinet selected by the legislature, but once installed it is not subject to parliament's confidence.

9.1
PRESIDENTIALISM DEFINED

9.1   Presidentialism Defined
9.2   Presidentialism with Separated Powers: the United States
9.3   Presidentialism in Parliamentary Systems: France
9.4   An Exceptional Case: Switzerland
9.5   Conclusion

**9.2
PRESIDENTIALISM WITH
SEPARATED POWERS:
THE UNITED STATES**

As noted in Chapter Seven, the American Constitution rests on the principles of republicanism, mixed government, and a separation of powers (employing checks and balances). The latter is the one with which we are most concerned here, because it establishes the independence of the presidency (and the cabinet) from the legislature, and this in turn has several important implications.

The President is not and cannot be a member of the legislature. The same is true of members of the cabinet (called secretaries, not ministers), who are appointed by the President. American cabinet secretaries are not responsible to the legislature, collectively or individually, but rather are individually responsible to the President. As a result, there is no body that can be identified (as in parliamentary systems) as the current government or the government of the day. In the United States reference is often made to **THE ADMINISTRATION** (and more commonly the "Reagan administration" or the "Clinton administration," etc.), which encompasses the President, cabinet, and White House officials. The task of each secretary is to oversee the administration of his or her government department and advise the President on the ability of the public service to deliver policy consistent with the administration's purposes. This means a role primarily of implementing policy determined elsewhere: either in the legislature or by presidential aides and advisers. This cabinet is not a collective executive, and for this reason rarely meets as a whole. Given the size of the American state, and in comparison with parliamentary executives, the American cabinet is small: thirteen secretaries, the President, Vice-President, and a few cabinet-level executives such as the head of the CIA and the ambassador to the United Nations bring the total to around 20 members.

In some ways the American counterpart to the parliamentary cabinet is as much contained in White House staff as it is in the American cabinet. White House officials number around 1,500 individuals, freshly appointed with each change in president, and hired to provide a range of support and advisory services to the chief executive. The organization and functioning of this bureaucracy is very much at the discretion of the President and will reflect his leadership philosophy and style. In this structure will be found the President's closest policy advisers, and these aides may often wield more influence on public policy than does the cabinet secretary of the relevant department.

Because of the separation of powers, the executive has no legislative standing, and can only have an impact on legislation by influencing legislators or appealing to those whose partisan or ideological attachments make them sympathetic to the executive's position. While the President in particular will not have difficulty finding members of Congress to sponsor legislation reflecting the policy aims of the administration, there is no guarantee of sufficient support to ensure passage. It has become not unusual for different parties to control the legislative and executive branches, and even where there is a party congruence between the White House and the Congress, the weakness of party discipline means there are no safe bets. While observers have noted that a strengthening of party voting (a situation in which a majority of Democrats oppose a majority of Republicans, or vice versa) on legislation is becoming more common in recent years, the situation is still a far cry from the virtual unanimity of party discipline that exists in most parliamentary systems. On the other hand, the defeat of any bill or measure in the legislature is simply that; there is no question of confidence or of the consequences associated with the lack of confidence in parliamentary regimes. Parties are weak in part because there is no requirement of responsible government, which works in parliamentary systems as a powerful incentive to create mechanisms of discipline. The weakness of parties means that party labels provide no infallible guide to the voting behaviour of legislators: Democrats may vote against legislation sponsored by a Democratic President or supported by the party leadership. Republicans might overwhelmingly support a bill in one chamber, but block its passage in the other house of Congress.

In the same sense that there is no government in this model, there is no head of government. The President is chief administrator and the head of state, performing both formal and political functions, the latter including foreign policy, defence, and considerable emergency powers. It is these latter powers, combined with the relative size and might of the American military on the world stage, that give the U.S. President such an international prominence. On the other hand, the lack of control over the legislature can mean much less domestic power than a prime minister wields in a parliamentary system. An outside observer might well conclude that the willingness of the United States to employ military solutions to problems abroad (e.g., Grenada, Panama, the Persian Gulf, etc.) has nothing to do with innate belligerence and everything to do with the fact that this is one area where the President can exercise power relatively unhindered by Congress or the Courts.

In contrast to the relative coherence or concentration of authority within parliamentary systems, the separation of powers in the American case creates what its critics describe as a fragmented government, and in many cases, a weak government. Its supporters, on the other hand, celebrate the American system as the epitome of **PLURALIST DEMOCRACY**. Whereas majoritarian parliamentary systems manufacture majorities, and proportionate systems put together a more legitimate consensus through coalition, in either case power is exercised in the period between elections by a fairly static majority. Those not in government, the minority, are left in most cases with very little voice in the policy-making process, and thus with ineffective representation. At its worst, this can become a tyranny of the majority over the minority. The designers of the American Constitution wished to avoid just this domination of a minority (they feared that men of property and substance would be submerged in the democratic mass) and thus fragmented power through the checks and balances of separated powers. As the term "pluralist" implies, power is centred nowhere within the American state, but is dispersed among various institutions, and diluted by being placed in many hands. As critics point out, the fragmentation of public power may in fact enhance the concentration of private power, and puts no barrier in the way of those with power, money, and influence in civil society from coming to have a disproportionate share of influence in all three branches of government (see Parenti, 1978, 1980).

One means by which political power is fragmented, and at the same time a means of balancing the executive and legislative branches of government, is the device of fixed, staggered elections. This balances the branches in that neither has the power to dismiss the other and call an election (in most parliamentary systems the executive can dissolve the legislature and seek early elections, and in Austria the legislature can dissolve itself). Members of the first chamber of Congress (the House of Representatives) serve a two-year term, and Senators (members of the second chamber) serve a six-year term, with one-third of the seats contested every two years. The presidential term of office is four years, and no President may serve more than two terms. Thus a Congress elected at the same time as the president may change radically halfway through his term, and a President re-elected may find that many of his congressional allies have gone down to defeat. In fact, it is normal for the President's party to lose seats in the midterm Congressional elections. This was dramatically the case, for example, in 1994, when the Democrats not only lost 52

House and 8 Senate seats, but also lost majority status in both houses for the first time in four decades. As a result, whereas the 103rd Congress had been dominated by the President's neo-liberal agenda (deficit reduction, economic stimulation, health-care reform), the 104th Congress was preoccupied with the resurgent Republican Party's conservative "Contract With America." There is, on the other hand, no government formation process, nor are there any of the difficult procedural or constitutional questions about dissolution or defeat of government that arise in parliamentary situations. The business of government tends to be conducted within the constraints provided by the fixed electoral terms and the corresponding congressional calendar.

Another institutional means of fragmenting power in the American system is the sharing of legislative power between two coequal legislative chambers. Because all legislation must secure majorities in both houses if it is to be forwarded to the President, this is referred to as a system of strong or "symmetrical" bicameralism. The House of Representatives is comprised of 435 members elected from single-member districts according to the principle of representation by population (with a minimum of one member per state). The Senate, by contrast, is elected on the basis of state representation, each state returning two senators, regardless of the size of the state (in the 104th Congress, 54 Senators, a sufficient number to pass legislation, came from states representing only 20 per cent of the national population). Although the two houses are coequal in the legislative process, they are not identical. Revenue bills must originate in the House of Representatives. The House can bring impeachment charges against the President, but only the Senate can try the case (as the world witnessed in late 1998 and early 1999). The Senate can scrutinize high-level appointments, and when the party opposing the President controls this house, it can make this process a very visible and potentially embarrassing experience for presidential nominees.

To the outside observer, one of the most striking characteristics of the fragmentation of powers in the American system is the elusiveness of public policy, elusive in three ways. First of all, it may simply not be possible to effect public policy, because political actors with conflicting policy preferences are able to thwart each other using the checks and vetos built into the system. Policy proposed by the President may not be able to marshall enough support in one or both houses of Congress. Legislation passed by Congress may fall to a presidential **VETO**. Presidents can veto legislation by sending it back to Congress with an explanation of the reasons for rejecting it. Congress may override the veto if the bill is passed again with a two-thirds majority in both houses. Only about 4 per cent of vetoed legislation is able to clear this hurdle. Legislation that passes may be implemented or administered by an indifferent or hostile executive in ways that thwart the legislators' intentions. This is often made possible by the vagueness of the legislation that is passed. The details necessary for implementation are often left to bureaucratic agencies to flesh out, on the grounds that the level of necessary technical expertise is found there.

Second, public policy is elusive because, in order to secure passage through so many possible veto points, a series of compromises and trade-offs is often necessary, diluting the effect or changing the outcomes of policy along the way. In recent Congresses, thousands of bills have been submitted by members every two years (up from 144 bills introduced in the 1st Congress). Only a small percentage survive to become laws, however, and those that do often bear little resemblance to their initial drafts. To become law, bills must pass in both houses, and at any point along this path, a failure to act is sufficient to kill a piece of legislation. The need to compromise and build coalitions of support inevitably blunts the edge of legislation and dilutes any ideological content. Astute legislators often attach "riders" to a bill in return for their support, amendments that often have nothing to do with the topic of the bill itself.

Third, public policy is elusive in the sense that it is often difficult for citizens to know who properly to credit for policy successes or determine who should shoulder the blame for policy failures. There will be no shortage of actors claiming to have played the crucial role in a popular policy, and no shortage of finger-pointing among political actors when there is dissatisfaction with the government's performance. This elusiveness of public policy, in all three senses, may well contribute to the large-scale public dissatisfaction with government and with politicians, and may account in part for the spectacularly low turnouts of voters in American elections. Ironically, in a testament to the strength of the American political culture, and the effectiveness of the socialization process, Americans seem to revere their constitution when it may be exactly this constitutional system that leads them to distrust their government and their political classes.

The weakness of a presidential system with separated powers was one of its attractions for those who designed it, insofar as they wished to avoid absolutism and tyranny. It also means that policy-making can be difficult and is often stymied by stalemate. As was noted in Chapter Seven, the successful export of the American system to other countries has been rare. Sartori (1994) lists eighteen countries outside the U.S. with presidential democracies; apart from the Philippines, all are in Latin America, and only three—Costa Rica (1949), Venezuela (1958), and Columbia (1974) —have been uninterruptedly democratic for more than 20 years. Sartori concludes as follows:

> Ironically, then, the belief that presidential systems are strong systems draws on the worst possible structural arrangements—a divided power defenseless against divided government—and fails to realize that the American system works, or has worked, *in spite* of its constitution—hardly *thanks to* its constitution. (1994: 89)

One reason for mistaking the presidential system as strong may be the misperceptions of the *American* President (i.e., as world leader, military commander, etc.) alluded to above. Another may be the misidentification of those systems where a strong President adds stability to (or is intended to stabilize) a parliamentary regime. Such is our next example of presidentialism.

A nother route to presidentialism is not in opposition to parliamentary systems, but alters the character of the dual executive that is common to such systems. As pointed out above, in normal parliamentary constitutions, the role of the head of state is largely formal, that is, ceremonial and procedural. It is the prime minister who exercises political authority in his or her capacity as head of government (i.e., chair of cabinet). It is not difficult to imagine (and we will explain it more precisely in a moment) a situation where the head of state retains, or is allocated, some of the political authority or discretionary powers that would otherwise fall to the prime minister. The question is: why do it?

In the case of France's **FIFTH REPUBLIC** (since 1958), the universal answer is that the creation of a strong presidency was an answer to the instability of the Fourth Republic (1946-58). In the thirteen years of the Fourth Republic, France had twenty-seven governments, beset with an overly fragmented party system and unstable coalitions further destabilized by divisive foreign policy

9.3
PRESIDENTIALISM
IN PARLIAMENTARY
SYSTEMS: FRANCE

questions, in particular the issue of Algerian independence. The constitution of the Fifth Republic, authored by Charles De Gaulle (its first President) and Michel Debré (the future Prime Minister), weakened the role of parliament and prime minister, and strengthened the presidency in several important ways, thus creating a unique dual executive or **DYARCHY**.

Since 1962, the President has been elected directly by the French people to a seven-year term, a term which is lengthy, but which guarantees an executive institution that is stable independent of possible parliamentary turnover or turmoil. The President in turn appoints the Prime Minister, and, depending on circumstances, the cabinet ministers. If sitting members of the legislature are appointed to cabinet, they must resign their legislative seats. The government, once installed, is responsible to the first chamber of the legislature, the National Assembly. A motion of censure (non-confidence) must be moved by at least one-tenth of the Assembly's deputies, and to succeed requires the approval of an absolute majority. The President also has the ability to dissolve parliament at any time and require elections, and may also dismiss the Prime Minister at will. In these, and several other ways, the French President has considerable control over both the government and the legislature. In addition, although the practice has fallen into disuse, the President has the ability to circumvent parliament and put questions directly to the people in a referendum. The French chief executive also has considerable emergency powers, and like the American President is commander-in-chief of the armed forces. Certainly, the office of president is much stronger in France than in the United States, given the control the French President wields over the legislature. On the other hand, the French President enjoys an independence from the legislature and a direct mandate conferred through popular election that parliamentary prime ministers lack.

Having said this, we should note that the pre-eminence of the French President is at its zenith when his political party also controls a majority in the legislature, a circumstance that has been the norm for most of the Fifth Republic. Some observers even doubted if this system of a dual executive could work if there were to be a strong parliamentary majority opposed to the President. However, successful cohabitation between a socialist President and a conservative Prime Minister and government occurred on two separate occasions during the 14 years of François Mitterrand's two-term presidency, and, at present, continues between a Conservative President (Chirac) and a Socialist Prime

Minister (Jospin). While the President appoints the Prime Minister, the realities of parliament do constrain this choice, especially when the electorate has given a clear mandate to one party or group of like-minded parties. One of Mitterand's greatest accomplishments may have been his demonstration, through his handling of conservative Prime Ministers Chirac and later Balladur, that the Fifth Republic system of a dual executive can work in France. In part, this has been true because of a willingness to recognize that the balance of power within the executive can shift between Prime Minister and President as circumstances vary.

In France, as elsewhere, there is a difference between the formal or legal constitution, and what we have called the constitution as the actual structure of authority—what Sartori calls the *material constitution*. It is worth noting that in the French constitution, the primary responsibility for public policy rests with the Prime Minister and cabinet. In practice, though, especially under De Gaulle, the material constitution was one in which the President's will prevailed over the Prime Minister and government. In describing "semi-presidential" systems, of which he believes France is the exemplar, Sartori makes the useful observation that the President "is not entitled to govern alone or directly, and therefore his will must be conveyed and processed via his government" (1994: 132). In this way it is possible to understand how, when the government comes from the President's party, the preponderance of policy-making power may rest with the President rather than the Prime Minister. Conversely, though, when the government comes from a party ideologically opposed to the President (as the government must when such a party clearly controls the legislature), the ability of the President to express his will via the government will be constrained. In these circumstances the Prime Minister's influence over policy-making is enhanced, or so Mitterand seemed to understand during his two periods of "cohabitation" with an ideological rival in government. When there is a double majority (the same party controls the presidency and the legislature), the material constitution tends to be in effect, and the President dominates; when there is a split majority, the formal constitution, which assigns policy to the Prime Minister and government, is adhered to more closely.

There is good reason to see the French union of a strong presidency with a parliamentary system as something idiosyncratic, designed to meet the particular problems and requirements of France, and managing to work within the political traditions and culture of France. Finland used to be described as another parliamentary system with strong presidentialism. As in France, the Finnish president appointed the prime minister, and could dissolve parliament and require elections. As in other countries the Finnish president has particular responsibility for the country's foreign relations and chairs cabinet meetings dealing with such issues. In 1991, a constitutional amendment removed the president's power to dissolve the legislature, but the system of indirect election through the device of an electoral college was replaced by direct election. On balance, Lijphart concludes, Finland is now "much closer to a parliamentary than a presidential system." (1999: 123). In 1996, Israel implemented direct election of the prime minister, an anomaly within parliamentary systems, which has the effect of making the prime minister more like a president in several respects, although Israel continues to have a president, elected by the Knesset (Israel's parliament), who serves as head of state.

As indicated earlier, strong presidents also exist in parliamentary systems in several of the new democracies to emerge out of Eastern Europe and the former Soviet Union. As these are all barely more than a decade old, it is premature to pass judgement on their effectiveness, and in many cases the exact nature of the relationship between presidency and the parliamentary executive is still not clear, or is clearly still evolving. The rationale for having a strong presidency in these countries is once again to counteract potential or perceived instability in the political system. In most of these countries, authoritarian regimes were in place for a considerable period, which means that the political culture has not developed or sustained the attitudes and practices that are associated with democratic politics. Similarly, political pluralism is new to these regimes; while they were once officially one-party systems, free elections have now produced extremely fragmented multi-party systems. In Poland, for example, the first truly free parliamentary elections returned 29 parties to the Sejm (Poland's legislature), the largest winning only 13.5 per cent of the seats. Over time, in such regimes, one expects parties with similar ideological leanings to merge and consolidate their support, while other parties (such as Poland's Beer Lovers Party) may eventually disappear. Clearly, though, forming a government in such fragmented parliaments is a challenge, and sustaining a coalition is always more difficult the more fragmented the party system. Not surprisingly, Polish President Lech Walesa and Russia's Boris Yeltsin both tried to emulate the French presidency in the early stages of their newly emerging democracies. Whether a strong presidency is merely a temporary expedient for these parliamentary systems until they establish institutional stability and loyalty to democratic traditions, or something that will persist as in the French Fifth Republic to date, is something too early to judge.

Among the world's democracies, Switzerland truly belongs in a class of its own. Considered individually and superficially, most of its constitutional features are not exceptional; other countries use referendums (although not to the extent the Swiss do), other countries are federal, other countries have grand coalitions, others have proportional representation. No other country, though, has the combination of elements that Switzerland does, and in the case of each of these elements considered closely, there is something unique about the way the Swiss experience it.

Alone among parliamentary systems, the Swiss is not one of responsible government: the executive cannot be defeated in the legislature, a feature that goes well with the four-year fixed term for parliament, and makes this executive quasi-presidential. Uniquely also, the size of the Swiss cabinet is fixed constitutionally, at seven members, who—like cabinet ministers in France or secretaries in the U.S.—cannot hold legislative seats. On the other hand, in keeping with parliamentary tradition, the composition of the Swiss cabinet is determined by the distribution of seats in the legislature among parties.

As we shall see in Chapter Thirteen, the Swiss have a unique system of proportional representation and have had an unusually stable party system. This, coupled with a convention that requires representation of Switzerland's linguistic communities in the cabinet, has led to a series of grand coalitions, in which the number of parties sharing in the executive and the number of seats each party takes remains unchanged election after election. Since 1959, in fact, the Free Democrats, Social Democrats, and Christian Democrats have each taken two executive seats, with the remaining seat going to the Swiss People's Party. In the 1999 election, there was a significant gain in the number of seats held by the most junior coalition partner, the Swiss People's Party (SVP), gains made largely at the expense of small extreme-right parties. The SVP, itself the most right-wing of the parties in government, is now the second largest party in the legislature and argued that its share of the executive should increase to two places. This would

9.4
AN EXCEPTIONAL
CASE: SWITZERLAND

KEY TERMS

the administration
cohabitation
consensual democracy
direct democracy
dyarchy
Fifth Republic
pluralist democracy
presidentialism
veto

have been the first change in the so-called "Magic Formula" that has apportioned seats on the Swiss executive for the past 40 years. The size of this executive is fixed by the constitution and creates a powerful, compact executive that cannot be removed by the legislature. Unlike other parliamentary systems, Switzerland does not have a true dual executive: there is no prime minister; members of the cabinet have equal rank; and duties of head of state (president) are filled by one of the cabinet members for a one-year term that rotates among the executive on the basis of seniority.

The relative permanence of the composition of the Swiss executive, barring any radical change in party support from the electorate, and the inability of the legislature to defeat the executive once installed are among the reasons Switzerland is seen to be a **CONSENSUAL DEMOCRACY** *par excellence*. The flip side of this is the lack of an effective parliamentary opposition, or mechanism to keep the executive accountable. Instead, the Swiss have a long tradition of **DIRECT DEMOCRACY** (see Chapter Fourteen) that balances grand coalition government with popular initiatives and referendums. Fittingly, perhaps, in a system where the people's representatives have little control over the executive, the task of keeping government accountable is one the people can exercise themselves. And, interestingly enough, in Switzerland they do so in ways that are often strikingly conservative.

9.5 CONCLUSION

What we have glimpsed in both this chapter and the previous is the great variety of constitutional arrangements that can exist within systems that otherwise have a great deal in common. Common to the systems in this chapter is a political executive that is neither drawn from nor responsible to the legislature. This is what characterizes a presidential executive, where such a president exercises more than the merely formal or procedural authority of a parliamentary head of state. In these cases the president replaces, rivals, or dominates the prime minister. Stepping back and excluding the United States, we can see the presidential regimes presented in this chapter as merely exceptional varieties of parliamentary systems. It remains the case that apart from the U.S. and the few stable Latin American examples of U.S.-style separation-of-powers systems, the world's democratic nations have followed the parliamentary route. In some cases, still a distinct minority of cases, this has also involved presidentialism, but a presidentialism without a separation of powers, and for that reason a presidentialism that might evolve into something resembling the more passive head of state we associate with "normal" parliamentary regimes. Portugal, for example, has abandoned its flirtation with strong presidentialism, and it may be that other parliamentary systems with strong presidents might do so also as they stabilize. At the end of the day we are left with a great variety of parliamentary systems, so much so that for almost every generalization there is at least one exception to the rule. The strongest distinction remains the one considered in the previous chapter: between systems that put power in the hands of one party (majoritarian) and those that tend to produce coalitions (proportionate). In the next chapter we will turn to a wholly different basis for distinguishing among democratic polities, namely the division of power between different levels of government, or what is known as federalism.

SOMETHING TO CONSIDER

Under what conditions might a strong presidency become a constitutional option for Canadians to consider seriously?

REFERENCES AND SUGGESTED READING

Gallagher, Michael, et al. 1995. *Representative Government in Modern Europe*, 2nd ed. New York: McGraw-Hill.

Lane, Jan-Erik, and Svante O. Ersson. 1991. *Politics and Society in Western Europe*, 2nd ed. London: Sage.

Lijphart, Arend. 1984. *Democracies: Patterns of Majoritarian and Consensus Government in Twenty-One Countries*. New Haven: Yale University Press.

——, ed. 1992. *Parliamentary versus Presidential Government*. Oxford: Oxford University Press.

——. 1999. *Patterns of Democracy: Government Forms and Performance in Thirty-Six Countries*. New Haven: Yale University Press.

Mahler, Gregory S. 1995. *Comparative Politics: An Institutional and Cross-National Approach*. Englewood Cliffs, NJ: Prentice Hall.

Mény, Yves. 1993. *Government and Politics in Western Europe*, 2nd ed. Oxford: Oxford University Press.

Parenti, Michael. 1978. *Power and the Powerless*. New York: St. Martin's Press.

——. 1980. *Democracy for the Few*, 3rd ed. New York: St. Martin's Press.

Sartori, Giovanni. 1994. *Comparative Constitutional Engineering*. New York: New York University Press.

Steiner, Jürg. 1995. *European Democracies*, 3rd ed. White Plains, NY: Longman.

10 federalism

Thus far we have examined *the* state, or *the* government. In actuality, the state is usually "segmented," that is, it operates at several levels. It would not be unusual for urban citizens in Canada to elect representatives to the national Parliament, to a provincial legislature, to a regional government, to a municipal government, to a school board, and even to a board of public utility trustees. Here, clearly, governments are several, and the state is multiple. Some of this multiplicity is captured by the term **FEDERALISM**; some of it is not. Either way—and we will see this more clearly very soon—this chapter deals with the reality that in almost every country, the state exists at different levels, and rarely are people subject to only one government. This is something that has no relation to the type of democratic system or government in place; Canada, the United States, Germany, and Switzerland are federal countries, and between them represent four different types of constitutional system.

Federalism seems to be one of the most difficult political terms to define—see Figure 10.1—and yet what most definitions seem to share comes down to three elements:

a) the state is divided between a national government and regional or sub-national governments,

b) the powers of government are constitutionally allocated between these two levels of government, and

c) each level of government possesses some autonomy from the other, meaning either that neither can destroy the other, that each has the final say in some area(s) of jurisdiction, or both.

10.1 FEDERALISM DEFINED

10.1 Federalism Defined
10.2 Why Federalism?
10.3 The Division of Powers
    10.3.1 Legislative powers
    10.3.2 Administrative powers
    10.3.3 Fiscal powers
10.4 Bicameralism in Federal States
10.5 Constitutional Amending Formulas
10.6 Quasi-Federalism, Home Rule, and Decentralization in a Unitary State
10.7 Supranational Federalism

DEFINITIONS OF FEDERALISM

Federalism is a political organization in which the activities of
government are divided between
regional government and a central
government in such a way that
each kind of government has some
activities on which it makes final
decisions.
— William H. Riker, in Greenstein
and Polsby, 1975: 101

A federal system of government
consists of autonomous units that
are tied together within one
country.
— Steiner, 1995: 123

In a formal sense, federalism can
be defined as a division of powers
between central and regional
governments such that neither is
subordinate to the other.
— Dyck, 1996: 69

In a federal system there are two
levels of government above the
local level, each enjoying sovereignty in certain specific areas.
— Mahler, 1995: 31

It is a political system in which
most or all of the structural
elements of the state ... are
duplicated at two levels, with both
sets of structures exercising effective control over the same territory
and population. Furthermore,
neither set of structures should be
able to abolish the other's jurisdiction over this territory or
population.
— Stevenson, 1989: 8

"the method of dividing powers
so that the general and regional
governments are each, within a
sphere, co-ordinate and independent."
— K.C. Wheare, 1953: 11

FIGURE 10.1

As noted, authority exists at more than one level in virtually every country (excepting perhaps micro-states or city-states); what makes for federalism—in our view—is the constitutional independence of two levels of government. The government of Canada cannot abolish the provinces, nor can the provinces dissolve Confederation and the national government that was so created in 1867. Municipal governments, by contrast, are entirely creatures of provincial government. The authority to make or abolish municipal governments is one of the powers of provincial government in the Canadian constitution. One way to understand this distinction is the notion of **DELEGATION**. Authority is delegated when it is transferred from one body to another, but the original body retains the right to take the authority back at any point in the future. Most of the authority that is exercised by public servants working in government bureaucracies is power delegated by the legislature, which, in theory, it could revoke at any time. Delegated authority or power is "on loan," however permanent this may seem. Municipal government is typically, as in Canada, delegated from a higher level of government; federal- ism, by contrast, means two levels of government, each exercising authority not delegated by the other.

Where there is only one sovereign level of government, that is, where all subordinate levels exercise delegated authority, a **UNITARY STATE** exists, as in Great Britain, where all sovereignty ultimately rests with Parliament. At the other extreme is a situation where the regional or sub-national governments are supreme, and the national authority is entirely their creation and servant. Such is a **CONFEDERATION**, and although the first Constitution of the United States embodied confederal principles, few if any exist in the world today. As we will see, calling Canada a confederation was a mislabelling. Between these two poles—a unitary state at one end, and a confederal state at the other—are all federal states, where each of the two levels of government is sovereign in some respect(s). Within this condition, though, there is an enormous range of possibilities, from systems where the weight of the central government is so dominant that it might as well be unitary (hence very *centralized*), to such a weak central government that it might as well be confederal (hence very *decentralized*). The range of possibilities is suggested by Figure 10.2.

On the other hand, what this obscures is the real possibility within unitary states for a considerable **DECENTRALIZATION** of authority through delegation to regional and/or municipal governments. In this way a formally unitary constitution might in

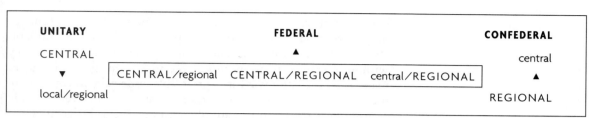

UNITARY	FEDERAL	CONFEDERAL
CENTRAL	▲	central
▼	CENTRAL/regional CENTRAL/REGIONAL central/REGIONAL	▲
local/regional		REGIONAL

FIGURE 10.2

fact allow a division of power much more decentralized than a federal constitution where the central government has clear dominance. The distinction made earlier between material and formal constitutions is useful here too. While the authority of subordinate governments may in fact be delegated, and this means it may legally be revoked or altered by the central government, the limitations imposed by the political traditions, expectations, fiscal realities, etc. may impose limits on the practical ability of the central government to "re-occupy" areas of jurisdiction once delegated.

It is also noteworthy that the federal dimension of a constitution is one that can be subject to considerable evolution or development over time. Canada began as a very centralized system, so much so that it was characterized by observers as (and formally, remains) **QUASI-FEDERAL**; it is now in practice one of the world's most decentralized federations. The United States, by contrast, began as a confederation, re-constitutionalized as a relatively decentralized federation, and became by the mid-twentieth century much more centralized than the Founding Fathers would ever have dreamed possible (or wise). Why federal systems are so flexible is something we will discuss after looking at the component features of federal constitutions. After discussing the features of systems which satisfy the definition of federalism, we will look at quasi-federal elements (including home rule), and then at decentralization within unitary states. What we must do first, though, is establish the rationale for structuring the state at more than one level.

10.2 WHY FEDERALISM?

Writing in 1995, Gregory Mahler noted that of 178 nation-states in the world, only twenty-one claimed to be federal, but included in these were five of the world's six largest countries (Russia, Canada, the United States, Brazil and Australia); he also noted that China, which is not federal, nonetheless has some federal characteristics (1995: 31). Intuitively, it makes sense that larger countries would have more than one level of government; to govern from one centre is simply not efficient or prudent. While administrative decentralization can achieve efficiency without creating an autonomous second level of government, in many cases the latter was often preferable, especially in days before modern communication and transportation. One very simple reason that large countries are likely to be federal is that they are often the product of a union of smaller territories, colonies, or even countries that have wished to retain some measure of autonomy in the new polity, and have achieved this through regional or subnational governments. This certainly describes the situation of Canada, the United States, and Australia, which each represent an amalgamation of separate colonies, and/or territories within a colony; and of Germany, which achieved political unity by uniting a great number of smaller principalities and states that collectively comprised a culturally Germanic nation. Stevenson notes that many observers of federalism "refuse to recognize as a federation any state that did not result from a union of previously separate entities which retained their identities after union" (1989: 11–12).

UNITS OF FEDERALISM

The national level of government in federal systems is sometimes called the central government, or the national government, or, as in Canada, the federal government. The subnational or regional governments go by a variety of names:

Canada	Provinces
Germany	Länder
Switzerland	Cantons
United States	States
Brazil	States
India	States
Australia	States

FIGURE 10.3

Two of the most powerful incentives for such separate entities to unite are economic reasons and fear of a common foreign enemy (or potential enemy). Both of these were behind the union of three British North American colonies into the federal Dominion of Canada: fear of annexation by the United States probably clinched the argument for union in many circles. There was a third factor in the Canadian case, which helped ensure that the new Dominion would be federal and not unitary, and this was the cultural and linguistic duality of the largest colony: Canada (which would become Ontario and Quebec). A French-Canadian majority and English-Canadian minority had been the result of uniting Upper and Lower Canada in 1841; by the 1860s the positions were reversed. Throughout this period, each section had equal representation, something the increasingly populous and predominantly English Canada West increasingly resented. Creating a federal system in the new Dominion and dividing the colony of Canada (once again) allowed its English- and French-speaking peoples to have secure majorities within the provinces of Ontario and Quebec, respectively. Giving provincial governments power over culturally sensitive matters such as education gave the French-Canadian minority a measure of security and autonomy within the larger English whole. As this illustrated, federalism can provide a means of safeguarding the interests of cultural or ethnic minorities without renouncing the benefits of inclusion within a larger union. Switzerland, with its three principal linguistic communities, is an even more striking example than Canada of a country that has employed federalism to safeguard cultural entities. Political and social tensions based on linguistic, economic, and cultural differences have also transformed Belgium from a unitary state to an extremely decentralized federal-like structure, and finally, in 1993, to a federal constitution.

It should be obvious by this point that federalism, if it entails the autonomy of both levels of government, will require a written constitution where this autonomy is articulated and entrenched. One of the key devices in a federal constitution is a division of powers between the two levels of government. Among the powers so divided will be the ability to make laws in certain fields (i.e., **JURISDICTIONS**), the power of administering laws, and the capacity to raise and spend money. This division is what is sometimes called the "federal bargain" between the two levels of government, and in a truly federal system, neither level of government can alter the federal bargain without the consent of the other level.

10.3 THE DIVISION OF POWERS

10.3.1 Legislative powers

Let us begin with the division of legislative powers, what Stevenson calls the "heart of any federal constitution" (1989: 30), perhaps so because the principle of the rule of law requires that important public policy have an ultimate basis in law. The term "division of powers" suggests that there is a fixed set of jurisdictions that we can simply apportion in some way (like a deck of cards, or Grandma's china dishes) between two parties. In fact it turns out that dividing powers between levels of government is more difficult than this, and it is problematic with respect to both the principle(s) on which the division is based, and the means used to accomplish it. Consider the principle first; one might assume it is simply a matter of assigning matters with a "national" dimension to the central government, and matters of a "regional" nature to the subnational governments. But what constitutes a "national" matter (remember that we are dealing with *subjects* of legislation, not particular cases)? Some matters, such as those connected to defence, foreign trade, treaties with foreign powers, currency, or the postal service, seem obviously national in character, and we would be surprised at not finding them assigned to the central government. Other subjects are not so clear cut: labour relations regulation, the environment, highway construction and maintenance, education—in each of these cases an argument could be made either way, and in the real world these are sometimes "national," sometimes "regional" responsibilities.

Matters are also complicated by the fact that the division of powers is a prime means of establishing which level of government will predominate—that is, how centralized or decentralized the system will be. When constitution-framers want a centralized constitution, they will try to give as many of the important powers, or certainly what they believe to be the most important powers, to the national government (as was attempted in Canada). By contrast, in Switzerland, which was originally (and is nominally still) a confederation, the cantons are in theory "sovereign" and legislate in most areas according to their internal constitutions. It often turns out that whether you see something as a "national" or "regional" matter depends on which level of government you happen to favour. As we will see shortly, federal systems also have a remarkable capacity to evolve from decentralized to centralized systems, and vice versa.

Assuming that one can establish a principle of dividing the powers between the two levels of government, the means of indicating this in the constitution are various. Put most simply, the headings of power (the subjects concerning which a government may make law, i.e., jurisdictions) must be enumerated in the constitution for one, or the other, or both levels of government. The simplest approach is to enumerate the powers of one level of government, and indicate that everything else belongs to its counterpart. By and large this is the approach of the American Constitution, which enumerates the powers of the national government, places certain prohibitions on both national and state governments, and indicates that all other powers "are reserved to the States, respectively, or to the people" (Tenth Amendment). The Tenth Amendment is an example of a **RESIDUAL CLAUSE**, i.e., one that indicates which level of government will receive powers not expressly allocated in the Constitution. This is an important device, since constitution-makers will not list every possible area of government activity, especially those yet to be invented. For example, both Canadian and American constitutions predate the invention of air travel, telecommunications, and nuclear power, each of which requires regulation by the state at some level. In the American case, then, the powers of the States are not enumerated, but residual, which on some interpretations at least implies State supremacy. On the other hand, in addition to its enumerated powers the government of the United States is given the power "to make all laws which shall be necessary and proper" for carrying out its enumerated powers (the so-called "elastic clause" of Section 8, Article I), something open to a very wide interpretation.

In Canada, we know that the Fathers of Confederation intended a highly centralized federal system, and rather than give the provinces residual power, the Constitution Act of 1867 enumerates 16 heads of provincial power, ending with "all Matters of a merely local or private Nature in the Province" (Section 92). Because of an accident of history, namely that Quebec had a different system of civil law from the rest of British North America, one of the provincial heads of power is "Property and Civil Rights in the Province" (92). Having enumerated the provincial heads of power, one might expect the constitution to simply assign all other powers, residually, to the federal government. The first part of Section 91 appears to do just this, stating that

> It shall be lawful for the Queen, by and with the Advice and Consent of the Senate and House of Commons [i.e. Parliament], to make Laws for the Peace, Order, and good Government of Canada, in relation to all Matters not coming within the Classes of Subjects by this Act assigned exclusively to the Provinces; (91)

Known as the "Peace, Order, and Good Government" clause (or POGG), this first part of Section 91 serves as the residual clause, but its intention has been clouded (or been left open to interpretation) by the addition of twenty-nine specific headings of power that are assigned exclusively to the government of Canada. It has been argued that these are not meant as illustrations of the POGG power, but specify jurisdictions of the federal government that might otherwise have been interpreted as falling under the provincial heading of "Property and Civil Rights"; but this will not explain all twenty-nine headings. Another view is that the Canadian constitution-makers were attempting an "exhaustive enumeration" of the powers of both levels of government, and intended POGG to cover anything omitted from the two lists of powers. At any rate, what Canadians were left with was a problematic residual clause; constitutional cases have often pitted the federal government's POGG against the provinces' "Property and Civil Rights" clause, and in some periods it was the latter that triumphed.

In Germany, the regional governments, the *Länder*, hold the residual power under Article 70 of the Basic Law, which means the power to legislate in areas not expressly granted to the federal government. In addition, and an element with no Canadian or American parallel, the *Länder* can also legislate in the expressly federal areas when and to the degree that the federal government has declined to do so (Article 72). On the other hand, three separate reasons that justify the federal government's taking over a legislative field from the *Länder* mean that the jurisdictions of the latter, while "exclusive," are hardly secure (see Meny, 1993: 201). The net result is a very large area of mutual jurisdiction, over which ultimately the federal government has final say. As we will see below, the balance between the German federal state and the *Länder* is more a function of the bicameral legislature than of the division of legislative powers.

The German example illustrates the possibility of **CONCURRENT** legislation, where both levels of government may occupy a field of jurisdiction. In Canada, for example, agriculture and immigration are areas the constitution expressly identifies as fields where both levels of government may legislate (95). If provincial and federal laws should conflict and the constitution specifies that the federal law will prevail, this is a statement of **PARAMOUNTCY**, one that addresses a matter *not* restricted to cases of concurrent jurisdiction. It might be that the levels of government, each legislating within its constitutionally defined jurisdictions, come into conflict—which law will prevail? In the United States, Article 6, clause 2 (the "supremacy clause"), states that "This Constitution, and the Laws of the United States ... shall be the supreme Law of the Land"; this is regarded as implying federal paramountcy. Section 109 of the Australian constitution explicitly states federal paramountcy, and the courts have adopted the same principle in Canada, although whether POGG provides justification of this is not fully clear (see Hogg, 1977: 102).

One point that deserves some attention is the tendency of federal constitutions to deviate from their original form, or from the balance originally intended. Canada, originally conceived as a very centralized federation, has become one of the world's most decentralized federal systems, while it is generally agreed that the United States has evolved in the opposite direction: from decentralized to centralized (or at least potentially so). There are several factors at work here. Obviously the character of a federal bargain can be altered deliberately through constitutional amendment, although this is made less likely by the requirement that such an amendment obtain the consent of both levels of government. In the United States, the Fourteenth, Sixteenth, and Seventeenth Amendments to the Constitution are seen to have limited states' rights.

Another powerful force in the Canadian and American systems has been judicial interpretation in response to constitutional challenges based on the division of powers. By declaring a subject to be within (*intra vires*) or beyond (*ultra vires*) the jurisdiction of one or the other level of government, Supreme Courts can transform the federal bargain, or indeed, halt its evolution. During the Depression of the 1930s in both Canada and the U.S., the Supreme Court ruled unconstitutional extensive social and economic legislation of the federal government on grounds that it encroached on the powers of the provinces and states, respectively. In fact, in both countries, there have been broad periods in which rulings from the Court have tended to favour the expansion of the relative power of one level of government or the other. It should also be noted that these cases were often the result of individuals challenging the jurisdictional constitutionality of a law, and not because one level of government was objecting to actions by the other.

Another important factor in the evolution of federalism has been social and economic change. As a result of new technologies or a changing economic structure or demographic transformation, powers that once seemed central or important to constitution-framers become less important, and matters once regarded as minor (or not yet foreseen) become of great importance. In Canada, for example, many areas were originally assigned to the provinces in the belief that they were not areas of national importance, nor did they require much government expenditure. Because of technological and social change, two such areas, health care and education, have become among the largest areas of government program spending. Similarly, roads and highways, which have ended up under provincial jurisdiction, would not have caused much consideration in the days before the invention and establishment of the automobile.

Finally, we should note that the balance of power between the levels of state within a federation will depend to a considerable degree on the use that governments make of the powers the constitution gives them, or of opportunities to expand or extend the boundaries of these powers. In the U.S., Franklin Roosevelt continued to push for expanded governmental powers despite rejection by the Supreme Court of his New Deal legislation, and after 1937 met with success. In Canada, decentralization occurred in part at least because strong provincial leaders were unwilling to have their governments play the "merely local" role that centralists such as John A. Macdonald had envisaged. As we have noted, the extent of the power of the German *Länder* is very much a function of the decision by the federal government to act in a field. Much of the twentieth century witnessed the tremendous expansion of government, and in most federal countries, this occurred at both levels of the state, national and subnational. The last decade or so has been marked by a retreat of government in the face of massive accumulated debts. In most cases this has meant a downsizing of government activity and spending, but not necessarily a change in *constitutional* powers. Nonetheless, in some cases, levels of government may look to offload responsibilities to their counterpart. This may be particularly relevant in cases, as we will see below, where the government's capacity to raise revenue does not match its spending responsibilities.

In short, a variety of factors combine to shape the ongoing evolution of the "federal bargain" within federal systems. The fact that this may lead to a deviation from the original settlement of powers upon the governments by the constitution does not make it wrong or right. It just happens, and what matters more than its fidelity to the intentions of "founding fathers" is its effect on the ability of the two levels of government to be responsive to the problems of their common citizenry.

10.3.2 Administrative powers

The Canadian and American constitutions appear to assume that it is normal for the level of government that makes laws in a particular field also to administer legislation in that jurisdiction. One explicit exception to this in the Canadian constitution is the field of justice; provinces have the power to make laws concerning "the administration of justice" (92.14) while "the criminal law" and "procedure in criminal matters" is a matter of federal jurisdiction (91.27). It is also possible for governments to delegate to one another the responsibility for administering legislation (which is technically known as "federal interdelegation"), but in the absence of such arrangements, and thus normally, the government that makes a law implements it.

Such is not the case in Germany, where Article 84 of the Basic Law establishes that the *Länder* will implement and administer laws passed by the federal government. Not only is executive responsibility for most (if not all) laws passed to the *Länder*, but also, according to Article 83 of the Basic Law, the *Länder* are empowered to execute federal laws "as matters of their own concern" (Meny, 1993: 209). This allows for considerable policy variance among the *Länder*, and *how* a program is delivered is very often as significant as any variable in determining its success. In this way, then, the legislative dominance of the German federal government is balanced by the administrative monopoly of the *Länder*. In 1989 *Länder* public servants outnumbered federal public servants in West Germany by a ratio of 5:1; in Canada, by comparison, the ratio of provincial to federal employees is almost 1:1.

10.3.3 Fiscal powers

As we all know very well, governments do more than make and enforce laws; they also (or as a result of legislation) spend money through programs, and collect taxes to fund their expenditures. The term "fiscal" directs our attention to the revenues and spending of governments. Just as the autonomy we associate with genuine federalism requires that each level of government be able to make laws in some areas without the consent of the other level of government, so, we might argue, federalism requires that each government have the authority to raise the revenues necessary to finance its expenditures. In the best of all possible worlds each government's revenue capacity (which is not the same as its revenue authority) will match its expenditure needs, but in the real world, for many reasons, this often is not the case. In some cases the constitution may allocate revenue sources (such as types of taxation) unequally between the levels of state, perhaps reflecting a judgement of unequal need. In Canada, because the federal government was seen to have most of the important responsibilities, it was given the ability to raise revenue by any system of taxation, while the provinces, with their more limited jurisdiction, were limited to direct taxes. As the balance shifted between the levels of government activity and responsibility, a gap developed in Canada as some of the most expensive responsibilities (health,

EQUALIZATION PAYMENTS

Equalization payments have existed in Canada since 1957 as a result of tax agreements negotiated between the federal and provincial governments, and are renegotiated every five years. In 1982, the principle of equalization was enshrined in the constitution, although not the formula on which it is calculated, perhaps because this has changed many times over the years.

Currently, provinces qualify for equalization payments (or not) if their revenue capacity falls below a benchmark obtained by averaging the revenue capacity for five provinces (British Columbia, Saskatchewan, Manitoba, Ontario, and Quebec) and summing for all provincial revenue sources (there are over 30 of these). In this calculation Alberta is excluded because of the volatile nature of its petroleum-based natural resource revenue, and the four poorest provinces are also omitted from the calculation. Typically, all provinces except Alberta, British Columbia, and Ontario end up qualifying for equalization payments, which are projected to total over $10 billion in fiscal 2000-01.

One myth that has developed around equalization is that this is a transfer from rich to poor provinces. This overlooks the fact that equalization payments are transfers from the federal government which raises its revenues in all ten provinces by various means. For example, some of the funds that the federal government raises through the GST, income tax, and customs duties (to name just three sources) in the province of Quebec, may well return to that province in the form of equalization payments.

The principle behind equalization payments is that of 'horizontal equity', which means that Canadians should be able to receive comparable levels of government services at comparable levels of taxation wherever they live.

FIGURE 10.4

education, social welfare) fell to the fiscally weaker level of government: the provinces. Even in cases where there is no constitutional distinction between the taxing powers of levels of state, there are some taxes that are associated with particular jurisdictions, or that for economic or political reasons are more easily collected at the national level. More often than not, for constitutional reasons or otherwise, central governments end up being better positioned fiscally than their regional counterparts—something we might call the **FISCAL IMBALANCE** of federalism. This has at least two significant consequences.

On the one hand it means that state or provincial governments are underfunded in relation to their responsibilities, and therefore look to federal governments to provide extra funding, or to take over some of the responsibilities. Conversely, federal governments can use their spending power to gain influence in areas of jurisdiction that otherwise are constitutionally barred to them. While national governments in all truly federal systems are prohibited from making laws in (at least some) regional government jurisdictions, there are usually no limits on the ability of federal governments to spend money in any area whatsoever. The Canadian government cannot legislate in the fields of education or health care, but it has been spending money in these areas for decades. National governments spend in provincial areas of responsibility by transferring money to the provincial governments, but rarely do so without attaching some conditions or requirements to its expenditure. In this way national governments gain "leverage" in policy fields otherwise denied them by the division of powers. Provincial or regional governments quite naturally resent federal intrusions into their policy areas, but their fiscal vulnerability leaves them little choice but to accept the conditions and receive the offered money. In 1980 the United States government funded 23 per cent of the expenditures of local and state governments (Janda, Berry, and Goldman, 1989: 121); Hague et al. report that 60 per cent of the Australian states' revenue comes from the federal government (1993: 273). In Canada in 1996, about 16 per cent of provincial revenues ($26.5 billion) came in the form of grants from the government of Canada (*Finances of the Nation 1997*, 8:3 and B:5).

The means by which fiscal **TRANSFERS** are made from one level to another are various. One useful distinction is between general purpose and specific purpose transfers, the former being transfers to the general revenue of the recipient government, the latter (called "grants-in-aid" in the U.S.) being monies targeted for specific programs or program areas. The most significant general purpose transfer in Canada is **EQUALIZATION** payments, which are designed to compensate provincial shortfalls in revenue capacity. A significant source of provincial monies, for example, is natural resource revenue, but while some provinces are very wealthy in terms of minerals and timber, others are not. Similarly, corporate income tax has great revenue potential in some provinces but not others. Equalization payments address these questions of regional economic disparity through transfers from the federal government to provinces whose revenue capacity falls below a national benchmark (see Figure 10.4).

In both Canada and the United States, the bulk of transfers from the federal government come in the form of specific purpose transfers, which normally (but not always) go to the individual provinces or states on an equal per capita basis. Here, too, it is useful to distinguish between **CONDITIONAL** grants and **BLOCK** grants, the former being funds to be spent in a particular area meeting a more or less stringent set of federally set conditions, the latter being monies intended for expenditure in particular policy areas, but over which the provinces exercise complete control. As noted, conditional grants are a means by which the federal government gains policy leverage in a field in which it has no constitutional legislative competence. The Canada Health Act, for example, penalizes provinces that allow doctors to bill patients in addition to the fees negotiated under provincial health insurance plans, or that allow parallel fee-for-service private clinics. Certain conditions also attach to the provincial expenditure of funds intended for social welfare. The justifications offered for these federal intrusions into provincial jurisdiction are twofold: on the one hand, the federal government cannot simply be expected to transfer funds to the provinces and receive nothing in return; some policy leverage is a reasonable exchange. Secondly, and perhaps more plausibly, the enforcement of national standards ensures that Canadians will enjoy comparable services or public goods wherever they happen to live. Another type of conditional grant is the **MATCHING GRANT** (or cost-sharing), where the federal government transfers funds to the provinces in an amount determined by the provincial governments' expenditures. The more provinces spend, the more they receive from the federal government. Many of the federal government's transfers for social welfare under the Canada Assistance Plan (CAP), for example, were matching grants. Such transfers represent a federal intrusion into provincial budgeting decisions, and while it is possible to argue that provinces need not accept such federal funds, political realities make such refusals unlikely. To be able to decline federal funds a province must have sufficient revenue sources of its own (which could well be going to other purposes) or be willing to explain to its citizens why it is not providing the service or program that other provinces are delivering.

In the Canadian experience of fiscal federalism, provinces have resented the intrusions of the federal government into their jurisdictions and the distortions placed upon their budgeting by conditional grants. Understandably, the provinces would like to receive the money without any strings attached, and have long lobbied for just that. On the other hand, the less control the federal government has over what is being done with its dollars, the less incentive there is for it to spend them. After all, a built-in disadvantage of spending through transfers is that the political credit tends to go to the government that is seen to deliver the service, not the one footing the bill. Over time, then, there has been a pattern of erosion; provinces have worked away at cutting the strings attached to the transfer of monies from the federal government with a fair measure of success. In return, though, the ending of conditions has often weakened the federal government's commitment to continuing to transfer funds. As the federal government has come under increasing pressure to deal with its deficit, transfers to the provinces become an attractive target for cost-cutting, particularly when the federal government gets less and less in return for these transfers, either in terms of political credit or policy leverage (coincidentally, in the early 1990s, the size of the federal deficit was almost the same as the combined federal transfers to the provinces).

In Canada, in 1977, arrangements known as Established Program Financing (EPF) replaced federal cost-sharing of provincial expenditures in areas of health and post-secondary education. EPF was block funding, and for the funding government (i.e., the federal), the switch from conditional to block funding was an exchange: a surrender of control over program delivery for firm control over the level of transfers. Under cost-sharing arrangements, where the federal government matches provincial expenditures, it is the provincial government's activity that determines the size of the transfer. Block funding is attractive to the federal government because it puts the size of transfers back in federal hands, and it is attractive to the provincial governments because there are no longer strings attached to the money (exceptional legislation like the Canada Health Act aside). In the past twenty years, the two largest federal transfers to the provinces have been EPF, and the Canada Assistance Plan (CAP), a set of shared-cost programs in social welfare fields. The size of CAP was driven by provincial expenditures, and in the early 1990s the Mulroney government put a ceiling on federal increases in CAP payments to the three wealthiest provinces (Alberta, British Columbia, and Ontario). As of April 1, 1996, CAP and EPF were both rolled into one transfer, the Canada Health and Social Transfer (CHST), which delivers virtually all of the federal government's social spending transfers to the provinces via block funding. Initially the federal government decreased transfers to the provinces under CHST, a move that is one of the drawbacks of block funding, and something particularly worrisome to the poorer provinces that are much more dependent on transfers from the federal government. This ultimately is the provinces' greatest concern about fiscal federalism; in no position to decline federal monies, the provinces become dependent on these transfers in order to deliver programs, and then are stuck trying to fund such programs after the federal government reduces or eliminates its funding for them. More recently, as the federal balance sheet has improved, transfers to the provinces have increased, but not to a level with which they are satisfied.

The difficult and complex issues of fiscal federalism have been the central arena for intergovernmental relations (the interactions between the two levels of government) in Canada in the postwar period. The other topic that brings federal and provincial politicians together regularly is the constitution and questions of national unity. Not surprisingly, many provincial politicians have tried to place the issue of the federal government's spending power on the constitutional agenda.

**10.4
BICAMERALISM IN
FEDERAL STATES**

Discussion of the division of powers directs our attention to federalism as a relationship between governments, federal and regional. Yet, as we have seen, an underlying rationale for having two levels of government may well be to represent different populations or cultures traditionally identified with the territorial sub-units. Representing the people in two different dimensions, national and subnational, can be accomplished, then, by having two levels of government, one corresponding to each dimension of society. It is also possible to represent the two dimensions of society *within the national government*; this is the function of a bicameral legislature and, more specifically, of the second chamber of a bicameral legislature in federal systems. In other words, in a federal polity, the second (or "upper") chamber of the legislature represents in some way the people or governments of the sub-national or regional states. (This is what Lijphart calls "incongruence"; the two chambers of the legislature are constituted on distinct bases, i.e., represent wholly different constituencies.)

In most bicameral democracies, the lower chamber, the one to which the government is responsible, is elected on the principle of **REPRESENTATION BY POPULATION**, sometimes articulated as 'one person, one vote'. If consistently adhered to, this principle will give the people of the country equal representation in the legislative chamber: each citizen's vote will carry the same weight. This also means that more populous regions or federal units will have a greater number of representatives than less populous areas. Thus in Canada, Ontario currently sends 103 MPs to the House of Commons, and Prince Edward Island sends four. In the United States, after the 1980 census, California had 45 representatives in the House of Representatives, while six states had just one. In federal countries, the second chamber usually serves to represent the regional or sub-national units in a more equal fashion.

The simplest way to do this is to give an equal number of seats to each unit. In the United States, each state elects two Senators, regardless of state population. In Germany, by contrast, each *Land* is represented in the *Bundesrat* by three, four, or five votes, depending on its population, and the votes in the *Bundesrat* are controlled by the *Land* governments, which means that this chamber is in fact a federal council representing the governments of the *Länder*, rather than a legislative chamber representing constituencies. Within federal democracies, the Canadian Senate is something of an anomaly. First of all, the Canadian Senate is a patronage chamber: the senators are chosen by the Prime Minister and tend to be party members rewarded for loyal service (they serve until age 75). Second, the Canadian Senate represents regions rather than provinces: prior to the incorporation of Newfoundland as the tenth province (with six Senate seats) in 1949, there were four regions with 24 senators each (Atlantic Canada, Quebec, Ontario, and the West), plus one for each of the Territories. This creates a very unequal representation in provincial terms, which satisfies almost no one (see Figure 10.5).

As important as the basis of representation in second chambers, and often related to it, is the power of the second chamber relative to the first or "lower" house. In parliamentary systems, normally the second chamber cannot bring down the government; the first chamber is the *confidence chamber*. For this reason, there is often a requirement that bills (i.e., legislative proposals) involving the expenditure of money be introduced in the first chamber, although this is also required in the U.S. Congress, which has no rules of confidence. The key issue here is whether or not the second chamber has the ability to veto or block legislation coming from the lower house. There is a strong argument to be made that second chambers that represent the regional states must have some such ability if they are to represent their constituencies effectively in the national government. This is what Lijphart calls "symmetry" between the chambers of the legislature; the combination of incongruence and symmetry creates what he calls "strong bicameralism." In other words, under such conditions, the two houses of the legislature have a relatively equal weight in the legislative process, or conversely, the upper house does not simply give formal approval to what emerges from the lower chamber. Of the five federal systems included in his study of 21 democracies, Lijphart concludes that four (Australia, Germany, Switzerland, and the United States) qualify as strongly bicameral; the one that does not is Canada (1984: 99).

It is important to remember, though, that the ability of the upper chamber to defeat or block legislation from the lower chamber must be matched by a willingness to do so. If party discipline is weak, then such a possibility is more or less continuous.

THE CANADIAN SENATE

A. In 1867, the original Canadian Senate represented three regions equally:

Nova Scotia	12 seats		
New Brunswick	12 seats		

Atlantic Canada	24 seats	**Quebec** 24 seats	**Ontario** 24 seats

TOTAL: 72 seats

B. The addition of Prince Edward Island required adjustment of the Atlantic bloc:

Nova Scotia	10 seats
New Brunswick	10 seats
P.E.I.	4 seats

Atlantic Canada	24 seats	**Quebec** 24 seats	**Ontario** 24 seats

TOTAL: 72 seats

C. The eventual addition of four Western provinces added to the regional symmetry but increased the provincial inequality:

		B.C.	6 seats
Nova Scotia	10 seats	Alberta	6 seats
New Brunswick	10 seats	Saskatchewan	6 seats
P.E.I.	4 seats	Manitoba	6 seats

Atlantic Canada	24 seats	**Quebec** 24 seats	**Ontario** 24 seats	**The West**	24 seats

TOTAL: 96 seats

D. Finally, the three Territories and Newfoundland round out the picture of a patchwork of representation for the subnational governments:

Newfoundland	6 seats	B.C.	6 seats
Nova Scotia	10 seats	Alberta	6 seats
New Brunswick	10 seats	Saskatchewan	6 seats
P.E.I.	4 seats	Manitoba	6 seats

Atlantic Canada	30 seats	**Quebec** 24 seats	**Ontario** 24 seats	**The West**	24 seats

Territories	Yukon	1 seat	
	Northwest Territories	1 seat	
	Nunavut	1 seat	**TOTAL:** 105 seats

FIGURE 10.5

The United States Congress provides perhaps the clearest example of two legislative chambers with more or less equal weight in the legislative process, so much so that most bills move through the two houses simultaneously, rather than sequentially, as is the parliamentary norm. A bill may survive either or neither chamber, but then again, bills in this system are not "government" bills and their fate has no bearing on the term of the political executive. In parliamentary systems, where the requirements of responsible government have produced strong parties, the conditions of strong bicameralism will tend to come into play only if the party or parties that control the government are in a minority in the upper chamber. In such a case, "the opposition" controls the second chamber.

In contrast to American bicameralism, in parliamentary Australia most legislation is government legislation, and any defeat presents implications (if not indications) of non-confidence. In 1975, the opposition controlled the Australian Senate and refused passage to the Labour government's appropriations bills (which authorize government expenditures) when they were received from the lower chamber. In the view of the opposition, this constituted a vote of non-confidence in the government, whose resignation it demanded. The Prime Minister and his party argued that parliamentary government requires the confidence of the lower chamber only, a position which is true by convention in some democracies, and constitutionally established in others. On the other hand, a government that cannot get parliamentary authorization for its expenditures is a government that cannot govern. In a move that remains controversial, the Governor-General dismissed the Labour government and ordered new elections for both houses of the Australian parliament, elections won by the opposition Liberal–Country coalition. Significantly, it is the "incongruence" of the two chambers in a federal system that leads to the possibility that the majority in either chamber could be controlled by a different party or group of parties, something made more likely when elections for the chambers take place at different times.

Part of the difficulty in the Australian case was the lack of clarity concerning the significance of a defeat in the second chamber for the survival of the government. Such a problem does not exist in Germany. Constitutionally, only the lower or first chamber (the *Bundestag*) can defeat the government, so any defeat of legislation by the second chamber (the *Bundesrat*) is simply that. In addition, the veto exercised by the *Bundesrat* is qualified: it is an absolute veto only on matters that touch on the interests of the *Länder*. On all other matters, the lower house may override the veto of the upper chamber with a second vote of its own. This means that on non-*Länder* issues, the veto of the second house is a very limited **SUSPENSIVE VETO**. Such a device gives a measure of power, but not the ultimate ability to thwart the government. This is particularly attractive where the second chamber lacks the

A FEUDAL CHAMBER

Prior to reform at the end of 1999, the composition of the British House of Lords was as follows:

Hereditary Peers	759
Life Peers (appointed)	485
Law Lords	28
Archbishops and Bishops	26
Total	1,298

Of the total 1,298 Lords, 103 were women (16 hereditary, 87 life). Of the hereditary peers, 298 were declared Conservative supporters and 17 Labour supporters. Among the life peers, the declared Conservatives outnumbered the Labourites 173 to 153.

FIGURE 10.6

democratic legitimacy of the first or popularly elected chamber. In (non-federal) Britain, for example, the House of Lords is a remnant of the days of feudal aristocracy, being composed of a mixture of hereditary and life (appointed) peers. Such a representation of class and privilege is difficult to reconcile with the norms of democracy and egalitarianism that have been proclaimed (if not fully realized) in the twentieth century and, not surprisingly, is unique to Britain. At any rate, since 1911, the House of Lords has had only a suspensive veto over legislation, and in 1949 the length of that suspensive period was reduced from two years to one.

Traditionally in favour of the abolition of the second chamber, the Labour Party moderated its stance in the early 1990s to one of seriously reforming the House. Since 1996, Labour leader Tony Blair has advocated a two-stage process, beginning with the removal of hereditary peers. In 1999, the government introduced the House of Lords Bill, which would have removed all seats for hereditary peers. In order to speed passage of the bill in the face of opposition from the Conservative-dominated life peers, the government agreed to a compromise by which 92 seats for hereditary peers would remain, at least until the second stage of reform of the chamber is decided upon. The second stage of reform is to be informed by a royal commission that will hold hearings and gather opinion on what further steps should be taken to modernize the House of Lords and make it more democratic. It may very well be that the reform of the House of Lords will be influenced by the other major constitutional project of the Blair government: devolution of power to Scotland and Wales (discussed below).

Canada's upper chamber represents an unsatisfactory compromise between the British second chamber, which protects privilege and the status quo against democracy and change (the conservative function), and the American Senate, which represents the regional units of state (the federal function). It has been pointed out that Canada's Senate was designed as a chamber of "sober second thought" in order to protect the interests of property against possible incursions by the policies of a popularly elected (and therefore intemperate) lower house. For that reason, Canadian senators were, and remain, appointed by the Governor-General on the advice of the Prime Minister. Such an appointed body offends the principles of democracy, but it also fails to perform the federal function of a second chamber adequately, because the Prime Minister's appointees can hardly be said to represent either the provincial populations or the provincial governments.

In short, because of changing values, the Canadian Senate cannot be said to enjoy much legitimacy in either the Canadian state or the Canadian public, and it is for this reason that Canada has weak bicameralism. Legally, according to the written constitution, the Senate's powers are almost equivalent to those of the House of Commons. Money bills must originate in the House, and since 1982 the Senate's veto over constitutional motions is limited to a six-month suspensive veto; in all other respects the Senate has full legal power, and any veto it exercises over legislation from the House of Commons is real. Once again, though, we confront the difference between the written and the material constitution: while the Senate has considerable legal powers, its diminished legitimacy in a democratic age means that it is less willing to veto to thwart the people's elected representatives. One notable exception, which only proves the point, was the willingness of the Senate to oppose the Conservative government's Goods and Services Tax (GST) in 1990, the Liberal senators arguing that *they* were upholding the democracy by opposing what was a clearly very unpopular measure. Prime Minister Mulroney used a provision of the constitution to appoint eight extra senators and give his party a majority in the second chamber to ensure the tax bill's passage. Although this provoked considerable uproar, the constitutional provision had been designed for just such a situation, although it had never been used before. It should perhaps also be noted that, given Canada's propensity to periods of one-party dominance (the tendency for one party to win a disproportionate share of elections over time), prime ministers have usually been able to ensure that their party also controls a majority in the Senate.

One consequence of the lack of perceived legitimacy of the Senate is that Canada has not faced a crisis such as the Australian situation of 1975. The rare instances when the Senate defeats legislation coming from the House of Commons are not seen to have implications of confidence, and the Senate has avoided defeating any legislation that might be seen to have such an import. A more subtle tactic is for the Senate to amend legislation and send it back to the House of Commons. If such legislation comes back a second time in its original form, the senators are likely to give it reluctant passage. Not surprisingly, there has been no shortage of calls to reform the Canadian Senate, and most focus on improving its capability of representing the provinces (i.e., their peoples, or their governments). It is difficult to argue with the proposition that if the Senate cannot perform the function of representing the provinces adequately, it has no reason for existing.

10.5 CONSTITUTIONAL AMENDING FORMULAS

Given the autonomy of each level of government from its counterpart, constitutional change takes on added significance in federal systems. More specifically, in a federal system we would expect that any constitutional amendment affecting both levels of government, national and regional, would require the consent of both levels of government, or of a majority of the people polled directly. In addition, where consent of both levels of government is required, the degree of regional government consent needs to be specified. Hence, in federal countries, the importance of the constitutional **AMENDING FORMULA**, which outlines the nature of the consent necessary to alter the constitution, and under what conditions.

Amending formulas may be simple or complex, and they may be rigid or flexible, and there is no necessary link between these two dimensions. The American amendment process is fairly simple, but turns out in practice to be rigid; over 10,000 amendments have been proposed since 1787, but only 26 have passed (10 of which constituted the Bill of Rights, and were passed in 1789). A constitutional amendment can be proposed at the federal level or at the state level. In the former case a proposal must receive a two-thirds vote in both houses of Congress to proceed. Alternatively, a proposal may be made by a national convention called for that purpose if requested by two-thirds (34) of the 50 states. In fact, this latter method of proposal has never been used. Once proposed, an amendment must be **RATIFIED**, which requires approval by three-quarters of the states, approval either by the state legislatures or by constitutional conventions held in the states. It is up to Congress to choose the method of ratification, and ratification by conventions was used only once (to end Prohibition). It should perhaps also be noted that at each stage, by either means, the margin of approval is much greater than a simple majority (50 per cent plus one); this is common to constitutional votes and reflects the belief that the basic rules should not be constantly changing.

By contrast, the Basic Law of Germany has a simple and flexible amending procedure: a vote of two-thirds of the members of both houses of the federal legislature. In this case, the provision that the members of the *Bundesrat* are delegates of the *Länder*

CHANGING THE CONSTITUTION: CANADA

The procedure for amending the Canadian constitution is contained in Part V of the Constitution Act, 1982. There are in fact several procedures that may apply as the circumstances dictate, and these may be summarized as follows:

Amendment begins with a resolution passed by the House of Commons, the Senate, or a provincial legislative assembly.

The **GENERAL AMENDING PROCEDURE** (Section 38) requires the consent of Parliament and the legislatures of two-thirds of the provinces, these provinces containing at least 50 per cent of the national population at the last census. This is known as the "7/50" rule, seven provinces being two-thirds of the total.

In five areas (such as the office of the Queen, or the composition of the Supreme Court), amendment requires **UNANIMOUS** approval of Parliament and the ten provincial legislatures.

In six areas (such as the powers of the Senate, or the creation of a new province) amendment must take place under the general procedure (s. 38). In other matters, amendment that affects all the provinces must take place by the general amending procedure, or, if the amendment affects some but not all provinces, it requires the consent of Parliament and those provinces affected.

Parliament may amend the constitution with respect to the executive government of Canada or to the Senate and House of Commons (44), and provincial legislatures may amend their own constitutions (45).

Amendments made under the general procedure must receive the required minimum consent within three years of the passage of the resolution initiating the amendment procedure. If the minimum consent is obtained, the amendment does not take effect until at least one year after the passage of the resolution initiating the amendment, except when all eleven governments have passed the resolution.

Amendments made under the general procedure that diminish the legislative power of a province do not apply to any province that has not given its consent.

If after 180 days of passage of a resolution by the House of Commons the Senate has not also approved, the amendment may be made without Senate consent by a second passage in the House of Commons.

FIGURE 10.7

governments makes such a simple procedure capable of securing the consent of both levels of state. As a result it has been possible for the German constitution, although less than 50 years old, to be amended with great frequency. Interestingly, though, parts of the German constitution cannot be amended, including the existence of a federal system, and some fundamental individual rights.

Australia and Switzerland, each in their own way, provide examples of federal systems where the people have a direct role in the constitutional amendment process. In Australia, the normal procedure is for a proposal receiving a majority in both Houses of Parliament to be submitted to the people for ratification through a referendum. In cases where a proposal passes one House but not the other, it may, if passed a second time by the original chamber, be submitted by the Governor-General to the public in a referendum. To succeed, a proposal must receive a majority of all votes cast in the country, as well as a majority of the votes cast in a majority of the states (i.e., a "double majority"). In Switzerland, the procedures by which a proposal may be put to the chambers of parliament and/or to the people are much more complicated, in part because of the possibility that a full or partial revision of the constitution may be requested by a portion of the public (see also Chapter 14). At the end of the day, though, constitutional change requires popular ratification, and as in Australia, it must receive a double majority: a national majority, and a majority in a majority of the cantons. Most recently, in the 1999 referendum asking Australians whether they wished to replace the Queen as head of state with a republican constitution, the measure was defeated nationally by a margin of 55 per cent to 45 per cent, and in five of the six Australian states.

Once again, on this matter as in others, Canada represents a rather unique experience. For 115 years, amendment of much of the Canadian constitution—and certainly anything touching upon a dimension of federalism—could be done only by the Parliament of Great Britain. Canada's original written constitution, the British North America Act of 1867, was an act of the British Parliament, and as such could be changed only by that legislature. In time, the convention developed that the British government would change the Canadian constitution only at the request of Canadian governments, and there were numerous occasions (including any time after the Statute of Westminster in 1931) when the British government would have gladly turned the Canadian constitution over to Canadian governments. The stumbling block remained the inability of the Canadian federal government and provincial governments to agree on an amending formula, and this despite several serious attempts in the postwar period to find an acceptable solution. The history of these attempts and the reasons why success was finally achieved in 1982 are beyond our scope here, but the complexity of the amending formula in its different categories and classes of amendment indicates something of the difficulties that were involved (see Figure 10.7).

As in the United States and Germany, and unlike Switzerland and Australia, constitutional amendment in Canada is a matter for governments, not the direct decision of the people. In some cases governments can act alone. In other cases, the national government and one or more provinces may act together in ways that affect only themselves. To date, these are the only kinds of amendment that have succeeded under the amending formula, but one could argue that it is premature to judge the rigidity or flexibility of the general amending formula (the so-called "7/50" rule) or the unanimity provisions. For example, both Quebec and Newfoundland have sought and received the support of the federal government for amendments to the constitution that allowed them to replace their denominational school boards. On the other hand, two significant and relatively comprehensive attempts at constitutional change in Canada have failed: the Meech Lake Accord of 1987, which expired in 1990, and the Charlottetown Accord, which was defeated in a (non-binding) national plebescite in 1992. The latter was the first case of a national vote on a constitutional question, and though it was non-binding on the federal government and most provinces, it may have created an expectation that the public should be consulted on any future significant constitutional reforms.

One of the little ironies of constitutional politics is that a faulty or unpopular amending formula can be changed only by using that very formula. It is also generally easier to make a flexible formula more rigid than a rigid formula more flexible. If the Meech Lake Accord had succeeded, Canada's amending formula would have been made even more rigid by increasing the number of classes of subjects requiring unanimous approval by the federal Parliament and all 10 provincial legislatures—in effect giving each province a veto over these types of constitutional change. The Charlottetown Accord did not address the amending formula.

In the preceding sections we have employed a fairly orthodox definition of federalism, which insists that the two levels of government—national and regional—must be autonomous of each other, and we have indicated several ways in which this autonomy can be achieved. In this section we want to consider several situations that do not satisfy the strict definition of federalism, but that have a similar effect or may accomplish the same purposes as federalism.

Over the years many observers have argued that Canada is not a truly federal state, but is at best "quasi-federal." This judgement stems from several features of the Constitution (or British North America) Act of 1867. As we have indicated, the intention of the constitution-framers was a strong central government overseeing provincial administrations that would serve to address largely "local" matters. To this end, the federal government was given several means of vetoing or interfering with provincial government legislation, what might be called collectively the *federal means of subordination* within the Canadian constitution.

10.6 QUASI-FEDERALISM, HOME RULE, AND DECENTRALIZATION IN A UNITARY STATE

For example, each province has a Lieutenant-Governor, the provincial counterpart of the Governor-General, but the Lieutenant-Governor is appointed by and remains an agent of the federal government. Among the powers of the Lieutenant-Governor is the ability to refuse to give assent to provincial legislation, and to reserve the bill for consideration by the federal government. This power of **RESERVATION**, has been exercised only four times since 1920, and not since 1961. As early as 1882, Prime Minister Macdonald issued a minute-in-council stating that apart from "a case of extreme necessity," reservation should only be made upon instructions from the federal government. Moreover, the federal government has the power of **DISALLOWANCE**, which is essentially a veto of provincial legislation (within a year of its passage), which may or may not follow its reservation by the Lieutenant-Governor. No provincial legislation has been disallowed since 1943 (see also Reesor, 1992: 203).

With reservation and disallowance we confront again the difference between the material and the written constitution. Legally, disallowance and reservation remain a possibility, although constitutional observers usually note that they have "fallen into disuse," and state that it is inconceivable for them ever to be employed again. One very good reason for this is the political rebuke that such an action constitutes to the electorate of the province concerned. Nonetheless, the possibility of a sovereigntist government in Quebec attempting to legislate a secession from Canada within the current constitutional framework might provide a conceivable context for using reservation and disallowance, even though such an exercise would in all likelihood be merely symbolic. At the moment, and perhaps for all time, the federal means of subordination in the Canadian constitution remain dormant.

Another issue raised by the Canadian experience of federalism is the possibility of **ASYMMETRICAL FEDERALISM**, where symmetry has to do not with the relationship of the two houses of a bicameral parliament (as in Lijphart), but with the relationship between the federal government and the provinces. Most federal systems are characterized (at least constitutionally) by a symmetrical relationship between the national state and the regional states. That is to say, the powers or privileges that one province has are the same as the powers or privileges of any other province. As noted, in Canada the heading "property and civil right" is a provincial head of power because of the unique civil law in Quebec, and the constitutional treatment of education has much to do with Quebec's unique cultural situation. In theory, the constitution-framers could have given powers over property and civil rights, and education, to Quebec but not to the other provinces. This would have been an asymmetrical federal bargain, and contrary to usual federal practice. In recent times, though, the question of an asymmetrical federalism has arisen in Canada in terms of possible "special status" for Quebec. The argument here is that because of Quebec's uniqueness within Canada, there is a justifiable basis for extending powers or recognition to Quebec and not to the other provinces. Understandably, this is not a big seller with the other provinces, but on at least two occasions, all provincial premiers have agreed to constitutional proposals that would have recognized Quebec as a "distinct society." This agreement may have been forthcoming because a distinct society clause does not give Quebec any new constitutional powers, but invites the courts to consider certain factors of the Quebec identity (e.g., its unique language, culture, and civil law) as relevant to judgements concerning constitutional cases that affect Quebec. Of course asymmetrical federalism generally, and special status for Quebec specifically, run counter to the norm of "provincial equality" that has come to prominence in recent decades. It is also possible though, to achieve the same ends as special status by extra-constitutional means. The federal government can negotiate (and on many occasions has negotiated) agreements with one or more provinces that are unique to it (or them). The Quebec Pension Plan, negotiated in 1964 when the federal government established the Canada Pension Plan (in which all other provinces participate), is a case in point. When the Meech Lake Accord failed to receive approvals necessary for ratification, there were suggestions that the federal government could negotiate the same terms on a bilateral basis with Quebec. The problem with such **ADMINISTRATIVE SPECIAL STATUS** is that there is no guarantee that all future governments will be equally disposed to continue the relationship. Nonetheless, the point is that important dimensions of federalism can be accomplished by extra-constitutional means, in particular through administrative agreements between political executives.

HOME RULE is another concept closely related to federalism, and exists when a territory or region within a unitary state achieves autonomy or special status. In other words, a particular government exists in this region, but not others. The obvious basis for such an asymmetry is clearly cultural, focusing on a minority language, ethnicity, or religion. The Finnish island of Åland, which has a large Swedish-speaking population, has extensive autonomy or home rule, including a parliament with powers over health policy, education, and environmental policy (Lane and Ersson, 1991: 219). Similarly, in Denmark, the Faroe Islands and Greenland both have their own legislature and executive.

In Britain, the Labour government that came to power in 1997 was committed to devolving power to the regions: Scotland, Wales, and depending on the progress of peace initiatives, Northern Ireland. After publishing White Papers on its proposals for each region, the government held a referendum in September 1997 in each region on proceeding with the devolution proposals. Legislation was then introduced and passed creating a Scottish Parliament and a Welsh Assembly outlining the devolution of powers to each body. The Scottish Parliament has powers over a wide range of policy issues from health, education, and economic development to criminal and civil justice. Its revenue capacity consists of a limited ability to vary the rate of income tax from that set by Westminster. The Welsh Assembly by contrast, has no taxation powers and very limited legal authority (essentially assuming the powers previously exercised by the Welsh Office at Westminster). In May 1999, the first elections were held for the new regional legislatures, the Labour Party finishing first in each case but failing to gain a majority in the proportional electoral systems employed (see Chapter 13). The first government formed in the Scottish Parliament was a coalition between Labour and the Liberal Democrats. In December 1999, after progress in the peace talks between the major players in Northern Ireland, London once again devolved powers to the provincial parliament at Belfast. This restored home rule to the province, which had lost this autonomy in 1972, when the British government imposed direct rule in response to escalating violence. The first government in Northern Ireland in 27 years was composed of a coalition of four parties, two Protestant and two Catholic, which between them controlled 90 of the Northern Ireland Assembly's 108 seats. Although it is too early to tell where devolution will eventually lead the British state, in some respects it has the potential to be the most radical transformation of that country's political system since the Glorious Revolution of 1688.

Finally, we should note the trend within even centralized unitary states for a decentralization of power. In some cases this is the result of ideology, but there is a strongly pragmatic basis to decentralization: as the size and extent of the state have grown, it has become more difficult or inefficient to try to govern from one centre. Decentralization often entails establishing administrative districts and corresponding offices for the purposes of administering the programs and enforcing the laws made by the national government. In this sense the state is decentralized but not the government as there are no regional legislatures or separate structures of representation. Decentralization of the administrative or bureaucratic apparatus can also provide a basis, though, for the development of **AUTONOMY** in other ways. Spain, constitutionally a unitary state, has for many years endured nationalist or separatist pressures from various ethnic divisions, and in some regions (most notably the Basque) there has been terrorism and violence. The response of the Spanish government has been to create a system of regional governments, and in areas where unrest has been greatest, to negotiate considerable autonomy for the regional governments. Spain now has a system of 17 autonomous regional governments, each with its own executive and legislature, but the powers enjoyed by each depends on agreements negotiated with the Spanish state. Four of the most nationalist regions—Catalonia, the Basque Country, Galicia, and Andalusia —have achieved a considerable degree of autonomy. Thus, although Spain is not strictly speaking a federal system, it contains considerable degrees of asymmetrical regional autonomy, attaining in some cases what might be considered home rule. In the Scandinavian countries, decentralization has been achieved not by creating regional governments, but by delegating to and increasing the autonomy of local governments.

What all of the examples in this section demonstrate is that while the number of countries that qualify as federal may be few when the definitions are strictly applied, there are any number of ways in which political systems may incorporate elements of federalism, or apply federal solutions to their problems, without actually adopting federalism. It is our hunch, moreover, that formally or informally, federalism is something of which the world's citizens are going to see more, rather than less, in the coming decades.

In the second half of the twentieth century, the emergence and development of the European Community/Union has presented the possibility that federalism cannot only arise within a nation (e.g., Belgium), or through the union of political units into a nation-state (e.g., Canada, the U.S.), but also serve as a system for governing associated sovereign nation-states. What began as a

**10.7
SUPRANATIONAL
FEDERALISM**

KEY TERMS

amending formula
asymmetrical federalism
autonomy
bicameralism
block grants
confederation
concurrency
conditional grants
congruence
decentralization
delegation
devolution
disallowance
division of powers
equalization
federalism
fiscal imbalance
home rule
jurisdiction
matching grant
paramountcy
quasi-federal
ratification
representation by population
reservation
residual clause
special status
suspensive veto
symmetry
transfers
unitary state

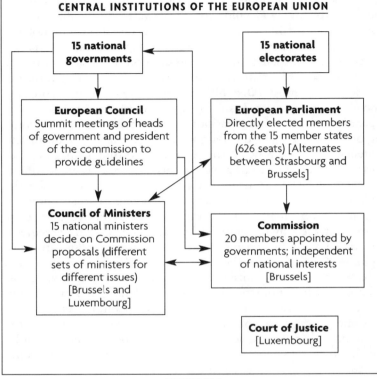

CENTRAL INSTITUTIONS OF THE EUROPEAN UNION

15 national governments

15 national electorates

European Council
Summit meetings of heads of government and president of the commission to provide guidelines

European Parliament
Directly elected members from the 15 member states (626 seats) [Alternates between Strasbourg and Brussels]

Council of Ministers
15 national ministers decide on Commission proposals (different sets of ministers for different issues) [Brussels and Luxembourg]

Commission
20 members appointed by governments; independent of national interests [Brussels]

Court of Justice
[Luxembourg]

FIGURE 10.8

limited trade association among six nations (the European Coal and Steel Community, created in 1951) became a commitment to the creation of a common market and united policies on matters such as transportation and agriculture (the European Economic Community, created in 1957, and consolidated in 1967), and evolved into a commitment to a common currency, customs union, and further political unity (the European Union, based on the Maastricht Treaty of 1991). Along the way, membership has expanded from the original six members (France, Germany, Italy, Belgium, Netherlands, Luxembourg) to nine in 1973 (adding Britain, Denmark, and Ireland), to 12 by the mid-1980s (Greece, Portugal, and Spain), and most recently to 15 with the additions of Austria, Finland, and Sweden in 1995. Another 12 countries have applied for entry, with Cyprus, the Czech Republic, Estonia, Hungary, Poland, and Slovenia on a fast track that could see entry as early as 2003.

As the scope of the European Union has enlarged and as expansion of membership has accelerated, this has raised questions about the present and future government of the association. At present, there are four main political institutions, as well as a Court of Justice. The complexity of the relationships between these is outlined in Figure 10.8. The authority of the EU's institutions springs from two sources. Every five years the national electorates of each member state elect members to the European Parliament, which has 626 seats. These seats are apportioned among the member states according to population, but in an inexact fashion that over-represents the smaller members. The powers of the Parliament vary, being largely advisory with respect to legislation, much more significant in dealing with the EU budget, and formidable on matters such as the admission of new member states.

The Commission, which is both like and unlike a "cabinet or government," consists of 20 members appointed by the member states. Each assumes a portfolio concerned with a particular policy field. The Commission must be approved by the Parliament before taking office, and may also be dismissed by the Parliament. Although the Commission is responsible for initiating legislation, its proposals may be overruled by the Council (see below) and it may be requested by the Council to draft proposals on a particular subject. Similarly, while the Commission is the body that monitors compliance by member states with EU policies, its ability to enforce implementation is weak. The authority of the Commission was not helped by events in March 1999, when the entire Commission was forced to resign after the release of a damning report that detailed widespread corruption in the practices of its members.

The most powerful body with respect to policy-making is the Council of Ministers, which represents the governments of the member states. Each country's seat is filled by a minister from its government, and which minister attends depends on the topic under discussion. One meeting might bring together all the transportation ministers to discuss trucking regulations; another might involve all health ministers considering home-care standards. On all issues except the EU's budget, the Council is the final step in the decision-making process.

Finally, the European Council is a summit meeting of the heads of government of the member states, and meets twice yearly to set the direction of the Union and deal with thorny issues that have defied solution elsewhere. Gallagher et al. (1995: 99) note that since 1975, "virtually all the major steps forward taken by the EC ... have been initiated by the European Council or, at the very

REFERENCES AND SUGGESTED READING

Burgess, Michael, and Alain-G. Gagnon. 1993. *Comparative Federalism and Federation*. Toronto: University of Toronto Press.

Dyck, Perry Rand. 1996. *Canadian Politics: Critical Approaches*. Scarborough, Ont.: Nelson.

Elazar, Daniel. 1987. *Exploring Federalism*. Tuscaloosa: University of Alabama Press.

Gallagher, Michael, et al. 1995. *Representative government in Modern Europe*, 2nd ed. New York: McGraw-Hill.

Greenstein, Fred I., and Nelson Polsby. 1975. *Handbook of Political Science*. Reading, Mass.: Addison-Wesley.

Hague, Rod, et al. 1992. *Comparative Government. An Introduction*, 3rd ed. London: Macmillan.

Hogg, Peter. 1977. *Constitutional Law of Canada*. Toronto: Carswell.

Janda, Kenneth, et al. 1989. *The Challenge of Democracy*, 2nd ed. Boston: Houghton-Mifflin.

Lijphart, Arend. 1984. *Democracies: Patterns of Majoritarian and Consensus Government in Twenty-One Countries*. New Haven: Yale University Press.

Mahler, Gregory S. 1995. *Comparative Politics: An Institutional and Cross-National Approach*. Englewood Cliffs, NJ: Prentice Hall.

Mény, Yves. 1993. *Government and Politics in Western Europe*, 2nd ed. Oxford: Oxford University Press.

Reesor, Bayard. 1992. *The Canadian Constitution in Historical Perspective*. Scarborough, Ont.: Prentice Hall.

Rocher, François, and Miriam Smith, eds. 1995. *New Trends in Canadian Federalism*. Peterborough, Ont.: Broadview Press.

Shugarman, David, and Reg Whitaker, eds. 1989. *Federalism and Political Community*. Peterborough, Ont.: Broadview Press.

Steiner, Jürg. 1995. *European Democracies*, 3rd ed. New York: Longmans.

Stevenson, Garth. 1989. *Unfulfilled Union*, 3rd ed. Toronto: Gage.

Wheare, K.C. 1953. *Federal Government*. London: Oxford University Press.

least, have needed the backing of the European Council to get going." The same authors note that the authority of this body is largely political, not legal.

As the above description of EU institutions implies, the EU is much more of a confederation than a federation, in that member states actually have surrendered very little of their national sovereignty to the larger body, and each is free to withdraw from the Union at any time. It may be, in fact, that the EU is the world's most successful example of a confederation in operation; it is certainly the largest. Many of the issues critical to the future of the EU—from further economic and political integration, to expansion in Eastern Europe, to the establishment of a European defence force—will hinge on whether or not the Union will continue to be a confederation, or member states will surrender more authority to the Union's institutions, in particular, to the European Parliament. The implications are significant either way. British Prime Minister Thatcher, for example, having triumphed over the Labour Party and rolled back social democratic policies, was loath to have her government's work undone by EU institutions in which social democratic forces held (or might hold) the majority of positions. This tension between domestic sovereignty and the inclinations of the larger community could, of course, work with any ideology or issue at stake.

SOMETHING TO CONSIDER

What is an appropriate balance of power between the national government and the sub-national governments (the provinces)? Need this be the same for every province?

Consider the pros and cons of a North American (or even North and South American) Union modelled on the example of the European Union.

IV

THE POLITICAL PROCESS

The concern of this section and the next is with what links the institutions of the state that we have been examining to the wider environment, and most especially to the citizens whom these institutions exist to serve.

That, of course, is a very democratic conception of the relationship between institutions and society, and reflects an ideal that is always only partially realized. Nonetheless, it is to democracy that we turn in this section, or more generally, to the political process which, in the societies where our students live, is a democratic political process.

Simply put, the political process comprises the behaviours and machinery that deliver inputs to the state. These inputs consist of particular demands for policy, and of individuals (political candidates) who claim to be committed to the delivery of particular policies on behalf of their supporters. After discussing the ideas and conditions of democracy we will turn to cleavages, the societal divisions and identities that underlie the struggle for control of government. Then we will examine the actual machinery by which this competition is conducted in contemporary democracies—the electoral and party systems. Finally, on the basis that democracy in this day and age requires organization and presupposes representation, we will compare alternative vehicles of representation and process of delivering demands to the state.

11 democracy

We live in a democratic age, but democracy remains a problematic variable in our modern political experience. Increasingly, the modern state must be democratic to be legitimate; yet, at the same time, the impression persists that often our institutions present a democratic façade behind which a largely undemocratic politics persists. Our political culture is effectively democratic; ideologies that are elitist and anti-democratic remain at the margins, but to some degree, the unanimous voice for democracy within our political culture is institutionally constrained. Once scarce positions of power and authority are determined through competition in a democratic political process, it is difficult for any anti-democratic ideology to flourish. If one rejects democracy, one rejects the judgement of the voters, and sensible voters will reject anti-democratic parties and politicians. On the other hand, widespread public suspicion of politicians or dissatisfaction with political institutions sometimes leads to reforms, which in the process diminish rather than enhance democracy. In a democracy, all voices are democratic because this is the language of political success, but it is also possible for rhetoric to mask an indifference or hostility to the public will.

Democratic institutions sustain and reinforce a democratic political culture, but the converse is also true—a political culture shapes institutions, and from this angle, democracy can be seen as the logical working out of some notions implicit in liberalism. According to liberal theory, government (like society) is a contrivance for the welfare of individuals; who better to assess this government, or to approve it, than the individuals themselves? And since for liberal theory, all individuals are (at least in the abstract) identical, this means the consent of *all* individuals. The

11.1 INTRODUCTION

11.1   Introduction
11.2   Democracy Defined
11.3   Distrust of Democracy
11.4   From Representative Government to Representative Democracy
11.5   Representative Democracy Considered
11.6   The Costs and Benefits of Democracy
11.7   The Prospects For Democracy
       11.7.1   Enriching democracy
       11.7.2   Consolidating democracy

liberal revolution, with its emphasis on *rational* government, undermined both traditional and charismatic grounds of obligation. In their place liberal theory put the notion of the **CONSENT OF THE GOVERNED**, and within liberal theory this consent changed from something hypothetical (see Hobbes) to something tacit (see Locke) to something expressed (see Rousseau). In practice, the category of "those whose consent is necessary to confer legitimacy" was gradually extended from a small class of property owners to all adults of self-sufficient rationality. This expansion (which will be examined more fully below) reflected a tension between the democratic logic within liberalism and the suspicion of democracy held by most elites, liberals included. The actual state of democracy within the modern age (the present time included) represents a compromise or trade-off between the logic for democracy and the social and cultural impediments to its actualization.

In this chapter we examine this compromise more closely, consider the constraints within which democracy is or is not possible, and ponder the future prospects for democracy. Our first task, though, is to define our terms more precisely.

11.2
DEMOCRACY DEFINED

By democracy, Aristotle meant the "rule of the Many," and democracy is commonly contrasted in classical literature with the "rule of the Few" (aristocracy) and the "rule of One" (monarchy). Today, "democracy" is usually understood as it translates literally: the "rule of the *people*," as implied in Lincoln's famous phrase about a government "of the people, by the people, and for the people." As we noted in Chapter One, democracy is a form of **POPULAR SOVEREIGNTY**: the idea that the authority of the state derives from the people who are governed. What distinguishes democracy is its insistence that the authority of the state not only *derives* from the public, but ultimately *rests with* the public in one fashion or another. In some way, the people must actually be involved in the exercise of the authority of the state, or those who exercise the authority of the state must be accountable to the people. Democracy is subversive of power by insisting that authority ultimately belongs to the ruled, not the rulers.

How do the people rule in a democracy? When societies were smaller and the scope of government was much less than it has become today, it was conceivable that "the people" might exercise authority themselves. As communities became larger, more fragmented, and the tasks of the state became more complex, the direct participation of the people in government became increasingly impractical, and democracy came to mean the popular choice of delegates or representatives who govern *on behalf of* the people. In classical times, people still understood by democracy the direct participation of all citizens (i.e., male property-owners) in the task of government; since the liberal revolution, democracy has been generally understood as a form of **REPRESENTATIVE** government in which people choose their rulers. In contemporary democracies, much comes down to the quality of the "choice" that citizens have. Moreover, as Rousseau (the first major Western thinker to embrace democracy fully) recognized, if people choose representatives to rule them, there should be some means by which the people keep their representatives accountable.[1] In short, then, in **DIRECT DEMOCRACY**, citizens exercise authority and power personally; in **REPRESENTATIVE DEMOCRACY**, citizens choose delegates to exercise authority and power on their behalf—an exercise for which these delegates must answer to the people at some subsequent point in time.

Obviously, modern liberal democracies are examples of representative democracy, but there are also moments of direct democracy within these states, primarily through referendums and initiatives. Here the decision-making undertaken by elected representatives is supplemented by occasional direct participation by the citizenry, direct participation which may be more or less binding on the government (see also Chapter Fourteen).

The greatest opportunities for democracy thus seem to lie with the legislative function, which is sometimes exercised directly today through referendums and initiatives, but most often is carried out by elected representatives. The executive and judicial functions of the state have rarely been exercised directly by the body of citizens, and certainly not in modern times. Even a thorough democrat like Rousseau suggested that these tasks should be carried out by delegates of the people. In the modern era it has not been unusual for members of the executive to be elected, but commonly this applies only to the chief executive (especially in presidential systems) or heads of state. Most democracies are parliamentary, and if members of the executive are elected it is because of a fusion of powers; they are elected as legislators and subsequently join the cabinet (the political executive). Moreover, in the modern state, executive and judicial responsibilities are carried out by large bureaucracies staffed by professional public servants.

1. Rousseau was the first major thinker to embrace democracy fully in the sense that he recognized no distinctions of economic or social class that would exclude citizens from participating in the general will. Like many thinkers of his time, he did not believe women were fit for political life, and he would not have included them as participants in democracy. Full democracy for Rousseau entailed only complete adult male suffrage. Like most thinkers of his day, Rousseau did not actually *say* that women were to be excluded; he simply took for granted their non-participation. Thus, while "citizen" for Rousseau meant "male adult," today we can read his work and understand "citizen" to mean "all competent adults."

While the most immediate and involved participation of citizens in government is the direct democracy of referendums, even this is a limited activity. Unlike many cases where decision-making is the final act in a whole process involving debate, discourse, and amendment, voting in a referendum occurs quite apart from the process by which the question is formulated and brought forward for decision. The direct democracy of the referendum and initiative, and electing representatives, are examples of non-participatory democracy. **PARTICIPATORY DEMOCRACY**, which requires that citizens be involved in the discussion and informed debate that precedes decision-making, is the democracy of small societies, of town hall meetings, sometimes of the workplace, but something few see as a viable option for today's plural societies.

Clearly, then, democracy is something that may be present in a political system in a variety of ways and with various degrees of intensity. At the very least, to qualify as democratic, a system must present its citizens with the opportunity of selecting political elites in competitive, periodic elections. This is the very least, and it is possible for democracy to entail much more. We could construct a continuum beginning with an absence of public input and ending with a maximum of public involvement. Actual political systems or states fall somewhere on that continuum to the degree that they reflect these democratic elements. It should also be noted that most of the systems we recognize as democratic do not go very far beyond the minimum of holding periodic elections.

**11.3
DISTRUST OF
DEMOCRACY**

It is easy for citizens who have grown up within a democratic political system to take it for granted. Historically, though, the allegiance to democracy is rather recent, something perhaps obscured by our knowledge that a democracy existed in ancient Athens, one that was in some senses more direct and participatory than that of today. On the other hand, Athenian democracy was limited to a small body of citizens (who were property-owning males), and the democratic period in Athens was denounced by many of its leading citizens. Neither Aristotle nor Plato was a democrat, and it seems that few among the educated classes mourned the passing of democracy in ancient Greece. Early critics of democracy had at least two concerns. First of all, democracy was seen to be inherently unstable, to degenerate easily into **DEMAGOGUERY** and tyranny. The term "demagogue" indicates

MAJORITY RULE

Sometimes, democracy is erroneously defined as "majority rule." This is inaccurate because democracy may require consent of more than the majority, and often gets by with the consent of something less than the majority. It is quite possible to require unanimity, although this would diminish greatly the chances of accomplishing anything and is quite impractical in any but the smallest decision-making bodies. In such small assemblies, though, a demand for consensus may well require that all, not simply a bare majority, agree. (By convention, within the Westminster model of parliamentary government, cabinet decisions are supposed to be matters of consensus.) There are any number of degrees of consent between unanimity and a numerical majority (50 per cent plus one); the consent of two-thirds of the eligible voters is a common requirement for constitutional decisions. Even more common than levels of consent greater than a simple majority are levels that represent less than a majority. Sometimes a plurality (having more support than any other option or candidate or alternative) is sufficient. Many electoral systems will award victory on the basis of much less than a majority of the votes cast, and even an electoral majority may mean much less than a majority of the citizens (because all do not or cannot vote). Commonly a majority is required in the legislature to pass a motion, but this is simply a majority of those present, who may be but a handful of the legislators, and in turn represent only a very small portion of the citizen body. More important than the actual presence or absence of a numerical majority is adherence to three other notions that are intrinsic to democracy. One is the principle that the level of consent (whether a majority, plurality, two-thirds of the citizen body, etc.) be determined, agreed to, and a matter of public knowledge prior to the consent being polled. The second principle is that those who take part agree to abide by the outcome, regardless of which side of the issue they end up on. In other words, the process legitimizes all decisions, not simply those with which we agree. Third, this puts the onus on the winning side, and especially on governments that gain control of the policy process, to implement policies that all can at least live with, even if they don't approve of them.

FIGURE 11.1

someone who incites the crowd by playing upon its fears, vanity, or prejudice, and becomes its leader by such flattery or deceit. In ancient experience, these leaders, originally acclaimed by the people, came to exercise power absolutely and without restraint, thus becoming *tyrants*; Peru's popular autocrat Fujimori may be considered a contemporary example. For the ancients, tyranny was the worst form of government, being roughly equivalent to (and receiving the same scorn that we today would reserve for) personal dictatorship. A second fear was that democracy involves a rule by the larger part of the people *against* the lesser part, or what has been called in more recent times, a **TYRANNY OF THE MAJORITY**. Instead of being rule by all the people for the general welfare, democracy may become a rule by one class or group (albeit the largest) for its own interest, an interest that may involve exploiting or persecuting a minority.

Underlying these criticisms of democracy has very often been a relatively low opinion of "the people," that is to say, of ordinary citizens, who were assumed to be ignorant and irrational (an assumption that has informed elitist attitudes throughout the centuries). Accordingly, the argument runs, a certain amount of power must be kept in the hands of an enlightened elite to keep government from being usurped by a tyrant, or to shelter minority interests, or simply to protect the benefits and achievements of culture and civilization. We might point out that the fear of a "tyranny of the majority" has often been raised by a minority occupying economically, politically, or socially privileged positions. Nonetheless, in large plural societies, the possibility of a majority (particularly of a religious, linguistic, or ethnic nature) oppressing a minority *is* a potential problem for fully participatory models of democracy. In those societies where the unequal exercise of power also ensures that the mass of the population remains poor and uneducated, fears about the weaknesses of democracy may not be ungrounded, but it is the effects of undemocratic actions and policies that make democracy danger-ous in such instances. Not surprisingly, then, democracy remained a suspect form of government from the time of Aristotle until the late eighteenth century, when thinkers like Rousseau began to make a strong case for its legitimacy. It was a few generations later before reforms began to make representative liberal governments into representative liberal democratic governments. The dangers of democracy were less apparent once the general population began to be neither so poor nor so ignorant. Certainly the success of democracy in the United States in the nineteenth century did much to recommend it to other liberal nations.

**11.4
FROM REPRESENTATIVE
GOVERNMENT TO
REPRESENTATIVE
DEMOCRACY**

We have already observed the logical relationship between liberalism and democracy. Yet in the aftermath of the liberal revolution, this relationship was not fully obvious to liberal thinkers; it was overshadowed by their acceptance of the traditional criticisms of democracy. Instead of democracy, liberal thinkers were concerned to establish **REPRESENTATIVE GOVERN-MENT**, and to replace absolute monarchy with parliamentary sovereignty. This is obvious in the political writings of the foundational liberal thinkers, Thomas Hobbes and John Locke.

Hobbes was certainly no advocate of democracy, but it should be noted that he understood the term literally as the rule by (all) the people, which he considered an impossibility. None-theless, his justification of government was that in a "state of nature" individuals acting out of self-interest would create the Sovereign (the authority of the state) to protect them, and would create this authority through a covenant (agreement) of each individual with every other. This is very much like an argument for popular sovereignty in that the authority of the state is traced back to the interests of the subjects themselves. By virtue of the device of the covenant, Hobbes says more than once that the subjects are the "authors" of the Sovereign's actions. On the other hand this covenant is an entirely hypothetical event; the popular sovereignty Hobbes describes is only apparent.

Like Hobbes, Locke begins with a social contract, a mutual agreement among those who wish security and stability, but unlike Hobbes, Locke writes as if such a contract were a real historical event. The social contract is an agreement between the Sovereign and the subjects, so that for Locke, government has its origin in **THE CONSENT OF THE GOVERNED**. The unanimity of all participants in Hobbes's imaginary covenant is replaced by the more practical principle of majority rule in Locke's version. Locke argues that the legislative power should be in the hands of an assembly, a body of men who together make the law, but are also at the same time subject to it. It is important to note that Locke's theory does not (nor was it intended to) describe the workings of a democracy. But it does describe a liberal, parliamentary government, and articulates several of the ideas and conventions that have become integral to liberal, representative democracy. Like many philosophers, Locke believed that government requires rationality, and he would have restricted the political community to those who are rational; like many of his time, Locke believed that most people do not demonstrate sufficient rationality to merit rights of political participation. Those who did demonstrate such sufficient rationality were thought to be those with productive property. In this respect Locke did not challenge the existing arrangements which limited the right to vote for Parliament (and to sit in Parliament) to a small wealthy class, but rather the relationship between the legislature and the monarchy.

When representative government became democratic, this involved extending the **FRANCHISE** (the right to vote for representatives) from a small propertied class to virtually all adult citizens. This happened in stages, often in the face of much opposition and resistance, and was only completed in the twentieth century in most contemporary democracies. Among other things, these extensions of the democratic franchise involved (a) eliminating property qualifications as a condition of the franchise, (b) the recognition of women as persons equally entitled to political rights, (c) the removal of restrictions based on racial,

EDMUND BURKE ON THE REPRESENTATIVE

"Certainly, Gentlemen, it ought to be the happiness and glory of a representative to live in the strictest union, the closest correspondence, and the most unreserved communication with his constituents. Their wishes ought to have great weight with him; their opinions high respect; their business unremitted attention. It is his duty to sacrifice his repose, his pleasure, his satisfactions, to theirs, and above all, ever, and in all cases, to prefer their interest to his own. But his unbiased opinions, his mature judgement, his enlightened conscience, he ought not to sacrifice to you, to any man, or to any set of men living. These he does not derive from your pleasure, no, nor from the law and the constitution. They are a trust from Providence, for the abuse of which he is deeply answerable. Your representative owes you, not his industry only, but his judgement; and he betrays, instead of serving you, if he sacrifices it to your opinion.

... government and legislation are matters of reason and judgement, and not of inclination; and what sort of reason is that in which the deliberation precedes the discussion, in which one set of men deliberate and another decide, and where those who form the conclusion are perhaps three hundred miles distant from those who hear the arguments?

To deliver an opinion is the right of all men; that of constituents is a weighty and respectable opinion, which a representative ought always to rejoice to hear, and which he ought always most seriously to consider. But authoritative instructions, mandates issued, which a member is bound blindly and implicitly to obey, to vote, and to argue for, though contrary to the clearest conviction of his judgement and conscience; these are things utterly unknown to the laws of this land, and which arise from a fundamental mistake of the whole order and tenor of our constitution.

Parliament is not a congress of ambassadors from different and hostile interests, which interests each must maintain, as an agent and advocate, against other agents and advocates; but Parliament is a deliberative assembly of one nation, with one interest, that of the whole, where not local purposes, not local prejudices, ought to guide, but the general good, resulting from the general reason of the whole. You choose a member, indeed; but when you have chosen him, he is not a member of Bristol, but he is a member of Parliament. If the local constituent should have an interest or should form a hasty opinion evidently opposite to the real good of the rest of the community, the member for that place ought to be as far as any other from any endeavour to give it effect.... Your faithful friend, your devoted servant, I shall be to the end of my life: a flatterer you do not wish for."

— Speech to the Bristol Electors,
November 3, 1774

FIGURE 11.2

ethnic, or religious grounds, and (d) a lowering of age limits to present levels (see also Chapter Thirteen).

On the other hand, extending the right to vote did not alter the basic functioning of representative government; the same institutions, conventions, and practices continued to operate as before, with representatives perhaps even gaining more autonomy from the immediate demands of constituents as their constituencies became more pluralistic. Moreover, the significance of extending the franchise depends on the importance of the vote within the institutions of liberal representative government. Certainly, to gain the right to vote was important for citizens previously denied that right, but significant as much for the symbolic importance attached to full citizenship as for any power gained. Undeniably, each expansion of the franchise has required elected officials—singly or in parties—to be more responsive to the section of the electorate thus enfranchised than they might otherwise have been. Nonetheless, one reason this act of voting fails to carry more weight is the nature of the ongoing relationship between the voters and their representatives.

Elected representatives serve as members of a legislature. In its original configuration—as an assembly of feudal lords—Parliament consisted of members with no legal obligations to their retainers (constituents), bound only by a moral obligation to consider their well-being. So, today, apart from the necessity of facing constituents in periodic elections, legislators typically have no legal responsibilities to their constituents. This absence of accountability for the period between elections can be called **REPRESENTATIVE AUTONOMY**, and it is a feature of most contemporary democracies. The most eloquent defence of the autonomy of the elected representative is that provided by Edmund Burke in a 1776 letter to his constituents (see Figure 11.2).

The autonomy advocated by Burke is not mere freedom or licence: we say that the representative is "free" to follow his own judgement rather than that of his constituents, but we should note that as far as Burke was concerned, the representative is not free to do whatever he or she likes, but rather enjoys a freedom to use his or her reason to *judge* what is in the constituents' best interest. What Burke did not admit is that this creates a problem for constituents whose representative does not follow their opinions, judgements, etc. How do the constituents know whether or not the representative is making a thoughtful, informed decision about what is in their interest, or pursuing some other agenda—perhaps one of personal interest?

In defence of Burke, we might note that in an age before universal state-funded schooling, the level of education attained was more or less proportionate to wealth. The vast majority had little or no formal education and, one could argue, did not possess the tools to make rational, informed judgements. This social reality provided ammunition, not only for the autonomy of representatives, but against any notion of making the political system more democratic: how could one, in an increasingly complex and technical world, consider giving the vote to people who could neither read nor write? This also indicates that prior to universal, compulsory education, the class rule by the propertied interests could be defended on the basis of factors other than class—such as expertise, or education—which were nonetheless very much associated with class.

Within the world of parliamentary democracy we should make a further observation, namely that while representative autonomy describes the relationship between legislator and constituents, it does not account for the actions of representatives. Instead, our modern MPs are governed almost exclusively by the dictates of party discipline, which remains central to government stability. Individual autonomy only comes into full play with those rare issues on which a "free" vote is held—so-called matters of "conscience," such as capital punishment or abortion. In the United States, party discipline is much less rigid, and members are not at all bound to vote along party lines, although there are more alliances within parties than outside them. It could be argued, though, that the freedom from party discipline makes American legislators more susceptible to the influence of lobbyists, and not necessarily to the wishes of their constituents.

11.5 REPRESENTATIVE DEMOCRACY CONSIDERED

If we continue to regard democracy as "rule by the people," then critical examination suggests that liberal representative government, even with a universal franchise, presents a bare minimum of democracy. It does so only to the degree that citizens participate in the selection of rulers. We should acknowledge that this is often the extent of the participation that our liberal, representative democracy grants to its citizens. This also means that the justification of such a democracy comes down to the significance of a popular selection of political officials.

In classical liberal democratic theory, the selection of representatives through popular periodic elections is justified as an important and rational activity by which citizens transmit their preferences for policies or their position on issues by matching their self-interest to the stated positions or platforms of candidates and/or parties. In other words, in liberal democracies, informed and interested citizens employ their vote in a rational fashion in response to the issues of the day and the policy options articulated by competing electoral candidates. In this way, democracy ensures popular sovereignty by implementing the common will, or at least the will of the majority, once voters rationally select responsible individuals who govern on the basis of the mandate supplied by their supporters. Liberal theorists sometimes compare the functioning of the free market in the economy with the free exercise of the suffrage in democratic politics. In the market, demand by consumers is held to represent their rational choice of the objects corresponding to their self-interest, and the level of consumer demand will determine the supply of corresponding goods by producers. By analogy, political candidates fit the role of producers, competing to offer the best package of goods—i.e., policies or programs—that will respond to the demands or desires of voters (the consumers).

Several problems attend this depiction of **ELECTORAL ACTIVITY**, not the least of which is the large body of empirical evidence that reveals that it is not an accurate representation of actual citizen behaviour. Studies of political behaviour, for example, have indicated several characteristics of voters that run contrary to the portrait drawn by classical democratic theory. One is a lack of interest and involvement in the political process. The majority of citizens participate in the political system only by voting, choosing not to engage in any number of other voluntary activities such as running for office, campaigning on behalf of a candidate, writing to a representative, etc. Even more troubling to some is the low turnout in national elections where such participation is entirely voluntary. (In the U.S., where the onus is on citizens to register if they wish to vote, barely half the electorate participates in electing the President.) Indeed, in many Western democracies (e.g., Australia), voting is no longer a privilege or a right but a legal requirement enforced by penalties.

A further concern for classic liberal theorists is the finding that voting is often a very non-rational activity. In other words, voting behaviour is not primarily the result of an evaluation of the fit between self-interest and the policy options articulated by candidates, but rather is often the byproduct of other, non-rational factors such as socialization, habit, affect (emotion), misinformation, or manipulation. In addition, early social scientific voter studies identified unexpected anti-democratic or non-democratic attitudes. Many individuals seemed to display attitudes identified as authoritarian: in particular a deference to authority and a desire to exercise authority over others. Typically, such attitudes were identified among the "apathetic": the non-participators.

What are we to conclude from these empirical findings? Do they speak to us about the character of ordinary individuals and confirm the anti-democratic prejudices that have prevailed through so much of human history? Or do they tell us something about a society that permits little in the way of democracy and demands even less from its citizens? For example, given the autonomy of government from its citizens, the actual lack of direct input by citizens into decision-making, is there any reason for citizens to take an active, rational interest in politics? To take the time and effort to become informed about issues when there is little if any opportunity to employ that information? It is possible to argue that the behaviour of citizens very much reflects the opportunities given them (or not). It would seem that there are two sets of impediments to citizen participation: institutional, and cultural.

In the first place, the electoral machinery of many, if not most democracies, does not in any way register, let alone reward, a "rational" vote (where rational indicates a vote cast on the basis of a judicious consideration of policies, issues, and programs). The representative who is elected, or the leader of the party to which she belongs, has no real knowledge about why she received more votes than any other candidate. There is no way for you as a voter to indicate on your ballot that you support this party for its economic and foreign policies, but oppose its stand on social programs and legalized gambling. Nor is there any way to distinguish your ballot so informed, from mine, which supports the same party because of its promises on social programs and despite its economic policies. This lack of specificity in the way the ballot records one's support makes all talk by winning parties about having received a mandate to carry out specific policies most dubious (see also the discussion of electoral politics in Chapter Fourteen).

Ultimately, the democratic vote amounts to a transmission of trust or statement of faith rather than a set of instructions or directives. In this case, affect, habit, or socialization may be just as "rational" a basis for decision as any calculation of enlightened "self-interest." We should not expect voters to act rationally when the political process in which they are active does not encourage rationality, take notice of it, nor in some cases even permit it. But if, in both theory and practice, we recognize that governing requires rational decision-making, then it seems odd not to ask whether the participation of the people in the political system should not also entail rationality—and therefore a set of institutions and practices that permit, and indeed require, such rationality.

The institutional limitations to democracy are buttressed by cultural messages transmitted from generation to generation. We have seen above that political culture is an aggregate of the beliefs within a society or community about the political world, and identified the belief in democracy as a central feature of our contemporary political culture. At the same time this is a limited belief in democracy, just as the democracy of our institutions is a very limited form of public participation. Hand-in-hand with the belief in the rightness of democracy goes the age-old suspicion of "the public" or of its competence to judge how authority and power should be exercised. The phrase "too much democracy is dangerous" seems to capture this ambivalence: democracy is good, but kept within limits, not taken too far. This equivocal stance towards democracy is very often transmitted, if not reinforced, by the socialization process.

When empirical studies undermine the portrait of democratic voting as rational decision-making, they also undermine liberal democracy's traditional claims to legitimacy. If modern democracy claims to be *the* good form of government because it realizes popular sovereignty, and that sovereignty turns out on close examination to be largely symbolic or merely formal, then the claim to legitimacy is seriously undermined. If liberal democracy fails to give citizens an actual role in governing, and if it fails to encourage rational activity in the selection of rulers, what does it do?

A critical and historical examination of liberal (representative) democracy reveals that it remains a system of **ELITE DOMINANCE**. It differs from other systems in which elites dominate in that it has periodic elections in which some of the most prominent of those elites must compete for scarce positions of power and authority. In a representative democracy, these officials are chosen through periodic elections, and are in this way replaceable. This seems to be a long way from the characterization of democracy as "rule by the people"; in much twentieth-century theory, the emphasis shifted from saying that liberal democracies embody the popular will, to noting that they are more *stable* than other forms of government.[2] In other words, competition among political elites and their replacement through the electoral process mean that unpopular governments can be ousted without revolution or violence. At the same time, what we might well call the democratic myth continues to foster the view that popular inputs are closely reflected in the content of the law, of policies, and of programs. Such a view further enhances the state's claims to legitimacy and thereby its ability to rely on authority rather than power.

If liberal democracy is distinguished from other political arrangements by the popular selection of elites, then much depends upon the nature and significance of this selection process. Commonly, the modern process definition of democracy makes reference to "periodic, competitive" elections. But how

2. While this may seem odd, given the ability of authoritarian regimes and dictatorships to remain in power for long periods, the latter are much more likely than democracies to be subject to coups, civil wars, insurrections, and civil disobedience; whether or not these succeed in ousting rulers is (partly) beside the point.

competitive? The significance of competition is that it is supposed to make our choices more meaningful by increasing the range of options presented to us. The choices we confront may be more or less meaningful in a variety of ways. We might be concerned about the number of choices, the ideological diversity or range of choices offered, the clarity of competing positions advanced, the responsibility of candidates for positions advanced or to be implemented (i.e., is there any point evaluating the relative promises and commitments of candidates A and B, if there is no guarantee that the party leadership will listen to A or B, or allow them to follow through on promises made?), or the accuracy of the available information about the candidates or policy options at stake. As we will see in Chapter Thirteen there are very real differences in the electoral and party systems of liberal democracies, differences that affect both the quality of choice the voters can make and the quality of representation they receive. If the quality of choice with which citizens are presented is diminished for any reason, then, so too, is much of the value that can be claimed for liberal democracy.

11.6
THE COSTS AND
BENEFITS OF
DEMOCRACY

Our examination of political history and practice reveals an ambiguous commitment to democracy; the democracy we have is quite limited, and within the limited scope of electing representatives is often incomplete or compromised. At the same time our ideologies, our constitutions, and even our foreign policy rest on a formal commitment to democracy, however vaguely defined. What we have not done yet in this chapter is examine why it matters whether or not our politics is democratic, or whose interests are best served by having a democratic polity. If we can clarify these questions, then we may also illuminate why it matters (or doesn't) that our present experience of democratic politics is limited in the ways we have identified.

In the opening chapter it was suggested that one hallmark of the modern era in politics has been the replacement of traditional and charismatic forms of legitimacy with legal–rational grounds, and that these latter have come down to basically two: justice and popular sovereignty. These are alternate means of procuring legitimacy; a government will be seen as legitimate if it exercises authority correctly (justice), or because it implements a popular will or mandate. Consequently, it should not surprise us that virtually every government claims to provide justice, *and* to carry out the public will. This should alert us to the possibility that governments that are not democratic might claim to be so—and to the likelihood that governments will often be less democratic than they claim. The concept of legitimacy helps to explain what interest governments or rulers may have in democracy. Democracy, from the perspective of those in power, may be *a means of securing support for the exercise of power.* Those who enjoy the exercise of power and authority may wish for just enough democracy to grant them legitimacy, but not enough to put serious constraints on their exercise of authority and power. We have acknowledged that democracy is not the only means of realizing popular sovereignty, but have also suggested that anything less than the actual participation of the people in some way is only an "apparent" popular sovereignty. It may well be that it is in the interest of elites to have a popular sovereignty that is only apparent, rather than one that is effective. But it is harder to see that this is in the long-term interest of citizens.

The whole point of the liberal revolution against medieval authority was to secure individuals from the arbitrary exercise of power, and the kind of power justified by traditional or charismatic grounds could offer no such guarantee. There are two fundamental ways to be secure from arbitrary power: one is to constrain the use of power so that it cannot harm us, and the second is to exercise that power ourselves. The latter is the goal of democracy; the former is the aim of justice. Further, our commitment to democracy may be weak, or take second place, if justice appears to be doing the job of protecting our interests. This will be true particularly if justice seems more convenient or efficient than democracy. The critic of (more) democracy will point out, and often quite rightly, that democracy is expensive, that it slows down the work of government, that it is economically inefficient and tends to burden the marketplace, that it involves a commitment by citizens to activity that may not be attractive (or as attractive as other leisure pursuits), that it is simply too time-consuming, or that it presupposes a level of political knowledge and experience that citizens do not presently have (and that would be too expensive to provide). It is best, on these grounds, to keep government small, manageable, economic, and in the hands of experts. Such an argument gains strength when it can be demonstrated that justice secures us from the arbitrary or injurious use of that power by governmental elites. Given the establishment of constitutionalism, of the rule of law, and in particular the entrenchment of individual rights in common law and constitutional law, it is tempting to conclude that democracy has become something of a luxury, perhaps something superfluous. According to this argument, governments may best be kept honest by an appeal to the courts when our rights have been infringed—a method that is more efficient and convenient for the community at large (although it may not be for the individuals who must make such appeals) than wholesale political participation.

On the other hand, this last view overlooks the relationship between democracy and justice. Who protects, interprets, and defines our rights—politicians or judges? Can rights be secure if those who protect, interpret, and define them are not accountable to the public? Democracy is a possible means of keeping those who safeguard the citizens' rights accountable to the citizens. Similarly, social justice involves a variety of difficult decisions about the distribution of social values, the criteria by which distribution should take place, and about what kinds of inequalities should be tolerated. Who should make these decisions? If social justice is an entitlement of the people, rather than a gift from rulers, then perhaps there is a function for democracy here that is not optional. With political economy (see Chapter Seventeen below), we encounter various options concerning the degree to which the state should engage in regulating the market, or intervene in the economy generally. Who should determine the character of the state's management of economic life? Here some argue that democracy is a potential means by which the state can be made responsive to the needs of all classes, not merely those of the economic elite, or of the dominant economic class. Are they right? At the very least, justice issues point out the interest that citizens might have in democracy, regardless of whether it is convenient, or easy, or efficient.

**11.7
THE PROSPECTS FOR
DEMOCRACY**

The twentieth century has seen both the greatest advances towards popular democracy and some of the greatest repudiations of democracy. It has been remarked that at the end of the twentieth century democracy is the one great remaining ideology. It is worthwhile to step back and assess the prospects for democracy as a new century dawns. For this purpose it is useful to distinguish between those states in which democracy is more or less well established, and those in which the institutions and practices of democracy are new and potentially fragile.

11.7.1 Enriching democracy

Our discussion in this chapter and elsewhere in the book reflects a judgement that the nature of democracy in the established liberal democracies falls far short of the ideals of democracy that great political thinkers have articulated, and indeed, far short of the rhetoric politicians employ in these states to describe the state of contemporary democracy. Some of this distance between ideal and reality may reflect the work of social, economic, and political forces we have described:

- the increasing population of contemporary societies;
- a greater fragmentation of population and social roles;
- the greater complexity of government in such societies;
- the challenges of modernization and globalization, etc.

The sceptic may well argue that we enjoy about as much democracy as is reasonable to expect given the complexity of society today and the nature of the tasks governments are asked to perform.

On the other hand, in every age, and indeed in every political system, democratic or otherwise, there are powerful pressures towards the centralization of power, not least among them the desire of those who have authority for more. Without periodic reforms in the direction of strengthening the ability of the public to keep their rulers accountable, there is an almost inevitable erosion of popular sovereignty, *even as* the appearances and rhetoric of democracy are maintained and championed in a way that obscures their superficiality. In the established democracies we can ask what is the likelihood that popular participation will be further extended or strengthened? What are the constraints working against the growth of democracy, or perhaps, even towards its contraction?

In the past, democracy was often implemented or extended as the result of revolution, or as political leaders responded to public pressure or unrest. It is probably a safe generalization to say that those in power do not voluntarily relinquish any authority unless it is in their own interest to do so. Perhaps political parties committed to greater democratization will be elected in the future, or circumstances will arise to make greater democracy an attractive option to those in power. Revolution for a *more* democratic polity does not seem likely so long as Western economies are relatively healthy; people seem more likely to take radical political action when they have less to lose (or conversely, they have more at stake). This was one lesson learned quickly and dramatically in Eastern Europe in 1989-91 and, painfully, in Tiananmen Square in 1989. It is much easier, unfortunately, to be definite about the impediments to or constraints on realizing democracy within contemporary societies.

One challenge is the pluralistic character of modern societies. It is increasingly impossible to speak with any accuracy of "the people" or about *a* public will; there are typically several or many peoples and a variety of wills within the public. Such plurality presents at least three problems for democracy. One is the possibility that any democratic majority might systematically exclude a people or peoples, a result that can only be destabilizing over the long term. At the very least, the legitimacy of the state will quickly be eroded in the view of those who are consistently excluded from shaping its policies. Second, it may not be possible, given the institutions in place, to manufacture a majority, in which case the decisive voice is that of a plurality. Here, a minority ends up deciding for all, which may be unjust and may also be destabilizing. Finally, democracy has traditionally been a means of collective decision-making, which implies either a common interest or the ability to make the compromises necessary to find a solution satisfactory to various competing interests. As the plural character of society grows and is more sharply defined, compromises between competing interests may well become more difficult to reach; instead of a collective decision-making process, democracy becomes the arena for irreconcilable, competing voices seeking outright victory rather than compromise.

The increasingly complex world presents another set of challenges for democracy. It has helped to fuel the tremendous growth of government in this century. While there is much action and more rhetoric about making government smaller and simpler, success has been limited, and the utility of many cutbacks remains uncertain. Apart from the sheer size of government and the challenges that its "volume of business" presents for democracy, the business of government has become, like society at large, increasingly technical. Informed decision-making requires informed decision-makers, and democratic decision-making requires an informed citizenry. We are told that citizens are better informed and educated than ever before, especially in an age where Internet resources grow exponentially. But citizens are not always informed or educated about government, or politics, or about the substance of political decisions. Where the bulk of their information is received through a mass media primarily engaged in entertainment, there is reason to doubt that citizens are adequately informed for democratic decision-making. There are other means by which they can become so informed, but it is not obvious that all (or even a majority of) citizens are sufficiently interested to become so informed, or are willing to invest the time to do so.

Democracy carries an implicit endorsement of the political sphere; by inviting or even requiring citizens to participate in the exercise of authority and power, we indicate that this is an important, worthwhile activity. Such an approach and attitude can be traced back to Aristotle's view of humans as essentially political animals. For Aristotle, politics was a noble, worthy human activity (unlike making money, which was an activity fit for slaves). It is not much of an exaggeration to say that in our contemporary democracies the situation is reversed; making and spending money is celebrated, while politicians and political activity are despised and distrusted. Again there is an irony here: much of the public disenchantment with the political realm stems from its failure to be more democratic, or to be as democratic in practice as it is in theory. The public hears political promises made in order to gain its support; the public grows cynical as politicians in power backtrack or renege on their commitments. Political actors seek to manage public opinion in order to co-opt the minimal accountability they must submit to, and manage to alienate a wary public. In the process, the whole political process is discredited, and instead of agitating for more democracy, citizens turn away from the limited democracy they have.

There is also a danger to democracy in the common failure to distinguish adequately between government and state. In rejecting "big government" or calling for "less government," the activities of reformers may sometimes threaten the representative institutions and processes of democracy. The decade of the 1990s was one in which the growth of the state slowed, was halted, or in some cases was reversed. This was also the period in which the trend began towards smaller governments, in the strictest sense. In parliamentary countries, as noted in Chapter Eight, this meant smaller cabinets and leaner structures to support them. In many jurisdictions it has meant a move to smaller legislatures with fewer representatives to voice the public's will and keep the political executive accountable. While all these developments seem logically connected (e.g., having fewer cabinet ministers with policy agendas seems consistent with maintaining a leaner state), the benefits of smaller legislatures are not so obvious, and the latter may actually diminish the quality of democracy.

The fewer representatives there are, the more constituents each must serve—constituency size varies inversely with the number of legislators. The ability of legislators to give voice to or respond to constituents' concerns is compromised in more than one way. First, as the size of constituencies grows, the diversity of interests they contain is likely to rise, and the proportion of the representative's attention that any particular group can hope to receive is sure to diminish. Those interests that are better organized or have more resources will likely move to the head of the line, to the detriment of less advantaged groups. Second, as the number of members in the legislature is reduced, their additional parliamentary duties increase, leaving less time for addressing constituency concerns. Third, in smaller legislatures, the margin of any plurality that the government holds with respect to the opposition will be smaller rather than larger. This increases the possibility that the government might lose on votes held in the legislature, increasing the pressure on *all* members to adhere to the party line, regardless of whether that position meets the needs of their constituents.

In Canada, the Ontario Legislative Assembly illustrates some of these points. With the 1999 election, Ontario's parliament went from 130 seats to 103, a drop of 21 per cent. This increased the average constituency size from about 88,000 to almost 111,000. In 1995, the Conservative Party won 82 seats with 45 per cent of the vote, giving them a plurality of 34 seats over the combined opposition forces. After the 1999 election, on the basis of 45 per cent of the vote, the Conservatives held 59 seats, to 44 for the opposition, their plurality reduced to 15 seats. The cabinet sworn-in in 1999 numbered 25 (including the Premier), and 19 parliamentary assistants were appointed, leaving only 15 backbenchers, one of whom subsequently was elected Speaker of the Assembly. (This compares to the previous government in which there was a cabinet of 19, with 19 parliamentary assistants, leaving a total of 44 backbenchers.) In other words, in the smaller legislature (1999), 77.9 per cent of the Conservative caucus have extra ministry-related responsibilities, as opposed to only 46.3 per cent in the larger legislature (1995). In such a setting, the amount of time that government members have to hear and represent the concerns of the publics they represent is inevitably diminished.

While the downsizing of a provincial or state legislature on this scale is unusual, similar reductions in the machinery of democracy have taken place in countless municipalities, school boards, and other elected bodies across North America. Such actions often constitute an excellent example of "symbolic" politics, where the exercise of cutting government and bureaucracy is trumpeted as eliminating "waste" and "duplication." In fact, while the people lose representatives, and it becomes more difficult to hold those who do govern accountable, the fiscal savings achieved are minimal. In the Ontario government's fiscal plan for 1999–2000, the amount allocated to the Board of Internal Economy (which manages the offices of the Legislative Assembly) was $121 million, a large expenditure perhaps to you or me, but representing less than one-quarter of 1 per cent of the Ontario operating expenditure budget of $56.8 billion. In most of today's large post-industrial societies, democracy is an inexpensive proposition.

11.7.2   Consolidating democracy

There are probably no more than 40 to 45 states in which democracy is so firmly established that its overthrow or suspension is unthinkable, and this is many more than this could have been said of only 20 years ago. A much larger number of countries qualify as "democratic" today, but for them the experience, the institutions, and supports of democracy are too new, too fragile, or as yet inadequately constructed. In these states the challenge is not to implement the machinery of democracy but to establish the habits and norms within the political culture that will make other forms of government unacceptable. This is the work of consolidating democracy.

Samuel Huntington (1991) has described the growth of democracy in the world as having occurred in three waves. The first of these lasted from roughly 1828 to 1926, the second from 1943 to 1964, and the third, which has involved the largest number of democratizations, is dated from 1974. Scholars such as Larry Diamond (1999) speculate about whether or not the third wave is now over. This is not an idle question, for as Huntington showed, the first two waves of democratization were followed by reverse waves in which democratic regimes suffered breakdown, returning to authoritarian or dictatorial rule. Figure 11.3 shows the number of nation-states and democracies during this third wave of democratization.

	NO. COUNTRIES	NO. DEMOCRACIES	% DEMOCRACIES	AVERAGE FREEDOM SCORE
1974	145	39	26.9	4.47
1990	165	76	46.1	3.84
1997	191	117	61.3	3.58

FIGURE 11.3

The extent of the "third wave" of democratization is clear: an increase of 46 in the number of countries in 24 years; an increase of 78 in the number of democracies, and a corresponding increase in the proportion of democracies from 26.9 to 61.3 per cent.

One crucial issue here is what qualifies as a democracy. Innumerable definitions have been put forward to clarify the empirical use of this term; all applications remain ultimately a matter of judgement. The definition used in Figure 11.3 is based on the view of democracy as consisting of regular, contested elections. The two adjectives used in the last sentence are important. Elections held only at the whim of those in power do not constitute democracy; elections must have a constitutional or legally prescribed regularity that is beyond the control of those in power. Elections, to be democratically meaningful, must also be competitive. There must be more than one party with a legitimate opportunity of winning. Indeed, Diamond defines authoritarian regimes as those that lack "legal, independent opposition parties" and **PSEUDO-DEMOCRACIES** as those regimes that lack "an arena of contestation sufficiently fair that the ruling party can be turned out of power" (1999: 17, 15). In other words, if all the rules are stacked in favour of the party in power it may still be impossible for a legal, independent opposition party to win, ever. Mexico, until perhaps very recently, Senegal, and Singapore are cited as classic examples of pseudo-democracy.

The 117 countries listed as democratic in 1997 thus represent regimes with competitive, periodic elections, and in this sense they satisfy the criteria of **ELECTORAL DEMOCRACY**. Many scholars argue, though, that electoral democracy is a necessary condition, but not a sufficient condition of being democratic. The notion that having elections is sufficient to establish democracy is what Shmitter and Karl (1991) call the "electoral fallacy." The notion behind this view is that democratic choice must be meaningful, informed, unforced, and free of personal repercussions. These (and other) key variables have nothing to do with the machinery of elections and much more to do with the environment in which elections are contested. Incorruptible electoral officials, a free press, gender equality, confidentiality, public literacy, and civilian control of the military are just a few of the ingredients that must accompany elections if democracy is to be meaningful.

Many of the conditions of democracy are closely associated with the values, institutions, and practices of the liberal state that we have already discussed. Accordingly, Diamond and others make a distinction between those minimal democracies that contest periodic elections (electoral democracies) and those more complete democracies where elections are contested within an environment of civil and political freedom (liberal democracies). We would argue that this is not just a "Western" bias towards a type of democracy, but a recognition of the full range of conditions necessary to make democracy work. Interestingly, the most stable and long-lasting democracies have been those that qualify as liberal democracies, and those democracies most likely to backslide into pseudo-democracy or authoritarianism have been electoral democracies in which the institutions that provide citizens with liberty have yet to become firmly established in the political or civil society.

Admittedly, the conditions that distinguish liberal from electoral democracy are to some degree a matter of judgement, as is the determination of which regimes actually satisfy these conditions (or the degree to which they satisfy these). Diamond (1999) lists 10 conditions of liberal democracy that range from the vesting of authority in elected officials to whom the military is subordinate, to conditions of cultural, ethnic, and religious liberty, to an independent media, to freedom of association and expression, all of which imply an eleventh condition: constitutionalism. Many of these "liberal" elements of the developed industrial democracy have been discussed at length in this book. Since 1972, an organization called Freedom House has measured the status of civil and political liberty in countries around the world and published an annual report called *Freedom in the World: The Annual Survey of Political Rights and Civil Liberties.* The final column in Figure 11.3 (above) is the average freedom score of the countries for the selected years, and the data show an improvement in the scores throughout the period, although much less change between 1990 and 1997 than was the case between 1974 and 1990. Figure 11.4 shows the proportion of liberal and formal (i.e., electoral) democracies for selected years in the 1990s.

As the numbers in this table indicate, the proportion of electoral democracies that are also free (i.e., are liberal democracies) has remained constant through much of the 1990s, with a small

KEY TERMS

consent of the governed
demagoguery
democracy
direct democracy
electoral activity
elite dominance
franchise
majority rule
participatory democracy
popular sovereignty
representative autonomy
representative democracy
representative government
stability
tyranny of the majority

	FORMAL DEMOCRACIES NO. (%)	FREE STATES/ LIBERAL DEMOCRACIES NO. (%)	FREE STATES AS % OF FORMAL DEMOCRACIES	TOTAL NO.
1990	76 (46.1)	65 (39.4)	85.5	165
1992	99 (53.2)	75 (40.3)	75.8	186
1994	114 (59.7)	76 (39.8)	66.7	191
1996	118 (61.8)	79 (41.4)	67.0	191
1998	119 (62.0)	85 (44.3)	69.2	192

FIGURE 11.4

REFERENCES AND SUGGESTED READING

Barber, Benjamin R. 1984. *Strong Democracy: Participatory Politics for a New Age.* Berkeley: University of California Press.

Diamond, Larry. 1999. *Developing Democracy: Towards Consolidation.* Baltimore: Johns Hopkins University Press.

Held, David. 1987. *Models of Democracy.* Cambridge: Polity Press.

Huntington, Samuel P. 1991. *The Third Wave: Democratization in the Late Twentieth Century.* Norman: University of Oklahoma Press.

Jones, A.H.M. 1986. *Athenian Democracy.* Baltimore: Johns Hopkins University Press.

Macpherson, C.B. 1977. *The Life and Times of Liberal Democracy.* New York: Oxford University Press.

Mansfield, Jane. 1980. *Beyond Adversarial Democracy.* New York: Basic Books.

Parenti, Michael. 1978. *Power and the Powerless.* New York: St. Martin's Press.

——. 1980. *Democracy for the Few.* New York: St. Martin's Press.

Pateman, Carol. 1970. *Participation and Democratic Theory.* Cambridge: Cambridge University Press.

Schmitter, Philippe C., and Terry Lynn Karl. 1991. "What Democracy Is ... And Is Not," in *Journal of Democracy,* Summer 1991.

spurt of liberalization in 1998. Whether democracy continues to spread and become more stable in the coming years will depend on the ability of formally democratic regimes to foster the liberal conditions noted briefly above. As yet, almost 62 per cent of the world's population still lives in non-liberal democratic regimes. In addition, some countries considered liberal democratic (e.g., India, the Phillipines) continue to have large portions of their population living in poverty, illiteracy, and under the influence of societal norms (e.g., patriarchal cultures) that discourage democratic citizenship for many. In many cases the most certain guarantee of a future for democracy will be economic growth, but also, *and this is as true of established as of growing democracies*, a greater equalization of wealth and economic opportunity. These are concerns we return to in later chapters of this book.

It is certainly noteworthy that in the longest established democracies (and according to Freedom House's requirement of election by a universal adult suffrage, there were in 1900 *no* democracies yet) liberal political institutions and the creation of a civil society embodying at least moderate levels of liberal tolerance, middle-class affluence, and widespread literacy *preceded* the reforms that constituted democratization. In many of the world's newer democracies, another experiment is under way: namely, to establish democracy without or prior to the liberal foundations that most citizens in the West have come to take for granted.

SOMETHING TO CONSIDER

Implicit in this chapter (and indeed throughout this text) is a belief that democracy is a good towards which individuals and political communities should strive. Is this just a bias of the author, or are there objective grounds for this conclusion? Is it possible for there to be too much democracy?

Which is the lesser of two evils, an illiberal democracy or a liberal autocracy?

12
cleavages

A theme recurring in definitions of politics is the resolution of conflict, and we might well ask: conflict between whom, and over what? Part of the answer is contained in our observation about the character of most modern societies: they are pluralistic aggregations of several or many communities—their identity is multiple. The conflict that states must resolve is sometimes a dispute between individuals, but it is as often, and perhaps more importantly, about competition between different segments of society, and it is competition for influence, if not control, over the policy outputs that government delivers. In turning to cleavages in this chapter, we are looking at the bases of division within a society, the societal sources of the peaceful competition and conflict that are resolved through the political process. The fundamental nature of these divisions is captured by Lane and Ersson when they describe cleavages as "the so-called raw materials of politics which political parties mould by aligning themselves in a party system facing the electorate in competitive elections. Public institutions offer decision-making mechanisms for handling issues that somehow relate to the cleavages in the social structure" (1991: 11). Similarly, Gallagher et al. describe cleavages as "the actual substance of the social divisions that underpin contemporary ... politics" (1995: 210).

Building on the work of Lipset and Rokkan (1967), Gallagher et al. suggest that a cleavage involves three dimensions:

a) a "social division" between people in terms of some central characteristic,

b) a collective identification in terms of this social division, and

12.1
CLEAVAGES DEFINED

12.1 Cleavages Defined
12.2 Cleavages Examined
    12.2.1 Religious
    12.2.2 Ethno-linguistic
    12.2.3 Centre-periphery
    12.2.4 Urban-rural
    12.2.5 Class
12.3 Reinforcing and Cross-Cutting Cleavages
12.4 Case Study: Quebec within Canada

319

c) some organization that gives "institutional expression" to this collective identification. (1995: 210-11)

Each of these points deserves expansion. The first suggests that not only do people identify themselves in terms of a common characteristic, but also that this is a basis for distinguishing themselves from others who do not share in this defining criterion. There are, in fact, many different bases on which such divisions may rest, but the most compelling are those that are at least in some degree **ASCRIPTIVE**. This adjective designates characteristics in some way innate (race), or inherited (mother tongue), or (for at least one's formative years) involuntarily assigned (religion, class). This allows us to distinguish the identities on which cleavages rest from those identities or identifications more consciously selected or manufactured, such as an ideology, or a political party, or an interest group. Each of these latter may, in fact, be linked very closely to a cleavage (e.g., socialism and class; Christian Democratic parties and religion), but need not necessarily be so connected.

The second element of cleavages also indicates how the distinction made above is not entirely artificial. You could hardly belong to a political party or an interest group without being aware of or identifying yourself as a member of these organizations. It is entirely possible, if not in fact often the case, that we do *not* identify ourselves in terms of our race, or mother tongue, or class. We each have racial or ethnic, linguistic, and class characteristics, but may not see these as the things that determine who we are and what we want. Very often these characteristics become "visible" to us only in the presence of others whose characteristics are different. In this sense, a cleavage does not rest on the fact of difference, but on the *perception* of difference.

Third, though, the perception of difference is by itself not enough to make a cleavage politically relevant. The collective identification of people in terms of their common characteristic may lead to some political action, and this will in all likelihood express itself in some form of organization. This is where cleavages may link up with ideology, or political parties, or interest groups. Hence, members of the working class, conscious of their collective identity and interest, may adopt a socialist ideology, establish trade unions, support the social democratic party, etc. You will have noticed that something extra slipped into that last sentence, namely the addition of the words "and interest." We need this, or something like it, to explain how we get from consciousness of our identity in terms of a social characteristic to organization for political action on the basis of this identity. To be conscious of my religious or ethnic or class identity has no political significance unless it also means that I have an **INTEREST** that is connected to that identity, and that this interest is not being met, or is threatened, or requires protection, by the government. The division at the basis of a cleavage must be not simply a difference in identities, but a *difference in interests*, where interest directs us to what a group (or individual, for that matter) wants or believes it needs. The political interest of a group is in receiving the public policies it wants or needs, and enduring none that are contrary to its wants or needs. Differences in interest (whether real or perceived) are critical to the movement from collective identity to organization for political action. Where a collective identity fails to mobilize politically on behalf of some common interest the cleavage is only *latent*, in contrast to those that are *manifest* in the activity of other groups. This may become clearer if we look at some of the more common cleavages within modern societies.

Cleavages are the product of history: either significant changes in the nature of a society (a religious schism, the emergence of a new economic system, the impact of technology, etc.) have conspired to differentiate a people; or wars, conquests, or political union have put together different peoples into one society. By and large either or both of these are true of the cleavages considered below.

**12.2
CLEAVAGES EXAMINED**

12.2.1 Religious

One of the oldest cleavages in most Western democracies, and one that had much to do with the emergence of modern society in Western Europe and its dependencies, is that arising from religious difference: a cleavage that can most seriously threaten the peace and stability of a society. The Reformation in Europe led to, or served as an excuse for, a number of civil wars and wars between nation-states. Interestingly, even today most European countries remain overwhelmingly Catholic *or* Protestant, and it is not an exaggeration to say that in most of the world, religious pluralism is still either unknown or a source of tension. One need only think of the world's persistent trouble spots to identify clashes based, in whole or in part, on religious difference: the various parts of former Yugoslavia, Northern Ireland, Cyprus, Kashmir, Lebanon, etc. Elsewhere, the political questions have focused on the role of the state in protecting a religion's values or traditional practices. For a variety of historical reasons, countries where there is a strict constitutional separation of church and state—as in the United States—have been rare. If not constitutionally, then in practice, or perhaps traditionally in past practice, the state has tended to favour one religion or another in some of its policies, and this creates resentment or demand for equity from other religious denominations. In some European countries (and among some of the Christian right in the U.S.) the religious cleavage is not so much interdenominational as between those who continue to defend a wholly secular state and those who would make religious values once again part of official decision-making, or who seek to make public policy consistent with church teachings. In parts of the Islamic world, the question is reversed: namely, whether secularization of the state is possible. We should perhaps note that with the religious cleavage we are talking as much about a social identification as about any commitment to a particular spiritual creed. In many cases the conflict between adherents of rival faiths has little to do with theology or devotion, and everything to do with a way of life and identification within the community. In plural, secular North American society, religious belief and practice are often seen to be simply matters of personal choice; in many other societies religious affiliation has a much more collective and social character: religion cannot be so simply or neatly extricated from other aspects of life.

12.2.2 Ethno-linguistic

A variety of different but similar variables can be treated here. Despite the increasing doubts that scientists have with the concept of "race," we can easily note the existence of many societies in which race has been (Uganda) or remains (the U.S., South Africa, Indonesia) a significant cleavage. Most of these cleavages are the unhappy legacy of colonialism and imperialism. In many other cases, though, political union or conquests or dynastic marriages have joined different ethnic and linguistic communities (which are not so distinct "racially") in one society. English and French in Canada, Flemish and Walloon in Belgium, and French, German, and Italian in Switzerland are more striking examples of advanced democracies with a significant ethno-linguistic cleavage, but countries like Spain, France, and Britain also score high on ethnicity indexes (see Lane and Ersson, 1991: 75). It is important to understand that these cleavages are never just about language, but also about cultural differences rooted in or sustained through linguistic difference. In some cases, like the Scottish or Welsh in Britain, the cultural differences may in fact have survived the demise or decline of the native tongue. As we will discuss shortly, such ethno-linguistic cleavage seems rarely to exist in isolation, but is often linked to another, such as religion or class. In and of itself, the ethno-linguistic cleavage mobilizes its supporters around issues relevant to the survival of the culture: measures protecting and preserving use of the language, education, and other cultural supports. In some cases, freedom from discrimination or redress for historic injustices will also be high on the agenda. Most important is some kind of political power with which to guarantee favourable policies. For political majorities this is not a problem; ethno-linguistic minorities, though, will seek some manner of constitutional protection, special representation, and/or autonomy within the system. (See also the discussion of Quebec in Canada, section 12.4.)

12.2.3 Centre-periphery

This cleavage is a function of size (i.e., population) and distance (i.e., geography), in that without a significant separation of population there can, by definition, be no centre and periphery. As in all other cleavages, the difference *has to matter* in some way. Virtually all societies—city-states or micro-states excepted—have a centre, and what makes it the centre is not its location but its *centrality* within the society. It is the largest city or most populous region; it may be the political capital and/or the most economically developed and productive region. In most cases, then, this centrality will be a source of resentment to regions or areas that feel disadvantaged or excluded by not being at the centre. **METROPOLE** and **HINTERLAND** is another way of characterizing the halves of this cleavage, which is apt in that hinterland has the connotation of a region exploited or used for the benefit of the metropole, something very likely to cause resentment among those who inhabit the hinterland. Doug Owram (1987) has called the Canadian western provinces a "reluctant hinterland," suggesting that this perception of being

323

excluded from the Canadian economic and political centre lies at the heart of so-called "western alienation." Similar feelings may colour the attitudes of those in northern Britain with respect to the wealthier south, or those outlying regions of France *vis-à-vis* Paris. This implies that the cleavage is fuelled by a sense of economic disparity or deprivation, but that is clearly not the case in western Canada, where the strongest expressions of discontent come from two of the country's wealthiest provinces. The grievance seems to stem rather from being excluded from the economic and political decision-making that takes place in central Canada (Ottawa-Toronto-Montreal) where the central Canadian voices of Ontario and Quebec dominate, in part because of their larger populations. For their part, central Canadians sometimes suspect that western alienation persists because provincial political leaders call on historic grievances (often long settled) or exacerbate conflict with the central government as a means of building their own support.

At least to date, in the Canadian case, the centre-periphery cleavage has usually been about a periphery that would like to have greater weight or influence in the policy-making that goes on at the centre. In Italy, growth in the 1990s in support in northern provinces for political movements with separatist agendas points in a more disruptive direction. Italy is governed from Rome, situated in the more populous, but also poorer, southern half of the country. As in most modern countries, the Italian state performs a redistributive function, which in this case means that the industrialized urban north subsidizes the poor, more rural south. Northern support for separatist parties is an example of a wealthy hinterland seeking to be free from a needy metropole.

To a considerable degree, the centre-periphery cleavage accounts for what is commonly called "political regionalism," which exists whenever the identification with a particular territory within a larger geographic whole becomes a factor in political activity. By itself, though, identification with a particular territorial region will not be the basis for political action; something else must unite and motivate the people within this region. There are many cases where regionalism reflects, as it does in western Canada, a centre-periphery cleavage, but there are also cases where regionalism is based on a different kind of cleavage.

12.2.4 Urban-rural

The urban-rural cleavage illustrates an important point, namely that for a cleavage to play a significant role in a country's politics, there must be some measure of balance between the two sides of the division. To speak of an urban-rural cleavage in the Middle Ages, when there were few cities, would be rather pointless, but the same is just as true in many parts of the industrialized world today where more than 80 per cent of the population lives in cities. This does not mean that there is no contrast nor a conflict of interest between those who live in the cities and those who still live in the country, but the balance of power is so clearly held by urban dwellers that the cleavage is no longer significant in the larger play of politics. In many places the urban-suburban cleavage has become as relevant as the urban-rural one once was.

There remain pockets where this cleavage is capable of exerting an influence: within Europe in Scandinavia, and within Canada in Saskatchewan, for example. It has also been suggested that the rise of environmental consciousness, combined with an increase in the number of urban workers who commute from a home in the country, has given renewed strength to this cleavage in some cases, albeit with a different flavour from the days when the rural component was primarily—if not uniformly—agricultural in its interests. As technology-intensive agribusiness replaces traditional farming, an additional split in the rural population develops, pitting environmentalists and rural home-owners against agricultural producers.

12.2.5 Class

There are several compelling reasons for arguing that class has become the most significant of the cleavages in contemporary politics, and most observers would agree with Gallagher et al. that this has been especially true of Western European politics (1995: 214). It is even possible to see the rural-urban cleavage, in many cases, as rooted in class differences. Certainly not all countries are characterized by ethno-linguistic difference, or religious distinctions, or centre-periphery conflicts, but all have economic classes. Two factors must be kept in mind here, though: *how* we define and identify class; and the fact that class, like other bases of identity, may remain a *latent* cleavage.

Class, in any society, represents social stratifications that give differential access to resources and other societal goods. How these classes are to be defined and identified depends, in part, on perspective. Marx, for example, defined classes *structurally*, in terms of the organization of the means of economic production in any society, and believed that the capitalist mode of production created essentially two classes: owners and workers. Marx believed modern politics would become the class struggle between these two classes (and eventually the victory of the working class). In fact, in modern industrial (or now post-industrial) economies, the structure of capitalism is much more complex. In addition to owners and workers there are considerable numbers who are neither: the self-employed (whom Marx thought would be insignificant), the unemployed, those employed in public or quasi-public institutions, farmers, students, etc. Division *within* classes, or class fractions, can be as significant as the divisions between classes. Different segments of the business community (manufacturers versus retailers versus bankers, for example) have different needs and interests, above and beyond what they share in common. Similarly, workers of blue, white, and pink collars may be in as much competition and conflict with each other as with their bosses. An increasing fragmentation of the classes, considered structurally, puts impediments in the way of class politics. Sociologically, class is more likely to be considered today in terms of measures such as income, education, status, or composites that combine several of these. So to the extent that class has become an academic construct, it is less likely to form the basis of an identity on which a politics will be based.

It is possible, therefore, that however real class may be, it remains latent as a cleavage, and there are several reasons for this. One is the growth of a so-called "middle-class" society in the affluent world, combined with the strength of those ideologies and cultural beliefs that ignore or minimize the significance of class in such societies. Studies show that the overwhelming majority view themselves as members of the middle class, which may reflect in part the structural fragmentation noted above, as well as the relative affluence of all in these societies. It also means almost automatically that they cannot conceive of class as the basis on which their politics needs to be based. As with all cleavages, there must be a significant "other" or the basis of identity does not become politicized. In societies where strong cultural beliefs argue (contrary to all evidence) that individuals' social positions are the product of their hard work, intelligence, and initiative, to be disadvantaged in class terms can be a sign of failure. Certainly, in most European democracies, class is a significant cleavage, but it is much less so in North America, where political parties that campaign on behalf of a particular class are rare, and rarely successful. This is not to say that class is not an important variable in North American politics, only that it is not the primary identity informing the political consciousness and action of large segments of society.[1]

Any society will have a cleavage structure that will reflect some, but probably not all, of the cleavages discussed above. Across generations, the cleavages that matter may shift as technological, social, and demographic changes take effect. There may be other cleavages (like age) that remain latent but have the potential to manifest themselves at some future date. The constellation of cleavages operating in any given society has two significant relationships: one internal and one external. The latter is the relationship between the cleavages and the political organizations and institutions where behaviour occurs. As noted, a cleavage may account for the support given to a political party, to an interest group, or to the strength of an ideology within a political culture. Political parties, interest groups, and any other vehicles of representation will succeed or fail to obtain policies that respond to the needs of the segments of society they represent. In this way cleavages are either accommodated within the polity, or not. When a cleavage is most fully accommodated by responsive policies within a political community, the division represented by the cleavage ceases to be a basis for political mobilization. At worst, a cleavage that cannot be accommodated leads to civil war (see Yugoslavia) or partition (see the former Czechoslovakia). The ability of the society to accommodate or at least contain its cleavages will depend on features of the party system that we will be discussing below, in particular the electoral and party systems, which in turn shape the nature of party government. What also matters is the internal relationship, that of the cleavages to each other.

The crucial distinction here is between **REINFORCING** and **CROSS-CUTTING** cleavages. In the former case, two or more bases of identity (or difference) are shared by the same population. This means, in effect, that on virtually every issue the lines of opposition will separate the same groups from each other. In Austria, the Catholic population has tended to be more bourgeois; the work-

12.3 REINFORCING AND CROSS-CUTTING CLEAVAGES

1. Many studies of voting behaviour, for example, continue to use class to explain patterns and to answer questions such as "why do suburban residents vote differently from inner-city dwellers?" Or, "why have high-income blue-collar voters abandoned the NDP?" But the existence of patterns does not mean that underlying them is a conscious political identity formed in terms of class. To use one of Marx's terms, such patterns do not necessarily indicate "class consciousness."

REINFORCING CLEAVAGES

Catholic upper class	Anti-clerical working class

FIGURE 12.1

CROSS-CUTTING CLEAVAGES

Anti-clerical working class	Catholic working class
Anti-clerical business class	Catholic business class

FIGURE 12.2

ing class is generally anti-clerical (see Figure 12.1). This division led to a brief civil war in the 1930s. Even more strikingly, in Belgium, the Flemish population in the north and west is generally more affluent than the Francophone Walloons in the south and east parts of the country. Tension between the two groups exists here on at least three levels, and the effect of such reinforcement in the Belgian case has been a steady decentralization of the political system. Generally speaking, we would expect reinforcing cleavages to lead, all else being equal, to **FRAGMENTATION** of the polity, as happened in Czechoslovakia and Yugoslavia. At the very least, reinforcing cleavages will require a special effort by all parties to avoid destabilizing consequences.

The situation is easier where cleavages do not coincide so neatly. Consider a situation where there is a strong religious cleavage and a strong class cleavage, but each class is divided equally among those who fall on either side of the religious divide (see Figure 12.2). Here the cleavages offset each other perfectly: those who are united by religion are divided by economic class, and vice versa. On different issues, then, the majority and minority groups will not be identical. The more cross-cutting cleavages there are, the more political majorities will be shifting and temporary, favouring or alienating no particular group on a regular basis. In this way, cross-cutting cleavages can be stabilizing in a pluralistic society.

Cleavages draw our attention to the fragmentation of identity in modern societies. A central task for the political system of any such society is to contain or defuse the differences and contests of interest that emerge out of these various identities. This is perhaps the element of politics that is identified as the resolution of conflict, the engineering of consent, or the art of compromise. If one side of any division is always the "winner" in battles over policy, then the losing party will soon feel aggrieved, exploited, alienated. The long-term consequences of such an outcome are rarely good for a political community. What will make a big difference in determining whether such outcomes are likely is the capacity of the political process to provide representation to the various segments of society and in so doing provide a share in government and/or a voice in the policy process. To explore this further means moving from cleavages to the representative vehicles such as parties, organized groups, etc. It is our contention, though, that the nature of parties is itself determined by the electoral system in which parties compete, and by the party system that the electoral system has a large part in shaping. It is these institutional systems, electoral and party, that we will examine in the next chapter.

The dominant cleavage in Canadian politics has been an ethno-linguistic one, between English-speaking and French-speaking Canada. Given the territorial concentration of Canada's francophone population in Quebec (and adjacent areas of New Brunswick and Ontario), this cleavage also contributes to the country's second axis of conflict: regionalism. The English/French division, or what has come to be regarded as "the Quebec problem," is illustrative of many points about cleavages generally, and about this kind of cleavage in particular.

First, this is not a question primarily or solely about language; it is rather about cultural identity, about a people conscious of themselves as a collective entity bound together by culture, history, *and* language, and about the political demands arising out of this sense of being "a nation." Thus, there are real and significant differences between the political demands (or aspirations) of francophones *outside* Quebec, expectations largely focused on language and education rights, and the demands of the self-identified Québécois, whose fundamental concerns are about self-government or autonomy within the Canadian state.

Second, it is about the power of history, and culture, and community, and the old truism about the whole being greater than the sum of its parts. How else do we explain the survival of a French-speaking culture of 6 million people in an English continent of over 300 million, especially considering that Quebec was cut off from France more than 200 years ago and has had only a marginal relationship with that country in the intervening time? The Quebec people claim, with some justification, to be a nation, and a North American nation. French settlement began early in the seventeenth century, and today it is estimated that a majority of the province's francophones has descended from families settled in Quebec *before* conquest by the English in 1759-63. Québécois are proud of the uniqueness of their culture, not only in English-speaking North America but also in the francophone world.

These facts also point to the difficulty of labelling peoples in a way that is true to their identity. Growing up in English Canada, people of this author's generation would have referred to their francophone fellow citizens as "French Canadians." This is a misnomer, since French Canada ceased to exist in 1763, and the label

**12.4
CASE STUDY: QUEBEC
WITHIN CANADA**

"French" could be construed as implying a relationship to France, which also ceased to exist after 1763. By the same token, "English Canada" is no more accurate today, although it is significant that this term *was* accurate until well into the twentieth century, perhaps until the Statute of Westminster in 1931. In the respect of being independent of European authority *and* attachment, the French-speaking inhabitants of Quebec could truly claim to be the first Canadians. If, on the other hand, we use terms like English-Canadian and French-Canadian as short forms for English-speaking Canadians and French-speaking Canadians, we then swallow up a great many cultural distinctions, not simply within francophone Canada (the Québécois, the Acadians of New Brunswick, the francophone Métis of Saskatchewan, etc.) but also within anglophone Canada, *and* we ignore all those whose primary tongue is neither English nor French. The strategy of treating the cleavage we are discussing as simply or primarily about language (the thrust behind the official bilingualism policies of the Trudeau Liberals, *and* the perception of many of those most opposed to bilingualism) ultimately fails to accommodate this cleavage because it fails to address the fact that Quebec does constitute "a distinct society," whether or not this is recognized constitutionally.

In an earlier chapter, we described one type of nationalism as the demands of a people (i.e., a nation) for the political autonomy necessary to preserve its culture and way of life. Nationalism in Quebec has taken two forms, and to distinguish them we will employ one of those inadequate terms we noted earlier. French-Canadian nationalism, which covered the period from 1763 to 1960, emphasized survival: maintaining the integrity of language, culture, and custom, and avoiding the pressures for assimilation into a larger anglophone society. As early as 1774, Quebec received special status in British North America. The passage of the Quebec Act preserved the civil law code of New France and strengthened the status and power of the local seigneurs (quasi-feudal lords) and of the Catholic Church.

The latter move may be seen as the origin in Canada of the strategy of **ELITE ACCOMMODATION**—ruling a people by co-opting their leaders. Beginning with the union of Lower Canada (Quebec) and Upper Canada (Ontario) into the single colony of Canada in 1840, an element of consociational power-sharing was introduced, which continues in some largely informal respects still today. Many historians, and certainly Quebec historians, would agree that while the Québécois culture survived through the past two centuries, avoiding assimilation into anglophone North America, this survival came at a price. Prior to 1960, francophones in Quebec remained second-class citizens in their own homeland, dominated economically by a wealthy anglo-Canadian business class in Montreal and dominated socially by a conservative Catholic Church. Perhaps the most extreme expression of the sense of inferiority this created for Québécois was captured in the searing title of Pierre Vallières's 1967 book: *White Niggers of America (Nègres Blanc d'Amèrique)*.

In 1960, forces of social, economic, and political change, previously held in check by Quebec governments willing to continue the strategy of elite accommodation, launched what has come to be called the "Quiet Revolution." This was a time of transformation: notably, of a secularization of Quebec society, an expansion of the Quebec state, and the emergence of a new Québécois nationalism. Instead of ensuring the survival of their culture by remaining a traditional, conservative, church-dominated society, *les Québécois* were ready to take their place in urban, secular, liberal North American society, to become fully modern. The survival of their culture and language was to be guaranteed by political means, through the exercise of new or expanded authority.

In the past 40 years, Quebec society has been thoroughly transformed in virtually every respect, with the creation of a modern, activist state (symbolized by the giant projects of Hydro-Québec), the emergence of a francophone business and entrepreneurial class, and the enactment of Bill 101, the Charter of the French Language in Quebec, designed to make Quebec, so far as social and political realities permit, a unilingual, francophone society. The Quiet Revolution began with the slogan *"Maitres chez nous"*—"masters in our own house"—which was about the status of francophone Quebecers within their own province. The past 20 years have instead comprised an evolving debate about Quebec's place within Canada, a debate involving two camps: the federalists and the sovereigntists.

Since the election of the Parti Québécois to power in 1976, the movement for Quebec sovereignty has been at the forefront of Quebec and, as often as not, Canadian politics; the PQ has formed the government in Quebec or has been the official opposition since that time. Sovereigntists believe that Quebec's survival as a distinct society in North America depends on achieving that degree of self-government that comes with being a sovereign nation-state. So-called "soft" sovereigntists, such as the PQ's first Premier, René Lévesque, believe that Quebec's independence is

KEY TERMS

ascriptive variables
centre
class
cross-cutting cleavages
ethnicity
fragmentation
hinterland
identities
interest
language
latent cleavage
metropole
periphery
race
reinforcing cleavages
religion
urban-rural

only feasible if it can remain closely partnered with Canada for currency, customs, trade, defence, and other matters. Such a partnership (what Lévesque called "sovereignty-association") would be negotiated with Canada before or after a declaration of sovereignty. Hard-line sovereigntists advocate a unilateral declaration of independence, regardless of the willingness of Canada to negotiate terms or agree to subsequent forms of association. On two occasions Quebecers have gone to the polls for plebiscites that would have authorized the government of Quebec to take further steps towards securing independence from Canada. The No ("non") side won by a 60-40 margin in 1980, but barely eked out a victory in 1995, despite the overwhelming support of non-francophones.

Opposing the sovereigntists has been the "federalist" side, comprised of those who believe that Quebec's proper place remains within Canada. Part of this contingent includes the majority of anglo-Canada (inside and outside Quebec), which seems comfortable with the status quo. The bulk of francophone federalists within Quebec (traditionally represented by the Quebec Liberal Party) seek constitutional accommodation from the rest of Canada as the means of ensuring the survival of Quebec's distinct society within the federation. Since the 1980 referendum, the federalists' position (within francophone Quebec) has been articulated in terms of five "traditional demands" requiring constitutional change. Twice, all provincial premiers have agreed to accords that met or went most of the way to meeting these demands: in the Meech Lake Accord of 1984 and the Charlottetown Accord of 1992. Each failed to receive the popular support outside of Quebec that their passage required (politically, if not legally). It has been speculated that some of the "soft" sovereigntist vote comes from frustrated federalists hoping to force a better deal for Quebec from a recalcitrant English Canada.

Ironically, the "Quebec question" is not likely to go away until it receives some constitutional resolution, one way or another, but past failures have created a popular distaste for constitutional questions that is only surpassed by the wariness of politicians to test these waters again. In 1998, the Supreme Court of Canada ruled that the rest of Canada would be obligated to negotiate separation with the government of Quebec if it should receive a clear majority in favour of separation in a clearly worded question. In June 2000, the Parliament of Canada passed the government's so-called "Clarity Bill" (C-20), which "provides for the House of Commons to determine the clarity of a referendum question on the secession of a province and sets out some of the factors to be considered in making its determination." The Act also provides for the House of Commons to determine what constitutes a "clear majority" in the event of a referendum on separation, and establishes that any act of separation by a province would require a constitutional amendment necessitating negotiation by the government of Canada and all the provinces. The argument has been made in the past that ambiguous questions and a lack of clarity on just what might follow a sovereignty vote have misled Quebecers who have voted "yes" to sovereignty referenda. The strongest arguments against Quebec sovereignty today, though, are probably the economic costs such a separation would entail, not just for Quebec but for all of Canada.

SOMETHING TO CONSIDER

Some observers would suggest that in North America the class cleavage is not absent from politics: rather, it is simply that the advantaged classes are well mobilized and the disadvantaged are not. Is there evidence to support this conclusion?

Setting aside *how* it might happen, if the "Quebec question" were resolved to everyone's satisfaction, what issue(s) might take its place at the core of Canadian politics?

REFERENCES AND SUGGESTED READING

Gallagher, Michael, et al. 1995. *Representative Government in Modern Europe*. New York: McGraw-Hill.

Gibbins, Roger. 1994. *Conflict and Unity*, 3rd ed. Scarborough, Ont.: Nelson.

Lane, Jan-Erik, and Svante O. Ersson. 1991. *Politics and Society in Western Europe*. London: Sage.

Lipset, Seymour Martin, and Stein Rokkan. 1967. *Party Systems and Voter Alignments*. New York: Free Press.

Mény, Yves. 1993. *Government and Politics in Western Europe*, 2nd ed. Oxford: Oxford University Press.

Owram, Doug. 1987. "Reluctant Hinterland," in R.S. Blair and J.T. McLeod, eds., *The Canadian Political Tradition*. Scarborough, Ont.: Methuen, 1987.

13

electoral systems and party systems

In the modern age, most democracy is representative democracy, a term we have reserved for those systems in which citizens have the opportunity to vote for representatives in periodic, competitive elections. In Chapter Eleven we reflected on the significance of this kind of democracy; here we will extend that examination on the basis of a closer look at the institutional machinery of the electoral process and its consequences for vehicles of representation in the political process. After examining some technical issues that must be addressed by all systems, we will turn to perhaps the most significant variable within any country's political process: its electoral system. The electoral system in turn has enormous influence on the party system that operates in a country. The electoral and party systems will determine the kind of parliamentary system that tends to prevail (as discussed in Chapter Eight), and also influence the other vehicles of representation to which citizens turn for political organization.

It is possible for officials from all three "branches" of government, or types of governmental institution, to be subject to periodic election. In practice, though, most electoral politics, particularly at the national level, concerns choosing representatives to sit in the legislature, and in some bicameral legislatures, in both houses of the parliament. The only other commonly elected post in national government is that of president, and this is true of strong presidents in systems characterized by what we called presidentialism, and in some cases of presidents who serve as formal heads of state in parliamentary regimes. In the remainder of this chapter, then, our focus will be on the selection of representatives for the legislature, and, in most cases, will remain with the lower

13.1
THE BASICS

13.1   The Basics
13.2   Electoral Systems
13.3   Majoritarian Electoral Systems
       13.3.1   Single-member plurality
       13.3.2   Single-member majority
13.4   Proportionate Electoral Systems
13.5   PR: The "German-Style" System
13.6   Party Systems
13.7   Conclusion

SIZE OF LEGISLATURE AND AVERAGE CONSTITUENCY (LOWER CHAMBER IN BICAMERAL LEGISLATURES, JULY 1999)

Country	Seats	Population (millions)	Constituency Size (pop / seats)
Finland	200	5.2	26,000
Hungary	386	10.2	26,000
Sweden	349	8.9	26,000
Norway	165	4.4	27,000
Denmark	179	5.4	30,000
New Zealand	120	3.7	31,000
Greece	300	10.7	36,000
Portugal	230	9.9	43,000
Austria	183	8.1	44,000
Israel	120	5.7	48,000
Czech Rep.	200	10.3	51,000
Ireland	60	3.6	61,000
Belgium	150	10.2	68,000
Poland	460	38.6	84,000
Italy	630	56.7	90,000
U.K.	659	59.1	90,000
France	577	59.0	102,000
Canada	301	31.0	103,000
Netherlands	150	15.8	105,000
Spain	350	39.2	112,000
Germany	669	82.1	123,000
Australia	148	18.8	127,000
Japan	500	126.2	252,000
Russia	450	146.4	325,000
U.S.	435	272.6	627,000
India	545	1,000.8	1,836,000

FIGURE 13.1

or first chamber of the legislature (because of its role as the "confidence chamber" in parliamentary systems).

With regard to the last point, we should note that while different principles of representation exist, first chambers in bicameral systems and unitary legislatures are based on the principle of **REPRESENTATION BY POPULATION**. This is also known as the "one man (person), one vote" principle, which requires that each citizen's vote carry at least roughly the same weight as that of every other citizen. In practice this means that each member of the legislature should ideally represent the same number of citizens (constituents). Thus the territorial **SIZE** of each representative's district or **CONSTITUENCY** should be determined by population, and each should contain the same population. We say "should" because populations do not remain static, but shift through growth and migration. Periodically, then, constituency boundaries must change to keep the weight of each citizen's voice in the political process equal. This is one reason why in most (if not all) democracies, a regular census is taken.

We should also note that the redefinition of constituency (or riding) boundaries made necessary by demographic change provides an opportunity for any party that controls this process to maximize its own electoral chances in future elections. If in two adjacent constituencies the government won one riding by a two-to-one majority and lost the other by a slim margin, the temptation would be great to readjust the boundaries so that both ridings contained a simple majority of loyal supporters. Depending on circumstances, one might wish to concentrate one's opponents' supporters in one riding or disperse them more evenly through many ridings, in either case hoping to minimize their impact on one's own party's fortunes. This manipulation of electoral boundaries goes by the name **GERRYMANDERING**, an activity with much more potential in plurality systems than in proportionate ones. To avoid gerrymandering, the business of adjusting constituency boundaries is usually given to an all-party committee, or to a supposedly impartial judicial panel.

The point behind electoral boundary commissions and the broader principle of representation by population is that of fairness. Several other features of democratic systems are designed to provide fairness to the parties contesting the election. One is rules about the **FINANCING** of election campaigns, rules that for the most part today are designed (not to say that they succeed) to minimize the influence of wealthy private or corporate donors and encourage broad public financing of political parties. Here the reasoning is that parties which are heavily reliant on support from narrow or particular interests cannot be expected to be fully responsive to the wishes of the broader public, nor should any individual or group be able to "buy an election." In some European countries, there are severe restrictions on corporate or private contributions to political parties, which instead receive monies from the public treasury, usually in proportion to the vote share received in the most recent election. On the other hand, in most European countries, laws requiring political parties to disclose private sources of funding are either weak or non-existent (Gallagher et al., 1995: 260).

Just as there are rules about financing, so are there often restrictions concerning the use of the mass media and polling firms. In most European countries (except Germany, Italy, and Sweden), political parties cannot purchase **ADVERTISING** time on television, although in many cases they receive an allocation of free time for political broadcasts (Gallagher et al., 1995: 259). In Canada, political parties can purchase advertising time, but are limited to the share allocated to each registered party from six-and-a-half hours of prime time in the last 39 days of the campaign. The allocation is determined largely (but not exclusively) on the basis of the support received by each party in the previous election and the number of seats held in the House of Commons (see Figure 13.2). Parties also receive an amount of free time allocated in the same proportions. Not surprisingly, perhaps, there are no restrictions on the use of television in the United States. Another possible restriction is on the publication of public opinion **POLLS** during an election campaign (usually in the very final stages). In Canada, regulations that prohibited the publication of a poll or commissioned survey in the last three days of a federal election campaign were ruled unconstitutional by the Supreme Court of Canada. The new Canada Elections Act, passed in May 2000, prohibits the transmission to the public of the results of new election

TV TIME

Broadcast time allocated to the registered parties in the 2000 Canadian general election by order of the Broadcasting Arbitrator:

Party	Minutes
Liberal	113
Canadian Alliance	59.5
Progressive Conservative	48
Bloc Québécois	40.5
NDP	40.5
Natural Law	17
Green	15.5
Christian Heritage	14.5
Marxist-Leninist	14.5
Canadian Action	14.5
Communist	6
Marijuana Party	6
Total	390

To receive the above allocation, a party must have had candidates nominated in at least fifty electoral districts at the close of nominations.

FIGURE 13.2

SUFFRAGE FOR WOMEN

New Zealand	1893
Australia	1902
Canada	1918
Germany	1919
Sweden	1919
United States	1920
Britain	1928
Spain	1931
France	1944
Italy	1945
Japan	1945
Switzerland	1971

FIGURE 13.3

surveys during polling day. (Before being amended, the Bill would have banned polls during the last 48 hours of a campaign.) Such restrictions on the publication of polls are not uncommon in other democracies, where the period covered by the "gag-law" may be as long as a week.

Last but not least, we should consider the extent of the democratic **FRANCHISE** or the right to vote. Usually, but not always, the same rules determine who may or may not stand for election to office. Today, the franchise in the countries we recognize as democratic is **UNIVERSAL ADULT SUFFRAGE**, meaning that—with a few exceptions such as those in prison, or those deemed to be mentally incapacitated—all citizens above a certain age (usually 18 to 20) have the right to participate in elections as voters or candidates. The universality of voting rights today obscures how recently this universality has been achieved. Women did not receive the vote until just after the First World War in many cases, following the Second World War in countries such as France and Italy, and 1971 in Switzerland (see Figure 13.3). In contrast, New Zealand deserves credit for having extended the vote to women at a time when some countries still restricted the male vote to those holding sufficient property. At many different times the franchise has been withheld from people on the basis not only of gender, but also of race, religion, or ethnic origin. That voting is usually restricted to citizens, and that citizenship is seen to be incomplete without the right to vote, indicate the symbolic importance of elections, something that may be as significant as anything we can say about their representative capacity.

13.2
ELECTORAL SYSTEMS

An electoral system is a mechanism for transforming the preferences of citizens (votes) into an allocation of the offices at stake (seats in the legislature, a presidency) among the competing candidates—a sorting out of the winners and losers. In some ways an electoral system is a very simple institution, not much more than some rules and mathematical formulas (although the latter can challenge those less arithmetically-inclined). On the other hand, the consequences of electoral systems are considerable: for the party system, for the nature of representation that citizens receive, and for the nature of parliamentary government (discussed at greater length in Chapter Eight). Because these consequences are most clearly attached to the selection of representatives for the legislature, this will be our focus: the

ELECTORAL FORMULAS, DISTRICT MAGNITUDE, AND RESULTING SYSTEM

ELECTORAL FORMULA	DISTRICT MAGNITUDE	
	SINGLE-MEMBER (M = 1)	MULTI-MEMBER (M > 1)
PLURALITY	**Majoritarian** Britain, Canada, New Zealand (pre-1996), United States	**Majoritarian** Japan (pre-1996): this system had multi-member constituencies in which citizens cast one vote
MAJORITY	**Majoritarian** France, Australia	**None**
PROPORTIONATE	**Proportionate** Germany, Italy, Japan (1996), New Zealand (1996): although there are single-member districts, a second vote cast for party is used to ensure proportionality	**Proportionate** Austria, Belgium, Denmark, Greece, Iceland, Ireland, Luxembourg, Malta, Netherlands, Norway, Portugal, Spain, Sweden, Switzerland, and most East European democracies

FIGURE 13.4

electoral system as a means of translating votes (v) for competing candidates and parties into seats (s).

As in Chapter Eight, there is a distinction to be made between those systems that tend (or are designed) to produce a majority outcome, hence **MAJORITARIAN ELECTORAL SYSTEMS**, and those systems designed to distribute seats proportionately among parties, hence **PROPORTIONATE ELECTORAL SYSTEMS**. Behind these distinctions (which are based on outcomes) are two variables that describe the basic features of an electoral system. One is the number of candidates elected in each of the constituencies (electoral districts), what is sometimes known as **DISTRICT MAGNITUDE** (M). The universe of electoral systems can be divided into those having an M of 1, known as **SINGLE-MEMBER** systems, and those where M is greater than 1, **MULTI-MEMBER** systems. Canada, the United States, and Britain each have single-member systems, where citizens choose one candidate per riding or electoral district; it may surprise students from these countries to learn that in most of the world's democracies, citizens either choose two or more candidates in each riding, or cast separate votes for candidates and parties (a distinction explained below). The second variable is the **ELECTORAL FORMULA**, which is simply the rule by which the winner is (or winners are) determined. Three types of electoral formula are used: **PLURALITY**, which indicates that the candidate (or candidates) with more votes than any other(s) is declared the winner; **MAJORITY**, which requires a winning candidate to secure a majority of the votes cast; and **PRO-PORTIONATE**, which distributes seats among parties in roughly the proportion that the votes were cast. As may seem obvious, the plurality and majority formulas are usually associated with single-member systems, and the proportionate formula with multi-member systems. An overview of these variations is presented in Figure 13.4.

In comparing electoral system effects, again two broad variables can be noted. One is the amount of **DISPROPOR-TIONALITY**. In a perfectly proportionate system, the proportion of seats each party receives in the legislature is identical to the proportion of votes it received from the electorate; thus % s = % v. This is not simply a mathematical equation, but represents what some would argue is the ideal of **ELECTORAL JUSTICE**; where there is strict proportionality, the legislature reflects most accurately citizens' preferences; no party wins more or fewer seats than its share of the votes entitles it to. In this way, strict proportionality is extremely democratic. Although it is something rarely achieved, most proportionate systems come close, and some very close indeed.

The second outcome variable is something called the **EFFECTIVE THRESHOLD**. This will determine how much support a party needs in order to gain seats in the legislature and, as a result, influence business in the legislature. In some proportionate systems there is a **LEGAL THRESHOLD**, a level of support that a party must receive in order to be allocated its share of legislature seats. In Germany, Italy, and New Zealand, for example, the threshold is (with exceptions) 5 per cent. Where there is no legal requirement, the features of the electoral system itself will determine the "effective" threshold. In the Netherlands, for example, there is one national constituency of 150 seats; this means that any party that can win more than 0.67 per cent of the vote will be guaranteed a seat in the legislature—this is a very low effective threshold. In a single-member plurality system like Canada's, Lijphart calculates the effective threshold to be 35 per cent (1994: 17). This doesn't mean a party must win 35 per cent of the vote to win seats, but that this level of support is required for a party to be reasonably assured of receiving a proportion of seats matching or exceeding its level of support. What matters here is that a high effective threshold will discourage or penalize new or small parties; a low threshold will have the opposite effect, all else being equal. Now let us consider the major types of systems a little more closely.

These are systems that tend to produce a majority in the legislature for the winning party, or that are designed to ensure that the winning candidate has a majority of the votes cast in her riding. A legislative majority has the consequence of producing a single-party majority government (as discussed in Chapter Eight), and many observers equate such a government with political stability. Securing a majority for winning candidates (as in France and Australia) seems to agree nicely with the understanding of democracy as "majority rule." The problem, as we will see, is that in either case, the majority is in some way "**MANUFACTURED**" (or at least inflated).

13.3 MAJORITARIAN ELECTORAL SYSTEMS

13.3.1 Single-member plurality

The simplest system is **SINGLE-MEMBER PLURALITY (SMP)**, which is now common only to Canada, the United States, the United Kingdom, and a few formerly British territories. The simplicity of the system is often presented as one of its virtues: citizens can understand it easily. In each constituency, eligible voters select one from a list of competing candidates, and the candidate receiving more votes than any other is the winner. If there are only two candidates, as was once often the case (and in some cases—particularly in the U.S.—may still be), the winner will also have a majority of votes. But as the number of candidates rises, the level of support with which it is possible to win decreases (for three candidates it is 33 per cent +1 vote, for four candidates it is 25 per cent +1 vote, for five candidates it is 20 per cent +1 vote, etc.), and it becomes more likely that the winner will have received less than a majority of votes cast in the riding (hence the designation as a *plurality* system). This system is quite accurately described as a "**WINNER-TAKE-ALL**" system; since there is a single-member riding, there is just one "prize," which the winner receives no matter how large or small the margin of victory. The other candidates, no matter how close they were to the winning level of support, win nothing at all. This feature affects the outcome of SMP systems in several ways.

	District 1	District 2	District 3	District 4	District 5	Total
Party A	**1,500** v	**1,200** v	**800** v	**750** v	**668** v	4,918 v
Party B	400 v	750 v	750 v	700 v	666 v	3,266 v
Party C	100 v	50 v	450 v	550 v	666 v	1,816 v

TOTAL	%v	%s
Party A	49.18	100
Party B	32.66	0
Party C	18.16	0

FIGURE 13.5

First of all, it contributes to the likelihood of *disproportionality*; there is no necessary correspondence between the proportion of votes gained by each party and its share of legislative seats. This is because *in each riding* one party wins 100 per cent of the seats with something less than 100 per cent of the vote. When these results are added up nationally there is considerable chance of distortion, and no reason that these will somehow "balance out" among the parties. Figure 13.5 presents an extreme but by no means impossible example for a very small parliament of five ridings.

As this hypothetical example shows, even though Party A wins every riding by finishing ahead of its rivals, overall its share of the votes cast is actually less than 50 per cent. In such a situation, a majority of citizens voting expressed a preference for legislators from parties *other* than A, but receive no representation in the legislature. If the example seems extreme, it is noteworthy that in New Brunswick in 1987, the Liberals won all 58 seats in the legislature with the votes of only six of every 10 New Brunswickers. More recently, in the 1997 general election, the Liberals won 101 of the 103 seats (98.1 per cent) at stake in Ontario on the basis of having received 2,294,593 out of 4,633,700 votes cast (49.5 per cent). Figure 13.6 presents a hypothetical result for our five-seat parliament in which the party with the least support wins every seat but one, and the party with the most support is completely shut out.

The disproportionalities or distortions in outcome created by SMP systems are not random, but follow regular patterns. Because of the "winner-take-all" feature of the system, the party with the largest share of the votes tends (the previous example notwithstanding) to be "overpaid" by the system, receiving a larger share of seats than its share of vote would warrant. Correspondingly, when one party is overpaid, another (or more) must be penalized: in a two-party system this will be the second-place party, but where there are several parties it may be some or all of

	District 1	District 2	District 3	District 4	District 5	Total
Party A	**700** v	100 v	**820** v	**730** v	**880** v	3,230 v
Party B	690 v	800 v	600 v	630 v	720 v	**3,440** v
Party C	610 v	**1,100** v	580 v	640 v	400 v	3,330 v
TOTAL	**%v**	**%s**				
Party A	32.3	80				
Party B	34.4	0				
Party C	33.3	20				

FIGURE 13.6

these in varying degrees. This tendency to overcompensate the winning party at the expense of others is the feature that allows SMP systems to generate single-party majority governments, but these majorities are generally inflated (like the New Brunswick example), and are often manufactured (like the example in Figure 13.5). Canada has had 11 majority governments since 1945; of these only two had earned the support of more than 50 per cent of the electorate. Nine of 11 majority governments were "manufactured," meaning that a majority of the electorate had actually voted against the government. A majority government based on minority support is in some respects a "false" victory produced by SMP; on two occasions in Canadian history the party finishing second in voter support has received more seats in the legislature (1896, 1979). SMP is not necessarily responsive to changes in public opinion—parties can lose a little support and all their seats, or lose much support but few seats—and in some cases delivers a contrary result. At the very least, these kinds of results indicate that there is no necessary correspondence in this electoral system between inputs and outputs. If elections are to be a primary means for citizens to keep elites accountable, it seems curious to employ a system that fails to reflect accurately the public's expressed preferences.

The "winner-take-all" character of SMP is especially tough on new or small parties, and for this reason supports or sustains two-party systems in most cases (Canada being a notable exception). A new party can succeed only in ridings where it becomes *the* most popular party; by the same token a party that finishes second in every riding has no more to show for its effort than a party that finishes tenth in every riding. New or small parties with evenly distributed, weak to moderate support will win little or nothing, while new or small parties with regionally concentrated support can succeed, or even flourish, for a time. In this way SMP encourages regionalism or sectionalism, not only within the party system, but within parties themselves, which may seek to concentrate on areas where they already have support rather than seeking to strengthen their appeal in more marginal areas. Finally, SMP encourages **STRATEGIC VOTING**. This occurs when voters, anticipating a certain outcome, vote for a party other than their first choice, in an attempt to prevent that outcome. It may be difficult to find reasons to vote for a party that has no realistic chance (given available evidence) of winning the seat. In this way votes cast for any candidate other than the one who wins are "wasted" votes—they count for nothing in the outcome.

13.3.2 Single-member majority

In France and Australia, different electoral formulas have been combined with single-member districts to produce results that are majoritarian, but here in either case, a simple plurality of votes will not suffice to win the constituency. These are sometimes called **SINGLE-MEMBER MAJORITY (SMM)** systems, but this is only partially (and not necessarily) true of the French legislative elections.

The distinctive feature of the French system is a second round of voting (or what is sometimes called a "**RUN-OFF**") in constituencies where no candidate secures a majority of the votes cast in the initial round. The second vote occurs a week following the first. All candidates receiving less than 12.5 per cent of the vote in the first round are removed from the ballot for the second round. Whoever receives a plurality in the second round is the winner. In practice, this system encourages electoral co-operation among parties of the left and among parties of the right, parties within each group usually agreeing on whose candidate to support in the second round. This often has the result of reducing the number of effective candidates in the second round to two, which ensures that the winner has a majority of the votes cast. Nonetheless, this majority has also been manufactured: many will be forced to vote in the second round for a party that repre-

LEGISLATIVE ELECTION: FRANCE, 1997

Party	% Votes in Round 1	2	No. Seats	% Seats
PARTIES OF THE LEFT				
Communist	9.9	3.7	37	6.4
Socialist	23.5	38.6	246	42.6
Socialist Radical	1.4	2.2	13	2.3
Other Left	2.8	2.2	16	2.8
Greens	6.8	1.7	8	1.4
PARTIES OF THE RIGHT				
UDF	14.2	21.0	109	18.9
RPR	15.7	22.7	139	24.1
Other Right	6.6	2.4	8	1.4
National Front	14.9	5.7	1	0.2
Other	4.2	0.0	0	0
TOTAL			577	

FIGURE 13.7

sents their second or third choice, or not vote at all. Similarly, there is no necessary correspondence between voter preferences and final party standings in the legislature. Figure 13.7 demonstrates some of these features of the French system.

The effect of the second round of voting (or run-off) is to draw support from minor parties and concentrate it with the more dominant parties within each ideological division. For the second ballot, voting becomes more "strategic", it is based on a calculation of the probabilities of victory for the various remaining candidates. As for the final distribution of seats among the parties, the disproportionalities can be considerable. In 1997, the largest effect of the electoral system was to reward the ultra-right National Front, which collected almost 15 per cent of the first-round vote, with ultimately only one seat in the legislature. (In 1993, both the Socialists and the UDF finished the second round of voting with the support of 28.3 per cent of the vote, but the UDF gained 213 seats to the Socialists' 60. The RPF, which finished third in popular vote at 25.8 per cent, actually won the most seats: 247.) This electoral system has the virtue (like proportional representation) of presenting the electorate with a wide range of choices, at least initially, but the drawback (like the single-member plurality system) is that of generating no strict correspondence between strength of support and number of seats won.

The Australian single-member system employs what is called an alternative vote, by means of an **ORDINAL** or **PREFERENTIAL BALLOT**. This means that instead of choosing one among the available candidates, voters rank all the candidates in order of preference. If no candidate should secure a majority of first preference votes, then the candidate with the least number of first preference votes is eliminated, and his or her ballots redistributed among the remaining candidates on the basis of the second preferences indicated.

One is tempted to call the French and Australian systems idiosyncratic variations on the majoritarian theme, measuring marginally better than simple plurality systems with respect to disproportionality and effective threshold (see Figures 13.7 and 13.8); they are also less likely to manufacture a parliamentary

LEGISLATIVE ELECTION: AUSTRALIA, 1998

Party 1	% Votes	No. Seats	% Seats
Australian Labor Party	40.0	66	44.6
Liberal Party of Australia	34.1	64	43.2
National Party of Australia	5.3	16	10.8
Pauline Hanson's One Nation	8.4	—	—
Australian Democrats	5.1	—	—
Australian Greens	2.1	—	—
Others	1.7	2	1.4
TOTAL		**148**	

FIGURE 13.8

EFFECTS OF ELECTORAL FORMULAS ON DISPROPORTIONALITY AND PARTY SYSTEMS

Electoral formula	Dispropor-tionality (%)	Effective no. of elective parties	Effective no. of parliamentary parties	Frequency of parliamentary majorities	Frequency of manufactured majorities
Plurality (5)	13.56	3.09	2.04	0.93	0.71
Other majoritarian (2)	10.88	3.58	2.77	0.52	0.52
Proportionate (20)	4.27	4.07	3.56	0.20	0.12

The number in brackets indicates the number of countries on which the numbers for each formula are based. Adapted from Lijphart (1994: 96).

FIGURE 13.9

majority. The larger point, though, is that majoritarian systems, whether resting on plurality rules or not, are increasingly idiosyncratic in the democratic world, where the virtues of proportionality increasingly rule.

**13.4
PROPORTIONATE
ELECTORAL SYSTEMS**

The operation of plurality systems is easy to understand but the results can be puzzling; the outcome of proportionate systems, by contrast, is fairly transparent, but the various means employed to achieve this result can be complicated and confusing. The entire rationale of proportional representation systems is to distribute legislative seats among parties in proportions as true to their share of vote as is possible. This can be seen in the contrast, presented in Figure 13.9, between the distribution of seats and votes in plurality systems and in proportionate systems. There are three sets of distinctions we need to examine in order to understand how proportionate systems actually work: the nature of the multi-member constituency system, the type of electoral formula used, and the use of a second tier.

First of all, we have noted that proportionate systems often employ a multi-member constituency. The size of these constituencies can vary considerably, from three or four members up to a national constituency that effectively presents the whole legislature to each citizen (as in Israel and the Netherlands), but the normal range seems to be between five and 15 members returned to the legislature from each constituency. The larger the constituency the easier it will be to obtain a proportionate distribution of seats in the constituency. Consider an outcome like the following:

Party A 40 %	Party C 20 %
Party B 30 %	Party D 10 %

If there were four seats at stake here, the division might be one seat for each party (depending on the formula used), or two for Party A and one each for Party B and Party C. Neither division is very close to the actual proportions of support. With ten seats at stake, each party could receive exactly the proportion of seats warranted by its vote share: four for A, three for B, two for C, and one for D. The trade-off for securing greater proportionality through larger constituencies is a less direct relationship between representatives and their constituents.

Given the number of parties that may be contesting the election, multi-member constituencies obviously involve a different balloting environment than that of single-member plurality systems. In two countries, Ireland and Malta, the voters employ a **SINGLE TRANSFERABLE VOTE** (STV), which is (like the Australian ballot) an ordinal ballot in which voters rank the candidates in order of preference. Unlike the Australian case, though, here several candidates will be elected, so the ballot may be quite lengthy, and counting procedures quite complicated. One virtue of STV is that it gives the voters maximum freedom to choose among candidates of different parties and express their preferences for them.

Much more common in multi-member constituencies are **LIST SYSTEMS**, where voters choose between party lists. In a six-member constituency, then, each party contesting the election presents voters with a list of candidates for consideration (see Figure 13.11). List systems vary considerably with regard to the amount of choice they present to voters. In some cases, voters simply choose between one party's list or another's, the order of candidates in each case being set and fixed by the party. In other systems, voters are able to change the order of the candidates on the list. Control over the ranking of candidates is clearly crucial to their electability (and it is also a very effective means of exercising party discipline). Obviously, in a six-member riding, given proportionality, it is extremely unlikely that a party will elect all of its candidates; those at the top of the list will be the first elected. In the sample ballot shown, the party has attempted to increase the chances of electing its first candidate. Casting this ballot would give six votes to the Radical Party: two to B. Barker, and one to

A: PLURALITY SYSTEMS

Canada 2000

Party	% v	# s	% s
Liberal	40.8	172	57.1
Canadian Alliance	25.5	66	21.9
Progressive Conservative	12.2	12	4.0
Bloc Québécois	10.7	38	12.6
New Democratic Party	8.5	13	4.3
Total		301	

Britain 1997

Party	% v	# s	% s
Labour	43.2	418	64.4
Conservative	30.7	165	25.0
Liberal Democrats	16.8	46	7.0
Referendum	2.6	—	—
Scottish National	2.0	6	0.9
Ulster Unionist	0.8	10	1.5
Social Democratic and Labour	0.6	3	0.5
Playd Cymru/Party of Wales	0.5	4	0.6
Sinn Fein	0.4	2	0.3
Democratic Unionist	0.3	2	0.3
Other	2.0	3	0.5
Total		659	

B: PROPORTIONATE SYSTEMS

Belgium 1999

Party	% v	# s	% s
Flemish Liberals and Democrats	14.3	23	15.3
Christian People's (Flemish)	14.1	22	14.7
Socialists (Francophone)	10.1	19	12.7
Liberal Reformist	10.1	18	12.0
Flemish Bloc	9.9	15	10.0
Socialists (Flemish)	9.6	14	9.3
Francophone Ecologists	7.3	11	7.3
Flemish Ecologists	7.0	9	6.0
Christian Social (Francophone)	5.9	10	6.7
People's Union-ID21	5.6	8	5.3
National Front	1.5	1	0.7
Other	2.1	—	—
Total		150	

Czech Republic 1998

Party	% v	# s	% s
Social Democrats	32.3	74	37.0
Civic Democratic Party	27.7	63	31.5
Communists	11.0	24	12.0
Christian Democrats	9.0	20	10.0
Freedom Union	8.6	19	9.5
Rally for the Republic	3.9	—	—
Pensioners' Party	3.1	—	—
Democratic Union	1.4	—	—
Total		200	

Denmark 1998

Party	% v	# s	% s
Social Democrats	36.0	63	35.2
Liberals	24.0	42	23.5
Conservative People's Party	8.9	16	8.9
Socialists	7.5	13	7.3
Danish People's Party	7.4	13	7.3
Centre Democrats	4.3	8	4.5
Radical Left-Social Liberal	3.9	7	3.9
Unity List-The Red Greens	2.7	5	2.8
Christian People's Party	2.4	4	2.2
Progress Party	2.4	4	2.2
Others		4	2.2
Total		179	

Finland 1999

Party	% v	# s	% s
Social Democrats	22.9	51	25.5
Centre Party	22.4	48	24.0
National Coalition Party	21.0	46	23.0
Left-Wing Alliance	10.9	20	10.0
Swedish People's Party	5.1	11	5.5
Greens	7.3	11	5.5
Finnish Christian League	4.2	10	5.0
Others	1.2	3	1.5
Total		200	

Germany 1998

Party	% v	# s	% s
Social Democrats	40.9	298	44.5
C.D.U. / C.S.U.	35.1	245	36.6
Alliance 90-The Greens	6.7	47	7.0
Free Democrats	6.2	43	6.4
Party of Democratic Socialism	5.1	36	5.4
The Republicans	1.8	—	—
German People's Party	1.2	—	—
Total		669	

Greece 2000

Party	% v	# s	% s
Socialists	43.8	158	52.7
New Democracy	42.7	125	41.7
Communists	5.5	11	3.7
Left Coalition	3.2	6	2.0
Democratic Movement	2.7	—	—
Total		300	

Norway 1997

Party	% v	# s	% s
Labour	35.1	65	39.4
Progress	15.3	25	15.2
Christian People's Party	13.7	25	15.2
Conservatives	14.3	23	13.9
Centre	8.0	11	6.7
Socialist Left	5.9	9	5.5
Liberal	4.5	6	3.6
Others	3.3	1	0.6
Total		165	

Netherlands 1998

Party	% v	# s	% s
Labour Party	29.0	45	30.0
People's Party	24.7	38	25.3
Christian Democratic Appeal	18.4	29	19.3
Democrats 66	9.0	14	9.3
Green Left	7.3	11	7.3
Socialists	3.5	5	3.3
Reformation Political Federation	2.0	3	2.0
Reformed Political League	1.3	2	1.3
Political Reformed Party	1.8	3	2.0
Total		150	

Switzerland 1999

Party	% v	# s	% s
Swiss People's Party	22.6	44	22.0
Social Democrats	22.5	51	25.5
Free Democrats	19.9	43	21.5
Christian Democratic People's Party	15.8	35	17.5
Green Party	5.0	9	4.5
Liberal Party	2.3	6	3.0
Swiss Democrats	1.8	1	0.5
Evangelical People's Party	1.8	3	1.5
Federal Democratic Union	1.3	1	0.5
Swiss Labour Party	1.0	2	1.0
League of Ticenesians	0.9	2	1.0
Freedom Party	0.9	1	0.5
Alliance of Independents	0.7	1	0.5
Sol	0.5	1	0.5
Christian Social Party	0.4	1	0.5
Total:		200	

Poland 1997

Party	% v	# s	% s
Solidarity Electoral Action	33.8	201	43.7
Alliance of Democratic Left	27.1	164	35.7
Freedom Union	13.4	60	13.0
Polish People's Party	7.3	27	5.9
Reconstruction Movement	5.6	6	1.3
Union of Labour	4.4	—	—
Silesian Germans	.	2	0.4
Others	6.5	—	—
Total		460	

Russia 1999

Party	% v	# s	% s
Communists	24.3	113	25.1
Unity	23.2	72	16.0
Fatherland-All Russia	12.1	66	14.7
Union of Right Wing Forces	8.6	29	6.4
Zhirinovsky Bloc	6.0	17	3.7
Yabloko	6.0	21	4.7
Others and Independents	18.4	132	29.3
Total		450	

Spain 2000

Party	% v	# s	% s
People's Party	44.6	183	52.3
Socialists	34.1	125	35.7
United Left	5.5	8	2.3
Convergence and Union of Catalonia	4.2	15	4.3
Basque Nationalist	1.5	7	2.0
Galician Nationalist Bloc	1.3	3	0.9
Canarian Coalition	1.1	4	1.1
Andalusian	0.9	1	0.3
Republican Left of Catalonia	0.8	1	0.3
Catalonian Greens	0.5	1	0.3
Basque Solidarity	0.4	1	0.3
Aragonese Junta	0.3	1	0.3
Total		350	

Sweden 1998

Party	% v	# s	% s
Social Democrats	36.4	131	37.5
Moderates	22.9	82	23.5
Left-wing Party	12.0	43	12.3
Christian Democrats	11.8	42	12.0
Centre Party	5.1	18	5.2
People's Party Liberals	4.7	17	4.9
Greens	4.5	16	4.6
Total		349	

FIGURE 13.10

RADICAL
ballot October 21, 1999
Party: Radical   **List:** #02

**Election of
Six Members
of Parliament**
02.01 Barker, Brigitte
       Barker, Brigitte
02.02 Dali, Georg
02.03 Feingold, Isaac
02.04 Lewis, Cynthia
02.05 Zubac, Jan

FIGURE 13.11

each of the other candidates. Remember that the votes a party receives determine its share of the seats at stake, but in a list system the number of votes received by individual candidates determines (along with their ranking on the party lists) which members of that party will occupy any seats won. The maximum amount of flexibility is perhaps exhibited in the degree of choice that the Swiss system gives to voters. They may scratch names off a party ballot, and write in names of individuals from other parties, thus indicating that while they wish to support a particular party, they also want to influence the determination of which representatives are elected from the other parties. In addition, Swiss voters are given a blank ballot on which they may write the names of candidates from any of the party ballots supplied to them. As in so many other areas, though, Swiss practice here is exceptional rather than typical.

Perhaps the most complicated aspect of proportionate systems, and one that is only exciting to the specialist or the mathematically inclined, is the formula by which seats are allocated within the constituency. Various rules are applied to determine the allocation of seats within specific PR systems, and these differ in their overall tendency to favour small or large parties; however, compared with the disproportionalities of SMP, these variations are normally small. Two types of formula are used: highest averages (the D'Hondt and modified Sainte-Laguë systems) and largest remainders (the Hare, Droop, and Imperiali quotas being those in use). The application of these systems is rather complicated and not something we need to explore further here, but Figure 13.12 illustrates the different allocation of seats that each method would make for the same results in an eight-member constituency with 100,000 votes cast.

As may be obvious, while these methods award seats in a much more proportional way than a plurality or majoritarian formula, strict proportionality is still not achieved on a constituency basis unless the constituency (or district magnitude) is very large. As Figure 13.10 demonstrates, results in the Netherlands, which has one national constituency, are extremely proportional. Since most systems employ smaller constituencies, they often also use what is called a **SECOND TIER**. This means that not all seats are allocated through the balloting for candidates in the constituencies; some are held back for a second round of allocation, the purpose of which—generally—is to adjust for any disproportionalities created by the constituency allocation of seats (i.e., the first round). Countries employing a two-tier system

PROPORTIONAL ELECTORAL FORMULAS (APPLIED TO EIGHT-MEMBER CONSTITUENCY)

| Party | Votes | SEATS | | | | |
| | | Highest Averages | | Largest Remainders | | |
		D'Hondt	Sainte-Laguë	Hare	Droop	Imperiali
A	32,000	3	2	2	3	3
B	24,000	2	2	2	2	2
C	20,000	1	2	2	1	1
D	13,500	1	1	1	1	1
E	10,500	1	1	1	1	1

FIGURE 13.12

include Austria, Belgium, Denmark, Germany, Greece, Iceland, Italy, Malta, Norway, and Sweden. For the second tier, district magnitude is usually much larger than for the first tier, and often is a national constituency. The electoral formula also is usually different from that employed at the first tier. Depending on thresholds, legal or effective, the second tier may exclude smaller parties, or in fact ensure that they receive seats. The amount of disproportionality generated by the Greek system (see Figure 13.10) has a lot to do with the high threshold for participation in second-tier allocation of seats; this means the larger parties are rewarded. If, as is usually the case, the purpose of the second-tier seats is to eliminate disproportionalities created in the first-tier allocation, then the number of second-tier seats necessary will be determined by the level of disproportionality that the first tier generates. (The second-tier seats, for this reason, are often called **ADJUSTMENT SEATS**.) If the total discrepancy between share of votes and seats that parties ought to receive is small, then the second tier can be small, also. As a general rule, the smaller the first-tier constituencies, the larger the possibility of disproportionality, and hence the larger the second tier will need to be.

This brings us to what seems to be emerging as one of the more popular forms of proportional representation, a two-tier system that combines the virtue of single-member districts (i.e., attachment of a representative to a local constituency) with the justice of proportional outcomes. The model here is the German system, in which half of the seats for the Bundestag are elected by voters choosing a candidate in single-member constituencies. Victory in the local constituency requires simply a plurality of votes

13.5
PR: THE "GERMAN-STYLE" SYSTEM

SAMPLE CANADIAN BALLOT – GERMAN-STYLE ELECTORAL SYSTEM

HYPOTHETICAL BALLOT PAPER
(For the House of Commons, federal electoral
district of Westdale, 21 October 2001)

YOU HAVE TWO (2) VOTES

Mark here your first vote for the election of a constituency representative:				Mark here your second vote for the election of a provincial party list:	
1	ANDERSON, Helen lawyer [home address]	PC		PC	Progressive Conservatives: J. Clark, E. Wayne, ... H. Anderson	
2	WONG, William small business owner [home address]	LIB		LIB	Liberals: J. Chrétien, S. Copps, P. Martin, ... W. Wong	
3	ANDRIOTTI, John engineer [home address]	NDP		NDP	New Democratic Party: A. McDonough, S. Robinson, ... J. Andriotti	
4	JONES, Harry piano teacher [home address]	CA		CA	Canadian Alliance: S. Day, D. Grey, ... H. Jones	
5	RUSSOW, Joan teacher [home address]	GRN		GRN	Green Party: J. Russow, B. Hanson, K. LaRoche ...	

FIGURE 13.13

cast. At the same time, German voters cast a separate vote for the party of their choice. This allows them to select who they think is the best candidate without compromising their support for a national party. Figure 13.13 demonstrates what a German-style ballot might look like in a Canadian election. The "party vote" is used to determine the final allocation of seats in the legislature. Seats not allocated through the single-member districts (i.e., the other 50 per cent) are used as adjustment seats in a national constituency and are allocated in such a way that the *total* of seats in the Bundestag is proportionate to a party's support as registered by the party half of the ballot.

Consider, for example, a 200-seat legislature, in which 100 seats are filled by plurality rules applied in single-member districts (first tier), and 100 seats are adjustment seats constituting a national constituency (second tier). Votes cast for parties return the following result:

Liberal	35%		70
PC	25		50
CA	15	generating a final	30
BQ	15	total of seats =	30
NDP	10		20
Total:	100%		200 seats

In the 100 first-tier seats the results are:

Liberal	45
PC	4
CA	15
BQ	15
NDP	6

At the level of the single-member constituencies the Liberals and BQ have been overrewarded, the Alliance has received its proportionate share, and the PCs and NDP have been penalized by the plurality allocations (which, of course, is what happened in the past three general elections). Adjustment seats would compensate for the disproportionalities in the following manner:

Allocation	% v	Final Share Seats	less	1st-Tier Seats Won		2nd-Tier Allocation
Liberal	35	70	–	45	=	25
PC	25	50	–	4	=	46
CA	15	30	–	15	=	15
BQ	15	30	–	30	=	0
NDP	10	20	–	6	=	14
TOTAL		**200**	**=**	**100**	**+**	**100**

The German system has a legal threshold: parties that do not receive at least 5 per cent of the party vote are ineligible for second-tier seats, except if they win at least three first-tier seats. In the latter case they are entitled to a share of the second-tier seats that will deliver a proportionate result, even if their party vote was below the threshold. This is in fact what happened to the Party of Democratic Socialism in the 1994 election.

THE GERMAN ELECTION, 1998

Party	% v	1st-Tier Seats	2nd-Tier Seats	Total Seats	% Seats
Social Democrats	40.9	212	86	298	44.5
C.D.U. / C.S.U.	35.1	112	133	245	36.6
Alliance 90 / The Greens	6.7	—	47	47	7.0
Free Democrats	6.2	—	44	44	6.6
Party of Democratic Socialism	5.1	4	31	35	5.2
Republicans	1.8	—	—	—	—
German People's Party	1.2	—	—	—	—
Others	2.9	—	—	—	—
TOTAL				**669**	

FIGURE 13.14

One remaining puzzle, perhaps, is how the second- or upper-tier seats are actually allocated among party members. In the German case, each party ranks all its candidates, from party leader down. The upper-tier seats will go in order to those candidates on the party list who failed to win a lower-tier seat. This is another case where party control over candidate ranking can be a powerful tool of party discipline.

As noted above, the German system has been much copied recently, leading to what is now often called a "mixed-member" system. One difference, though, is that the ratio of lower- to upper-tier seats is rarely 1:1, as it is in Germany. Figure 13.15 shows election results in Italy, where the first tier single-member seats account for 75 per cent of the total. As in Germany, citizens cast two votes, one for a candidate in single-member districts awarded on the basis of plurality, and one for a party list for second-tier seats. As in Germany there is a threshold (5 per cent) that eliminates smaller parties from receiving second-tier seats. In Italy, though, the second-tier allocation fails to compensate fully for the disproportionalities of the lower tier, in part at least because the number of PR seats is too small to do the trick. For this reason the final allocations of seats to parties displays nowhere near the proportionality that we observed in the German case.

In Italy, the change from a list PR system to the two-tiered "mixed-member" system was designed to correct the extremely fragmented party system that was regarded as contributing to Italy's notorious political instability. Specifically, it was believed that single-member districts would force parties to consolidate, thus reducing the number of small and minor parties in the system, and this is in part why the proportion of single-member seats

THE ITALIAN ELECTION, 1996

Party	% v	1st-Tier Seats	2nd-Tier Seats	Total Seats	% Seats
Olive Tree[1]	34.8	246	38	284	45.1
Freedom Alliance[2]	42.1	169	77	246	39.0
Northern League	10.1	39	20	59	9.4
Refounded Communists	8.6	15	20	35	5.6
Others	4.4	6	—	6	0.1
TOTAL				**630**	

1. Olive Tree includes the Democratic Party of the Left, the Italian Popular Party-Prodi List, the Dini Italian Renewal List, Greens, and others.
2. Freedom Alliance includes the United Christian Democrats-Christian Democratic Centre, Forza Italiana, and the National Alliance.

FIGURE 13.15

is so high. Unfortunately, elections that have been held under this system have not had the desired effect of simplifying the party system, but have given Italy much less proportional results than were previously the norm.

In two other countries, a switch to a "mixed-member" PR system has been made in the attempt to address problems in the party system and parliament. In 1996, New Zealand held its first election under a new proportional system with 65 single-member seats and 55 proportional or adjustment seats. This is obviously very much like the German system, and transformed one of the few remaining plurality system countries into a member of the proportionate family. Significantly, this reform of the electoral system was approved by the people of New Zealand in a national referendum. The intent was to inject fairness and responsiveness into a system that tended to favour the two largest parties, which in turn were seen by many to be too much alike. Also at the end of 1996, Japan inaugurated a new electoral system with 300 single-member seats and 200 proportional seats chosen in eleven regional constituencies. Here the intent was to reform a multi-member plurality system that had been dominated by the (often corrupt) LDP. Japan, incidentally, is the only industrial democracy that requires voters to write in full the name of the candidate of their choice. The results of the first elections in the new systems in New Zealand and Japan are shown in Figure 13.16.

Finally, we might note that a large number of academics and an increasing number of voices in the political community have called for electoral reform in Canada along more proportionate

JAPAN/NEW ZEALAND NEW ELECTORAL SYSTEMS

Japan 1996

Party	% v	# s	% s
Liberal Democratic Party	32.8	239	47.8
New Frontier	28.0	156	31.2
Democratic Party of Japan	16.1	52	10.4
Communists	13.1	26	5.2
Social Democrats	6.4	15	3.0
Independents	4.4	9	1.8
New Party Sakigake	1.1	2	0.4
Democratic Reform Party	0.1	1	0.2
TOTAL		**200**	

New Zealand 1999 (1996)

Party	% v		# s		% s	
New Zealand Labour Party	38.7	28.3	49	37	40.8	30.8
New Zealand National Party	30.5	34.1	39	44	32.5	36.6
Alliance	7.7	10.1	10	13	8.3	10.8
ACT New Zealand	7.0	6.2	9	8	7.5	6.7
Green Party of Aotearoa	5.2	—	7	—	5.8	—
New Zealand First Party	4.3	13.1	5	17	4.2	14.2
United New Zealand	0.5	—	1	—	—	—
Other	4.6	6.6	—	1	—	0.8
TOTAL			**120**	**120**		

FIGURE 13.16

lines. Given Canada's geography and tradition of single-member constituencies, some version of the "German-style" system might well provide a reasonable alternative.

Consider, for example, the result of the general election of 1993 as shown in Figure 13.17. The appearance of two new parties (the Bloc Québécois and Reform) and the allocation of seats

2000 AND 1997 CANADIAN GENERAL ELECTIONS

Party	%v		#s		%s	
	2000	1997	2000	1997	2000	1997
Liberal	40.8	38.4	172	155	57.1	51.5
Reform / Canadian Alliance	25.5	19.4	66	60	21.9	19.9
Progressive Conservative (PC)	12.2	18.9	12	20	4.0	6.6
Bloc Québécois (BQ)	10.7	10.7	38	44	12.6	14.6
New Democratic Party (NDP)	8.5	11.0	13	21	4.3	7.0
Others	2.3	1.6	0	1	0.0	0.3
TOTAL				**301**		

FIGURE 13.17

CANADIAN GENERAL ELECTION (HYPOTHETICAL 400-SEAT CHAMBER)

2000 Party	% v	1st-Tier Seats	2nd-Tier Seats	Total Seats	% Seats
Liberal	40.8	172	—	172	43.0
Canadian Alliance	25.5	66	36	102	25.5
Progressive Conservative (PC)	12.2	12	37	49	12.2
Bloc Québécois (BQ)	10.7	38	5	43	10.7
New Democratic Party (NDP)	8.5	13	21	34	8.5
Others	2.3	—	—	—	0.0
TOTAL		**301**	**99**	**400**	

1997 Party	% v	1st-Tier Seats	2nd-Tier Seats	Total Seats	% Seats
Liberal	38.4	155	—	155	38.8
Reform	19.4	60	19	79	19.8
Progressive Conservative (PC)	18.9	20	57	77	19.3
New Democratic Party (NDP)	11	21	23	44	11
Bloc Québécois (BQ)	10.7	44	—	44	11
Others	1.6	1	—	1	0.3
TOTAL		**301**	**99**	**400**	

FIGURE 13.18

among five registered parties made this a somewhat unusual election, but the results also illustrate several typical features of Canada's plurality system. First of all, the system manufactured a parliamentary majority: the first place Liberals were overpaid by 19 per cent, winning 177 seats, a very strong majority, with only 41 per cent of the vote. The system also continued to favour parties with concentrated support, hence with a regional base. The strongest of these was the Bloc Québécois, which despite finishing fourth in popular vote, became the official opposition; the Bloc's support, of course, was entirely within the province of Quebec. The Reform Party, while fielding a national slate of candidates, continued to draw most of its support from western Canada, and in particular, from Alberta and British Columbia. A large collapse in support from traditional levels for both the NDP and Progressive Conservatives put these parties in fifth and third place, respectively, in vote totals, and as smaller parties (in this election) they were typically underpaid by the system. The Conservatives suffered from having weak, evenly distributed support; there was no regional concentration here, so that despite finishing third in votes, ahead of the Bloc and the NDP, this party barely managed to elect two MPs. The only party that the system treated

In the 2000 election, a marginal increase in national support for the Liberals led to a solid majority. The second place Canadian Alliance gained more support nationally, but did not win a correspondingly larger share of seats. Although the Bloc's vote share was constant, the collapse of Conservative support in Quebec led to gains for the Liberals. For the third consecutive election, the PCs finished third in vote, but last in seats. While the NDP won seats in six provinces, its support was concentrated in specific pockets across the country, largely those which its campaign had targeted.

at all "fairly" was Reform, and that is only true when national results are considered; on a provincial basis, Reform was overpaid in provinces where it did win seats and underpaid in other regions such as Ontario and some Atlantic provinces.

In the 1997 election, the Liberals again secured a manufactured majority in the House, but with a smaller plurality, and a majority somewhat less manufactured. In fact, with the exception of the NDP, all parties received a proportion of seats more in line with their proportion of vote. This was not only the second Canadian general election in which five parties won seats, but the first in which five parties won 10 per cent or more of the vote and 20 or more seats in the House of Commons. The 1997 election also produced less volatility—significant changes in the support for parties—than other recent national contests.

Suppose, though, that federal political leaders agreed to change Canada's electoral system to a more proportional system, and did so by adding 99 adjustment seats (an entirely arbitrary number) in 1997 and 2000. The results are shown in Figure 13.18. Notice that in either case the Liberals received more seats in the single-member ridings than their share of vote would entitle them to *even in a 400-seat legislature*. This is why the proportion of upper-tier seats must often be very high to adjust for lower-tier disproportionalities. On the other hand, assuming a threshold of 5 per cent, the parties and independents lumped together as "Others" would not receive any second-tier seats. Under this new system, it would be possible to bring the parties that were underpaid in the single-member tier up to a final allocation very close to their proportion of the vote.

In either case, the strong majority the Liberals gained under the plurality system would be reduced to a dominant minority position in a proportionate House. The PCs, who actually finished last in terms of seats in both elections, penalized for their weak and evenly distributed support, would actually finish third under a proportional system. The BQ would have finished last in 1997 and fourth in 2000, while the Reform Party would have been the official opposition in both Houses. Under these conditions, the Liberals could well try to govern as a minority government. In the context of Canada's plurality system, parties that "won" with a minority have governed alone until the next election, in the expectation that the system would then return to "normal" by manufacturing a majority. In the new proportionate system this would not be a wise assumption, and parties in a position such as the Liberals would probably seek a coalition partner. Interestingly, the results in Figure 13.18 show that the Liberals could form a majority coalition with any one of the other four parties. These results are based on the existing party system, but in all likelihood a new system would give incentives to new parties and alliances.

Electoral systems matter because of the outputs they deliver, which are first and foremost a party system and, out of that party system, a pattern of government formation. We discussed patterns of government formation in Chapter Eight, and in Chapter Fourteen will examine political parties as vehicles (among others) of representation. To conclude this chapter, though, we need to make some observations about party systems, where a party system is a "set of political parties operating within a nation [polity] in an organized pattern, described by a number of party-system properties" (Lane and Ersson, 1991: 175). This system, most observers agree, is something larger than the sum of its parts, for the behaviour and characteristics of individual parties are shaped by the systems within which they operate and, more specifically, by the properties of those systems. We will look at just three system properties: the size of the system, its ideological polarization, and its capacity to express distinct issue dimensions.

We have noted the principal features of plurality systems: their tendency to manufacture majorities by overrewarding winning parties; their overcompensation of regionally concentrated parties; and the penalization of parties with diffuse but moderate to weak strength. The "winner-take-all" character of such systems also puts a very large hurdle in the way of new parties: to win a seat, a new party must finish ahead of all the established parties in the riding. To gain 15, 20, or even 30 per cent of the vote is something of an accomplishment for a new party, particularly if it can do this in several or many ridings, and over the course of two or more elections. Nonetheless, this level of support is meaningless unless within specific ridings it means finishing first: there is no prize for finishing second, even if that has meant obtaining 49.99 per cent of the votes cast. Not surprisingly, then, most plurality systems tend to sustain a two-party system; Canada with its regionally based third (and sometimes fourth) parties is an exception to the rule.

Proportionate systems are almost uniformly associated with multi-party systems. The combination of several parties with more or less strict proportionality means that a one-party majority

13.6
PARTY SYSTEMS

**ELECTORAL SYSTEMS AND DISPROPORTIONALITY
MEASURED WITH GALLAGHER'S LEAST SQUARES INDEX (disP)**

Single Member Plurality		**PR (List Systems)**	
Election:	*disP*	*Election:*	*disP*
Britain 1997	17.12	Belgium 1999	2.69
Canada 2000	12.71	Czech Republic 1998	5.75
		Denmark 1998	0.73
Single Member Majority		Finland 1999	3.01
Election:	*disP*	Greece 2000	6.79
Australia 1998	10.84	Netherlands 1998	1.08
France 1997	5.54	Norway 1997	3.43
		Poland 1997	10.29
PR (Mixed Member)		Russia 1999	5.96
Election:	*disP*	Spain 2000	4.87
Germany 1998	3.17	Sweden 1998	0.94
Italy 1996	7.95	Switzerland 1999	3.02
Japan 1999	13.20		
New Zealand 1999	2.20		

FIGURE 13.19

is unlikely, and is almost never manufactured (see Figure 13.9). It is thus normal for the government in PR systems to be a coalition (see Chapter Eight). Defenders of plurality systems are usually quick to associate coalition government with instability, and point to Italy's series of short-lived governments since 1945 to demonstrate the undesirable side-effects of a proportionate system. There is, though, little conclusive evidence that PR (or coalition government) produces instability, or that the "instability" of changing governments has necessarily detrimental consequences. In many cases the "new" government contains many of the same partners as the "old." Where governments are single-party majorities, by contrast, government change may well mean significantly new directions for public policy. For every Italy, there is a Switzerland *and* a Germany *and* a Luxembourg, where stability and coalition seem on intimate terms. What is beyond dispute is the responsiveness of PR systems to changes in public opinion; any increase or decline in a party's support is immediately and accurately reflected in its legislative standing, a feature that is bound to affect the way parties behave towards their supporters and others. If the existing parties are unsatisfactory to significant portions of the population, then new parties appealing to those sections of the electorate will form, and are more likely to succeed under PR than SMP, the only barrier being the legal threshold (which may, of course, be a significant barrier). Regional parties are also unlikely to have a

EFFECTIVE NUMBER OF ELECTIVE AND LEGISLATIVE PARTIES

Election	Elective	Legislative	Election	Elective	Legislative
Single-Member Plurality (SMP)			*PR (List Systems)*		
Britain 1997	3.22	2.07	Belgium 1999	10.30	9.05
Canada 1997	4.09	2.98	Czech Republic 1998	4.73	3.71
Canada 2000	3.77	2.54	Denmark 1998	4.73	4.93
			Finland 1999	5.94	5.15
Single-Member Majority (SMM)			Greece 2000	2.63	2.21
Australia 1998	3.45	2.52	Netherlands 1998	5.14	4.81
France 1997	3.98	3.56	Norway 1997	5.05	4.36
			Poland 1997	4.74	2.95
PR (Mixed Member)			Russia 1999	7.04	8.48
Germany 1998	3.31	2.91	Spain 2000	3.12	2.48
Italy 1996	3.17	2.72	Sweden 1998	4.54	4.30
Japan 1999	4.25	2.94	Switzerland 1999	5.86	5.16
New Zealand 1999	3.87	3.45			

FIGURE 13.20

monopoly of representation in their region, as is often the case under plurality rules.

We have been referring to two-party and multi-party systems without defining our terms adequately. In fact, determining the "size" of a party system is not the same as simply counting the number of parties. In the case of the U.S. Congress, or the first several Canadian general elections, where there are (or were) in fact only two parties, the judgement that we are talking about two-party systems is rather obvious. But what about the situation where a third party emerges and wins a few seats; how does this change the picture? To say that the picture is unchanged until the third party becomes sufficiently large just invites the further question: what is sufficiently large? Such questions have prompted political scientists to generate an index that measures the **EFFECTIVE NUMBER OF PARTIES** based on a combination of their numbers *and* their relative strength. Thus the British Parliament (see Figure 13.10) contains what is virtually a two-party system, even though at least nine parties have representation, because the two largest parties hold almost 90 per cent of the seats between them.

In addition, we need to distinguish between **ELECTIVE PARTIES** and **LEGISLATIVE PARTIES.** In virtually every election there is a difference between the number of parties that contest the election and the number of parties that actually win seats in the legislature. The former are elective parties; the latter are legislative parties. As Figure 13.10 and other data presented indicate, the electoral system has a large effect on the difference between the number of elective and legislative parties. Generally speaking, the electoral system presents more hurdles to elective parties in a plurality system than in a proportionate system (this is known as Duverger's "mechanical effect"). At the same time this effect is compounding: voters who know that minor parties will not receive their share of seats in plurality systems will consider votes for these parties "wasted" and vote strategically for other parties they may in fact prefer less (this is known as Duverger's "psychological effect"). Figure 13.20 shows the effective numbers of elective and legislative parties for the election results that have been presented in this chapter. In the 1997 Canadian election the effective number of elective parties was 4.09, reduced to an effective number of 2.98 legislative parties; the corresponding reduction for the 2000 election was from 3.77 to 2.54 parties. We noted above the more even and proportionate distribution of strength of the parties (compared to 1993) in the 1997 Canadian election; this is reflected in the higher effective number of parties, both elective and legislative. Nonetheless, the electoral system still effectively reduced the party system by one whole party. Similarly, in the 1997 British general election the effective number of elective parties, 3.22, was reduced to 2.07 legislative parties. The point that Figure 13.20 illustrates is that the shrinkage from elective to legislative parties is generally much more severe in non-PR than in PR electoral systems. An exception to this is when a PR system, such as Greece's, has a large legal threshold, but generally PR electoral systems can be expected to generate multi-party systems in which the effective representation in the legislature strongly resembles the levels of support parties received in the election. Note, too, the two exceptional cases where the effective number of legislative parties is *greater* than the effective number of legislative parties: Denmark and Russia.

Perhaps even more significant than the number of parties in the system (but much more difficult to measure) is the degree of choice it presents to the voters. It hardly matters if there are two or twelve parties if the policy choices that they present to the voters are more or less indistinguishable. Conceptually, determining the degree of **POLARIZATION** entails plotting the position of parties on a right-left ideological scale and observing the patterns that result. Consider two very different situations within a two-party system:

Clearly situation A is very unpolarized, while B presents an extremely polarized scenario. It is not unfair to suggest that American politics has often resembled A, and B has at various times been true of British party politics (particularly at the start of Margaret Thatcher's tenure in office). Situation B offers a much clearer choice to voters than A, but a single-party government in B will be extremely distasteful to its non-supporters, while one could argue that it doesn't make much difference in A which party governs.

Similar patterns are common in multi-party systems, which, perhaps not surprisingly, can often be grouped into families—parties of the right, of the left, etc. Hence, we could substitute Germany for the U.S., noting that the two dominant right and left parties tend to converge on the centre, and for Britain substitute Italy with parties ranged across the ideological spectrum, from the refounded Communists on the left to the neo-fascists on the right. Here, too, is a contrast between political competition played out at the centre, and a contest covering a broader ideological range. It could be argued that, all else being equal, a party system that provides a range of ideological positions presents clearer choices to citizens and offers the conditions for a more meaningful political discourse about policy issues. Parties competing at the centre are more likely to craft platforms that do not differ greatly in substance, shifting attention to issues of character and personality of candidates and leaders.

It is useful to point out that not all competition is evenly balanced on either side of a "neutral" centre. By definition, whichever party controls the median voter is "at the centre" of the country's political culture. Hence, in Sweden, ranging the parties ideologically from left to right results in the following:

Left Party	Social Democrats	Greens	Centre	Liberals	Christian Democrats	Moderates
22	131	16	18	17	42	82

Interestingly, while the Centre party is indeed centrally located—three parties to its left, three to its right—the median

KEY TERMS

adjustment seats
categorical ballot
constituency size
disproportionality
district magnitude
effective number of parties
effective threshold
election financing
elective parties
electoral formula
electoral justice
electoral system
franchise
"German-style" PR
gerrymandering
issue dimensions
legal threshold
legislative parties
list system
majoritarian system
manufactured majority
multi-member constituency
ordinal ballot
parliamentary system
party system
plurality
polarization
political advertising
polling
preferential ballot
proportionate electoral systems
representation by population
"run-off"
second tier
single-member majority
single-member plurality
single-member riding
single transferable vote
strategic voting
universal adult suffrage
"winner take all"

vote in the legislature (halfway from either right or left) is controlled by Greens, and is one seat away from being controlled by the Social Democrats (as it was in the previous legislature). Effectively, this means that the Social Democrats are "in the centre." At the same time the strength of the Social Democrats and the distance between them and the second place Moderates at the far end of the spectrum suggests a fair degree of polarization in this party system. On a polarization index that generates an average for 16 European democracies of 3.1 in the period between 1945 and 1989, Lane and Ersson report a high of 5.1 for France and a low of 0.9 for Ireland (1991: 185).

It is also the case that the centre is not fixed, but moves in one direction or another as the political culture changes. There are differences between countries (in both the U.S. and Germany, the major parties converge on the centre, but the American centre is much to the right of the German centre), but also within countries over time. American parties have (almost) always competed at the centre for the middle-class voter, but most observers would probably agree that this centre has shifted considerably to the right in the last two decades—as, indeed, it has in most industrial democracies. To what degree this is a temporary reaction to the accumulated deficits that governments have faced in this period, or a real shift in ideology, remains to be seen.

Finally, we may note that the right-left classification of parties is itself suspect. On the one hand, the assessment of where a party falls on this scale is always a judgement call and not a matter of exact science. In addition, though, most right-left scales are largely concerned with party policy positions concerning socio-economic policy, issues that deal with what has been discussed as the class cleavage (see Chapter Twelve). As Lijphart (1994) argues, there are at least six other dimensions that play a role in at least some of the stable democracies we have been considering: the religious, cultural-ethnic, urban-rural, regime support, foreign policy, and post-materialist issue dimensions. Parties poles apart on questions of socio-economic policy may be close allies on the religious dimension, while a third set of allies links up on foreign policy questions. The presence of different issue dimensions poses intriguing challenges for government formation and explains many of the sources of internal division between coalition partners. Lijphart has calculated the number of relevant issue dimensions for twenty-two democracies in the 1945-1980 period, ranging from a low of 1.0 in Ireland, New Zealand, and the United States, to a high of 3.5 in France,

364

Norway, and Finland (1984: 130). Perhaps more striking is the fairly strong correlation he finds between the number of issue dimensions present and the number of effective parties. The higher the number of effective parties, the more issue dimensions a party system seems able to accommodate. This implies that multi-party systems will be better able to accommodate multiple issue dimensions (and thus, conceivably, accommodate social cleavages) than two-party (duopolistic) systems. This again suggests an advantage to proportional systems compared with single-member plurality electoral machinery.

13.7 CONCLUSION

To summarize, electoral systems determine the distribution of legislative seats among the competing political parties, and do so in a great variety of ways. The elective and legislative party systems created by the electoral system are significant outputs at the heart of democratic politics. The legislative party system will determine the government of the day, and distinct types of party systems lead to significantly different kinds of government, as discussed in Chapter Eight. At the same time, the nature of the elective party system and the degree to which popular preferences for political parties are reflected in the legislature will have a great influence on the organization and strategy of political parties, considered as actors in the drama of democracy. In the next chapter we will examine this aspect of political parties, namely, their competence as vehicles of representation, as well as some of the alternatives to political parties.

It has no doubt also become obvious that this text reflects a clear preference for proportionate systems over the single-member plurality systems that have dominated the Anglo-American world. To put the argument most simply, the plurality system emerged in a time that was much simpler, in social, political, and technological terms, but has little to recommend it to today's complex, fragmented societies. The principal virtue of plurality is its ability to return a majority government to parliament, but the degree to which this is in fact a virtue needs critical examination, particularly considered against the costs of manufacturing such a majority through a system that is by no means consistently responsive to the preferences of voters.

REFERENCES AND SUGGESTED READING

Bogdanor, Vernon, and David Butler, eds. 1983. *Democracy and Elections.* Cambridge: Cambridge University Press.

Duverger, Maurice. 1963. *Political Parties.* New York: Wiley.

Frizell, Alan, et al. 1985. *The Canadian General Election of 1984.* Ottawa: Carleton University Press.

——. 1989. *The Canadian General Election of 1988.* Ottawa: Carleton University Press.

——. 1994. *The Canadian General Election of 1994.* Ottawa: Carleton University Press.

Gallagher, Michael, et al. 1995. *Representative Government in Western Europe.* New York: McGraw-Hill.

Irvine, William. 1979. *Does Canada Need A New Electoral System?* Montreal and Kingston: McGill-Queen's University Press.

Johnston, J. Paul, and Harvey Pasis. 1990. *Representative and Electoral Systems.* Scarborough, Ont.: Prentice Hall.

Lakeman, Enid. 1974. *How Democracies Vote,* 4th ed. London: Faber & Faber.

Lane, Jan-Erik, and Svante O. Ersson. 1991. *Politics and Society in Western Europe.* London: Sage.

Lijphart, Arend. 1984. *Democracies: Patterns of Majoritarian and Consensus Government in Twenty-One Countries.* New Haven: Yale University Press.

——. 1994. *Electoral Systems and Party Systems: A Study of Twenty-Seven Democracies, 1945-1990.* Oxford: Oxford University Press.

Penniman, Howard, and Austin Ramney, eds. 1981. *Democracy at the Polls: A Comparative Study of Competitive National Elections.* Washington: American Enterprise Institute.

SOMETHING TO CONSIDER

Based on the last three federal elections in Canada, the most important effect on the party system of adoption of some form of PR in this country would not be an increase in the *number* of parties, but changes in their behaviour. What might these changes be?

What model of PR might work best with the other realities of Canadian politics? Consider list versus mixed-member systems, the size of a legal threshold, and whatever else might be important.

14

parties, organized groups,
and direct democracy

We have encountered various pieces of evidence of something that a few moments' reflection will confirm: that democracy in the age of mass society is necessarily representative. There is very little that you or I or anyone else can accomplish individually in today's political world; even if we have the inclination, and the time, we lack the ability to go it alone and succeed. Behind each successful individual stands an organization or network of organizations providing expertise, financial backing, communications, transportation, etc. Interestingly, in this sense, the candidate we elect is not simply representing us, the voters, or "our interests," but represents *to us* the whole organization of supporters, staff, and others whose passion, wit, and labour have sustained this candidacy. Ironically, this is increasingly true even as the predominance of television obscures to us anything except the images of the candidate.

In this chapter we will examine a few of the central questions surrounding some of the principal vehicles of representation upon which the political process of modern democracy depends. For simplicity's sake we will explore four contrasts:

a) between political parties and interest groups as organized vehicles of representation;
b) within political parties, between those that primarily serve their leaders and those that primarily serve the electorate;
c) within organized interests, between those that have an institutionalized role in the policy process (corporatism) and those that compete for policy influence (pluralism); and

14.1   Introduction
14.2   Political Parties
14.3   Organized Interests
14.4   Pluralism versus Corporatism
14.5   Direct Democracy
14.6   Conclusion

367

d) by contrast to the foregoing, the operation of direct democracy as an alternative to representative institutions.

The approach in this chapter is more macro-political than micro-political. That is to say, we want to understand first and foremost the significance of political parties to the political process of democracies, and will examine the internal working of parties, their strategies, problems, etc., only (or mainly) to the extent that they illuminate the former for us.

14.2
POLITICAL PARTIES

If democracy in the contemporary age is necessarily representative, then the politics of democratic (and some non-democratic) nation-states depends on the functioning of political parties. The observation that political parties are *institutionalized* within modern democratic systems is another way of saying the same thing. One reason parties have become so indispensable is that they perform a variety of functions central to the political process; some of these functions they perform consciously, and some are accomplished as by-products of the activity parties deliberately engage in. For example, parties consciously seek to organize the electorate by recruiting candidates, organizing campaigns, assisting voters with registration, arranging child care on polling day, etc. Less effectively, parties help to stimulate policy development through conventions, workshops, and debates. In the effort to construct broad bases of public support, parties may build bridges between disparate communities within society and help to balance competing interests. Parties engage in such activities more or less self-consciously in their pursuit of their own objectives; in the process they may accomplish much more for the political system. By engaging citizens within the political process and organizing opportunities for activity, debate, and dissent, parties may increase their feelings of efficacy and enhance the legitimacy of the political system. In a similar way, parties can be agents of socialization for the broader population, and organizations that recruit and groom future political leaders. As important, perhaps, as any of these, parties are said to simplify to a manageable level the range of issues and options presented to the public—the critic might well argue today that, collectively, parties have gone too far in this simplification of the political agenda.

It is important to grasp, then, that political parties serve many masters, or for the sake of argument, at least three: their leaders, their members, and the broader public. This is reflected in the different ways that political parties are described, defined, and evaluated. Consider the definitions in Figure 14.1. The over-whelming emphasis here is upon parties as means of securing scarce positions of authority and power. This puts the emphasis on the services that parties can provide for their leaders, what we might call their **MOBILIZATION FUNCTION**. This is an important part of the picture, for certainly the modern political campaign requires an extensive machinery to support it, to mobilize sup-porters, and to collect the financial supports required to finance television advertising, jet travel, professional pollsters, image con-sultants, etc. On the other hand, we should not expect leaders to be the only beneficiaries of party politics. The following discus-sion of parties by G. Bingham Powell emphasizes what parties can do for the political system at large and for citizens generally:

> Political parties are the institutions that link the voting choices of individual citizens with aggregate electoral outcomes in the competitive democracies. The parties set the alternatives offered to the citizens in elections and their organized activities can encourage both reg-istration and election-day turnout. The relationships between party systems and national cleavage structures should play a major role in shaping voting participation levels. (1982: 115)

This description indicates clearly how, in performing the mobilization function for leaders, parties perform what we might call an **ADMINISTRATION FUNCTION** for the political process or the electorate, considered collectively. In between the party lead-ers and the broad public at large, however, stands the party mem-bership: those individuals who actually join a party and sustain it with their labour, time, and money. The relationship of the party to its members is not included in any of the definitions provided so far. In this respect we might define parties as *voluntary organiza-tions that seek to further the interests and principles of their members through gaining elected office.* Like all the other definitions we have seen, this one is incomplete, but it presents a dimension lacking in the others, what we will call the **REPRESENTATION FUNCTION** of political parties. As organizations within the political process of democracies, political parties perform a mobilization function for leaders, a representation function for members, and an adminis-tration function for the political process at large.

PARTIES DEFINED

"Structured, articulated and hierarchical groups adapted to the struggle for power."
— Duverger, 1966

"They are agencies for the acquisition of power."
— Lawson, 1980

"… organizations designed to secure the power of the state for their leaders."
— Jackson and Jackson, 1990

"… an organizational means for governing the political system."
— Landes, 1987

FIGURE 14.1

It is possible to approach any of the issues relevant to the discussion of political parties in terms of these three functions, whether it be the process by which party leaders are selected, the rules of party finance, or whatever. For our discussion, though, we will focus on the possible tension between the mobilization function and the representation function. In other words, parties can operate primarily as **ELECTORAL VEHICLES**, in which case their primary purpose is to elect candidates or generate support for their leaders, *or* they can operate primarily as **AGENTS OF REPRE-SENTATION**, when their primary activities focus on furthering their members' interests. The immediate objection may be that this is an unnecessary dichotomy, that parties surely can be *both*. Indeed, but while this is possible, and maybe even desirable, it is not automatic. In the best of possible worlds, parties will succeed in electing their candidates *because* they are good agents of representation, but in the real world, it is quite possible that electoral success may hinge upon practices or strategies that are contrary to good representation. Many observers have noted, for example, that the modern television campaign emphasizes images of leadership and the politics of "character," rather than issues of policy, or favours 15-second "sound-bites" over detailed explanation or debate of policy positions. It is hard to see how these media-driven strategies enhance the party's ability to represent members' concerns or interests. Similarly, while parties cultivate members to provide organizational resources and financial support, they may also turn to pollsters for advice on how to pitch their campaign to the larger, less active public: the demands and ideas of party members in this context become a nuisance or a handicap. By the same token, it is also true that parties that cannot elect members to official positions will not be very effective in representing their members' concerns. This, too, can be a matter of degree; in some settings—e.g., minority or coalition government—parties may very well be able to influence public policy without controlling, or even participating in, the government. In short, while it is ideal that the party's mobilization and representation functions be complementary, it is also possible for them to be in tension.

Another way to approach the question of political parties is to consider, as Bingham Powell notes in the passage quoted above, their relationship to the cleavages within a society. The challenge in democracy is to mobilize the support of a majority of citizens for public policy, and within contemporary pluralistic societies this will involve building coalitions of diverse interests and identities. A key question is whether this coalition or majority-building takes place between parties (as in coalition government formation), or within parties. Where parties closely correspond to the cleavage structure of a society (i.e., their basis of support corresponds to class identities, or ethnic solidarities, or religious affiliations), it may be necessary and appropriate for majorities to be built through negotiation and bargaining between the elected representatives of the various communities represented by political parties. In such cases, it would appear that the representation function of parties is primary, and the mobilization function is limited by the constraints of the government formation process. The role of the electoral system will also be a key ingredient here, as we will see shortly.

A party may, on the other hand, attempt to transcend or bridge the cleavages of society by accommodating a broad coalition of supporters within its ranks (whether a pluralistic membership or simply a broad range of supporting voters). Such parties have been called "catch-all" (after Kirchheimer, 1966) parties or, more typically in Canada, **BROKERAGE PARTIES**. As both terms indicate, these are parties that seek to build support from very diverse sources within society, appealing to many constituencies at the same time. As might be expected, this means the party will be, to say the least, quite flexible about its ideology or long-term policy commitments. The authors of *Absent Mandate* (Clarke et al., 1996: 16), an ongoing study of Canadian electoral politics, describe Canada's brokerage parties as having the following characteristics:

a) they "re-create coalitions at each election,"
b) they "constantly compete for the same policy space and the same votes,"
c) they present voters with "appeals to narrow interests, and proposals that tinker with existing arrangements," rather than "a clear choice between worldviews and the political projects that follow from them,"
d) they "practise inconsistency as they search for electorally successful formulae," and
e) they "organize around leaders rather than around political principles and ideologies."

There is much more that follows from a politics practised by brokerage parties, but the sketch just presented highlights the elements that lead many observers to conclude that brokerage parties have developed to win elections, but function poorly as agents of representation. To the extent that they *do* articulate policies, these will stand on no clearly principled foundation, but appeal to the diversity of interests whose support the party is seeking. The brokerage party courts everyone, and if it does so with policy, this means promising something to each interest it hopes to represent. The difficulty comes with delivering such a program once it is elected. It is one thing on the campaign trail to claim to be the party that can best represent farmers *and* small businessmen *and* the financial community *and* the unemployed *and* middle-class suburbanites; but policy-making in office will involve choices that favour some of these interests and disappoint others. This is one reason why the brokerage party must "re-create" its coalition at each election, which in turn explains its unwillingness to be pinned down to long-term agendas by either ideology or other principled positions. Hence also, the attraction, where possible, of turning from policy specifics to an emphasis on the party leader, and a campaign focused on images of leadership. This, as we discuss more fully below, also dovetails neatly with the development of television politics.

The implication is that brokerage parties succeed electorally but fail in several respects at providing good representation to citizens. Yet both of these observations need qualification. First, we should acknowledge that brokerage parties can perform an important function within the polity, namely that of knitting together diverse communities that are otherwise in tension or have conflicting interests. In this way, the brokerage party builds bridges across the societal cleavages that otherwise fracture the political community. Given the division of Canada into two dominant linguistic communities, the relative strength of these two communities, and the nature of the electoral system, it has been impossible to gain control of government (a parliamentary majority) without significant support from both halves of Canada's dualism. This has been true in Canada since the 1840s, and the two parties to have governed in Canadian history thus far, the Progressive Conservatives and the Liberals, have often been characterized as brokerage parties—certainly they have acted as such during their periods of success. During much of Canadian history, the reins of power have fallen into the hands of whichever party could capture a majority (or significant support) in both Quebec and Ontario (something that reinforced perceptions elsewhere of "central Canadian domination"). This was certainly the case during the period of Conservative domination between 1867 and 1896. After western Canadian provinces were settled and incorporated

PARTISAN INSTABILITY

A relatively simple measure of partisan instability (or volatility) in the party system is found by summing the absolute values of the changes in party support from one election to the next and then dividing by the number of parties.

For example, consider the change in party support in the Canadian elections 1988-93:

Party	1988 %v	1993 %v	Difference
PCs	43	16	27
Liberals	32	41	9
NDP	20	7	13
Reform	0	19	19
BQ	0	14	14
Total			82/2 = 41
Average per party			8.2

These results represent one of the most radical shifts in voter support in any election, anywhere, let alone the most dramatic set of changes in Canadian political experience.

To put them in context, compare the resulting average of 8.2 per party with the data in the following table, which presents volatility per party (considering parties with 3 per cent or more of the vote) for various countries for the two most recent elections.

Country (Elections)	Average Volatility (no. of parties)	
Britain (1992 – 1997)	3.45	(3)
Canada (1997 – 2000)	1.75	(5)
Czech Republic (1996 – 1998)	1.39	(7)
Denmark (1994 – 1998)	1.30	(9)
Germany (1994 – 1998)	1.29	(5)
Netherlands (1994 – 1998)	2.12	(7)
New Zealand (1996 – 1999)	2.60	(6)
Spain (1993 – 1996)	0.79	(4)
Sweden (1994 – 1998)	2.04	(7)

FIGURE 14.2

into Confederation, a Quebec-western alliance became an alternative base from which to govern, as demonstrated initially by Laurier (1896-1911) and most recently by the two-term government of Brian Mulroney (1984-93). When Conservative support collapsed, this bridge between the West and Quebec was shattered, large portions of western Conservative support going to the Reform Party, and much of the Conservative Quebec base going to the Bloc Québécois. Therefore, after the 1993 and 1997 elections, the Liberals remained the only party with national representation, facing a handful of regionally based foes.

When parties can bridge societal cleavages successfully, they can play an important unifying or integrating function within the political system. Not surprisingly, building such bridges may mean downplaying ideology, being flexible about policy solutions to potentially divisive issues, and placing the emphasis on leaders. It is important to think of leaders in the plural, because the bridge between different segments of society is built in part by assuring each segment that it will have strong spokespersons in the government and therein their guarantee that policy will not compromise their interest(s). From the Macdonald-Cartier partnership of the

In the 2000 election, only the Liberals won seats in every province. The PCs and NDP won in six provinces, the Canadian Alliance in five.

373

1860s to the St. Laurent-Howe partnership of the 1950s, this ability to "broker" or pull together English and French Canada has been critical to political success. It is clear, though, that sometime in the 1960s brokerage politics began to change. For one thing, the emphasis became less on the party leader as simply the pre-eminent member of a team of strong regional players (e.g., Pearson) and more on the leader as the prima donna on the basis of whose performance the party's fortunes would succeed (Trudeau, Mulroney) or fail (Stanfield, Clark, Turner). R.K. Carty (1988) has characterized Canadian party politics since 1963 as the age of "electronic" politics, which includes not just television but also the use of public opinion-polling as a tool for agenda-building and shaping campaign strategy: "Most important is the capacity to build a sophisticated political machine that, using the modern electronic technologies of polling, communication and constant monitoring, can mobilize a national constituency" (Thorburn, 1991: 138). It is not difficult to see how a politics based on constructing images of political leadership and a platform of issues based on the results of public-opinion polling will reinforce many of the features identified above as central to brokerage politics. Clearly, the party needs to be able to be flexible enough to respond to shifting currents of public opinion (bearing in mind what was said earlier about public opinion being as much constructed as measured), and certainly its focus is on the wider public, not merely (or even primarily) the concerns of its loyal dues-paying members. What is significant is that in the electronic age this becomes true of every party, while at the same time the ability of parties actually to perform the integrating function once associated with brokerage politics seems ever weaker. The authors of *Absent Mandate* have identified three consequences of brokerage politics: **POLICY BLANDNESS**, emphasis on leaders, and **PARTISAN INSTABILITY**. The latter refers to the willingness of voters to shift their support from one party to another, something that introduces a considerable volatility to the political process (see Figure 14.2). Clearly, these three consequences of brokerage politics are intimately linked:

Policy Blandness

↗   ↘

Emphasis on Leaders   ←   Partisan Instability

The refusal of parties to distinguish themselves in terms of ideology or long-term policy commitments forces the attention of both strategists and voters elsewhere, and in the age of electronic politics this means the focus falls on leaders. Parties are thus only as popular as their leaders (or as popular as the images associated with their leaders), and because parties change leaders or their leaders' public image changes, their popularity is inevitably volatile. This means that the attachment of voters to any party is weak; their vote is essentially "up for grabs." Instead of addressing the concerns (i.e., representing the interests) of a stable, long-term following, parties seek the approval of the flexible electorate.

The second qualification we must make is to the observation that brokerage parties succeed electorally; they do so only in part, and to some degree because of the electoral system. The success of brokerage parties can be measured negatively by the presence of parties based on a particular societal cleavage, whether of class, or region, or language. In Canada since 1921, significant numbers of seats have been won at the federal level by the Progressive, Co-operative Commonwealth Federation, Social Credit, New Democratic, Reform, and Bloc Québécois parties, none of which has yet been transformed into a successful brokerage party. While these parties have been able to win seats, usually through a regionally concentrated support, none has participated in government, and only four times—the Progressives in 1921, the Bloc Québécois in 1993, the Reform Party in 1997, and the Canadian Alliance in 2000—has one finished as high as second place.

At the same time, we may expect the electoral system to play a role here. In pluralistic societies, the brokerage party succeeds by building a coalition of supporters drawn from diverse segments of society, segments with often diverging interests. Now all else being equal, we would expect members of a particular societal interest (say labour, or agriculture, or small business) to receive better representation from a party of their own than from a party representing them and several other interests. In other words, why would a party that claims to represent everyone be more attractive than a party that just represents you? One reason might be that it stands a better chance of forming the government, which is certainly true in plurality systems with their tendency to manufacture majorities. The brokerage party needs only to seek the support of a coalition comprising some 40 to 44 per cent of the vote to secure a majority government in a plurality system. In a proportionate system, though, the brokerage party will not be assured of a place in government, and certainly will not have a majority government, unless it can secure the support of 50 per cent of the electorate or more. Such a level of support for one party in a multi-party system is very rare. If, as in most proportionate systems, the norm is a coalition government, then a party that represents a narrower segment of society may be just as likely as the brokerage party to participate in government, but more likely to provide good representation.

Consider the position of farmers, whose interests may clash with those of consumers, food processors, wholesalers and retailers, bankers, etc. Are they better represented by a party of their own or by throwing their support behind a party that also claims to represent bankers, consumers, retailers, etc.? In a plurality system, a focused agrarian party is likely to win few seats, and those only in areas where the farm vote is concentrated. At best they will be a minor party within the opposition, with little voice in public policy. By supporting the brokerage party at least they may have a spokesperson within the government who is committed to their cause and will argue for it when it is threatened by policies favouring other interests. In a proportionate system, the share of seats won by the agrarian party will correspond to the share of the vote the agrarian party can draw. This party may be one of the partners in a coalition government formed after the election; in that event, the agrarian party's share of cabinet will most likely be (or include) the agriculture ministry and thus considerable control over agricultural policy. This kind of opportunity in proportionate systems for small, focused parties presents a challenge to (and perhaps limits) the success of parties trying to practise brokerage politics in such systems.

In the 1950s Maurice Duverger made a distinction about party organization, which many have appropriated, between **CADRE** and **MASS** parties. At the risk of oversimplification, cadre parties are controlled by the parliamentary representatives, are run from the top down by regional and local elites, and organize to mobilize support at election time, but are largely dormant (outside of parliament) between elections. Mass parties, by contrast, depend on a large, loyal membership, which remains active in the period between elections, employs a full-time secretariat of professional workers and organizers, and keeps the parliamentary wing accountable to the broader membership. For a variety of social, economic, and historical reasons, Duverger associated cadre organization with conservative parties rooted in the status quo, and mass parties with left-wing political movements. The two traditional brokerage parties in Canada—the Liberals and

Conservatives—have often displayed features of cadre organization, while the various third parties have more resembled
Duverger's mass parties. In keeping with earlier observations, we
would suggest that most parties today exhibit a mix of cadre and
mass characteristics. To the extent that campaigning has focused
on party leaders, and has come to rely on television advertising
and opinion sampling, this means a centralization of control over
the campaign in the hands of the party elite and the paid
professionals who provide modern communication and public
relations expertise. On the other hand, the expense of the modern
campaign requires parties to recruit members or at least large
numbers of adherents who can be solicited for financial
contributions. Again, electronic technology has allowed parties to
perfect mass mailing and canvassing techniques that build a base of
mass support (if not actual membership) without the nuisance of
an actively participating mass membership. Parties want to be free
of the actual demands of loyal members in order to pursue the
more flexible demands of the uncommitted larger public. In short,
parties want support (financial and political) on the order of a mass
party, but seek to centralize control of agenda-formation and
policy direction on the order of a cadre party. It is difficult to
escape the conclusion that parties continue to perfect their
techniques as electoral vehicles while stagnating or deteriorating as
agents of representation.

Parties practise electoral politics within the rules or constraints of a particular electoral system. In the background there
are also the political culture, the patterns of socialization, the tools
of influence for shaping public opinion, parties' and leaders' per-
formances, and many other variables. In short, at several points in
this book we have touched upon the variables that feed into the
modern electoral campaign. Any further detailed examination is
beyond our scope here, but there is no shortage of good and
accessible material on this topic. A few summarizing observations
must suffice.

First, the modern campaign has become increasingly
sophisticated and professional as it has become increasingly
focused on the use of mass communications technology, in
particular of public opinion polling, and of television. This has
meant several things:

- a focus on leadership and images associated with the
  personality of the leader rather than a clear, detailed
  articulation of policy;

- a decreasing emphasis on local candidates, on the potential cabinet team the party is offering, and a decreasing public influence for party notables other than the leader;
- increasingly centralized campaigns directed from party headquarters, and essentially run by professional consultants, specialists in polling, advertising, marketing, media management, and image creation;
- a corresponding need for considerable sums of money to finance such professional, technology-intensive campaigns—hence mass-mailing and telephone solicitation efforts;
- an increasingly superficial politics, superficial in the desire to avoid commitment to long-term positions and in the poverty of detailed information actually shared about likely policy outcomes; and
- in the absence of anything positive to offer, a negative style of campaigning that seeks to demonstrate the weakness of opponents rather than one's own strengths.

This kind of politics must share at least some—if not the largest portion—of the blame for some of the features of our political process:

- voters are cynical and distrustful of politicians, as well as of government generally;
- journalists practise judgemental journalism and become participants in the political campaign rather than conduits by which political candidates speak to voters;
- partisan attachments are weak and highly flexible; and
- politics becomes less a matter of public discourse about means and ends, and more a matter of mass psychology and attempted manipulation of public opinion.

What is perhaps most troubling about this situation is the difficulty of imagining what might happen to change things for the better. It is not surprising, then, that citizens have sometimes looked for alternative agents of representation, such as interest groups, or have sought to participate directly without mediation, as in some of the instruments of direct democracy.

An alternative to the political party, and one with potentially great significance, is the **INTEREST GROUP**, or **ORGANIZED INTEREST**. Like parties, organized interests are voluntary organizations that seek to further the interests of their members, but unlike parties they seek to accomplish this not by winning election to political office, but by influencing policy-makers (this influence, as we shall see, may be exerted in a number of ways). This small but critical difference between political party and organized interest leads to several others. For the most part, interest groups are not as institutionalized as political parties, and where they are institutionalized it is in different ways (see the discussion of corporatism below). While many political parties gear up for elections and all but disappear in the between times, organized interests engage in a more regular calendar of activity, and may mobilize most intensely at any point in the political cycle, being driven by policy considerations. Whereas citizens are unlikely to belong to more than one political party, and at election time are forced to choose between parties, there is no limitation to their membership in, activity on behalf of, or support for organized interests. Multiple membership may mean that citizens simultaneously support groups that are competing or in conflict, as well as those more obviously complementary. The flip side is that the claim of groups to represent a particular size of constituency in society may often be a very partial representation.

The validity of these observations may depend on the types of organized group with which we are dealing. One distinction is between groups that organize around an issue (e.g., saving wetlands, opposing political imprisonment and torture, either side of the abortion issue, etc.) and those that are institutional or structural, that is, representing an interest determined by the structure or organization of society or the economy (e.g., labour federations, chambers of commerce, professional associations, etc.). But apart from subject matter, does this distinction stand for anything else? The idea that **ISSUE GROUPS** will be temporary and loose collections of a mobilized public while institutionalized groups are permanent structures organized and served by a bureaucracy cannot be supported; issue groups are often as permanent and as bureaucratized as any structural associations.

On the other hand, when it comes to the functions that organized interests perform, there may be real differences between issue and **STRUCTURAL GROUPS**. By definition, as it were, all groups have the role of trying to influence policy-makers, seeking government action on a problem experienced by or of interest to

14.3
ORGANIZED INTERESTS

members, or trying to block or modify policies perceived as contrary to members' interests. In addition, though, and this we suggest is more likely to be true of the structural group than the issue group, organized interests may provide support and information to members, offer training and educational programs, provide access to a variety of professional services, and, in some cases, regulate and discipline members. This last point indicates that, like other institutions, the functions performed by organized interests may not affect just these groups and their members; in particular, organized groups can be very useful for policy-makers and administrators. The resources that groups command and employ to influence public policy can in turn be tapped into by policy-makers looking for alternative sources of expertise, for reaction to policy proposals, or for means of mobilizing a particular segment of the population. In the case of self-regulating professional associations, actual governmental authority has been delegated from the state to recognized organizations.

While organized interests serve a variety of purposes, then, what still interests us most, politically speaking, is their activity to influence public policy; this is where we must assess their significance as vehicles of political representation. Here, too, the strategies of groups are various, and the activity of any particular group is less likely to be a choice between these strategies than a calculated mix of each of them. One set of strategies concerns offering or threatening to withhold from policy-makers certain scarce resources that groups have at their disposal. These resources may be the votes of the group's members, or financial contri- butions, or co-operation in the implementation or enforcement of particular policies. If policy-makers are not influenced directly by the incentives or disincentives that groups can put before them, they may be more influenced by the larger public, and a second set of strategies concerns spreading the group's concerns to society at large through information or advertising campaigns, demon- strations, or even acts of civil disobedience. Perhaps more effective than either of these avenues is to have an "inside track" —that is, to be able, through a good working relationship with policy-makers, to exercise influence through consultation. This may be the payoff, as it were, for being a source of information, advice, feedback, and support to policy-makers: the group's interests are taken into consideration as a key variable in policy formulation. This is why policy communities and policy networks have become so important within public policy literature today (see Chapter Fifteen).

The activity of trying to influence politicians generally, and policy-makers more specifically, is often indicated by the term **LOBBYING**, which involves making a representation to political officials (elected or otherwise) on behalf of a group, interest, or company. Lobbying can be an important part of the job of the officers or paid employees of interest groups, and organized interests with sufficient resources will employ their own full-time lobbyists—called "in-house lobbyists." On the other hand, there are professional lobbyists not committed to any particular cause, but who sell their expertise and their political connections as a professional service. It is this last aspect of the lobbyists' activity that worries outside observers and critics of the political and policy process: that in using their connections to provide privileged access to the viewpoints of their paying clients, lobbyists are subverting the democratic process. Consequently, the greater the apparent influence of lobbyists, the greater the calls for public registration of lobbyists and disclosure of their clients and of the issue for which they have been hired. Legislation regulating lobbying in Canada was passed in 1989, requiring both in-house and professional lobbyists to register and file returns disclosing their clients and their concerns. Many observers have complained that the regulations in Canada are much weaker than those in place in the United States. On the other hand, lobbying plays a much larger role in U.S. politics and has been prominent for a longer time.

The difference between lobbying in the U.S. and Canada reflects an important dimension to this whole issue: namely, the environment within which organized interests are active. Since groups seek to influence policy, it is important to distinguish the number and nature of the **ACCESS POINTS** where influence can be exerted. A system of separated powers such as in the United States, with weak (undisciplined) parties and no responsible government requirements, has many more access points and they are found at a lower "level" in the hierarchy of elected officials than is the case in a parliamentary system such as Canada's, particularly when this entails a one-party majority government. In the U.S., for example, because party discipline is weak, the vote of any senator or congressman is to some degree "up for grabs," and there is no member of Congress who is not important enough to be lobbied. In Canada, by contrast, policy is made in the cabinet, and unless one hopes to engineer a rare caucus revolt, there is not much to be gained by lobbying backbench MPs. On the other hand, those who cannot get a hearing from cabinet ministers, or from officials in the Prime Minister's Office or senior public servants, will be forced to lobby MPs. In Canada, in short, the access points are fewer and higher up in the system. Canada represents a fairly closed system for organized interests; the U.S., a very open system. In Canada, if organized interests cannot ultimately gain the ear of cabinet-level decision-makers (by whatever path), their chance of influencing policy is slight. In the U.S. there are many more targets of influence, but then this applies for all groups and it will be easier to stop a policy from going ahead than to get a new policy implemented—all those access points are also potential **VETO POINTS**. Not surprisingly, there is a considerable current of resentment in U.S. politics directed towards interest group activity and any party or leader who is seen to be in the pocket of "special interests"—however these might be defined.

Finally, it is also possible to raise questions about the accountability of organized interests: How democratic are these organizations? How well do they represent their constituents? Here there is considerable difference among organized interests; some may indeed demonstrate a leadership clearly representative of and accountable to the membership, but others may simply solicit members' money and support without inviting or indeed allowing any input over decisions about the issues that supposedly unite them. In other words, interest groups are no worse or better than other organizations. On this dimension, it may well be that structural or professional groups are more democratic than issue groups, the bulk of whose members often remain anonymous individuals on the other side of a mailing list and who may never meet one another.

14.4 PLURALISM VERSUS CORPORATISM

The degree to which organized interests are able to influence policy is not only an empirical question, but also a normative one. The discussion of groups in the previous section made reference only to settings where their participation in policy is informal, and the product of competition with other groups for influence on the policy process. This is the reality described by (and usually advocated by) *pluralists*.

PLURALISM presents group activity in the political process as a competition of multiple elites. There are numerous groups of varying strength, whose leaders bargain, compete, and compromise in the effort to shape public policy. By and large, pluralists have no difficulty regarding the competition of organized groups as legitimate. The only normative question they consider important is one of fairness; are the terms on which such groups compete balanced? If so, then no one interest or set of interests will be able to dominate, and policy outputs generally, over time, will represent a compromise between the favoured positions of different interests. In the minds of some, this is as close to the "will of the majority" or the "common good" as any other mechanism is likely to produce in today's complex societies. Pluralism takes a *laissez-faire* approach to the competition of groups for influence in the political system. It is not surprising, then, that pluralism has been championed most strongly in the United States, where the roots of pluralism are traced back to the early Federalists, in particular to James Madison. Critics argue, of course, that the playing field of organized interests is *not* level, that interest group activities— whether lobbying, or mobilizing public opinion—are expensive, and that the advantage will be with those who have resources.

In **CORPORATISM**, the place of organized interests is not left to haphazard competition, but is institutionalized. In other words, what distinguishes corporatism is the regular, official participation of organized interests in the formation of public policy. (Obviously the degree of corporatism can vary, depending on the degree to which interest group participation in policy formation is formalized.) Most of the countries ranked medium to high in corporatism are found in Western Europe (especially Switzerland, Norway, Sweden, Austria, the Netherlands, and Belgium). Typically, corporatism involves trilateral negotiation and consensus between representatives of the state, the business community, and organized labour. It is possible for other actors such as farmers or consumers to be involved also. In any case, the non-state actors are agents of **PEAK ASSOCIATIONS**, which are granted a representational monopoly. This means that interest groups are organized hierarchically on the basis of functional interests (like labour, business, etc.), and **UMBRELLA ORGANIZATIONS** covering each functional group are accorded status by the state in the policy process. This usually means there is an extra-parliamentary institution or forum (a council, or chamber, etc.) where these interests meet, negotiate, and come to decisions. The aim of corporatism clearly is to ensure that all major interests are involved in the formation of a social consensus on policy—which should also increase the likelihood that that policy will be acceptable to the public at large. Those interests that fall outside the functional or institutionally recognized categories will obviously not be included here.

In countries where corporatism is weak or non-existent, the term has a bad reputation, being linked to fascism, or to authoritarian one-party states. This is called **STATE CORPORATISM**, and should be distinguished from the **SOCIETAL CORPORATISM** of Western Europe, which is entirely compatible with political pluralism. Also, and not surprisingly, in countries where organized labour is weak and business interests are strong, like the United States, corporatism is not seen to be an attractive option.[1]

What distinguishes pluralism and corporatism are the nature of the interaction among competing non-state elites and the nature of the interaction between non-state and state actors. Both are essentially about the role of elites in the policy process. Regardless of their concern with consensus, or a fair representation of social diversity, or balanced competition, neither is fundamentally democratic in the sense of inviting or requiring participation by non-elites. If democracy is not possible in the longer term in our changing world, or if the degree of democracy possible will always be constrained by other factors, then pluralism or corporatism (or something in between?) may be important alternatives. In either case the organized group provides an alternative mode of representation to that provided by the political party. Another, less-travelled, route is to bypass representation and involve the citizenry directly in decision-making.

1. Note that corporatism is not a system dominated by the business corporation. Rather, it attempts to treat the entire society as a "corporation"— i.e., as a single, united body.

14.5 DIRECT DEMOCRACY

Among Western democracies, only the U.S. and the Netherlands have not held a national referendum, but few countries use this device regularly and only four (France, Denmark, Australia, and Switzerland) have held more than ten. **DIRECT DEMOCRACY** is known but not trusted, or if you like, is common but infrequent. Direct democracy refers to instruments that involve direct citizen participation or input on questions of policy. The device of direct democracy most commonly employed is the referendum, but some important distinctions are often collapsed by applying this term to all instances of popular voting on questions rather than for candidates.

First of all, it is useful to distinguish between those votes that are binding upon the state and those that are only consultative. Those which compel the government to act, or by a negative vote veto a government action, are properly **REFERENDUMS**; those votes that the government may legally ignore (whether positive or negative) are more properly called **PLEBISCITES**. On the basis of this distinction, all three national referendums in Canada—including the most recent, the 1992 vote on a constitutional package called the Charlottetown Accord—were, properly speaking, plebiscites. On the other hand, in democratic states it would not be politically prudent to proceed contrary to the result of a plebiscite; had governments in Canada proceeded to enact the Charlottetown Accord despite the negative vote, they would have invited a popular backlash, which would probably have manifested itself in the next election. To a large degree, then, a plebiscite today probably carries as much force as a referendum in countries with a democratic tradition. Another difference, though, is that while the decision to hold a plebiscite is always (since it is consultative) at the discretion of the government, referendums are often mandatory, particularly in countries where constitutional change requires popular ratification (e.g., Australia, Switzerland).

Secondly, it is important to distinguish those cases where the question originates with the state (most referendums or plebiscites) from those where the question emerges from the public—an **INITIATIVE**. An initiative is a device allowing a segment of the public to force a question to be placed before the wider population. At the very least, it usually requires collecting a specified number or proportion of signatures within a limited time period (say, 150,000 signatures in 90 days, or 50,000 signatures in 45 days, etc.). In addition, there may be procedures to ensure that the question put before the public is constitutional, and in some jurisdictions (e.g., Switzerland) the government may also present the public with a counter-proposal. While initiatives are popular in many American states, Switzerland is the only country that employs them with any frequency on a national level, and here they are limited to proposals for revision of the constitution. Popular initiative has placed a matter on the national ballot three times in Italy, and once in Austria.

Similar to the initiative is the **ABROGATIVE REFERENDUM** (or popular veto), by which a petition gathered in much the same manner as an initiative forces an act of parliamentary legislation to face popular ratification (or defeat) in a referendum. This is usually possible only in a limited period of time after the passage of legislation, and obviously will be resorted to by opponents of the law in question. In Denmark, such a vote may be requested by one-third of the members of the legislature except for laws concerning finance and international law. The very existence of this device might well cause governments to avoid passing legislation it knows is unpopular—it is difficult to imagine a measure such as the Canadian GST (Goods and Services Tax) being passed in a country with an abrogative referendum. In short, the abrogative referendum is like the initiative except that it seeks to negate a governmental action, whereas the initiative seeks to force governmental action (or inaction).

There are any number of reasons why people choose to bypass representation and employ direct democracy instruments, although we should note that in all cases this is supplementary or complementary to the processes of representative government, not replacing them. Most commonly, referendums seem to meet one of two needs. The first is to give legitimacy to a decision, the scope or status of which is too large or too important to be decided by representatives on the people's behalf. Hence the common use of referendums to ratify constitutional changes, and in some countries constitutional change *must* be ratified in a referendum—in Australia and Switzerland, which are federal countries, the referendum must win a majority nationally *and* a majority in a majority of the states or cantons. Similarly, entry into the European Economic Community has required a successful referendum on the question in each potential member country; in the most recent expansion, which saw the admission of Austria, Finland, and Sweden, the people of Norway rejected membership in a binding referendum.

A second basis for direct democracy is to locate responsibility for deciding questions of a politically sensitive or potentially divisive nature squarely with the public; in this way parties can avoid internal division over an issue, or being forever identified with a decision that might be unacceptable to a significant segment of the population. Questions that deal with moral issues have often been decided directly; in Italy and Ireland, abortion and divorce have been addressed by referendum. Earlier in this century, questions about the prohibition (or ending of the prohibition) of the sale of alcohol were commonly addressed in popular ballots. Of Canada's three national plebiscites, one addressed constitutional questions (1992), one concerned conscription of soldiers (1942), and one was about prohibition of alcohol (1898). There have also been 21 non-binding provincial plebiscites on the sale or prohibition of alcohol.

Switzerland's politics present special conditions that provide a compelling basis for direct democracy, and thus it is no accident that this country leads the world in the variety and frequency of its use of direct instruments. Simply put, Switzerland has been governed for many years by a grand coalition of the four leading parties in parliament. Every election returns the same four parties to office. This means that there is no effective parliamentary opposition to the government. The referendum and initiative thus place the people themselves in the oppositional role of providing a check on the government through these direct instruments.

Of course it is also possible that the Swiss have just come to believe in the value of direct democracy, and principle is another reason for advocating non-representative decision-making. In Canada, the official platform of the Reform Party (now Canadian Alliance Party) called for referendums, initiatives, and even the use of an initiative-like process to recall elected MPs and force them to face a by-election in the period between general elections. It is no accident that the loudest call for direct democracy has come from Canada's populist conservative party; observers have long noted that the general tenor of direct democracy is conservative. Public opinion is generally slow to embrace new causes, wary of change, and always resistant to new expenditures and/or taxes. For those wishing to limit the size of the state, or to achieve significant downsizing, direct questions on tax cuts and other fiscal measures seem a promising strategy.

Depending on your ideological perspective, then, the conservative character of direct democracy (and Switzerland is famously conservative) can be seen as a virtue or a defect. A variety of other concerns are raised about the feasibility or desirability of direct democracy. Clearly, there are practical limits to the type of issue that can be addressed by referendum; only some matters are capable of being addressed by a question that permits only "yes" or "no" responses. In forcing categorical responses, the referendum also forces decisions and thereby may exclude the possibility of compromise or consensus. As in all situations where the majority has clear control of the outcome, minorities may feel threatened by direct democracy. In the 1942 Canadian plebiscite on conscription, for example, the national "Yes" vote (affirming the possibility of conscription) was 63.7 per cent, but in Quebec was 29 per cent, reflecting very different attitudes towards Canada's war participation by English-speaking and French-speaking Canadians. A different issue concerns the expertise or competence of the general public; if referendums appeal to common sense, how informed or educated is that common sense? This critique may rest on the possibly dubious assumption that the decisions of representatives are always well-informed. At any rate, the onus of educating the citizens on the pros and cons of the issue at stake usually falls to the groups

KEY TERMS

abrogative referendum
access points
administrative function
agents of representation
brokerage parties
cadre parties
corporatism
direct democracy
electoral vehicles
electronic politics
initiatives
interest groups
issue groups
lobbying
mass parties
mobilization function
organized interests
partisan instability
peak associations
pluralism
political parties
referendum
representative function
structural groups
umbrella organization
veto points

REFERENCES AND SUGGESTED READING

Boyer, Patrick. 1992. *Direct Democracy in Canada: The History and Future of Referendums*. Toronto: Dundurn.

Butler, David, and Austin Ranney, eds. 1978. *Referendums*. Washington: American Enterprise Institute.

Carty, R.K. 1988. *Canadian Political Party Systems*. Peterborough, Ont.: Broadview Press.

Clarke, Harold D., et al. 1996. *Absent Mandate*, 3rd ed. Toronto: Gage.

Duverger, Maurice. 1966. *Political Parties*. London: Methuen.

Esberey, Joy, and Grace Skogstad. 1991. "Organized Interests," in Robert Krause and R.H. Wagenberg, eds., *Introductory Readings in Canadian Government*. Mississauga, Ont.: Copp Clark Pitman.

Jackson, Robert J., and Doreen Jackson. 1990. *Politics in Canada*, 2nd ed. Scarborough, Ont.: Prentice Hall.

campaigning on either side of the issue. This last point directs us to perhaps a more serious set of issues: namely, the rules governing campaigning in direct democracy, and whether or not some interests are advantaged here.

If there are no rules, then the referendum campaign becomes a free-for-all in which those with the most influence are advantaged, and in all likelihood this will be those with the most resources to spend on advertising, polling, and the other tools of mass communication. In many jurisdictions, referendum legislation requires the establishment and registration of "umbrella" organizations for both sides of the question, and these organizations in turn are subject to regulations concerning financing, expenditures, advertising, etc. The effectiveness of these rules in creating an open, fair, and informative campaign varies considerably.

In short, in addition to the principled belief that "the people should decide," there are many practical reasons why referendums or initiatives may be desirable, and provide important enhancement to the processes of representative government. At the same time, there are clear limitations to the feasibility of such mass instruments, and they are always likely to be supplementary rather than form the basis of modern democracy. The ability of such instruments to provide citizens with "good government" will ultimately depend on the citizens themselves and their preparation for sound decision-making. Here, no less than in voting for representatives, what will matter is the quality of information on which citizens depend, the activity of the mass media, the distribution of resources among competing actors, and the susceptibility or immunity of the public to manipulation.

14.6 CONCLUSION

Just as we have all become used to the fact that our governments are several, that the state exists at several levels, so too in modern society it is probably good that we have many vehicles of representation at our disposal. Although they may sometimes compete among themselves, these vehicles ultimately serve us in different ways, in different contexts. We are not in a position of having to choose between political parties, organized interests, or direct instruments of decision-making, but ideally live in a polity where we have the opportunity to employ each as the context and issues seem to require. None of these will serve us perfectly; the point, perhaps, is to recognize how the ways in which they do serve us can bear improvement, and seek to generate the will to make such improvements.

It should also be clear that in contemporary society political activity is organized activity. Whether we are talking about parties, interest groups, or the campaign organizations that support one side of a referendum question, organization is critical to the marshalling and employment of the resources that are necessary to communicate and persuade a mass public. This is the inevitable consequence of the size and complexity of the communities in which we live today. The challenge is to ensure that the representative organizations remain responsive and accountable to those they claim to represent.

SOMETHING TO CONSIDER

How might the continued growth of the Internet affect the evolution of (a) political parties, (b) organized interests, and (c) direct democracy?

To what degree is it impossible to have either meaningful representation or truly informed direct democracy in mass societies dominated by electronic media and an ethic of consumerism?

Kirchheimer, Otto. 1966. *Poltics, Law, and Social Change*. New York: Columbia University Press.

Landes, Richard. 1987. *The Canadian Polity*, 2nd ed. Scarborough, Ont.: Prentice Hall.

Lawson, Kay. 1980. *Political Parties and Linkage*. New Haven: Yale University Press.

Lehmbruch, Gerhard, and Phillip Schmitter. 1982. *Patterns of Corporatist Policy-Making*. Beverley Hills, Calif.: Sage.

Mair, Peter. 1990. *The West European Party System*. Oxford: Oxford University Press.

Powell, G. Bingham. 1982. *Contemporary Democracies*. Cambridge, Mass.: Harvard University Press.

Pross, Paul. 1986. *Groups, Politics, and Public Policy*. Toronto: Oxford University Press.

Tanguay, A. Brian, and Alain-G. Gagnon, eds. 1996. *Canadian Parties in Transition*, 2nd ed. Toronto: Nelson.

Thorburn, H.G. 1985. *Interest Groups in the Canadian Federal System*. Toronto: University of Toronto Press.

——, ed. 1991. *Party Politics in Canada*, 6th ed. Scarborough, Ont.: Prentice Hall.

Wearing, Joseph. 1991. *The Ballot and Its Message: Voting in Canada*. Toronto: Copp Clark Pitman.

Wilson, Graham K. 1981. *Interest Groups in the United States*. Oxford: Clarendon Press.

V

GOVERNING

In describing constitutional models and government institutions, as was our focus in Section III, it is all too easy to lose sight of the fact that these structures are really *places where something is happening*. Politics is dynamic, a complex of related and interrelated activities taking place within or by means of the structures that we identify as institutions. Where activity or behaviour is regular or rule-governed we tend to speak in terms of process, and the focus of political study is very often (if not generally) on what is happening within the various processes we have identified. In Section IV we examined key elements in the political process, the "input" side of the political system. The flip-side or complement of this is the processes that concern the "outputs" of government. Here we discover the actual exercise of authority and power of the state by those within the government in ways that affect those outside the government, namely citizens. Giving these governmental outputs a more general label, namely *policy*, we will first discuss the nature of the policy process, and then the role of two key institutions of the state—the legislature and the bureaucracy—in the formulation and delivery, respectively, of policy. Second, we will examine the role of a different set of important actors, namely the judiciary, and the ability of the courts to set the boundaries of public policy through their performance of *judicial review*. Our interest in policy, though, is not merely with the process, but is also substantive: what are the actual policies of states, and how do they make a difference to the lives of citizens? Put another way: what do governments *do*? These are questions that, pursued with any degree of comprehension, would take us well beyond the scope of this text. We will examine the expansion and contraction of the postwar welfare state in order to provide a brief overview of some of the

391

shifting currents of social and economic policy in the twentieth century. This also will serve as an introduction to many of the basic issues of *political economy*.

15

public policy, legislation, and the bureaucracy

People look to the state to solve problems, or to take action on pressing issues; this is what is meant by saying that the political process delivers "demands" to the state. In fact, a considerable area of ideological debate concerns what kinds of demands should be made of the state, or what kinds of tasks the state should be set to do. In a variety of ways, and for several purposes, it is useful to think of the state as an ensemble of resources organized for solving problems. In recent decades an increasing focus has been on this problem-solving activity of the state, its organization for doing so, its efficacy and efficiency, its co-ordination and rationales. This focus constitutes the study of public policy.

Leslie Pal has defined policy as "a course of action or inaction chosen by public authorities to address a given problem or set of problems" (1992: 2). Several aspects of this definition are worth highlighting, and some of them are more problematic than might first appear obvious. First, there is the idea that policy can involve action *or* the decision *not* to act; there may indeed be problems decision-makers consider, but are unable or unwilling to tackle. The obvious difficulty is in determining when inaction is the result of a deliberate decision, and for this reason most policy studies focus on the actions rather than the inactions of the state. As an example of policy as inaction, though, consider a government pressured to "do something" about unemployment, which then announces that it will leave job creation to the private-sector forces of the marketplace.

Second, where action *is* chosen, it is "a course" of action, implying a relatively coherent or co-ordinated set of different interventions. As noted, policy is made in response to problems in the environment of the policy actors, and it will involve decisions

15.1
PUBLIC POLICY DEFINED

15.1 Public Policy Defined
15.2 Policy Communities and Policy Networks
15.3 Elements of Policy-Making
    15.3.1 Agenda formation
    15.3.2 Decision-making
    15.3.3 Instrument choice
    15.3.4 Implementation
    15.3.5 Evaluation
15.4 The Legislative Process
15.5 The Bureaucracy
15.6 Conclusion

393

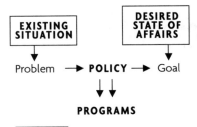

FIGURE 15.1

at various levels. At its most basic, a policy decision is about whether or not to become involved, and the decision to address a particular problem will in all likelihood involve identification of some goal or purpose, however vaguely it might be articulated (e.g., to reduce health-care costs). Policy, then, is a commitment to certain ends, and at the next level will involve identification and selection of various means for achieving these purposes. To describe policy as a "course of action" presents the reality that the means governments employ to achieve their purposes are usually several, ideally co-ordinated into a coherent strategy of action. Much of what governments do in the modern world, whether it involves providing services, transferring resources, facilitating private actions, or delivering public goods, is captured by the term **PROGRAMS**. Student loans, legal aid, and employee retraining schemes are examples of government programs. Policy is broader and more fundamental: it is the decision to have programs (or not), the decision about what kind and mix of programs to have, the selection of the goals and objectives that programs should meet, and often, it is the decision to change or abandon existing programs. Programs are the means or instruments through which governments implement policy.

What students of public policy are (and, we would argue, all citizens should be) interested in is how and by what means specific policies come to be chosen and implemented. It is in this context that we sometimes speak of a **POLICY PROCESS**, a set of stages linking the behaviour of individuals within various institutional structures and producing as an outcome some identifiable public policies. Obviously, within any state such a process will depend on the institutional structure, the political culture, the experience of political actors, the resources available, and any number of other relevant factors.

The definition of public policy, the designation of a policy process, and indeed much of the study and literature on public policy rest on the notion that governmental outputs are deliberately chosen, that someone is "in charge," that there is control over what emerges. Simply put, this is less certain than it appears, depending on a variety of circumstances, and it may be more accurate to say that the degree of control implied by the discussion of public policy is more or less so rather than absolutely so. To give just one example of why this assumption is problematic, consider simply the number of actors and institutions involved in deciding, designing, and delivering policy; the more diffuse the authority involved, the less control will rest anywhere identifiable

394

within the whole. In this respect, policy may often be a by-product of the activity of any number of actors, rather than the product of a coherent process.

Two useful concepts for understanding the world of public policy are the ideas of a **POLICY COMMUNITY** and of **POLICY NETWORKS**. A policy community is all those actors, governmental and private, who "have a continuing stake in, and knowledge about, any given policy field or issue" (Doern and Phidd, 1992: 76-77). In other words, for any **POLICY SECTOR**, such as health care, or education, or defence policy, etc., there will be a cluster of institutions, associations, and individuals who have an ongoing interest in whatever policy is made in this sector. The policy community is quite often further divided into the **SUB-GOVERN-MENT** and the **ATTENTIVE PUBLIC** (Pross, 1992: 120). This is largely equivalent to a distinction between those who make policy and those who attempt to influence policy-makers. The sub-government will be a relatively small group that includes the minister of the relevant department, senior departmental bureaucrats, officials from central co-ordinating agencies or departments, and sometimes key parliamentarians or representatives from institutionalized interest organizations. These individuals are linked by their responsibility (in one shape or another) for policy. Of course, the nature of the sub-government will depend very much on the constitutional arrangement of the institutions of state, the organization of governmental departments, the structure of cabinet decision-making, and a variety of other institutional considerations.

The attentive public is a much larger collection of individuals and organizations whose interests are affected by policy decisions in this sector. The most important segment of the attentive public will usually be the organized interests concerned. These may be issue groups, professional associations, and corporate interests. Academics, private institution scholars, and journalists will be another key component. Officials of other governments, domestic or foreign, opposition politicians, and interested individuals with no institutional affiliation may round out the policy community. What they all have in common is their interest in the policy sector, of course, but also their willingness, if not eagerness, to influence policy outcomes. Importantly, though, many of these segments of the policy community will have opposing

15.2
POLICY COMMUNITIES AND POLICY NETWORKS

perspectives or be seeking very different and incompatible solutions to their problems. A key determinant of any policy will be which voices within the attentive public succeed in gaining the attention and the sympathy of those who matter within the sub-government.

Consider a policy sector such as health care. Interested actors in this policy community's attentive public will include doctors' associations, nurses' associations, and various unions representing health-care workers. These groups may well be united in their opposition to cuts in health-care funding. On the other hand, once such cuts are unavoidable, it may be that these groups will oppose each other in the attempt to minimize the impact of such cuts on their own members. In a world of shrinking health-care budgets, more money for doctors means less for nurses, or means hospitals trying to contract out ancillary services to lower-paying non-unionized contractors. Other members of the health policy attentive public will include pharmaceutical companies, and within Canada there has been a bitter division and battle for control over public policy between brand-name and generic drug producers. One of the issues raised by this rivalry is the cost of medication, which may bring into the policy community actors normally found elsewhere, such as anti-poverty groups or seniors' associations. The size of the attentive public within a policy community will fluctuate partly in response to the level of activity within that sector. Some groups are always there; others will become involved only when the fate of a particular policy in which they have taken an interest is still being determined. For example, Susan Phillips reports that the Mulroney government's proposed Child Care Act of 1988 brought opposition from "among others, the Canadian Day Care Advocacy Association (CDCA), major unions—including the Canadian Labour Congress, Public Service Alliance of Canada, Canadian Union of Public Employees, and the National Union of Provincial government employees— the Canadian Teachers' Federation, the Federation of Nurses, National Anti-Poverty Organization, Canadian Jewish Congress, Canadian Federation of Students, National Council of Welfare, Canadian Advisory Council on the Status of Women and women's groups (notably the National Action Committee on the Status of Women)" (1989: 172).

Given the potential enormity and fluidity of the policy community, the second central notion, that of *policy networks,* is very useful. A policy network describes the relationships that develop between the sub-government and actors, particularly organized groups, in the attentive public. We have noted that many within the attentive public will bring opposing interests to the table, so to speak; Pross suggests that networks bring together people with common ideas and approaches to policy: "Just as a village divides into camps over divisive issues, so policy communities divide into networks" (1992: 120). Coleman and Skogstad (1990) have provided an influential treatment of networks, focusing on the structural characteristics of the relationship between the state (sub-government) and organizational interests (groups). Pal explains this: "The central variables in the relationship are the degree of autonomy and concentration of power among state agencies, and the degree of concentration or coordination of interests on the societal side" (1992: 111). Because these networks are determined only in part by the institutional structure of the state, they will vary from policy community to policy community depending also a great deal on the makeup of the particular attentive publics involved. Ultimately, mapping these networks is useful in explaining, in part, how some segments within society succeed in exerting influence on the formation of public policy, and, perhaps, why some are not so successful.

It follows from what was said above that there is not *one* policy process, but many. Indeed, some observers argue that policy is the product of essentially unco-ordinated, unstructured activities. Nonetheless, whether the policy process is structured or unstructured, coherent or chaotic, there remain five stages in the emergence of policy that may be distinguished analytically.

15.3 ELEMENTS OF POLICY-MAKING

15.3.1   Agenda formation

At several points throughout the text, we have viewed the state as a problem-solving mechanism, and policy as deliberate decisions to act (or not) in response to societal problems. A basic issue is the matter of *whose* problems catch the attention of policy-makers and receive their response. This stage of the policy process is often identified as the business of agenda formation. An agenda is a list of things to be done; in public policy we want to know who controls that list, whose problems get on that list (and whose don't), how the order of items for action is determined and by whom, and even whose view of the problem is reflected by its formulation on the agenda and the responses considered. Various approaches have been taken to these questions, and we can touch upon only a couple of these briefly. One is to distinguish between the **PUBLIC AGENDA** (the problem is highly visible and the public is interested) and the **FORMAL AGENDA** (policy-makers have noticed the problem and included it for consideration), and examine the relationship between the two. Clearly, policy requires that an issue reach the formal agenda, and it may or may not do so by first becoming an important item on the public agenda (see Cobb, Cobb, and Ross, 1976).

The idea of the policy community may be useful here, particularly if we consider that most issues that are candidates for policy consideration are probably identified and articulated first either within the attentive public by an interested group or within the sub-government. Consider an issue initiated by an organized group within the attentive public of a policy community, say the demand of child-care advocates for the conversion of commercial day care into non-profit care. The nature of the policy network(s) within this community (i.e., the links with the sub-government) may determine whether this group is able to place its issue on the formal agenda. If the association of commercial child-care operators has sufficient influence, it may be able to block this issue from proceeding any further. At this point child-care advocates opposed to commercial care may resort to a public awareness campaign to generate broader support for their position and, by placing the issue on the public agenda, hope to obtain the attention of policy-makers. Some groups may succeed at influencing policy-makers only by influencing the broader public first and mobilizing public demand for policy action. Other groups may wish to influence policy-makers without arousing the attention of other interested parties in the public. Various strategies of moving issues from the public to the formal agenda, or onto the formal agenda while bypassing the public agenda, will be involved here.

Some issues will originate with state actors, who may be able to use their privileged access to the sub-government to place their concerns on the formal agenda. Assuming that these issues receive a policy response, policy-makers must also decide whether the policies in question require public support for their successful resolution. If so, the challenge will be to move the issue from the formal to the public agenda and build support for it there. If not, the issue may be dealt with without its ever achieving prominence on the public agenda.

The issues that receive entrance to the formal agenda will vary, as will the prominence they receive on that agenda, according to a variety of factors. Obviously, the ideology of those in government, and of those who advise them, is one important aspect (there is no point lobbying for increased spending on social programs from a government committed to downsizing and rolling back the welfare state), but there are others also. In most societies and political systems the agenda of the rich and powerful receives careful attention, in part simply because of the strategic power within capitalist economies of those whose investment and employment decisions will have an impact on the popularity of governments judged for the state of the economy over which they preside. Changing demographics (the structure of the population) can also be significant, as can the constraints placed on policy-makers by the health of the economy, the degree of government indebtedness, and the amount of time remaining before the next election.

Finally, we should note that managing to place one's concern or issue on the formal agenda is no guarantee (a) that the government will take action, or (b) that by choosing to take action it will implement the solutions preferred by those who originally sought the response. Indeed, entrance onto the broader public agenda or the formal agenda may be the precise moment when the group responsible for initiating and specifying an issue loses control of it.

15.3.2 Decision-making

Placing an issue on the formal agenda entails a commitment eventually to decide its fate. In other words, the arrival of a problem on the official agenda ultimately means a policy decision concerning its resolution (and such a decision may well be to take no action, and to leave the problem unsolved). A point of some debate among students of public policy concerns the model of decision-making that most accurately depicts the policy-making reality. At one end is the **RATIONALIST** model, which proposes an orderly process of identifying, evaluating, and matching ends in a "rational" manner that satisfies criteria such as efficiency, efficacy, etc. In this model, the goal of policy-makers is to identify and implement the best possible solution to the problem at hand. In contrast is the **INCREMENTALIST** or **PLURALIST EXCHANGE** model, according to which policy is a by-product of competition among interested parties, emerging as a result of conflict, bargaining, and trade-offs. What results here is a compromise between competing ideas of what is best, or indeed, between the opposing positions of self-interested actors; rather than the "best" policy, this model generates what is the most practical or feasible given the circumstances that constrain policy-makers.

The difference between these models is sometimes presented as the ideal versus the real: the rationalist model describing how policy should be made, and the incrementalist model describing how it in fact *is* made. However, the supporters of the incrementalist model point not only to its empirical accuracy, but argue that it is actually preferable to the rationalist model. For one thing, the rationalist model rests on various assumptions about information, knowledge, and resources that policy-makers are unlikely to find met in the real world. Above all, rationalist decision-making implies a degree of control that is incompatible with most policy environments—consider the complexity and potential fragmentation of not only the policy community but also the sub-government. If rationalist decision-making were possible, it would certainly create the possibility of very radical change, unconstrained by anything but the desire to implement the "best" solution. The very constrained nature of actual policy-making, which makes the incrementalist model more empirically attractive, is also a reason why its adherents argue its superiority: we cannot predict the success or failure of our policies with any great accuracy, radical changes are unnecessarily disruptive and potentially destabilizing, and policy-making that proceeds in small ("incremental") steps from existing practices is more prudent and likely to produce long-term successes. Clearly the incrementalist model has a "conservative" element, while the rationalist model has the potential to be radical.

Interestingly, the incrementalist model has been most closely associated with Charles Lindblom, an American political scientist, and it is arguable that this model is particularly applicable to policy-making in the U.S., given the fragmentation and dispersion of power within the American system. In other institutional environments where policy-making is more concentrated, some degree of rationalist decision-making may be feasible. Certainly, radical and deliberate shifts in policy *do* occur in regimes, and should not surprise us in majoritarian parliamentary systems—Margaret Thatcher's so-called "revolution" in public policy in the 1980s in Britain is a good case in point. This association of rationalist decision-making with one of the late twentieth century's most celebrated conservatives perhaps is not wholly accidental. In many jurisdictions, conservative governments have tried to bring market-based models of governance into practice, including the formulation of annual "business plans" for ministries. A typical business plan will identify "core businesses," report on achievements over the previous year, and establish objectives for the coming year, as well as performance measures or targets by which success or failure in meeting those objectives will be gauged. This is very much in the mode of rationalist policy-making and reflects the hierarchical corporate structure, where strategic decisions are taken at the top and the organization is managed with a view to their implementation. It is also a model that works best in the political world when there are fewer impediments such as effective opposition parties, critical media attention, bureaucratic discretion, or mobilized citizen protest. In other words, it is not very compatible with any kind of democracy that delivers inputs in the period *between* elections.

As noted, forced to choose between these two models of decision-making, most observers would probably agree that the incrementalist model depicts actual policy-making more realistically. Many, though, have looked for other models, some of which fall somewhere between the extremes presented by the rationalist and incrementalist variants. One alternative is Amitai Etzioni's "mixed scanning," which proposes that long-term or more fundamental decisions are made in an essentially rationalist fashion, while detailed decisions about means or implementation are more incrementally achieved. There is something intuitively attractive about this: the decision to launch a new social program, for example, surely must be made deliberately, and not simply emerge as a by-product of pluralist exchange among political actors; the details about how to realize the objectives of this program may, on the other hand, be concluded through just such a process. Another variation is provided by Herbert Simon's notion of "satisficing," which is in some ways a less ambitious or more realistic application of the rationalist decision-making process. Instead of arriving at *the best* solution, policy-makers aim for something *satisfactory*, an adjective that implies a compromise between what is ideal and what is practical.

Whatever the model, policy requires decision-making, and this involves a variety of types of decision. Most generally, there is a decision to consider a problem as a candidate for attempted solution, and then, a decision about whether or not to commit the government to action in response to this issue. Where the decision is a "go" for action, at some level, in some way, certain objectives or ends will be cited as the justification for or intent of the government's policy. The next stage, perhaps the most crucial, will be deciding what particular means will be used to achieve the policy goals.

15.3.3 Instrument choice

In choosing to act or not, policy-makers consider specific actions, and in doing so evaluate a variety of possible instruments for achieving their goals. Most simply, instruments are the various kinds of exercise of authority that governments have at their disposal, from regulations and laws, to penalties like imprisonment or fines, to taxation, to the provision of public goods like education or services like postal delivery, etc. In the policy process, instrument choice presupposes that ends have been identified and that it is a matter of choosing the means best suited to their achievement; in practice the distinction may not be so clear, and choosing between means may in fact be a way of choosing different ends. Any number of factors may determine the choice of instruments. Ideology will dispose some political parties towards certain instruments and against others: socialists have traditionally been comfortable with public enterprises, while neo-conservatives would privatize as much of government as is feasible. Cost or difficulty of implementation may also be key considerations: the rationalist view of decision-making would place the emphasis in instrument choice on efficiency, that is, on the instrument or combination of instruments that will most closely achieve the desired objectives while incurring the least cost. It is possible, though, to distinguish between **TECHNICAL EFFICIENCY** and **POLITICAL EFFICIENCY**.

Technical efficiency is fairly straightforward: the ability of an instrument to achieve objectives without an undue or unreasonable expenditure of resources. If the goal of child-care policy is to increase the number of available spaces, then the technical efficiency of promoting commercial versus not-for-profit establishments will simply come down to which strategy creates more new spaces. If, in addition, the policy goal is to improve the quality of care provided, then the tendency of profit or non-profit care to deliver high staff-to-child ratios, or employ staff with early childhood education training, etc., must also be measured. Political efficiency, by contrast, has to do with the benefits or costs of the policy instrument for the policy-makers: will the use of an instrument create goodwill among a particular constituency that will come in handy later, or will it cost the governing party key votes in the next election? For example, the GST introduced by the Mulroney government is an example of a policy instrument that may well have been high in technical efficiency, accomplishing certain goals with respect to fairness and revenue generation, but at the same time low in political efficiency, given the costs to the government in terms of immediate popularity and long-term credibility. In almost any policy environment, the political efficiency of instruments will be as much a part of the calculation as their technical efficiency, if not more so. It is also worth noting that instrument choice may be constrained by matters of law, tradition, or resources.

There are almost as many catalogues of the kinds of instrument available to policy-makers as there are writers on the topic, but typical categories include **EXHORTATION** (advertised guidelines), **TAXATION** (the GST), **EXPENDITURE** (government money for subway construction), **REGULATION** (anti-noise bylaw), **SUBSIDY** (free prescriptions for seniors), **GRANT** (arts funding), **SELF-REGULATION** (delegation to professional associations), and **DIRECT PROVISION** (national parks). These instruments differ in the way they employ resources; some—like regulation—tend to be less expensive than others—like expenditure. They also vary in terms of the amount of coercion or force involved; exhortation is low in its coercive content, while taxation and regulation are high. These are the ingredients in designing programs to fulfil the policy objectives identified.

It should also be clear that in most cases a policy does not involve choosing *an* instrument, but a bundle or mix of various instruments; this is one reason why policy has been defined as a *course* of action, involving moving on several fronts at once. A government wishing to reduce the public health costs associated with smoking could simultaneously employ a public education campaign (exhortation), impose restrictions on the sale of products to minors and on advertising (regulation), establish punitive taxes (taxation), and subsidize farmers who shift production from tobacco to other crops (expenditure/subsidy).

15.3.4 Implementation

At some point, the decision-making and the design of policy must give way to the delivery and implementation of these decisions. Here policy is turned over from its designers and architects to the administrators who execute policy in their exercise of bureaucratic power. A variety of theories and approaches may be employed to examine the actual experience of policy administration, and some common themes recur. One is that the distinction between policy-making and policy administration is somewhat artificial; policy administrators are not only frequently involved in the design and decision stages, but policy is also effectively made by administrators in the ways they choose to implement the program entrusted to them. Some observers use the term "**SLIPPAGE**" to describe the difference between the intentions of policy-makers and the actual results brought about by policy administrators. Others note that "perfect implementation" depends on a variety of conditions not likely to be found in the real world; this alerts us to the possibility that slippage need not be the result of deliberate decisions by public servants to sabotage policy-makers' intentions, but may simply be an inevitable consequence of the complexity of policy in today's world. Again, knowledge by policy-makers of the ways in which policy is likely (or not) to be changed by administrators in the process of implementation may in turn influence instrument choice or other design considerations.

We noted above that policy will involve a variety of decisions, beginning with the most general and becoming increasingly specific and concrete. We should acknowledge in this regard that the policy/administration distinction is something of a fiction. The more general and fundamental the decision, the more we expect it to be made by elected officials, i.e., cabinet ministers, keeping in mind that these decisions will in all likelihood have benefited from consultation with and advice provided by senior administrators in the ministers' departments. At some level of decision-making, as we move from principles to the details, the bulk of discretion will pass to the public servants whose expertise and experience provide them with the resources to solve the practical problems of implementation. In other words, some decisions are clearly the business of policy-making and some decisions are clearly the nitty-gritty of implementation; to pretend there is a neat line that can be drawn between them is just that: a pretense.

15.3.5 Evaluation

Finally, it is suggested that the policy process is incomplete without a stage for follow-up, where the degree to which the policy has met expectations or goals can be formally assessed. This stage of evaluation is not without controversy. On the one hand there are debates concerning the methods of evaluation: What are the criteria by which policies should be assessed? What quantitative or qualitative methods are most useful? Is evaluation best done by experts or by the general public? A second set of issues concerns the value of conducting formal evaluation of policy: Does evaluation lead to revision? Do policy-makers pay attention to the results of evaluation? Generally, scepticism about evaluation is closely associated with adherence to the incrementalist view of policy as the product of pluralist exchange. On the other hand, for the rationalist paradigm of policy-making, evaluation is necessary to allow policy-makers to receive feedback, and from there consider revision or redesign. If policy-making is a form of problem-solving, then evaluation is intended to provide information about how well problems have in fact been solved by the adoption of policies, information that might well be useful for other similar situations. As in many areas, in policy there is also a powerful disincentive for evaluation: it may draw attention to failures, mistakes, or miscalculations, an attention that will not be appreciated by those who have responsibility for the policy.

The impression we do *not* want to leave is that policy is made according to a simple five-step process; on the contrary, we have been examining five elements or dimensions of public policy that will be present in one fashion or another in most policy environments. At the same time, the actual "process" by which policy is made will vary by country, by policy sector, and even by specific policy cases—no two instances of policy are alike. This is one reason why many treatments of public policy are case studies.

In countries where the rule of law has become a firmly entrenched constitutional norm, all policy will rest ultimately on some authority grounded in law. In cases where the legislative authority for policy is already clear and complete, policy-makers will transmit instructions to departmental or agency officials to fulfil the policy's intentions; this is the move from decisions about instruments to their implementation (as described above). Within a parliamentary context, this means that the cabinet, or ministers individually, deliver instructions to public servants to change operating procedures, rules, etc. In many cases, though, policy decisions require a change in the law to authorize public officials to act, or require new legislative authority altogether. Institutionally, this means that between decisions about policy and their implementation by the bureaucracy (see below, 15.5), they must receive legislative authorization, which, momentarily at least, puts the fate of policy in the hands of the legislature.

**15.4
THE LEGISLATIVE
PROCESS**

The degree to which the legislature plays an active role in determining policy outcomes, or, conversely, is reduced to giving ratification to decisions reached elsewhere, depends for the most part on the type of constitutional system. In the United States, not only the fate of policy, but the very shape and details of policy often are determined on the floor of the legislature or in its committees. In most parliamentary systems, particularly when the executive (single party *or* coalition) controls a majority in the legislature, policy decisions are made by cabinet and presented when necessary to the legislature for approval. It is not normally expected that the legislature will defeat government policy, nor modify it in any significant way in the legislative process. Nonetheless, the principles of the rule of law, representation, and democracy combine to place significance on the activity of the legislature in formulating and legitimizing the laws, which are a primary instrument of authority and power.

Our first observation must be that the legislative process depends very much on the constitutional model involved; legislating is very different in a system with separated powers and weak parties than it is in a system with fused powers and strong parties. At the same time, there are many elements that are also common to legislative processes regardless of constitutional model. A legislative process is a set of decisions concerning a proposal for a new law, or a proposal to amend an existing law or laws. Such proposals are often known as "bills."

The constitutional model defines who can introduce these bills; in parliamentary systems legislation can be introduced by individual members of parliament, or by members of the government (i.e., the cabinet). Government bills occupy the greatest part of the parliamentary legislature's time and attention and are usually the only bills passed (in Canada, *only* government bills can involve the expenditure of public monies). In a separated powers system, there are no "government" members: all legislators may introduce bills, and every legislator will do so.

Once introduced, a bill will go through a variety of stages whose mix will differ from legislature to legislature; nonetheless, there are some common elements involved. These amount to various opportunities for careful examination of the contents of legislation, discussion and debate over its merits or weaknesses, change to its contents through amendment, and decision over its fate through votes. These opportunities are governed by quite strict procedural rules, and take place in public so that formal law-making can be witnessed by the people. Cable television channels that telecast such proceedings make this true today as never before (although, ironically, in an age in which the mass media generally pay less and less attention to the substance of legislative debate). As indicated, the specific order and arrangement of the stages of the legislative process differ from country to country. We will discuss some of the common stages that are found, and then briefly contrast the Canadian and American processes as examples of legislating within parliamentary and separated powers systems, respectively.

a) Presentation

Before anything can happen, a legislative proposal must be put before the members of the legislature. In the British parliamentary tradition this involves a series of Readings, which originally were quite literally that; in an age before general literacy, proposals would be read aloud for the benefit of all members. Obviously, today it is not necessary to read bills to the members, but the stages called "Readings" persist. The first stage in a legislative process is typically *introduction*, in which a bill is presented, print-ed, and distributed to members of the legislature. Normally the bill will not proceed to the next stage of the process until some later point in the parliamentary calendar, so that members may have time to acquaint themselves with the bill's substance.

b) Debate

An essential part of rational decision-making is the chance for people to speak for or against a proposal. In this way the strengths and weaknesses of the proposal have the best chance of being uncovered and, presumably, their illumination can lead to better decisions. **DEBATE** is significant not only because legislators have a chance to discuss and argue the relative merits and demerits, but also so that the public has the opportunity to learn of the bill and hear from its supporters and critics.

c) Scrutiny and testimony

For the same set of reasons that debate is important, so is the opportunity for **SCRUTINY** and **TESTIMONY**: scrutiny being the close examination of the bill in all its details, and testimony being the opportunity for legislators to hear the views of others with an interest in the bill, such as those who would be affected by it, or those who might have to administer it, or experts in the subject area the bill concerns. This stage of the consideration of a bill is normally done in **LEGISLATIVE COMMITTEE**, and thus not on the floor of the legislature. The committee is better situated than the whole legislature to perform detailed examination of the contents of the bill, and committee hearings provide an opportunity for non-parliamentarians to speak about a proposal.

d) Amendment

One result of the debate and scrutiny a proposal receives may well be ideas about improvement, or second thoughts by the sponsors about what will achieve their purposes: in either case, or for other reasons, there is often a need to change or amend a proposal. Opportunity for **AMENDMENT** suggests that the legislature is really engaged in taking a proposal and making law from it. As will become clearer below, this is more true in some legislatures than others. At any rate, even though amendments may fail, the opportunity for opponents of a bill to propose amendments is important, because it allows the public to judge their representatives not only on the basis of what is done, but on what was proposed and then ultimately ignored or defeated.

e) Decision

Eventually, there will have to be a time of decision, and a determination of whether the bill lives or dies. In fact, there are usually several stages of decision in the legislative process, and this is something that enhances the legitimacy of the bill by demonstrating that its passage was not the result of coincidence or an accident of fate. Depending on the system, and on the nature of bills, it may be desirable that some proposals be rejected sooner rather than later, and in this way the finite time of the legislature is not consumed by unnecessary labour. In some systems there is an "approval in principle," which indicates consent to the idea behind the bill, but as yet no commitment to the specifics. In theory, this is simply asking "Is this a good idea?" and should streamline the process by weeding out those ideas not receiving adequate support, allowing the legislature to concentrate on the "good" ideas. In practice, as we shall see, this proves not always to be the case.

f) Procedure

In addition to the above elements of a legislative process, there are some common procedural devices or issues involved. One is the use of committees for performing one or more of the stages in the legislative process, in particular that of scrutiny and testimony. Such committees are drawn from the legislature and meet separately; their composition usually reflects proportionally the balance of parties within the legislature as a whole. A second procedural point concerns bicameral legislatures and whether or not a bill proceeds through both chambers concurrently (as in the U.S.) or consecutively (as in Canada and most parliamentary systems). A further set of questions concerns whether each chamber has equal weight in the legislative process. In some systems, certain types of bill must originate in a specific chamber (e.g., in Canada, bills that involve government expenditure—money bills—must be introduced in the House of Commons, the "lower" chamber). In most bicameral systems the approval of both chambers is necessary for a bill's passage, but there are cases where one house (the British House of Lords, for example) can only delay legislation from its counterpart, what is called a suspensive veto. Where both chambers approve a bill, they may nonetheless amend it in the process, and in doing so produce different versions that require reconciliation, which usually involves the activity of a committee drawn from both chambers.

Once a bill has passed through all the stages of approval by the legislature, it may require further consent by the formal executive: the head of state in a parliamentary system, or the chief political executive in a system of separated powers. In the former case, such **EXECUTIVE ASSENT** is more or less automatic. In the U.S., on the other hand, the President has the ability to **VETO** legislation, and the legislature in turn may overturn a presidential veto with a two-thirds majority. Usually with the granting of executive assent, the bill has become law; however, it may be necessary to indicate further when the law will come into effect (and there can be very good reasons for delaying this final step). In Canada, this last step is called proclamation, and is made by the head of state on the advice of the government. There have been instances where legislation has passed the legislature and received assent, but has never been proclaimed into force as law. Once proclaimed, or brought into effect, a law is no longer the object of the legislature (unless there are subsequent proposals to amend the law), but passes to the executive for administration and enforcement, or to the courts for interpretation or judicial review. In addition to these post-legislative stages, in some systems direct democracy may allow citizens to challenge the law through an initiative (see Chapter Fourteen).

Because of strong party discipline and the majority position of the government, most bills introduced into the legislature in a parliamentary system become law. In addition, it is unusual for more than one bill on the same subject to be introduced at any one time, and bills in bicameral systems tend to go through the two houses in sequence, proceeding from the lower to the upper chamber. The picture is very different in the U.S. system. It may be useful to consider the American legislative process as something of an obstacle course; many bills (often several on the same topic) are introduced into Congress, but a small fraction of these succeed in surmounting all the obstacles. The legislative process is characterized by a series of veto points that filter out or select which bills will proceed to the next stage. So while the two processes can look not dissimilar (see Figure 15.2), the reality of the processes is very different. It is worthwhile to stress again the essential points of this difference.

The most significant feature of the parliamentary legislative process is its dominance by the executive (the cabinet) and its

THE LEGISLATIVE PROCESS

CANADA

Legislative Stage	Function
First Reading	Introduction
Second Reading	Debate/Approval in Principle
Committee Stage	Scrutiny and Testimony
Report Stage	Amendment/Decision
Third Reading	Decision
Process repeated in other House of Parliament	
Royal Assent	Executive Assent
Proclamation	Inform and Put Into Effect

UNITED STATES

Legislative Stage	Function
Introduction	Introduction
Subcommittee	Scrutiny and Testimony
Committee	Debate/Amendment/Decision
House Rules Committee*	
House/Senate	Debate/Amendment/Decision
Conference Committee	Harmonization
Full House/Senate	Decision
Executive Signature/Veto	Executive Assent

* In the House of Representatives only, the Rules Committee sets the parameters of debate and amendment concerning the bill when it is considered by the full House.

FIGURE 15.2

subjection to party discipline. This means that, given a majority government, the legislature has a very limited role in determining the content of legislation, and there are few impediments to the passage of government bills. This is why parliamentary systems are identified with strong government; the only obstacle in the way of the fulfilment of the government's legislative agenda is time. In a typical majority situation, given party discipline, the parliamentary opposition will never succeed in defeating government legislation or in forcing its amendments to government bills. The most that the opposition can do is delay the passage of bills by using as much of the scarce time on the parliamentary calendar as possible, maximizing the length of debate, proposing amendments that the government must take time to defeat, and employing any other procedural manoeuvres. As party discipline becomes stronger in legislatures, minority opposition is more and more reduced to obstructionist tactics, and the debate and decision of the legislature is less and less a matter of constructive law-making. For a government in power, there are two ways around the delaying tactics of the opposition: one is to employ procedural weapons such as strict rules governing debate (time allocation) or even closure (which ends debate and brings immediate decision); a second is to make concessions such as accepting an amendment or two, or dropping a controversial clause, in order to secure the opposition's co-operation. By and large, a majority government in a parliamentary system is assured of the passage of its legislative program, and of the passage of legislation in essentially the same form that the cabinet minister responsible originally presented it to the legislature.

By contrast, the legislature in a system with separated powers and weak parties is much more chaotic and fluid. Here the legislature actually does legislate, and is not simply legitimizing proposals approved by the executive. As noted above, in this system each legislator may introduce legislation, and virtually each one will do so, some prodigiously. The passage of none of these proposals is assured, and defeat is a real possibility at each point of decision along the legislative path. In contrast to the parliamentary model, where a significant portion of legislation introduced will also be passed, here most bills will be defeated at one or another point in the legislative process. Thus, while the two models differ considerably regarding the number of bills introduced, they are much more alike in terms of their legislative output. Instead of resting on party discipline, bills in the U.S. often command a consensus that cuts across party lines. Bargaining and compromise is the name of the game, as is the collection and expenditure of favours, or debts owed for past support.

It is also worth noting the different roles played in each model by committees, and by the head of state. In both cases, committees do the work of detailed scrutiny and of hearing testimony concerning bills. In the parliamentary model this usually occurs *after* the legislature has given approval in principle, meaning commitment to some sort of action on the bill has been made. In practice, and given that committees are also very much creatures of party discipline, bills are reported back to the legislature much as they were when sent to committee. In the U.S. legislature, the committee, and sometimes first the subcommittee, serves as an important gatekeeper, censor, or editor: eliminating bills, consolidating bills of similar intent into one, or rewriting bills to suit the committee's own views on the subject. Committees play a most important role here, and the chairmanship of such committees (and subcommittees) is a position of considerable influence.

A similar distinction between systems concerns the head of state. In the parliamentary model, legislation that passes the legislature requires approval by the head of state, but this approval is a formality: it is always given. Failure to give such consent would create a constitutional crisis and is virtually unthinkable. In the U.S., by contrast, bills passing the legislature come to the President for approval, but here nothing is automatic. The President may sign the bill into law, or refuse to sign and have the bill become law without executive approval, or veto the bill. In reply, the legislature may override the presidential veto by repassing the bill by a two-thirds majority in each chamber. Here we see the operation of the checks and balances associated with separated branches of government.

In the end, the significance of the legislative process will depend greatly on the system in which it operates. At one extreme a very active legislature subject to a minimum of executive control may have a relatively free hand to make policy through the legislative process; at the other extreme a legislature dominated by the executive will do little more than ratify the legislative proposals of that executive. In both cases, though, the legislature's most important function is to make the authorization of policy a public act, which proceeds by means of procedures that allow for scrutiny, criticism, and opposition. These procedures may seem often to be mere formalities, but they are at the heart of our legal-rational notions of legitimacy. To some degree also, the legislative process is as significant not for what it does, but for what it prevents: namely the arbitrary, unopposable implementation of policy through secret means. However much our governments control the policy and legislative processes, they are forced to do their business in public, where a vigilant opposition and mass media (assuming these are vigilant) are able to hold the government to the judgement of public opinion.

A t the end of the day, after Parliament has issued legislation, or on the basis of instructions issued directly by the cabinet, policy comes to the bureaucracy for implementation. The contact that most of us have with government is in respect to one of the many programs or services it provides, and the human dimension of that contact is with our interaction with public servants, the employees of the state. The terms **"BUREAUCRACY," "CIVIL SERVICE,"** and **"PUBLIC SERVICE"** have become somewhat interchangeable: all represent that veritable army of full- and part-time employees of the state who staff its various departments, agencies,

15.5
THE BUREAUCRACY

**GENERAL GOVERNMENT
EMPLOYMENT, SELECTED OECD
COUNTRIES, AS A PERCENTAGE
OF TOTAL EMPLOYMENT**

Country	1980	1997	Change 1980-97
Sweden	30.7	31.5	+ 0.8
Norway	24.1	31	+ 6.9
Denmark	28	30.2	+ 2.2
Finland	19.3	25.7	+ 6.4
France	20.6	24.9	+ 4.3
Canada	20	20.6	+ 0.6
Belgium	18.9	18.7	– 0.2
Poland	na	18.4	na
Italy	15.4	17.5	+ 2.1
Spain	9.3	15.6	+ 6.3
U.S.	16.4	15.1	– 1.3
Australia	17.4	14.5	– 2.9
N. Zealand	17.8	13.7	– 4.1
Germany	14.6	12.9	– 1.7
Greece	9.5	12.7	+ 3.2
Ireland	14.2	12.2	– 2
Neth.	13.4	11	– 2.4
Japan	8.8	8.3	– 0.5
Hungary	na	7.2	na
Czech Rep.	na	5.2	na

FIGURE 15.3

and enterprises. Although the term "bureaucracy" is sometimes used by people pejoratively, implying needless layers of staffing and closely associated with the infamous "red tape," the term itself comes from sociology and describes a structure of authority (a hierarchical, rule-governed system in which individuals perform specialized tasks) that is in fact common to all modern organizations, from the corporation to the university to the trade union.

The twentieth century has been the century of public-sector bureaucracy. Meny reports that the Italian civil service grew from 50,000 at the end of the nineteenth century to almost two million by 1992, and Britain's from 20,000 in the early nineteenth century to 500,000 in the early 1990s (1993: 277). In the United States, in 1997, the federal civil service totalled 2.8 million, the state bureaucracy 4.73 million, and local officials 12 million, for a total of 19.5 million. Statistics Canada reports public administration employment figures for 1998 of 220,000 federal employees, 202,000 provincial employees, and 247,000 local public servants, for a total of 669,000. Figure 15.3 presents the relative size of public services in selected OECD countries over the last two decades. It is instructive to note in which countries public-sector employment rose and in which it fell, keeping in mind that the figures represent a percentage of total employment (which may itself have risen or fallen across this period). Obviously, the size of the bureaucracy reflects the growth in governmental activity in the twentieth century, particularly the development of the postwar welfare state. At the same time, the last 10 to 15 years have also been a time in which many governments have attempted to scale back the state, sometimes for ideological reasons, often because of the pressures of mounting government debt. Clearly one target for downsizing has been the public payroll, but to date in most countries while the public service has not grown in recent years, neither has it shrunk much.

If the growth of the public sector has reflected the growth of the state in this century, it has also embodied a much more diversified and complicated state: just who counts as a public servant is not an easy matter to define. As noted above, Statistics Canada reported 220,000 federal employees for 1998. The Treasury Board, which is the official employer of federal bureaucrats, reports a full-time equivalent of 183,068 for 1999 (compared to 239,668 in 1992). The RCMP uniformed personnel numbered 17,656 (compared to 19,911 in 1992), military personnel, 91,970 (in 1998, compared to 115,320 in 1992), and employees of federal Crown corporations, 71,023 (152,383 in 1992). In each of these areas, the number of employees has declined over the last decade, most dramatically in the area of Crown corporations, reflecting the privatization of many government enterprises, the largest of these being the Canadian National Railway.

One reason it matters who is or is not a public servant is the professionalization of public service that has accompanied the emergence of the modern state. Once upon a time, most government jobs were **PATRONAGE** appointments, which is to say that one of the great benefits of winning elections and forming governments was the ability to give employment to one's supporters, friends, family, etc. A change in governing party often meant a wholesale change in the public service from supporters and friends of one party to the supporters and friends of the newly triumphant party. With the growth of government, and with the increasing complexity and specialization of the tasks of government, there was an increasing need—increasingly recognized—for permanence, the development of expertise, and promotion on the basis of merit: in short for a *professional* public service.

All advanced democracies today employ a professional public service, a distinction that involves several components. First of all, entrance to the public service and promotion within its ranks are based on merit, that is, demonstrated ability and accomplishment, not personal connections or political ties. The degree to which and the means by which this is enforced vary from country to country. Usually, entrance to the public service is gained on the basis of competitive, public examinations. In some countries (e.g., France, Italy, and Germany) the examinations favour those with specialized knowledge, often those with particular legal training; in other countries (e.g., Britain and Canada) generalists are more commonly sought. The **MERIT PRINCIPLE** was established by law in Canada in 1918. On the other hand, any number of senior administrative posts are still filled by appointment by the Prime Minister and cabinet, including deputy ministers and heads and members of agencies, boards, and commissions.

A second principle is that the public service should be non-partisan or **POLITICALLY NEUTRAL**. This is based in part on the notion that a clear distinction can be made between decisions of policy (which are political and should be left to elected, publicly accountable officials) and their implementation (which is non-political, and should be carried out in a disinterested, efficient manner by professionals). In practice this has often meant clear rules or even laws restricting public servants from engaging in partisan political activity, but interesting variations exist. In

KEY TERMS

agenda formation
amendment formation
attentive public
bureaucracy
civil service
debate
decision-making
direct provision
evaluation
executive assent
exhortation
expenditure
formal agenda
grant
implementation
incrementalism
instruments
legislative committee
legislative process
merit principle
mixed scanning
patronage
pluralist exchange
policy community
policy network
policy sector
political efficiency
political neutrality
procedural tactics
programs
public agenda
public policy
public service
rationalism
regulation
satisfaction
scrutiny
self-regulation
slippage
sub-government
subsidy
taxation
technical efficiency
testimony
veto

REFERENCES AND SUGGESTED READING

Atkinson, Michael M. 1993. *Governing Canada: Institutions and Public Policy.* Toronto: Harcourt Brace Jovanovich.

Brooks, Stephen. 1989. *Public Policy in Canada*, 3rd ed. Toronto: Oxford University Press.

Campbell, Robert M., and Leslie A. Pal. 1994. *The Real Worlds of Canadian Politics: Cases in Process and Policy*, 3rd ed. Peterborough, Ont.: Broadview Press.

Cobb, Roger, Jennie Keith-Ross, and Marc Howard Ross. 1976. "Agenda-Building as a Comparative Political Process," in *American Political Science Review*, vol. 70.

Coleman, William, and Grace Skogstad. 1990. *Policy Communities and Public Policy in Canada: A Structural Approach.* Mississauga, Ont.: Copp Clark Pitman.

Doern, G. Bruce, and Richard W. Phidd. 1992. *Canadian Public Policy: Ideas, Structure, Process*, 2nd ed. Toronto: Nelson.

Etzioni, A. 1968. *The Active Society.* New York: Free Press.

Harrop, Martin, ed. 1992. *Power and Politics in Liberal Democracies.* Cambridge: Cambridge University Press.

Canada, restrictions on the partisan activity of public servants were challenged successfully on the basis of the Charter of Rights and Freedoms, except in the case of senior bureaucrats, whom the Court ruled should continue to be seen to have no partisan attachments. On the other hand, it is precisely at the senior levels of the bureaucracy where politicization of the bureaucracy matters most, and politicization may mean other things than partisan attachment. As a consequence, often the top-ranking public servants, i.e., the deputy ministers, are replaced by incoming governments who suspect these deputies may be too closely aligned with the previous government or (more importantly) with its policies.

If public servants adequately perform their duties in an impartial, disinterested manner, then they should be secure in their employment, not subject to the whims of political superiors. A professional public servant is a career public servant, and just as in other walks of life, the loyal, competent performance of duties should be rewarded with secure employment. On the other hand, in all sectors of society in recent years, employment has not been secure; for various reasons downsizing has been occurring in both private and public sectors. Public-sector cuts often involve eliminating public-sector jobs, eliminating bureaucracies, imposing salary freezes, etc. One consequence has been increasing activity by public-sector unions, and an increased level of political activity from public servants who find themselves on the receiving end of the negative effects of policy decisions made by their political masters.

The model of a professional public service is, of course, an ideal that is realized in different settings and under different governments to a greater or lesser degree. Each country has its own traditions and expectations about public-sector management and performance. In any country the model probably works less well when the state itself is the object of public policy, because public servants have a real, abiding interest in the state, an interest they cannot be expected to set aside easily, if indeed at all.

15.6 CONCLUSION

Our concern in this chapter has been with the processes of governing, which ultimately can be subsumed under the heading of public policy. We have tried to outline the role of the various institutions in the making and implementation of policy, and on many topics we have barely scratched the surface. The emphasis here has been on personnel and procedure; on the "who" and the "how." An altogether different approach, and perhaps the most popular today, focuses on the substance of public policy. In some cases this involves tracing the career of particular policies through the process from genesis to implementation and realization; in other cases it is a comparative look at policies in a particular sector across different jurisdictions. Some people become specialists in a particular area of public policy: social policy, economic policy, defence policy, etc. Our look at the substance of public policy in Chapter Seventeen focuses on the complex of policies associated with the emergence, expansion, and (lately) contraction of the welfare state in advanced industrial democracies. In doing so, we combine a concern with the substance of public policy with an introduction to some of the concepts and questions of *political economy*.

There remains one institution or "branch" of the state that we have not considered in our discussion of policy so far: the courts. This in part reflects an important distinction, namely that the determination of public policy is a political act; indeed, it is the essence of what democratic politics is about. The courts are supposed to be apolitical, independent of, and removed from, the political fray. Nonetheless, as a result of the liberal notions of justice that underlie Western democratic practice, in particular the principle of *constitutionalism*, the courts are asked from time to time to rule on the constitutionality of the legislation that authorizes the activity of the state. In delivering such judgements, the courts become active in the policy process. It is to this dimension that we now turn.

Mény, Yves. 1993. *Government and Politics in Western Europe*, 2nd ed. Oxford: Oxford University Press.

Pal, Leslie A. 1992. *Public Policy Analysis: An Introduction*, 2nd ed. Toronto: Nelson.

Phillips, Susan. 1989. "Rock-A-Bye, Brian: The National Strategy on Child Care," in Katherine Graham, ed. *How Ottawa Spends: 1989-90*. Ottawa: Carleton University Press.

Pross, A. Paul. 1992. *Group Politics and Public Policy*, 2nd ed. Toronto: Oxford University Press.

Simon, Herbert A. 1965. *Administrative Behaviour*, 2nd ed. New York: Free Press.

SOMETHING TO CONSIDER

Why is it that the most visible decision-making process—what we have called the legislative process—seems mostly a formality, while those processes in which the most crucial decisions are made—within the bureaucracy and in the cabinet and central agencies—are mostly invisible to the general public? Does this have any implications for democracy? Are there ways to make it otherwise? How likely is it that either might ever take place?

16

justice, law, and politics

JUSTICE is one of the oldest concepts in political discourse. Plato's *Republic*, which is essentially concerned with the question "what is justice?," is still taught as the first great text of the Western political tradition. In the modern age, justice has become a central standard by which policies of governments are judged, and very often is something on which the legitimacy of states rests. Our political tradition is rich in terms of the understandings of justice that have been presented, acted upon, or put forward for consideration. There are two elements common to these various conceptions of justice: a normative element and a specifically political dimension. The normative dimension means that we intend our statements about justice to be evaluative: to provide standards by which we measure the appropriateness of actions and behaviours, policies and programs. Where there is a consensus about the claims of justice, they are not merely evaluative, but regulative: measures will be taken to ensure adherence to the standards provided by justice.

Justice is also political. Loosely stated, justice is a set of normative principles concerning the relationship between the state and its individuals, and those relationships between individuals in which the state or society at large has taken an interest. Thus much of the content of justice deals with the exercise of authority or power by the state, and with what individuals have a right to claim or expect from the state. In virtually any society, justice is also concerned with certain kinds of relations between individuals. Criminal and civil law each concerns a separate class of actions between individuals. It is entirely possible that what is an issue of private morality in one society, such as adultery or personal insult, may be regarded as a public issue subject to authoritative sanctions

16.1 JUSTICE DEFINED

16.1 Justice Defined
16.2 The Rule of Law
16.3 Rights
16.4 Equality
16.5 Justice and Institutions
    16.5.1 Parliamentary supremacy
    16.5.2 Judicial review
    16.5.3 Balancing Parliament and the courts
16.6 Conclusion

419

THE VENDETTA: ROUGH JUSTICE?

We may note, recalling our discussion of anthropology in Chapter Two, that in less complex societies where the state has not emerged, binding decisions are reached and enforced by means other than government. In such communities, justice will be concerned with these alternative means, and the types of matters with which they deal.

An example to consider is the vendetta; that is, the customary response in certain societies or cultures to an act such as murder is not apprehension and punishment of the murderer by the state, but rather a restitution that involves taking the life of the murderer or of one of his family by a member of the victim's family. In societies where this is the accepted and expected response to murder, is the vendetta a concept of justice or not? According to our definition, it might not be seen as a matter of justice, since the authority of the state (or whatever process or institution that

makes and enforces decisions) is not actively involved. It is not unusual, however, to view customs such as the vendetta as culturally and historically specific acts of justice. One way to accept this view and remain consistent to our definition is to say that, in the case of vendetta, the community has delegated to injured individuals the authority to punish or sanction the offending party. Standing in the background behind the individual act of vengeance in this case is the approval and indeed the expectation of the community for this response. This makes the case vastly different from those individual actions to which society is indifferent. It may very well be that in pre-state cultures, much of the enforcement of societal or public norms is in a similar way delegated to individuals who occupy no "official" capacity. With the development of the state and its monopoly on coercive sanctions, the responsibility for maintaining community standards of justice is no longer delegated, but executed directly by state officials.

FIGURE 16.1

in another society. In the latter case, this may indicate a moral consensus that the state has been entrusted with enforcing, or that the state has taken upon itself to enforce. Whichever is the case, the involvement of the power or authority of the state makes the matter one of justice.

As the example of the vendetta shows (see Figure 16.1), it may be difficult to draw the line between public morality and justice. This is in part because notions of justice are often informed or governed by the moral and/or religious doctrines prevailing in the community. Students in Western societies may very well take for granted the notion that justice is distinct from religious or moral beliefs, but this distinction (like the distinction between religion and morality) is a product of the historical development that distinguishes and explains Western culture. In other cultures, it may be difficult, if not impossible, to distinguish clearly between religious and moral beliefs, public and private morality, issues that concern justice and those that do not. However, operating within the context of Western liberal society, we will use the term *justice* to refer to *normative principles concerning the exercise of authority and power.*

In saying this, we have answered the question in only the broadest and most general sense. More commonly, discussions of justice concern specific principles. Should rewards be distributed on the basis of merit, or of need? Should discriminations be made on the basis of race, language, or creed? Is ignorance of the law an excuse from its sanctions? Should individuals accused of crime be required to prove their innocence, or the accusers required to prove the guilt of the accused? Answers to these questions assume or draw upon specific principles of justice, and each is susceptible of various formulations. In what follows, we will examine three concepts that have become central for modern liberal society— the rule of law, rights, and equality. This is the historical order in which these three principles were articulated and received recognition, something reflected in the degree of consensus that has been achieved about their suitability. While it is rare in our society to hear the rule of law disputed as a valid regulative principle, it is still possible to find sceptics about rights, and there is still considerable disagreement about the validity of equality as a principle of justice, or, among those who believe in equality, much uncertainty about what it requires. In this second sense, then, the question "what is justice?" is really asking "what are the correct principles of justice?"

Finally, even with consensus obtained about the principles of justice, there may yet be debate about whether or not policies, laws, or actions conform to those principles. It is one thing to articulate the elements contained in the principle of the rule of law, but another still to determine whether or not specific legal practices or legislative procedures meet these standards. People who agree that justice demands equality may disagree completely on whether affirmative action is consistent with or contrary to the principle of equality. At this third level, the question "what is justice?" concerns the application of the principles in concrete, everyday situations. This certainly complicates things, for the applications of justice principles will be as numerous as the concrete situations or problems that arise in a society and in which the state or the community has taken an interest. One of the differences underlying civil law versus codified law, for example, is different assumptions or propositions concerning the application of abstract principles to empirical cases.

Our normative discourse concerning justice, then, may not be about the principles of justice, but rather about their proper application, or even about their applicability. In any given situation, how do we know which principle of justice to apply? Should individual rights be our prime consideration, even when the exercise of those rights leads to inequality, or should the claims of equality justify setting aside or overlooking individual rights? Should restitution or deterrence be the principle guiding criminal sanctions? Should welfare be treated as a matter of individual right, or as a question of the proper distribution of societal goods? It is not our concern here to provide the answers to such questions, but instead to stress the complexity of what is involved in that familiar concept, justice.

To summarize, we can consider the question "what is justice?" to be meaningful in at least three distinct but related ways, moving from the most general and abstract to the more concrete and empirical. At any or all three levels, in any given society, there may be considerable consensus, or vigorous debate, or a combination of the two. Thus justice entails

a) *normative conceptions* concerning the political realm, most commonly addressing the proper exercise of authority and the proper objects of authority;

b) *specific principles* indicating how authority should be exercised and with what it should or should not be concerned (e.g., rule of law, rights, fairness, equity, equality, etc.); and

c) *concrete applications* of specific principles to particular situations, problems, policies, laws, procedures, actions, behaviour, etc.

16.2 THE RULE OF LAW

The **RULE OF LAW** as we know it today emerges as a principle of justice in liberal society, although law itself has of course been with us for many more centuries than liberal society. The *Concise Oxford English Dictionary* describes law as "[the] body of enacted or customary rules recognized by a community as binding," or "one of these rules" (1982: 568); on this basis, we might observe that all political communities or societies possess law. Even if, like Hobbes, we reserve the term for those rules that are made binding through the enforcement of coercive sanctions, we will have to admit that there has been law as long as there have been states (since the state is distinguished by the centralization of authority necessary to make and enforce rules or decisions upon the community). The rule of law, then, has nothing to do with the presence or absence of law, and everything to do with the nature or use of law. The rule of law places certain requirements upon lawmakers and demands certain qualities of law itself.

Discussion of the rule of law in our philosophic tradition goes back to Aristotle, who asks "the old question, Which is preferable, the rule of the best man or the rule of the best law?"

(Bk. III, Ch.16).[1] Aristotle's answer is both, government by the best men *and* the best laws; but the issue then breaks down into at least three questions: Who are the best men to rule? What are the best laws with which to govern? and In which cases should men rather than laws govern? Behind these questions stands Aristotle's observation that laws or rules are relatively inflexible: this is their advantage in that they provide us with a standard or procedure to follow in cases that are alike, and by acting in accordance with them we are able to be consistent. The inflexibility of rules is also their disadvantage when they do not permit us to take into account different circumstances or considerations. The law against theft, for example, does not distinguish between the single mother in a society with inadequate social assistance who steals to feed her children and the well-paid bank employee who steals to cover his gambling debts. Aristotle's concern is that justice sometimes requires a distinction and a flexibility that is not given by the law: "Among the matters which cannot be included in laws are all those which are generally decided by deliberation" (III, 16). (In our own society, flexibility is not achieved by allowing officials to set aside the law and decide according to the situation, but rather in the allowance given to magistrates in sentencing to take into account particular circumstances and individual conditions. In many North American jurisdictions in recent years there has been a move to eliminate this flexibility by prescribing mandatory sentences.) Thus, Aristotle indicates the need for laws, *and* for individuals able to make proper decisions when the law is inappropriate or too rigid:

> it is obvious that to rule by the letter of the law or out of a book is not the best method. On the other hand, rulers cannot do without a general principle to guide them; it provides something which, being without personal feelings, is better than that which by its nature does feel.... It seems clear then that there must be a lawgiver—the ruler himself, but also that laws must be laid down, which shall be binding in all cases, except those in which they fail to meet the situation. (III, 15)

We should stress that Aristotle would only set aside the rule of law for the rule of the *best* men: those with wisdom, good judgement, moderation, and a variety of other virtues. This rule of the best men is never something that can be done by one man: "it is preferable that law should rule than any single one of the

1. Any reference to Aristotle's *Politics* is to the T.A. Sinclair translation (1962).

citizens" (III, 16). The best form of government, and the one most consistent with justice, is the "rule of the best men, true aristocracy," a government by "the majority who are all good" (III, 15).

By the time of the liberal revolution, experience and history had come to place the distinction between rule of men and rule of law in a different light. The feudal system had established rule by a class of nobility, and the rise of the nation-state brought government by absolute hereditary monarchy. It was obvious that rulers were determined by chance, by tradition, by war or intrigue, by accidents of birth and death, but by no means on the basis of their enlightenment, their virtue, or their judgement. Lunatics, idiots, and children at various times inherited the office of sovereign, and even the most enlightened monarch remained just one individual whose word (reflecting his/her whims, passions, and prejudices) became law for a nation and its people. The "rule of men," which Aristotle had seen as the exercise of judgement by wise and virtuous men in situations not best dealt with by inflexible rules, had by Hobbes's day frequently come to mean simply a personal authority. Authority was viewed by medieval rulers as their own personal property, as something belonging to them (or to their family), sanctioned by tradition or by God's blessing (the "divine right" of kings).

Through much of the Middle Ages and the Renaissance, a rudimentary framework of law prescribed penalties for particular harms, and means for establishing innocence or guilt. By modern standards this framework was extremely narrow in scope, and its dictates could be—and frequently were—overridden on the authority of a nobleman or monarch. The fact that such rulers used the instrument of law did not hide the fact that their decisions often reflected purely personal criteria and dispositions. The rule of men was in this way personal, irregular, particular, and arbitrary. Because it was a product often of only personal criteria, it was also very unpredictable.

In contrast to such arbitrary rule or government, the ideal of a rule of law came to represent something impersonal, regular, universal, rule-governed, and (because based on public criteria) something also more predictable. In the background here stands the Enlightenment, with its call to set aside tradition and establish rational institutions and processes, and also the emerging market economy, with its need for rational, predictable, uniform rules and policies. While the rule of men had not turned out in practice to match the ideal Aristotle had called for, contemporary notions of the rule of law match his expectations: "[i]n law you have the intellect without the passions" (III, 16). "Laws ... prescribe the rules by which the rulers shall rule and shall restrain those that transgress the laws" (IV, 1).

The *rule of law* is the principle that *obliges everyone, including those in power, to obey formal, public, neutral rules of behaviour.* In theory, the rule of law requires that citizens be governed by consistent, publicly known, impartial rules *and* that those who exercise authority do so by publicly known, impartial, and consistent rules. In practice, implementing the principle of the rule of law means establishing procedures by which authority is exercised. Consequently, we can identify the "rule of law" as a principle of **PROCEDURAL JUSTICE**, and one that has come to command general consensus within Western political culture. There are at least five elements we can identify as requirements of the rule of law:

LEGAL CULPABILITY. One is punished only for breaking a law—that is, for what one has done or failed to do—and is subject to uniform, known sanctions. Simply displeasing or annoying those in authority should not be grounds for action.

PUBLIC LAW. The law must be publicly known, in that it would be unjust to find one responsible for breaking a rule of which one was ignorant. This places two obligations: one on the state, to publish all laws, and another on the person, to become informed about the laws that apply to citizens. This lies behind the idea that "ignorance of the law is no excuse from its penalties."

VALID LAW. Hobbes argued that it is not enough for the law to be published; there must be a sign that indicates it is actually the Sovereign's will, a real enough concern in a day before mass media of communication. This sign could be use of a royal seal or stamp, or today the use of official state letterhead, but in the final analysis we know the law is genuine and not counterfeit when it is made according to known and accepted procedures. This is one function performed by the legislative stages through which all legislative proposals must pass (recall above).

UNIVERSALITY. It must be possible to enforce or apply the law to everyone, including those who exercise power and/or authority. Our lawmakers and law-enforcers must be no less subject to the law than ordinary citizens.

IMPARTIALITY. All individuals stand equal before the law, and on this basis only relevant criteria, such as guilt or innocence, are applied. The personal prejudices or interests of judges should never play a role in proceedings, nor should individuals be judged on the basis of their personal attributes. This is the idea that lies behind the image that "justice is blind." That is to say, if justice is impartial, it takes no notice of irrelevant differences such as race, religious creed, age, gender, etc., but rather treats all individuals as identical abstract legal personalities. In this sense it might be said that the state does not need to know *who* we are, only *that* we are. Before the state, all stand equally as abstract legal entities or persons.

If these five elements seem extremely obvious, this is in part because they have become so embedded in our legal and political practice, and in part because we have lost acquaintance with states where the exercise of authority conforms to different criteria. This dominance of the rule of law as a regulative principle of procedural justice is part of what it means to say that we live in a society with legal-rational legitimacy.

There are also at least four institutional conditions that seem necessary accessories to the rule of law:

A CONSTITUTION. As noted in Chapter Seven, a constitution is a body of fundamental laws concerning the exercise of authority and the relation between the state and the people. Some such body of rules is necessary if the requirement of universality is to be met.

AN INDEPENDENT JUDICIARY. It is essential, if impartiality is to be maintained, and if rulers are also to be subject to the law, that judges be free from the influence or power wielded by officials of the state. Judges must be able to decide cases on the basis of the issues at hand, not out of concern for the wishes of third parties who take an interest. Neither should the state nor its officials be able to influence proceedings to which they are a party, either as plaintiff or defendant.

A PUBLIC LEGISLATURE. For Aristotle, the virtue of law is that it is dispassionate, not distracted by personal passions and feeling. For this very reason, though, he thought it necessary that law emerge from a consensus of the wise and just individuals in a society. On the other hand, one of the weaknesses in Hobbes's theory is that it would leave the law to the judgement and reason (let alone arbitrary passions and whims) of only one individual, the absolute monarch. The practical solution to this problem in Hobbes's England was the transfer of legislative power from the monarch to a legislative assembly (Parliament). Law became the product of the collective effort of legislators, operating within a set of rules or procedures. The advantages of a group here are important. A group needs rules and procedures to operate effectively, and such rules can provide for greater fairness, openness, and even flexibility than might otherwise be the case. The establishment of such rules and procedures also allows for debate, reflection, and reconsideration of proposed laws. In short, quality of law is enhanced—all else being equal—by the procedural requirements practically entailed by delegating legislative power to a group rather than an individual. In order to meet the requirements of validity and publicity, it is necessary that law-making itself occur in public. Only in this way can citizens have any certainty that good and correct procedures have in fact been followed.

CIVILIAN CONTROL OF THE POLICE AND MILITARY. The state is commonly identified as that body that has a monopoly of coercion: that is, only the state may legally force behaviour or actions, and only the state may use force to punish violations of the law. The body that employs force to uphold the law within the state is the police, and the body that employs force to defend the state against foreign aggression or encroachment is the military. It is noteworthy that two cases where the rule of law is violated are captured by the terms "police state" and "military dictatorship." What has happened in these situations is the collapse of the distinction between law-makers and law-enforcers. There are many reasons why it is generally accepted in liberal cultures that those who enforce the law should not make the law, but rather serve or be answerable to those who do make the law. Some of these reasons have to do with democracy, or our notion of rights (i.e., the concern that there should be limits on the legitimate use of force), and some have to do with our notions of law as impartial, public, and predictable.

In summary, then, the rule of law involves the articulation and establishment of legal-rational principles governing the exercise of authority and power, and the development of procedures and rules conforming to those principles. The rule of law is thus a set of regulative concepts, existing as standards by which we can measure the performance of the state and its officials, and providing a basis for increasing the likelihood that citizens will receive a fair, impartial, and consistent treatment whenever authority is exercised. At the same time, we might recall Aristotle's concern that authorities possess the flexibility to deal with individual cases as they merit, and not be hampered in this fashion by rigid rules. We see this concern addressed in the discretion given to magistrates in sentencing, to executives to pardon or commute sentences, and in other ways in which officials are granted discretion in the exercise of their power. Most often, though, this leeway or flexibility is itself today something proscribed and confined by laws.

16.3 RIGHTS

The rule of law is a *procedural* rather than a *substantive* principle. That is to say it deals with *how* the law is made, rather than with *what* the law concerns. The rule of law is concerned with the recipe, but not the meal that emerges, with the grading practices of a course rather than its curriculum, with the rules of a sport, but not with the game itself. This is why we said that the rule of law only "provides a basis for increasing the likelihood" that citizens receive justice; it is, in and of itself, no guarantee. It is still quite possible to make bad laws using proper procedures. Establishing correct procedures may lessen the likelihood that we will be governed arbitrarily or unfairly, but it says nothing about what kind of laws should or should not be made, only that they be made according to a certain set of rules.[2] For the most part, the rule of law is silent concerning the *content* of the law. Does the law ban all abortions or permit all abortions? Does it forbid religious practice or allow the private ownership of semi-automatic weapons? Does it permit pollution of the environment or limit public nudity? None of these questions, or an infinite number of others, can be answered on the basis of the principle of the rule of law.

2. By analogy, elections are also procedures by which citizens determine who will gain positions of authority, and it has been argued that elections are a better procedure for determining the ruling class than other alternatives that have been used. Elections, however, do not guarantee good government.

Rights, however, are very much about the content of the law. They are *entitlements that citizens can claim against the state and other individuals,* which therefore confine the content of the law within certain established limits. Rights are an attempt to remove or at least reduce the possibility that the government will make unjust laws, or exercise power legally but unjustly. Rights state that there are certain subjects about which the government may not legislate, certain freedoms that the government may not abridge, or certain actions that the state may not take. If nothing else, the story of justice in the twentieth century narrates the triumph of rights. Almost every issue that receives attention is presented by at least one of the interested parties as a question of rights. We live in an age in which people speak seriously about rights for animals, an age in which governments have legislated such rights. The discourse on rights has become so ingrained that to challenge the notion of animal rights, let alone the sense of speaking about individual rights, is for many people unthinkable.[3]

As often happens when a term becomes extremely commonplace, "rights" is used by people to mean many different things, but some key elements are clear. Most generally, the centrality of rights to modern political discourse represents a triumph of certain kinds of individualism on one hand, and the decline of community on the other. The concept of rights is a specifically modern notion, the liberal counterpart to **MEDIEVAL RIGHT**, and is a central product of the liberal revolution that replaces the feudal community with modern civil society.

In feudal communities, individuals enjoyed rights and could claim redress for **ENTITLEMENTS** denied. But in such communities your right or my right would be legitimate because of its agreement with "the Right," the objective moral order upon which the community was agreed, and which governed its relations. In this context, rights were not properties of individuals, but were enjoyed by individuals by virtue of their membership in a moral community, by virtue of their collective participation in "what is right." An individual who was not of the community could not be said to have rights—for this reason there was no difficulty with the idea of foreigners as slaves. At the same time, rights were particular. Because feudal communities were inegalitarian, highly differentiated structures, rights would depend on one's "station"—i.e., as peasant, soldier, nobleman, or priest. Rights were thus derived from *right,* and served as part of the glue binding together the social whole. Just as rights served to establish properly the place of the individual within the community, so too

3. Nonetheless, some very good arguments invite us to rethink what we are doing in employing the language of rights, arguments challenging some of the assumptions and notions underlying that language. See especially Edward Andrew, *Shylock's Rights* (1988), and Alasdair MacIntyre, *After Virtue* (1984).

4. Rights are commonly enumerated in a "code." When such a code is placed in the constitution it is said to be "entrenched," because amendment is thereby made more difficult. A rights code may also be embodied in ordinary statute, but then it is easily amended, repealed, or added to by subsequent legislative activity. An entrenched rights code (e.g., in Canada the Charter of Rights and Freedoms, or in the U.S. the Bill of Rights) typically takes precedence over any statute codes (for example, those codes applied by Human Rights Commissions, such as the Ontario Human Rights Code), which must then conform to the entrenched code.

5. Most organized groups (see Chapter Fourteen) are groups in the sense used here: aggregates of individuals united by a common interest. Some groups are *also* communities, when the members share a set of fundamental values, norms, and practices; the interests pursued by such groups may in fact be collective or community interests.

did duties. If my right here is what I am morally entitled to as peasant, king, or artisan, then my duty is what I am obliged to do as peasant, king, or artisan. Individuals' rights and duties were inseparable halves of the communal whole embodied in the notion of *Right*.

In liberal society, by contrast, individuals have rights (or claim redress for denied entitlements) that are often presented and understood as inalienable individual properties. Rights are claims that you or I make, and that some other party such as the state or another individual is required to respect. What justifies these claims is no longer a shared notion of "what is right," for none may exist, but rather legal definition. Rights are legal entities, embodied in law, whether statute or common, or in the device of an entrenched constitutional code.[4] Regardless of the different moral beliefs citizens may have, their rights are recognized through the legal rules that govern the society. Because these rights are the property of individuals *per se*, and not as members of a community, they are universal rather than particular, at least in theory. The abstract individual created by the notion of an impartial rule of law is also the bearer of rights. This separation of rights from community is what informs declarations of the "Rights of Man," or the United Nations' Universal Declaration of Human Rights. Finally, because rights have become legal (and political) rather than moral claims, they are no longer seen to be contingent upon or tied to the performance of duties.

The distinction between medieval Right and liberal rights is not simply philosophical, but characterizes two different ways in which individuals are reconciled within the social whole. Right has to do with the shared moral vision of a community, while rights is a legal-political means of establishing relations between state and individual, and between individual and individual in a secular, often pluralistic society. We will not debate the relative merits of Right versus rights here, but simply suggest that Right is only relevant to members of a community, and community in the strict sense (discussed in Chapter One) is not a feature of contemporary liberal societies. Elsewhere in this text we have referred to groups, i.e., aggregates of individuals united by interest. Most groups are intent on securing rights for their members; some justify this by claims about "what is right."[5]

The liberal argument that rights are inalienable properties of individuals that other parties (including the state) must respect, and the enshrinement of individual rights in entrenched codes, together tend to obscure the political nature of rights. Consider the question, "to what rights are you entitled?" One answer is to talk about what you *should* receive, that is, what is yours by *right,* and this returns us to notions about "what is right"; in this sense, rights are moral entitlements. It is also possible to talk about what each of us is entitled to in fact, which requires reference to the law that defines or entrenches entitlements. This will vary from polity to polity, each with its own definition of legal entitlements. For example, the American Constitution appears to give citizens the right to bear arms; Canadians know they have no such entitlement (note that neither position is the same as saying that citizens should bear arms, or that it is not right for citizens to bear arms, etc.). The rights actually enjoyed are defined by law, and law is itself a political act, the result of humans legislating. As such, rights exist only so long as the legislation that defines them remains in force, and even entrenched rights codes can be changed through subsequent political actions. In this way, you and I enjoy rights not as individuals possessing inalienable properties, but in our capacity as members of a polity. The status of the rights we enjoy will ultimately depend upon the political decisions made within our state, and thus upon the distribution of the power to make such decisions.

We will subsequently consider rights to be legal entitlements enjoyed by individuals with respect to other parties, i.e., other individuals or the state. The objects of rights are of basically three kinds:

FREEDOMS These are negative entitlements, which require the other party to refrain from interference with individual action or behaviour. Examples: freedom of expression, freedom of association, etc.

PROTECTIONS These, too, are negative entitlements, which require some party (usually the state) to protect us from harm that others might inflict, intentionally or otherwise. Examples: human rights codes, environmental protection legislation, labour laws.

BENEFITS Positive entitlement to specific goods, services, or resources. Examples: minority language services, social assistance payments, family support payments.

Although the actual distribution of freedoms, protections, and benefits within societies is of interest to us, we are more concerned here with the means by which citizens acquire rights and the institutions that define and enforce rights. In fact, how these latter issues are addressed is more likely than anything to determine the claims, both negative and positive, that citizens may successfully make.

**16.4
EQUALITY**

In our look at ideology (Chapter Five), we noted the spread—however unevenly and incomplete—of the idea of equality within liberal democracy in the last century. This has involved the movement from a naïve belief among early liberals in an equality of opportunity that required no state assistance, to the recognition that anything approaching a "level playing field" requires the activity of the government as a levelling agent. Eventually, liberalism moved from focusing on individuals as abstract units, to considering them collectively, and to considering the distribution of values or goods within the community or society as a whole. Most generally we talk about *wealth, power* (or authority), and *status* as the usual values with which distributional justice is concerned. Perhaps in our own society we could also include specific public goods such as education and health care. In short, attention within liberal democracies has increasingly turned to principles of **SOCIAL JUSTICE**, one of which is equality. Concern within liberal democracies for social justice has found concrete expression in a wide variety of measures, from progressive income tax, to selective grants for post-secondary education, to affirmative action hiring programs.

Behind the concern for social justice stands the observation that individuals are not by and large the authors of their own fate, but determine their own outcomes only within the opportunities and with the advantages that the particular circumstances of their birth and life afford them. The distribution of these opportunities and advantages is in large part the outcome of social arrangements and forces ultimately resting on the exercise or abstention of authority. On this argument, then, it is not enough that authority be exercised within the rule of law and in respect of rights, but that the state do all that it can to ensure a just distribution of social goods and benefits. What then constitutes a just distribution? About this there is considerable debate. It is not at all obvious to everyone that an equal distribution is the most just distribution, nor do those who endorse equality agree about what it means.

BLIND JUSTICE

One liberal who has contributed greatly to the debate concerning social justice is John Rawls (*A Theory of Justice*: 1971). Like many of his predecessors, Rawls asks us to imagine social arrangements as the result of a contract that we enter into with other individuals. However, we determine the nature of this contract behind a "veil of ignorance" concerning where we will be situated in that society.

At present, most of us are well aware of our social position or standing, and could imagine social arrangements by which our position or standing would be improved. Rawls's question is "what set of arrangements would we construct if we didn't know where we might end up, or if it was entirely up to chance which position we came to occupy?" Rawls concludes that our self-interest would lead us to establish arrangements consistent with equality. In other words, if equality is the principle of justice governing our social arrangements, it does not matter which social position we occupy; we are left no better or worse off than others. The one exception to equality this argument allows is that any inequality must tend to the benefit of those currently least advantaged. In other words, any unequal employment of authority must work to improve the positions of those who are disadvantaged by the current working of the social arrangements. For Rawls, then, justice consists of initial conditions of equality and action to correct or compensate for any inequalities that arise.

FIGURE 16.2

We should also observe that in reality, patterns of distribution are largely the result of social customs and individual transactions in which competing interests and judgements of utility are worked out. Justice is not primarily or often a central consideration. Moreover, patterns of distribution are reinforced and maintained by institutions and social structures that individuals come to inhabit, having little say or control over these institutions or structures. Inequalities are passed on from generation to generation, and it is simply not true to say that at any moment in time, the people of a society have freely chosen the patterns of distribution that prevail. It is possible to argue, however, that only such consent could make these patterns of distribution "right" or "just." In this view, social justice requires democracy, whether in order to preserve or maintain a condition of equality, whether to work towards the transformation of an inegalitarian society into one more consistent with equality, or whether simply to ensure that the inegalitarian distributions in society are the product not of custom, coercion, or ignorance, but rather of universal, informed consent.

Of the three principles of justice that have emerged since the liberal revolution, equality is the most recent, and the one to which allegiance is yet most tenuous. It may be premature still to judge whether or not equality is a practical or desirable option for humanity, or in what shape it is such.

**16.5
JUSTICE AND
INSTITUTIONS**

Justice does not simply consist in defining and reaching a consensus about principles; it also concerns the application and embodiment of principles within institutions and processes of the state. A good illustration of this is the question of the articulation and defence of rights within liberal democracies. Consideration of who should define and defend rights generally falls upon two alternatives: legislators in their capacity as lawmakers, or judges in their role of interpreting the law. Within the parliamentary tradition, this is a distinction between elected representatives and non-elected officials appointed by the political executive. To put the definition and protection of rights into the hands of one or the other of these is to choose between *parliamentary supremacy* and *judicial review*.

16.5.1   Parliamentary supremacy

This doctrine (discussed briefly in Chapter Seven) is best reflected by the English constitution, for it lies at the heart of the model of parliamentary government created by the Whig revolution of 1688. As the second Earl of Pembroke is supposed to have said: "A parliament can do any thing but make a man a woman, and a woman a man." This means that the legislature is supreme, in two senses: (1) there is no other institution that can overturn its decisions, and (2) there is no fundamental body of law or precepts to which the legislature's decisions must conform. Anything that is possible falls within the legislative competence of Parliament. The role of the judiciary in this context is to interpret the meaning of the law it receives from Parliament and apply it to relevant cases. If Parliament should disagree with the interpretation that the courts give to the law as it stands, it need only amend the law to match its intentions less ambiguously. Ultimately, then, the rights of citizens depend upon the political activity of legislators; their security is the degree to which lawmakers must consider the possibility of a withdrawal of support in the next election. Rights are secured through the political process, and those who dominate the political process will be more successful in ensuring that the law protects their rights. If the political process favours those with economic power, then they will be more secure in their rights than those whose rights require the limitation of economic power (i.e., labour, the unemployed, etc.). In a truly democratic system, whoever constitutes the majority should be most adept at securing protection in law for

COMPOSITION OF THE SUPREME COURTS OF CANADA AND THE U.S.

CANADA

Justice	Year Appointed	Year Born[†]	Nominated By
The Right Hon. Beverley McLachlin, Chief Justice	1989[*]	1943	B. Mulroney
Madam Justice Claire L'Heureux-Dubé	1987	1927	B. Mulroney
Mr. Justice Charles Doherty Gonthier	1989	1928	B. Mulroney
Mr. Justice Frank Iacobucci	1991	1937	B. Mulroney
Mr. Justice John C. Major	1992	1931	B. Mulroney
Mr. Justice Michel Bastarache	1997	1947	J. Chrétien
Mr. Justice William Ian Corneil Binnie	1998	1939	J. Chrétien
Madam Justice Louise Arbour	1999	1947	J. Chrétien
Mr. Justice Louis LeBel	2000	1939	J. Chrétien

[*] Appointed Chief Justice, January 7, 2000.   [†] Canadian Supreme Court Justices serve until age 75.

UNITED STATES

Justice	Year Appointed	Year Born[†]	Nominated By
Chief Justice William H. Rehnquist	1972[*]	1924	R. Nixon
Justice John Paul Stevens	1975	1920	G. Ford
Justice Sandra Day O'Connor	1981	1930	R. Reagan
Justice Antonin Scalia	1986	1936	R. Reagan
Justice Anthony Kennedy	1988	1936	R. Reagan
Justice David H. Souter	1990	1939	G. Bush
Justice Clarence Thomas	1991	1948	G. Bush
Justice Ruth Bader Ginsburg	1993	1933	W. Clinton
Justice Stephen G. Breyer	1994	1938	W. Clinton

[*] Appointed Chief Justice, 1999.   [†] United States Supreme Court Justices are appointed for life.

FIGURE 16.3

their rights, and in a majoritarian democracy, minorities may have no such protections.

16.5.2 Judicial review

Judicial review involves two elements: (1) a written constitution, including an entrenched rights code (e.g., the U.S. Bill of Rights, the Canadian Charter of Rights and Freedoms), and (2) a Supreme Court empowered to reject legislation that it judges to be contrary to the constitution. In this system the court acts as a check on the legislature, protecting the rights of citizens as defined within the constitutional document. The status of rights will thus depend not only on their original articulation in the written document, but also on the patterns of interpretation taken by the court.

Where there is judicial review (and to the extent that judicial review is possible), parliamentary supremacy has been eliminated; the courts have the ability to second-guess policy-makers by subjecting their acts to scrutiny on the basis of the written constitution. Judicial review means a replacement of parliamentary sovereignty with constitutional sovereignty. In theory the final word (in a democracy) remains with the people; if the constitution becomes a roadblock to popular or necessary legislation, it is always possible to amend the constitution. In practice, though, this is often difficult, and this is precisely why rights that are defined by the written constitution are said to be *entrenched*.

We have noted that with parliamentary sovereignty there is the danger of a legislative majority oppressing a minority. The entrenchment of rights and the provision of judicial review allow an independent institution (i.e., the courts) to protect minorities against the actions of a legislatively represented majority. It is not, though, a guarantee of such protection, nor does it ensure that the minorities that receive the protection afforded by judicial review are those that actually need it. Just as securing rights through the political process requires having the resources on which political success rests, securing rights through the courts (i.e., successfully challenging the constitutionality of a law) requires legal resources, namely legal expertise and the ability to fund a sustained legal challenge. We need to remember that in common-law systems at least (the Anglo-American world), a constitutional challenge is not really won or lost until the high or supreme court has delivered its judgement (which binds all lower courts). The possibility that a successful challenge might involve three separate trials (court of first instance, court of appeal, supreme court) means that the protection of rights through a written constitutional document may favour those with resources: either wealthy individuals or corporations, or organized groups that pool the more meagre resources of their members.

One concern with judicial review is the unaccountability of the judges who finally rule on the constitutionality of legislation. Although in the U.S. many judges are elected (and therefore politically accountable), this is not true of the Supreme Court justices, who are appointed for life by the President. In Canada, similarly, the Prime Minister appoints justices who serve until age 75. To a certain degree this unaccountability is a necessary by-product of the principle of **JUDICIAL INDEPENDENCE**, which requires that courts be free from political influence (particularly any pressure from the government of the day). In the U.S., the President's nominees to the court face hearings and approval by the Senate, an example of the checks and balances in this system. The consequence, though, has been to politicize the appointment process. In 1987, the nomination of Judge Robert Bork was rejected by the Senate on the basis of what were perceived to be extremely conservative positions held by the candidate. One of George Bush's nominations, that of Judge Clarence Thomas, was ratified by the Senate only after much controversy and hearings investigating claims of sexual harassment. It may seem appropriate that if justices are to be making political decisions, they should be chosen at least partly on political grounds, but then why not simply leave the definition and protection of rights with properly political bodies (the legislature and executive)? The length of tenure for judges means that political opinions consistent with public values at the time of appointment may increasingly fall out of step; appointment for life to the Court often saddles subsequent generations with the political values of a preceding era.

None of this would matter if the decisions the Court makes were simply (as many citizens seem to regard them) findings of fact and as legal questions, merely "objective," "scientific" matters for which nothing else is relevant but legal expertise and judicial experience. As countless observers have noted, in particular legal scholars, in performing judicial review the courts are making political decisions. They may be hearing legal arguments and rendering legal decisions on the basis of legal precedents, but the content of what is being decided through these legal means is very often extremely political. The simple reason for this is that the phrases contained in any constitutional code of rights are often so vague as to require considerable interpretation by the courts before they can be applied to particular cases. Judges individually, and courts collectively, gain a reputation for the styles of inter-pretation that they favour. One common distinction is between **JUDICIAL ACTIVISM** and **RESTRAINT**. There are two different ways of understanding this, one of which focuses on outcomes, the other on the actual style of interpretation. Russell et al. (1989: 19) argue that the distinction refers either to the willingness of the court to set aside legislative or executive acts as unconstitutional or, conversely, to a reluctance to do so:

Activism refers to judicial vigour in enforcing constitutional limitations on the other branches of government and a readiness to veto the policies of those
branches of government on constitutional grounds.
Self-restraint connotes a judicial predisposition to find
room within the constitution for the policies of democratically accountable decision-makers.

A different application of these terms is made by Landes,
who sees restraint as indicated when "the courts take a very
narrow view of their own powers of interpretation ... the judges
seek to divine the literal and intended meaning of the initial
constitution," while activism "reflects a willingness on the part of
judges to use their powers vigorously, if necessary, to take a broad
view of any powers delineated in the constitution" (1995: 255). It
is not clear that these two competing applications of judicial
activism and judicial restraint can be reconciled. Certainly in some
circumstances, a narrow (restrained) interpretation could lead to
support for governmental actions (e.g., ruling that "freedom of
peaceful assembly" does not entail the picketing by public servants
of courthouses), while in other circumstances it could lead to
judicial review of legislation (e.g., the "right to the enjoyment of
property" is improperly infringed by environmental regulations).
Similarly, a broad, "between the lines" interpretation could,
depending on circumstances, enlarge the legislative competence
of the state, or limit it on behalf of individuals. At any rate, what
either set of distinctions should make clear is that there is no
neutral, objective middle ground that we should expect the courts
to be in a position to articulate simply because they contain
judges, not elected politicians.

16.5.3   Balancing Parliament and the courts

When it comes to the entrenchment of rights in the constitution,
as with the nature of the Senate and federalism generally, Canada
has displayed its mixed parentage, in this case a product of British
tradition of parliamentary sovereignty and the American practice
of full judicial review. As a federal country, Canada has since 1867
had the experience of partial or limited judicial review with
respect to interpretation of the division of powers between the
two levels of government protected by the written constitution.
This limited the courts, though, to consideration of the jurisdic-

tional competence of each level of government, that is, the question: "Is the subject matter of this provincial (or federal) legislation something that falls within the jurisdictions assigned by the constitution to the provincial (or federal) governments?" Anything found to be unconstitutional in this way would be unconstitutional *only for that level of government*, and could, conceivably, be enacted by the other level of government, falling within its jurisdiction. It was only with the addition of the Charter of Rights and Freedoms to the Canadian constitution in 1982 that full judicial review became possible, but even here there are two interesting provisions that preserve some measure of parliamentary supremacy (or hold out the possibility of doing so).

The opening section, subtitled the "Guarantee of Rights and Freedoms," notes that the rights contained in the Charter are subject to reasonable limits if these are made by law, and are justifiable in a free and democratic society. It may seem odd to begin a rights code by describing how these rights may be limited, but this simply reflects an awareness of the reality that *all* (or almost all) rights, no matter how categorically defined, become subject in practice to some limitation. My freedom of speech does not extend to libel; my freedom of religion will extend much farther to beliefs than to actions or practices. What Section 1 does is ensure that whatever limitations are put on my rights, they will be subject to three qualifications: they must be contained in law, they must serve a justifiable purpose (i.e., consistent with freedom and democracy), and they must be reasonable (which the Supreme Court has further defined in terms of proportionality). The Supreme Court has also established that the onus is on the government to demonstrate that the limitations of right satisfy Section 1, not on the individual to prove that the limitations do not satisfy those conditions.

Even more of a concession to parliamentary supremacy, at least potentially, is found in Section 33 of the Charter, the so-called "notwithstanding clause." This is an example of a "legislative override"; it allows either level of government, in passing legislation, to invoke this clause and thereby escape judicial review with respect to certain specified portions of the Charter. In other words, this section allows legislatures to enact laws in contravention of certain sections (2, 7-15) of the Charter, thus restoring, in these spheres at least, full parliamentary sovereignty. Any legislation that invokes the notwithstanding clause is valid only for five years, which is the normal maximum life of a parliament. In this way a government that sets aside the Charter in passing legislation will be forced to receive a fresh mandate from the electorate before re-enacting such legislation.

In Canada, then, both judicial review and parliamentary sovereignty remain viable avenues by which citizens can attempt to secure or protect their rights. Whether this will offer the best of both worlds, or the worst, will depend on the behaviour of politicians and justices, and upon the influences exerted upon them through the political process.

16.6 CONCLUSION

KEY TERMS

benefits
entitlement
equality
freedoms
impartiality
judicial activism
judicial independence
judicial restraint
judicial review
justice
legal culpability
legislative override
medieval Right
parliamentary supremacy
procedural justice
protections
public law
rights
rights code
rule of law
social justice
universality
valid law
vendetta

The language and concerns of justice occupy a large part of the political terrain in liberal democracies. Competing conceptions express notions of what is right when it comes to the exercise of power and authority, and various institutions make concrete the mechanisms and procedures for realizing and securing these notions. Common to the rule of law, rights, and equality as notions of justice is the depersonalization of authority that accompanied the transformation from feudalism to liberal modernity in Western Europe. Particularly in the case of the rule of law and rights, but perhaps in the ways that equality is embodied in rights and other legal instruments, there is a tendency in liberal notions of justice to look for a procedure, a formula, or a process which by being followed or invoked will ensure that justice ensues. This reflects the concern with the bias, discrimination, or prejudice that can result when too much discretion is given to those in positions of authority. At the same time, we may do well at times to recall Aristotle's teaching that justice is never wholly a matter of applying the rules, but is sometimes something that also calls for our wisdom and judgement applied to the particularities or circumstances before us.

Perhaps related to the search for an impersonal, impartial justice, but also connected to the broad degree of public consensus (or lack of dispute) over their essential aptness, the rule of law and rights have largely departed from the political realm, almost entirely with the former, and increasingly with rights as they are further judicialized. As argued above, this should not obscure to us that political decisions continue to be made, particularly when it comes to rights, even though the forum for decision-making (i.e., the courts) is not generally seen to be political. It is also worth noting that there remain important subjects that, even though understood as rights questions, are *not* constitutionalized, but are left to legislatures to determine and define, and are thus still understood to be legitimate political questions. For example, however much the Charter has transformed justice and politics in Canada since 1982, we do well to remember that it applies only to the activities of the two constitutionally protected levels of government. The rights of Canadians with respect to each other, of employees with respect to employers, of consumers with respect to corporations: all of these are rights (insofar as they are rights) defined in ordinary legislation. Entrenched rights codes such as the Charter put limits on the power of the state, but we do well to remember that there are significant sources of private power in our world, also. One legitimate concern with entrenching rights is that it has the potential to limit the state from making policies that shift the balance of private power in society—which, obviously, is also why some are very pleased to constitutionalize rights. At the beginning of the twenty-first century, the role of the state in society and the relationship of public power to private power have come very much into question as a result of shifting political and economic realities. It is this relationship that we explore in the next chapters.

SOMETHING TO CONSIDER

Justice is supposedly blind. What is the necessary truth contained in this metaphor? What are the effects of mass media saturated with stories of crime (in news, dramas, and documentaries) on popular understanding of the principle of the "rule of law"? Consider the contrast between the abstract idea that each of us has a "legal personality" and the literal presentation of all suspects in the media of popular culture.

REFERENCES AND SUGGESTED READING

Andrew, Edward. 1988. *Shylock's Rights*. Toronto: University of Toronto Press.

Benn, S.I., and R.S. Peters. 1959. *Social Principles and the Democratic State*. London: Unwin.

Dworkin, Ronald. 1977. *Taking Rights Seriously*. London: Duckworth.

Green, Phillip. 1981. *The Pursuit of Inequality*. New York: Pantheon.

Greene, Ian. 1989. *The Charter of Rights*. Toronto: James Lorimer.

Landes, Ronald. 1995. *The Canadian Polity*, 4th ed. Scarborough, Ont.: Prentice Hall.

MacIntyre, Alasdair. 1984. *After Virtue*, 2nd ed. Notre Dame, Ind.: Notre Dame University Press.

Mandel, Michael. 1989. *The Charter of Rights and the Legalization of Politics in Canada*. Toronto: Wall and Thompson.

Rawls, John. 1971. *A Theory of Justice*. Cambridge, Mass.: Harvard University Press.

Russell, Peter. 1987. *The Judiciary in Canada: The Third Branch of Government*. Toronto: McGraw-Hill Ryerson.

Russell, Peter, et al. 1989. *Federalism and the Charter: Leading Constitutional Decisions*. Ottawa: Carleton University Press.

17

the rise (and fall) of the welfare state

A variety of themes examined in earlier chapters converge here. In the last chapter we noted that questions of justice sometimes turn upon the notion of equality (or inequality), and one factor determining the **DISTRIBUTION** of material resources in society is the relative weight of the market economy and of the state, respectively, in allocation. In our treatment of ideology in Chapter Five, we observed the convergence of the mainstream ideologies around the notion of a private property market economy. Economic policy, or the particular relationship between the state and the market, remains a fundamental dimension along which ideologies distinguish themselves. In a democracy, citizens may seek to enhance their security—that is, their continued assurance of the means of life, if not of material well-being—by requiring particular social and economic policies in return for their political support. While disagreement may be widespread about the proper role of the state in the economy, all expect it to do something.

It is important to emphasize that how the state performs its function (limited or extensive) of economic management is very much influenced by the presence or absence of democracy. Only in the twentieth century, as democracy took root, did the modern state acknowledge responsibility for management of the economy, and only in the age of democracy has the extensive level of activity associated with the term "welfare state" arisen. Charles Lindblom has noted that while market society has arisen in nondemocratic regimes, liberal democracy has survived only in market societies, something which in itself invites exploration of the linkages between politics and economics (Lindblom, 1977: 5).

17.1
INTRODUCTION

17.1   Introduction
17.2   Market Society
17.3   Liberalism and *Laissez-faire*
17.4   Critiques of Market Society
17.5   Ideological Compromise: The Welfare State
17.6   Rolling Back the Welfare State
17.7   After the Welfare State?

We should also note that a distinct approach to the study of politics, namely **POLITICAL ECONOMY**, explores the links between politics and economics. A stronger sense of the term implies a conviction that politics is essentially about economic questions, or, that politics cannot be understood without reference to economic variables, or even, that political issues not immediately perceived to be economic are often determined by economic considerations. Within economics, the term "political economy" denotes a specific tradition in economic theory that held that the source of all value is human labour. Adam Smith, David Ricardo, James Mill, and Karl Marx were classical political economy theorists, but contemporary economics focuses instead on the nature of **MARKETS** and the values assigned to things by markets (see Howlett, Netherton, and Ramesh, 1999).

Not surprisingly, political scientists and economists often have very different views of the relationship between politics and economics. Some (but by no means all) political scientists argue that the economy should be subordinate to political purposes or goals. The National Policy of the Macdonald Conservatives reflected a belief in the primacy of politics over economics, that market forces should be subject to political decisions and interests; the government committed itself to supporting the construction of a national railway and intervened in market relations by erecting a tariff barrier to protect infant Canadian industries. Most (but not all) economists argue instead that economics should be autonomous from political direction, that market forces should be given free rein to determine outcomes. There are three fundamental questions at stake here in modern market societies:

a) What is the proper role of the state with respect to the market?
b) Who benefits most from a regulated or unregulated market? and
c) Is the "efficient use of resources" (as the economist defines "efficient") the most appropriate criterion for judging public policies?

17.2 MARKET SOCIETY

The context of our discussion is the predominance of a private property market economy, which indicates two dimensions of economic life: how resources are allocated, and who owns the principal means of economic production. In market societies, resources are primarily allocated in one of two ways: by **PRIVATE TRANSACTIONS** in which individuals purchase goods or services from others, or by the **AUTHORITATIVE TRANSFER** of these by the state. In other words, resources are largely allocated either by the market or by the authority of government. What we call "the market" is simply the aggregation of individual transactions, or the purchase and sale by individuals of goods, services, and labour. In a completely "free" or unregulated market, resource allocation occurs through non-authoritative relations, i.e., private exchanges governed only by the "natural" laws of the market (i.e., supply and demand). Almost all societies beyond a minimal level of development have had a market (i.e., private exchanges), but a market economy exists only where the bulk of production occurs for the purpose of market activity (as opposed, for example, to economies where production occurs for immediate consumption or for authoritative allocation).

Beyond the allocation of resources, political economy is concerned with how goods are produced in a society. How, for example, are the materials of nature cultivated or transformed to produce what humans can use, consume, or possess? Agriculture is a set of such processes, industry is another. Both rely on the progressive development of technology: new ways of accomplishing the practical tasks of humanity. The kinds and levels of production are as important in characterizing an economy as the allocation of resources, and here too the policies and laws implemented by the state can be crucial. The tariff of Macdonald's National Policy was designed to provide protection for Canadian manufacturers. Critics of this policy argue that it was an uneconomical allocation of resources, artificially inflating the costs of goods to support a non-competitive manufacturing sector. Supporters point to the jobs created by such industry and argue that these justify the higher prices. At any rate, modern market economies have been characterized by technologically intensive manufacturing processes and an increasingly large "service" sector, including activities developing and employing "information" technology.

A related but separate issue is the matter of ownership in an economy; is it something vested in individuals, somehow shared as in a co-operative, or held by citizens in common through the state? Ownership is twofold: on the one hand it reflects the title to possession of the goods, services, and labour that are exchanged (or not) in the marketplace. In this respect almost everyone owns something. More crucial, though, is who owns the processes of production by which the objects of exchange are created. While there remain other possibilities, such as co-operatives, the usual distinction here is between **PRIVATE PROPERTY**, where the means of production are owned by (some of) the individuals in society, and **PUBLIC PROPERTY**, where ownership is held by the state, on behalf of the people.

In contemporary Western societies that rely on markets for allocation, the production of goods is generally associated with private property. Modern market economies are consumer societies in which most individuals procure the means of life through purchases. (In addition, as levels of disposable income have risen, the quantity and quality of goods consumed have become about much more than the provision of mere necessities.) Furthermore, most individuals in a modern market economy are also employees who sell their labour to a corporation, to a government institution, or to other individuals. There is thus a modern market in labour as well as in goods, products, or raw materials. In this way the market is central to the life of virtually everyone in modern society.

The modern market economy servicing a consumer society and organizing the largest part of socially productive labour did not come about all at once. It is the result of several centuries of development, of the emergence and development of technology, of the organization and employment of labour by capital, and of many other processes and techniques that have had to be invented, learned, used, and perfected. Moreover, all this was not spontaneous, but rather was the result of countless laws, policies, and programs implemented by governments, and often secured after much struggle among competing interests over the shape of these policies or laws.

The growth and dominance of the market required a revolutionary transformation of the economic system that had governed medieval society, an economic revolution that had profound political consequences. In brief, the new market economy required two developments: (a) that individuals be removed from the structures of medieval society in order to be "free" to be active in the market (consumers and/or buyers or sellers of labour); and (b) that political authority be exercised in ways consistent with, and supportive of, the needs of the market. These correspond with the two ideological themes stressed by supporters of the market ever since the seventeenth century: (1) that government *respect the autonomy of the market,* and (2) that government *provide market interests with the structure of law, services, and incentives* deemed optimal for market activity, that is, with *support.*

MARKET AUTONOMY is the demand that the primary (if not only) allocation of resources be done through the market (private, voluntary transactions between individuals), and that the laws and regulations made by the state interfere as little as possible with the operation of market forces (such as the determination of price through "supply" and "demand"). The second theme, **MARKET SUPPORT**, is the demand that the state provide the conditions or infrastructure necessary for individuals to be able to produce, buy, and sell in the market, conditions such as a stable currency, enforcement of contracts, freedom from theft or extortion, etc. While the exchanges that characterize market economies are private, voluntary transactions, these rely in turn on a public system of involuntary laws that enforce contracts, protect property from theft, and settle disputes over title. The state has a very important role in establishing the framework of law in which market activity can occur, and in establishing thereby how this market activity will occur. It would certainly be possible to have a market without a supportive state, but not the extensive economic activity we recognize as a market society. The question put properly is not *whether* the state should make policies that affect the market, but rather *how* the state's policies should affect the market. This is where matters become controversial, not least because of differing evaluations both of the market and of who benefits most from its operation.

LIBERALISM was the original ideology of market society, embracing new economic developments and arguing for the conditions of rational government and economic (social) liberty conducive to the progressive development of market forces. Liberalism was also flexible enough to demand of the state policies corresponding to the nature of the market and the needs of its dominant producers. In the works of some of the early liberals, it is possible to see demands for market support and for the creation of a rational government under the rule of law that would provide the framework of order and appropriate policies for an emerging market economy. As the liberal state replaced the absolutist monarchy of feudalism and as the market became more securely established, liberal thinkers turned their emphasis to policies stressing the need for market autonomy.

By the end of the eighteenth century these policies were most eloquently summed up in Adam Smith's landmark treatise

17.3
LIBERALISM AND *LAISSEZ-FAIRE*

The Wealth of Nations; the doctrine of economic liberalism represented by this work came to be known as **LAISSEZ-FAIRE**. As this term suggests, the emphasis was on leaving the market as unfettered by **REGULATION** and state interference as possible, and the reason for this was to maximize competition among producers, consumers, and labourers. This competition, it was argued, would result in the most efficient and productive use of resources, an economy by which the interests of all would best be served.

According to the model, markets are not only efficient but progressive: competition improves the standard of living of all by lowering prices that consumers pay for goods, improving the quality of products, encouraging research that produces beneficial goods and by-products, productively employing the resources of society, and increasing the level of wages paid workers. All this is the unintended consequence of rational self-interested activity in the marketplace; such results, Smith said, were the product of "an invisible hand." According to Smith, the beneficial social effects of individual actions will not be produced if governments interfere in the market or artificially determine its outcomes. Therefore, this ideal model seeks what has been called a **MINIMAL STATE**, one that interferes least with the supposed "free" nature of markets. This model works because of the assumptions made about competition and the incentives or penalties imposed by competition between producers and buyers and sellers. Therefore, anything that inhibits this competition is deemed harmful and likely to reduce efficiency. The policy that would remove or resist restrictions on trade and thereby completely open markets to competition was known as *laissez-faire*, a term often employed, and used here, to refer to the political economic doctrine of a maximum amount of market autonomy and, correspondingly, of a minimal state.

While the *laissez-faire* doctrine calls for a minimal state, it nonetheless relies on this state to perform some important roles, and to perform them in ways that benefit entrepreneurs or producers. For Adam Smith, these functions were as follows: the administration of justice, the provision of defence, the provision of public works (necessary to facilitate economic activity), and the reform of "various institutional and legal impediments to the system of natural liberty" (Skinner, 1970: 79).

By the nineteenth century, *laissez-faire* had become the dominant economic theory of liberalism and was to become the effective economic policy of the British government, managing what was then the world's most advanced market economy. This last point is important: *laissez-faire* was adopted in Britain when this nation had the most efficient and developed industrial economy in the world and therefore could compete with any state on favourable terms. Where industry is less efficient, or must cope with higher production costs, the commitment to *laissez-faire* will be less strong, and tariffs or other forms of protectionism more popular. *Laissez-faire* was originally the doctrine of successful industrial capitalism; it is therefore not necessarily the optimal policy for less competitive industrial economies, or for other segments of the economy, i.e., merchant capital, finance capital, farmers, or (especially) workers. Thus, while *laissez-faire* became the economic theory of classical liberalism, we should not be surprised that other ideologies were critical of this policy and its effects.

Market society has been criticized from any number of directions for its effects on collective and individual human existence. At the risk of caricature, some of these critiques might be summarized as follows:

17.4 CRITIQUES OF MARKET SOCIETY

- the conservative (i.e., tory) identifies market society with progress and believes progress is corrosive of what is eternal, valuable, and worthy of respect;
- the socialist, by contrast, believes in progress and believes that progress requires proceeding beyond market society in our social and political-economic development;
- the feminist identifies the market with the perpetuation of patriarchal structures and attitudes, and argues for a radically different organization of production and a correspondingly revised set of attitudes about production;
- the environmentalist identifies market society with the destruction of the planetary biosphere.

Other objections are raised against market society, often with compelling force, although critics may not be clear about a possible alternative. For example, modern market societies are sometimes criticized for their narrow view of "the good life," with their stress on consumption and pleasure rather than on the development of abilities or on creative human activity. In this view, market society is not just a means of organizing economic life; it organizes our entire life, determining our priorities and values in a narrow fashion. These are important issues and difficult questions, some of which take us beyond the sphere of political economy.

Tories who supported the agrarian feudal economy of the medieval period tended to view the new market economy as disruptive of established relations and practices. This was not simply a matter of disrupting feudal relations, but also of displacing the landed aristocracy with a new class of capitalists. In some nations the opposition between tory and liberal reflected a distinction between country and city. Market society was associated with urbanization, secularization, commercialism, materialism, and anything else that challenged traditional ways and institutions. Nonetheless, eventually many, if not most, tories came to accept (and often prosper in) the market economy.

The rise of industrial capitalism in the nineteenth century and its operation within the bounds of the minimal state had a dramatic effect on the class of industrial workers that it brought into being. It is no accident that the nineteenth century saw the rise of the rival political economic doctrine of socialism. The most formidable socialist critic of the market system or **CAPITALISM** was Karl Marx. Marx regarded his work as consistent with the tradition of political economy that included such orthodox market advocates as Adam Smith, David Ricardo, and John Stuart Mill. More than any socialist before him, Marx's critique was based on a close acquaintance with the workings of capitalism and an appreciation of the productive powers it had developed. His critique consisted of roughly five main points.

Instead of the liberal approach of treating market society as simply an association of individuals entering into private economic transactions, Marx analysed it in terms of **CLASSES**, where class is determined by the position occupied by individuals within the productive process. Marx argued that industrial capitalism creates a two-class society, divided between the **PROLETARIAT** (workers) and the **BOURGEOISIE** (owners). The latter own or control the **MEANS OF PRODUCTION** and hire labour power for a wage payment; the former consists of those who sell their labour to the owners (who are owners of capital, hence *capitalists*). The capitalist and the wage labourer stand at opposite ends of the capitalist mode of production. In time, Marx believed, all other classes in society would disappear, and social life would be dominated by the *class conflict* between these two remaining classes.

Marx also argued that the relationship between bourgeoisie and proletariat is exploitive, that is, the worker is paid less than full value for his/her labour by the capitalist, and this surplus extracted from the worker is the source of profits and capital. At various points, Marx also suggested that the capitalist treatment of labour in the effort to maximize profits is dehumanizing, alienating individuals from the full expression of their humanity in creative, self-directed activity.

As capitalism progressed, Marx believed, the proletariat would become conscious of itself as an oppressed class, that is, become aware of its collective exploitation by the capitalist class. This would lead to a revolution—which Marx thought might even occur by democratic means (the election of a proletarian party)—which would replace class-divided society with a classless community that would organize on socialist principles the economic machinery created by capitalism.

Politically, Marx believed that the chief impediment to socialism was the existence of the state operating as an instrument of the bourgeoisie. That is to say, the government in capitalist societies not only creates the conditions necessary for capitalism to flourish, but supports and promotes the ideas and ideology that support that economic system. This helps prevent workers from gaining revolutionary class consciousness; instead, they accept the legitimacy of the very system that exploits them.

From his analysis of capitalism, Marx concluded that capitalism would self-destruct because of its own internal contradictions; the product of this would be a socialist revolution led by a class-conscious proletariat. These contradictions within capitalism have to do largely with the business cycle (a somewhat cyclical pattern of growth and decline) that in Marx's lifetime had regularly brought market economies into periods of economic depression that seemed increasingly acute and protracted. Marx believed the revolution could very well occur in the most developed industrial societies, like England or Germany.

Marx's critique (which is much more complicated than what has been presented), like the models of orthodox economists, was based on a variety of assumptions. It was also based on the social and economic realities of the time when Marx was writing, in the middle of the nineteenth century. Industrial capitalism had created an urban working class of factory laborers dependent upon market activity for their existence. Nineteenth-century capitalism *was* exploitive: real wages were lower after the Industrial Revolution than before, urban labourers had much less security than peasants had enjoyed, and the working conditions imposed by industrial capitalism were generally abominable. At one point it was normal for every man, woman, and child over the age of four or five to work a 12- to 14-hour day for a subsistence wage (the minimum necessary to feed and clothe workers). The state could very well be seen as an instrument for the preservation and support of the interests of the economic elite, especially as long as those who could vote and/or stand for office had to own sufficient property. The nineteenth century gave evidence of increasing **CLASS-CON-SCIOUSNESS** on the part of labourers, who attempted to organize to protect their interests, forming working men's associations, unions, working-class political parties, etc. Capitalism also regularly exhibited the swings of the business cycle, in which periods of expansion and prosperity were regularly followed by periods of contraction and poverty.

There is little of substance in Marx's critique of British industrial society to illuminate what alternative economic system he thought could take its place. Clearly, the private ownership of the productive processes would be replaced with collective ownership by (or in the name of) the people (workers). Marx also seemed to believe that the state should play a transitional role in managing the change from a market economy to a socialist system, and that when this transition was complete, the state would "wither away," having become redundant. The basic point for Marx was that socialism would inherit the tremendous productive forces created by the market system, but organize productive labour in a way so as to eliminate class division and the effects of class exploitation.

The economic systems established in the former Soviet Union and East European countries in the guise of Marxist-Leninism replaced private ownership of production with centralized state ownership, where the state was monopolized by the Communist Party (ostensibly on behalf of the proletariat). It is these **COMMAND ECONOMIES** that have collapsed in the last two decades, and that are presently being reformed into market systems. The failure of these Marxist-Leninist regimes owes little if anything to Marx, and does nothing to invalidate his analysis of nineteenth-century capitalism or to discredit his reflections on the nature of human creative activity. As with Adam Smith, the limits of Marx's insights into market society are found in his theory, not in the deeds of his disciples.

Whatever the strengths of Marx's analysis of mature, developed, industrial capitalism, his prognosis regarding its future health and development was flawed in two principal respects. First, Marx overestimated the revolutionary potential of the working class, whose members generally seem more concerned with improving their own living conditions *within* the existing social framework than with embarking upon a grand social experiment. Second, Marx underestimated the ability of capitalism to reform itself without abandoning its basic commitment to private property, or to the market as the principal means of allocating resources and values.

The reform of capitalism, which Marx could not have foreseen, entailed moving away from the ideal of *laissez-faire* and, from the middle of the nineteenth century, increasingly involved the state in economic affairs, something that accelerated dramatically after the Depression of the 1930s. While the existence of socialism as a rival economic ideology no doubt influenced liberal theory, the reform of *laissez-faire* was largely the result of pressures internal to developed market economies.

One consequence of economic liberalism and its emphasis on market autonomy is to suggest that politics must take second place to economics. Some conservatives, by contrast, will argue that economics should take second place to politics. Thus even while embracing a private property market economy, it is possible for conservatives to argue that the state has a role in directing and shaping the activities of the market for the larger good of the community. One economist who argued this point, and who has largely been ignored in the English-speaking world, was Friedrich List.

List's fundamental point was to argue that the unorganized individual pursuit of self-interest will not necessarily lead to the greater good of all. Rather, it is requisite for the state to encourage, regulate, erect tariffs if necessary—in short, the state should play an active role in shaping the economy. As List wrote in *The National System of Political Economy* (1837),

> The cosmopolitan theorists [e.g., Smith, Ricardo] do not question the importance of industrial expansion. They assume, however, that this can be achieved by adopting the policy of free trade and by leaving individuals to pursue their own private interests. They believe that in such circumstances a country will automatically secure the development of those branches of manufacture which are best suited to its own particular situation. They consider that government action to stimulate the establishment of industries does more harm than good....

The lessons of history justify our opposition to the assertion that states reach economic maturity most rapidly if left to their own devices ... the growth of industries is a process that may take hundreds of years to complete and one should not ascribe to sheer chance what a nation has achieved through its laws and institutions. In England Edward III created the manufacture of woollen cloth and Elizabeth founded the mercantile marine and foreign trade. In France Colbert was responsible for all that a great power needs to develop its economy. Following these examples every responsible government should strive to remove those obstacles that hinder the progress of civilisation and should stimulate the growth of those economic forces that a nation carries in its bosom.

As this passage indicates, List was an **ECONOMIC NATIONALIST**, in opposition to the internationalist (free trade) policies of economic liberalism (*laissez-faire*). James Fallows has pointed out that in Japan the economic ideology of List has been much more influential than the work of Adam Smith ("How the World Works" in *Atlantic Monthly*, December 1993). List's *The National System of Political Economy* is a non-socialist counterpoint to Adam Smith's *The Wealth of Nations*.

In most Western nations, and certainly in the English-speaking democracies, conservatives have remained economic liberals, i.e., they have continued to support the minimal state of *laissez-faire*. By contrast, liberalism, in reforming itself, abandoned *laissez-faire* economics. It did so in part because *laissez-faire* turned out to work less well in practice than in theory, and in part because the coming of political democracy forced liberalism to accommodate the interests of those least well served by *laissez-faire*.

The political economic position of *laissez-faire* rests on an economic model, and as a model it necessarily abstracts from real life to postulate ideal conditions that may never actually be found, and in many cases or respects may be impossible to obtain. The model assumes that participants in economic transactions have perfect information, make wholly rational decisions, are equally free to engage in transactions or not, do so under conditions of ideal competition, etc. These and other assumptions are not realized in the real economic world. This divergence should not surprise us: the point of models is to make abstractions from real conditions for the purpose of comparison, manipulation, or other study. What became problematic for liberals was that the divergences between the real experience of *laissez-faire* and its ideal operation made it difficult to justify the minimal state, particularly from a liberal perspective. Most importantly, the divergence between how markets operate ideally and how they work in practice is a cost that does not fall on those in the best position to absorb it, or is a benefit that accrues to those least in need of it (and often is both of these together). Not surprisingly, this is why advocates of *laissez-faire* economics in the nineteenth century were often very suspicious of democracy, fearing it would deliver political power to those least advantaged, if not actually disadvantaged, by market society, who might use the state to replace or regulate market mechanisms.

For example, the economic *model* accepts that inequality accompanies a capitalist market economy, an inequality rationalized on two grounds. One is the claim that a market economy will generate prosperity for all and that it is better to be unequal and secure than to be equal and poor. The second is that the "invisible hand" of the unregulated market will improve the position of the least advantaged by providing for full employment and by constantly increasing the price of labour while decreasing the margins of profit. In this way inequality is diminished over time. Both these arguments, which rest on certain theoretical assumptions, are not confirmed by experience. Full employment and an increasing price for labour are conditions that *laissez-faire* meets only occasionally, if at all. Very often, considerable unemployment and periods of low or diminishing wages exist. The claim that policies increasing or sustaining market autonomy will benefit everyone needs always to be examined critically in light of the possibility that only some interests will benefit or will benefit disproportionately (*and* that these interests will not be those most in need of the benefit). These are considerations to which liberalism is particularly vulnerable, since it claims not to discriminate between individuals, but to give all equal regard. If liberalism is indifferent to the treatment by the market of the poor and working classes, then it risks justifying Marx's claim that it is simply the ideology of the propertied classes passing itself off as something more universal.

Market society is the best alternative for the poor and the lesser advantaged only under certain conditions, and it appears that unregulated markets cannot sustain these conditions indefinitely. The supposed benefits that accrue from the efficiency a market system promotes are accompanied by the costs of weeding

FEDERAL GOVERNMENT EXPENDITURES AND DEFICITS IN CANADA ($ MILLIONS)

Year	Expenditures on goods & services	Transfers to persons/ business	Debt charges	Grants to other govt.	Total Expend.	Surplus or Deficit (−)
1943	3,735	276	246	148	4,412	−1,795
1960	2,656	2,271	753	994	6,746	−229
1970	4,995	4,793	1,862	3,397	15,291	247
1980	14,893	22,891	9,897	12,831	61,316	−10,663
1985	24,359	41,091	24,620	21,746	114,661	−31,424
1990	31,068	48,744	41,453	26,781	152,734	−25,492
1994	32,444	55,160	40,126	30,540	168,845	−28,504
1996	30,480	54,570	45,306	27,776	169,917	−15,938

Sources: National Accounts; Statistics Canada; Canadian Tax Foundation.

TABLE 17.1

PRINCIPAL REVENUE SOURCES: FEDERAL GOVERNMENT ($ MILLIONS)

Year	Personal Income Tax	Corporate Income Tax	Other Taxes	Total Revenue
1943	630	636	973	2,469
1960	1,917	1,308	2,121	6,517
1970	6,302	2,276	5,168	15,538
1980	19,131	8,406	16,579	50,653
1985	32,141	9,560	31,479	83,237
1990	58,056	11,655	41,708	127,242
1994	58,877	12,108	54,542	140,341
1996	67,975	14,268	54,933	153,979

Sources: National Accounts; Statistics Canada; Canadian Tax Foundation.

TABLE 17.2

REVENUE AND EXPENDITURE, ALL LEVELS OF GOVERNMENT, CALENDAR YEAR 1996 ($ MILLIONS)

	Federal	Provincial	Local	Hospitals	CPP/QPP	Total
Revenue from own sources	153,979	140,403	37,400	1,575	19,796	353,153
Plus grants from other govt.		26,510	29,429	22,156		78,199
Total revenue	153,979	167,017	66,829	23,731	19,796	431,352
Expenditure for own purposes	142,141	116,249	62,925	24,194	22,070	367,579
Plus grants to other govt.		27,776	50,299	124		78,199
Total expenditure	169,917	166,548	63,049	24,194	22,070	445,778
Surplus or deficit (−)	−15,938	469	3,780	−463	−2,274	−14,426

Source: Finances of the Nation 1997.

TABLE 17.3

GENERAL GOVERNMENT REVENUE IN G-7 NATIONS AND SELECTED OTHERS (AS % OF NOMINAL GDP)

Country	1980	1990	2000*
Belgium	48.1	47.9	49.1
Canada	36.5	42.1	42.5
France	45.6	47.7	49.8
Germany	43.7	41.8	45.6
Greece	32.0	34.9	47.2
Ireland	34.1	35.0	32.9
Italy	33.5	42.1	45.9
Japan	27.6	34.2	30.5
New Zealand	—	44.0	40.3
Norway	49.3	52.3	51.4
Sweden	53.6	60.5	56.8
Switzerland	43.3	48.6	57.6
United Kingdom	—	40.3	40.3
United States	28.7	29.3	30.8

* Estimate or projection.
Source: OECD National Accounts.

TABLE 17.4

SURPLUSES OR DEFICITS (−) FOR GENERAL GOVERNMENT IN G-7 NATIONS AND SELECTED OTHERS (AS % OF NOMINAL GDP)

Country	1980	1990	2000*
Belgium	−8.6	−5.4	−0.9
Canada	−3.1	−4.5	1.6
France	0.0	−1.6	−1.7
Germany	−2.9	−2.0	−1.2
Greece	−2.6	−16.1	−1.6
Ireland	−11.7	−2.8	3.8
Italy	−8.3	−11.0	−1.6
Japan	−4.4	2.9	−7.9
New Zealand	—	−4.7	0.6
Norway	5.4	2.6	6.5
Sweden	−3.9	4.0	2.1
United Kingdom	−3.3	−1.5	0.8
United States	−2.6	−4.3	0.9

* Estimate or projection.
Source: OECD National Accounts.

TABLE 17.6

GENERAL GOVERNMENT EXPENDITURES IN G-7 NATIONS AND SELECTED OTHERS (AS % OF NOMINAL GDP)

Country	1980	1990	2000*
Belgium	56.5	53.3	50.0
Canada	39.6	46.7	40.9
France	45.6	49.3	51.5
Germany	46.5	43.8	46.8
Greece	34.5	51.0	48.7
Ireland	45.9	37.8	29.2
Italy	41.8	53.1	47.5
Japan	32.0	31.3	38.4
New Zealand	—	48.8	39.7
Norway	43.9	49.7	44.9
Sweden	57.4	56.4	54.7
Switzerland	—	41.0	50.0
United Kingdom	—	41.8	39.5
United States	31.3	33.6	29.9

* Estimate or projection.
Source: OECD National Accounts.

TABLE 17.5

UNEMPLOYMENT RATES, SELECTED OECD COUNTRIES (AS % OF TOTAL LABOUR FORCE)

Country	1980	1990	1997
Belgium	—	7.2	12.7
Canada	—	8.1	9.4
France	6.4	7.0	12.6
Germany	—	7.2	11.1
Greece	4.0	7.0	10.4
Ireland	—	12.9	10.8
Italy	7.6	11.0	12.1
Japan	2.0	2.1	3.2
New Zealand	—	7.8	6.0
Norway	1.7	5.2	4.5
Sweden	2.0	1.6	8.1
Switzerland	—	1.8	5.4
United Kingdom	—	6.8	6.1
United States	7.0	5.6	5.0

Source: World Bank Statistics.

TABLE 17.7

INFLATION RATES, SELECTED OECD COUNTRIES (AS % OF ANNUAL CPI GROWTH)

Country	1980-90	1990-97
Belgium	4.2	2.2
Canada	5.3	1.8
France	5.8	2.0
Germany	2.2	3.0
Greece	18.7	11.7
Ireland	6.8	2.2
Italy	9.1	4.5
Japan	1.7	1.0
New Zealand	10.9	2.0
Norway	7.4	2.1
Sweden	7.0	2.9
Switzerland	2.9	2.3
United Kingdom	5.8	3.0
United States	4.2	2.9

Source: World Bank Statistics.

TABLE 17.8

PER CAPITA GDP, 1997, SELECTED OECD COUNTRIES (US $)

Country	Current Exchange Rates	Current Purchasing Power Parities
Belgium	23,820	23,242
Canada	20,064	23,761
France	23,798	21,293
Germany	25,470	22,049
Greece	11,438	13,912
Ireland	21,104	20,634
Italy	19,913	21,265
Japan	33,212	24,574
New Zealand	17,272	17,846
Norway	34,815	26,771
Sweden	25,746	20,439
Switzerland	35,897	25,902
United Kingdom	21,740	20,483
United States	29,326	29,326
Mexico	4,298	7,697
Czech Republic	5,050	13,087
Hungary	4,461	9,875
Poland	3,509	7,487
Turkey	2,979	6,463

Source: World Bank Statistics.

TABLE 17.9

out inefficient or outmoded production: competition produces losers as well as winners. It may be true that "in the long run" everyone is better off, and that conditions are improved for all. But who pays the short-term costs? How short is that short term? How temporary are the human costs of paying that short-term economic cost? Consider, for example, an economic downturn—what is today called a "recession" and what used to be experienced as a "depression." Someone must pay the costs of this economic contraction as firms declare bankruptcy and close their doors, as unemployment grows and welfare rolls swell. It may be, as the economist observes, that inefficient producers are being eliminated, that surviving producers and new firms will be forced to be more efficient and that, in this way, eventually all will benefit, but who pays this cost of restructuring? Clearly the owners of the firms that close or are put into receivership lose their investment, but that is generally all they lose. At the very least they will retreat from their investments before their own survival is threatened. The employee, however, is likely to have no surplus: the wage is all that stands between her and the food bank or the unemployment line. The greater economic cost may well be borne by the employer or owner, but the more immediate and human cost is often borne by the worker. Increasing efficiency (the epitome of market rationality) may well mean fewer jobs if it involves improving technology or automation, and there is no reason that this improved efficiency will somehow necessarily result in job creation that sustains those displaced by this rationalization.

The nineteenth century offered considerable real world experience of *laissez-faire*, and it was obvious that often the condition of the working classes was not progressively improving, that often it was the poor and working classes were that most devastated by the periodic economic contractions and restructurings of the market economy. During the latter half of this same century, trade unions, working men's (and women's) associations, and socialist parties began to form and grow. In the late nineteenth century and the first decades of the twentieth century, the franchise was extended to all (or almost all) adults. In 1917, the Bolshevik Revolution put a government in power in Russia dedicated to creating a communist utopia, a classless society, and it would not be clear for some time that this effort was doomed to fail. It is not surprising, then, that reform liberalism abandoned *laissez-faire* economics in search of a political economic policy that might plausibly benefit all members of society. The pragmatic argument that moved them was something like the following.

The kind of market society that can be justified as the best available system for all will be one that can minimize the imposition of the costs of its restructurings, downturns, or modernizations on those who are least advantaged within that system under the best of conditions. This will involve action by the state and will therefore not be true to *laissez-faire* policy of maximal market autonomy and a minimal state. Something more than the minimal state may not be in the interest of producers, entrepreneurs, or investors (although it can be argued that it is), but that is a question of their economic interest, and politically these individuals are only one set of voices seeking policies conducive to their interest. From a political rather than economic standpoint and from the perspective of democracy, it is only reasonable to demand that if those least advantaged in a market society are to be expected to pay the short-term economic costs (which may entail long-term human costs) for the purported long-term benefits of improved efficiency, their consent to this payment should first be obtained. If they should have the opportunity for input on political economic questions, we would not be surprised if they support a state that manages changes in the market economy for the benefit of all, if not primarily for the least advantaged groups. As a result, in the twentieth century, in almost every advanced market economy, *laissez-faire* economic policy was exchanged for something called the **WELFARE STATE**.

17.5 IDEOLOGICAL COMPROMISE: THE WELFARE STATE

The distance travelled in the transition from *laissez-faire* capitalism to the twentieth century welfare state was enormous (although not all countries took the same path or took it so far), but it is important to understand that this transition did not challenge the *primary* reliance on the market as the allocator of resources. Nor did it challenge the private ownership of productive property or the dependence of the majority of individuals on a wage that they receive for their labour. A strong argument can be made, and has been made by supporters and critics, that the welfare state did much to preserve and strengthen the market economy in the twentieth century. The reform of capitalism entailed by the welfare state undermined the appeal of those who sought to replace private property capitalism with a collectivist alternative.

Most generally, the welfare state is an **ACTIVIST STATE**, a state intentionally involved in the economic life of the nation, that performs economic management functions with specific social and political goals in mind. Ringen (1987) emphasizes the **REDISTRIBUTIVE** character of the welfare state: its attempt to eliminate poverty and create equality through a system of taxes and transfers. This characterization is more accurate of the Scandinavian welfare states with which Ringen was most familiar than the welfare state in other states (particularly Canada and the United States).[1] By contrast, Mishra talks about the welfare state as a "three-pronged attack on want and dependency" (1990: 18), involving (a) a government commitment to **FULL EMPLOYMENT**, (b) the delivery of **UNIVERSAL SOCIAL PROGRAMS**, such as health care and education, and (c) the provision of a "safety net" of assistance for those in need, or what others have referred to as **INCOME MAINTENANCE** schemes.

Mishra sees the welfare state as the result of a postwar consensus among the interests of business, labour, and government; others—like Ringen—claim that such a consensus never

1. A transfer is a payment from government to individuals or corporations, and as such has the potential to be strongly redistributive if the class of individuals receiving transfers is largely distinct from the class of individuals paying for them through taxes and other levies. In practice, though, many transfers are universal, eliminating much of their redistributive impact.

existed, that business interests always resisted the elements of the welfare state. The truth may well be somewhere in between; a balance of political forces in the postwar period, coupled with a prolonged period of sustained economic growth, made the welfare state "affordable." Part of the difficulty here may be that the welfare state was not so much one conscious policy aim, but rather the result of countless different policy decisions, sometimes only loosely connected or co-ordinated with each other. As a result, the welfare state came in many varieties, ranging from small welfare states in the United States and Switzerland to large welfare states in France and Sweden. The "size" of welfare states is simply the share of a nation's economy that can be accounted for by government non-military activity (spending or revenue). Size, however, is relative here; in all advanced industrial democracies in the twentieth century the role played by the state with respect to the private property market economy changed significantly. The welfare state was a product of these various departures from *laissez-faire* capitalism.

One of the earliest liberal strategies was to reform the market economy through regulations. These were designed to correct the worst abuses of the capital-labour relationship or to compensate for other consequences of market activity; they did not replace that relationship or alter the fundamental nature of that activity. Many such regulations would be taken for granted today: the elimination of child labour, minimum wage laws, health and safety regulations, limits on the length of the working day. More recent (and often more controversial) regulations concern issues such as pay equity, smoke-free space, and environmental safeguards.

A second significant reform was recognition of the legitimacy of **TRADE UNIONS**, formed by workers beginning in the nineteenth century in an effort to improve their conditions within *laissez-faire* capitalism. The union aggregates the minimal power of individual labourers so that they can bargain collectively on more equitable terms with management. The trade union does not threaten or change the capitalist wage-labour relationship, but accepts it as legitimate and, in fact, strengthens it insofar as organization provides a route for grievance *within* the structure of market society. As Lenin recognized, trade union activity is not *revolutionary*, and experience has shown that unions can be very conservative organizations. Unions (like market society) do not "just happen," but require legislation and enforcement of the rights of organization, the legitimization and regulation of the collective bargaining process, and a variety of other supports from the state. Labour law varies greatly from country to country, reflecting in part differences in the strength of the working classes and in part differences in political culture. In many countries, the rise of trade unions and their eventual legal recognition occurred only after considerable and often violent struggle.

The welfare state was also a child of democracy. In the last quarter of the nineteenth century and the first quarter of the twentieth century, most societies with a developed market economy became representative democracies with full adult suffrage. A political party advocating *laissez-faire* in a representative democracy with full adult suffrage must convince a sufficient portion of the working and middle classes that the minimal state is in their best interest. In the latter half of the nineteenth century and early in the twentieth, many members of the working and middle classes had experiences that convinced them to the contrary. Extending the vote to members of the working and middle classes thus made it possible for there to be middle- or working-class parties and also made it more likely that all parties would begin to support regulation of the market economy.

The state in market societies grew significantly in the twentieth century, in part, perhaps, in response to pressures generated by representative democracy. Many circumstances and factors were involved here, from the role of the state in fighting and then rebuilding after two world wars, to the response of the state to the Depression of the 1930s, to the demand for services and the need for infrastructure created by social and technological change, which seems to have proceeded at an accelerating pace.

As important as any of these was the adoption of **KEYNESIAN** fiscal policy. Following the war and in the attempt to avoid more periods of pronounced stagnation like the Depression of the 1930s, governments in market societies adopted the fiscal policy John Maynard Keynes had recommended in *The General Theory of Employment, Interest and Money* (1936). (The very success of Keynesian and other economic management policies sometimes allows us to forget just how radical the shifts from periods of prosperity to prolonged periods of economic stagnation once were.) Keynes argued that the periodic slumps experienced by capitalism arise from a combination of overproduction and insufficient demand—that there is not enough money to keep the exchange of goods and labour in equilibrium. What Keynes proposed was the concept of **DEMAND MANAGEMENT**, whereby governments would stimulate consumer demand in slow times and put a brake

462

on its acceleration in good times, thereby evening out the cycle. Governments could accomplish both strategies by adjusting their spending and taxation. Until this time, governments' practice, apart from exigencies such as war, had been to run balanced accounts: government expenditures would equal government revenues. Keynes had proposed instead that when the economy slows down, the government should spend more money than it collects. By putting more money into the economy than is taken out, the government would stimulate flagging demand and production. It would also accumulate a deficit on its books, i.e., go into debt. Conversely, when the economy is booming, Keynes proposed that the government collect more money than it spends, thus removing demand from the system and slowing down economic expansion. The surplus accumulated in good years should erase the **DEFICITS** accumulated in lean times. To varying degrees, Western industrial nations adopted Keynes's strategy of demand management, although they often found that it was easier to accumulate deficits than surpluses.

The growth of the state with regard to the economy takes many forms, from public works programs (building highways, bridges, hydroelectric dams, etc.) to assuming ownership of companies. The increase in the size of the state has its own impact by increasing the number of employees, the scale of government purchases in the economy, and so on. Another area of economic influence by the state is the transfers it makes to citizens: income payments or the provision of goods such as health care or education. These payments are central to the welfare state, and they are made for several reasons. One is to provide relief to those who become disadvantaged, often through no fault of their own, sometimes because of the inability of the market economy to sustain them. Another is to alleviate some of the inequality the market system tends to reproduce. These payments are also a means by which governments can inject money into the economy when it stagnates. They take many forms and have come about over many decades. Like other phenomena, the welfare state varied from one advanced industrial country to another under the influence of history, political culture, and economic circumstance. The net effect of all of these developments was the creation of a significant **PUBLIC SECTOR**, which characterized all modern welfare states.

Now, whether or not Mishra is accurate in describing the welfare state as a compromise among the interests of business, labour, and the state, it is clear that in many ways the welfare state represented a compromise or even consensus among ideologies. Reform liberals, social democrats, and even market tories (or European Christian Democrats) could find reason to agree on the continued justification of the welfare state, even though they might disagree on its optimal size or on the particular programs it should encompass. Standing outside this consensus were those economic liberals (i.e., conservatives) advocating a return to the minimal state and those radical socialists (i.e., communists) still convinced that a private property market economy can and should be overthrown. While such radical socialists are difficult to find today in any great number, economic liberalism has made such a significant comeback that many observers came to see the contemporary welfare state as a state in crisis, if not a state whose day was done. As is so often the case in ideology, what shifted was the context, and the result is that a question that seemed more or less settled a few decades ago—the proper role of the state in the economy—once again became central to ideological debate.

17.6 ROLLING BACK THE WELFARE STATE

For a considerable period after World War II, the Keynesian welfare state seemed to be working; market economies were able to achieve relatively stable economic growth in conditions of relatively full employment and low inflation. At the same time government services and transfers continued to be introduced and enriched. After 1970, for a variety of reasons, the Keynesian strategy and all that was associated with it seemed to be failing. While previously there had been a trade-off between unemployment and **INFLATION**, allowing governments to tackle one of these conditions at the expense of the other, after 1970 *both* inflation and unemployment persisted (what was called "stagflation"). Behind this period of economic turmoil were the oil crisis triggered by a deliberate reduction in output by the OPEC nations, the movement of the world currency system to floating exchange rates, and the increasing shift of industrial production from developed to developing world labour markets. These and other factors led to a prolonged period of government deficits, which in turn led to ever-larger levels of accumulated indebtedness. Keynesian economics fell out of favour with economists and was replaced by **MONETARISM**. Instead of practising demand management, governments attempted to influence the rate of economic growth through their control of the money supply (hence "supply-side economics") and the use of instruments such as interest-rate policy. This meant the end of the commitment to full employment economies in favour of policies focused on fighting inflation. Until quite recently, in most advanced economies, unemployment remained high, often at double-digit levels.

While governments were no longer committed to Keynesian policies, they continued to spend more than they were raising in revenue. There was considerable debate about why deficits seemed so irreversible. Certainly governments found it difficult to cut expenditures, and the difficult economic times that arose since the mid-1970s made it more difficult to cut social welfare expenditures. The end of a full employment economy meant that more people required or were eligible for income maintenance, either through unemployment insurance or general social assistance. At the same time, in economically depressed times it is difficult to raise more revenue to match continued spending commitments. In an age of transnational corporations and increasingly free trade, it is relatively easy for wealthy individuals and corporations to move investments away from jurisdictions that impose higher taxes (or the threats of capital to move to another locale seem more plausible). The middle class came to bear an increasingly higher proportion of the tax burden, but in turn began to demonstrate its willingness to punish governments that tax too highly.

While the debate about the causes and the cures of government deficits continued, the seriousness of the mounting debt-load was increasingly recognized by left and right alike. Once upon a time, one could distinguish adherents of ideologies by their attitude towards deficits, fiscal conservatives (economic liberals) abhorring them and reform liberals and social democrats dismissing them as short-term expedients that could be paid down at some point in the future (presumably once the economy turned around). The practical problem with sustained deficits is that governments must at least meet interest payments on the debt they have accumulated over the years. As the level of this debt rises, the interest payments consume an ever larger portion of government expenditure, inhibiting the ability of governments to pay for the policies to which they are committed. More and more government revenue goes to pay bondholders and other investors from whom governments have borrowed, and proportionately less is spent on services or transfers to the public. This situation compelled even reform liberals and democratic socialists who still might be committed to Keynesianism in principle to question the ability of governments to continue to finance deficits.

Given the difficulty governments experienced in trying to increase revenues, deficit reduction or elimination appeared to require reductions in government spending. This meant reducing the size of the public sector, cutting back or eliminating government programs, or reducing government transfers. The fiscal crisis that many states experienced placed the continued shape (if not existence) of the welfare state in question. In the debate about how to downsize government and about the impact of this exercise on the welfare state, competing ideologies collided.

Fiscal conservatives found in the mounting debt of governments ammunition for their argument that the welfare state ought to be dismantled. The so-called neo-conservative revolution of the Thatcher and Reagan decade (the 1980s) was premised on this basis (although government deficits rose under the Reagan administration, largely because of military outlays). Many elements of the Gingrich Republicans' "Contract with America" (mid-1990s) involved a rolling back of the public sector (and we need to remember that among developed nations, the United States has always had one of the smallest public sectors). Liberals who once participated in the design and expansion of the welfare state began to discuss the need to reform the welfare state, to redesign programs, to "do more with less." At one point, the only defence of the postwar welfare state as it had come to be known came from the left, from democratic socialists or social democrats. A generation earlier these groups would have argued that the welfare state did not go far enough in redressing inequalities created by a market economy. Most recently, even socialists, when in power, have found themselves holding the line or cutting back on government expenditures. The so-called "Third Way" of Tony Blair and other contemporary social democrats has involved a serious rethinking of the assumptions behind the welfare state. To a large degree the question that dominated throughout most of the twentieth century—"how large the state?"—seemed to become "how small the state?"

It is difficult, perhaps, to appreciate today that for much of the twentieth century the question was "whether markets?"—a question that experience and history seem to have answered resoundingly in the affirmative. Today the question seems more along the lines of "whither markets?"—in other words, what shape will market society take in the coming years, what political challenges will this raise, and how will they be resolved? How will the relationship of the state to the economy be defined? Conservatives and conservative liberals will argue for more market autonomy. This is not necessarily the demand for a classic *laissez-faire* economy with a minimal state; in the present realities this may not even be feasible, let alone desirable, and many (but by no means all) supporters of market autonomy recognize this. Their concern is rather to generate more autonomy, less government activity, less regulation, less extensive or expensive social programs, and, as a result of all these reductions in the role of the state, to create greater investment and greater opportunities for investors. The justification for this increase in market autonomy continues to hinge on the claim that all will benefit from this autonomy, if not equally, then at least in ways substantial enough in the long term to justify hardship in the short term. The evidence to support this claim is, at the least, rather thin. Moreover, while the current economic orthodoxy appears to be for a less rather than more active state, signalled particularly by the commitment to "free" or "unmanaged" trade and the creation of larger common markets, some supporters of market capitalism (particularly outside the English-speaking world) still believe in the continued viability (if not necessity) of promoting a national economy through an active state. Here the emphasis is not on market autonomy, but on market support.

For another group, too, the solution is not less government activity but an activist role for the state in economic management. This may mean an emphasis on job creation through public works, or increased regulation of the economy, or expanding the network of social services, or even government ownership of key sectors of the economy. Here, too, the justification is the belief that in this way the power of the state can provide economic opportunity, if not equality, for everyone, and only in this expanded role can the state counter the tendencies of the market to generate inequality and frustrate opportunities.

Finally, there are those who do not call for an expansion of the state's activity but for a refinement or redefinition of that role with respect to the market. This may mean neither abandoning nor expanding social programs, but redesigning them to meet the double end of serving those in need without needlessly expending resources. For a country such as Canada, the future may involve drawing on the experience of such countries as Germany and Japan, where the role of the state is much more closely linked to participation by both business and labour interests in shaping policy goals and in implementing programs to meet the challenges of a changing world. On the other hand, the nature of labour itself is changing so much that the status of the trade union may soon be in as much doubt as the status of the activist welfare state.

The ultimate question remains: who benefits from the shape of the state that comes after the welfare state?

**17.7
AFTER THE
WELFARE STATE?**

At the beginning of 2000, the recent political climate (in North America certainly, but also in parts of Europe and Australasia) has favoured those who sought to roll back the welfare state. This is in part because of the general acceptance that continued deficit financing and ever-increasing accumulated debt are unacceptable, in part also because politicians have been able to capitalize on "tax fatigue," and in part because of a resentment of the disadvantaged or non-working poor by the working middle class. These last two are related and require some further explanation.

As noted, a large portion of the tax burden was shifted in the last quarter of the twentieth century from wealthy individuals and corporations to the middle class. For this reason, tax cuts have often been a winning strategy for neo-conservative politicians and a populist plank for election campaigns. While such cuts appeal to the taxpaying working and middle classes, the irony is that in many cases the bulk of the benefit has been enjoyed by the upper-middle and upper classes. One rationale offered for this upward redistribution of wealth is that it puts more money in the hands of those likely to invest it productively and thereby stimulate economic growth, higher employment, etc. There is considerable dispute over whether this happens, and much evidence suggests the contrary—Canadians need merely remember the "jobless recovery" of the much of the 1990s. There is every reason to believe that the real reason for tax cuts is not to put money in the hands of taxpayers, but to force the state to shrink and to make it difficult for it to grow in the future. A tax cut in an age weary of deficits *forces* government downsizing, and in particular focuses attention on the government spending programs associated with the welfare state.

In most welfare states, these spending programs can be divided into two categories (Mishra, 1990): universal social services such as education and health care, which, by definition, benefit all or all can claim; and income maintenance programs, targeted at those least advantaged within society. In most cases, and contrary to what seems elementary fairness or justice, the immediate target for spending reductions has been the income maintenance programs that support the most disadvantaged. It is difficult to escape the conclusion that this segment is targeted because it is the most politically marginal portion of the electorate, less likely to vote, and in all likelihood less likely to vote for the party cutting their supports. The rationalization of this strategy takes many forms: arguing that the need of this segment is exaggerated, or that their benefits are too generous, or that high numbers of the poor are simply "taking advantage of the system" in one way or another. While the evidence for all these claims is slight (or dubious), it is often compelling enough to those working- and middle-class taxpayers who resent the apparent existence of a lazy or undeserving underclass supported by state transfers. In many jurisdictions the levels of social assistance have been reduced, unemployment insurance programs have been made more stringent, and workfare has been introduced.[2]

In many cases, however, the demand for smaller government moved on from income maintenance to the universal social services at the heart of the welfare state. Education and health care are the two largest areas of such expenditure, and these areas are more politically sensitive and hence difficult to cut: the constituency that benefits from and identifies with these programs is much broader and better organized than the disadvantaged on social assistance. Here, a tax cut may provide the sugar-coating to make the bitter pills of cutbacks more palatable.

As noted earlier, Ringen suggested that the purpose of the welfare state was redistribution, which, along with eliminating poverty, would create greater economic equality. It is not accidental that Ringen is a Swede, for the Swedish welfare state is the world's most extensive and came closest to meeting this characterization. In most other welfare states, while poverty may have been diminished, there is little evidence that equality was created; in Canada the data are quite clear that the welfare state tended to stabilize the distribution of wealth. The share of income of the bottom and top quintiles changed little between 1957 and 1987. Interestingly, though, in every country in which the welfare state has been rolled back through tax and spending reductions, thus moving back in the direction of the minimal state, there has been an increase in inequality, a polarization with significant implications. It is no accident that this has happened; from the time of Adam Smith it has been understood that a market economy, left unregulated, tends to redistribute wealth upward. This should not be surprising, since those with capital and income will be better positioned to take advantage of economic opportunities than

2. Interestingly, those who believe that people on welfare should be put to work for their benefits are often those who express a concern for child poverty and profess the belief that children should be raised by their mothers; in fact, in most jurisdictions the majority of social assistance recipients are children under the age of eighteen, a large proportion of whom are being raised by a single parent, almost always the mother.

KEY TERMS

authoritative allocation
bourgeoisie
business cycle
capitalism
command economy
consumer society
deficits
demand management
distribution
economic nationalism
fiscal policy
full employment
income maintenance
inflation
Keynesianism
laissez-faire
market
market autonomy
market society
market support
means of production
minimal state
monetarism
monetary policy
political economy
private property
proletariat
public property
redistribution
regulation
social programs
supply management
tax fatigue
trade union
transactions
transfers
welfare state
workfare

those without, better able to purchase the expertise or services that will help them maintain and augment their economically privileged positions. No natural mechanism within the market is going to halt this upward accumulation of wealth. To some degree, and in some countries more than in others, the welfare state balanced this upward transfer of wealth by the market with the redistributive impact of income maintenance and universal social programs. In a few countries such as Norway and Sweden this may have led to greater socio-economic equality; in most countries it kept existing inequalities from widening. As the redistributive programs of the welfare state have been downsized, reformed, or eliminated, the consequence has been an increasing inequality within almost all advanced industrial societies, a development that should be of surprise to no one. The more important question is whether it should be a development that no one (or no politically significant number) finds alarming?

A society that becomes more unequal also becomes more fragmented and, in the long term, less stable politically; crime becomes a more common response to social and economic despair. It is tempting to think that political equality (i.e., democracy) provides a natural feedback mechanism; that is, that those who are disadvantaged by increasing inequality will be able to use their right to vote to pressure political parties for policies that will heal division, address inequities, and meet basic needs universally. There are two flaws with this. One, as we have seen throughout much of this text, is the incomplete character of the democracy citizens inhabit, particularly in those countries without proportional representation and in those countries where corporate interests have an undue influence over the political process or where the political process lacks the ability (or the will) to provide citizens with the kinds of serious information they need to make informed, meaningful choices. The second flaw is to imagine that political equality can persist (if it could ever exist) in the face of economic inequality. Modern politics does not come cheaply, and those with resources will usually manage much better than those without in shaping (if not controlling) the political agenda.

On the other hand, just as the pendulum swung since the mid-1970s towards neo-conservatism, the elimination of Keynesian policies, and the downsizing of the postwar welfare state, the very "successes" of this shift to the right may lead it eventually to swing in the other direction. In Canada and the U.S., the federal governments of each and a majority of the provinces and states have moved from budget deficits into surplus positions. While the

470

accumulated debt of these governments remains to be reduced, it is also true that as the economy grows that debt will shrink as a share of each jurisdiction's wealth; it will be easier to finance that accumulated debt even as it is being eliminated. We have reached the stage, in most of North America at least, where governments are no longer constrained by deficits and debt in the way they have been for the previous two decades. This also creates the possibility that the question "how small the state?" can become "how small *or large* the state?" The debate is already engaged between those who call for tax reductions and those who advocate renewed government activity.

There is no reason to think that the state of tomorrow will or even should look like the postwar welfare state. It is possible, though, to consider that in an age where governments are not constrained by fiscal realities, they will be constrained more by the political forces at work within their environment. It is not unreasonable to expect that those who have been disadvantaged or inconvenienced by government cutbacks and program reductions will agitate for more rather than less government activity. Certainly, public opinion surveys have shown that Canadians continue to place a premium on strong government funding of health care and education. In some quarters it also has been evident for a long time that an "infrastructure deficit" has accumulated; roads, sanitation systems, bridges and canals, and other products of public works programs in the 1930s, 1940s, and 1950s need renewal and augmentation that will cost hundreds of billions of dollars.

It may be that many citizens will prefer to pay less taxes to government than to receive more services. On the other hand, public goods such as health care and education address real needs, and it may not be so obvious to many that these services can be provided for privately in an adequate or equitable fashion. A very real consideration is the reality that we live in community with others. We may well judge that a community in which all are whole, healthy, and have an adequate opportunity at happiness is preferable to one in which some have these basic goods at the expense of others. In a democracy, it is always legitimate for the people to turn to the government to solve those problems for which there appears no private solution. In the "age of deficits," economics managed to assert its primacy over politics; whether economics or politics or citizens are in control in the time after deficits yet remains to be seen. Much of the makeover of contemporary government that has accompanied the shift from times of deficit financing to today's surpluses has been possible because

REFERENCES AND SUGGESTED READING

Friedman, Milton. 1963. *Capitalism and Freedom*. Chicago: University of Chicago Press.

Galbraith, John Kenneth. 1973. *Economics and the Public Purpose*. Boston: Houghton Mifflin.

Heilbroner, Robert L. 1970. *Between Capitalism and Socialism*. New York: Random House.

Howe, Irving, ed. 1982. *Beyond the Welfare State*. New York: Schocken Books.

Howlett, Michael, Alex Netherton, and M. Ramesh. 1999. *The Political Economy of Canada: An Introduction*, 2nd ed. Toronto: Oxford University Press.

Lindblom, Charles. 1979. *Politics and Markets*. New York: Basic Books.

List, Friedrich. 1837. *The National System of Political Economy*.

Marx, Karl. 1849. *Wage Labour and Capital*.

Mishra, Ramesh. 1990. *The Welfare State in Capitalist Society*. Toronto: University of Toronto Press.

Novack, Michael. 1982. *The Spirit of Democratic Capitalism*. New York: Simon & Shuster.

Ringen, Stein. 1987. *The Possibility of Politics*. Oxford: Clarendon Press.

Schumpeter, Joseph A. 1962. *Capitalism, Socialism, and Democracy*. New York: Harper & Row.

Smith, Adam. 1776. *The Wealth of Nations*.

of one of the longest periods of sustained economic growth in North America. No one can say how long that will last, and only a very few believe that the cyclical nature of private property market economies has been made a thing of the past. Once economic recession returns, all the answers about the relationship between the state and markets, which have seemed so settled in the past 10 years, will once again become questions.

SOMETHING TO CONSIDER

Conservative critics will argue that the welfare state has survived quite well, especially when one considers how little government expenditures have shrunk, if at all, in most of the countries concerned. Has the rhetoric about "less government" been just that? Is the significant fact not the shrinking of the state but the end of its growth? Who is benefiting from the state's expenditures today? What conclusions can you draw from the various statistical tables presented in this chapter?

VI
concluding

18
politics in a global context

For the most part, discussion in the preceding chapters has been about what happens *within* nation-states and about the relationships between peoples and their states. We have, from time to time, made note of the wider world and of how forces quite diverse in character, collected under the heading of **GLOBALIZATION**, have impact upon us and throw up new challenges to nations and to governments. There is no turning back; the days of a people quietly going about their business and choosing to avoid or refusing to engage the rest of the world are gone for all but a few isolated societies (and whether this means they are blessed or accursed is another matter altogether). The extreme reaction from governments around the world to the inclusion of Joerg Haider's Freedom Party in the Austrian coalition government in early 2000 is just one example of how anybody's business is now considered everybody's business.

Ten years ago, few were using the term "globalization"; today it is employed to explain almost everything. To the degree that intra- or international forces *do* increasingly make a difference to the quality of our lives, it is only natural and appropriate that the attention of the media, of academics, and of political activists has turned "outward." Nothing to date symbolizes this more, perhaps, than the scope of the protests that accompanied the meetings of the World Trade Organization in Seattle in late 1999. One overriding message that protestors brought to the streets was their dissatisfaction with losing control of their lives to unaccountable global organizations and corporations. Perhaps implicit in that reaction was the recognition that those who pay no attention to the changing nature of global politics risk giving control over the decisions that will shape their lives to strangers. The degree to

18.1
INTRODUCTION

18.1   Introduction
18.2   The "End" of Empire?
18.3   Haves and Have-Nots
18.4   A Clash of Civilizations or a Convergence of Cultures?
18.5   Sovereignty, Security, Sustainability
18.6   Conclusion: Smashing the Crystal Ball

475

which we do this already *within* our political communities is surely bad enough.

This chapter is no substitute for a good course in international relations, or developing world studies, or international political economy, but it is an attempt to provide an overview of issues that are and will continue to be shaping the changing world within which nation-states and their citizens hope to flourish.

**18.2
THE "END" OF EMPIRE?**

In the 1960s, maps were still commonly in use in which pink-coloured countries were (or once were) portions of the British Empire, green represented those large parts of Africa still under French control, and so on. The twentieth century began with a world divided among empires, and only at its end did it become a world in which formal imperialism seemed finally dead. World War I was a struggle born of imperialist rivalries and ambitions among European powers, and it has been suggested that this contest only really ended in 1989. For the first half of the twentieth century, until the end of World War II, empires were the remnants of European colonialism in the preceding 300 years or so. After 1945 there was a significant **DECOLONIZATION** as former colonies in Indochina, Africa, and Latin America forcefully claimed or were granted their independence. The member states of the United Nations numbered 50 in 1945, and rose to 116 in 1965 and 185 by 1995 (Kelleher and Klein, 1999: 12).

At the same time, in the post-World War II era, empire was re-created on a new basis symbolized by the partition of Europe and the creation of the Iron Curtain dividing the allies of the United States on the one side from the satellites and allies of the Soviet Union on the other. The **COLD WAR** was a sustained period of superpower rivalry that led to a nuclear **ARMS RACE** and shaped the economic, political, and social priorities of these countries and their allies for almost 40 years. It also gave us the terms **FIRST WORLD** (the industrial democracies allied with the United States), **SECOND WORLD** (the U.S.S.R. and its allies), and the **THIRD WORLD** (encompassing all the **DEVELOPING WORLD** nations that, in theory, were aligned with neither bloc). One says "in theory" because in the so-called Third World some of the most intense competition between the superpowers occurred, each attempting to expand its sphere of influence and, where possible, to establish **CLIENT STATES** willing to do its bidding on strategic matters. The actual interests of the developing world peoples were often missing from the equation.

It is difficult to appreciate from today's vantage point the impact of the Cold War on the politics of nation-states in the decades of the 1950s, 1960s, and 1970s, impact not just because of what items were moved to the head of the political agenda but also because of those left off the list altogether. The arms race diverted billions of dollars to military spending, and, as a result, had various other consequences of a social, political, and economic nature. Already by the end of the 1950s, President Eisenhower warned of the pernicious consequences of the development of a "military-industrial complex" in the United States. One could debate endlessly whether the resources dedicated to the space program and to the development of ever more sophisticated weaponry were actually a boon to the American economy, providing a steady source of demand that helped counter the normal fluctuations of the business cycle and generating any number of technological spinoffs that found their application in the consumer economy. On the other hand, it is tempting to wonder about the degree to which it might really have been possible to eradicate poverty and inequality and make advances in medicine had the same resources been devoted to social programs and non-military research. Conversely, the arms race placed a very different and proportionately larger burden on the Soviet Union, which came out of World War II in much worse shape than the U.S. Had the Soviet Union been able to turn the resources it spent on military production and maintenance to the production of consumer goods instead, the fate of the Communist command economy might have turned out quite differently. By the same token, had there been no Cold War, development in the Third World might have come about at a very different pace and with very different outcomes than the largely unstable, often corrupt, and largely ineffectual governments in place in too many of these countries for much of the postwar period.

The point of these observations is not to play the game of the history that might have been, but to point to the fact that empire is rarely, if ever, beneficial for the conquered or colonized, and is often of dubious benefit to the conquerors and colonizers. The popular overthrow of Communist governments in Eastern Europe and the Soviet Union and the dissolution of the latter into its component republics have seemingly put an end to the bipolar world of capitalist and communist blocs. Whatever the differences remaining between these states on a variety of issues, all First and formerly Second World nation-states are now at least formally committed to market economies and democracy, and it is said that market economy democracies do not go to war with one another. The end of the Cold War has left the United States as the one dominant superpower, a position that might lead many of its traditional opponents to worry about the possibility of the U.S. asserting its power to establish a position of world dominance or hegemony. While this view overlooks a number of important factors, such as the increasing political unity of a growing European Union, the modernizing economy and military of China, and the emergence of nuclear players such as India, Pakistan, Israel, and perhaps Iraq or Iran, two other conditions make this less likely. One is the strong strain of isolationism in the American political culture—the very real opposition to involvement in engagements where U.S. interests are not clearly and immediately threatened. The other is the growing dominance of American economic and cultural power, which makes military and political dominance seem less necessary in and of itself.

One theme of this text has been that power comes in different forms. In modern, non-totalitarian, non-authoritarian states, there is always a mix of public and private power. We have noted that within the nation-state, a minimal or diminished state makes room for an expanded or growing sphere of private power. This was the imperative that led to the creation of liberal states in the first place: to restrict the absolute power of monarchies and thereby create a safe space for an emerging market economy to grow and flourish. When the state weakens or retreats, the dominant forces in civil society advance. This may well be beneficial to all, but if private power is concentrated among only a few, or in the wrong hands, then it may well be as capable of oppression and injustice as any unaccountable public authority. History might judge the rise of the commercial and enterprising classes in Britain after the Glorious Revolution as a progressive and beneficial development (although the displaced agrarian and exploited urban classes might have disagreed); current wisdom is that the ascendancy of organized crime in contemporary Russia is pernicious to the survival of democracy and the maturation of a market system in that country. On this basis, then, the absence of political or military empire in today's world should not blind us to the possibility of other kinds of empire, particularly the economic and cultural empires that lie within and are being forged within the phenomena associated with *globalization*.

The term "globalization" has been given a broad range of definitions, but they all suggest the internationalizing of human activity across a broad spectrum of fields in ways that ignore or transcend nation-state borders. Less and less of the world is remote to us, whether in communications or travel, or politically, socially, and culturally. Many factors have contributed to or are part of globalization:

- an international monetary system of flexible exchange rates;
- movement towards freer trade;
- continued growth of multinational corporations;
- the expanding application of digital communications technologies;
- a steady pattern of corporate mergers and consolidations;
- the growth of multinational and international governmental and non-governmental organizations; and
- the development of a truly global mass media.

The phrase we used previously, that "anybody's business is everybody's business," is a handy metaphor for understanding the result of globalization and also for the ambivalence that many have towards this set of phenomena. Does the spread of technology and knowledge to every corner of the earth hold the promise of eradicating disease, poverty, exploitation, and misery? Or does it threaten to commodify everything, to make all interaction nothing more than a subspecies of commerce? The Internet, which more than anything is *the* technology of globalization, attracts the same uncertainty: is this a powerful tool for the spread of information and knowledge that can be put to progressive purposes, or is it increasingly just another medium of entertainment, another form of marketplace? Some of the specifically political issues generated by a wider awareness of the pace of globalization are discussed in the next three sections.

The first issue is whether the direction in which the contemporary world is headed is shared by all. Despite rhetoric to the contrary, the peoples who are involved in the new information economy and its bounty are the most economically, educationally, and technologically advantaged. There are literally millions of people who have never used a telephone, let alone a modem connection. The World Wide Web is very much a "First

18.3 HAVES AND HAVE-NOTS

World" Wide Web. There are enormous gaps in income and other resources between the developed and developing nations, the "haves" and "have-nots," and there are growing gaps within most nations, developing and developed alike, between the rich and the poor. "From 1960 to 1991, the richest 20% of the world's population increased their share of total global wealth from 70% to 85%, while the poorest 20% saw their global share fall from a meagre 2.3% to a disgraceful 1.4%. By 1991 more than 85% of the world's population received only 15% of its income" (Keegan, 1996).

Table 18.1 shows, for selected countries, various ways of measuring the distribution of income or inequality/equality. Columns A and B show the 1998 per capita income measured in purchasing power parity (PPP) and the rank of each country (out of a total of 210). Differences would be even more pronounced using nominal GDP (Switzerland = $40,080; Sierra Leone = $140); PPP adjusts for different costs of living and per capita income in international dollars. As is stands, the per capita income in the U.S. is 75 times that in Sierra Leone. Within the developed world, the top national income is about twice that of the bottom; among developing countries the difference is about 35 times.

Column C presents the **GINI COEFFICIENT**, which measures the distribution of wealth within a country. With perfectly equal distribution the Gini value is 0; with maximum inequality its value is 100. The lowest values in the world are in some of the most developed welfare states (Norway, Sweden, Belgium, Germany) and in Poland. Gini numbers also indicate that developing world countries are not only poor but have some of the most unequal distributions of wealth. It is one thing to note that the average per capita income in Mali is $720, another to imagine that over half this income is received by the richest 20 per cent of the population. This lowers the average annual income for the other 80 per cent to $396. Note, too, that among the developed countries the United States has the highest Gini value, indicating the most unequal distribution of wealth.

Column D expresses the societal inequality in a less abstract way, expressing the ratio of the income of the wealthiest 10 per cent to that of the poorest 10 per cent. Thus the wealthiest 10 per cent (or decile) of Americans have 19 times as much income as the poorest 10 per cent. By comparison, the top decile of Norwegians have only five times as much income as the poorest decile. As the Gini numbers predict, the distance between richest and poorest deciles is even greater (as a rule) in the developing countries than

MEASURING THE DISTRIBUTION OF INCOME AND EQUALITY, SELECTED COUNTRIES

Country	Per Capita Income (PPP)	World Rank	Gini	Ratio% of national income (top 10% to bottom 10%)	Bottom Quintile	Top Quintile
	A	B	C	D	E	F
United States	29,340	3	40.1	19.0	4.8	45.2
Switzerland	26,620	7	36.1	9.9	7.4	43.5
Norway	24,290	8	25.2	5.2	10.0	35.3
Canada	24,050	9	31.5	8.5	7.5	39.3
Belgium	23,480	12	25.0	5.5	9.5	34.5
France	22,320	17	32.7	10.0	7.2	40.1
Netherlands	21,620	19	31.5	8.5	8.0	39.9
Germany	20,810	20	28.1	6.1	9.0	37.1
United Kingdom	20,640	22	32.6	10.3	7.1	39.8
Italy	20,200	24	31.2	8.2	7.6	38.9
Sweden	19,480	27	25.0	5.4	9.6	34.5
Ireland	18,340	30	35.9	11.0	6.7	42.9
Spain	16,060	38	32.5	9.0	7.5	40.3
Chile	12,890	53	56.5	32.9	3.5	61.0
Mexico	8,190	71	53.7	30.6	3.6	58.2
South Africa	6,990	79	59.3	41.7	2.9	64.8
Poland	6,740	83	27.2	5.5	9.3	36.6
Ecuador	4,630	100	46.6	16.3	4.2	55.7
Russia	3,950	110	48.0	26.7	4.2	52.8
Philippines	3,540	122	42.9	14.0	5.9	49.6
China	3,220	119	41.5	14.0	5.5	47.5
Bolivia	2,820	140	42.0	13.8	5.6	48.2
India	1,700	163	29.7	6.1	9.2	39.3
Gambia	1,430	174	47.8	25.1	4.4	52.8
Bangladesh	1,100	188	28.3	5.8	9.4	37.9
Burkina Faso	1,020	191	48.2	18.0	5.5	55.0
Mali	720	204	50.5	22.4	4.6	56.2
Ethiopia	500	208	40.0	11.2	7.1	47.7
Sierra Leone	390	210	62.9	87.2	1.1	63.4

Source: World Bank Development Indicators database, as of July 1, 1999, at: http:/www/worldbank.org

FIGURE 18.1

in most developed world societies. One might even suggest that the United States has the distribution curve of a developing world state, not that of a mature developed world economy.

Finally, Columns E and F show the proportions of income for the bottom and top **QUINTILES** in each country. Quintiles represent a 20 per cent slice of the population, once it has been sorted by income from top to bottom. If, for example, there were perfect equality of income, the share of income of each quintile would be 20.0 per cent. It is easy to see the degree of inequality by assessing how far each quintile falls above or below this 20 per cent mark. Patterns here are similar to those observed in the other measures. The bottom quintile has the largest share of income in the developed countries with large welfare states, but even here, the highest (in Norway) is no more than 10 per cent. By contrast, the top quintile has no less than 34 per cent in all states, and in the developing world is often above 50 per cent. Once again, the United States has the lowest value for the bottom quintile in the developed world and the highest value for the top quintile.

One factor contributing to the growth of inequality in advanced post-industrial societies is the reduction in social programs and other redistributive activities associated with the welfare state. Technology and the skill sets necessary to exploit technology and turn it to advantage are more likely to be available to those with economic resources than to those without. This will be true in all societies, rich and poor alike. Those lacking education (and the accompanying motivations that education can provide) may well access new technologies mainly for entertainment or leisure purposes. For this segment of society, the new technologies of globalization are more significant in structuring their consumption than their production. And if the unequal parcelling of the benefits of new technology is true within the developed nation-states, it is even more characteristic of the effects of globalization as measured *between* nation-states:

> globalization has meant increased integration for the Organization for Economic Cooperation and Development (OECD) countries, yet this process has also involved increasing marginalization of a number of Third World countries or parts of countries. Integration in the core and fragmentation of large parts of the periphery have gone hand in hand." (Holm and Sørensen, 1995: 1)

Similarly, Lopez, Smith, and Pagnucco (1995: 36) note that:

> States in the North and West, with strong economies and functioning democracies, will reap the economic benefits of globalization and realize the social and political rewards of transnational movements.... But for many people in Southern states, with limited resources, lesser development, and no democratic

political tradition, the prospect of enjoying equal benefits will grow more remote.

One of the consistent challenges in the second half of the twentieth century was (as it continues to be) the development of the developing world. The difficult questions as to *how* to accomplish this are made more intractable by confusion over the best answer to a prior query: what *is* "development"? Is development about how to turn developing world countries into advanced industrial societies, or is it about eliminating disease, squalid living conditions, and exploitation by private or political power, and about providing basic levels of education, health care, and economic subsistence?

To answer either yes or no to the first question (that development means becoming a Western market democracy) invites criticism. To affirm the proposition is to be open to the charge of "Eurocentrism" or more simply "imperialism," imposing Western standards on developing world states. Moreover, the record so far seems to suggest that apart from a few newly industrializing countries, catching up to the West is simply not very likely in the foreseeable future for less-developed countries. And if it were, what would be the impact of the accompanying levels of consumption and production on the environment? These and other considerations suggest that if greater global equality is to be attained it will require as much change on the part of the developed countries as it will from the developing states. On the other hand, to reject the ideas of modernization and marketization for these states can be seen as simply an excuse to continue the unequal relations by which the developed nations not only control a disproportionate share of the world's resources, but also exploit whatever share the developing world has. In a similar vein, those states that have for decades contributed with their pollution to the changing world environment are hardly in a position to say to the developing world that its economic development is unsustainable. If, as the second question posed above suggests, development is about providing the tools and knowledge necessary to ensure the provision of a certain quality of life, regardless of ultimate economic or political destination, how is this to be brought about?

Three perspectives have tended to dominate thinking on the problem of "underdevelopment" in the Third World. Two of these share the ultimate goal of creating modern industrial/post-industrial societies, but differ on the means necessary to achieve this. **LIBERAL** economists argue for opening developing world economies to the discipline and creative incentives of the competitive marketplace. Developing countries need to create the conditions that will attract foreign investment, lead to the growth of exports (specifically in those commodities or products in which the country has a comparative advantage), and stimulate private entrepreneurship. In many cases, outside assistance to these nations has been conditional on the implementation of market-friendly policies. Large-scale aid is not so much delivered country-to-country these days, but through international organizations like the World Bank and the International Monetary Fund (IMF). The latter, in particular, requires recipients of aid to accept conditions premised on liberal economic theory.

The liberal economic approach to development has been criticized because it skews policies and priorities in ways that may be detrimental to the immediate needs of the people in less-developed countries. Gearing agriculture to export production rather than meeting basic subsistence needs, downsizing state bureaucracy in ways that eliminate social development, and privatization that concentrates resources in the hands of an economic elite are examples of policies that impose short-term pain in the prospect (and it is only a prospect) of longer-term gain.

The adherents of **DEPENDENCY THEORY** and the advocates of **SUSTAINABLE DEVELOPMENT** agree with these criticisms of liberal theory but would go further, and each approach champions different solutions. Dependency theory points to the unequal relationship between the developed and developing countries and suggests that a so-called "free" market system simply continues to bring benefits to the developed world at the expense of the developing. In economic terms, this follows from the notion that for market competition to be beneficial, it must occur between relatively equal competitors; in the real world, opening developing world economies to foreign investment and market competition only perpetuates the dependency of the "third" world on the "first." In political terms, this is sometimes referred to as **NEO-COLONIALISM**.

Dependency theorists argue, then, that countries of the developing world need to use the power of the state to compensate for their disadvantaged position within the world economy. This essentially means a variety of interventions in the market, that is, the provision of economic and social programs designed to supplement the market system. Subsidizing local producers to compete more effectively, using tariffs to protect domestic markets, and employing tax policies that favour national over foreign entrepreneurs are examples of possible strategies that do not necessarily oppose a market system but attempt to turn it to the advantage of the developing state. In some respects, the programs that dependency theory promotes bear more resemblance to the economic ideas of Friedrich List than to those of Adam Smith (discussed in Chapter 17).

The adherents of **SUSTAINABLE DEVELOPMENT** share the antipathy of dependency theorists to international economic liberalism, but also reject the dependency theorists' belief that marketization and industrialization are necessarily good for developing world countries. From this perspective, development means providing people with the tools and knowledge to be able to meet their basic needs in a sustainable way. It means improving agricultural practices in order to feed families; improving literacy, schooling, and basic knowledge of hygiene, health care, and family planning; using technologies that are compatible with the level of education, local infrastructure, and labour force.

This approach to development is carried out at the micro rather than the macro level, and it is implemented through local projects. Its goal is not economic growth, but to meet human needs, regardless of the ultimate success or failure of any attempts to become integrated into world markets (and most advocates of this kind of development are sceptical about the ability of developing world countries to achieve that integration). In this respect, notwithstanding the goal of sustainability, its attention is on the immediate and short term: improving people's lives now, not imposing more hardship on them for the prospect of future progress. Sustainable local projects that meet people's immediate needs are the actual means by which many (if not most) **NON-GOVERNMENTAL ORGANIZATIONS** (NGOs) carry out their work in the developing world. The criticism that will be brought against this approach is not that it doesn't work, for there are countless success stories, but that it is necessarily small-scale and doesn't provide the means of improving the lives of a country's entire population the way that systemic economic change might.

There are no easy answers to the problems posed by global inequality and the challenges of development, nor is it an option for those in the affluent countries simply to ignore these difficult challenges as insoluble. Globalization teaches us daily that what happens elsewhere, almost anywhere in the world, has the potential to impact on our lives here, wherever here happens to be.

18.4
A CLASH OF
CIVILIZATIONS OR A
CONVERGENCE OF
CULTURES?

For many, the increasing globalization of trade, the penetration of technology to and through all societies, and the shrinking of space and time through modern means of communication, information, and transportation point to an erasure of differences, a harmonization of ways of life and of practices, and perhaps even to the kind of world community implied in McLuhan's phrase "a global village." Against this, some (see Huntington, 1997) stress the continued relevance of cultural difference, indeed, not just its relevance but its ability to divide, oppose, and ultimately engage peoples in conflict. As Huntington has argued, modernization and Westernization are different things: technological adaptation is not the same as cultural colonization—or is it? The jury is still out, and the clash between materialist and idealist explanations seems as old as thought itself.

Our focus throughout this text has been the societies and institutions of **LIBERAL DEMOCRACY**, for the simple reason that this is the political environment of our readers. This means, of course, that much of the material covered here has a limited applicability: to the countries of Western Europe; to the "new world" states of Australia, Canada, New Zealand, and the United States; and in some respects to Israel, Japan, and states re-emerging from authoritarian rule into democracy, such as Chile and Argentina. What these countries share is stable systems of representative democracy, a commitment to liberal notions of justice such as the rule of law and the protection of individual rights, and advanced market economies aptly described in many (though not all) cases as "post-industrial" rather than industrial. To varying degrees, these societies endorse individualism and the freedoms associated with the individual; they are generally pluralistic, tolerant societies rooted (Israel and Japan excepted) in a Christian tradition that in many cases has been transformed into post-Christian secularism. This is a description, not a justification or an endorsement of any of the particulars of liberal democracy or of the package as a whole.

The differences within these countries on any one of these variables may often be considerable, but differences between these countries and others are greater still; what they have in common remains considerable and significant. Obviously, the nature and politics of these societies have great import for those living within their borders. The really big question, and one to which we keep returning, is whether they have any relevance for the rest of the world. After all, the countries we have included amount to less than 15 per cent of the world's nation-states. Their share of the world's population is about 14 per cent and declining. Their share of the world's wealth (measured in gross domestic product) is close to 80 per cent and rising. (According to World Bank figures, the combined GDP of the G-7 countries—the U.S., Japan, Germany, France, Italy, Britain, and Canada—accounted for two-thirds of world GDP in the early 1990s.)

For whatever reasons, liberal democratic countries have represented the conjunction of a certain type of politics—liberal and democratic—with a certain kind of economic system—private property, (post-)industrial market capitalism. (In more general terms, these societies have generally been characterized by a level of material affluence that, apart from oil-exporting countries and a few micro-states, has been attained only by advanced capitalist economies. The dream of nineteenth-century socialists—to combine the productive capacity of capitalism with a collectivist organization of production and distribution—has yet to prove feasible in any form.) Whether or not this political and economic conjunction rests on or is in any way connected to the common cultural heritage of most of these liberal democracies is another question altogether (but one that the example of Japan and, more recently, the newly industrializing countries of Asia may be seen as answering).

One set of difficult questions concerns whether (or to what degree) any of these elements of the liberal democratic world can be exported or should be exported to the rest of the world. Obviously, many of those raised within the liberal democratic world will have a bias towards democracy, liberal (political and economic) values, the materialist and consumerist habits of members of market society, and the attitudes and beliefs that correspond to a highly technological society. To assume that all countries will inevitably or naturally "evolve" into liberal democracies is a naïvely **ETHNOCENTRIC** (or culturally biased) fallacy. Similarly, to assume that liberal democracy is a superior form of socio-economic and political organization that all countries would be fortunate to adopt is rather presumptuous. It is useful, though, on each of these dimensions—political, economic, and cultural— to consider to what degree liberal democratic ideas have penetrated or polluted (depending on one's perspective) the rest of the world, and to what degree they are likely to continue to do so.

We noted earlier that considerably less than half the world's nation-states are liberal democracies. The proportion of the world's citizens who have lived their entire lives in a liberal democracy or who were socialized within a democracy is much smaller still. Part of this, as we have seen, is definitional: if we define democracy by the presence of elections, then a much higher proportion of states is democratic. In many cases, though, elections are a façade, can be rigged or bought, or, even when the process is fair and legitimate, can deliver an unstable regime susceptible to coups, civil war, or rebellion. Similarly, we have noted the argument that democracy is not possible without social and political pluralism, or without key institutions and qualities of civil society: free media and general literacy and education. In some countries the machinery of elections may be in place without the supporting conditions that democracy requires: democratic machinery may mask an undemocratic political reality. In many of these cases, the political culture of democracy has yet to be established, and both individuals and parties of an authoritarian character have sometimes taken advantage of the democratic process. Where democracy is weak or has not become part of the political agenda, the effective reality is an **AUTHORITARIAN** political system, and about that we have as yet said too little, especially since a majority of the world's people live in authoritarian regimes.

The word "authoritarian" may seem an ironic choice to indicate regimes where the maintenance of order and stability often depends much more on power than on authority. This is only sometimes true, however, and often only partially true. We need to realize that while authoritarian regimes are not legitimate from the perspective of those holding liberal democratic values, they may well be regarded as legitimate by their own citizens on the basis of other (typically non-Western) values. While authoritarian regimes are, by definition, not democratic, they sometimes *claim* to be democratic and often appeal to the principle of *popular sovereignty,* claiming that their policies and actions are consistent with the will of the people or that their policies provide what the people need. Almost without exception, these regimes will claim to provide "justice" for their citizens, and it is often their norms of justice, or the applications that they make of these norms, that clash with the values of liberal democracy.

While there is no *one* authoritarian vision, perspective, or program, what authoritarian regimes have in common is a commitment by those in power not to relinquish it. Indeed, one might define an authoritarian regime as *one in which there is no regular and peaceful means of replacing the existing political elite with another.* Typically, those who occupy top political offices have not been elected to them or, having once been elected, have since suspended or abolished democratic political processes. This means that they have become unaccountable to the public. Democracy provides a means by which the public can peacefully replace those who rule them; such an avenue is missing in an authoritarian regime, and the replacement of rulers often requires violence (coups, assassinations, revolutions, etc.).

In regimes where rulers do not expect to give an accounting of their actions to the public, they often act as if they are outside the law or above it. The application of the rule of law may also be suspect; widespread corruption among the police, the military, and even judicial authorities is not uncommon. If the liberal understanding of the rule of law is foreign to the practice of authoritarian regimes, the liberal respect for and reliance upon individual rights is almost inconceivable; limits on the state are, by definition, contrary to the nature of authoritarian regimes. A result of authoritarian disdain for the liberal rule of law and respect for individual rights is a very incomplete comprehension of "the individual" as an abstract unit of legal personality. Consequently, those who fall afoul of the law (or more accurately, and thereby emphasizing our point, fall afoul of "the authorities") in authoritarian regimes are often subjected to treatment regarded as abusive by liberal standards.

Perhaps not surprisingly, the commitment to equality is even weaker in authoritarian regimes than it is in democracies. Any thorough belief in equality is sure to undermine the justifications that sustain rulers in their permanent monopoly of power. It might well be objected that in some authoritarian systems, including but not restricted to those that have drawn on Marxist-Leninism, there is a strong commitment to social and economic equality. While this is true, we may make two qualifications. One is that such a commitment has often turned out to be stronger in theory than in practice: the classless society remains a goal to be realized rather than a present reality. The other is that in such societies *political* inequality is total and will accept no challenge. The driving imperative for most authoritarian regimes is to maintain a hold on power. In this respect they are profoundly conservative of a status quo.

A further important distinction concerns the place of religion within the authoritarian state. Often, authoritarian regimes do not acknowledge the separation of church and state that, in the Western liberal democracies, was a legacy of the Reformation and the Enlightenment. Public policy, on this view, should neither reflect nor favour the influence of any particular religious creed. This separation of church and state was in part simply a practical recognition of growing religious diversity in Western culture, a diversity that began with the Reformation. It has also sometimes been the case in Western nations that the more religiously homogeneous the population, the less perfectly and completely the separation of church and state has been realized. In authoritarian regimes, religion is often a source of justification (sometimes *the* source) for the rulers' power. Here there may be a high degree of conformity between the civil and religious laws, or the authority of the state may be used to enforce religious edicts and to ensure religious conformity—particularly where the dominant religion takes a **FUNDAMENTALIST** form (a strict, literal reading of sacred texts and tenets). In such systems the degree of religious tolerance will be low, if it exists at all. The case of religion illustrates a more general observation, namely, that authoritarian regimes are less likely to celebrate plurality within their society and more likely to work to maintain, or even forcibly create, a homogeneity within the population in terms of language, culture, religion, and sometimes even ethnicity.

Authoritarianism, then, is a term indicating a broad category of political regimes characterized by a government whose ruling members are not accountable to those they rule. (A typology would include dictatorships, monarchies, juntas, theocracies, and dynasties.) Permanence in office may seem to indicate stability, but there are two senses in which this is misleading. Precisely because authoritarian rulers are not regularly replaced by peaceful means, their governments are susceptible to violent challenges such as insurrection or revolution. At the same time, the fear of this happening and the attempt to stifle any competition lead to repressive actions and agencies (secret police, bureaus of censorship, etc.) that impose stability through coercion and intimidation. Most importantly, authoritarian rulers will seek to justify their hold on power in order to stabilize their regimes. Their distaste for public involvement in decision-making or in selecting rulers goes hand in hand with a desire to receive public approval of their actions and policies.

The desire to achieve legitimacy, not only in the eyes of their citizens but before the world, sometimes leads authoritarian regimes to democracy, or rather, to the façade of democratic elections. In many states, elections *do* take place, but they do not meet the standards that most observers regard as satisfying the criteria of democracy. The most obvious example is elections in which there is no choice: the people are allowed to cast a ballot, but there is only one candidate. Or they are allowed to choose among candidates, but all candidates belong to the same ruling party. What amounts to the same thing is elections in which there is a choice among candidates and parties but, nonetheless, the ruling party is guaranteed victory—through corruption or fraud, special rules, or control of other institutions such as the mass media, the police, etc. (Mexico is a well-known example of a state with contested elections that always managed [until July 2000] to return the ruling party to power.)

The turn towards democracy, however much a sham it may turn out to be in practice, can lead to the demand for genuine processes, for real public participation in the selection of rulers and the policies they will implement. In deigning to use electoral machinery to try to secure legitimacy, authoritarian regimes may start down a slippery slope that leads to the end of authoritarian politics. Two other factors also contribute. One is the sheer volume of democratically elected governments; as more of the world's nation-states employ the machinery of democracy, this puts pressure on the remaining holdouts to come on side. Another incentive is the prospect of improving economic relations with wealthy democratic regimes that find political ties with dictators and juntas embarrassing. As the Cold War recedes into memory, this may be increasingly true: the U.S. and its allies once propped up many right-wing dictatorships simply because they were "on our side," i.e., friendly to capital and hostile to forces of radical social reform.

On another level, the challenges of developing versus developed worlds, of democratic expansion and consolidation, of world population growth, of environmental depletion and degradation, and of ethnic wars lead many to suggest that the nation-state has become somewhat obsolete. Insofar as the forces creating change—transnational corporations, global markets, new communication and information technologies—are international or global in scope, exploitation of their possibilities and implementing solutions to the problems they create seem to require global solutions: the activity of international organizations or institutions. The same can be said of problems that, quite apart from the technologies associated with globalization, have become truly transnational issues: damage to the environment and a

**18.5
SOVEREIGNTY,
SECURITY,
SUSTAINABILITY**

KEY TERMS

arms race
authoritarianism
blocs
client states
Cold War
decolonization
dependency theory
developed world
developing world
development
ethnocentrism
First World
fundamentalism
Gini coefficient
globalization
international governmental
organizations
liberal economics
neo-colonialism
non-governmental organizations
(NGOs)
quintiles
Second World
sustainable development
Third World

changing world climate, population growth, the international movement and accommodation of refugees.

For some, the principal actors on the world stage now are, and will increasingly be, **BLOCS** of nations. These may be security alliances like NATO, which despite the demise of the Cold War shows no signs of disbanding but instead seems intent on expansion, even at the risk of antagonizing Russia. Perhaps more importantly, these blocs are frequently economic alliances or trading associations, like the NAFTA countries or the **EUROPEAN COMMUNITY**. We have observed the importance of international quasi-governmental organizations such as the World Bank and the IMF. Whether these transnational structures are a stepping stone to some form of global governance more effective than the **UNITED NATIONS** has been, or simply new units that will serve as the basis of future rivalries or even strife, it is too soon to say. Optimists and pessimists will each see different possibilities, and it may be that as yet none is foreclosed.

It is clear, however, that whether or not it is being diminished, the nature of national **SOVEREIGNTY** is changing. To become integrated into a world economy in a climate of freer trade and flexible exchange rates is to tap into the opportunities for growth and flourishing that international markets provide, but also to be subject to the shocks and surprises dealt by international forces. To adapt a phrase, in the global economy no nation is an island; survival requires trade, trade requires access to markets, and access to markets comes through membership in trading blocs. Committing to the terms of a trade treaty is to surrender sovereignty, or at least to accept limits on the kinds of policy that the state can implement. The world's most established trading bloc—the European Community—has found that economic alliance has required increasing political harmonization, which means that members agree to a common course of action or delegate authority to a supranational governing body.

In strategic terms, too, the world has changed. In the postwar, Cold War world, armed conflicts ("hot" wars) primarily were escalated disputes over territory or civil wars into which other parties may or may not have been drawn. Whatever else these were, they were disputes over sovereignty, over who was in control of a given territory. When issues other than sovereignty arose, such as the treatment of minority peoples within a state, other nations expressed concerns but did not actively intervene. Increasingly, towards the end of the twentieth century, the reasons for armed conflict seem to have shifted. Other nations

492

have declared an interest in local territorial squabbles (Iraq and Kuwait), or have intervened in civil wars (former Yugoslavia), or have sought to prevent the large-scale suffering of masses of innocent civilians (Rwanda, Kosovo). To a degree that seems unprecedented, the international community is taking a greater interest in what happens within the boundaries of nation-states, and has shown an increased willingness to take action.

In part this reflects the broadening of the economic interests of each state within a globalizing economy. Everyone understands that the United Nations action against Iraq had nothing to do with preserving democracy in Kuwait (which did not and does not exist) and everything to do with the security of the world's oil supply. As an integrated global economy develops, dependent on trade, wars that involve any of the states integrated into that economy will be seen as tiresome and potentially destabilizing, contrary to the interests of all the other states. The market values stability and predictability as it moves in and out of equilibrium. It should not surprise us if the states with an increasingly common economic interest in the world economy that connects them should also find the collective will to intervene to end or otherwise resolve bothersome conflicts elsewhere.

In our view, none of this means the irrelevance or impending demise of the nation-state. We saw earlier that the state in almost all countries exists at a variety of levels, whether formally autonomous in a federal form or not. This, we suspect, will be true of the future, only more so, and increasingly it may be the case that the nation-state is no longer the ultimate level of governance. It may well be that the twenty-first century will increasingly be engaged not with the question "what should the state do (or not)?" but with the question "at what level of organization should the state do what it does?" The more complicated government becomes, which seems a corollary of the increasing complexity of society, the more important it is that citizens have an understanding of how and what it is doing—and the means to keep it accountable to their needs and aspirations.

A t the beginning of the twenty-first century, one might be expected to close by predicting where the political world, in all its varieties, is headed. If the past teaches anything, however, it is the impossibility of predicting the future. Few could have guessed in 1988, say, that within three years, communism would

18.6
CONCLUSION: SMASHING THE CRYSTAL BALL

REFERENCES AND SUGGESTED READING

Holm, Hans Henrik, and Goerg Sørenson, eds. 1995. *Whose World Order? Uneven Globalization and the End of the Cold War.* Boulder, Colo.: Westview Press.

Huntington, Samuel. 1997. *The Clash Of Civilizations.* Keegan.

Kelleher, Ann, and Laura Klein. 1999. *Global Perspectives.* Upper Saddle River, NJ: Prentice Hall.

Lopez, George A., Jackie G. Smith, and Ron Pagnucco. 1995. "The Global Tide," *Bulletin of the Atomic Scientists* (July-August).

have collapsed throughout Eastern Europe and the former Soviet Union. This was perhaps the most significant political development of the past quarter-century, and no one is in a position to say as yet what it will all mean in the long term. After the fact, looking back, one can trace the developments and forces that explain the events that transpired. There are probably many changes and movements under way today that will account for the great changes we will witness in the next decades, but can barely guess at today.

What will be the ultimate impact of the growth of a market economy in China? Will this lead to political freedom also? Will democracy in China come peacefully or otherwise? Where will the civil unrest gradually engulfing more and more of sub-Saharan Africa eventually lead that continent? What technological developments in the next 15 years will transform our lives in the developed world to the degree that the Internet has in the past decade or more? Will all share in any benefits brought about by technological advance, or will the gulf between rich and poor continue to grow? At what point will the changes in world climate cease to be "merely" environmental issues and come to be seen as serious political challenges facing the world's governments? Will the need to address ecological issues be recognized before it is too late for political authorities to make a difference? Will the European Union continue to expand its borders and consolidate its political power, and could this ultimately mean a challenge to the economic dominance of the United States? Will Canada continue to be integrated into a larger North American economy and culture so that eventually sovereignty is more formal than effective? Will Russia continue to drift further into anarchy and chaos, or will the pendulum swing in the other direction entirely and an authoritarian regime be re-established? What will be the impact of continued ethnic and religious unrest and violence in Indonesia, one of the world's most populous states? Will the trend towards a less well-informed and increasingly alienated citizenry continue in developed democracies? Will the development of these issues turn out to be the opposite of that implied in each of these questions? How long will it be before these speculations seem terribly "dated" or "quaint"? Perhaps the most relevant questions will turn out to be those we haven't even thought to ask.

SOMETHING TO CONSIDER

Is sustainable development, as discussed above in the context of the developing world, an idea that also ought to be adapted to the developed world? Is sustainable development compatible with an economic model that seeks ever greater levels of consumption?

Are there any "natural limits" to the growth of inequality, either within or between political communities?

Can the development and application of technology outstrip the capacity of the social and political system to respond to the changing circumstances this technology creates?

APPENDICES

the canadian constitution (selections)

The Constitution of Canada is contained in the Constitution Acts 1867 to 1982. We reproduce here three segments of that constitution embodying elements referred to in the text.

1. THE DIVISION OF POWERS

As we discussed in Chapter 10, the constitution of any federal country must allocate jurisdictions between the levels of government. The relevant sections of the Canadian constitution follow (from the Constitution Act, 1867, Consolidated with Amendments).

91. Legislative Authority of Parliament of Canada. It shall be Lawful for the Queen, by and with the Advice and Consent of the Senate and the House of Commons, to make Laws for the Peace, Order and Good Government of Canada, in relation to all Matters not coming within the Classes of Subjects by this Act assigned exclusively to the Legislatures of the Provinces; and for greater Certainty, but not so as to restrict the Generality of the foregoing Terms of the Section, it is hereby declared that (notwithstanding anything in this Act) the exclusive Legislative Authority of the Parliament of Canada extends to all Matters coming within the Classes of Subjects hereinafter enumerated; that is to say,

Powers of the Parliament

1. Repealed.
1A. The Public Debt and Property.
2. The Regulation of Trade and Commerce.
2A. Unemployment insurance.
3. The Raising of Money by any Mode or System of Taxation.

4. The borrowing of Money on the Public Credit.
5. Postal Service.
6. The Census and Statistics.
7. Militia, Military and Naval Service, and Defence.
8. The fixing of and providing for the Salaries and Allowances of Civil and other Officers of the Government of Canada.
9. Beacons, Buoys, Lighthouses, and Sable Island.
10. Navigation and Shipping.
11. Quarantine and the Establishment and Maintenance of Marine Hospitals.
12. Sea Coast and Inland Fisheries.
13. Ferries between a Province and any British or Foreign Country or between Two Provinces.
14. Currency and Coinage.
15. Banking, Incorporation of Banks, and the Issue of Paper Money.
16. Savings Banks.
17. Weights and Measures.
18. Bills of Exchange and Promissory Notes.
19. Interest.
20. Legal Tender.
21. Bankruptcy and Insolvency.
22. Patents of Invention and Discovery.
23. Copyrights.
24. Indians, and Lands reserved for the Indians.
25. Naturalization and Aliens.
26. Marriage and Divorce.
27. The Criminal Law, except for the Constitution of Courts of Criminal Jurisdiction, but including the Procedure in Criminal Matters.
28. The Establishment, Maintenance, and Management of Penitentiaries.
29. Such Classes of Subjects as are expressly excepted in the Enumeration of the Classes of Subjects by this Act assigned exclusively to the Legislatures of the Provinces.

And any Matter coming within any of the Classes of Subjects enumerated in this Section shall not be deemed to come within the Class of matters of a local or private Nature comprised in the Enumeration of the Classes of Subjects by this Act assigned exclusively to the Legislatures of the Provinces.

92. Subjects of exclusive Provincial Legislation. In each Province the Legislature may exclusively make Laws in relation to Matters coming within the Classes of Subject next hereinafter enumerated; that is to say,

Exclusive Powers of Provincial Legislatures

1. Repealed.
2. Direct Taxation within the Province in order to the raising of a Revenue for Provincial Purposes.
3. The borrowing of Money on the sole Credit of the Province.
4. The Establishment and Tenure of Provincial Offices and the Appointment and Payment of Provincial Officers.
5. The Management and Sale of the Public Lands belonging to the Province and of the Timber and Wood thereon.
6. The Establishment, Maintenance, and Management of Public and Reformatory Prisons in and for the Province.
7. The Establishment, Maintenance, and Management of Hospitals, Asylums, Charities, and Eleemosynary Institutions in and for the Province, other than Marine Hospitals.
8. Municipal Institutions in the Province.
9. Shop, Saloon, Tavern, Auctioneer, and other Licences in order to the raising of a Revenue for Provincial, Local, or Municipal Purposes.
10. Local Works and Undertakings other than such as are of the following classes:
    (a) Lines of Steam or other Ships, Railways, Canals, Telegraphs, and other Works and Undertakings connecting the Province with any other or others of the Province, or extending beyond the Limits of the Province:
    (b) Lines of Steam Ships between the Province and any British or Foreign Country:
    (c) Such Works as, although wholly situate within the Province, are before or after their Execution declared by the Parliament of Canada to be for the general Advantage of Canada or for the Advantage of Two or more of the Provinces.
11. The Incorporation of Companies with Provincial Objects.
12. The Solemnization of Marriage in the Province.
13. Property and Civil Rights within the Province.

14. The Administration of Justice in the Province, including the Constitution, Maintenance, and Organization of Provincial Courts, both of Civil and of Criminal Jurisdiction, and including Procedure in Civil Matters in those Courts.

15. The Imposition of Punishment by Fine, Penalty, or Imprisonment for enforcing any Law of the Province made in relation to any Matter coming within any of the Classes of Subjects enumerated in this Section.

16. Generally all Matters of a merely local or private Nature in the Province.

92 A. Non-Renewable Natural Resources, Forestry Resources and Electrical Energy

Laws respecting non-renewable natural resources, forestry resources and electrical energy

(1) In each province, the legislature may exclusively make laws in relation to

(a) exploration for non-renewable natural resources in the province;

(b) development, conservation and management of non-renewable natural resources and forestry resources in the province, including laws in relation to the rate of primary production therefrom; and

(c) development, conservation and management of sites and facilities in the province for the generation and production of electrical energy.

Export from provinces of resources

(2) In each province, the legislature may make laws in relation to the export from the province to another part of Canada of the primary production from non-renewable natural resources and forestry resources in the province and the productions from facilities in the province for the generation of electrical energy, but such laws may not authorize or provide for discrimination in prices or supplies exported to another part of Canada.

Authority of Parliament

(3) Nothing in subsection (2) derogates from the authority of Parliament to enact laws in relation to the matters referred to in that subsection and, where such a law of Parliament and a law of a province conflict, the law of Parliament prevails to the extent of the conflict.

(4) In each province, the legislature may make laws in relation to the raising of money by any mode or system of taxation in respect of

    (*a*) non-renewable natural resources and forestry resources in the province and the primary production therefrom, and

    (*b*) sites and facilities in the province for the generation of electrical energy and the production therefrom, whether or not such production is exported in whole or in part from the province, but such laws may not authorize or provide for taxation that differentiates between production exported to another part of Canada and production not exported from the province.

Taxation of resources

(5) The expression "primary production" has the meaning assigned in the Sixth Schedule.

"primary production"

(6) Nothing in subsections (1) to (5) derogates from any powers or rights that a legislature or government of a province had immediately before the coming into force of this section.

Existing powers of rights

93. Education

In and for each Province the Legislature may exclusively make Laws in relation to Education, subject and according to the following Provisions:

Legislation respecting Education

(1) Nothing in any such Law shall prejudicially affect any Right or Privilege with respect to Denominational Schools which any Class of Persons have by Law in the Province at the Union:

(2) All the Powers, Privileges, and Duties at the Union by Law conferred and imposed in Upper Canada on the Separate Schools and School Trustees of the Queen's Roman Catholic Subjects shall be and the same are hereby extended to the Dissentient Schools of the Queen's Protestant and Roman Catholic Subjects in Quebec:

(3) Where in any Province a System of Separate or Dissentient Schools exists by Law at the Union or is thereafter established by the Legislature of the Province, an Appeal shall lie to the Governor General in Council from any Act or Decision of any Provincial Authority affecting any Right or Privilege of the Protestant or

Roman Catholic Minority of the Queen's Subjects in relation to education:

(4) In case any such Provincial Law as from Time to Time seems to the Governor General in Council requisite for the due Execution of the Provisions of this Section is not made, or in case any Decision of the Governor General in Council on any appeal under this Section is not duly executed by the proper Provincial Authority in that behalf, then and in every such Case, and as far only as the Circumstances of each Case require, the Parliament of Canada may make remedial Laws for the due Execution of the Provisions of this Section and of any Decision of the Governor General in Council under this Section.

94. Uniformity of Laws in Ontario, Nova Scotia and New Brunswick

Legislation for Uniformity of Laws in Three Provinces

Notwithstanding anything in this Act, the Parliament of Canada may make Provision for the Uniformity of all or any of the Laws relative to Property and Civil Rights in Ontario, Nova Scotia, and New Brunswick, and of the Procedure of all or any of the Courts of Those Three Provinces, and from and after the passing of any Act in that Behalf the Power of the Parliament of Canada to make Laws in relation to any Matter comprised in any such Act shall, notwithstanding anything in this Act, be unrestricted; but any Act of the Parliament of Canada making Provision for such Uniformity shall not have effect in any Province unless and until it is adopted and enacted as Law by the Legislature thereof.

94. Old age Pensions

Legislation respecting old age pensions and supplementary benefits

A. The Parliament of Canada may make laws in relation to old age pensions and supplementary benefits, including survivors' and disability benefits irrespective of age, but no such law shall affect the operation of any law present or future of a provincial legislature in relation to any such matter.

95. Agriculture and Immigration

In each Province the Legislature may make Laws in relation to Agriculture in the Province, and to Immigration into the Province; and it is hereby declared that the Parliament of Canada may from Time to Time make Laws in relation to Agriculture in all of any of the Provinces, and to Immigration into all or any of the Provinces; and any Law of the Legislature of a Province relative to Agriculture or Immigration shall have effect in and for the Province as long and as far only as it is not repugnant to any Act of the Parliament of Canada.

Concurrent Powers of Legislation respecting Agriculture, etc.

109. All Lands, Mines, Minerals and Royalties belonging to the Several Provinces of Canada, Nova Scotia, and New Brunswick at the Union, and all Sums then due or payable for such Lands, Mines, Minerals or Royalties, shall belong to the several Provinces of Ontario, Quebec, Nova Scotia and New Brunswick in which the same are situate or arise, subject to any Trusts existing in respect thereof, and to any Interest other than that of the Province in same.

Property in Lands, Mines, etc.

2. THE CHARTER OF RIGHTS AND FREEDOMS

As we discussed above, particularly in Chapter 16, in 1982 the Canadian constitution was amended to include an entrenched rights code, redefining the relationship between citizens and the state and greatly expanding the scope for judicial review. The Charter of Rights and Freedoms, from the Constitution Act, 1982, follows.

Canadian Charter of Rights and Freedoms

Whereas Canada is founded upon principles that recognize the supremacy of God and the rule of law:

GUARANTEE OF RIGHTS AND FREEDOMS

1. The *Canadian Charter of Rights and Freedoms* guarantees the rights and freedoms set out in it subject only to such reasonable limits prescribed by law as can be demonstrably justified in a free and democratic society.

Rights and freedoms in Canada

FUNDAMENTAL FREEDOMS

Fundamental freedoms

2. Everyone has the following fundamental freedoms:

a) freedom of conscience and religion;
b) freedom of thought, belief, opinion and expression, including freedom of the press and other media of communication;
c) freedom of peaceful assembly; and
d) freedom of association.

DEMOCRATIC RIGHTS

Democratic rights of citizens

3. Every citizen of Canada has the right to vote in an election of members of the House of Commons or of a legislative assembly and to be qualified for membership therein.

Maximum duration of legislative bodies

4. (1) No House of Commons and no legislative assembly shall continue for longer than five years from the date fixed for the return of the writs of a general election of its members.

Continuation in special circumstances

(2) In time of real or apprehended war, invasion or insurrection, a House of Commons may be continued by Parliament and a legislative assembly may be continued by the legislature beyond five years if such continuation is not opposed by the votes of more than one-third of the members of the House of Commons or the legislative assembly, as the case may be.

Annual sitting of legislative bodies

5. There shall be a sitting of Parliament and of each legislature at least once every twelve months

MOBILITY RIGHTS

Mobility of citizens

6. (1) Every citizen of Canada has the right to enter, remain in and leave Canada.

Rights to move and gain livelihood

(2) Every citizen of Canada and every person who has the status of a permanent resident of Canada has the right

a) to move to and take up residence in any province; and
b) to pursue the gaining of a livelihood in any province.

Limitation

(3) The rights specified in subsection (2) are subject to

a) any laws or practices of general application in force in a province other than those that discriminate among persons primarily on the basis of province of present or previous residence; and

b) any laws providing for reasonable residency requirements as a qualification for the receipt of publicly provided social services.

(4) Subsections (2) and (3) do not preclude any law, program or activity that has as its object the amelioration in a province of conditions of individuals in that province who are socially or economically disadvantaged if the rate of employment in that province is below the rate of employment in Canada.

Affirmative action programs

LEGAL RIGHTS

7. Everyone has the right to life, liberty and security of the person and the right not to be deprived thereof except in accordance with the principles of fundamental justice.

Life, liberty and security of person

8. Everyone has the right to be secure against unreasonable search or seizure.

Search or seizure

9. Everyone has the right not to be arbitrarily detained or imprisoned.

Detention or imprisonment

10. Everyone has the right on arrest or detention

Arrest or detention

a) to be informed promptly of the reasons therefor;
b) to retain and instruct counsel without delay and to be informed of that right; and
c) to have the validity of the detention determined by way of *habeas corpus* and to be released if the detention is not lawful.

11. Any person charged with an offence has the right

Proceedings in criminal and penal matters

a) to be informed without unreasonable delay of the specific offence;
b) to be tried within a reasonable time;
c) not to be compelled to be a witness in proceedings against that person in respect of the offence;

d) to be presumed innocent until proven guilty according to law in a fair and public hearing by an independent and impartial tribunal;

e) not to be denied reasonable bail without just cause;

f) except in the case of an offence under military law tried before a military tribunal, to the benefit of trial by jury where the maximum punishment for the offence is imprisonment for five years or a more severe punishment;

g) not to be found guilty on account of any act or omission unless, at the time of the act or omission, it constituted an offence under Canadian or international law or was criminal according to the general principles of law recognized by the community of nations;

h) if finally acquitted of the offence, not to be tried for it again and, if finally found guilty and punished for the offence, not to be tried or punished for it again; and

i) if found guilty of the offence and if the punishment for the offence has been varied between the time of commission and the time of sentencing, to the benefit of the lesser punishment.

Treatment or punishment   **12.** Everyone has the right not to be subjected to any cruel and unusual treatment or punishment.

Self-crimination   **13.** A witness who testifies in any proceedings has the right not to have any incriminating evidence so given used to incriminate that witness in any other proceedings, except in a prosecution for perjury or for the giving of contradictory evidence.

Interpreter   **14.** A party or witness in any proceedings who does not understand or speak the language in which the proceedings are conducted or who is deaf has the right to the assistance of an interpreter.

EQUALITY RIGHTS

Equality before and under law and equal protection and benefit of law   **15.** (1) Every individual is equal before and under the law and has the right to the equal protection and equal benefit of the law without discrimination and, in particular, without discrimination based on race, national or ethnic origin, colour, religion, sex, age or mental or physical disability.

(2) Subsection (1) does not preclude any law, program or activity that has as its object the amelioration of conditions of disadvantaged individuals or groups including those that are disadvantaged because of race, national or ethnic origin, colour, religion, sex, age or mental or physical disability.

Affirmative action programs

OFFICIAL LANGUAGES OF CANADA

16. (1) English and French are the official languages of Canada and have equality of status and equal rights and privileges as to their use in all institutions of the Parliament and government of Canada.

Official languages of Canada

(2) English and French are the official languages of New Brunswick and have equality of status and equal rights and privileges as to their use in all institutions of the legislature and government of New Brunswick.

Official languages of New Brunswick

(3) Nothing in this Charter limits the authority of Parliament or a legislature to advance the equality of status or use of English and French.

Advancement of status and use

16.1 (1) The English linguistic community and the French linguistic community in New Brunswick have equality of status and equal rights and privileges, including the right to distinct educational institutions and such distinct cultural institutions as are necessary for the preservation and promotion of those communities.

English and French linguistic communities in New Brunswick

(2) The role of the legislature and government of New Brunswick to preserve and promote the status, rights and privileges referred to in subsection (1) is affirmed.

Role of the legislature and government of New Brunswick

17. (1) Everyone has the right to use English or French in any debates and other proceedings of Parliament.

Proceedings of Parliament

(2) Everyone has the right to use English or French in any debates and other proceedings of the legislature of New Brunswick.

Proceedings of New Brunswick legislature

18. (1) The statutes, records and journals of Parliament shall be printed and published in English and French and both language versions are equally authoritative.

Parliamentary statutes and records

New Brunswick
statutes and records

(2) The statutes, records and journals of the legislature of New Brunswick shall be printed and published in English and French and both language versions are equally authoritative.

Proceedings in courts
established by Parliament

19. (1) Either English or French may be used by any person in, or in any pleading in or process issuing from, any court established by Parliament.

Proceedings in New
Brunswick courts

(2) Either English or French may be used by any person in, or in any pleading in or process issuing from, any court of New Brunswick.

Communications by public
with federal institutions

20. (1) Any member of the public in Canada has the right to communicate with, and to receive available services from, any head or central office of an institution of the Parliament or government of Canada in English or French, and has the same right with respect to any other office of any such institution where

a) there is a significant demand for communications with and services from that office in such language; or
b) due to the nature of the office, it is reasonable that communications with and services from that office be available in both English and French.

Communications by
public with New
Brunswick institutions

(2) Any member of the public in New Brunswick has the right to communicate with, and to receive available services from, any office of an institution of the legislature or government of New Brunswick in English or French.

Continuation of existing
constitutional provisions

21. Nothing in sections 16 to 20 abrogates or derogates from any right, privilege or obligation with respect to the English and French languages, or either of them, that exists or is continued by virtue of any other provision of the Constitution of Canada.

Rights and privileges
preserved

22. Nothing in sections 16 to 20 abrogates or derogates from any legal or customary right or privilege acquired or enjoyed either before or after the coming into force of this Charter with respect to any language that is not English or French.

MINORITY LANGUAGE EDUCATIONAL RIGHTS

23. (1) Citizens of Canada

    a) whose first language learned and still understood is that of the English or French linguistic minority population of the province in which they reside, or

    b) who have received their primary school instruction in Canada in English or French and reside in a province where the language in which they received that instruction is the language of the English or French linguistic minority population of the province,

have the right to have their children receive primary and secondary school instruction in that language in that province.

Language of instruction

(2) Citizens of Canada of whom any child has received or is receiving primary or secondary school instruction in English or French in Canada, have the right to have all their children receive primary and secondary school instruction in the same language.

Continuity of language instruction

(3) The right of citizens of Canada under subsections (1) and (2) to have their children receive primary and secondary school instruction in the language of the English or French linguistic minority population of a province

Application where numbers warrant

    a) applies wherever in the province the number of children of citizens who have such a right is sufficient to warrant the provision to them out of public funds of minority language instruction; and

    b) includes, where the number of those children so warrants, the right to have them receive that instruction in minority language educational facilities provided out of public funds.

ENFORCEMENT

24. (1) Anyone whose rights or freedoms, as guaranteed by this Charter, have been infringed or denied may apply to a court of competent jurisdiction to obtain such remedy as the court considers appropriate and just in the circumstances.

Enforcement of guaranteed rights and freedoms

Exclusion of evidence bringing administration of justice into disrepute

(2) Where, in proceedings under subsection (1), a court concludes that evidence was obtained in a manner that infringed or denied any rights or freedoms guaranteed by this Charter, the evidence shall be excluded if it is established that, having regard to all the circumstances, the admission of it in the proceedings would bring the administration of justice into disrepute.

GENERAL

Aboriginal rights and freedoms not affected by Charter

25. The guarantee in this Charter of certain rights and freedoms shall not be construed so as to abrogate or derogate from any aboriginal, treaty or other rights or freedoms that pertain to the aboriginal peoples of Canada including

    a) any rights or freedoms that have been recognized by the Royal Proclamation of October 7, 1763; and
    b) any rights or freedoms that now exist by way of land claims agreements or may be so acquired.

Other rights and freedoms not affected by Charter

26. The guarantee in this Charter of certain rights and freedoms shall not be construed as denying the existence of any other rights or freedoms that exist in Canada.

Multicultural heritage

27. This Charter shall be interpreted in a manner consistent with the preservation and enhancement of the multicultural heritage of Canadians.

Rights guaranteed equally to both sexes

28. Notwithstanding anything in this Charter, the rights and freedoms referred to in it are guaranteed equally to male and female persons.

Rights respecting certain schools preserved

29. Nothing in this Charter abrogates or derogates from any rights or privileges guaranteed by or under the Constitution of Canada in respect of denominational, separate or dissentient schools.

Application to territories and territorial authorities

30. A reference in this Charter to a Province or to the legislative assembly or legislature of a province shall be deemed to include a reference to the Yukon Territory and the Northwest Territories, or to the appropriate legislative authority thereof, as the case may be.

Legislative powers not extended

31. Nothing in this Charter extends the legislative powers of any body or authority.

APPLICATION OF CHARTER

32. (1) This Charter applies

Application
of Charter

a) to the Parliament and government of Canada in respect of all matters within the authority of Parliament including all matters relating to the Yukon Territory and Northwest Territories; and
b) to the legislature and government of each province in respect of all matters within the authority of the legislature of each province.

(2) Notwithstanding subsection (1), section 15 shall not have effect until three years after this section comes into force.

Exception

33. (1) Parliament or the legislature of a province may expressly declare in an Act of Parliament or of the legislature, as the case may be, that the Act or a provision thereof shall operate notwithstanding a provision included in section 2 or sections 7 to 15 of this Charter.

Exception where
express declaration

(2) An Act or a provision of an Act in respect of which a declaration made under this section is in effect shall have such operation as it would have but for the provision of this Charter referred to in the declaration.

Operation
of exception

(3) A declaration made under subsection (1) shall cease to have effect five years after it comes into force or on such earlier date as may be specified in the declaration.

Five year limitation

(4) Parliament or the legislature of a province may re-enact a declaration made under subsection (1).

Re-enactment

(5) Subsection (3) applies in respect of a re-enactment made under subsection (4).

Five year limitation

34. This Part may be cited as the *Canadian Charter of Rights and Freedoms*.

Citation

3. THE CONSTITUTIONAL AMENDING FORMULAS

As we noted in Chapter 13, constitutions need to change from time to time. We also noted, in Chapter 10, that in a federal state there must be a stipulated degree of consent between levels of government over constitutional change that affects their interests. We described the current amending procedures for the Canadian Constitution in Chapter 7; here we present the actual selections from the Constitution Act, 1982.

General procedure for amending Constitution of Canada

38. (1) An amendment to the Constitution of Canada may be made by proclamation issued by the Governor General under the Great Seal of Canada where so authorized by

(a) resolutions of the Senate and House of Commons; and
(b) resolutions of the legislative assemblies of at least two-thirds of the provinces that have, in the aggregate, according to the then latest general census, at least fifty per cent of all the population of all the provinces.

Majority of members

(2) An amendment made under subsection (1) that derogates from the legislative powers, the proprietary rights or any other rights or privileges of the legislature or government of a province shall require a resolution supported by a majority of the members of each of the Senate, the House of Commons and the legislative assemblies required under subsection (1).

Expression of dissent

(3) An amendment referred to in subsection (2) shall not have effect in a province the legislative assembly of which has expressed its dissent thereto by resolution supported by a majority of its members prior to the issue of the proclamation to which the amendment relates unless that legislative assembly, subsequently, by resolution supported by a majority of its members, revokes its dissent and authorizes the amendment.

Revocation of dissent

(4) A resolution of dissent made for the purposes of subsection (3) may be revoked at any time before or after the issue of the proclamation to which it relates.

Restriction on proclamation

39. (1) A proclamation shall not be issued under subsection 38(1) before the expiration of one year from the adoption of the resolution initiating the amendment procedure thereunder, unless the

legislative assembly of each province has previously adopted a resolution of assent or dissent.

(2) A proclamation shall not be issued under subsection 38(1) after
the expiration of three years from the adoption of the resolution
initiating the amendment procedure thereunder.

Idem

40. Where an amendment is made under subsection 38(1) that
transfers provincial legislative powers relating to education or
other cultural matters from provincial legislatures to Parliament,
Canada shall provide reasonable compensation to any province to
which the amendment does not apply.

Compensation

41. An amendment to the Constitution of Canada in relation to
the following matters may be made by proclamation issued by the
Governor General under the Great Seal of Canada only where
authorized by resolutions of the Senate and House of Commons
and of the legislative assemblies of each province:

*Amendment by
unanimous consent*

(a) the office of the Queen, the Governor General and the
Lieutenant Governor of a province;
(b) the right of a province to a number of members in the
House of Commons not less than the number of Senators
by which the province is entitled to be represented at the
time this Part comes into force;
(c) subject to section 43, the use of the English or the French
language;
(d) the composition of the Supreme Court of Canada; and
(e) an amendment to this Part.

42. (1) An amendment to the Constitution of Canada in relation
to the following matters may be made only in accordance with
subsection 38(1):

*Amendment by
general procedure*

(a) the principle of proportionate representation of the
provinces in the House of Commons prescribed by the
Constitution of Canada;
(b) the powers of the Senate and the method of selecting
Senators;
(c) the number of members by which a province is entitled
to be represented in the Senate and the residence
qualifications of Senators;

(d) subject to paragraph 41(d), the Supreme Court of Canada;

(e) the extension of existing provinces into the territories; and

(f) notwithstanding any other law or practice, the establishment of new provinces.

Exception

(2) Subsections 38(2) to 38(4) do not apply in respect of amendments in relation to matters referred to in subsection (1).

Amendment of provisions relating to some but not all provinces

43. An amendment to the Constitution of Canada in relation to any provision that applies to one or more, but not all, provinces, including

(a) any alteration to boundaries between provinces, and

(b) any amendment to any provisions that relate to the use of the English or the French language within a province,

may be made by proclamation issued by the Governor General under the Great Seal of Canada only where so authorized by resolutions of the Senate and House of Commons and of the legislative assembly of each province to which the amendment applies.

Amendments by Parliament

44. Subject to sections 41 and 42, Parliament may exclusively make laws amending the Constitution of Canada in relation to executive government of Canada or the Senate and House of Commons.

Amendments by provincial legislatures

45. Subject to section 41, the legislature of each province may exclusively make laws amending the constitution of the province.

Initiation of amendment procedures

46. (1) The procedures for amendment under sections 38, 41, 42, and 43 may be initiated either by the Senate or the House of Commons or by the legislative assembly of province.

Revocation of authorization

(2) A resolution of assent made for the purposes of this Part may be revoked at any time before the issue of a proclamation authorized by it.

Amendments without Senate resolution

47. (1) An amendment to the Constitution of Canada made by proclamation under section 38, 41, 42, or 43 may be made without a resolution of the Senate authorizing the issue of the proclamation if, within one hundred and eighty days after the adoption by the House of Commons of a resolution authorizing its issue, the Senate has not adopted such a resolution and if, at any time after the expiration of that period, the House of Commons again adopts the resolution.

(2) Any period when Parliament is prorogued or dissolved shall not be counted in computing the one hundred and eighty day period referred to in subsection (1). **Computation of period**

48. The Queen's Privy Council for Canada shall advise the Governor General to issue a proclamation under this Part forthwith on the adoption of the resolution required for an amendment made by proclamation under this part. **Advice to issue proclamation**

49. A constitutional conference composed of the Prime Minister of Canada and the first ministers of the provinces shall be convened by the Prime Minister of Canada within fifteen years after this Part comes into force to review the provisions of this Part. **Constitutional conference**

canadian federal election results, 1867-2000

Each party entry: seats won (% of total seats) % of popular vote · disproportionality

Year	Seats	Conservatives	Liberals	Others
1867	181	**108** (60) 50.1 +9.9	72 (40) 49 –0.09	1 (0.5) 0.8 –0.3
1872	200	**104** (52) 49.9 +2.1	96 (48) 48 0	0 (0) 1.2 –1.2
1874	206	67 (32.4) 45.4 –12.9	**138** (67) 53.8 +13.2	1 (0.5) 2.5 –2.0
1878	206	**142** (68.9) 52.5 +16.4	64 (31.1) 46.3 –15.2	0 (0) 1.1 –1.1
1882	211	**139** (65.9) 50.7 +15.2	71 (33.6) 46.8 –13.2	1 (0.5)
1887	215	**126** (58.6) 50.2 +8.4	89 (41.4) 48.7 –6.3	0 (0) 1.8 –1.8
1891	215	**121** (56.3) 51.1 +5.2	94 (43.7) 47.1 –3.4	0 (0) 1.3 –1.3
1896	213	88 (41.3) 46.1 –4.8	**118** (55.4) 45.1 +10.3	7 (3.3) 8.8 –5.5
1900	213	80 (37.6) 47.4 –9.8	**133** (62.4) 51.2 +11.2	0 (0)
1904	214	75 (35) 46.4 –11.4	**138** (64.5) 52 +12.5	1 (0.5) 1.5 –1.0
1908	221	85 (38.5) 46.9 –8.4	**135** (61.1) 50.4 +10.7	1 (0.4) 2.7 –2.3
1911	221	**134** (60.6) 50.9 +9.7	87 (39.4) 47.7 –8.3	0 (0) 1.4 –1.4

Year	Seats	Government	Opposition	Others
1917	235	**153** (65.1) 57 +8.1	82 (34.9) 39.9 –5.0	0 (0) 3.7 –3.1

Year	Seats	Conservatives	Liberals	Progressives	Others
1921	235	50 (21.3) 30.3 –9.0	**116m** (49.4) 40.7 +8.7	64 (27.2) 22.9 +4.3	5 (2.1) 6.1 –4.0
1925	245	116 (47.3) 46.5 +0.8	**99m** (40.4) 39.9 +0.5	24 (9.8) 8.9 +0.9	6 (2.4) 4.7 –2.3
1926	245	91 (37.1) 45.3 –8.2	**128** (52.2) 46.1 +6.1	20 (8.2) 5.3 +2.9	6 (2.4) 3.4 –1.0
1930	245	**137** (55.9) 48.8 +7.1	91 (37.1) 45.2 –8.1	12 (4.9) 2.8 +2.1	5 (2.0) 3.2 –1.2

Each cell lists: seats (% of seats) vote % [seat % − vote %]

Year	Seats	Conservatives	Liberals	CCF	Social Credit	Others
1935	245	40 (16.3) 29.6 −13.3	173 (70.6) 44.8 +25.8	7 (2.9) 8.8 −5.9	17 (6.9) 4.1 +2.8	8 (3.3) 12.6 −9.3
1940	245	40 (16.3) 30.7 −14.4	181 (73.9) 51.5 +22.4	8 (3.3) 8.5 −5.2	10 (4.1) 2.7 +1.4	6 (2.4) 6.6 −4.2
1945	245	67 (27.3) 27.4 −0.1	125 (51.0) 40.9 +10.1	28 (11.4) 15.6 −4.2	13 (5.4) 4.1 +1.3	12 (4.9) 12.1 −7.2
1949	262	41 (15.6) 29.7 −14.1	193 (73.7) 49.5 +24.2	13 (5.0) 13.4 −8.4	10 (3.8) 2.3 +1.5	5 (1.9) 5.1 −3.2
1953	265	51 (19.2) 31.0 −11.8	171 (64.5) 48.8 +15.7	23 (8.7) 11.3 −2.6	15 (5.7) 5.4 +0.3	5 (1.9) 3.5 −1.6
1957	265	112m (42.3) 38.1 +4.2	105 (39.6) 40.9 −1.3	25 (9.4) 10.7 −1.3	19 (7.2) 6.6 +0.6	4 (1.5) 2.8 −1.3
1958	265	208 (78.5) 53.6 +24.9	49 (18.5) 33.6 −15.1	8 (3.0) 9.5 −6.5	0 (0.0) 2.6 −2.6	0 (0.0) 0.7 −0.7

Year	Seats	Conservatives	Liberals	NDP	Social Credit	Others
1962	265	116m (43.8) 37.3 +6.5	100 (37.7) 37.2 +0.5	19 (7.2) 13.5 −6.3	30 (11.3) 11.7 −0.4	0 (0.0) 0.4 −0.4
1963	265	95 (35.8) 32.8 +3.0	129m (48.7) 41.7 +7.0	17 (6.4) 13.1 −6.7	24 (9.1) 11.9 −2.8	0 (0.0) 0.4 −0.4
1965	265	97 (32.4) 36.6 +4.2	131m (49.4) 40.2 +9.2	21 (7.9) 17.9 −10.0	14 (5.3) 8.4 −3.1	2 (0.8) 1.2 −0.4
1968	264	72 (27.3) 31.4 −4.1	155 (58.7) 45.5 +13.2	22 (8.3) 17.0 −8.7	14 (5.3) 4.4 +0.9	1 (0.4) 1.7 −1.3
1972	264	107 (40.5) 35.0 +5.5	109m (41.3) 38.5 +2.8	31 (11.7) 17.7 −6.0	15 (5.7) 7.6 −1.9	2 (0.8) 1.2 −0.4
1974	264	95 (36.0) 35.4 +0.6	141 (53.4) 43.2 +10.2	16 (6.1) 15.4 −9.3	11 (4.2) 5.1 −0.9	1 (0.4) 0.9 −0.5
1979	282	136m (48.2) 35.9 +12.3	114 (40.4) 40.1 +0.3	26 (9.2) 17.9 −8.7	6 (2.1) 4.6 −2.5	0 (0.0) 2.3 −2.3
1980	282	103 (36.5) 33.0 +3.5	147 (52.1) 44.0 +8.1	32 (11.3) 20.0 −8.7	0 (0.0) 1.6 −1.6	0 (0.0) 1.4 −1.4

Year	Seats	Conservatives	Liberals	NDP	Reform / Alliance	Bloc Québécois
1984	282	211 (75.0) 50.0 +25.0	40 (14.0) 28.0 −14.0	30 (11.0) 19.0 −8.0		
1988	295	169 (57.2) 43.0 +14.3	83 (28.1) 32.0 −3.9	43 (14.5) 20.0 −5.5	0 (0.0) 3.0 −3.0	
1993	295	2 (0.7) 16.0 −15.3	177 (60.0) 41.0 +19.0	9 (3.1) 7.0 −3.9	52 (17.6) 19.0 −1.4	54 (18.3) 14.0 +4.3
1997	301	20 (6.6) 18.8 −12.2	155 (51.5) 38.5 +13.0	21 (7.0) 11.0 −4.0	60 (19.9) 19.4 +0.5	44 (14.6) 10.7 +3.9
2000	301	12 (4.0) 12.2 −8.2	172 (57.1) 40.8 +16.3	13 (4.3) 8.5 −4.2	66 (21.9) 25.5 −3.6	38 (12.6) 10.7 +1.9

1917: In October 1917, Western (pro-conscription) Liberals joined the Borden Conservatives in a wartime coalition or Union government, which contested the December election against the anti-conscription Liberals under Laurier. Note that the term of the Twelfth Parliament had been extended by the BNA Act, 1916 (repealed by the Statute Law Revision Act, 1927).

index

abrogative referendum, 385-86
access points, 381-82
activist state, 134, 136, 204, 331, 460, 467
adjustment seats, 351-52, 358
administrative function/power, 189, 207, 270, 369
administrative special status, 287
advertising, 171
Age of Print, 176
agenda-building, 374, 397
agents of representation, 370, 372, 377-78
alienation, 113, 130, 148, 313, 451
amending procedure, 213, 282-85
American Revolution, 76
anarchism, 145-47
apathy, 305
Aquinas, Thomas, 86, 96-99, 116
Argentina, 486
aristocracy, 92, 112, 142, 194, 196, 201, 206
Aristotle, 17, 42, 64, 85, 86, 88, 89, 90-96, 98, 99, 100, 116, 206, 296, 298, 300, 313, 422-24, 427, 440
arms race, 476-77
asymmetrical federalism, 286-87
atomism, 49, 102
attentive public, 395-98
attitudes, 162
Australia, 192, 194, 198, 214, 222, 234, 235, 244, 263-64, 273, 279, 283-84, 305,

336, 338-39, 344, 360-61, 384-85, 386, 414, 486
Austria, 194, 198, 222, 234, 239, 290, 327, 336, 339, 351, 383, 385-86, 475
authoritarian(ism), 37, 142, 194, 196, 256, 315-17, 384, 486, 488-91
authority, 18, 22-25, 26-27, 28, 30, 44, 55-57, 59-60, 68, 86, 105, 106, 127, 146, 211, 215, 262, 301, 307, 309, 311, 313, 369, 391, 406, 414, 419
depersonalization of, 29, 57-58, 60, 77, 187, 262, 288, 440
discretionary, 194
formal, 194

backbenchers, 239, 243, 314
Bacon, Frances, 89
bands, 54-56, 59-60
Bangladesh, 481
Basic Law, 213, 268, 271, 282
behaviouralism, 46-47
Belarus, 236
Belgium, 194-95, 198, 222, 228, 234-35, 239, 289, 290, 322, 328, 336, 339, 348, 351, 360-61, 383, 414, 457-58, 480-81
beliefs, 161, 166
benefits, 431
Bentham, Jeremy, 89, 115
Bernstein, Eduard, 141, 143

bicameral legislature, 193, 244, 268, 276-82, 286, 409
Bill 101, 331
Bill of Rights, 208, 216, 282, 430, 435
bills, 406-07, 408
block grants, 273, 275
Bolivia, 481
Bolshevik Revolution, 459
bourgeoisie, 450-51
branches of government, 206, 209
Brazil, 263
Britain, 192-95, 198-202, 213-14, 219, 222, 234, 239, 262, 280, 284, 288, 290, 323-24, 336, 338-39, 341, 348, 360-63, 415, 449, 451, 458, 478, 481, 487
British North America (BNA) Act, 211, 284
brokerage parties, 371-76
Bundesrat, 277, 279, 282
Bundestag, 279, 351-52
bureaucracy, 57, 64, 81, 189, 207, 210, 391, 406, 413-16
Burke, Edmund, 89, 108, 111-12, 128, 137, 302-03
Burkina Faso, 481
business cycle, 451-52

cabinet, 30, 196, 200-01, 203, 207, 217-18, 222, 223, 227, 229, 238-42, 243, 248, 253, 257, 297, 314, 381, 395, 405-06, 415

inner, 241
cadre parties, 376-77
Canada Assistance Plan (CAP),
    274-75
Canada Health and Social
    Transfer (CHST), 275
capitalist society, 113, 114, 129,
    130, 144, 150, 326, 450-55
caretaker government, 230-31
Catholic Church, 66-67, 69-71,
    73, 97-98, 331
caucus, 218, 243
centralization of authority/
    power, 55-56, 59
Charlottetown Accord (1992),
    285, 332, 385
Charter of Rights and Freedoms,
    135, 216, 416, 430, 435,
    439, 441
checks and balances, 78, 206,
    208, 210, 215, 233, 238,
    244, 248, 250, 413
chiefdom, 54-57, 60, 66
Chile, 481, 486
China, 263, 478, 481, 494
Christian Democracy, 138-39,
    320, 464
church, the, 79, 127, 167
Cicero, 89
citizen(ship), 36, 38, 85, 91, 95,
    110, 170, 173, 196, 216,
    245, 252, 293, 304-06,
    308-10, 312-13, 317-18,
    338, 363, 369, 391, 434
city state, 64
civil society, 33-37, 79, 134, 170,
    185, 317-18, 478, 488
class, 80, 92, 120, 129, 156, 299,
    303, 310, 320-21, 323,
    326, 328, 450
    cleavage, 364, 371, 375
    conflict, 450
    consciousness, 141, 452
    defined, 51
classical antiquity, 63-66
cleavages, 293, 319-33, 369-73
    centre-periphery, 323-24
    class, 325-27
    cross-cutting, 327-28
    ethno-linguistic, 89, 322-23,
        329, 371
    latent, 321, 325-27

manifest, 321, 327
reinforcing, 327-28
religious, 321-22, 371
urban-rural, 325
client states, 476
closure, 412
coalition, 225, 229, 234, 256,
    288, 358, 360
    executive, 223-24, 232
    government, 223, 224, 226,
        228, 233, 242, 364, 376
coercion, 23, 54, 57, 60, 146
cognitive ideas, 161
cohabitation, 254-55
Cold War, 121, 476, 491-92
collective executive, 201
collective ownership, 452
collective responsibility, 218
Columbia, 209
command economies, 452
common law, 214
communism, 131, 140-45, 150,
    464
community, 17, 18, 19-21, 25,
    27, 33, 35, 42-43, 51, 53-
    58, 60, 68, 101, 108, 109,
    126, 127, 146, 147, 159-
    60, 162, 329, 422, 429-30
comparative analysis, 47-48
competitive, periodic elections,
    245, 298, 304, 307, 316,
    319
concentrated powers, 200-04
concurrent legislation, 268
conditional grants, 273-75
confederal state, 262
confederation, 206, 262, 266, 292
Congress, 206, 249, 251-52, 278
consensual democracy, 258
conservatism, 111-13, 125-27,
    132, 152-53, 166, 402,
    449, 454, 464
    defined, 125
constituency size, 314, 336
constitution, 21, 96, 187, 198,
    204, 205-06, 211-16, 430,
    438
    American, 205, 208, 210, 213,
        126, 248, 266, 269, 431
    Canadian, 284
    defined, 211
    formal, 211, 215, 263

German, 283
Constitution Act, 211, 213, 267,
    285
constitutional
    amendment, 282
    change, 30, 32, 269
    court, 198, 212
    ethic, 212
    monarchy, 194-95
    systems, 190-200, 261, 391,
        406
constitutionalism, 28, 77, 81,
    123, 127, 211-16, 309,
    317, 417, 426
constructive non-confidence, 232
consumer society, 78-79, 117, 446
convention, 202, 216, 227, 237,
    284
    defined, 214
corporatism, 367, 382-84
Costa Rica, 209
cost-sharing, 275
Council of Ministers, 290-91
Court of Justice, 291
custom, 24, 127, 433
Cyprus, 209, 290, 322
Czech Republic, 204, 290, 336,
    348, 360-61, 414
Czechoslovakia, 327-28

deference to authority, 164, 305
deficit reduction, 466
deficits, 457, 463, 465, 471
delegation of authority, 262, 270,
    380
demand management, 462
democracy, 27-29, 32-33, 37, 44,
    77, 90-91, 92, 110, 115-
    16, 127, 130, 135, 141,
    158, 162, 164, 168, 174,
    196, 245, 280, 293, 295-
    318, 382, 384, 401, 406,
    433, 443, 455, 459, 462,
    470-71, 478, 487-91, 494
    defined, 296-98
    direct, 148, 158, 297-98
    electoral, 32, 316-17
    representative, 112, 124, 169,
        213, 297, 301, 307, 335,
        368, 462, 486
democratic franchise, 338
democratization, 78, 193, 315-18

Denmark, 192, 194, 198, 221, 234-35, 239, 288, 290, 336, 339, 348, 351, 360-62, 384-85, 414
dependency theory, 484-85
Descartes, René, 89
developing world, 166, 476-77, 483-85, 491
development, 80, 151, 483-85
sustainable, 151
devolution, 280, 288
Dewey, John, 135, 137
Diamond, Larry, 315
direct democracy, 368, 378, 384-85, 410
defined, 384
direct election of PM, 256
disallowance, 286
disproportionality, 340, 342, 345-46, 351, 358
dissolution, 230, 251
distinct society, 287, 329, 331
distribution, 432-33, 443
district magnitude, 339, 351
divine right of kings, 67, 424
division of labour, 109, 113
division of powers, 265-76
Dominican Republic, 209
double majority, 283-84
dual executive, 195-96, 218, 253-55, 258
Duverger's "mechanical" effect, 362
Duverger's "psychological" effect, 362
dyarchy, 254

Easton, David, 47, 162
ecology, 151
economic liberalism, 453-54, 464-65
economic management, 443
economic nationalism, 454
Ecuador, 209, 481
effective number of parties, 346, 361
effective threshold, 340, 345
efficacy, 36, 162
elections, 30, 81, 204, 250, 488, 490-91
elective parties, 346, 361-62, 365
electoral

campaign, 337, 377
fallacy, 316
formula, 339, 346, 350-51
justice, 340
systems, 219, 221, 293, 327-28, 335-66
vehicles, 370, 377
electronic politics, 374-75
elite accommodation, 329, 331
elite dominance, 307
elites, 300, 310, 382, 384
Engels, Friedrich, 113, 129, 130, 133
English Civil War, 101, 107, 200
Enlightenment, 69, 71-72, 73, 75, 77-78, 125, 196, 424, 489
entitlements, 429
entrenched provisions, 214, 216
environmentalism, 151-53, 449
equality, 28, 44, 72, 85, 108, 110, 130, 129, 133-34, 164, 421, 432-33, 440, 443, 460, 489
equalization payments, 272-73
Established Program Financing (EPF), 275
Estonia, 290
Ethiopia, 481
ethnocentricity, 487
European
Community, 289, 386, 492
Council, 290-91
Parliament, 290-91
Union, 290-92, 494
executive, 190, 191, 193-97, 206, 207
assent, 410
dominance, 204, 244, 410
function/power, 189, 190, 193, 201, 217, 297
veto, 410

factions, 203, 205
family, the, 34-35, 79, 167
federal autonomy, 285, 289
federal interdelegation, 270
federal means of subordination, 285-86
federalism, 215-16, 240, 261-92, 438
defined, 261-62
fiscal, 272-74

federalists, 332
feminism, 120, 149-50, 156, 449
feudal (or medieval) society, 63-64, 66-69, 72, 75, 76, 78, 88, 97, 101, 106, 122, 126, 128, 130, 153, 424, 429, 446-47
Finland, 198, 221, 234-35, 239, 244, 287, 290, 336, 348, 360-61, 365, 386, 414
First World, 476-80
fiscal conservatism, 140, 465-66
fixed elections, 230-31, 251, 257
flexible elections, 231
flexible electorate, 375
formal agenda, 398-99
formal executive, defined, 195
formateur, 228
France, 192, 194, 198-99, 215, 222, 233-35, 239, 244, 253-57, 290, 323-24, 336, 338-39, 344, 360-61, 364, 384, 414-15, 458, 461, 487
franchise, 135, 301
free press, 170, 174, 204, 316-17, 488
free vote, 304
freedom. See liberty
Freedom House, 317
French Revolution, 75, 111, 131
Friedrich List, 453, 485
full employment, 455, 460, 464-65
functions of the state, 188, 199
fusion of powers, 197, 200, 201, 202-03, 214-15, 217, 406

Gambia, 481
GDP, 458, 487
gender, 149
equality, 316
general amending formula, 284
Gerbner, George, 168
"German-style" system, 351-59
Germany, 192, 194, 198, 213, 221, 230, 232-35, 239, 244, 261, 268, 271, 276-79, 282, 284, 290, 336-40, 348, 351, 360-61, 363-64, 414-15, 451, 458, 467, 480-81, 487
gerrymandering, 336

Gini coefficient, 480
global warming, 210
globalization, 37-38, 79, 117, 165, 311, 475, 478-79, 482, 486, 491
Glorious (Whig) Revolution, 76, 101, 107, 478
government, 18, 19, 21, 29-30, 43, 54-59, 66, 77, 80, 101, 103-05, 110, 115, 117, 123, 127, 162, 170, 174, 181, 187, 190, 193, 222, 225, 261, 266, 289, 295-97, 300-01, 309, 311-13, 365, 391, 415, 445
    defeat, 218
    defined, 29
    expenditures, 240, 457
    formation process, 226, 236, 251, 364, 371
    representative, 78, 107, 115, 116, 124, 133, 135, 137, 297, 300, 302, 386
    revenues, 457
Governor-General, 195, 237, 279-80, 283
grand coalition, 257, 386
Greece, 194, 222, 228, 235, 290, 336, 339, 349, 351, 360-62, 414, 458

head of government, 194, 196, 202, 218, 227, 249
head of state, 194-95, 196-97, 227-28, 230, 235-38, 247, 249, 253, 256, 258-59, 297, 410, 412
Hegel, G.W.F., 87, 89, 108, 113, 129
high court, 198, 212
highest averages, 350
Hobbes, 89, 101-09, 115-16, 296, 300-01, 422, 424, 427
home rule, 287-88
House of Commons, 203
    Canada, 281, 409
    U.K., 193, 200-02
House of Lords, 193, 201, 206, 280, 409
House of Representatives, 193, 207, 250-51

human nature, 42, 87, 114, 116, 132, 136
Hungary, 290, 336, 414
Huntington, Samuel, 315, 486

Iceland, 194, 198, 221, 234-35, 339, 351
idealism, 91, 113
identity, 320-21
ideological consensus, 121, 145
ideology, 80, 113, 119-58, 320, 327, 372-73, 399, 402, 443, 464
    defined, 119
impeachment, 251
imperialism, 79, 322, 483
income maintenance, 460, 465, 468, 470
income quintiles, 210, 481-82
incongruence, 276-77
incrementalist model, 399-401, 405
India, 222, 318, 336, 478, 481
individualism, 122, 124, 429, 486
Indonesia, 322, 494
industrial democracy, 209
Industrial Revolution, 74, 78, 128, 451
industrialization, 485
inequality, 109, 126, 136, 138, 210, 455, 469, 480, 482
inflation, 464-65
    rates, 458
informateur, 228
initiatives, 148, 297, 385-87
inputs, 47, 391
institutions, 30, 81, 101, 106, 132, 167, 185, 190, 199, 205, 215, 293, 295, 306, 391, 396, 434
instrument choice, 402-04
instrumental reason, 100, 102
interest group, 181, 320, 327-28, 367, 378, 379-84, 389, 395, 398
intergovernmental relations, 275
International Monetary Fund (IMF), 484, 492
international relations, 37-38
investiture vote, 228-29, 237
invisible hand, 448, 455
Iran, 478, 493

Iraq, 478, 493
Ireland, 194, 198, 222, 228, 234-35, 239, 290, 336, 339, 347, 364, 386, 414, 458, 481
isolationism, 478
Israel, 192, 194, 198, 222, 228, 336, 478, 486
issue dimensions, 364
issue groups, 379-80, 382
Italy, 192, 194, 198, 221, 228, 233-34, 239, 290, 324, 336-40, 351, 354-55, 360-61, 363, 385-86, 414-54, 481, 487

Japan, 192, 194, 198, 222, 336, 338-39, 355, 360-61, 414, 458, 467, 486-87
judgemental journalism, 176-77, 378
judicial
    activism, 437-38
    function, 189-90, 297
    independence, 78, 197, 437
    interpretation, 269
    restraint, 437-38
    review, 198-99, 204, 208, 214, 216, 245, 391, 410, 434, 435-38, 439-40
judiciary, 190-91, 197-99, 209, 391, 434
    independent, 426
jurisdiction, 22, 265
justice, 27-29, 30-33, 44, 77, 85, 91, 164, 185, 197, 308-10, 419-41, 443
    defined, 419-21

Kashmir, 322
Keynesianism, 462
kinship, 55, 57, 132
Kosovo, 493

laissez-faire, 124, 127, 134-37, 140, 447-49, 453-55, 459-62, 467
language, 320, 375, 142, 145
largest remainders, 350
Laver, Michael, 21, 35, 54
law, 28, 30, 34-35, 43, 58, 60, 66, 68, 96, 105-06, 109,

165, 188, 189, 197, 211, 214, 410, 419-41, 434
rule of, 19, 27-28, 31, 72, 77, 81, 96
leadership, 54, 56, 372-75, 377
Lebanon, 322
legal culpability, 425
legal threshold, 340, 351, 353, 360
legislative
  branch, 206
  confidence, 201, 217, 222, 230
  defeat, 231, 235
  function/power, 188, 190, 207, 297, 301
  parties, 361-62, 365
  process, 406-13
legislature, 29, 124, 190-92, 203, 207, 210, 214, 217, 222, 239, 247-49, 301, 303, 391, 406, 434
  defined, 192
legitimacy, 25-27, 28-29, 30, 32, 60, 66, 104, 109, 110, 146, 163, 178, 281, 307, 309, 312, 368, 386, 409, 419, 491
  charismatic, 26, 60, 67, 296, 308
  legal-rational, 26, 60, 77, 308, 413, 426
  traditional, 26, 60
Lenin, V.I., 113, 140, 461
liberal
  democracy, 30, 59, 174, 307, 317, 432, 443, 486-87
  economics, 483-84
  modernity, 63-64, 69, 88, 440
  revolution, 64, 75, 77, 101, 126, 128, 134, 193, 211, 296, 300, 309, 424, 429, 433
  society, 81, 420, 422
liberal-conservatism, 136-40
liberalism, 101, 108, 113-15, 122, 128, 131-32, 137, 152-53, 155, 191, 296, 300, 432, 447-50, 466
  classic, 122-25
  reform, 133-36, 144, 459, 464-65

libertarianism, 147, 208
liberty, 44, 70, 72, 105, 108-10, 116-17, 122-24, 133-34, 146, 147
Lindblom, Charles, 400, 443
list systems, 347
lobbying, 304, 381, 383
Locke, John, 89, 101, 106-07, 109, 122-23, 16, 135, 205, 296, 300-01
Luther, Martin, 69, 89
Luxembourg, 194, 198, 217, 222, 234-35, 239, 290, 339, 360

Maastricht Treaty, 290
Machiavelli, 89, 96, 99-101, 116
MacIntyre, Alasdair, 97, 429
Madison, James, 205-06, 208, 383
majoritarian systems, 217, 219, 221-22, 225, 236, 339, 341-46
majority government, 222, 226-27, 230, 235-36, 365, 412
majority rule, 107, 164, 299-301
Mali, 480-81
Malta, 222, 235, 339, 347, 351
manufactured majority, 220, 312, 341, 343-44, 346, 357-59, 365, 375
market, the, 310, 444-45, 447, 453, 472
  autonomy, 124, 446-47, 453, 455, 459, 467
  economy, 34-35, 37, 69, 72-75, 79, 130, 138, 140, 443, 452, 455, 478
  society, 78, 127, 444-47, 449
  support, 446-47
Marx, Karl, 51, 62, 86, 89, 108, 113, 116-17, 120, 128-30, 133, 140, 146, 326, 444, 450-56
Marxism, 120, 131, 144, 156
Marxist-Leninism, 452, 489
Maslow, Abraham, 50-51
mass media, 79, 169, 173, 177, 182, 313, 337, 388, 407, 479
mass parties, 376-77
mass society, 117, 165
matching grants, 274

material constitution, 211, 215, 255, 263, 281
maximum term of office, 231
means of production, 450
median voter, 363
medieval society. See feudal society
Meech Lake Accord (1984), 285, 287, 332
Mexico, 316, 481, 491
Mill, James, 89, 113, 115, 124, 444
Mill, John Stuart, 89, 114, 116, 124, 126, 134, 450
minimal state, 134, 136, 137, 140, 448, 455, 459, 464, 467, 469
Ministry, the, 201, 229, 239-40
minority government, 223, 225-29, 231, 233, 235, 358
mixed government, 206
mixed-member system, 354, 360-61
mobilization function, 369-70
modernization, 148-50, 311, 483
monarchy, 67, 69, 104, 108, 206, 301, 447
  absolute, 109, 187, 191, 193-94, 196, 204, 424, 427
monetarism, 464
multi-member
  constituencies, 346-47
  majority, 224
  systems, 339-40
multi-party system, 220-21, 244, 256, 359, 365, 376

nation, 21-22, 153-54, 329
  defined, 22
National Assembly (Fr.), 254
National Policy, 444-45
nationalism, 132, 153-55
  economic, 127
  French Canadian, 329
  Quebecois, 331
nationalization, 143-44
nation-building, 154-55
nation-state, 22, 37-38, 64, 69, 100, 154, 165, 195, 478, 482, 491, 493
NATO, 492
natural law, 98-100

Netherlands, 192, 194, 198-99, 217, 221, 234-35, 239, 290, 336, 339-40, 349, 360-61, 383-84, 414, 481
New Deal, 121, 209, 270
"New Labour", 144
New Zealand, 192, 194, 198, 214, 222, 234-35, 336, 338-40, 355, 360-61, 364, 414, 458, 486
non-confidence, 228, 279
non-governmental organizations (NGOs), 485
Northern Ireland, 288, 322
Norway, 192, 194, 198, 217, 221, 230, 234-35, 239, 336, 339, 349, 351, 360-61, 365, 383, 386, 414, 458, 470, 480-82
notwithstanding clause, 439

Oakeshott, Michael, 127, 129, 137
obligation, 25-27, 59, 66
   See also legitimacy
office, 55, 57, 215
official bilingualism, 329
one-party dominance, 281
Organization for Economic Cooperation and Development (OECD), 482
organized interests, 397, 430
outputs, 47, 391

Pakistan, 478
paramountcy, 268
pariah party, 227
Parliament (U.K.), 361
parliamentary
   calendar, 407
   government, 338
   parties, 218, 346
   procedure, 203
   secretaries, 240
   supremacy, 76, 200, 434, 436, 438, 440
   systems, 197, 199, 200-04, 209-10, 217, 225-26, 236, 242-43, 247, 253, 256-57, 279, 335, 406, 410-11
Parti Quebecois, 331
partisan instability, 373-74, 378

party discipline, 203-04, 208, 222, 227, 242, 244, 249, 277, 304, 354, 410-12
party systems, 219, 221, 293, 327-28, 338, 354, 359-65
   defined, 359
patriarchy, 94, 12, 149, 150, 156
patronage, 81, 415
Peace, Order, and Good Government, 267-68
peak associations, 383
Peru, 299
Philippines, 318, 481
Plato, 44, 64, 88, 89, 90-96, 100, 298, 419
plebescite, 285, 384-85
pluralism, 52, 70, 147, 160, 367, 382-84, 488
pluralist democracy, 250
pluralistic society, 300, 312, 319, 328, 370, 375
plurality, 221-22, 225
   systems, 336, 339, 348, 359, 375-76
Poland, 194, 215, 236, 244, 290, 336, 349, 360-61, 414, 480-81
polarization, 362, 364
policy
   administration, 404
   blandness, 374
   committees, 242
   communities, 380, 395-97, 398, 400
   decision, 399
   defined, 188
   evaluation, 405
   implementation, 404
   instruments, 402
   networks, 380, 395-97
   process, 391
   sector, 395
policy-makers, 398, 400
policy-making, 188, 242, 244, 379-80, 397-406
polis, 68, 90, 95, 98
political
   agenda, 368
   anthropology, 53-59
   culture, 33, 80, 159-83, 233, 240, 253, 256, 295, 306, 315, 377, 488

economy, 310, 392, 444
efficiency, 402-03
executive, 195, 218, 247, 258
good, 51
neutrality, 415
participation, 162
parties, 181, 218, 223, 319-20, 327-28, 365, 367, 368-79, 389
philosophy, 88-118
pluralism, 256
process, 31-32, 80, 293, 319, 335, 368, 391, 434
politics
   comparative, 121
   defined, 18
   empirical, 41, 45-49
   normative, 41-45
   study of, 61-62,
   women in, 150
polling, 179, 337, 374, 377
popular sovereignty, 28, 30, 38, 72, 106-07, 110, 123, 178, 185, 205, 296, 301, 304, 307-09, 311, 488
populism, 147-49
portfolios, 239, 291
Portugal, 194, 222, 228, 235, 290, 336, 339, 359
Postman, Neil, 171-74
power, 18, 22-25, 27, 30, 44, 55, 57, 59-60, 68-69, 86, 100, 102, 104, 127, 146, 211, 307, 309, 311, 313, 369, 391, 406, 419, 478, 483
precedent, 214
President (U.S.), 248-51, 437
presidential veto, 251-52, 413
Presidentialism (FR), 247-53
   defined, 247
presidents, 196-97, 199, 235, 236, 247-59, 297, 335
prime minister, 29, 194, 200-02, 203-04, 215, 218, 227, 229-31, 234, 236, 238-42, 243, 247, 253, 258, 280, 415
principles of justice, 421
private power, 174, 441
private property, 107, 109, 130, 280, 443-46, 453, 460, 487
procedural justice, 425-26

processes, 30, 187-88, 215
proletariat, 141-42, 450-52
propaganda, 24
proportional representation,
219-20, 222-23, 226, 257,
288, 360-61
proportionate systems, 217, 221-
22, 238, 336, 339-40, 346-
51, 365, 375
protections, 431
Protestantism, 70-71
provincial equality, 287
pseudo-democracies, 316-17
public
agenda, 398-99
broadcasting, 172
choice theory, 49-50
enterprise, 402
goods, 188-93, 471
law, 425
morality, 420
opinion, 117, 134, 161, 178,
204, 313, 360, 378, 383,
387
ownership, 130, 143
policy, 181, 202, 204, 238,
241, 243, 248-49, 251-52,
255, 265, 291, 370, 372-
73, 377, 380, 393-417, 489
property, 446
sector, 463
service/servants, 30, 81, 271,
297, 405, 413-16
works, 463
Putnam, Robert, 36

quasi-federalism, 263, 285-89
Quebec, 329-33
Quebec Act, 329
Quebec Act (1774), 76
Quiet Revolution, 76, 331

ratification, 282, 284,
rationalist model, 399-401, 405
Rawls, John, 433
recall, 148
redistribution, 56-57, 130, 144,
460, 469-70, 482
reference, 169, 199
referendum, 148, 178, 254, 257,
297-98, 355, 384-87, 389
constitutional, 283

Reform Party, 149
Reformation, 69-71, 73, 75, 321,
489-90
regional
governments, 289
parties, 360
regionalism, 323-24, 329, 343
regulation, 403, 448, 461
religion, 21, 33-34, 73, 75, 136,
138-41, 320-21, 323, 328,
420, 489-90
Religious Right, 139-41
Renaissance, 69, 100, 424
representation, 328, 335, 338,
406
by population, 193, 251, 276,
336-37
representative autonomy, 302-04
representative function, 369-70
representatives, 314
republicanism, 77, 100, 248
reservation, 286
residual clause, 266
residual power, 267-68
responsible government, 78, 123,
201-04, 214, 217, 222-23,
242-44, 249, 257, 279
defined, 201
revenue capacity, 271, 288
revolution, 140-41, 307, 311,
451, 490
Ricardo, David, 113, 444, 450
rights, 28, 31, 44, 72, 78, 81,
117, 123, 130, 133, 135,
309-10, 421, 428-32, 434,
436, 439, 440, 486, 489
code, 198, 206, 430, 437
defined, 429
Rousseau, J.J., 89, 108-11, 116,
168, 296-97, 300,
rule of law, 137, 212, 265, 309,
405-06, 421, 422-28, 432,
440, 486, 489
defined, 197, 425
Russia, 194, 236, 244, 263, 336,
349, 360-62, 478, 481,
492, 494
Rwanda, 493

St. Augustine, 89, 97-98
Scholasticism, 71, 128
Scottish Parliament, 288

second chamber, 244, 276
Second International, 141
second tier, 346, 350, 354
Second World, 476-78
sectionalism, 343
secularization, 331, 450
self-determination, 153, 155
semi-presidentialism, 255
Senate
Australian, 279
Canadian, 277-78, 280-82,
438
U.S., 193, 207, 250-51, 280,
437
Senegal, 316
separation of powers, 107, 123,
191-92, 197, 200-03, 204-
09, 210, 247-48, 250, 258,
381, 406, 410, 412
Sierra Leone, 480-81
Singapore, 316
single member systems, 339-41,
344-46, 360-61, 365
single transferable vote, 347
single-party government, 242,
343
single-party majority, 225, 360
Slovenia, 290
Smith, Adam, 89, 113, 135, 444,
447-48, 450, 452, 454,
469, 485
social
contract, 106, 301
democracy, 114, 131, 140-45,
464-66
justice, 210, 310, 432
mobility, 68
programs, 460, 468, 470, 482
socialism, 113-14, 128-31, 132-
33, 136, 140-45, 152-53,
155, 320, 402, 449-53, 487
socialization, 157, 165, 252,
305-6, 368, 377
agents of, 167
societies, pre-industrial, 53-59
society, 18, 19-21, 29, 53, 56, 60,
88, 103, 160-64, 187
Socrates, 91-92
South Africa, 322, 481
South Korea, 209
sovereigntists, 331

sovereignty, 44, 191, 331, 333, 492
sovereignty-association, 332
Soviet Union, 213, 222, 452, 477, 494
Spain, 194, 222, 228, 235-36, 289, 290, 323, 336, 338-39, 349, 360-61, 414, 481
special status, 287
specific purpose transfers, 273
spin doctors, 176-77
stability, 229, 234, 360, 490, 493
state, 18, 19, 21-22, 29-33, 37-38, 54-59, 80, 100, 103, 105, 123, 127, 134, 139, 140, 145, 162, 163, 170, 190-91, 201, 261, 289, 293, 296, 301, 307, 310, 313, 322, 388, 391, 419, 422, 441, 443-44, 447, 451-53, 462, 466, 472, 478, 489, 493
    defined, 29
    totalitarian, 33
    versus civil society, 33-37, 79
state, of nature, 102-06, 108, 146
Statue of Westminster, 284, 329
statutes, 214
strategic voting, 344-45
strong bicameralism, 244, 251, 279
strong government, 204, 210, 245, 411
strong parties, 203
strong presidency, 194, 215, 244, 253, 256
structural groups, 379-80, 382
subgovernment, 395-96, 398, 400
supporters, 163-69
supranational federalism, 289-92
supreme court, 198, 200, 206, 212, 435
Supreme Court (U.S.), 207-09, 269, 435
Supreme Court of Canada, 332, 337, 435, 439
suspensive veto, 279-81, 409
sustainable development, 484-85
Sweden, 192, 194-95, 198-99, 221, 224, 230, 234, 239, 290, 336-39, 349, 351, 360-61, 363-64, 383, 386,

414, 458, 461, 469-70, 480-81
Switzerland, 192, 198, 222, 232-33, 235, 238, 244, 257-58, 261, 266, 277, 283, 322, 338-39, 349-50, 360-61, 383-87, 458, 461, 480-81
"symbolic" politics, 315
symmetrical bicameralism, 251

tax fatigue, 468
taxation, 271, 403
technical efficiency, 402-03
technology, 269, 479, 482
television, 160, 170, 174, 177, 370, 374, 377
Television Age, 169, 176
termination of government, 228-30, 234-35
terms of office, 208
territoriality, 22
Third International, 142
Third World, 476-77, 483
tolerance, 128
tory(ism), 126, 131, 450, 464
totalitarian(ism), 142
trade unions, 459, 461
tradition, 67, 111-12, 126, 127-28, 136, 139-40, 150, 196, 450
traditional legitimacy, 296, 308
transnational corporations, 465, 479
tribe, 54-57, 60
Trotsky, Leon, 142-43
Trudeaumania, 169
two party system, 221, 343, 359
tyranny, 92
tyranny of the majority, 250, 299-300

Uganda, 322
Ukraine, 236
umbrella organizations, 383
unemployment, 455, 458, 465
    rates, 457
unicameral legislature, 193
unitary state, 262, 298
United Nations, 476, 492-93
United States, 191-92, 194, 196, 198, 200, 205-08, 209, 213-14, 219, 244, 247-53, 261, 263-70, 273, 276-79,

282, 284, 304-05, 322, 336-39, 341, 364, 381-85, 400, 406, 409-10, 413-14, 436-37, 458, 461, 476-81, 486-87, 491, 494
    Congress, 361
    legislature, 412
    President, 413
universal adult suffrage, 338
Universal Declaration of Human Rights, 430
universality, 426
unwritten constitution, 216
upper-tier seats, 354
urbanization, 450
utilitarianism, 115

"value free" inquiry, 46, 156
values, 164, 166
vanguard, 141-42
vehicles of representation, 365, 380, 388
vendetta, 420
Venezuela, 209
veto points, 382, 410

Wales, 288
wasted votes, 344
weak bicameralism, 281
weak government, 208-10, 250
weak parties, 207, 381, 407, 412
weak president, 194
Weber, Max, 26-27, 29, 60
welfare, 140, 295
    state, 35-36, 135-36, 144, 391, 443, 460-72, 482
welfare, individual, 103-04
Welsh Assembly, 288
"Western Alienation", 324
Whig Revolution, 123, 200, 202, 288, 434
White House, 207, 248
"winner take all", 341, 359
World Bank, 484, 492
World Trade Organization (WTO), 475
written constitution, 265, 281

Yugoslavia, 322, 327-28, 493